Al-Kafi
Volume 6 of 8

English Translation

Al-Kafi

Volume 6 of 8

(Fru' al-Kafi)

English Translation

Second Edition

Compiled by
Thiqatu al-Islam, Abu Ja'far Muhammad
ibn Ya'qub al-Kulayni

Translated by
Muhammad Sarwar

Published by
The Islamic Seminary Inc.
www.theislamicseminary.org

The Islamic Seminary Inc., New York
© 2015 by The Islamic Seminary Inc.
All rights reserved
Second Edition 2015
Printed in the United States of America.

ISBN: 978-0-9914308-9-5

Al-Kafi, Volume 6 of 8. English Translation – 2nd ed.
Jamadi al-Awwal 1436
February 2015

Note to Readers

Dear respected readers, please note the following:

The English translation of this volume from Kitab al-Kafi is now, by the will of Allah, in your hands. It was only because of the beauty of the words of Ahl al-Bayt *'Alayhim al-Salam* that made it all possible. The magnitude of this project had become quite large and complex due to two language texts and it was sometimes difficult to handle.

All comments, suggestions and corrections will be very much appreciated. In fact it will be your participation in the good cause and rewarding in the sight of Allah, most Majestic, most Glorious. Please e-mail your comments, suggestions or corrections to: info@theislamicseminary.org.

With thanks,

The Islamic Seminary
www.theislamicseminary.org

Contents

Part Two: The Book of Talaq (Divorces)

Part Three: The Book of Hunting

Part Four: The Book of Slaughtering Animals for Food

Part Five: The Book of Food

Part Six: The Book of Drinks

Part Seven: The Book of Dresses, Beautification and Kindness

Part Eight: The Book of Domestic Animals

An Outline of the Number of Volumes, Sections and Sub-divisions of Kitab al-Kafi

Part 1 - Al-'Usul (Principles)

Volume 1

This part of the book consists of *Ahadith* on the principles of beliefs and it is called 'Usul (principles) in *al-Kafi*.

The sections or chapters in volume 1 are as follows:

1. The Book of Intelligence and Ignorance (*Kitab al-'Aql wa al-Jahl*)
2. The Book of the Excellence of Knowledge (*Kitabu Fad al-'Ilm*)
3. The Book on Oneness of Allah (*Kitab al-Tawhid*)
4. The Book about the people who possess Divine Authority (*Kitab al-Hujja*)

Volume 2

Sections or Chapters in Volume 2:

5. The Book on Belief and Disbelief (*Kitab al-'Iman wa al-Kufr*)
6. The Book on Prayers (*Kitab al-Du'a'*)
7. The Book on the Excellence of the Holy Quran (*Kitabu Fadl al-Quran*)
8. The Book of Social Discipline (*Kitab al-'Ishra*)

PART 2 - Al-*Furu'* (Branches)

Volumes 3-7

This part consists of *Ahadith* on Islamic practical laws such as:

> The acts of worship (*'Ibadat*)
>
> Business transactions (*mu'amalat*)
>
> Judicial laws (*al-Qada'*)

Furu' al-Kafi (volume 3 – 7): The rules of conduct, the practical laws of the Islamic system, consists of the following:

9. The Book of Laws of Cleanliness (*Kitab al-Tahara*)
10. The Book of Laws of Menstruation (*Kitab al-Hayd*)
11. The Book of Laws about the dying people and their burials (*Kitab al-Jana'iz*)
12. The Book of Laws of Prayer (*Kitab al-Salat*)
13. The Book of Laws of Charities, Taxes (*Kitab al-Zakat*)
14. The Book of Laws of Fasting (*Kitab al-Siyam*)

15. The Book of Laws of Pilgrimage (*Kitab al- Hajj*)
16. The Book of Laws of Defense (*Kitab al-Jihad*)
17. The Book of Laws of Business (*Kitab al-Ma'ishah*)
18. The Book of Laws of Marriage (*Kitab al-Nikah*)
19. The Book of Laws about New-born (*Kitab al-'Aqiqa*)
20. The Book of Laws of Divorce (*Kitab al-Talaq*)
21. The Book of Laws of Emancipation of Slaves (*Kitab al-'Itq wa al-Tadbir wa al-Mukataba*)
22. The Book of Laws of Hunting (*Kitab al-Sayd*)
23. The Book of Laws of Slaughtering Animals for food (*Kitab al-Dhaba'ih*)
24. The Book of Laws of Foods (*Kitab al-At'imah*)
25. The Book of Laws of Drinks (*Kitab al-Ashriba*)
26. The Book of Laws of Dresses, Beautifying and the Ideal of Manhood (*Kitab al-Zay wa al-Tajammul*)
27. The Book of Laws of Animal Farming and Poultry (*Kitab al-Dawajin*)
28. The Book of Laws of Wills (*Kitab al-Wasaya'*)
29. The Book of Laws of Inheritances (*Kitab al-Mawarith*)
30. The Book of Laws of Penalties (*Kitab al-Hudud*)
31. The Book of Laws of Restitution for Bodily Injuries (*Kitab al-Diyat*)
32. The Book of Laws of Testimony and Witnessing (*Kitab al-Shahadat*)
33. The Book of Judicial Laws (*Kitab al-Qada' wa al-Ahkam*)
34. The Book of Laws of Oaths, Vows and Expiation (*Kitab al-'Ayman wa al-Nudbur wa al-Kaffarat*)

PART 3 - Al-Rawdah (Garden of Flowers (Hadith))

Volume 8

This part consists of miscellaneous *Ahadith* of both the *'Usul* and *Furu'* of *al-Kafi*. The topics are not arranged and organized as in the other volumes. The chapters are not in alphabetical order of *Ahadith* or narrators.

This volume comprises about six hundred *Hadith* on various topics and is a treasure of knowledge of the matters of belief, spiritual discipline, interpretations of many verses of the Holy Quran, accounts of the noble manners of the Holy Prophet and infallible members of his family and information about the system of this and the next life.

In the Name of Allah, the Beneficent, the Merciful

Part One:
The Book of 'Aqiqah (Offering Animal Sacrifice for a Newborn Child)

Chapter 1 - Excellence of Son

H 10241, Ch. 1, h 1

Ali ibn Ibrahim has narrated from his father from al-Nawfaliy from al-Sakuniy who has said the following:

"Abu 'Abd Allah, *'Alayhi al-Salam,* has said that the Messenger of Allah, *O Allah, grant compensation to Muhammad and his family worthy of their services to Your cause,* has said, 'A virtuous son is a sweet smelling flower from Allah which Allah distributes among His servants. My sweet smelling flowers in this world are al-Hassan and al-Husayn whom I have named after the names of two grandsons in banu Israel, called Shabbar and Shabiyr.'"

H 10242, Ch. 1, h 2

A number of our people have narrated from Ahmad ibn Muhammad from 'Uthman ibn 'Isa from ibn Muskan from certain persons of our people who has said the following:

"Ali ibn al-Husayn, *'Alayhi al-Salam,* has said, 'It is of prosperity and good fortune of a man to have sons who help and support him.'"

H 10243, Ch. 1, h 3

A number of our people have narrated from Ahmad ibn Muhammad from al-Qasim ibn Yahya from his grandfather al-Hassan ibn Rashid from Muhammad ibn Muslim who has said the following:

"Abu 'Abd Allah, *'Alayhi al-Salam,* has said that the Messenger of Allah, *O Allah, grant compensation to Muhammad and his family worthy of their services to Your cause,* has said, 'You (my followers) should bring up more children because I will claim to have the majority with you among the nations tomorrow (on the Day of Judgment).'"

H 10244, Ch. 1, h 4

Ali ibn Ibrahim has narrated from his father from ibn abu 'Umayr from 'Abd Allah ibn Sinan who has said the following:

"Abu 'Abd Allah, *'Alayhi al-Salam*, has said, 'When Yusuf *'Alayhi al-Salam*, met his brother, he asked him, 'How could you marry women after me?' He replied, 'My father commanded me and said, 'If you like to have such a number of children who can make the earth heavy with *Tasbih* (Allah is free of all defects) you must do so.'"

H 10245, Ch. 1, h 5

Abu Ali al-Ash'ariy has narrated from Muhammad ibn 'Abd al-Jabbar from Safwan ibn Yahya from Ishaq ibn 'Ammar who has said the following:

"Abu 'Abd Allah, *'Alayhi al-Salam,* has said that so and so -whose name he (the Imam) mentioned- once said, 'I was not interested in children until I stood in al-'Arafat and there was a young man next to me who prayed and wept, saying, "O Lord, my parents, (grant blessings to) my parents." Hearing this made me interested in children.'"

H 10246, Ch. 1, h 6

A number of our people have narrated from Ahmad ibn Muhammad from ibn Khalid from his father in a *mursal* manner has said, the following:

"Abu 'Abd Allah, *'Alayhi al-Salam,* has said that the Messenger of Allah, *O Allah, grant compensation to Muhammad and his family worthy of their services to Your cause,* has said, 'Of good fortune and prosperity of a man is his having the virtuous son.'"

H 10247, Ch. 1, h 7

It is narrated from the narrator of the previous *Hadith* from Bakr ibn Salih who has said the following:

"I once wrote to abu al-Hassan, *'Alayhi al-Salam,* saying, 'I have avoided praying for a son for five years because my wife dislikes it and says that bringing up a child is very difficult because of lack of resources.' He (the Imam), *'Alayhi al-Salam,* wrote to me, 'Ask for them (children): Allah, most Majestic, most Glorious, will grant them sustenance.'"

H 10248, Ch. 1, h 8

Muhammad ibn Yahya has narrated from Ahmad ibn Muhammad ibn 'Isa from Muhammad ibn Yahya from Talhah ibn Zayd who has said the following:

"Abu 'Abd Allah, *'Alayhi al-Salam,* has said, 'Children of believing people are named before Allah, as intercessors with accepted intercession. When they become twelve years old they can have good deeds and when they mature then sins are written against them.'"

H 10249, Ch. 1, h 9

Ali ibn Ibrahim has narrated from his father from al-Nawfaliy from al-Sakuniy who has said the following:

"Abu 'Abd Allah, *'Alayhi al-Salam,* has said that `Amir al-Mu'minin would read, '. . . I am afraid for my dependents after me,' (19:6) meaning that he had no heirs until Allah granted him (an heir) after his becoming very old.'"

H 10250, Ch. 1, h 10

Ali ibn Ibrahim has narrated from his father from al-Nawfaliy from al-Sakuniy who has said the following:

"Abu 'Abd Allah, *'Alayhi al-Salam,* has said that the Messenger of Allah, *O Allah, grant compensation to Muhammad and his family worthy of their services to Your cause,* has said, 'A virtuous son is a sweet smelling flower from the flowers of paradise.'"

H 10251, Ch. 1, h 11

Through the same chain of narrators as that of the previous *Hadith*, the following is narrated:

"Abu 'Abd Allah, *'Alayhi al-Salam,* has said that the Messenger of Allah, *O*

Allah, grant compensation to Muhammad and his family worthy of their services to Your cause, has said, 'It is of the prosperity and good fortune of a man to have the virtuous son.'"

H 10252, Ch. 1, h 12

A number of our people have narrated from Ahmad ibn Muhammad from ibn Khalid from Sharif ibn Sabiq from al-Fadl ibn abu al-Qurrah who has said the following:

"Abu 'Abd Allah, *'Alayhi al-Salam,* has said that the Messenger of Allah, *O Allah, grant compensation to Muhammad and his family worthy of their services to Your cause,* has said the following: 'Jesus, son of Marry, once passed by a grave wherein its dweller suffered a great suffering. He passed by the same grave afterward but found the dweller was not suffering. He asked, "O Lord, I passed by this grave a year ago when he was suffering a great suffering and this year I passed by his grave but he did not suffer." Allah then revealed to him that his virtuous son became mature who repaired a road and gave shelter to an orphan, so I forgave him because of what his son has done.' The Messenger of Allah then said, 'It is of the inheritance of Allah, most Majestic, most Glorious, for His believing servant in the form of a virtuous son who worships Him after the death of his father' and he (the Imam) then read the verse of the Quran about Zakariya, '. . . O Lord, grant me from You an heir who will inherit me and the people of Ya'qub. O Lord, make him to please You.'"

Chapter 2 - Resemblance of a Child

H 10253, Ch. 2, h 1

Ali ibn Ibrahim has narrated from his father from al-Nawfaliy from al-Sakuniy who has said the following:

"Abu 'Abd Allah, *'Alayhi al-Salam,* has said that the Messenger of Allah, *O Allah, grant compensation to Muhammad and his family worthy of their services to Your cause,* has said, 'It is of the bounties of Allah for a man to have a son who resembles him.'"

H 10254, Ch. 2, h 2

Ali ibn Ibrahim has narrated from his father from ibn abu 'Umayr from Hisham ibn al-Muthanna' from Sadir who has said the following:

"Abu Ja'far, *'Alayhi al-Salam,* has said, 'It is of good fortune of a man to have a son who resembles his father, physically, morally and in his nature.'"

H 10255, Ch. 2, h 3

Muhammad ibn Yahya has narrated from Salmah ibn al-Khattab from al-Hassan ibn Ali ibn Yaqtin from Yunus ibn Ya'qub from a man who has said the following:

"I once heard abu al-Hassan, *'Alayhi al-Salam,* saying, 'Fortunate is the man who does not die before seeing a successor of his own self.'"

Chapter 3 - Excellence of Daughters

H 10256, Ch. 3, h 1

A number of our people have narrated from Ahmad ibn Muhammad ibn Khalid from Muhammad ibn 'Isma'il ibn Bazi' from Ibrahim ibn Mehzam from Ibrahim al-Karkhiy from a trustworthy man who narrated from certain persons of our people who have said the following:

"I married in al-Madinah and abu 'Abd Allah, *'Alayhi al-Salam,* asked me, 'How is your married life?' I replied, 'Every good thing that a man can see in a woman I found with her but she betrayed me.' He (the Imam) asked, 'How did she do so?' I replied, 'She gave birth to a girl.' He (the Imam) said, 'You may have disliked her but Allah, most Majestic, most Glorious, says, 'Regardless of how you feel about your parents or children, you do not know which of them is more beneficial to you. Allah is All-knowing and All-wise. (4:11)'"

H 10257, Ch. 3, h 2

Ali ibn Ibrahim has narrated from his father from ibn abu 'Umayr from Hammad ibn 'Uthaman who has said the following:

"Abu 'Abd Allah, *'Alayhi al-Salam,* has said, 'The Messenger of Allah, *O Allah, grant compensation to Muhammad and his family worthy of their services to Your cause,* was a father of daughters.'"

H 10258, Ch. 3, h 3

Muhammad ibn Yahya has narrated from Ahmad ibn Muhammad ibn 'Isa from Ali ibn al-Hakam from Aban ibn 'Uthman from Muhammad al-Wasitiy who has said the following:

"Abu 'Abd Allah, *'Alayhi al-Salam,* has said, 'Ibrahim, *'Alayhi al-Salam* prayed to his Lord to give him a daughter who will weep and mourn for him after his death.'"

H 10259, Ch. 3, h 4

Ali ibn Ibrahim has narrated from his father from and Muhammad ibn 'Isma'il has narrated from al-Fadl ibn Shadhan from all from ibn abu 'Umayr from Hisham ibn al-Hakam from Jarud who has said the following:

"I once said to abu 'Abd Allah, *'Alayhi al-Salam,* that I have several daughters. He (the Imam) said, 'Perhaps you wish that they die. You must take notice that if you wished that they die and they died, you will have no reward and will meet Allah, most Majestic, most Glorious, as a disobedient person.'"

H 10260, Ch. 3, h 5

Ali ibn Ibrahim has narrated from his father from al-Nawfaliy from al-Sakuniy who has said the following:

"Abu 'Abd Allah, *'Alayhi al-Salam,* has said that the Messenger of Allah, *O Allah, grant compensation to Muhammad and his family worthy of their services to Your cause,* has said, 'The best of children are daughters, who are kind, serving, comforting, blessed and nursing (their parents).'"

H 10261, Ch. 3, h 6

A number of our people have narrated from Ahmad ibn Muhammad from ibn Khalid from Ali ibn al-Hakam from abu al-'Abbas al-Zayyat from Hamzah ibn Humran in a marfu' manner has said the following:

"A man once was with the Holy Prophet, *O Allah, grant compensation to*

Muhammad and his family worthy of their services to Your cause, he informed him about the birth of a child but his face changed. The Holy Prophet asked him, 'What is the matter with you?' He (the Messenger of Allah) said, 'Say that it is good.' He then said, 'I left and my wife was in labor. I am informed that she has given birth to a girl.' The Holy Prophet said, 'The earth carries her weight, the sky provides her shadow, Allah gives her sustenance and she is a sweet smelling flower: you enjoy her fragrance.' He (the Messenger of Allah) then said this to his companions: 'One who has one daughter carries a heavy load, one who has two daughters is like scorched land that begs for rain from Allah and one who has three daughters is exempt from Jihad (serving in the army) and all hardships. One who has four daughters, then O slaves of Allah you must help him, O slaves of Allah you must give him a loan and O slaves of Allah you must have mercy on him.'"

H 10262, Ch. 3, h 7

It is narrated from the narrator of the previous *Hadith* from Ali ibn Muhammad al-Qasaniy from Sulayman ibn Ja'far al-Ja'fariy who has said the following:

"This is a narration of abu al-Hassan, al-Rida', *'Alayhi al-Salam,* from the Messenger of Allah, *O Allah, grant compensation to Muhammad and his family worthy of their services to Your cause.* He (the Messenger of Allah) , has said, 'Allah, most Blessed, most High, is kinder to female than to male, and whoever of men brings happiness to a female relative Allah, most High, will make him happy on the Day of Judgment.'"

H 10263, Ch. 3, h 8

It is narrated from the narrator of the previous *Hadith* from certain persons who narrated to him from Ahmad ibn 'Abd al-Rahim from certain persons of his people who has said the following:

"Abu 'Abd Allah, *'Alayhi al-Salam,* has said, 'Daughters are good deeds and sons are bounties. Reward comes only from good deeds and for bounties one will be held for questioning.'"

H 10264, Ch. 3, h 9

Ahmad ibn Muhammad al-'Asemiy has narrated from Ali ibn al-Hassan al-Taymuliy from Ali ibn Asbat from his father from al-Jarud ibn al-Mundhir who has said the following:

"Abu 'Abd Allah, *'Alayhi al-Salam,* once said to me, 'I am told a girl is born to you whom you dislike. What has she brought upon you? She is a sweet smelling flower you enjoy and her sustenance is guaranteed, besides, the Messenger of Allah was a father of girls.'"

H 10265, Ch. 3, h 10

Ali ibn Ibrahim has narrated from his father from ibn abu 'Umayr from Hisham ibn al-Hakam from 'Umar ibn Yazid who has said the following:

"Abu 'Abd Allah, *'Alayhi al-Salam,* has said that the Messenger of Allah, *O Allah, grant compensation to Muhammad and his family worthy of their services to Your cause,* has said, 'One who supports three daughters or three sisters, paradise becomes obligatory for him.' It then was asked, 'O Messenger of Allah, what happens if one supports just two?' He (the Messenger of Allah) replied, 'Even if they are just two.' It then was asked, 'O Messenger of Allah, what happens if it is only one?' He (the Messenger of Allah) replied, 'Even if she is just one.'"

H 10266, Ch. 3, h 11

A number of our people have narrated from Ahmad ibn Muhammad ibn Khalid from a number of his people from al-Hassan ibn Ali ibn Yusuf from al-Husayn ibn Sa'id al-Lakhmiy who has said the following:

"To a certain persons of our people a girl was born and he visited abu 'Abd Allah, *'Alayhi al-Salam,* who saw him disappointed. Abu 'Abd Allah, *'Alayhi al-Salam,* said to him, 'Consider if Allah, most Blessed, most High, sent revelation to you which said, "Do you want Me to choose for you or you want to choose for yourself," what would you say?' He replied, 'I would say, O Lord, You choose for me.' He (the Imam) said, 'If so then it is Allah, most High who has chosen for you.' He (the narrator) has said that he (the Imam) then said, 'The boy whom the learned man with Musa killed -- and is mentioned in the words of Allah, most Majestic, most Glorious, '. . . We wanted to replace him with a child better than him in purity and nearer as relatives' -- Allah replaced him with a girl who gave birth to seventy prophets.'"

H 10267, Ch. 3, h 12

A number of our people have narrated from Ahmad ibn Muhammad from al-Husayn ibn Musa from Ahmad ibn al-Fadl who has said the following:

"Abu 'Abd Allah, *'Alayhi al-Salam,* has said, 'Sons are bounties and daughters are good deeds, Allah questions one about the bounties but for the good deeds He gives good rewards.'"

Chapter 4 - Prayer and Appeal before Allah for a Son

H 10268, Ch. 4, h 1

Ali ibn Ibrahim has narrated from Salih ibn al-Sindiy, from Ja'far ibn Bashir al-Khazzaz from Ali ibn abu Hamzah from abu Basir who has said the following:

"Abu 'Abd Allah, *'Alayhi al-Salam,* has said, 'If the birth of a child for one of you is delayed, he should say this prayer, 'O Lord, do not leave me all by myself- and You are the best heir- alone and frightened so that my thoughts about a child reduce my thanks (to You). Grant me truthful consequences (successors) of male (children) and female ones who comfort me in my apprehension and I can find tranquility with them in my loneliness and thank You upon completion of bounties, O Magnanimous, O Great and O giver of greatness. Thereafter grant me good health and the ability to thank You until You take me to the stage where You will be pleased with me in truthfulness of words, safe return of trust and keeping the promise.'"

H 10269, Ch. 4, h 2

Muhammad ibn Yahya has narrated from Ahmad ibn Muhammad from Ali ibn al-Hakam from Sayf ibn 'Amirah from abu Bakr al-Hadramiy from al-Harith al-Nasriy who has said the following:

"I once said to abu 'Abd Allah, *'Alayhi al-Salam,* that I belong to a family that is extinct and I do not have any children. He (the Imam) said, 'Pray when you are in *Sajdah* (prostration), '[My Lord, grant me from Your dominion an heir who will inherit me]. O Lord, grant me fine offspring from Your dominion; You hear the prayers. O Lord, do not leave me alone and You are the best heir.' He (the narrator) has said that I followed the instruction, then Ali and al-Husayn (my sons) were born.'"

H 10270, Ch. 4, h 3

Muhammad ibn Yahya has narrated from Ahmad ibn Muhammad from Ali ibn al-Hakam from a man from Muhammad ibn Muslim who has said the following:

"Abu 'Abd Allah, *'Alayhi al-Salam,* has said, 'One who wishes for pregnancy should perform two *Rak'at Salat* (prayer) after Friday *Salat* (prayer) with long *Ruku'* (bowing down on one's knees) and *Sajdah* (prostration): then say, "O Lord, I ask and appeal before You as Zakariya had done. O Lord, do not leave me alone by myself –You are the best heir. O Lord, grant me from Your dominion fine offspring; You hear the prayer. O Lord, by Your name I have made her lawful and in Your trust I have taken her. If You have determined a child in her womb make it a son, a blessed one, [a clean one] and do not allow Satan to have a share or portion in him."'"

H 10271, Ch. 4, h 4

Ali ibn Ibrahim has narrated from his father from ibn abu 'Umayr from certain persons of his people who has said the following:

"Once al-Abrash al-Kalbiy complained before abu Ja'far, *'Alayhi al-Salam,* and said that he did not have any child and asked him (the Imam) to teach him something. He (the Imam) said, say, 'I ask forgiveness from Allah, my Lord and return to Him in repentance' one hundred times every day and every night, because Allah says, 'Ask forgiveness from your Lord; He is forgiving. . . . He helps you by means of your wealth and sons.'" (71:10)

H 10272, Ch. 4, h 5

Al-Husayn ibn Muhammad has narrated from Ahmad ibn Muhammad from al-Sayyariy from 'Abd al-Rahman ibn abu Najran from Sulayman ibn Ja'far from a Shaykh from al-Madinah from Zurarah who has said the following:

"Abu Ja'far, *'Alayhi al-Salam,* has said, 'Once I wanted to visit Hisham ibn 'Abd al-Malik but permission for a meeting was delayed and I felt worried.' He 'Abd al-Malik had a guard who was wealthy but had no children. Abu Ja'far, *'Alayhi al-Salam,* asked him, 'If you can arrange a meeting with Hisham I will teach you a prayer and you will have a child.' The guard agreed and arranged a meeting between him (the Imam) and Hisham who complied with all that he (the Imam) asked. When the meeting was over the guard said, 'I pray to Allah to keep my soul in service for your cause, the prayer that you had mentioned.' He (the Imam) said, 'Everyday in the morning and evening, say seventy times, *Tasbih* (Allah is free of all defects).' Then say, 'I ask forgiveness from Allah, my Lord and return to Him in repentance' ten times then *Tasbih* (Allah is free of all defects) nine times and finish the tenth with, 'I ask forgiveness from Allah, my Lord and return to Him in repentance.' Then say the words of Allah, most Majestic, most Glorious, 'Ask forgiveness from your Lord; He is forgiving. He sends you abundant rain from the sky. He helps you by means of your wealth and sons. He makes for you gardens and canals.' (71:12) The guard followed the instruction and he was granted a great many children. He thereafter kept good relations with abu Ja'far, *'Alayhi al-Salam.* Sulayman has said, 'I also said those prayers and I had married the daughter of my uncle but there was a delay in the birth of a son for me from her. I taught her also the prayer; then a son was born to me and the woman believed that whenever she wanted she could become pregnant after saying the prayer. I taught to more than one person of banu Hashim who did not have children: then many children were born to them. All praise belongs to Allah.'"

H 10273, Ch. 4, h 6

A number of our people have narrated from Sahl ibn Ziyad from Ya'qub ibn Yazid from Muhammad Shu'ayb from al-Nadr ibn Shu'ayb from Sa'id ibn Yasar who has said the following:

"A man once said to abu 'Abd Allah, *'Alayhi al-Salam,* 'We wish to have a child but the birth of a child has not happened for us.' He (the Imam) instructed him to say, 'I ask forgiveness from Allah, my Lord and return to Him in repentance' one hundred times just before it is dawn. If you forget; do its Qada' (compensatory prayer for it)."'

H 10274, Ch. 4, h 7

It is narrated from the narrator of the previous *Hadith* from certain persons of our people who has said the following:

"Once, a man complained before abu 'Abd Allah, *'Alayhi al-Salam,* saying, 'The birth of a child does not take place for us.' He (the Imam) said, 'When going to bed with your wife say, 'O Lord, if You grant me a son I will name him Muhammad.' He (the narrator) has said that he followed the instruction, then a son was born to him.'"

H 10275, Ch. 4, h 8

Muhammad ibn Yahya has narrated from Ahmad ibn Muhammad from Ali ibn al-Hakam from 'Isma'il ibn 'Abd al-Khaliq from certain persons of our people from abu 'Ubaydah who has said the following:

"I was sixty years old and had no children. I went to perform *al-Hajj* then visited abu 'Abd Allah, *'Alayhi al-Salam,* and complained about not having any child. He (the Imam) asked, 'Has any child ever been born to you?' I replied, 'No, it has not happened.' He (the Imam) said, 'When you go to Iraq marry a woman and it does not matter if she is not Sawa'. I then asked, 'What is Sawa'?' He (the Imam) said, 'It is a woman who has certain degree of ugliness because such women give birth to more children and say this prayer. I hope Allah will grant you male and female children, 'O Lord, do not leave me one, lonely and afraid, so that my thoughts reduce my thanking You. O Lord, (I appeal before You to) grant me comfort, truthful male successors and female ones in whom I can seek tranquility against fear, comfort against loneliness and thank You for completion of bounties. O Magnanimous, O Great , O the One who grants (favors), grant me with every successor goodness until You take me as far as You will be pleased with me in truthful words, safe return of trust and keeping the promise.'"

H 10276, Ch. 4, h 9

Muhammad ibn Yahya has narrated from Ahmad ibn Muhammad from al-'Abbas ibn Ma'ruf from Ali ibn Mahziyar from Muhammad ibn Rashid who has said the following:

"Hisham ibn Ibrahim narrated to me that he complained before abu al-Hassan, *'Alayhi al-Salam,* about not having a child. He (the Imam) commanded him to raise his voice with Adhan in his house. He has said, 'I followed the instruction: then Allah removed my shortcoming and my children became many.' Muhammad ibn Rashid has said, 'I remained ill all the time as well as a group of my servants and family (wife), so I would remain alone at home without anyone to help. I heard it from Hisham, I then practiced it and Allah removed the illnesses from me and my family. All praise belongs to Allah.'"

H 10277, Ch. 4, h 10

Ahmad ibn Muhammad al-'Asemiy has narrated from Ali ibn al-Hassan al-Taymuliy from 'Amr ibn 'Uthman from abu Jamilah who has said the following:

"Once, a man from Khurasan in al-Rabadhah said to abu 'Abd Allah, *'Alayhi al-Salam,* 'I pray to Allah to keep my soul in service for your cause, I have not been granted any children.' He (the Imam) said, 'When you return to your country and then decide to go to bed with your wife then read, 'When the companion of fish went away in anger he thought that We will not apply any measures against him. He then in the dark called, "I testify that no one other than You deserves worship. You are free of all defects. I have been of those who wrong themselves." Read up to three verses, you will be granted a child by the will of Allah.'"

H 10278, Ch. 4, h 11

A number of our people have narrated from Sahl ibn Ziyad from Musa ibn Ja'far from 'Amr ibn Sa'id from Muhammad ibn 'Umar ['Amr] who has said the following:

"I never had a child . I went to Makkah and did not have any children. A man met me and gave good news of the birth of a boy to me. I then went on and visited Ali ibn al-Husayn, *'Alayhi al-Salam.* When I went before him (the Imam), he (the Imam) asked, 'How are you and how is your son?' I said, 'I pray to Allah to keep my soul in service for your cause, I left home but I did not have a son. My neighbor met me and said, "A boy is born to you ."' He (the Imam) smiled and asked, 'Have you given him a name?' I replied, 'No, I have not given him a name.' He (the Imam) said, 'Name him Ali; whenever a delay would take place in giving birth of any of my father's girls he would ask her to keep her intention to name him Ali, then without much delay she would give birth to a boy.'"

H 10279, Ch. 4, h 12

Al-Husayn from Muhammad has narrated from Mu'alla' ibn Muhammad from al-Hassan ibn Ali from Aban ibn 'Uthman from Hariz from Muhammad ibn Muslim who has said the following:

"Abu Ja'far, *'Alayhi al-Salam,* has said, 'When you want to have a son then at the time of your going to bed with your wife say, "O Lord, grant me a son, make him pious, without any deficiency or extra in his physical condition and make his consequences in goodness."'"

Chapter 5 - If When Pregnant one Keeps Her Intention to Name the Child Muhammad or Ali the Child will be a Boy: and the Prayer for it

H 10280, Ch. 5, h 1

Muhammad ibn Yahya has narrated from Ahmad ibn Muhammad ibn 'Isa from 'Abd al-Rahman ibn abu Najran from al-Husayn ibn Ahmad al-Minqariy from certain persons of our people who have said the following:

"Abu 'Abd Allah, *'Alayhi al-Salam,* has said, 'If the wife of one you is pregnant, during the fourth month ask her to face al-Qiblah (al-Ka'bah) and read verse 255 of Chapter two, then tap on her side and say, 'O Lord, I have named him Muhammad.' Allah will make him a boy. If he keeps the name as he had promised Allah grants him blessings but if he changes his mind about the name Allah will have the choice to decide to keep the child alive or take him back.'"

H 10281, Ch. 5, h 2

It is narrated from the narrator of the previous *Hadith* from Muhammad ibn Ali from Ali ibn al-Hakam from al-Husayn ibn Sa'id who has said the following:

"Once ibn Ghaylan al-Mada'iniy and I visited abu al-Hassan, al-Rida', *'Alayhi al-Salam,* and ibn Ghaylan said to him (the Imam), 'I pray to Allah to keep you well, I have been informed that if one's wife is pregnant and he keeps his intention to name him Muhammad a son then is born to him.' He (the Imam) said, 'If one's wife is pregnant and he keeps in his intention to name him Ali, (in this case also) a son will born to him.' He (the Imam) then said, 'Ali and Muhammad is one thing.' He then said, 'I pray to Allah to keep you well, I left my wife pregnant, please pray to Allah to make him a boy.' He (the Imam) bent down his head for a long time; then raised his head and said, 'Name him Ali because it is good for his long life.' We then entered Makkah and a letter came from al-Mada'in saying, "A boy is born to him."'"

H 10282, Ch. 5, h 3

Ali ibn Ibrahim has narrated from his father from 'Isma'il ibn Marrar from Yunus from Ishaq ibn 'Ammar who has said the following:

"Abu 'Abd Allah, *'Alayhi al-Salam,* has said, 'Anyone whose wife is pregnant and he keeps in his intention to name him Muhammad, the child will be a boy by the will of Allah.' He (the Imam) said, 'There are three and all of them are Muhammad, Muhammad, Muhammad.' Abu 'Abd Allah, *'Alayhi al-Salam,* in another *Hadith* has said, 'He should hold her hand and turn her to al-Qiblah (al-Ka'bah) during the fourth month and say, "O Lord, I have named him Muhammad." A boy will be born to him but if he changes his name he will be taken away from him.'"

H 10283, Ch. 5, h 4

A number of our people have narrated from Sahl ibn Ziyad from certain persons of our people in a *marfu'* manner who has said the following:

"The Messenger of Allah, *O Allah, grant compensation to Muhammad and his family worthy of their services to Your cause,* has said, 'If one's wife is pregnant and he keeps in his intention to name him Muhammad or Ali, a boy will be born to him.'"

Chapter 6 - Beginning of the Creation of a Human Being and His Turning in His Mother's Womb

H 10284, Ch. 6, h 1

Muhammad ibn Yahya has narrated from Ahmad ibn Muhammad and Ali ibn Ibrahim has narrated from his father from all from al-Hassan ibn Mahbub from Muhammad ibn al-Nu'man from Salam ibn al-Mustanir who has said the following:

"I once asked abu Ja'far, *'Alayhi al-Salam,* about the words of Allah, most Majestic, most Glorious, '. . . created and not created . . .' (22:5) He (the Imam) said, 'Created are those whom Allah created in the back of Adam, *'Alayhi al-Salam.* He made them to promise and make a covenant. Then He allowed them to move through the backs of men and wombs of women. They are the ones who come out in the world so that they are asked about the covenant. His words 'not created' refer to every strand or trace that Allah did not create in the back of Adam, *'Alayhi al-Salam* when He created the particles and made them to form the covenant. They were the seeds that were not allowed to take place in the womb or were aborted before the spirit was blown in them as well as life and continued life.'"

H 10285, Ch. 6, h 2

It is narrated from the narrator of the previous *Hadith* from Ahmad ibn Muhammad from al-Husayn ibn Sa'id from Hammad ibn 'Isa from Hariz from those whom he has mentioned who has said the following:

"I once asked one of the two Imam, (abu Ja'far or abu 'Abd Allah), *'Alayhim al-Salam,* about the words of Allah, most Majestic, most Glorious, 'He knows what every female bears and what the wombs decrease (spoil) and what they increase (dispose).' (13:8) He (the Imam) said, 'Decrease' is every pregnancy before nine months and 'increase' is what is more than nine months. Whenever a woman experiences pure blood discharge during her pregnancy a similar number of days are increased in the length of her pregnancy.'"

H 10286, Ch. 6, h 3

Muhammad ibn Yahya has narrated from Ahmad ibn Muhammad from ibn Faddal from al-Hassan ibn al-Jahm who has said the following:

"Abu Ja'far, *'Alayhi al-Salam,* has said, 'Sperm in the womb after forty days becomes a clot and after forty days thereafter it becomes an embryo. When four months are complete Allah sends two creating angels and they ask, "O Lord, what do You want to create? Do You want to create a male or a female." They then receive the command. Thereafter they ask, "O Lord, do You want him to be virtuous or a wicked one?" They then receive the command. They ask, "O Lord, how much is the length of his life, how much is his sustenance, everything of his condition and the number of such things?" They write the covenant between his eyes. When the time of pregnancy is complete, Allah sends an angel who scolds him harshly. He comes out but has already forgotten the covenant.' Al-Hassan ibn al-Jahm has said, that I then asked him (the Imam), 'Will Allah because of prayer change female to a male and a male into a female?' He (the Imam) said,

11

'Allah can do whatever He wants.'"

H 10287, Ch. 6, h 4

Muhammad ibn Yahya has narrated from Ahmad ibn Muhammad and Ali ibn Ibrahim has narrated from his father all from ibn Mahbub from ibn Ri'ab from Zurarah who has said the following:

"Abu Ja'far, *'Alayhi al-Salam,* has said, 'When Allah, most Majestic, most Glorious, wants to create the seed which has formed the covenant when taken from the back of Adam or what appears to Him, (due to *al-Bada'*) He places it in the womb and moves the man to go to bed with the woman (his wife). He inspires the womb to open its door so that His creature can enter in it and His authoritative determination and measure. The womb opens its door and the seed reaches the womb, then turns back and forth for forty days, then it becomes a clot, then an embryo in forty days, then a piece of flesh in which veins spread like a net. Then Allah sends two creative angels in the womb who make in the womb as Allah wills. They enter inside the woman through her mouth until they reach her womb. In it (the seed) is the old spirit transferred from the backs of men to the wombs of women, then they blow in it the spirit of life and continued life and carve for him ears, eyes, all of his parts and all the inside by the permission of Allah. Then Allah sends revelation to the two angels that says, 'Write upon him My authoritative command of determination and measures and stipulate for me a change of plan (al-bada') in what you write.' They then ask, 'What must we write, O Lord?' Allah then reveals to them to raise their heads to the head of his mother.' They then raise their heads and find a tablet knocking [informing] from the forehead of his mother. They look at it and find in it his shape, fashion, duration of his life, his covenant of being a virtuous or a wicked one and all of his characteristics.' He (the Imam) then said, 'One of them dictates, the other writes all that is in the tablet and stipulates the condition of change of plan (al-bada'). They seal the book and place it between his two eyes, then they make him stand up in the belly of his mother.' He (the Imam) said, 'He perhaps turns insolent and changes and this only happens with insolent and disobedient ones. When it is time for his coming out Allah, most Majestic, most Glorious, inspires the womb to open its door so that His creature can come out to His earth so that His command is applied to him; it is time for him to come out.' He (the Imam) then said, 'The womb then opens the door of the child and Allah sends an angel called a reprimanding one, who reprimands him and it makes him feel shocked. His head turns downward and his feet upward thus Allah makes it easy for the child to come out as well as for the woman.' He (the Imam) then said, 'When he stops the angel reproaches him again which gives him a shock again. He then falls on the ground crying and upset because of the reproach.'"

H 10288, Ch. 6, h 5

Muhammad ibn Yahya has narrated from Ahmad ibn Muhammad from al-Husayn ibn Sa'id from Muhammad ibn al-Fudayl from abu Hamzah who has said the following:

"I once asked abu Ja'far, *'Alayhi al-Salam,* about the creation. He (the Imam) said, 'When Allah, most Blessed, most High, created the creation from clay He poured them as arrows are poured, took out the Muslim ones, made him fortunate and made the unbeliever wicked ones. When the seed falls angels receive it and give it its shape then they ask, 'O Lord, do You want it to be a male or female? ' The Lord, most Majestic, most Glorious, then says whatever He wants.' The two then say, 'Blessed is Allah the best Creator.' It then is placed inside her and it moves back and forth for nine days in every vein and joint. Inside from her to the womb there are three locks. One lock is for the upper side parallel to the bellybutton from the right side, the other lock is from the midsection and another lock is lower in the womb. After nine days, it is placed in the upper lock where it remains for three months and at this time, the woman experiences disgust and nausea. Thereafter it comes down to the middle lock and remains there for three months. The bellybutton of the child connects to a group of veins and all of the veins of the woman from which food enters as well as drinks by the way of these groups of veins. Then the child descends down to the third lock where the child remains for another three months and this completes nine months. The woman then undergoes childlabor and with every pain a vein of the veins disconnect from the bellybutton of the child. When pain starts his hand rests on his bellybutton and he falls on the ground with his hands spread and thereafter his sustenance is by the way of his mouth.'"

H 10289, Ch. 6, h 6

Muhammad ibn Yahya has narrated from Ahmad ibn Muhammad from Muhammad ibn al-Husayn from Muhammad ibn 'Isma'il or others who has said the following:

"I once asked abu Ja'far, *'Alayhi al-Salam,* saying, 'I pray to Allah to keep my soul in service for your cause, can a pregnant woman pray to Allah to make the child inside her a well formed boy?' He (the Imam) said, 'She can do so from conception up to the fourth month. Up to forty nights it is sperm, for another forty nights it is a clot and for another forty nights it is an embryo, thereafter Allah sends two creative angles who ask, "O Lord, what must we create, a male or female, fortunate or unfortunate?" Their question is then answered. They then ask, "O Lord, what is his sustenance, when is the time of his death and what is the length of his life?" It all then is told to them and his covenant is between his eyes to which he looks. He still is inside his mother until the time of his coming out draws near. Allah, most Majestic, most Glorious, sends an angel who drives him out with reproach that sends him into shock and he forgets the covenant.'"

H 10290, Ch. 6, h 7

Muhammad ibn Yahya has narrated from Ahmad ibn Muhammad and Ali ibn Ibrahim has narrated from his father from ibn Mahbub from ibn Ri'ab from Zurarah ibn 'A'yan who has said the following:

"I once heard abu Ja'far, *'Alayhi al-Salam,* saying, 'When the seed falls in the womb it settles there for forty days, remains as a clot for forty days and as an embryo for another forty days. Allah then sends two creative angels with instruction to create him, as Allah wants it to be. It can be a male or a female. They shape him and write down the duration of his life, the time of his death, that he is a fortunate or unfortunate. The two must write down between his eyes the covenant of Allah, which He has taken from him in the condition of being particles. When the time for his coming out from the belly of his mother draws near; Allah sends an angel called admonisher who admonishes him that sends him into shock. He forgets the covenant and falls on the ground weeping

13

because of the admonition of the angel.'"

Chapter 7 - When a Woman Gives Birth to More than one Child

H 10291, Ch. 7, h 1

Muhammad ibn Yahya and others have narrated from Ahmad ibn Muhammad ibn 'Isa from Ahmad ibn Muhammad from ibn abu Nasr from `Isma'il ibn 'Umar from Shu'ayb al-'Aqarqufiy who has said the following:

"Abu 'Abd Allah, *'Alayhi al-Salam,* has said, 'The womb has four ways in whichever way the seed (water) finds the path thereof comes a child, one child, two children , three children or four children . In (through) one way only one child can come and no more.'"

H 10292, Ch. 7, h 2

Ali ibn Muhammad has narrated from in a *marfu'* manner from Muhammad ibn Humran who has said the following:

"Abu 'Abd Allah, *'Alayhi al-Salam,* has said, 'Allah has created four receptacles for the womb. Whatever is from the first is for the father, whatever is from the second is from the mother, whatever is from the third is from the paternal uncles and whatever is from the fourth is from the maternal uncles (in gender or shape).'"

Chapter 8 - Discipline to Follow During Childbirth

H 10293, Ch. 8, h 1

Muhammad ibn Yahya has narrated from 'Abd Allah ibn Muhammad from his father from 'Abd Allah ibn al-Mughirah from ibn Muskan from Jabir who has said the following:

"At the time of the birth of a child, Ali ibn al-Husayn, *'Alayhi al-Salam,* would say, 'Send all women out of the house; they must not be the first to look at the privacy [genitals].'"

Chapter 9 - Congratulation for Childbirth

H 10294, Ch. 9, h 1

A number of our people have narrated from Ahmad ibn Muhammad from ibn Khalid from his father from Muhammad ibn Sinan from al-Husayn from Murazim from his brother who has said the following:

"A man once said to abu 'Abd Allah, *'Alayhi al-Salam,* 'A boy is born to me.' He (the Imam) said, 'May Allah enable you to thank the Benefactor, bless you with the gift and make him to grow up to manhood! May Allah grant you the chance to enjoy his virtuous deeds!'"

H 10295, Ch. 9, h 2

Ali ibn Muhammad ibn Bandar has narrated from Ibrahim ibn Ishaq al-Ahmar from 'Abd Allah ibn Hammad from abu Maryam al-Ansariy from abu Barzah al-Aslamiy who has said the following:

"A child was born to al-Husayn ibn Ali, *'Alayhi al-Salam,* and Quraysh came to congratulate him (the Imam) and said, 'Congratulations to you for the birth of the rider (the knight).' He (the Imam) said, 'What kind of expression is this!

Say, "May Allah enable you to thank the Benefactor for the blessed gift, may Allah make him to grow up to manhood and may Allah give you the chance to enjoy his good deeds!'"

H 10296, Ch. 9, h 3

A number of our people have narrated from Ahmad ibn Muhammad from Bakr ibn Salih from those whom he has mentioned who has said the following:

"Once a man congratulated another man saying, 'Congratulation for the birth of the rider (the knight).' Al-Hassan, *'Alayhi al-Salam,* said, 'How would you know if he will be a rider or walking on foot?' He asked, 'I pray to Allah to keep my soul in service for your cause, what I should say?' He (the Imam) said, 'Say, "May Allah enable you to thank the Benefactor. May the gift be a blessing for you and may Allah make him to grow up to manhood! May Allah give you the chance to enjoy his good deeds."'"

Chapter 10 - Names and Titles

H 10297, Ch. 10, h 1

A number of our people have narrated from Ahmad ibn Muhammad ibn 'Isa from ibn Faddal from abu Ishaq, Tha'labah ibn Maymun from a man whom he has mentioned who has said the following:

"Abu Ja'far, *'Alayhi al-Salam,* has said, 'The truest name is that which expresses one's slavery to (Allah) and the best of them are names of the Prophets.'"

H 10298, Ch. 10, h 2

A number of our people have narrated from Ahmad ibn Muhammad from al-Qasim ibn Yahya from his grandfather al-Hassan ibn Rashid from abu Basir who has said the following:

"Abu 'Abd Allah, *'Alayhi al-Salam,* has said, 'My father narrated to me from my grandfather that `Amir al-Mu'minin has said, 'Name your children before they are born: and if you do not know they are male or female, then name them with such names that are good for both male and female. In case a child is miscarried, when that child will meet you on the Day of Judgment, whom you had not given a name, it will say to his father, 'I wish you had named me.' The Messenger of Allah had named Muhsin before his birth.'"*

H 10299, Ch. 10, h 3

A number of our people have narrated from Ahmad ibn Muhammad from ibn Khalid from Muhammad ibn Ali from Muhammad ibn al-Fudayl from Musa ibn Bakr who has said the following:

"The first good thing that a father can do to his children is to give them good names. You must find a good name for (each of) your children.'"

H 10300, Ch. 10, h 4

Ahmad ibn Muhammad has narrated from certain persons of our people from those whom he has mentioned who have said the following:

"Abu 'Abd Allah, *'Alayhi al-Salam,* has said, 'We name every child born to us Muhammad and after seven days if we like we change or keep the same name.'"

H 10301, Ch. 10, h 5

Muhammad ibn Yahya has narrated from Ahmad ibn Muhammad from Ali ibn al-Hakam from ibn Mayyah from Fulan ibn Hamid ibn Hamid who has said the following:

"I asked abu 'Abd Allah, *'Alayhi al-Salam,* for advice about the name of my child and he (the Imam) said, 'Name him with the names that express slavery (to Allah).' He then asked, 'Which ones are they?' He (the Imam) said, "'Abd al-Rahman.'"

H 10302, Ch. 10, h 6
Al-Husayn ibn Muhammad has narrated from Mu'alla' ibn Muhammad from Sulayman ibn Sama'ah from his uncle 'Asem al-Kuziy who has said the following:

"Abu 'Abd Allah, *'Alayhi al-Salam,* has said that the Messenger of Allah, *O Allah, grant compensation to Muhammad and his family worthy of their services to Your cause,* has said, 'If four sons are born to someone and he does not name even one of them with my name he has done injustice to me.'"

H 10303, Ch. 10, h 7
Muhammad ibn Yahya has narrated from Ahmad ibn Muhammad formal-Barqiy from 'Abd al-Rahman ibn Muhammad al-'Arzamiy who has said the following:

"Mu'awiyah appointed Marwan ibn al-Hakam as his agent in al-Madinah and ordered him to pay a certain salary to the young people of Quraysh which he did. Ali ibn al-Husayn, *'Alayhim al-Salam,* has said, 'I went to him and he asked, 'What is your name?' I replied, 'It is Ali ibn al-Husayn.' He then asked, 'What is the name of your brother?' I replied, 'It is Ali.' He said, 'Ali and Ali. Is it that your father does not want to leave any of his children without naming them all Ali?' He paid me a certain amount. I returned to my father and informed him of what had happened. He (the Imam) said, 'Woe is upon the son of al-Zarqa', the leather- treating man. Even if one hundred sons will be born to me I will not give anyone of them any other name except Ali.'"

H 10304, Ch. 10, h 8
A number of our people have narrated from Ahmad ibn Muhammad from Bakr ibn Salih from Sulayman al-Ja'fariy who has said the following:

"I once heard abu al-Hassan, *'Alayhi al-Salam,* saying, 'Poverty does not enter a house wherein a person's name is Muhammad or Ahmad or Ali or al-Hassan or al-Husayn or Ja'far or Talib or 'Abd Allah or Fatimah of the women.'"

H 10305, Ch. 10, h 9
Ali ibn Ibrahim has narrated from his father from Ja'far ibn Muhammad al-Ash'ariy from ibn al-Qaddah who has said the following:

"Abu 'Abd Allah, *'Alayhi al-Salam,* has said that once a man came to the Holy Prophet, *O Allah, grant compensation to Muhammad and his family worthy of their services to Your cause,* and said, 'O Messenger of Allah, a son is born to me. What must I name him?' He (the Messenger of Allah) said, 'Name him with the name which is most beloved to Hamzah.'"

H 10306, Ch. 10, h 10
Ali ibn Ibrahim has narrated from his father from 'Abd Allah ibn al-Husayn ibn Zayd ibn Ali ibn al-Husayn from his father who has said the following:

"This is a narration of abu 'Abd Allah, *'Alayhi al-Salam,* from the Messenger of Allah, *O Allah, grant compensation to Muhammad and his family worthy of their services to Your cause.* He (the Messenger of Allah) has said, 'You should give yourselves good names; on the Day of Judgment you will be called with your names: O so and so son of so and so, stand up to your light and stand up, O so and so son of so and so, you have no light.'"

H 10307, Ch. 10, h 11

Ali ibn Ibrahim has narrated from his father from Salih al-Sindiy from Ja'far ibn Bashir from Sa'id ibn Khuthaym from Mu'ammar ibn Khuthaym who has said the following:

"Abu Ja'far, *'Alayhi al-Salam,* once asked me, 'What is your *Kunyah* (father of so and so or son of so and so)?' I replied, 'I have no *Kunyah* yet; I have no son or wife or daughter.' He (the Imam) asked, 'What keeps you from having one?' I replied, 'It is a *Hadith* which is narrated from Ali, *'Alayhi al-Salam.*' He (the Imam) asked, 'What is it?' I replied, 'Ali, *'Alayhi al-Salam,* has said, "If one adopts a *Kunyah* and he does not have a wife he then is father of *al-Ja'r* (dried up dung).'" Abu Ja'far, *'Alayhi al-Salam,* then said that it is forged and it is not of *Hadith* of Ali, *'Alayhi al-Salam.* We give *Kunyah* to our children in their childhood for fear of bad names being ascribed to them.'"

H 10308, Ch. 10, h 12

Al-Husayn ibn Muhammad has narrated from Mu'alla' ibn Muhammad from Muhammad ibn Muslim from al-Husayn ibn Nasr from his father from 'Amr ibn Shamir from Jabir who has said the following:

"Abu Ja'far, *'Alayhi al-Salam,* once wanted to visit one of his followers because he was ill. He (the Imam) told me to follow him and I followed him (the Imam). When he (the Imam) arrived at his door his small son came out and abu Ja'far, *'Alayhi al-Salam,* asked, 'What is your name?' He replied, 'It is Muhammad.' He (the Imam) asked, 'What is your *Kunyah*?' He replied, 'It is Ali.' Abu Ja'far, *'Alayhi al-Salam,* then said, 'You have fortified yourself against Satan very intensely. When Satan hears someone calling O Muhammad, O Ali, Satan melts like lead until he hears someone calling with the names of our enemies; he becomes excited and swaggers.'"

H 10309, Ch. 10, h 13

A number of our people have narrated from Ahmad ibn Khalid from Muhammad ibn 'Isa from Safwan ibn in a *marfu'* manner who has said the following:

"Abu Ja'far, or abu 'Abd Allah, *'Alayhi al-Salam,* has stated this *Hadith.* 'This is 'Muhammad' (the Messenger of Allah) who has given them permission to name themselves with his name. However, who has given them permission to name themselves 'Yasin' which is the name of the Holy Prophet, *O Allah, grant compensation to Muhammad and his family worthy of their services to Your cause*)?'"

H 10310, Ch. 10, h 14

Ali ibn Ibrahim has narrated from his father from ibn abu 'Umayr from Hammad ibn 'Uthaman who has said the following:

"Abu 'Abd Allah, *'Alayhi al-Salam,* has said that the Messenger of Allah asked for a sahifah (a book) and he (the Messenger of Allah) wanted to prohibit the use of certain names to use. He (the Messenger of Allah) passed away but he (the Messenger of Allah) did not mention them. Of such names are al-Hakam and Hakim, Khalid and Malik. He (the Imam) said that such names are six or seven and it is not permissible to use them.'"

H 10311, Ch. 10, h 15
Ali ibn Ibrahim has narrated from his father from al-Nawfaliy from al-Sakuniy who has said the following:

"Abu 'Abd Allah, *'Alayhi al-Salam,* has said that the Messenger of Allah, *O Allah, grant compensation to Muhammad and his family worthy of their services to Your cause,* prohibited four *Kunyah* like abu 'Isa, abu al-Hakam, abu Malik, abu al-Qasim if the name is Muhammad.'"

H 10312, Ch. 10, h 16
Muhammad ibn Yahya has narrated from Muhammad ibn al-Husayn from Muhammad ibn 'Abd Allah ibn Hilal from al-'Ala' ibn Razin from Muhammad ibn Muslim who has said the following:

"Abu Ja'far, *'Alayhi al-Salam,* has said, 'The most hated names to Allah, most Majestic, most Glorious, are Harith, Malik and Khalid.'"

H 10313, Ch. 10, h 17
Muhammad ibn al-Husayn has narrated from Ja'far ibn Bashir from ibn Bukayr from Zurarah who has said the following:

"I once heard abu Ja'far, *'Alayhi al-Salam,* saying, 'A man would come to Ali ibn al-Husayn, *'Alayhi al-Salam,* and his *Kunyah* was abu Murrah. When asking for permission at the door he would say, 'This is abu Murrah at the door.' Ali ibn al-Husayn, *'Alayhi al-Salam,* said to him, 'I swear you to Allah that when you come to our door do not say, 'This is abu Murrah at the door (it is *Kunyah* of Satan).'"

Chapter 11 - Complete Creation

H 10314, Ch. 11, h 1
A number of our people have narrated from Ahmad ibn Muhammad ibn Khalid from certain persons of our people from Muhammad ibn Sinan from those whom he has mentioned who has said the following:

"Ali ibn al-Husayn, *'Alayhi al-Salam,* has said, 'When one receives the news of the birth of his child one must not ask, "Is it a boy or a girl?' One must ask, 'Is it of complete physical condition?' If the child is of complete physical condition one must say, 'All praise belongs to Allah who has not created from me a defective child.'"

Chapter 12 - Foods Preferable for a Pregnant or a Woman during Childbirth to Eat

H 10315, Ch. 12, h 1
Muhammad ibn Yahya has narrated from Salmah ibn al-Khattab from 'Uthman ibn 'Abd al-Rahman from Sharahbil ibn Muslim who has said the following:

"He (the Imam), *'Alayhi al-Salam,* has said, 'A pregnant woman should eat quince because the child grows up of fine smell and clear color.'"

H 10316, Ch. 12, h 2
Muhammad ibn Yahya has narrated from Ali ibn al-Hassan al-Taymuliy, from al-Husayn ibn Hashim from abu Ayyub al-Khazzaz from Muhammad ibn Muslim who has said the following:

"Abu 'Abd Allah, *'Alayhi al-Salam,* while looking at a beautiful boy said, 'It seems the father of this boy had been eating quince.'"

H 10317, Ch. 12, h 3
Muhammad ibn Yahya has narrated from Ahmad ibn Muhammad ibn 'Isa from 'Abd al-'Aziz ibn Hassan from Zurarah who has said the following:

"Abu 'Abd Allah, *'Alayhi al-Salam,* has said that `Amir al-Mu'minin, *'Alayhi al-Salam,* has said, 'The best of your dates are al-Barniy, feed them to your women during their childbirth; your children will grow up intelligent and forbearing.'"

H 10318, Ch. 12, h 4
A number of our people have narrated from Ahmad ibn Muhammad from ibn Khalid from A number of his people from Ali ibn Asbat from his uncle Ya'qub ibn Salim in a *marfu'* manner from `Amir al-Mu'minin, *'Alayhi al-Salam,* who has said the following:

"The Messenger of Allah, *O Allah, grant compensation to Muhammad and his family worthy of their services to Your cause,* has said, 'The first thing that women should eat is fresh dates; Allah, most High, said to Maryam, '. . . shake the twig of the palm tree; fresh dates will fall on you to be picked up.' (19:24) It then was asked, 'O Messenger of Allah, what happens if it is not the season of fresh dates?' He (the Messenger of Allah) said, 'If this is not available then it is seven pieces of dates of the dates of al-Madinah, and if that is not available then seven pieces of dates of the dates of other cities. Allah, most Majestic, most Glorious, says, "I swear by My majesty, Glory, greatness and the height of My place that if a woman during her childbirth eats fresh dates, her child, a boy or girl, will grow up forbearing and tolerant."'"

H 10319, Ch. 12, h 5
It is narrated from the narrator of the previous *Hadith* from Muhammad ibn Ali from abu Sa'id (walking faster like running slowly)'d al-Shamiy from Salih ibn 'Uqbah who has said the following:

"I once heard abu 'Abd Allah, *'Alayhi al-Salam,* saying, 'Feed your women with al-Barniy (dates) during their childbirth; your children will grow up forbearing.'"

H 10320, Ch. 12, h 6
Muhammad ibn Yahya has narrated from Muhammad ibn al-Husayn from Muhammad ibn Qabisah from 'Abd Allah al-Naysaburiy from Harun ibn Muslim from abu Musa from abu al-'Ala' al-Shamiy from Sufyan al-Thawriy from abu Ziyad from al-Hassan ibn Ali, *'Alayhi al-Salam,* who has said the following:

"The Messenger of Allah, *O Allah, grant compensation to Muhammad and his family worthy of their services to Your cause,* has said, 'Feed your women, during their pregnancy, frankincense; if a child receives frankincense for nourishment in the mother's womb it strengthens the heart of the child and increases the reasoning power of the child. If the child is a male he grows up brave and if the child is female her posterior will grow large which is favorable to her husband.'"

H 10321, Ch. 12, h 7
A number of our people have narrated from Sahl ibn Ziyad from Muhammad ibn Ali from Muhammad ibn Sinan who has said the following:

"Al-Rida', *'Alayhi al-Salam,* has stated this *Hadith.* 'You should feed male frankincense to your pregnant women; if the child in her womb is a male he will grow up of intelligent heart, learned and brave; and if the child is female she will grow up of good moral behavior (beautiful) and of large posterior which will be favorable to her husband.'"

Chapter 13 - Special Treatments for the Newborn

H 10322, Ch. 13, h 1
Muhammad ibn Yahya has narrated from Ahmad ibn Muhammad from ibn Faddal from abu `Isma`il al-Sayqal from abu Yahya al-Raziy who has said the following:

"Abu 'Abd Allah, *'Alayhi al-Salam,* once asked, 'When a child is born what do you do for the child?' I replied, 'I do not know what we should do.' He (the Imam) said, 'Take *Jawshir* [Persian Arabicized word for cow milk] of the size of a lentil and warm it up with water then drop it in the nostrils of the child; two drops in the right and one drop in the left; say Adhan in the right ear and Iqamah in the left ear. You should do it before cutting off the umbilical cord. This protects the child against shock and seizure.'"

H 10323, Ch. 13, h 2
Al-Husayn from Muhammad has narrated from Mu'alla' ibn Muhammad from al-Hassan ibn Ali from Aban from Hafs al-Kunasiy who has said the following:

"Abu 'Abd Allah, *'Alayhi al-Salam,* has said, 'Instruct the doctor or someone involved to say *Salat* (prayer) in the right ear of the child to protect the child against the effect of insanity or the Jinn that follows human beings.'"

H 10324, Ch. 13, h 3
Ali ibn Ibrahim has narrated from his father from `Isma`il ibn Marrar from Yunus from certain persons of his people who have said the following:

"Abu Ja'far, *'Alayhi al-Salam,* has said, 'Drops of water from Euphrates or water from the sky should be dropped in the newborn's mouth and Iqamah should be said in his ear.'"

H 10325, Ch. 13, h 4
In another *Hadith* it is said, 'You should drop water from Euphrates and soil from the grave of al-Husayn, *'Alayhi al-Salam,* or water from the sky in the mouth of your newborn ones.'"

H 10326, Ch. 13, h 5
A number of our people have narrated from Ahmad ibn Muhammad from al-Qasim ibn Yahya from his grandfather al-Hassan ibn Rashid from abu Basir who has said the following:

"Abu 'Abd Allah, *'Alayhi al-Salam,* has said that `Amir al-Mu'minin, *'Alayhi al-Salam,* has said, 'Feed your newborn children dates because the Holy Prophet, *O Allah, grant compensation to Muhammad and his family worthy of their services to Your cause,* did so with al-Hassan and al-Husayn, *'Alayhim al-Salam.'*"

H 10327, Ch. 13, h 6
Ali ibn Ibrahim has narrated from his father from al-Nawfaliy from al-Sakuniy who has said the following:

"Abu 'Abd Allah, *'Alayhi al-Salam*, has stated this *Hadith*. 'The Messenger of Allah, *O Allah, grant compensation to Muhammad and his family worthy of their services to Your cause*, has said, 'One must say Adhan for *Salat* (prayer) in the right ear of a newborn child and Iqamah in the left ear to protect the child from Satan, condemned to be stoned.'"

Chapter 14 - Al-'Aqiqah and its Being Obligatory

H 10328, Ch. 14, h 1
Muhammad ibn Yahya has narrated from Ahmad ibn Muhammad from Ali ibn al-Hakam from Ali ibn abu Hamzah from the virtuous servant (of Allah), *'Alayhi al-Salam*, who has said the following:
"He (the virtuous servant of Allah, the Imam), *'Alayhi al-Salam*, has said, ''*Aqiqah* is obligatory when a child is born to one, and if he likes to give him a name on that day he can do so.'"

H 10329, Ch. 14, h 2
Al-Husayn from Muhammad has narrated from Mu'alla' ibn Muhammad and Muhammad ibn Yahya has narrated from Ahmad ibn Muhammad all from al-Washsha' from Ahmad ibn 'A'idh from abu Khadijah who has said the following:
"Abu 'Abd Allah, *'Alayhi al-Salam*, has said, 'Every newborn child is safeguarded with *'Aqiqah*.'"

H 10330, Ch. 14, h 3
Muhammad ibn Yahya has narrated from Muhammad ibn al-Husayn from Musa ibn Sa'dan from 'Abd Allah ibn al-Qasim from 'Abd Allah ibn Sinan from 'Umar ibn Yazid who has said the following:
"I once said to abu 'Abd Allah, *'Alayhi al-Salam*, 'I by Allah do not know if my father had made *'Aqiqah* for me or not.' He (the narrator) has said, 'Abu 'Abd Allah, *'Alayhi al-Salam*, commanded me and I made *'Aqiqah* for myself when I was an old man.' 'Umar has said, 'I heard abu 'Abd Allah, *'Alayhi al-Salam*, saying, "Every man is safeguarded with his *'Aqiqah* and *'Aqiqah* is more urgently needed than *Adhiyah* (sacrifice animal)."'"

H 10331, Ch. 14, h 4
Muhammad ibn Yahya has narrated from Muhammad ibn Ahmad from Ahmad ibn al-Hassan from 'Amr ibn Sa'id from Musaddiq ibn Sadaqah from 'Ammar ibn Musa al-Sabatiy who has said the following:
"Abu 'Abd Allah, *'Alayhi al-Salam*, has said, 'Every newborn is safeguarded with *'Aqiqah*.'"

H 10332, Ch. 14, h 5
Ali ibn Ibrahim has narrated from his father from 'Isma'il ibn Marrar from Yunus from abu Basir who has said the following:
"I once asked abu 'Abd Allah, *'Alayhi al-Salam*, about *'Aqiqah*: if it is obligatory or not. He (the Imam) said, 'Yes, it is obligatory.'"

H 10333, Ch. 14, h 6
Abu Ali al-Ash'ariy has narrated from Muhammad ibn 'Abd al-Jabbar from Safwan from 'Abd Allah ibn Bukayr who has said the following:
"Once I was with abu 'Abd Allah, *'Alayhi al-Salam*, when a messenger from his

uncle came and said, 'Your uncle says, "We tried to find *'Aqiqah* but could not find one. Do you think our giving its price in charity is sufficient?"' He (the Imam) said, 'No, Allah loves feeding of food and slaughtering animals (to feeding the needy).'"

H 10334, Ch. 14, h 7
Ali ibn Ibrahim has narrated from his father from ibn abu 'Umayr from abu al-Mighra' from Ali who has said the following:
"Abu 'Abd Allah, *'Alayhi al-Salam,* has said, ' *'Aqiqah* is obligatory.'"

H 10335, Ch. 14, h 8
Ali has narrated from father from 'Isma'il ibn Marrar from Yunus and ibn abu 'Umayr all from abu Ayyub al-Khazzaz from Muhammad ibn Muslim who has said the following:
"Two sons at the same time were born to abu Ja'far, *'Alayhi al-Salam.* He (the Imam) instructed Zayd ibn Ali to buy two fat healthy sheep (or camels) for *'Aqiqah.* At that time prices were high. He bought one and buying another became difficult. He said to abu Ja'far, *'Alayhi al-Salam,* 'Buying another is difficult, so you should give its price in charity.' He (the Imam) said, 'I will not seek to find one until it becomes possible for you; Allah, most Majestic, most Glorious, loves slaughtering of animals to feed the needy.'"

H 10336, Ch. 14, h 9
Al-Husayn ibn Muhammad has narrated from Mu'alla' ibn Muhammad has narrated from Mu'alla' ibn Muhammad from al-Washsha' from 'Abd Allah ibn Sinan from Mu'adh al-farra' who has said the following:
"Abu 'Abd Allah, *'Alayhi al-Salam,* has said, 'The boy is safeguarded on the seventh day from his birth with giving him a name and slaughtering of a ram for *'Aqiqah.*' He (the Imam) then said, 'Fatimah *'Alayha al-Salam,* shaved (the heads) of her two sons and gave in charity of silver by the weight of their hair.'"

Chapter 15 - 'Aqiqah for Boys or Girls is the Same

H 10337, Ch. 15, h 1
A number of our people have narrated from Ahmad ibn Muhammad from ibn Khalid from 'Uthman ibn 'Isa from Sama'ah who has said the following:
"I once asked him (the Imam), *'Alayhi al-Salam,* about *'Aqiqah* and he (the Imam) said, 'It is the same for both male and female.'"

H 10338, Ch. 15, h 2
Abu Ali al-Ash'ariy has narrated from Muhammad 'Abd al-Jabbar and Muhammad ibn 'Isma'il has narrated from al-Fadl ibn Shadhan from all Safwan from Mansur ibn Hazim who has said the following:
"Abu 'Abd Allah, *'Alayhi al-Salam,* has said, ' *'Aqiqah* for boys and girls is the same.'"

H 10339, Ch. 15, h 3
Ali ibn Ibrahim has narrated from his father from 'Isma'il ibn Marrar Yunus from ibn Muskan who has said the following:
"I once asked abu 'Abd Allah, *'Alayhi al-Salam,* about *'Aqiqah* and he (the Imam) said, ' *'Aqiqah* for a boy and a girl is the same, one ram for this and one

ram for this.'"

H 10340, Ch. 15, h 4
A number of our people have narrated from Ahmad ibn Muhammad from al-Husayn ibn Sa'id from Hammad ibn Shu'ayb from abu Basir who has said the following:

"Abu 'Abd Allah, *'Alayhi al-Salam,* has said, ''*Aqiqah* for a boy or a girl is one ram.'"

Chapter 16 - 'Aqiqah is not Obligatory on One who Cannot Find

H 10341, Ch. 16, h 1
Ali ibn Muhammad has narrated from Salih ibn abu Hammad from Muhammad ibn abu Hamzah from Safwan from Ishaq ibn 'Ammar who has said the following:

"I once asked abu al-Hassan, *'Alayhi al-Salam,* about *'Aqiqah* for one who is affluent and one who is poor. He (the Imam) said, 'It is not necessary for one who cannot find anything.'"

H 10342, Ch. 16, h 2
Ali ibn Ibrahim has narrated from his father from 'Isma'il ibn Marrar from Yunus from Ishaq ibn 'Ammar who has said the following:

"I once asked abu Ibrahim, *'Alayhi al-Salam,* about *'Aqiqah* for one who is affluent and one who is poor. He (the Imam) said, 'It is not necessary for one who cannot find anything.'"

Chapter 17 - On the Seventh Day from Birth the Newborn's Head is Shaved and a Name is Given to Him

H 10343, Ch. 17, h 1
Humayd ibn Ziyad has narrated from ibn Sama'ah from ibn Jabalah and Ali ibn Muhammad has narrated from Salih ibn abu Hammad from 'Abd Allah ibn Jabalah from 'Abd Allah ibn Sinan who has said the following:

"Abu 'Abd Allah, *'Alayhi al-Salam,* has stated this *Hadith.* 'On the seventh day from birth offer *'Aqiqah,* shave the head of the child and give in charity an amount of silver equal to the weight of his hairs and cut the meat of *'Aqiqah* without breaking any bones, then cook the meat and invite a group of Muslims to be served.'"

H 10344, Ch. 17, h 2
It is narrated from the narrator of the previous *Hadith* from al-Hassan ibn Hammad ibn 'Udays from Ishaq ibn 'Ammar who has said the following:

"I once asked abu 'Abd Allah, *'Alayhi al-Salam,* 'What should we do first?' He (the Imam) said, 'First shave his head, then offer *'Aqiqah* and give in charity of silver equal to the weight of his hairs. All of this should be done in one place.'"

H 10345, Ch. 17, h 3
Ali ibn Ibrahim has narrated from his father from 'Isma'il ibn Marrar from Yunus from abu Basir who has said the following:

"I once asked abu 'Abd Allah, *'Alayhi al-Salam,* about *'Aqiqah*: if it is obligatory. He (the Imam) said, 'Yes, *'Aqiqah* must be offered for him, his head is shaved when he is seven days old and his hairs are weighed with silver or gold to be given in charity. One-fourth of the sheep is served to *al-Qabilah* (the special nurse, doctor). The animal for *'Aqiqah* should be a sheep or Badanah (camel of a certain age).'"

(*Al-Qabilah* according to hadith number three, chapter ninety-three is a nurse who helps a woman to give birth and also thereafter not the one who helps one to give birth only and then moves away.)

H 10346, Ch. 17, h 4

It is narrated from the narrator of the previous *Hadith* from a man from abu Ja'far, *'Alayhi al-Salam*, who has said the following:

"When it is the seventh day of childbirth in your home, a boy or a girl you must offer an *'Aqiqah* in the form of slaughtering a ram for a boy and an ewe for a girl. When you offer an *'Aqiqah* for him, feed *al-Qabilah* (the special nurse, doctor) thereof. You can give the child a name on the seventh day.'"

H 10347, Ch. 17, h 5

Al-Husayn from Muhammad has narrated from Mu'alla' ibn Muhammad from al-Hassan ibn Ali from Aban from Hafs al-Kunasiy who has said the following:

"Abu 'Abd Allah, *'Alayhi al-Salam*, has said, 'When a child is born, *'Aqiqah* must be offered for him, his head should be shaved and equal to the weight of his hairs leaf (of silver) should be given in charity. The leg and hip of the animal slaughtered for *'Aqiqah* should be given to *al-Qabilah* (the special nurse, doctor). A group of Muslims should be invited to be served with meat of *'Aqiqah* and the boy should be given a name.'"

H 10348, Ch. 17, h 6

A number of our people have narrated from Ahmad ibn Muhammad from ibn Khalid and Ali ibn Ibrahim has narrated from his father from 'Uthman ibn 'Isa from Sama'ah who has said the following:

"Abu 'Abd Allah, *'Alayhi al-Salam*, has said, 'For a child *'Aqiqah* must be offered, his head is shaved on the seventh day and equal to the weight of his hairs silver or gold should be given in charity. One leg and hip of the animal slaughtered for *'Aqiqah* should be given to *al-Qabilah* (the special nurse, doctor). The animal accepted as *'Aqiqah* can be a badanah (camel) or a sheep.'"

H 10349, Ch. 17, h 7

A number of our people have narrated from Ahmad ibn Muhammad from Ali ibn al-Hakam from Ali ibn abu Hamzah from abu Basir who has said the following:

"Abu 'Abd Allah, *'Alayhi al-Salam*, has said, 'If a boy or a girl is born to you, on the seventh day offer an *'Aqiqah*, a sheep or a camel and eat of its meat, feed others and give him a name. Shave his head on the seventh day and equal to the weight of his hairs give silver or gold in charity. You should give to the doctor something thereof. Whatever of these (sheep or camel, silver or gold) you did is sufficient.'"

H 10350, Ch. 17, h 8

Muhammad ibn Yahya has narrated from Ahmad ibn Muhammad from Muhammad ibn 'Isma'il and al-Husayn ibn Sa'id all from Muhammad ibn al-Fudayl from abu al-Sabbah al-Kinaniy who has said the following:

"I once asked abu 'Abd Allah, *'Alayhi al-Salam,* about the newborn child: when to offer *'Aqiqah,* shave his head, give in charity equal to the weight of his hair and give him a name.' He (the Imam) said, 'All of such things can be done on the seventh day from his birth.'"

H 10351, Ch. 17, h 9

Muhammad ibn Yahya has narrated from Ahmad ibn Muhammad from Ahmad ibn al-Hassan ibn Ali from 'Abd Allah ibn 'Amir ibn Sa'id from Musaddiq ibn Sadaqah from 'Ammar ibn Musa who has said the following:

"I once asked abu 'Abd Allah, *'Alayhi al-Salam,* about *'Aqiqah* and a newborn. He (the Imam) has stated this *Hadith.* 'When a child is seven days old a name with which Allah, most Majestic, most Glorious, has named him must be given to him, then his head must be shaved and equal to the weight of his hairs gold or silver should be given in charity. A ram should be slaughtered, and if a ram is not available then whatever is sufficient for an animal offering during *al-Hajj* is sufficient for *'Aqiqah.* If this is not available then a lamb of the same year is sufficient. *Al-Qabilah* (the special nurse, doctor) should be given one-fourth of the meat thereof. If there is no *al-Qabilah* then it is up to the mother to whomever she wants to give and ten Muslims should be fed. If there are more than ten it is better. *'Aqiqah* is obligatory if one is affluent or even if one is poor; he must do so when he is able to manage; and if *'Aqiqah* is not done for one until he offers an offering animal during *al-Hajj,* it then is sufficient for *'Aqiqah.'* He (the Imam) then said, 'If *al-Qabilah* (the special nurse, doctor) is a Jewish woman who does not eat meat of the animal slaughtered by Muslims then one-fourth of the price of the animal for *'Aqiqah* should be given to her.'"

H 10352, Ch. 17, h 10

Abu Ali al-Ash'ariy has narrated from Muhammad ibn 'Abd al-Jabbar from Safwan from abu Basir who has said the following:

"About a newborn abu 'Abd Allah, *'Alayhi al-Salam,* has stated this *Hadith.* 'The child must be given a name on the seventh day, *'Aqiqah* must be offered, his head shaved, silver equal to the weight of his hairs should be given in charity, one leg and hip should be sent to *al-Qabilah* (the special nurse, doctor), and the rest of the meat should be used for food and as charity.'"

H 10353, Ch. 17, h 11

A number of our people have narrated from Ahmad ibn Muhammad from ibn Khalid from his father from Zakariya ibn Adam from al-Kahiliy who has said the following:

"Abu 'Abd Allah, *'Alayhi al-Salam,* has said, 'On the seventh day from the birth of a child *'Aqiqah* must be offered. One leg and hip of the animal offered as *'Aqiqah* should be given to *al-Qabilah* (the special nurse, doctor) and the bones should not be broken.'"

H 10354, Ch. 17, h 12

Al-Husayn from Muhammad has narrated from Mu'alla' ibn Muhammad from al-Washsha' from Aban from Hafs al-Kunasiy who has said the following:

"Abu 'Abd Allah, *'Alayhi al-Salam,* has stated this *Hadith.* 'When *'Aqiqah* is offered for a child, his head is shaved, equal to the weight of his hair charity is given, one leg and hip is given to *al-Qabilah* (the special nurse, doctor), Muslims should be invited and when they are served they should pray for the boy. A name can be given to the child on the seventh day of his birth.'"

Chapter 18 - 'Aqiqah is not Equal to al-`Adhiyah (animal offered as sacrificial offering during al-Hajj) and it is Sufficient in Place of 'Aqiqah

H 10355, Ch. 18, h 1

Muhammad ibn Yahya has narrated from Ahmad ibn Muhammad from al-'Abbas ibn M'aruf from Safwan 'Abd al-Rahman ibn *al-Hajj*aj from Minhal al-Qammat who has said the following:

"Once I said to abu 'Abd Allah, *'Alayhi al-Salam,* that our people can find animals for *'Aqiqah* when Arabs are around. They can find ram but in other seasons such an animal is difficult to find and it is expensive for them. He (the Imam) said, 'It is only a sheep and it is not like the sacrificial offering for *al-Hajj.* Anything is sufficient for it.'"

H 10356, Ch. 18, h 2

Ali ibn Muhammad has narrated from Salih ibn abu Hammad from Muhammad ibn Ziyad from al-Kahiliy from Murazim who has said the following:

"Abu 'Abd Allah, *'Alayhi al-Salam,* has said, '*'Aqiqah* is not like the animal offering for *al-Hajj.* The fat one is better for *'Aqiqah.*'"

Chapter 19 - Words to Say on 'Aqiqah

H 10357, Ch. 19, h 1

Ali ibn Ibrahim has narrated from his father and Ali ibn Muhammad from Salih ibn abu Hammad all from ibn abu 'Umayr and Safwan from Ibrahim al-Karkhiy who has said the following:

"Abu 'Abd Allah, *'Alayhi al-Salam,* has said, 'When you offer *'Aqiqah* say, 'In the name of Allah and with Allah; it is an *'Aqiqah* for so and so. Its flesh is for his flesh, its blood for his blood and its bones for his bones. O Lord, make it a protection for Muhammad and family of Muhammad, *O Allah, grant compensation to Muhammad and his family worthy of their services to Your cause.*'"

H 10358, Ch. 19, h 2

Ali ibn Ibrahim has narrated from his father from 'Isma'il ibn Marrar from Yunus from certain persons of his people who have said the following:

"Abu Ja'far, *'Alayhi al-Salam,* has said, 'When you slaughter the animal for *'Aqiqah,* say, "In the name of Allah, with Allah, all praise belongs to Allah and Allah is greater than can be described. (It is) the expression of (our) belief in Allah, praise in favor of the Messenger of Allah, *O Allah, grant compensation to Muhammad and his family worthy of their services to Your cause,* keeping up with His command and an expression of thanks for His sustenance and due to the knowledge about His generosity to us, people of the family." If the newborn is a male then say, "O Lord, You have granted us a boy. You know best about your gift and the favor is from You. Please accept all that we do according to Your *Sunnah* and the *Sunnah* of Your prophet, *O Allah, grant compensation to Muhammad and his family worthy of their services to Your cause.* Drive away and repel Satan, the one condemned to be stoned, from us. Blood is shed for Your sake, there is no partner for You and all praise belongs to Allah, Lord of the worlds.""""

H 10359, Ch. 19, h 3
A number of our people have narrated from Sahl ibn Ziyad from certain persons of his people in a *marfu'* manner who has said the following:

"Abu 'Abd Allah, *'Alayhi al-Salam,* has instructed to say on *'Aqiqah* - he (the narrator) mentioned the prayer in *Hadith* number two above with this addition: 'O Lord, its flesh is for his flesh, its blood is for his blood, its bones for his bones, its hairs for his hairs and its skin is for his skin. O Lord, make it a protection for so and so son of so and so.'"

H 10360, Ch. 19, h 4
Muhammad ibn Yahya has narrated from Ahmad ibn Muhammad from Ahmad ibn al-Hassan from 'Amr in Sa'id from Musaddiq ibn Sadaqah from 'Ammar ibn Musa who has said the following:

"Abu 'Abd Allah, *'Alayhi al-Salam,* has said that when you decide to slaughter the animal for *'Aqiqah* say, 'O my people I denounce what you consider partners (of Allah). I turn my face to the One who has invented the skies and earth, purely in obedience to Him and I am not a pagan. My *Salat* (prayer), acts of worship, life and death are in obedience to the Lord of the worlds. Allah does not have any partners. This is what I am commanded to do and believe and I am the first to submit to the will of Allah. O Lord, (it is) from You, for You, in the name of Allah, Allah is great beyond description. O Lord, *O Allah, grant compensation to Muhammad and his family worthy of their services to Your cause,* and accept from so and so son of so and so ' – mention the name of the newborn then slaughter the offering for *'Aqiqah.*"

H 10361, Ch. 19, h 5
Muhammad ibn Yahya has narrated from Ahmad ibn Muhammad from Ali ibn Sulayman ibn Rashid from al-Hassan ibn Ali ibn Yaqtin from Muhammad ibn Hashim from Muhammad ibn Marid who has said the following:

"Abu 'Abd Allah, *'Alayhi al-Salam,* has said to say this when offering *'Aqiqah,* 'O Lord, it is from You and for You is what You have granted. O Lord, accept it from us on the *Sunnah* of Your prophet, *O Allah, grant compensation to Muhammad and his family worthy of their services to Your cause.* We seek refuge with Allah against Satan, condemned to be stoned.' Thereafter mention the name of the newborn , then slaughter the offering for *'Aqiqah* and say, 'For You I have spilled the blood and no one is Your partner. All praise belongs to Allah, Cherisher of the worlds. O Lord, drive away Satan, condemned to be stoned.'"

H 10362, Ch. 19, h 6

A number of our people have narrated from Ahmad ibn Muhammad from ibn Khalid from his father from Zakariya ibn Adam from al-Kahiliy who has said the following:

"Abu 'Abd Allah, *'Alayhi al-Salam,* has said that when you offer *'Aqiqah* say, 'I turn my face to the One who has invented the skies and earth, purely in obedience to Him and I am not a pagan. My *Salat* (prayer), acts of worship, life and death are all in obedience to Allah, Cherisher of the worlds who has no partner. O Lord, it is from You and for You. O Lord, this is from so and so son of so and so.'"

Chapter 20 - The Mother should not Eat from the Meat of 'Aqiqah

H 10363, Ch. 20, h 1

A number of our people have narrated from Ahmad ibn abu 'Abd Allah from his father from 'Abd Allah ibn al-Mughirah from ibn Muskan from those whom he has mentioned who has said the following:

"Abu 'Abd Allah, *'Alayhi al-Salam,* has said, 'The mother of the newborn should not eat from the meat of *'Aqiqah* but it is not harmful if she gives to the needy neighbor.'"

H 10364, Ch. 20, h 2

Al-Husayn from Muhammad has narrated from Mu'alla' ibn Muhammad and Muhammad ibn Yahya from Ahmad ibn Muhammad all from al-Washsha' from Ahmad ibn 'A'idh from abu Khadijah who has said the following:

"Abu 'Abd Allah, *'Alayhi al-Salam,* has said, 'He or any of his dependents should not eat from the meat of *'Aqiqah.* One-third of the meat is for *al-Qabilah* (the special nurse). If the special nurse is the mother of the father of the newborn or a family member, then there is nothing for such nurse. It should be made in parts, cooked and distributed. It should be given only to those who are of the people of *Walayah* (people who believe in the divine authority of *'A'immah*).' He (the Imam) said, 'Everyone can eat from the meat of *'Aqiqah* except the mother.'"

H 10365, Ch. 20, h 3

A number of our people have narrated from Ahmad ibn Muhammad from ibn Khalid from his father from Zakariya ibn Adam from al-Kahiliy who has said the following:

"Abu 'Abd Allah, *'Alayhi al-Salam,* has said, 'Mother of the newborn must not be fed anything from the meat of *'Aqiqah.'"*

Chapter 21 - The Messenger of Allah, O Allah, grant compensation to Muhammad and his family worthy of their services to Your cause, and Fatimah, 'Alayha al-Salam, Offered 'Aqiqah for al-Hassan and al-Husayn

H 10366, Ch. 21, h 1

Ali ibn Ibrahim has narrated from his father from 'Isma'il ibn Marrar from Yunus from certain persons of his people who have said the following:

"Abu 'Abd Allah, *'Alayhi al-Salam,* has said that the Messenger of Allah, *O Allah, grant compensation to Muhammad and his family worthy of their services to Your cause,* offered *'Aqiqah* for al-Hassan with his own hands and said, "In the name of Allah. It is an *'Aqiqah* for al-Hassan." He (the Messenger of Allah) also said, "O Lord, its bones are for his bones, its flesh for his flesh, its blood for his blood and its hairs for his hairs. O Lord, make it a protection for Muhammad and his family.""""

H 10367, Ch. 21, h 2
Muhammad ibn Yahya has narrated from Ahmad ibn Muhammad from Ali ibn al-Hakam from Mu'awiyah ibn Wahab who has said the following:

"Abu 'Abd Allah, *'Alayhi al-Salam,* has said that Fatimah, *'Alayha al-Salam,* offered *'Aqiqah* for her two sons, shaved their heads on the seventh day, and gave in charity equal to the weight of their hairs of leaf (silver or gold).' He (the Imam) has said that people would stain the head of the child with the blood of the animal for *'Aqiqah* and my father would say that it is a practice of pagans.'"

H 10368, Ch. 21, h 3
A number of our people have narrated from Ahmad ibn Muhammad from al-Husayn ibn Sa'id from Hammad ibn 'Isa from 'Asem al-Kuziy who has said the following:

"I once heard abu 'Abd Allah, *'Alayhi al-Salam,* narrating from his father that the Messenger of Allah, *O Allah, grant compensation to Muhammad and his family worthy of their services to Your cause,* offered *'Aqiqah* for al-Hassan, *'Alayhi al-Salam.* It was a ram and one ram for al-Husayn, *'Alayhi al-Salam.* He (the Messenger of Allah) gave something to *al-Qabilah* (the special nurse), shaved their heads on the seventh day, weighed their hairs and equal to its weight gave in charity.' He (the narrator) has said, 'I asked him (the Imam), 'Is blood taken to stain the head of the child?' He (the Imam) said, 'That is *shirk* (considering things partners of Allah), a practice of pagans.' I then said, 'Allah is free of all defects. Is it *shirk*?' He (the Imam) said, 'If it is not *shirk* it certainly was a practice in the time of ignorance and Islam has prohibited it.'"

H 10369, Ch. 21, h 4
Ali ibn Ibrahim has narrated from his father from ibn abu 'Umayr from Jamil ibn Darraj who has said the following:

"I once asked abu 'Abd Allah, *'Alayhi al-Salam,* about the *'Aqiqah,* shaving, giving a name to the newborn and that which one should come first. He (the Imam) said, 'All of it should be done in one hour, shaving, slaughtering the animal offered for *'Aqiqah* and naming the child.' He (the Imam) then mentioned what Fatimah, *'Alayha al-Salam,* had done for her children. He (the Imam) then said, 'The hairs are weighed and equal to its weight silver is given in charity.'"

H 10370, Ch. 21, h 5
Al-Husayn from Muhammad has narrated from Mu'alla' ibn Muhammad from certain persons of his people from Aban from Yahya ibn abu al-'Ala' who has said the following:

"Abu 'Abd Allah, *'Alayhi al-Salam,* has stated this *Hadith.* 'The Messenger of Allah, *O Allah, grant compensation to Muhammad and his family worthy of their services to Your cause,* named al-Hassan and al-Husayn, *'Alayhim al-*

Salam, on the seventh day from their birth, offered a sheep for *'Aqiqah*, one leg of the sheep was sent to *al-Qabilah* (the special nurse) and the rest was kept. They ate thereof and gave as a gift to neighbors. Fatimah, *'Alayha al-Salam,* shaved their heads and gave in charity silver by the weight of the hairs.'"

H 10371, Ch. 21, h 6

Ali ibn Ibrahim has narrated from his father from al-Husayn ibn Khalid who has said the following:

"I once asked al-Rida', *'Alayhi al-Salam,* about when to offer congratulations for the birth of a child. He (the Imam) stated this *Hadith.* 'It was the birth of al-Hassan ibn Ali, *'Alayhi al-Salam.* Jibril descended to congratulate the Holy Prophet, *O Allah, grant compensation to Muhammad and his family worthy of their services to Your cause,* on the seventh day and instructed to name him and give him a *Kunyah,* shave his head, offer *'Aqiqah* for him and pierce a hole in his ear. When al-Husayn, *'Alayhi al-Salam,* was born Jibril came on the seventh day and instructed similarly.' He (the Imam) then said, 'They both had two bunches of hairs on the left middle side of their head and the hole was in their right ear on the loop and on the left one it was on the top of the ear. Earring was in the right ear and *al-Shanf* (earring) on the left ear.' It is narrated that the Holy Prophet, *O Allah, grant compensation to Muhammad and his family worthy of their services to Your cause,* left two bunches of hairs on the middle of their head and it is more correct than al-Qarn (the left middle of the head).'"

Chapter 22 - Abu Talib Offered 'Aqiqah for the Holy Prophet, *O Allah, Grant Compensation to Muhammad and his Family Worthy of their Services to Your Cause*

H 10372, Ch. 22, h 1

Ali ibn Muhammad ibn Bandar has narrated from Ibrahim ibn Ishaq al-Ahmar from Ahmad ibn al-Hassan from abu al-'Abbas from Ja'far ibn 'Isma'il from Idris from abu al-Sa'ib who has said the following:

"Abu 'Abd Allah, *'Alayhi al-Salam,* has narrated from his father who has said that abu Talib offered *'Aqiqah* for the Messenger of Allah, *O Allah, grant compensation to Muhammad and his family worthy of their services to Your cause,* on the seventh day and invited members of his family who asked, 'What is this?' He replied, 'It is *'Aqiqah* for Ahmad.' They asked, 'Why have you named him Ahmad?' He replied, 'I have named him Ahmad because of the praises of the inhabitants of the sky and the earth for him.'"

Chapter 23 - Cleansing, Circumcision

H 10373, Ch. 23, h 1

Ali ibn Ibrahim has narrated from Harun ibn Muslim from Mas'adah ibn Sadaqah who has said the following:

"Abu 'Abd Allah, *'Alayhi al-Salam,* has said, 'Circumcise your children on the seventh day from their birth; it is more clean and allows the flesh to grow quicker. The earth dislikes the urine of one who is not circumcised.'"

Through the same chain of narrators as that of the previous *Hadith* the following is narrated:

"Abu 'Abd Allah, *'Alayhi al-Salam,* has said, 'Piercing a hole in the ear of a boy is of *Sunnah* and circumcision on the seventh day is of *Sunnah.*'"

H 10374, Ch. 23, h 2

Ali has narrated from his father from al-Nawfaliy from al-Sakuniy who has said the following:

"Abu 'Abd Allah, *'Alayhi al-Salam,* has said that the Messenger of Allah. *O Allah, grant compensation to Muhammad and his family worthy of their services to Your cause,* has said, 'Cleanse (circumcise) your children on the seventh day of their birth; it is more clean and allows the flesh to grow quicker. The land remains unclean for forty days because of the urine of an uncircumcised man.'"

H 10375, Ch. 23, h 3

Muhammad ibn Yahya and Muhammad ibn 'Abd Allah have narrated from 'Abd Allah ibn Ja'far who has said the following:

"I once wrote to abu Muhammad, *'Alayhi al-Salam,* that it is narrated from the two truthful Imam, *'Alayhim al-Salam,* who have said, 'Circumcise your children on the seventh day from their birth; the earth cries before Allah because of the urine of an uncircumcised person.' I pray to Allah to keep my soul in service for your cause, people performing circumcision in our city are not very knowledgeable and they do not do it on the seventh day but there is a Jewish person; if it is permissible for a Jewish person to circumcise children of Muslims or not by the will of Allah. He (the Imam) signed the answer that said, 'It is of *Sunnah* to circumcise on the seventh day, so do not oppose the *Sunnah* by the will of Allah.'"

H 10376, Ch. 23, h 4

Muhammad ibn Yahya has narrated from Ahmad ibn Muhammad from ibn Mahbub from Muhammad ibn Qaza'ah who has said the following:

"I once said to abu 'Abd Allah, *'Alayhi al-Salam,* 'We are told that Ibrahim *'Alayhi al-Salam* circumcised with an adze on a base. He (the Imam) said, 'Allah is free of all defects, it is not the way they say it is. They have lied against Ibrahim.' I then asked, 'How did it happen?' He (the Imam) said, 'In the case of the prophets, *'Alayhim al-Salam,* it would drop off on its own as well as their umbilical cord on the seventh day. When a child was born to Ibrahim, *'Alayhi al-Salam,* from Hagar, Sarah reproached her as slave-girls are reproached and she wept. It caused her an intense feeling and when `Isma'il saw her weep he also wept because of her weeping. Ibrahim came in and asked `Isma'il, 'What has made you weep?' `Isma'il replied, "Sarah reproached my mother with such and such words. She wept and I also wept." Ibrahim then stood on his place for prayer, spoke to his Lord and asked to make it drop from Hagar. Allah caused it to drop off. When Sarah gave birth to Ishaq and it became the seventh day the umbilical cord of Ishaq fell off but not the cover to be circumcised. Sarah became frightened thereby. When Ibrahim came in she said, 'O Ibrahim, what is this incident which has taken place with the family of Ibrahim and the children of prophets? This is your son Ishaq. His umbilical cord has fallen off but not his circumcision place.' Ibrahim stood in the place of his prayer, spoke to his Lord and asked, 'O Lord, what is this incident that has taken place in the family of Ibrahim and the children of prophets? This is my son Ishaq. His umbilical cord has fallen off but not his circumcision place. Allah, most High, sent him revelation that said, 'O Ibrahim this is because when Sarah reproached Hagar I then swore not to allow the circumcision place of one of the children of the prophets to fall off because of Sarah's reproaching Hagar. Thus circumcise Ishaq with iron and make him to feel the heat of iron.' He (the Imam) said, 'Ibrahim circumcised him with iron; then the tradition continued in the children of Ishaq thereafter.'"

H 10377, Ch. 23, h 5

It is narrated from the narrator of the previous *Hadith* from Ahmad ibn Muhammad ibn 'Isa from 'Abd Allah ibn Sinan who has said the following:

"Abu 'Abd Allah, *'Alayhi al-Salam,* has said, 'Piercing the ears of a boy is of the *Sunnah* as well as his circumcision.'"

H 10378, Ch. 23, h 6

It is narrated from the narrator of the previous *Hadith* from Ahmad ibn Muhammad from al-Husayn ibn Sa'id from Fadalah ibn Ayyub from al-Qasim ibn Burayd from abu Basir who has said the following:

"Abu 'Abd Allah, *'Alayhi al-Salam,* has said, 'Of the *Sunnah* of prophets is draining *al-Istinja`* (one's urine) and circumcision.'"

H 10379, Ch. 23, h 7

It is narrated from the narrator of the previous *Hadith* from Ahmad ibn Muhammad from al-Hassan ibn Ali ibn Yaqtin from his brother al-Husayn from his father Ali ibn Yaqtin who has said the following:

"I once asked abu al-Hassan, *'Alayhi al-Salam,* about circumcision of a child, if on the seventh day is of *Sunnah* or it can be delayed and which one is better. He (the Imam) said, 'On the seventh day is of *Sunnah* but delaying is not harmful.'"

H 10380, Ch. 23, h 8

Ali ibn Ibrahim has narrated from his father from ibn abu 'Umayr from Hisham ibn Salim who has said the following:

"Abu 'Abd Allah, *'Alayhi al-Salam,* has said, 'Circumcision is of pure obedience to Allah.'"

H 10381, Ch. 23, h 9

A number of our people have narrated from Ahmad ibn abu 'Abd Allah from his father from 'Abd Allah ibn al-Mughirah from those whom he has mentioned who has said the following:

"Abu 'Abd Allah, *'Alayhi al-Salam,* has said, 'For a newborn *'Aqiqah* is offered on the seventh day and the child is circumcised.'"

H 10382, Ch. 23, h 10

Ali ibn Ibrahim has narrated from his father from al-Nawfaliy from al-Sakuniy who has said the following:

"Abu 'Abd Allah, *'Alayhi al-Salam,* has said that `Amir al-Mu'minin has said, 'If a man becomes a Muslim he must circumcise even if he is eighty years old.'"

Chapter 24 - Lowering for Girls

H 10383, Ch. 24, h 1
Muhammad ibn Yahya has narrated from Ahmad ibn Muhammad from ibn Mahbub from ibn Ri'ab from abu Basir who has said the following:

"I once asked abu Ja'far, *'Alayhi al-Salam,* about the case of a girl who is taken as captive from the pagan's land then she becomes Muslim and she is asked for Khafd but we are not able against a woman. He (the Imam) said, 'Circumcision is for men and not for women.'" (*It a is reference to lowering or reducing female clitoris*)

H 10384, Ch. 24, h 2
Muhammad ibn Yahya has narrated from Ahmad ibn Muhammad ibn 'Isa from 'Abd Allah ibn Sinan who has said the following:

"Abu 'Abd Allah, *'Alayhi al-Salam,* has said, 'Circumcision for boys is because of *Sunnah* but circumcision for girls is not because of *Sunnah.*'"

H 10385, Ch. 24, h 3
Ali ibn Ibrahim has narrated from his father from Harun ibn Muslim from Mas'adah ibn Sadaqah who has said the following:

"Abu 'Abd Allah, *'Alayhi al-Salam,* has said, 'Reducing for girls is a noble trait but it is not of the *Sunnah* or obligatory; however, a noble trait is a very preferred matter.'"

H 10386, Ch. 24, h 4
A number of our people have narrated from Ahmad ibn Muhammad from al-Husayn ibn Sa'id from certain persons of his people from 'Abd Allah ibn Sinan who has said the following:

"Abu 'Abd Allah, *'Alayhi al-Salam,* has said, 'Circumcision for man is of *Sunnah* and it is a noble trait for women.'"

H 10387, Ch. 24, h 5
A number of our people have narrated from Sahl ibn Ziyad from Ali ibn Asbat from Khalaf ibn Hammad from 'Amr ibn Thabit who has said the following:

"Abu 'Abd Allah, *'Alayhi al-Salam,* has said that there was a woman called 'Umm Taybah and she lowered girls. The Messenger of Allah, *O Allah, grant compensation to Muhammad and his family worthy of their services to Your cause,* called her and said, 'O 'Umm Taybah, when you lower a woman make it (as little as) a scratch but do not be excessive. It clears the color and is more enjoyable to the husband.'"

H 10388, Ch. 24, h 6
A number of our people have narrated from Ahmad ibn Muhammad ibn 'Isa from Ahmad ibn Muhammad, from ibn abu Nasr from Harun ibn al-Jahm from Muhammad ibn Muslim who has said the following:

"Abu 'Abd Allah, *'Alayhi al-Salam,* has said that when women migrated to the Messenger of Allah, *O Allah, grant compensation to Muhammad and his family worthy of their services to Your cause,* among them was a woman called 'Umm Habib who lowered girls. When the Messenger of Allah saw her, he (the Messenger of Allah) asked her, 'O 'Umm Habib, do you still do what you did before?' She replied, 'Yes, O Messenger of Allah, unless it is unlawful and you prohibit me.' He (the Messenger of Allah) said, 'No, I do not prohibit. Come closer to me so I can instruct you.' She has said, 'I then went closer to him (the Messenger of Allah) and he (the Messenger of Allah) said, "O 'Umm Habib, when you do it, do not be excessive to cut it from its root, only make it (the cut as little as) a scratch; it is more clearing for the face and enjoyable for the husband."'

Chapter 25 - After Seven Days from Birth Shaving is not Required

H 10389, Ch. 25, h 1
Muhammad ibn Yahya has narrated from al-'Amrakiy ibn Ali from Ali ibn Ja'far from his brother abu al-Hassan, *'Alayhi al-Salam,* who has said the following:

"I once asked abu al-Hassan, *'Alayhi al-Salam,* about the newborn: if shaving his head after seven days from his birth is required. He (the Imam) said, 'When seven days pass shaving is not required.'"

H 10390, Ch. 25, h 2
Ali ibn Muhammad has narrated from Salih ibn abu Hammad from Ali ibn al-Hassan ibn Ribat from Dharih al-Muharibiy who has said the following:

"Abu 'Abd Allah, *'Alayhi al-Salam,* has said, 'When seven days from the birth of a child pass, then it is not *'Aqiqah* (the way it should have been).'"

Chapter 26 - The Rare Ahadith

H 10391, Ch. 26, h 1
Muhammad ibn Yahya has narrated from Ahmad ibn Muhammad ibn 'Isa from Muhammad ibn Khalid from Sa'd ibn Sa'd from Idris ibn 'Abd Allah who has said the following:

"I once asked abu 'Abd Allah, *'Alayhi al-Salam,* about the case of a child who dies on the seventh day: if *'Aqiqah* is still necessary. He (the Imam) said, 'If he dies before *al-Zuhr 'Aqiqah* is not required; but if he dies after *al-Zuhr* then *'Aqiqah* is required.'"

H 10392, Ch. 26, h 2
Muhammad ibn Yahya has narrated from Ahmad ibn Muhammad from Muhammad ibn Sinan from abu Harun Mawla' ale Al-Ja'dah who has said the following:

"I would often sit with abu 'Abd Allah, *'Alayhi al-Salam,* in al-Madinah and he (the Imam) found me absent for a few days. When I went to visit him (the Imam) he (the Imam) asked, 'I have not seen you for many days, O abu Harun.' I said that a boy is born to me. He (the Imam) said, 'May Allah make him a blessing for you! What have you named him?' I replied, 'I have named him Muhammad.' He (the Imam) lowered his face to the ground saying, Muhammad, Muhammad, Muhammad, until his face almost touched the ground. He (the Imam) then said, 'My soul, my children, my family, my father and all the inhabitants of earth, all of them are sacrifices for the Messenger of Allah, *O Allah, grant compensation to Muhammad and his family worthy of their services to Your cause.* You must not abuse him (the child), beat him or misbehave with him. Take notice, O abu Harun, that there is no house on earth wherein someone is named Muhammad but that it speaks of the glory of Allah.' He (the Imam) then asked me, 'Have you offered *'Aqiqah* for him?' He (the narrator) has said, 'I remained quiet. He (the Imam) found me quiet and thought that I have not offered *'Aqiqah* yet. He (the Imam) said, 'O Musadif, come closer to me.' I by Allah did not hear what he (the Imam) said to him except that I guessed he (the Imam) instructed him to give something to me. I then wanted to stand up and he (the Imam) then said to me, 'Wait O abu Harun as you are.' Musadif then brought for me three dinars and placed them in my hand and said, 'O abu Harun, you can go and buy two rams, make sure they are fat, then slaughter and use them for food.'"

H 10393, Ch. 26, h 3
A number of our people have narrated from Ahmad ibn Muhammad ibn Khalid and Ali ibn Ibrahim has narrated from his father from 'Uthman ibn 'Isa from Sama'ah who has said the following:

"I once asked him (the Imam), *'Alayhi al-Salam,* about the case of a man who had not offered *'Aqiqah* for any of his children until they all grew up as young boys or grown up men. He (the Imam) said, 'If he offers sacrifice for them or they themselves offer sacrifice it then is sufficient for *'Aqiqah.* He (the Imam) said that the Messenger of Allah, *O Allah, grant compensation to Muhammad and his family worthy of their services to Your cause,* has said, 'The newborn is under the mortgage of *'Aqiqah* and it is up to the parents to free him or leave him under such mortgage.'"

Chapter 27 - Shaving Certain Parts of the Head of a Newborn and Leaving other Parts

H 10394, Ch. 27, h 1
Ali ibn Ibrahim has narrated from his father from al-Nawfaliy from al-Sakuniy who has said the following:

"Abu 'Abd Allah, *'Alayhi al-Salam,* has said that `Amir al-Mu'minin said, 'Do not shave the heads of children in *al-Qaza'* and *al-Qaza'* meaning to shave certain parts and leave other parts.'"

H 10395, Ch. 27, h 2
Ali ibn Ibrahim has narrated from his father from Abu Ja'far ibn Muhammad al-Ash'ariy from ibn al-Qaddah who has narrated the following:

"Abu 'Abd Allah, *'Alayhi al-Salam,* disliked shaving the head of a child a little and leaving the top middle of the head unshaved, which is called *al-Qaza'.*"

H 10396, Ch. 27, h 3
Ali ibn Ibrahim has narrated from his father from Ja'far ibn Muhammad al-Ash'ariy from ibn al-Qaddah who has said the following:

"Abu 'Abd Allah, *'Alayhi al-Salam,* has stated this *Hadith.* 'Once a child was brought to the Messenger of Allah, *O Allah, grant compensation to Muhammad and his family worthy of their services to Your cause,* so that he (the Messenger of Allah) might pray for him but the child had *Qanazi'* and he (the Messenger of Allah) refused to pray for him. He (the Messenger of Allah) instructed them to shave his head entirely. The Messenger of Allah commanded to shave belly hairs .'"

Chapter 28 - Breastfeeding

H 10397, Ch. 28, h 1
Muhammad ibn Yahya has narrated from Ahmad ibn Muhammad from Muhammad ibn Yahya from Talhah ibn Zayd who has said the following:

"Abu 'Abd Allah, *'Alayhi al-Salam,* has said that `Amir al-Mu'minin has said, 'No other milk has a greater blessing for the child as the milk of his mother does.'"

H 10398, Ch. 28, h 2
Muhammad ibn Yahya has narrated from Salmah ibn al-Khattab from Muhammad ibn Musa from Muhammad ibn al-'Abbas ibn al-Walid from his father from 'Umm Ishaq daughter of Sulayman who has said the following:

"Abu 'Abd Allah, *'Alayhi al-Salam,* once looked to me when I was breastfeeding one of my sons, Muhammad or Ishaq and he (the Imam) said, 'O 'Umm Ishaq, do not breastfeed him from one breast only. Breastfeed him from both breasts; one is food and the other is the drink for him.'"

H 10399, Ch. 28, h 3
Muhammad has narrated from Ahmad ibn Muhammad ibn 'Isa from Muhammad ibn Sinan from 'Ammar ibn Marwan from Sama'ah who has said the following:

"Abu 'Abd Allah, *'Alayhi al-Salam,* has said, 'Breastfeeding is for twenty-one months. Breastfeeding for less than this is injustice to the child.'"

H 10400, Ch. 28, h 4
Ali ibn Ibrahim has narrated from his father and Ali Muhammad al-Qasaniy from al-Qasim ibn Muhammad al-Jawhariy from Sulayman ibn Dawud al-Minqariy who has said the following:

"Once abu 'Abd Allah, *'Alayhi al-Salam,* was asked about breastfeeding. He (the Imam) said, 'A free woman cannot be forced to breastfeed; but the mother (who is a slave-girl) of child can be made to breastfeed.'"

H 10401, Ch. 28, h 5
Ali has narrated from his father from ibn abu 'Umayr from certain persons of our people from ibn abu Ya'fur who has said the following:

"Abu 'Abd Allah, *'Alayhi al-Salam,* has said that `Amir al-Mu'minin issued a judgment about the case of a man who had died, had left behind a child and they had found someone to breastfeed him. He (the Imam) said that the wages for breastfeeding must be paid from what the child has inherited from his father and mother.'"

H 10402, Ch. 28, h 6
Muhammad ibn Yahya has narrated from Ahmad ibn Muhammad from Muhammad ibn 'Isma'il and al-Husayn ibn Sa'id all from Muhammad ibn al-Fudayl from abu al-Sabbah al-Kinaniy who has said the following:

"I once asked abu 'Abd Allah, *'Alayhi al-Salam,* about the words of Allah, most Majestic, most Glorious, '. . . a mother must not be harmed because of her child nor must a father be harmed because of his child.' (2:232) He (the Imam) said, 'This is a reference to the case of breastfeeding woman when man persued her for going to bed with her she refused saying, "I cannot allow you to go to bed with me because I may become pregnant and kill my child."' It also refers to the case of the woman who asked a man for going to bed with her but he refused saying, "I am afraid that after going to bed with you then I will kill my child"; so he would not go to bed with her. Allah, most Majestic, most Glorious, prohibited man's harming the woman or woman's harming the man.'"

Ali ibn Ibrahim has narrated from his father from ibn abu 'Umayr from Hammad from al-Halabiy who has narrated a similar *Hadith* with this addition:

"About His words, '. ... an heir has similar responsibilities . . .' (2:232), he (the Imam) said, 'An heir must not harm the child or his mother during breastfeeding and she also must not take more than two complete years for breastfeeding the child. If they decide to wean the child by mutual agreement and consent before two years it is fine and separation is weaning.'"

H 10403, Ch. 28, h 7
Muhammad ibn Yahya has narrated from Ahmad ibn Muhammad from al-Hassan ibn Mahbub from ibn Sinan who has said the following:
"I once asked abu 'Abd Allah, *'Alayhi al-Salam,* about the case of a man who dies and leaves behind a woman with a child from the deceased and she gives the child to her servant for breastfeeding. She then asks the executor of the will to pay for the breastfeeding wages. He (the Imam) said, 'She deserves an equivalent wages and the executor of the will cannot take the child away from her until he grows up. He then delivers his assets to him.

H 10404, Ch. 28, h 8
Muhammad ibn Yahya has narrated from Ahmad ibn Muhammad from Muhammad ibn Khalid from Sa'd ibn Sa'd al-Ash'ariy who has said the following:
"I once asked al-Rida', *'Alayhi al-Salam,* about the case of a child; if he can be breastfed for more than two years. He (the Imam) said, 'It is two years.' I then asked, 'If the child is breastfed for more than two years do parents owe anything?' He (the Imam) said, 'No, they do not owe anything.

Chapter 29 - The Liability of the Breastfeeder

H 10405, Ch. 29, h 1
Muhammad ibn Yahya has narrated from Ahmad ibn Muhammad from ibn Mahbub from Jamil ibn Darraj and Hammad from Sulayman ibn Khalid who has said the following:
"I once asked abu 'Abd Allah, *'Alayhi al-Salam,* about the case of a man who hires a breastfeeding woman for his child and gives the child to her. The breastfeeding woman takes the child and gives him to another breastfeeding woman who remains away for a while. The man then asks for his child, the first breastfeeding woman confesses to her giving the child to another breastfeeding woman on hire and confesses to her taking the child from his father and that she has given him to another breastfeeding woman. He (the Imam) said, 'She must pay blood money or return the child.'"

H 10406, Ch. 29, h 2

Ibn Mahbub has narrated from Jamil ibn Salih from Sulayman ibn Khalid who has said the following:

"About the case of a man who hires a breastfeeding woman, who disappears with the child for many years, but then she brings the child to his family but the mother refuses to accept the child. The family thinks that they do not know him. He (the Imam) said, 'She is not responsible for anything; the breastfeeding woman is not liable.'"

Chapter 30 - The Preferable and Non-preferable Milk

H 10407, Ch. 30, h 1

Muhammad ibn Yahya has narrated from Ahmad ibn Muhammad ibn Faddal from ibn Bukayr from 'Ubayd Allah al-Halabiy who has said the following:

"I once asked abu 'Abd Allah, *'Alayhi al-Salam,* about the case of a woman who has given birth because of fornication; if I can hire her for breastfeeding. He (the Imam) said, 'Do not hire her for breastfeeding as well as her daughter.'"

H 10408, Ch. 30, h 2

Muhammad ibn Yahya has narrated from Ahmad ibn Muhammad from Ali ibn al-Hakam from 'Abd Allah ibn Yahya al-Kahiliy from 'Abd Allah ibn Hilal who has said the following:

"I once asked abu 'Abd Allah, *'Alayhi al-Salam,* if a Zoroastrian woman can be hired for breastfeeding a child. He (the Imam) said, 'No, however, she can be of the people of the book.'"

H 10409, Ch. 30, h 3

It is narrated from the narrator of the previous *Hadith* from al-Kahiliy from 'Abd Allah ibn Hilal who has said the following:

"Abu 'Abd Allah, *'Alayhi al-Salam,* has said, 'When they breastfeed for you do not allow them to drink wine.'"

H 10410, Ch. 30, h 4

Humayd ibn Ziyad al-Husayn from Muhammad ibn Sama'ah from more than one person from Aban ibn 'Uthman from 'Abd al-Rahman ibn abu 'Abd Allah who has said the following:

"I once asked abu 'Abd Allah, *'Alayhi al-Salam,* if it is proper to hire a Jewish or a Christian or a pagan woman for breastfeeding. He (the Imam) said, 'It is not unlawful but do not allow them to drink wine.'"

H 10411, Ch. 30, h 5

Ali ibn Ibrahim has narrated from his father, from Hammad from Hariz from Muhammad ibn Muslim who has said the following:

"Abu Ja'far, *'Alayhi al-Salam,* has said, 'The milk of a Jewish, a Christian or a Zoroastrian woman is more likeable to me than the milk of a woman because of fornication.' He (the Imam) would not consider it unlawful if the breastfeeding woman is a slave-girl who has committed fornication and her master gives permission."

H 10412, Ch. 30, h 6

A number of our people have narrated from Sahl ibn Ziyad Ahmad ibn Muhammad from ibn abu Nasr from Hammad ibn 'Uthaman from Ishaq ibn 'Ammar who has said the following:

"I once asked abu al-Hassan, *'Alayhi al-Salam,* about the case of a boy who impregnated my slave-girl who then gave birth and we needed her milk. If I give permission, will her milk be fine? He (the Imam) said, 'Yes, it will be fine.'"

H 10413, Ch. 30, h 7
Ali ibn Ibrahim has narrated from his father from ibn abu 'Umayr from Hisham ibn Salim and Jamil ibn Darraj and Sa'd ibn abu Khalaf who has said the following:

"About the case of a woman who has a servant who has committed fornication and we need her milk. He (the Imam) said, 'Instruct her to give permission, the milk will be fine.'"

H 10414, Ch. 30, h 8
Ali ibn Ibrahim has narrated from his father from ibn abu Najran from 'Asem ibn Hamid from Muhammad ibn Qays who has said the following:

"This is a narration of abu Ja'far, *'Alayhi al-Salam,* from the Messenger of Allah, *O Allah, grant compensation to Muhammad and his family worthy of their services to Your cause.* He (the Messenger of Allah) has said, 'You must not hire a dimwitted woman for breastfeeding; the milk spreads and the boy is drawn to the milk, that is, to the frivolity and dimwittedness of the breastfeeding woman.'"

H 10415, Ch. 30, h 9
Ali has narrated from Harun ibn Muslim from Mas'adah who has said the following:

"Abu 'Abd Allah, *'Alayhi al-Salam,* has said that `Amir al-Mu'minin would say, 'Do not hire a dimwitted woman for breastfeeding: milk overpowers natural manners. The Messenger of Allah has said, "Do not hire a dimwitted woman for breastfeeding; with such milk the child grows up."'"

H 10416, Ch. 30, h 10
Muhammad ibn Yahya has narrated from Ahmad ibn Muhammad from Muhammad ibn Yahya from Ghiyath ibn Ibrahim who has said the following:

"Abu 'Abd Allah, *'Alayhi al-Salam,* has said that `Amir al-Mu'minin has said, 'Pay proper attention to who breastfeeds your children: a child grows up with such milk.'"

H 10417, Ch. 30, h 11
Muhammad ibn Yahya has narrated from al-'Amrakiy ibn Ali from Ali ibn Ja'far from his brother, abu al-Hassan, *'Alayhi al-Salam,* who has said the following:

"I once asked abu al-Hassan, *'Alayhi al-Salam,* about the case of a woman who has given birth because of fornication; if it is proper to hire her for breastfeeding. He (the Imam) said, 'It is not proper as well as the milk of her daughter who is born out of wedlock.'"

H 10418, Ch. 30, h 12
Muhammad ibn Yahya has narrated from Ahmad ibn Muhammad from al-'Abbas ibn Ma'ruf Hammad ibn 'Isa from al-Haytham from Muhammad ibn Marwan who has said the following:

"Abu Ja'far, *'Alayhi al-Salam,* once said to me, 'You can use the milk of a horse for your child but you must remain on your guard against the milk of a fornicator; milk may spread.'"

H 10419, Ch. 30, h 13

Ahmad ibn Muhammad has narrated from al-ʿAbbas ibn Maʾruf from Safwan ibn Yahya from Ribʿiy from Fudayl from Zurarah who has said the following:

"Abu Jaʿfar, *ʿAlayhi al-Salam,* has said, 'You must find a clean breastfeeding woman because milk may spread (its bad effects).'"

H 10420, Ch. 30, h 14

Abu Ali al-Ashʿariy has narrated from Muhammad ibn ʿAbd al-Jabbar from Safwan from Saʿid ibn Yasar who has said the following:

"Abu ʿAbd Allah, *ʿAlayhi al-Salam,* has said, 'Do not hire a Zoroastrian woman for breastfeeding your child, however, you may hire a Jewish, a Christian woman who must not drink wine and you must not allow them to do so.'"

Chapter 31 - The One Who has More Priority for the Custody of a Small Child

H 10421, Ch. 31, h 1

Al-Husayn from Muhammad has narrated from Muʿallaʾ ibn Muhammad from al-Hassan ibn Ali al-Washshaʾ from Aban from Fadl abu al-ʿAbbas who has said the following:

"I once asked abu ʿAbd Allah, *ʿAlayhi al-Salam,* if a man has more right for the custody of a child or woman. He (the Imam) said, 'No, the man has more right. If a divorced woman asks for breastfeeding her child for the same price as others, then she has more right for breastfeeding.'"

H 10422, Ch. 31, h 2

Muhammad ibn Yahya has narrated from Ahmad ibn Muhammad from Muhammad ibn ʿIsmaʾil has narrated from Muhammad ibn al-Fudayl from abu al-Sabbah al-Kinaniy who has said the following:

"Abu ʿAbd Allah, *ʿAlayhi al-Salam,* has stated this *Hadith.* 'When a man divorces his wife, who is pregnant, he must provide her maintenance until she gives birth. When she gives birth he must pay her wages and must not harm her unless he finds someone who does it for less; but if she agrees with the lesser wages then she has more right to breastfeeding her child until the child is weaned.'"

H 10423, Ch. 31, h 3

Ali ibn Ibrahim has narrated from Ali ibn Muhammad al-Qasaniy from al-Qasim ibn Muhammad from al-Minqariy from those whom he has mentioned who has said the following:

"Once, abu ʿAbd Allah, *ʿAlayhi al-Salam,* was asked about the case of a man who divorces his wife. They have a child, which one of them has more right for the child? He (the Imam) said, 'The woman has more right as long as she does not marry.'"

H 10424, Ch. 31, h 4

Abu Ali al-Ashʿariy has narrated from al-Hassan ibn Ali from al-ʿAbbas ibn ʿAmir from Dawud ibn al-Hasin who has said the following:

"Abu ʿAbd Allah, *ʿAlayhi al-Salam,* has said, 'Mothers must breastfeed their children' means that a child during breastfeeding period is between the two parents in equal manners. When the child is weaned then the father has more right about him than the mother. When the father dies then the mother has more

40

right than the relatives. If the father finds a breastfeeding woman who asks four dirham, for example, and the mother says that she will not do for less than five dirham, he can take the child away from her unless she is more kind and better for the child.'"

H 10425, Ch. 31, h 5
Muhammad ibn Yahya has narrated from Ahmad ibn Muhammad from ibn Mahbub from Dawud al-Raqqiy who has said the following:

"I once asked abu 'Abd Allah, *'Alayhi al-Salam,* about the case of a free woman who has married a slave who has given birth to several children. She is then divorced and then does not stay with her children but marries another man. The slave then finds out about her marriage. He wants to take his children from her saying that he has more right than the mother has since she has married. He (the Imam) said, 'The slave has no right to take the children from her even if she has married until the slave becomes free; she has more right about her children than the slave as long as he is owned and when he becomes free then he has more right.'"

Chapter 32 - Growth of a Child

H 10426, Ch. 32, h 1
Muhammad ibn Yahya has narrated from Ahmad ibn Muhammad ibn 'Isa from abu Muhammad al-Mada'iniy from 'A'idh ibn Habib Bayya' al-Harawiy from 'Isa ibn Zayd in a *marfu'* manner who has said the following:

"Abu 'Abd Allah, *'Alayhi al-Salam,* has stated this *Hadith.* 'Children's milk teeth are replaced in seven years. They must be instructed to perform *Salat* (prayer) at the age of nine years, their bed must be separated at the age of ten, they experience wet dream at the age of fourteen, their growth in length stops at the age of twenty-two and their growth of reason stops at the age twenty-eight except experiences.'"

H 10427, Ch. 32, h 2
Muhammad ibn Yahya has narrated from Muhammad ibn Ahmad from Musa ibn 'Umar from Ali ibn al-Husayn (ibn al-Hassan) al-Darir from Hammad ibn 'Isa who has said the following:

"Abu 'Abd Allah, *'Alayhi al-Salam,* has said that `Amir al-Mu'minin, *'Alayhi al-Salam,* has said, 'A child grows every year by four fingers of his own fingers.'"

H 10428, Ch. 32, h 3
Ali ibn Ibrahim has narrated from his father from al-Nawfaliy from al-Sakuniy who has said the following:

"Abu 'Abd Allah, *'Alayhi al-Salam,* has narrated from his father, *'Alayhi al-Salam,* who has said, that a boy cannot impregnate until his breast becomes round and the smell of his armpit rises strong.'"

Chapter 33 - Disciplines for a Child

H 10429, Ch. 33, h 1

Ali ibn Ibrahim has narrated from Muhammad ibn 'Isa ibn 'Ubayd from Yunus from a man who has said the following:

"Abu 'Abd Allah, *'Alayhi al-Salam,* has said, 'Allow your child to play for seven years and keep him with yourself for another seven years (to practice and behave as you do) if he succeeds; otherwise, he is of the ones in whom there is nothing good.'"

H 10430, Ch. 33, h 2

A number of our people have narrated from Ahmad ibn Muhammad from ibn Khalid from A number of our people have narrated from Ali ibn Asbat from Yunus ibn Ya'qub who has said the following:

"Abu 'Abd Allah, *'Alayhi al-Salam,* has stated this *Hadith.* 'You should give your child time until he is six years old, then keep him with yourself (to practice and behave as you do) for another seven years; teach him your disciplines and moral manners, to see if he accepts and is established in good manners; otherwise, leave him alone (there is not much in him to hope for).'"

H 10431, Ch. 33, h 3

Ahmad ibn Muhammad has narrated from Muhammad al-'Asemiy from Ali ibn al-Hassan from Ali ibn Asbat from his uncle Ya'qub ibn Salim who has said the following:

"Abu 'Abd Allah, *'Alayhi al-Salam,* has said, 'A boy can play for seven years, learn how to read and write for another seven years and learn the lawful and unlawful matters in another seven years.'"

H 10432, Ch. 33, h 4

Ali ibn Asbat has narrated from his uncle Ya'qub ibn Salim in a *marfu'* manner who has said the following:

"'Amir al-Mu'minin, *'Alayhi al-Salam,* has said that the Messenger of Allah, *O Allah, grant compensation to Muhammad and his family worthy of their services to Your cause,* has said, 'You should teach your children swimming and sharp shooting.'"

H 10433, Ch. 33, h 5

A number of our people have narrated from Ahmad ibn Muhammad from ibn Khalid from Muhammad ibn Ali from 'Umar ibn 'Abd al-'Aziz from a man from Jamil ibn Darraj and others who has said the following:

"Abu 'Abd Allah, *'Alayhi al-Salam,* has said, 'You should hasten (take the initiative) to teach *Hadith* to your children before *al-Murji'ah* (name of a sect) takes control over their mind and belief.'"

H 10434, Ch. 33, h 6

Ali ibn Ibrahim has narrated from his father from and A number of our people have narrated from Sahl ibn Ziyad from Ja'far ibn Muhammad al-Ash'ariy from ibn al-Qaddah who has said the following:

"Abu 'Abd Allah, *'Alayhi al-Salam,* has said, 'When boys become ten years old, their bed must be separated from women.'"

H 10435, Ch. 33, h 7

Through the same chain of narrators as that of the previous *Hadith*, the following is narrated:

"Abu 'Abd Allah, *'Alayhi al-Salam,* has said, 'We instruct children to perform two *Salat* (prayer) together, one *Salat* (prayer) soon after the other, like *al-Zuhr* and *al-'Asr, al-Maghrib* and *al-'Isha'* as long as they have valid wudu before they get busy.'"

H 10436, Ch. 33, h 8

Muhammad ibn Yahya has narrated from Ahmad ibn Muhammad from Muhammad ibn Yahya from Ghiyath ibn Ibrahim who has said the following:

"Abu 'Abd Allah, *'Alayhi al-Salam,* has said that `Amir al-Mu'minin, *'Alayhi al-Salam,* has said, 'You must discipline an orphan as you discipline your own child and deal with him as you would deal with your own child (in matters of discipline).'"

Chapter 34 - The Rights of Children

H 10437, Ch. 34, h 1

Ali ibn Ibrahim has narrated from Muhammad ibn 'Isa from Yunus from Durust who has said the following:

"Abu al-Hassan, Musa, *'Alayhi al-Salam,* has said that once a man came to the Messenger of Allah, *O Allah, grant compensation to Muhammad and his family worthy of their services to Your cause,* and asked, 'O Messenger of Allah, what is the right of my son, this one?' He (the Messenger of Allah) said, 'You should give him a good name and teach him with discipline, a good and fruitful subject.'"

H 10438, Ch. 34, h 2

Muhammad ibn Yahya has narrated from Ahmad ibn Muhammad from Mu'ammar ibn Khallad who has said the following:

"Dawud ibn Zurbiy complained against his son before abu al-Hassan, *'Alayhi al-Salam,* because of what he had destroyed. He (the Imam) said, 'Reform and reclaim him; a value of a hundred thousand is not important compared to the bounty that Allah has bestowed up on you.'"

H 10439, Ch. 34, h 3

Ali ibn Ibrahim has narrated from his father from al-Nawfaliy from al-Sakuniy who has said the following:

"Abu 'Abd Allah, *'Alayhi al-Salam,* has said that the Messenger of Allah, *O Allah, grant compensation to Muhammad and his family worthy of their services to Your cause,* has said, 'May Allah grant forgiveness to the parents who support their children in their kindness and virtuous deeds.'"

H 10440, Ch. 34, h 4

Ali ibn Ibrahim has narrated from his father from 'Abd Allah ibn al-Mughirah from 'Abd Allah ibn Sinan who has said the following:

"Abu 'Abd Allah, *'Alayhi al-Salam,* has said that the Messenger of Allah, *O Allah, grant compensation to Muhammad and his family worthy of their services to Your cause,* once performed *Salat* (prayer) of *al-Zuhr* with people and made the two last *Rak'at* light. When he (the Messenger of Allah) completed, people asked if something has happened during *Salat* (prayer). He (the Messenger of Allah) asked, 'Why do you ask such question?' They replied, 'You made the last two *Rak'at* light.' He (the Messenger of Allah) said, 'Did you not hear crying of the child?'"

H 10441, Ch. 34, h 5

It is narrated from the narrator of the previous *Hadith* from Muhammad ibn Sinan from abu Khalid al-Wasitiy from Zayd ibn Ali from his father from his grandfather who has said the following:

"The Messenger of Allah, *O Allah, grant compensation to Muhammad and his family worthy of their services to Your cause,* has said, 'What parents' declaring their children as disobedient entails for parents is exactly what children's disobeying their parents entails for the children (both cases are extremely harmful)."

H 10442, Ch. 34, h 6

Ali ibn Muhammad has narrated from ibn Jumhur from his father from Fadalah ibn Ayyub from ibn al-Sakuniy who has said the following:

"I once went to visit abu 'Abd Allah, *'Alayhi al-Salam,* who found me sad and depressed. He (the Imam) then asked, 'O Sakuniy, what has made you so depressed?' I replied, 'Aminah (a daughter) is born to me.' He (the Imam) said, 'O Sakuniy, the earth carries her weight and Allah grants her sustenance. She lives in a lifetime which is other than your lifetime (her lifetime does not reduce your lifetime) and she eats from a sustenance which is other than your sustenance' – he (the Imam) by Allah removed my depression- and asked, 'What name have you given to her?' I replied, 'It is Fatimah.' He (the Imam) said, 'Ah! Ah! (It is an expression and reminder of one's nostalgia). He (the Imam) then placed his hand over his forehead, then stated this *Hadith.* 'The Messenger of Allah, *O Allah, grant compensation to Muhammad and his family worthy of their services to Your cause,* has said, "Of the rights of a son on his father is to respect and honor his mother, give him a good name, teach him the book of Allah, cleanse him (by circumcision) and teach him swimming. If it is a girl, he must respect her mother, give her a good name, teach her Chapter twenty-four of the Quran, not Chapter twelve, he must not lodge her in chambers, and send her very early to the house of her husband." Since you have named her Fatimah, you must not abuse, condemn or subject her to physical abuse.'"

Chapter 35 - Kindness to Children

H 10443, Ch. 35, h 1

A number of our people have narrated from Ahmad ibn Muhammad from ibn Khalid from Sharif ibn Sabiq from al-Fadl ibn abu Qurrah who has said the following:

"Abu 'Abd Allah, *'Alayhi al-Salam,* has stated this *Hadith.* 'The Messenger of Allah, *O Allah, grant compensation to Muhammad and his family worthy of their services to Your cause,* has said, 'One who kisses his son, Allah, most Majestic, most Glorious, writes down for him one good deed and one who makes him happy Allah will make him happy on the Day of Judgment. One who teach him al-Quran his parents will be called on the Day of Judgment and will be then dressed with two dresses which will make the faces of the people of paradise bright because of the light shining from those dresses.'"

H 10444, Ch. 35, h 2
Muhammad ibn Yahya has narrated from Ahmad ibn Muhammad ibn 'Isa from abu Talib in a marfu' manner who has said the following:

"Abu 'Abd Allah, *'Alayhi al-Salam,* has said that a man from al-Ansar (people of al-Madinah) once asked him (the Messenger of Allah), 'To whom should I be kind?' He (the Messenger of Allah) said, 'Be kind to your parents.' He said, 'They have passed away.' He (the Messenger of Allah) said, 'Be kind to your children.'"

H 10445, Ch. 35, h 3
Ahmad ibn Muhammad has narrated from Ali ibn Faddal from 'Abd Allah ibn Muhammad al-Bajaliy who has said the following:

"Abu 'Abd Allah, *'Alayhi al-Salam,* has said that the Messenger of Allah, *O Allah, grant compensation to Muhammad and his family worthy of their services to Your cause,* has said, 'You must love children and be kind to them. If you promise them, then keep your promise because they do not know anyone except you who provides them sustenance.'"

H 10446, Ch. 35, h 4
Ibn Faddal has narrated from abu Jamilah from Sa'd ibn Tarif from al-Asbagh ibn Nubatah who has said the following:

"'Amir al-Mu'minin, *'Alayhi al-Salam,* has said, 'One who has a child, he is in love ardently.'"

H 10447, Ch. 35, h 5
Ali ibn Ibrahim has narrated from his father from ibn abu 'Umayr from those whom he has mentioned who has said the following:

"Abu 'Abd Allah, *'Alayhi al-Salam,* has said, 'Allah will have mercy on (His) slave because of his intense love for his children.'"

H 10448, Ch. 35, h 6
A number of our people have narrated from Ahmad ibn Muhammad from ibn Mahbub servant from Ali ibn al-Hassan ibn Ribat from Yunus ibn Ribat who has said the following:

"Abu 'Abd Allah, *'Alayhi al-Salam,* has said that the Messenger of Allah, *O Allah, grant compensation to Muhammad and his family worthy of their services to Your cause,* has said, 'Allah grants mercy to one who supports his children in virtuous deeds.' He (the narrator) has said that he then asked, 'How does he support him in virtuous deeds.' He (the Imam) said, 'He accepts what he can do and bypasses what is difficult for him. He does not impose on him what is beyond his ability; between him and the limits of disbelief there is no more than entering in disobedience and cutting off the good relations among relatives.' He (the Imam) then said that the Messenger of Allah has said, 'Paradise is pleasant. Allah has made it pleasant as well as its fragrance which reaches a distance of two thousand years but one who is disobedient to parents, one who has cut off good relations with relatives and one who displays haughtiness and arrogance cannot find and sense the fragrance of paradise.'"

H 10449, Ch. 35, h 7

Ali ibn Muhammad ibn Bandar has narrated from Ahmad ibn abu 'Abd Allah from A number of our people have narrated from al-Hassan ibn Ali ibn Yusuf al-Azdiy from a man who has said the following:

"He (the Imam), *'Alayhi al-Salam,* has said that once a man came to the Messenger of Allah, *O Allah, grant compensation to Muhammad and his family worthy of their services to Your cause,* and said, 'I have never kissed a child.' When he left, the Messenger of Allah said, 'This man to me is one of the people of hellfire.'"

H 10450, Ch. 35, h 8

A number of our people have narrated from Ahmad ibn Muhammad from Ali ibn al-Hakam from Kulayb al-Saydawiy who has said the following:

"Abu al-Hassan, *'Alayhi al-Salam,* once said to me, 'When you promise children something, then you must keep your promise because they see you as the only one who provides them sustenance. Allah, most Majestic, most Glorious, does not become as angrier as He does for women and children.'"

H 10451, Ch. 35, h 9

Abu Ali al-Ash'ariy has narrated from Muhammad ibn 'Abd al-Jabbar from Safwan from Dharih who has said the following:

"Abu 'Abd Allah, *'Alayhi al-Salam,* has said, 'A child is a trial (mischief, attraction).'"

Chapter 36 - Giving Preference to One Child Over the Others

H 10452, Ch. 36, h 1

Muhammad ibn Yahya has narrated from Ahmad ibn Muhammad ibn Khalid from Sa'd ibn Sa'd al-Ash'ariy who has said the following:

"I once asked al-Rida', *'Alayhi al-Salam,* about the case of a man who loves certain ones of his children more than others and gives preference to certain ones among them over the others. He (the Imam) said, 'Yes, abu 'Abd Allah, *'Alayhi al-Salam,* gave a present to Muhammad; so also did abu al-Hassan, *'Alayhi al-Salam,* by gifting something to Ahmad and I went to collect them for him because he was a child.' I then said, 'I pray to Allah to keep my soul in service for your cause, can one love his daughters more than his sons?' He (the Imam) said, 'Sons and daughters are the same in this matter, in fact, it depends up on how they are in the sight of Allah, most Majestic, most Glorious.'"

Chapter 37 - Intelligence of a Boy and Signs of his Nobility

H 10453, Ch. 37, h 1

Muhammad ibn Yahya has narrated from Ahmad ibn Muhammad and Ali ibn Ibrahim has narrated from his father from all from ibn Mahbub from Khalil ibn 'Amr al-Yashkuriy from Jamil ibn Darraj who has said the following:

"Abu 'Abd Allah, *'Alayhi al-Salam,* has said that 'Amir al-Mu'minin has said, 'If a boy's scrotum is relaxed, his penis is small, his eyes are relaxed; then there is hope for goodness to come from him, as well as hope in safety from his evil. On the other hand if a boy whose scrotum is hard, his penis is large and has piercing eyes, he then is one in whose goodness there is no hope nor safety from his evil.'"

H 10454, Ch. 37, h 2

Ali ibn Muhammad ibn Bandar from his father from Muhammad ibn Ali al-Hamadaniy from abu Sa'd al-Shamiy who has said that Salih ibn 'Uqbah narrated to me saying the following:

"I heard the virtuous servant of Allah saying, 'It is preferable to involve a child in difficult tasks when he is small, so he can be forbearing when he grows up.' He (the Imam) then said, 'It is not proper to be other than as such.'"

H 10455, Ch. 37, h 3

It is narrated that the most intelligent child is the one who hates al-Kuttab (the writers) school the most.'"

Chapter 38 - Rare Ahadith

H 10456, Ch. 38, h 1

Abu Ali al-Ash'ariy has narrated from narrated from Muhammad ibn Hassan from al-Husayn ibn Muhammad al-Nawfaliy from children of Nawfil ibn 'Abd al-Muttalib, narrated to me Muhammad ibn Ja'far from Muhammad ibn Ali ibn 'Isa from 'Abd Allah al-'Amriy from his father from his grandfather who has said the following:

"'Amir al-Mu'minin, '*Alayhi al-Salam,* has said about the illness that a child may suffer, 'It is expiation for his parents.'"

H 10457, Ch. 38, h 2

A number of our people have narrated from Ahmad ibn abu 'Abd Allah from his father from Wahab who has said the following:

"Abu 'Abd Allah, '*Alayhi al-Salam,* has said that `Amir al-Mu'minin has said, 'A child (born after) six, seven or nine months lives but one who is born after eight months cannot live.'"

H 10458, Ch. 38, h 3

Ali ibn Muhammad has narrated from Salih ibn abu Hammad from Yunus ibn Ibrahim from 'Abd al-Rahman ibn Sayabah from those who narrated to him who has said the following:

"I once asked abu Ja'far, '*Alayhi al-Salam,* about how long a child can remain in the mother's womb because people say that a child may remain in mother's womb for many years. He (the Imam) said, 'They speak a lie. The ultimate time is nine months and it is no more even for a while because if the child remains for more than a sa'ah, (while), his mother will be dead before he comes out.'"

H 10459, Ch. 38, h 4

Abu Ali al-Ash'ariy has narrated from Muhammad ibn 'Abd al-Jabbar from *al-Hajj*al from Tha'labah from Zurarah who has said the following:

"One of the two Imam, (abu Ja'far or abu 'Abd Allah), '*Alayhim al-Salam,* has said, '*Al-Qabilah* (the doctor) is immune and not liable.'"

H 10460, Ch. 38, h 5

Muhammad Yahya has narrated from Muhammad ibn al-Husayn from Ya'qub ibn Yazid from ibn abu 'Umayr from Muhammad ibn Muslim who has said the following:

"Once I was with abu 'Abd Allah, *'Alayhi al-Salam,* when Yunus ibn Ya'qub came in and I found him moaning. Abu 'Abd Allah, *'Alayhi al-Salam,* asked him, 'Why are you moaning?' He replied, 'I have a child and I suffered last night the whole night because of him.' Abu 'Abd Allah, *'Alayhi al-Salam,* has stated this *Hadith.* 'O Yunus, my father, Muhammad ibn Ali, *'Alayhi al-Salam,* narrated to me from his ancestors from my great, great, great, great grandfather, the Messenger of Allah, *O Allah, grant compensation to Muhammad and his family worthy of their services to Your cause,* that Jibril came to him when he found the Messenger of Allah and Ali moaning. Jibril asked, 'O beloved of Allah, how is it that I find you moaning?' The Messenger of Allah replied, 'We have two children and because of their weeping we have suffered.' Jibril said, 'O Muhammad, be patient. Very soon, a nation of followers for them will be raised and the weeping of one of them will mean, "No one other than Allah alone deserves worship," up to seven years. From the age of seven onward is asking forgiveness for their parents until they become of age (of maturity). Thereafter, whatever good deeds they do will be for their parents and whatever bad deeds they do will not be against their parents.'"

H 10461, Ch. 38, h 6

Muhammad ibn Yahya has narrated from Ali ibn Ibrahim al-Ja'fariy from Hamdan ibn Ishaq who has said the following:

"I had a son who had bladder (kidney) stone and it was said to me that it has no medicine except operating and I operated, then the child died. The Shi'ah said, 'You have caused the death of your son. I then wrote to abu al-Hassan al-'Askariy, *'Alayhi al-Salam.* He (the Imam) signed the answer that said, 'O Ahmad, you are not responsible for what you have done. You tried to cure him and his death (the appointed time) was in what you did.'"

H 10462, Ch. 38, h 7

A number of our people have narrated from Sahl ibn Ziyad from Ali ibn al-Hakam from 'Abd Allah ibn Jundab from Sufyan ibn al-Simt who has said the following:

"Abu 'Abd Allah, *'Alayhi al-Salam,* once said to me, 'When a child becomes four months old then perform cupping every month in the depression in the back of the child; it reduces his saliva and the temperature from his head.'"

H 10463, Ch. 38, h 8

Muhammad ibn Yahya has narrated from Ahmad ibn Muhammad ibn 'Isa from Ali ibn Ahmad ibn 'Ushaym from certain persons of his people who has said the following:

"Twin boys were born to a man and abu 'Abd Allah, *'Alayhi al-Salam,* congratulated and asked him who is the older?' He replied, 'The one who came out first is the older one. Abu 'Abd Allah, *'Alayhi al-Salam,* said, 'No, the one who came out last is the older one because she conceived him first, and this one entered on him and he could not come out before he came out so the one who comes out last is the older one.'"

End of the Book of *'Aqiqah,* all praise belongs to Allah cherisher of the worlds, followed by the Book of Talaq (divorces).

Part Two:
The Book of Talaq (Divorces)

Chapter 1 - Detestability of Divorcing a Cooperating Wife

H 10464, Ch. 1, h 1

Narrated to us certain persons of our people from Ahmad ibn Muhammad from ibn Faddal from abu Jamilah from Sa'd ibn Tarif who has said the following:

"Abu Ja'far, *'Alayhi al-Salam,* has said that once the Messenger of Allah, *O Allah, grant compensation to Muhammad and his family worthy of their services to Your cause,* passed by a man and asked, 'How is your wife doing?' He said, 'I have divorced her, O Messenger of Allah.' He (the Messenger of Allah) asked, 'Did you do it without her misbehaving?' He replied, 'Yes, it was without her misbehaving.' He (the Imam) said that he married and the Holy Prophet, passed by and asked, 'Have you got married?' He replied, 'Yes, I have married.' He (the Messenger of Allah) afterward asked, 'How is your wife?' He replied, 'I have divorced her.' He (the Messenger of Allah) asked, 'Did you divorce her without her misbehaving?' He replied, 'Yes, it was without her misbehaving.' The man then got married and the Holy Prophet, passed by and asked, 'Have you got married?' Afterward he (the Messenger of Allah) asked about his wife and he replied, 'I divorced her.' He (the Messenger of Allah) asked, 'Did you do without her misbehaving?' He replied, 'Yes, it was without her misbehaving.' The Messenger of Allah then said, 'Allah, most Majestic, most Glorious, hates or condemns every man who divorces hastily (like an epicure who keeps tasting this and that food) and every woman who is as such.'"

H 10465, Ch. 1, h 2

Ali ibn Ibrahim has narrated from his father from ibn abu 'Umayr from more than one person who has said the following:

"Abu 'Abd Allah, *'Alayhi al-Salam,* has said, 'Of whatever Allah, most Majestic, most Glorious, has made lawful nothing is more hateful to Him than divorce. Allah hates those who divorce very often in a hasty manner (like an epicure who keeps tasting this and that food).'"

H 10466, Ch. 1, h 3

Muhammad ibn Yahya has narrated from Muhammad ibn al-Husayn from 'Abd al-Rahman n Muhammad from abu Khadijah who has said the following:

"Abu 'Abd Allah, *'Alayhi al-Salam,* has said, 'Allah, most Majestic, most Glorious, loves the house in which there is a wedding and He hates the house where divorce takes place. There is nothing more hateful to Allah, most Majestic, most Glorious, than divorce.'"

H 10467, Ch. 1, h 4

Muhammad ibn Yahya has narrated from Ahmad ibn Muhammad from Muhammad ibn Yahya from Talhah ibn Zayd who has said the following:

"I once heard abu 'Abd Allah, *'Alayhi al-Salam,* saying, 'Allah hates those who divorce very often in big haste (like an epicure who keeps tasting this and that food).'"

H 10468, Ch. 1, h 5

Through the same chain of narrators as that of the previous *Hadith*, the following is narrated:

"Abu 'Abd Allah, *'Alayhi al-Salam,* has said that the Holy Prophet, was informed about abu Ayyub's divorcing his wife. The Messenger of Allah, *O Allah, grant compensation to Muhammad and his family worthy of their services to Your cause,* then said, 'Divorcing 'Umm (mother of) Ayyub is a sin.'"

Chapter 2 - Divorcing an Uncooperative Wife

H 10469, Ch. 2, h 1

A number of our people have narrated from Ahmad ibn Muhammad from 'Uthman ibn 'Isa from a man who has said the following:

"Abu Ja'far, *'Alayhi al-Salam,* had a wife whom he (the Imam) liked and loved. One day he (the Imam) divorced her and he was sad about it. A certain person of his followers asked, 'Why did you divorce her?' He (the Imam) replied, 'I mentioned Ali, *'Alayhi al-Salam,* before her and she reduced him (the Imam). I did not like touching a burning piece of charcoal of the charcoal of hell with my skin.'"

H 10470, Ch. 2, h 2

Muhammad ibn al-Husayn has narrated from Ibrahim ibn Ishaq al-Ahmar from 'Abd Allah ibn Hammad Khattab ibn Salmah who has said the following:

"I had a wife who believed (in the divine authority of *'A'immah*) and so also was her father, but she had very bad moral behaviors and I did not like to divorce her because of her belief and the belief of her father. I met abu al-Hassan, Musa, *'Alayhi al-Salam,* and I wanted to ask him (the Imam) if divorcing her is proper saying, 'I pray to Allah to keep my soul in service for your cause, I need an answer to a question and I like to ask you.' He (the Imam) said, 'Come tomorrow at the time of *al-Zuhr Salat* (prayer). He (the narrator) has said, 'After performing *al-Zuhr Salat* (prayer) I went to see him (the Imam) and I found that he (the Imam) had completed his *Salat* (prayer) and he was sitting. I went inside and sat in front of him (the Imam). He (the Imam) initiated speaking to me and said, 'O Khattab, my father made me marry a daughter of my uncle and her moral behaviors were very bad. My father sometimes would close the door on both of us in the hope that I may meet her, instead of climbing the wall to run away. When my father passed away I divorced her.' I (the narrator) then said to myself, 'Allah is Greater than can be described, He (the Imam) has answered my question before I could even ask him (the Imam).'"

H 10471, Ch. 2, h 3

Ahmad ibn Mehran has narrated from Muhammad ibn Ali from 'Umar ibn 'Abd al-'Aziz from Khattab ibn Salmah who has said the following:

"I once went to see him, abu al-Hassan, Musa, *'Alayhi al-Salam,* and complain before him against my wife because of her bad moral behaviors. He (the Imam) initiating to speak to me said, 'One time my father arranged for me the marriage to a woman who had very bad moral behaviors and I complained before him against her. He said, 'What stops you from divorcing her? Allah has already given you such authority.' I (the narrator) then said to myself, 'You (Imam) by Allah have provided relief and a way out for me.'"

H 10472, Ch. 2, h 4

Humayd ibn Ziyad has narrated from al-Hassan ibn Muhammad ibn Sama'ah from Muhammad ibn Ziyad ibn 'Isa from 'Abd Allah ibn Sinan who has said the following:

"Abu 'Abd Allah, *'Alayhi al-Salam,* has said that `Amir al-Mu'minin, *'Alayhi al-Salam,* once from the pulpit said, 'Do not give in marriage to al-Hassan because he is a man who divorces very often.' A man from Hamadan stood up and said, 'Yes, we will give to him in marriage, by Allah, because he is the grandson of the Messenger of Allah, *O Allah, grant compensation to Muhammad and his family worthy of their services to Your cause,* and the son of `Amir al-Mu'minin, *'Alayhi al-Salam.* He may keep if he likes or divorce if he so wills.'"

H 10473, Ch. 2, h 5

A number of our people have narrated from Ahmad ibn Muhammad from Muhammad ibn `Isma'il ibn Bazi' from Ja'far ibn Bashir from Yahya ibn abu al-'Ala' who has said the following:

"Abu 'Abd Allah, *'Alayhi al-Salam,* has said, 'Al-Hassan ibn Ali, *'Alayhi al-Salam,* divorced fifty women. Ali, *'Alayhi al-Salam,* stood in al-Kufah and said, 'O people of al-Kufah do not give in marriage to al-Hassan because he divorces very often.' A man stood up and said, 'Yes, we will give to him in marriage, by Allah, because he is the grandson of the Messenger of Allah, *O Allah, grant compensation to Muhammad and his family worthy of their services to Your cause,* and the son of Fatimah, *'Alayha al-Salam.* He may keep if he likes or divorces if he so wills.'"

H 10474, Ch. 2, h 6

Al-Husayn from Muhammad has narrated from Mu'alla' ibn Muhammad from al-Washsha' from 'Abd Allah ibn Sinan from al-Walid ibn Sabih who has said the following:

"I once heard abu 'Abd Allah, *'Alayhi al-Salam,* saying, 'The prayers of three kinds of people are returned to them without a favorable answer. One of such people is one who prays against his wife to whom he is unjust and it is said to him, 'Have we not given you the authority to divorce her?'"

Chapter 3 - People Do not Remain Straight in Matters of Divorce without the Sword

H 10475, Ch. 3, h 1

Humayd ibn Ziyad from al-Hassan ibn Muhammad from al-Hassan ibn Hudhayfah, from Mu'ammar ibn ('Ata' ibn) Washik who has said the following:

"I once heard abu Ja'far, *'Alayhi al-Salam,* saying, 'People do not behave properly in matters of divorce without the sword. If you govern them, you can return them to the book of Allah, most Majestic, most Glorious.' He (the narrator) has said that al-Mithamiy from Muhammad ibn abu Hamzah from his narrators narrated guessing that this *Hadith* is from abu 'Abd Allah, *'Alayhi al-Salam.*'"

H 10476, Ch. 3, h 2

It is narrated from the narrator of the previous *Hadith* from 'Abd Allah ibn Jabalah from abu al-Mighra', from Sama'ah from abu Basir who has said the following:

"Abu Ja'far, *'Alayhi al-Salam,* has said, 'Were I to govern the people I would teach them how to divorce, thereafter I would make the back of the violators painful. Those who divorce against the *Sunnah* must be returned to the book of Allah, most Majestic, most Glorious, despite their opposing.'"

H 10477, Ch. 3, h 3

A number of our people have narrated from Sahl ibn Ziyad from Ahmad ibn Muhammad from ibn abu Nasr from Muhammad ibn Sama'ah from 'Umar ibn Mu'ammar ibn'Ata' ibn Washik who has said the following:

"I once heard abu Ja'far, *'Alayhi al-Salam,* saying, 'In matters of divorce people do not behave properly without the sword. Had I been governing them I would return them to the book of Allah, most Majestic, most Glorious.'"

H 10478, Ch. 3, h 4

Ahmad has said that certain persons of our people have narrated from abu 'Abd Allah, *'Alayhi al-Salam,* and Muhammad ibn Sama'ah from the virtuous servant (of Allah) has said the following:

"Had I been governing people I would teach them how to finalize a divorce case and thereafter make the violators to suffer pain.'"

H 10479, Ch. 3, h 5

Muhammad ibn Yahya has narrated from Ahmad ibn Muhammad from certain persons of our people from Aban from abu Basir who has said the following:

"I once heard abu Ja'far, *'Alayhi al-Salam,* saying, 'Had the affairs of people been in my hands I would straighten them with the sword and whip until they divorced with waiting period as Allah, most Majestic, most Glorious, has commanded.'"

Chapter 4 - The Divorces Not According to the Book and Sunnah

H 10480, Ch. 4, h 1

A number of our people have narrated from Sahl ibn Ziyad and Ali ibn Ibrahim has narrated from his father from all from Ahmad ibn Muhammad from ibn abu Nasr from Aban from abu Basir from ''Amr ibn Riyah who has said the following:

"I once said to abu Ja'far, *'Alayhi al-Salam,* 'Have you said that one who does not divorce according to the book and al-*Sunnah* his divorce is not valid?' Abu Ja'far, *'Alayhi al-Salam,* replied, 'I have not said so, in fact, Allah, most Majestic, most Glorious, has said it. By Allah, were we to give you fatwas with injustice we would become worse than you; Allah, most Majestic, most Glorious, says, 'Would that their Rabbis and Ahbar prohibit them from their sinful words and consuming what is filthy. . . .' (5:63)"

H 10481, Ch. 4, h 2

A number of our people have narrated from Sahl ibn Ziyad from Ahmad ibn Muhammad from ibn abu Nasr from 'Abd al-Karim from 'Abd Allah ibn Sulayman al-Sayrafiy who has said the following:

"Abu Ja'far, *'Alayhi al-Salam,* has said, 'Whatever is not according to the book of Allah, most Majestic, most Glorious, is returned to the book of Allah, most Majestic, most Glorious, and al-*Sunnah*.'"

H 10482, Ch. 4, h 3

Muhammad ibn 'Isma'il has narrated from al-Fadl ibn Shadhan from Safwan ibn Yahya from 'Abd Allah ibn Muskan from Muhammad al-Halabiy who has said the following:

"I once asked abu 'Abd Allah, *'Alayhi al-Salam,* about the case of a man who divorces his wife when she experiences *Hayd* (menses). He (the Imam) said, 'A divorce which is not according to *Sunnah* is invalid.' I then asked, 'What happens if a man divorces his wife three times in one place and time?' He (the Imam) said, 'It must be returned to *Sunnah*.'"

H 10483, Ch. 4, h 4

Humayd ibn Ziyad has narrated from al-Hassan ibn Muhammad from 'Abd Allah ibn Jabalah from abu al=Mighra' from Sama'ah from abu Basir who has said the following:

"Abu Ja'far, *'Alayhi al-Salam,* has said, 'One who does not divorce according to *Sunnah* must be returned to the book of Allah, most Majestic, most Glorious, even though he may refuse.'"

H 10484, Ch. 4, h 5

Ali ibn Ibrahim has narrated from his father from certain persons of his people from 'Abd Allah ibn Sinan who has said the following:

"I once asked abu 'Abd Allah, *'Alayhi al-Salam,* about the case of a divorce which is not with waiting period. He (the Imam) said, 'It must be returned to the book of Allah, most Majestic, most Glorious.'"

H 10485, Ch. 4, h 6

A number of our people have narrated from Sahl ibn Ziyad from Ahmad ibn Muhammad from ibn abu Nasr from 'Abd al-Karim from al-Halabiy who has said the following:

"I once asked abu 'Abd Allah, *'Alayhi al-Salam,* about the case of a man who divorces his wife during her experiencing *Hayd* (menses). He (the Imam) said, 'It is a divorce which is not according to *Sunnah*.'"

H 10486, Ch. 4, h 7

Ali ibn Ibrahim has narrated from his father from ibn abu 'Umayr from abu Ayyub from Muhammad ibn Muslim who has said the following:

"Abu Ja'far, *'Alayhi al-Salam,* has said, 'If one divorces his wife in one place and time three times when she is experiencing *Hayd* (menses) such divorce does not have any valid effect. A valid divorce is that which Allah, most Majestic, most Glorious, has commanded. Whoever does otherwise it is not a divorce. Ibn 'Umar divorced his wife three times in one place and time when she experienced *Hayd* (menses). The Holy Prophet, *O Allah, grant compensation to Muhammad and his family worthy of their services to Your cause,* commanded him to go to bed with her and ignore that kind of divorce.' He (the Imam) said, 'A man once came to 'Amir al-Mu'minin, *'Alayhi al-Salam,* and said, 'O 'Amir al-Mu'minin, I have divorced my wife.' He (the Imam) asked, 'Do you have witnesses?' he replied, 'No, I do not have any witnesses.' He (the Imam) said, 'You must disregard it.'"

H 10487, Ch. 4, h 8

Muhammad ibn Ja'far abu al-'Abbas has narrated from Ayyub ibn Nuh from Safwan from Ya'qub ibn Shu'ayb who has said that I heard abu Basir saying the following:

"I once asked abu Ja'far, *'Alayhi al-Salam*, about the case of a woman who is not divorced according to *Sunnah* and said that they are a family and no one knows them. He (the Imam) said, 'It does not have any valid effect.'"

H 10488, Ch. 4, h 9

A number of our people have narrated from Ahmad ibn Muhammad from al-Husayn ibn Sa'id, from al-Nadr ibn Suwayd from Muhammad ibn abu Hamzah from Sa'id al-A'raj who has said the following:

"I once heard abu 'Abd Allah, *'Alayhi al-Salam*, state this *Hadith*. 'Ibn 'Umar divorced his wife three times at the same place and time when she experienced *Hayd* (menses). He asked the Messenger of Allah, *O Allah, grant compensation to Muhammad and his family worthy of their services to Your cause*, and he commanded him to go back to his wife.' I then said, 'People say that he divorced only once when she experienced *Hayd* (menses).' He (the Imam) asked, 'What for, then, did he ask the Messenger of Allah if he was able to go back to her? They speak a lie. He divorced three times at the same place and time, then the Messenger of Allah commanded him to go back to her and then divorce her if he wanted or keep her if he so willed.'"

H 10489, Ch. 4, h 10

Muhammad ibn Yahya has narrated from Ahmad ibn Muhammad from Ali ibn al-Hakam from Musa ibn Bakr from Zurarah who has said the following:

"Abu Ja'far, *'Alayhi al-Salam*, was asked about the case of a woman who hears that the man has divorced her but he denies it: if she can stay with him. He (the Imam) said, 'Yes, because divorce without witness is not a divorce, also divorce without waiting period is not a divorce. It is not lawful to divorce without witnesses and without waiting period that Allah, most Majestic, most Glorious, has commanded to do.'"

H 10490, Ch. 4, h 11

Ali ibn Ibrahim has narrated from his father from Hammad ibn 'Isa from ibn 'Udhaynah from Zurarah and Muhammad ibn Muslim and Bukayr ibn 'A'yan and Burayd and Fudayl and 'Isma'il al-Azraq and Mu'ammar ibn Yahya from abu Ja'far and abu 'Abd Allah, *'Alayhim al-Salam*, who has said the following:

"When a man during a woman's experiencing blood discharge because of childbirth or after going to bed with her divorces, such divorce is not a valid divorce. A divorce at such time when commencing waiting period is possible and valid, that it is in a menses-free time but without the presence of two just witnesses, such divorce also is not a valid divorce.'"

H 10491, Ch. 4, h 12

Abu Ali al-Ash'ariy has narrated from Muhammad ibn 'Abd al-Jabbar from Safwan ibn Yahya from Ishaq ibn 'Ammar who has said the following:

"I once asked abu al-Hassan, (Musa), *'Alayhi al-Salam*, about the case of a man who divorces his wife in a menses-free period during which he has not gone to bed with her. He then goes back to her on the same day, then divorces her: if it becomes irrevocable with three divorces during one menses-free period. He (the

Imam) said, 'He has opposed the *Sunnah*.' I then asked, 'Is it necessary after going back to his wife to divorce her in another menses-free period of time?' He (the Imam) replied, 'Yes, it is necessary.' I said, 'So that he can go to bed with her?' He (the Imam) replied, 'Yes, he can do so.'"

H 10492, Ch. 4, h 13
Muhammad ibn Yahya has narrated from Ahmad ibn Muhammad from Muhammad ibn `Isma'il ibn Bazi' from Muhammad ibn al-Fudayl from abu al-Sabbah al-Kinaniy who has said the following:

"Abu 'Abd Allah, *'Alayhi al-Salam*, has said, 'If one divorces his wife without witnesses it does not become of any valid effect.'"

H 10493, Ch. 4, h 14
Sahl has narrated from Ahmad ibn Muhammad from Muhammad ibn Sama'ah from 'Umar ibn Yazid from Muhammad ibn Muslim who has said the following:

"Once, a man in al-Kufah came to `Amir al-Mu'minin, *'Alayhi al-Salam*, and said, 'I have divorced my wife after she became clean from her *Hayd* (menses) and before I went to bed with her.' `Amir al-Mu'minin asked, 'Did you ask two just men to witness as Allah, most Majestic, most Glorious, has commanded to do?' He replied, 'No, I did not do so.' He (the Imam) said, 'Your divorce in not valid.'"

H 10494, Ch. 4, h 15
Ali ibn Ibrahim has narrated from his father from ibn abu 'Umayr from Hammad from al-Halabiy who has said the following:

"Abu 'Abd Allah, *'Alayhi al-Salam*, has said, 'If one divorces his wife three times at the same place and time it does not become of any valid effect. The Messenger of Allah, *O Allah, grant compensation to Muhammad and his family worthy of their services to Your cause*, rejected the divorce of 'Abd Allah ibn 'Umar when he divorced his wife with three divorces when she experienced *Hayd* (menses). The Messenger of Allah called it an invalid divorce saying, 'Whatever is against the book of Allah, most Majestic, most Glorious, must return to the book of Allah, most Majestic, most Glorious.' He (the Messenger of Allah) said, 'Divorce without waiting period is not valid.'"

H 10495, Ch. 4, h 16
Abu Ali al-Ash'ariy has narrated from Muhammad ibn 'Abd al-Jabbar from Muhammad ibn `Isma'il ibn Bazi' from Ali ibn al-Nu'man from Sa'id al-A'raj who has said the following:

"I once said to abu 'Abd Allah, *'Alayhi al-Salam*, 'I asked 'Amr ibn 'Ubayd about the divorce of 'Abd Allah ibn 'Umar and he said, "He divorced her once when she experienced *Hayd* (menses)."' Abu 'Abd Allah, *'Alayhi al-Salam*, said, 'Why did you not say to him, "If he divorced her once during her experiencing *Hayd* (menses) or when she did not experience *Hayd* (menses), he had more authority to go back to his wife.' I said, 'I did say so.' He (the Imam) then said, 'He has not spoken the truth, may Allah condemn him. He divorced three times but the Messenger of Allah, *O Allah, grant compensation to Muhammad and his family worthy of their services to Your cause*, rejected it and said, "You can keep your wife or divorce her according to *Sunnah* if you wanted."'"

H 10496, Ch. 4, h 17

Ali ibn Ibrahim has narrated from his father from ibn abu 'Umayr from 'Umar ibn 'Udhaynah from Bukayr and others who has said the following:

"Abu Ja'far, *'Alayhi al-Salam,* has said, 'Every divorce without waiting period is not a valid divorce, or divorce during her experiencing *Hayd* (menses), Nifas (childbirth), after going to bed with her before her *Hayd* (menses), such divorces are not valid. If one divorces with waiting period more than once the extra one does not have any valid effect. If one divorces with waiting period without just witnesses, it also is not a divorce and women's witnessing is not sufficient.'"

H 10497, Ch. 4, h 18

Ali ibn Ibrahim has narrated from his father from ibn abu 'Umayr from 'Umar ibn 'Udhaynah from Zurarah who has said the following:

"Once, I was with abu Ja'far, *'Alayhi al-Salam,* when, Nafi' Mawla' ibn 'Umar came to visit him (the Imam). Abu Ja'far, *'Alayhi al-Salam,* asked him, 'Are you the one who believes that ibn 'Umar divorced his wife once during her experiencing *Hayd* (menses) and the Messenger of Allah, *O Allah, grant compensation to Muhammad and his family worthy of their services to Your cause,* commanded 'Umar to ask him to go back to his wife?' He replied, 'Yes, that is correct.' He (the Imam) said, 'You have spoken a lie against ibn 'Umar, by Allah, besides whom no one deserves worship. I heard ibn 'Umar saying, "I divorced her during the time of the Messenger of Allah, three divorces but the Messenger of Allah reversed it on me and I kept her after divorce." O Nafi' you must have fear of Allah and do not narrate falsehood against ibn 'Umar.'"

Chapter 5 - Divorce Does not Take Place unless Once has the Intention to Divorce

H 10498, Ch. 5, h 1

Ali ibn Ibrahim has narrated from his father from ibn abu 'Umayr from certain persons of his people from ibn Bukayr from Zurarah who has said the following:

"Abu 'Abd Allah, *'Alayhi al-Salam,* has said, 'It is not a divorce unless it is intended to be a divorce.'"

H 10499, Ch. 5, h 2

Muhammad ibn Yahya has narrated from Ahmad ibn Muhammad from ibn Faddal from ibn Bukayr from Zurarah from al-Yasa' from abu 'Abd Allah, *'Alayhi al-Salam,* from 'Abd al-Wahid ibn al-Mukhtar from abu Ja'far, *'Alayhi al-Salam,* who has said the following:

"One of the two Imam, (abu Ja'far or abu 'Abd Allah), *'Alayhi al-Salam,* has said, 'It is not a divorce unless it is intended to be a divorce.'"

H 10500, Ch. 5, h 3

Muhammad ibn Yahya has narrated from Ahmad ibn Muhammad and Ali ibn Ibrahim has narrated from his father from 'Abd al-Rahman ibn abu Najran from 'Abd Allah ibn Bukayr from Zurarah from al-Yasa' who has said the following:

"I once heard abu Ja'far, *'Alayhi al-Salam,* has stated this *Hadith.* 'Divorce, which is not according to *Sunnah,* is not a divorce. A divorce is not according to *Sunnah* if it is not pronounced in the presence of two just witnesses, in a menses-free period in which the husband has not gone to bed with her. If a man divorces his wife in a menses-free period during which he has not gone to bed with her but it is not in presence (of two just) witnesses, such divorce is not a valid divorce. If a man divorces his wife according to *Sunnah*, in a menses-free period in which he has not gone to bed with her and pronounces it in the presence of witnesses but has not intended it to be a divorce it also is not a valid divorce.'"

Chapter 6 - There Cannot be Divorce before Marriage

H 10501, Ch. 6, h 1

Muhammad ibn Yahya has narrated from Ahmad ibn Muhammad and Muhammad ibn al-Husayn from Muhammad ibn `Isma'il ibn Bazi' from Mansur ibn Yunus from Hamzah ibn Humran from 'Abd Allah ibn Sulayman from his father Sulayman who has said the following:

"Once I was in the Masjid when Ali ibn al-Husayn, *'Alayhim al-Salam*, came in but I could not recognize him properly; so I asked about him and I was told about his name so others and I stood up for him, we surrounded him (the Imam) and offered him (the Imam) greeting of peace. A man then said, 'I pray to Allah to keep you well, what is your view about a man who mentions a woman exactly and on the day of his marriage says three times that she is divorced then he decides to marry her: if he can do so.' He (the Imam) said, 'Divorce is only after marriage.'"

H 10502, Ch. 6, h 2

A number of our people have narrated from Ahmad ibn Muhammad from and Ali ibn Ibrahim has narrated from his father from 'Uthman ibn 'Isa from Sama'ah who has said the following:

"I once asked him (the Imam), *'Alayhi al-Salam,* about the case of a man who says that on the day I will get married to so and so she is divorced. He (the Imam) said, 'It does not have any valid effect until he has a binding marriage.'"

H 10503, Ch. 6, h 3

A number of our people have narrated from Ahmad ibn Muhammad ibn 'Isa from al-Husayn ibn Sa'id from Hammad ibn 'Isa from Shu'ayb ibn Ya'qub who has said the following:

"Abu 'Abd Allah, *'Alayhi al-Salam,* has said, 'Those who were before us would say, 'Setting free of a slave or divorce does not have any valid effect until a man has an ownership and marriage.'"

H 10504, Ch. 6, h 4

Muhammad ibn Ja'far al-Razzaz has narrated from Ayyub ibn Nuh and Abu Ali al-Ash'ariy has narrated from Muhammad ibn 'Abd al-Jabbar from Safwan ibn Yahya from Hariz from Hamzah ibn Humran from 'Abd Allah ibn Sulayman from his father who has said the following:

"Once I was in the Masjid when Ali ibn al-Husayn, *'Alayhi al-Salam,* came and I could not recognize him. He (the Imam) had a black turban and he had allowed both ends of the turban to hang down between his two shoulders. I then asked a man sitting near me, 'Who is this Shaykh?' He asked, 'Why did you not ask me about people other than this shaykh coming in the Masjid?' I replied, 'Because I did not see anyone else entering the Masjid look as good as this Shaykh and his condition in my eyes, thus I asked you.' He then said, 'This is Ali ibn al-Husayn, *'Alayhi al-Salam.*' The man, others and I stood up. We surrounded him (the Imam) and offered greetings of peace. A man then said, 'I pray to Allah to keep you well, what is your view about a man who mentions a woman exactly and on the day of his marriage says three times that she is divorced but then he decides to marry her: if he can do so.' He (the Imam) said, 'Divorce is only after marriage.' 'Abd Allah has said that my father and I visited abu 'Abd Allah, Ja'far ibn Muhammad, *'Alayhim al-Salam*, and my father narrated this *Hadith* to him (the Imam). Abu 'Abd Allah, *'Alayhi al-Salam,* asked, 'Will you testify that this is a *Hadith* of Ali ibn al-Husayn, *'Alayhi al-Salam*?' He replied, 'Yes I will do so.'"

H 10505, Ch. 6, h 5

Ali ibn Ibrahim has narrated from his father from ibn abu Najran from 'Asem ibn Hamid from Muhammad ibn Qays who has said the following:

"I once asked abu Ja'far, *'Alayhi al-Salam,* about the case of a man who says, 'If I marry so and so woman she is divorced; if I buy so and so slave, he is free and if I buy this cloth it is for the destitute. He (the Imam) said, 'It does not have any valid effect; he cannot divorce until he is married and owns. He cannot give charity except what he owns.'"

Chapter 7 - Divorce in Writing

H 10506, Ch. 7, h 1

Muhammad ibn Yahya has narrated from Ahmad ibn Muhammad from al-Hassan ibn Mahbub from abu Hamzah al-Thumaliy who has said the following:

"I once asked abu Ja'far, *'Alayhi al-Salam,* about the case of a man who says to another man, 'O so and so write to my wife her divorce or to my slave that he is free; if it is a divorce and setting free of a slave. He (the Imam) said, 'It is not a divorce or freedom until he says by his own tongue or his own handwriting and with the intention to divorce or set a slave free. This can happen by counting new moons and in the presence of witnesses when he is absent from his family.'"

H 10507, Ch. 7, h 2

Ali ibn Ibrahim has narrated from his father from Hammad ibn 'Isa or ibn abu 'Umayr from ibn 'Udhaynah from Zurarah who has said the following:

"I once asked abu Ja'far, *'Alayhi al-Salam,* about the case of a man who divorces his wife in writing or sets free his slave; he then changes his mind and deletes it. He (the Imam) said, 'It is not a divorce or setting free of a slave until he pronounces it through his mouth.'"

Chapter 8 - Explanation of Divorce with Waiting Period and what Makes Divorce Binding

H 10508, Ch. 8, h 1

Abu Ali al-Ash'ariy has narrated from Muhammad ibn 'Abd al-Jabbar and Muhammad ibn Ja'far abu al-'Abbas al-Razzaz from abu Ayyub ibn Nuh and Ali ibn Ibrahim has narrated from his father all from Safwan ibn Yahya from ibn Muskan from Muhammad ibn Muslim who has said the following:

"Abu Ja'far, *'Alayhi al-Salam,* has said, 'Divorce according to *Sunnah* is the divorce which one pronounces once in a menses-free period during which sexual intercourse has not taken place. It is pronounced in the presence of two witnesses and leaves her until her menses-free period is over. When this period is over she becomes stranger to him and he is one of those who may propose marriage; if he likes he can marry or not marry. If he decides to go back to his wife there must be a witness to bear witness to his going back to his wife before her menses-free period is over so that she remains with him within the first divorce.' He (the narrator) has said that abu Basir narrated from abu 'Abd Allah, *'Alayhi al-Salam,* who stated this about the words of Allah, most Majestic, most Glorious. 'Divorce is twice, thereafter one must keep her in proper manner or in kindness allow her to go.' (2:229) He (the Imam) has said that it is the second divorce and allowing with kindness to go.'"

H 10509, Ch. 8, h 2

A number of our people have narrated from Sahl ibn Ziyad Ahmad ibn Muhammad from Muhammad ibn Yahya has narrated from Ahmad ibn Muhammad Ahmad ibn Muhammad and Ali ibn Ibrahim has narrated from his father all from al-Hassan ibn Mahbub from ibn Ri'ab from Zurarah who has said the following:

"Abu Ja'far, *'Alayhi al-Salam,* has said, 'Divorce which is not according to *Sunnah* or not with waiting period does not have any valid effect.' Zurarah has said that I then asked abu Ja'far, *'Alayhi al-Salam,* 'Please explain to me divorce according to *Sunnah* and divorce with waiting period.' He (the Imam) said, 'For divorce according to *Sunnah* the man must wait until she experiences *Hayd* (menses) and becomes clean from *Hayd* (menses). When this happens he can divorce her in the presence of two witnesses without going to bed with her; then he leaves her until she experiences *Hayd* (menses) twice and her waiting period becomes complete. On her experiencing the third *Hayd* (menses) she becomes stranger to him. He then is one of those who may propose marriage; if he wants he can marry or not to marry. He must pay her maintenance as long as she is in her waiting period and they inherit each other during the waiting period.' He (the Imam) said, 'Divorce with waiting period is the divorce which Allah, most Majestic, most Glorious, has mentioned, '. . . .divorce them with waiting period and keep a count of the waiting period.' (65:2) For this kind of divorce if a man wants to divorce his wife he must wait until she experiences *Hayd* (menses) and become clean of *Hayd* (menses) then divorce her one divorce in the presence of two just witnesses without going to bed with her. He then can go back to her on the same day if he likes or after several days or before she experiences *Hayd* (menses). He must have a witness for his going back to her. He can go to bed with her and live with her until she experiences *Hayd* (menses). When she experiences *Hayd* (menses) and becomes clean, divorce her in the presence of witnesses without going to bed with her. He then can go back to her again anytime he likes before she experiences *Hayd* (menses) for the third *Hayd* (menses). When she becomes clean of the third *Hayd* (menses) he divorces her in the presence of witness for the third time without sexual intercourse. When he does this she becomes stranger to him and he cannot marry her again before she marries another man.' He (the Imam) was asked, 'What happens if she does not experience *Hayd* (menses)?' He (the Imam) said, 'In such case she is divorced according to *Sunnah.*'"

H 10510, Ch. 8, h 3

Ibn Mahbub has narrated from ibn Bukayr from Zurarah who has said the following:

"I once heard abu Ja'far, *'Alayhi al-Salam,* saying, 'If a man wants to divorce his wife I like if he does so in the form of divorce according to *Sunnah.*' He (the narrator) has said that he (the Imam) then said, 'This is that about which Allah, most Majestic, most Glorious, has said, '. . . perhaps Allah thereafter will cause something to happen.' (65:2) It means after divorce and waiting period a marriage with him, before the advance of the case to a marriage with another man. He (the Imam) said, 'How vast is the justice and time for them! He must divorce her in a *Hayd* (menses)-free period without sexual intercourse one divorce in the presence of witnesses then leave her until three months or three *Hayd* (menses) then he becomes one of those who may propose marriage.'"

H 10511, Ch. 8, h 4

Ali ibn Ibrahim has narrated from his father from ibn abu Najran or others from ibn Muskan from abu Basir who has said the following:

"I once asked abu 'Abd Allah, *'Alayhi al-Salam,* about the divorce according to *Sunnah.* He (the Imam) said, 'For divorce according to *Sunnah* when a man wants to divorce his wife he must leave her, if he has gone to bed with her, until she experiences *Hayd* (menses), then becomes clean. When she becomes clean he can divorce her once in the presence of two witnesses then leave her for three cycles of *Hayd* (menses). When three *Hayd* (menses)-free periods are over she becomes stranger to him and he becomes one of those who may propose for marriage. He can marry if he wants or not marry. If he marries with a new mahr (dower) she can live with him for the two remaining chances when only one is complete. If he divorces her once more in the presence of two witnesses, in a *Hayd* (menses)-free period, without sexual intercourse and then leaves her until her *Hayd* (menses)-free periods are over. If they are over before he goes back to her she then becomes stranger to him with control on her affairs and is free to marry. Her previous husband is now one of those who may propose for marriage if he likes to marry or not to marry. If he marries with a new marriage with a new mahr (dower) she can live with him for one more chance. Two chances are complete. If he decides to divorce her once more, she then is not lawful for him until she marries another man.

"For divorce with the choice to go back to her he waits until she experiences *Hayd* (menses) and becomes clean, he arranges two witnesses for divorce; then goes back to her and to bed with her then waits for the next *Hayd* (menses)-free period. When she experiences *Hayd* (menses) and becomes clean, he arranges two witnesses for divorce, after which he goes back to go to bed with her. He then waits until after her *Hayd* (menses)-free period she experiences *Hayd* (menses) and becomes clean. He then arranges for two witnesses for another divorce and thereafter she becomes unlawful for him to marry forever until she marries another man. She must complete a waiting period for three *Hayd* (menses)-free periods from the day of the third divorce. If he divorces once in a *Hayd* (menses)-free period in the presence of witnesses and waits until she experiences *Hayd* (menses) and becomes clean then divorces her before he goes back to her the second divorce is not a divorce. It is because he has divorced one who is divorced; she was a divorced woman from her husband and out of his authority until he goes back to her. When he goes back to her then marriage comes in his authority until he divorces for the third time. Upon divorcing her for the third time, the authority to go back to her goes out of his hand. When he divorces her in a *Hayd* (menses)-free period, in the presence of witnesses, then goes back to her and waits until one *Hayd* (menses)-free period ends without sexual intercourse. She then experience *Hayd* (menses) and becomes clean then he divorces her before sexual intercourse after going back to her his divorce as such is not a divorce. It is because he has divorced her for the second time in the first *Hayd* (menses)-free period and a *Hayd* (menses)-free period cannot be broken without sexual intercourse after going back to her. In the same way, the third divorce cannot take place except by going back to her. After going back then she experiences *Hayd* (menses) and a *Hayd* (menses)-free period. He then divorces in the presence of witnesses until there is *Hayd* (menses)-free period after every divorce with sexual intercourse is a *Hayd* (menses)-free period and cleansing by sexual intercourse then divorce takes place in the presence of witnesses.'"

H 10512, Ch. 8, h 5

Abu Ali al-Ash'ariy has narrated from Muhammad ibn 'Abd al-Jabbar, from Safwan ibn Yahya. A number of our people have narrated from Sahl ibn Ziyad from Muhammad ibn Yahya who has narrated from Ahmad ibn Muhammad. Ali ibn Ibrahim has narrated from his father all of them from Ahmad ibn Muhammad ibn abu Nasr, from 'Abd al-Karim, all from al-Hassan ibn Ziyad, who has said the following:

"I once asked abu 'Abd Allah, *'Alayhi al-Salam,* about the divorce according to *Sunnah* and how a man can divorce his wife. He (the Imam) said, 'He must divorce her in a *Hayd* (menses)-free period at a time when she can commence her waiting period, in the presence of witnesses without going to bed with her. If he divorces her once then leaves until her waiting period is complete, she then becomes stranger to him and he is one of those who may propose marriage. If he goes back to her she then is with him for two more divorces. If he divorces her for the second time and leaves until her waiting period is complete, she becomes stranger to him. If he arranges witness for his going back to her before her waiting period is complete she is then with him after two divorces and one more is left. If he divorces her for the third time she becomes stranger to him and is not lawful for him until she marries another man. She inherits him during the waiting period of the two previous divorces in which he had the right to go back to her.'"

H 10513, Ch. 8, h 6

Ali ibn Ibrahim has narrated from his father from and Ahmad ibn Muhammad from ibn abu Nasr who has said the following:

"I once asked abu al-Hassan, *'Alayhi al-Salam,* about the case of a man who divorces his wife in the presence of two just witnesses after going to bed with her. He (the Imam) said, 'It is not a divorce,' I then asked saying, 'I pray to Allah to keep my soul in service for your cause, how is divorce according to *Sunnah*?' He (the Imam) said, 'He divorces her after she becomes clean of *Hayd* (menses) in the presence of two just witnesses before going to bed with her as Allah, most Majestic, most Glorious, has said in His book. (65:2) If it is against what Allah has said it must be returned to the book of Allah, most Majestic, most Glorious.' I then asked, 'What happens if he divorces, in the presence of one witness and two women, during a *Hayd* (menses)-free period in which he has not gone to bed with her?' He (the Imam) said, 'Witnessing of women is not permissible in the case of divorce, however, it can be accepted along with other witnesses in a man-slaughter case if she is present.' I then asked, 'What happens if two Nasibiy men (people hostile to *'A'immah*) bear witness in the case of divorce, is it a divorce?' He (the Imam) said, 'Whoever is born on al-Fitrah (proper belief) his testimony is accepted in the case of divorce after it is known that he does good deeds.'"

H 10514, Ch. 8, h 7
Ali ibn Ibrahim has narrated from his father from ibn abu 'Umayr from ibn 'Udhaynah from ibn Bukayr and others who has said the following:

"Abu Ja'far, *'Alayhi al-Salam,* has stated this *Hadith.* 'The divorce which Allah, most Majestic, most Glorious, in His book has commanded to be formed and that which the Messenger of Allah, *O Allah, grant compensation to Muhammad and his family worthy of their services to Your cause,* has established is that the man must remain away from the woman. When she experiences *Hayd* (menses) and becomes clean of her *Hayd* (menses), he must arrange two just witnesses for one divorce when she is clean of *Hayd* (menses) and sexual intercourse has not taken place. He has the right to go back to her as long as three menses cycles have not expired. Divorce other than being in this manner is invalid and is not a divorce.'"

H 10515, Ch. 8, h 8
A number of our people have narrated from Sahl ibn Ziyad Ahmad ibn Muhammad from ibn abu Nasr from Jamil ibn Darraj from Zurarah who has said the following:

"Divorce according to *Sunnah* takes place when the woman is clean of *Hayd* (menses) and is divorced in her place in the presence of witnesses without sexual intercourse. If he decides to go back to her he must arrange for witness to his going back (reversing his pronouncement of divorce).'"

H 10516, Ch. 8, h 9
Humayd ibn Ziyad from al-Hassan ibn Muhammad from 'Abd Allah ibn Sinan who has said the following:

"Abu 'Abd Allah, *'Alayhi al-Salam,* has said that 'Amir al-Mu'minin has said, 'If a man decides to divorce he must do so before her waiting period without sexual intercourse. If he divorces once then leaves until her waiting period is complete, he then can be one of those who may propose marriage if he so wills. If he goes back to her before waiting period is complete or afterward, she can live with him after one divorce. If he divorces a second time also he then proposes marriage as others may do, in case he did not go back before the end of waiting period, if he wants he can go back to her if he so wills before waiting period is complete and if he did then she is with him after two divorces. If he divorces her for the third time then she is not lawful for him before marriage with another man. She inherits and is inherited if one of them dies as long as she experiences *Hayd* (menses) after the two first divorces.'"

Chapter 9 - The Necessary Expressions to Pronounce with the Decision to Divorce

H 10517, Ch. 9, h 1
Humayd ibn Ziyad has narrated from al-Hassan ibn Muhammad ibn Sama'ah from ibn Ribat and Ali ibn Ibrahim has narrated from his father from ibn abu 'Umayr all from ibn 'Udhaynah from Muhammad ibn Muslim who has said the following:

"I once asked abu Ja'far, *'Alayhi al-Salam,* about the case of a man who says to his wife, 'You are unlawful for me, you are stranger to me, you are cut off, you are free and your way is clear.' He (the Imam) said, 'All of such expressions do not have any valid effect in the form of divorce. Divorce is when one just before waiting period, after her becoming clean from *Hayd* (menses) without sexual intercourse says, *'Anti Taliq* (you are let go, divorced) or *'I'tady* (commence waiting period) intending thereby *Talaq* (divorce) which must be in the presence of two witnesses.'"

H 10518, Ch. 9, h 2
Ali ibn Ibrahim has narrated from his father from ibn abu 'Umayr from Hammad from al-Halabiy who has said the following:

"Abu 'Abd Allah, *'Alayhi al-Salam,* has said, 'Divorce takes place when he says, *'I'tady* (commence waiting period) or says, *'Anti Taliq* (you are let go, divorced).'"

H 10519, Ch. 9, h 3
Ali ibn Ibrahim has narrated from his father and A number of our people have narrated from Sahl ibn Ziyad from ibn abu Najran from 'Asem ibn Hamid from Muhammad ibn Qays who has said the following:

"Abu Ja'far, *'Alayhi al-Salam,* has said, 'Divorce with waiting period is that by which a man divorces his wife whenever she is clean of *Hayd* (menses) and sends her a message to commence her waiting period because so and so has divorced her.' He (the Imam) said, 'He has the authority to go back to her as long as waiting period is not complete.'"

H 10520, Ch. 9, h 4
Humayd ibn Ziyad has narrated from ibn Sama'ah from Muhammad ibn Ziyad from 'Abd Allah ibn Sinan who has said the following:

"Abu 'Abd Allah, *'Alayhi al-Salam,* has said, 'He (the husband) can send a message to his wife saying, 'You must commence your waiting period because so and so has departed you.'

"Ibn Sama'ah has said that the meaning of the words of the messenger, 'You must commence your waiting period because so and so has departed you,' is that he has divorced you because there is no departing without divorce.

"Humayd ibn Ziyad has narrated from ibn Sama'ah from Ali ibn al-Hassan al-T`atriy who has said that what is unanimously agreed upon to say for divorce is to say, '*Anti Taliq*' (you are let go, divorced) or "*I'tadi*' (you must commence your waiting period). He has mentioned that he asked Muhammad ibn Hamzah about how to arrange witnesses for his word, '*I'tadi*' (you must commence your waiting period). He said that one must say, 'Bear witness '*I'tadi*' (commence waiting period).' Ibn Sama'ah has said, 'Muhammad ibn abu Hamzah has made a mistake in saying, 'Bear witness ' '*I'tadi*' (commence waiting period).' Al-Hassan ibn Sama'ah has said that it is proper to come with witnesses to her place or take her to the witnesses to their homes and this is not possible to happen. Allah, most Majestic, most Glorious, does not make it obligatory on His slaves. Al-Hassan has said, 'Divorce is nothing other than what Bukayr ibn 'A'yan has narrated that one must say to her when she is clean of *Hayd* (menses) without sexual intercourse '*Anti Taliq*' (you are let go) or ' '*I'tadi*' (commence waiting period) in the presence of two witnesses. All other expressions are invalid.'"

Chapter 10 - Three Talaq (Divorce) in Hayd (menses) Free Period in the Presence of Witnesses in One place and Time or More is One Talaq

H 10521, Ch. 10, h 1
A number of our people have narrated from Ahmad ibn Muhammad from Sahl ibn Ziyad from Ahmad ibn Muhammad from ibn abu Nasr from Jamil ibn Darraj from Zurarah who has said the following:

"I once asked one of the two Imam, (abu Ja'far or abu 'Abd Allah), '*Alayhim al-Salam,* about the case of a man who divorces his wife three times in one place and time or [more] when she is clean of *Hayd* (menses). He (the Imam) said, 'It is only one.'"

H 10522, Ch. 10, h 2
Ali ibn Ibrahim has narrated from his father from ibn abu 'Umayr from Jamil from Zurarah who has said the following:

"I once asked one of the two Imam, (abu Ja'far or abu 'Abd Allah), '*Alayhi al-Salam,* about the case of a man who divorces his wife in a *Hayd* (menses)-free period in one place and time three times. He (the Imam) said, 'It is one.'"

H 10523, Ch. 10, h 3
Abu Ali al-Ash'ariy has narrated from Muhammad ibn 'Abd al-Jabbar and Muhammad ibn Ja'far from abu al-'Abbas al-Razzaz from abu Ayyub ibn Nuh all from Safwan from Mansur ibn Hazim from abu Basir al-Asadiy and Muhammad ibn Ali al-Halabiy and 'Umar ibn Hanzalah who has said the following:

"Abu 'Abd Allah, '*Alayhi al-Salam,* has said, 'Divorce three times in non-waiting period (without waiting period) if she is clean from *Hayd* (menses) counts as one, but if she is not clean of *Hayd* (menses) then it (divorce) does not have any valid effect.'"

H 10524, Ch. 10, h 4
Humayd ibn Ziyad has narrated from al-Hassan ibn Muhammad ibn Sama'ah from Ja'far ibn Sama'ah and Ali ibn Khalid from 'Abd al-Karim ibn 'Amr from 'Amr ibn al-Bara' who has said the following:

"I once said to abu 'Abd Allah, *'Alayhi al-Salam,* 'Our people say that if one divorces (pronounces the expression for divorce) his wife once or one hundred times it counts only one divorce.' It has been narrated to us from you that your ancestors, *'Alayhim al-Salam,* have stated this *Hadith.* 'If one divorces his wife (at one time and place) once or one hundred times it counts only one divorce." He (the Imam) said, 'It is just as it is narrated to you.'""

Chapter 11 - The Case of One who Arranges Witnesses Separately or Divorces in the Presence of a People but Does not Ask them to Bear Witness

H 10525, Ch. 11, h 1
Ali ibn Ibrahim has narrated from his father from Ahmad ibn Muhammad from ibn abu Nasr who has said the following:

"I once asked abu al-Hassan, *'Alayhi al-Salam,* about the case of a man who divorces his wife in a *Hayd* (menses)-free period and without sexual intercourse and asks one man to bear witness on that day, then after five days asks another man to bear witness. He (the Imam) said, 'He is commanded to arrange witnesses together.'"

H 10526, Ch. 11, h 2
Muhammad ibn Yahya has narrated from Ahmad ibn Muhammad from Ali Ahmad ibn 'Ushaym who has said the following:

"I once asked him (the Imam), *'Alayhi al-Salam,* about the case of a man whose wife becomes clean of *Hayd* (menses) and he says, 'So and so is *'Taliq'* (let go, divorced) and a people hears his statement but he does not say, "Bear witness"; if divorce takes place or not. He (the Imam) said, 'Yes, it is bearing witness. Can she be left in suspense?'"

H 10527, Ch. 11, h 3
Ali ibn Ibrahim has narrated from his father from Ahmad ibn Muhammad from ibn abu Nasr who has said the following:

"I once asked abu al-Hassan, *'Alayhi al-Salam,* about the case of a man whose wife becomes clean of *Hayd* (menses) and he comes to a group of people and says, 'So and so is *'Taliq'* (let go, divorced)' if divorce takes place or not but he has not asked them to bear witness. He (the Imam) said, 'Yes, divorce takes place.'"

H 10528, Ch. 11, h 4
Ali ibn Ibrahim has narrated from his father from Safwan ibn Yahya who has said the following:

"Abu al-Hassan, al-Rida', *'Alayhi al-Salam,* was asked about the case of a man whose wife becomes clean of *Hayd* (menses) and he says this: 'So and so is *'Taliq'* (let go, divorced) and a people hears his statement but he does not ask them to bear witness: if divorce takes place or not, he (the Imam) said, 'Yes, is bearing witness.'"

Chapter 12 - Appointing Witness to Divorce Two Women with One word

H 10529, Ch. 12, h 1
Ali ibn Ibrahim has narrated from his father from Ahmad ibn Muhammad from ibn Bukayr from Zurarah who has said the following:

"I once asked abu Ja'far, *'Alayhi al-Salam,* about the case of a man who arranges for the presence of two just witnesses. He then brings two of his wives who both are clean of *Hayd* (menses) and has not gone to bed with them; then says, 'Bear witness that these two my wives are *'Taliq'* (let go, divorced) and they are clean of *Hayd* (menses): if divorce takes place or not. He (the Imam) said, 'Yes, it is a valid divorce.'"

Chapter 13 - Arranging Witness for Revocation of Divorce

H 10530, Ch. 13, h 1
Ali ibn Ibrahim has narrated from his father from ibn abu 'Umayr from Hammad from al-Halabiy who has said the following:

"About the case of a man who goes back to his wife without witness, abu 'Abd Allah, *'Alayhi al-Salam,* has said, 'I like if he arranged for witness; however, what he has done is not unlawful.'"

H 10531, Ch. 13, h 2
Muhammad ibn Yahya has narrated from Ahmad ibn Muhammad from Ali ibn al-Hakam from Musa ibn Bakr from Zurarah who has said the following:

"Abu Ja'far, *'Alayhi al-Salam,* has stated this *Hadith*. 'Divorce must take place in the presence of two men as well as one's going back to his divorced wife. If he is ignorant (of the need for witness) and goes to bed with his wife, he must also appoint witness for what has happened; she still is his wife. If he had not done (pronounced divorce) in the presence of witnesses, his divorce as such does not have any valid effect.'"

H 10532, Ch. 13, h 3
Ali ibn Ibrahim has narrated from his father from ibn abu 'Umayr from ibn 'Udhaynah from Zurarah and Muhammad ibn Muslim who has said the following:

"Abu Ja'far, *'Alayhi al-Salam,* has said, 'Divorce does not take place without witnesses, however, going back to one's wife without witnesses is lawful but having witnesses for it is better.'"

H 10533, Ch. 13, h 4
Al-Husayn from Muhammad has narrated from Mu'alla' ibn Muhammad from certain persons of his people from Aban from Muhammad ibn Muslim who has said the following:

"About the case of a man who divorces his wife, abu Ja'far, *'Alayhi al-Salam,* has said, 'Although it is proper to arrange for witness about one's going back to one's wife before the expiration of waiting period, but if one is ignorant one should arrange for witness when he comes to know. However, I do not see any harm in what he has done. Many people, when in need of witnesses, at the time of marriage do not find witnesses for what has happened about their affair. I do not see anything harmful in it but if one finds witness it is better.'"

H 10534, Ch. 13, h 5

Muhammad ibn Yahya has narrated from Ahmad ibn Muhammad Ali ibn al-Hakam from al-'Ala' from Muhammad ibn Muslim who has said the following:

"I once asked one of the two Imam, (abu Ja'far or abu 'Abd Allah), *'Alayhim al-Salam,* about the case of a man who divorces his wife once. He (the Imam) said, 'He has the authority to go back to her before the expiration of waiting period.' I then asked about if he does not arrange witnesses to his going back. He (the Imam) said, 'He must do so.' I then asked, 'What happens if he is not attentive to it?' He (the Imam) said, 'He must find witness when he remembers; witness is because of inheritance.'"

Chapter 14 - Revocation of Divorce without Going to Bed is not Valid

H 10535, Ch. 14, h 1

A number of our people have narrated from Sahl ibn Ziyad and Ali ibn Ibrahim has narrated, from his father from ibn abu Nasr from 'Abd al-Karim from abu Basir who has said the following:

"Abu 'Abd Allah, *'Alayhi al-Salam,* has said, 'Going back to one's wife is to go to bed with her, otherwise, it is counted as one divorce.'"

H 10536, Ch. 14, h 2

Ali has narrated from his father and Muhammad ibn 'Isma'il has narrated from al-Fadl ibn Shadhan all from ibn abu 'Umayr from 'Abd al-Rahman ibn *al-Hajj*aj who has said the following:

"About the case of a man who divorces his wife, abu 'Abd Allah, *'Alayhi al-Salam,* has said, 'He has the right to go back to his wife. Another divorce cannot take place unless he touches her (goes to bed with her).'"

H 10537, Ch. 14, h 3

Ali has narrated from his father from ibn abu 'Umayr from ibn 'Udhaynah from Bukayr who has said the following:

"I once heard abu Ja'far, *'Alayhi al-Salam,* saying, 'If one divorces his wife in the presence of two just witnesses at a time when commencement of waiting period is possible, he then cannot divorce her before the end of waiting period unless he goes back to her.'"

H 10538, Ch. 14, h 4

Abu Ali al-Ash'ariy has narrated from Muhammad ibn 'Abd al-Jabbar from Safwan and Muhammad ibn 'Isma'il has narrated from al-Fadl ibn Shadhan from Safwan from Ishaq ibn 'Ammar who has said the following:

"I once asked abu Ibrahim, *'Alayhi al-Salam,* about the case of a man who divorces his wife in a *Hayd* (menses)-free period and without sexual intercourse; then goes back to her on the same day then divorces her with three divorces in one *Hayd* (menses)-free period. He (the Imam) said, 'It is against *Sunnah.*' I then asked, 'Is it not the case that if he goes back to her to divorce her he must do so in a *Hayd* (menses)-free period?' He (the Imam) replied, 'Yes, that is correct.' I then said, 'So that he can go to bed with her.' He (the Imam) said, 'Yes, that is correct.'"

H 10539, Ch. 14, h 5

Humayd ibn Ziyad has narrated from ibn Sama'ah from Safwan from ibn Muskan from Ishaq ibn 'Ammar who has said the following:

"Abu al-Hassan, *'Alayhi al-Salam,* has said, 'Going back is going to bed with her, otherwise, it is only one divorce.'"

Chapter 15

H 10540, Ch. 15, h 1

Muhammad ibn Yahya has narrated from Ahmad ibn Muhammad from ibn Mahbub from abu Wallad al-Hannat who has said the following:

"I once asked abu 'Abd Allah, *'Alayhi al-Salam,* about the case of a woman who claims that her husband has divorced her once in the manner of divorce which requires a waiting period. That it has taken place in the presence of witnesses in a *Hayd* (menses)-free period and without going to bed, but the husband denies it. He (the Imam) said, 'If his denying is before the expiration of waiting period it is (his Ruju') going back to her but if it is after the expiration of waiting period, then it is the task of the Imam to separate them from each other after establishing testimony and after oath. His denying after the expiration of waiting period places him in the position of one of those who may propose marriage with her.'"

H 10541, Ch. 15, h 2

Muhammad ibn Yahya has narrated from Ahmad ibn Muhammad ibn Khalid from Sa'd ibn Sa'd from al-Marzuban who has said the following:

"I once asked al-Rida', *'Alayhi al-Salam,* about the case of a man who says to his wife, *'I'tadi'* (you must commence waiting period); I have opened your way. In few days he arranges witness for his going back to her; then remains absent from her before going to bed with her until months pass from the waiting period or more. What do you command in the case?' He (the Imam) said, 'Since he has arranged for witness about his going back to his wife, she is his wife.'"

H 10542, Ch. 15, h 3

Ali ibn Ibrahim has narrated from his father from ibn abu Najran from 'Asem ibn Hamid from Muhammad ibn Qays who has said the following:

"About the case of a man, who divorces his wife in the presence of two witnesses, and then arranges for witness about his going back to his wife privately without her knowledge. He asks the witnesses to keep it secret from her so she remains uninformed about his revoking the divorce until her waiting period is complete. Abu Ja'far, *'Alayhi al-Salam,* has said, 'She will have the choice to remarry him or someone else. If she marries before learning about the revocation of divorce for which witness was arranged by her husband, then the one who divorced her has no way to her and the other husband is more rightful in the case.'"

Chapter 16

H 10543, Ch. 16, h 1
Humayd ibn Ziyad has narrated from ibn Sama'ah from more than one person from Aban from Zurarah who has said the following:

"About the case of a man who divorces his wife one divorce, then leaves her for three months minus one day then revokes the divorce in a session then divorces her, then at the end of the third month does so again. He (the narrator) has said that one of the two Imam, (abu Ja'far or abu 'Abd Allah), *'Alayhim al-Salam,* has said, if he has gone to bed she can count the waiting period from the last divorce; if he has divorced without going back then it does not have any valid effect.'"

Chapter 17 - One Who is not Lawful for her Husband without Marriage to another Man

H 10544, Ch. 17, h 1
Ali ibn Ibrahim has narrated from his father from al-Hassan ibn Mahbub from ibn Ri'ab from abu Basir who has said the following:

"I once asked abu Ja'far, *'Alayhi al-Salam,* about the case of a divorce after the husband cannot marry without her being married to another man. He (the Imam) said, 'I can inform you about the woman who was with me and I wanted to divorce her and how I did. I left her until she experienced *Hayd* (menses) and became clean of *Hayd* (menses). I divorced her in the presence of two witnesses without going to bed with her. I then left her until waiting period was almost to expire. I went back to bed with her and then left her until she experienced *Hayd* (menses) and became clean, I then divorced her in a *Hayd* (menses)-free period in the presence of two witnesses without going to be with her then left her until her waiting period was almost expire. I then went back to go to bed with her until she experienced *Hayd* (menses) and became clean of her *Hayd* (menses). I then divorced her in a *Hayd* (menses)-free period in the presence of witnesses without going to bed with her. I did so with her because I was not interested in her.'"

H 10545, Ch. 17, h 2
A number of our people have narrated from Sahl ibn Ziyad from ibn abu and Humayd ibn Ziyad from ibn Sama'ah from Ja'far ibn Sama'ah and Ali ibn Khalid from 'Abd al-Karim from abu Basir who has said the following:

"I once asked abu 'Abd Allah, *'Alayhi al-Salam,* about the case of a woman who cannot become lawful in marriage for her previous husband without marriage with another man. He (the Imam) said, 'She is a woman who is divorced, then her husband goes back to her, then is divorced then he goes back to her, then is divorced. She becomes unlawful for him in marriage unless she marries another man.' He (the Imam) said that going back to her must be for going to bed with her, otherwise, it is only one divorce.'"

H 10546, Ch. 17, h 3

Muhammad ibn Ja'far al-Razzaz has narrated from Ayyub ibn Nuh and Abu Ali al-Ash'ariy has narrated from Muhammad ibn 'Abd al-Jabbar and Muhammad ibn 'Isma'il has narrated from al-Fadl ibn Shadhan from and Humayd ibn Ziyad from Sama'ah all from Safwan from ibn Muskan from abu Basir who has said the following:

"I once asked abu 'Abd Allah, *'Alayhi al-Salam,* about the case of a woman who cannot become lawful for her previous husband in marriage without marriage with another man. He (the Imam) said, 'She is a woman who is divorced and he goes back to her, then divorces her then goes back to her, then divorces for the third time. She becomes unlawful for him in marriage until she marries another man who tastes her honey (goes to bed with her).'"

H 10547, Ch. 17, h 4

Safwan has narrated from Musa ibn Bakr from Zurarah who has said the following:

"Abu Ja'far, *'Alayhi al-Salam,* has said, 'If a man divorces his wife once then goes back to her after her waiting period is complete, when he divorces her for the third time she cannot become lawful for him in marriage until she marries another man. If another man marries her then divorces her but does not go to bed with her or dies, she does not become lawful for her previous husband until another man tastes her honey (goes to bed after a marriage with her).'"

H 10548, Ch. 17, h 5

Safwan has narrated from ibn Muskan from abu Basir who has said the following:

"About the case of a woman who is divorced for the third time, abu 'Abd Allah, *'Alayhi al-Salam,* has said, 'She cannot become lawful in marriage for her previous husband until she marries another man who tastes her honey (goes to bed with her).'"

H 10549, Ch. 17, h 6

A number of our people have narrated from Sahl ibn Ziyad from Ali ibn Asbat from Ali ibn al-Fadl al-Wasitiy who has said the following:

"I once wrote to al-Rida', *'Alayhi al-Salam,* and asked, 'A man has divorced his wife as such that she cannot become lawful for him in marriage without marriage with another man; but a boy who is not mature married her. He (the Imam) replied, 'No, until he becomes mature.' I then wrote and asked, 'What is the limit of maturity?' He (the Imam) replied, 'It is that which makes it obligatory for believers to execute penalties.'"

Chapter 18 - Issues that Validate and Invalidate Divorce

H 10550, Ch. 18, h 1

Ali ibn Ibrahim has narrated from his father from ibn abu 'Umayr from 'Abd al-Malik ibn al-Mughirah from Shu'ayb al-Haddad from Mu'alla' ibn al-Khunays who has said the following:

"There is a man who divorces his wife and does not go back to her until three *Hayd* (menses) are complete, then marries her then divorces her and leaves until three *Hayd* (menses) are complete and does not go back to her to touch her. Abu 'Abd Allah, *'Alayhi al-Salam,* has said, 'He can marry forever as long as he does not go back to her to touch'"

H 10551, Ch. 18, h 2

Humayd ibn Ziyad has narrated from 'Ubayd Allah ibn Ahmad from ibn 'Umayr from 'Abd Allah ibn al-Mughirah from Shu'ayb al-Hadad from Mu'alla' ibn al-Khunays who has said the following:

"There is a man who divorces his wife, then does not go back to her until three cycles of *Hayd* (menses) are complete, then divorces and leaves her until three cycles of *Hayd* (menses) are complete then marries her then divorces without going back to her and leaves until three cycles of *Hayd* (menses) are complete. Abu 'Abd Allah, *'Alayhi al-Salam,* has said, 'He can marry her forever as long as he does not go back and touch her.' Ibn Bukayr and his companions were of this opinion and 'Abd Allah ibn al-Mughirah narrated it to me that he asked, 'On what basis do you say so?' He replied, 'I say so on the basis of *Hadith* narrated by Rifa'ah who has narrated from abu 'Abd Allah, *'Alayhi al-Salam,* that it destroys what is passed. He (the narrator) has said, that Rifa'ah has only said, 'He divorced, then another man married her, then divorced; then the first man married her and this destroys the first *'Talaq'* (divorce).'"

H 10552, Ch. 18, h 3

Humayd ibn Ziyad has narrated from Sama'ah from Muhammad ibn Ziyad and Safwan from Rifa'ah who has said the following:

"I once asked abu 'Abd Allah, *'Alayhi al-Salam,* about the case of a man who divorces his wife and she becomes a stranger to him because of the expiration of her waiting period; then another man marries her who divorces her also; then she marries the first husband; if it destroys the first divorce. He (the Imam) said, 'Yes, it destroys the first divorce.' Ibn Sama'ah has said that ibn Bukayr would say, 'If a divorced woman is divorced by her husband, then leaves her until she becomes stranger to him, then marries her, she then can live with him on the basis of a new divorce. Ibn Sama'ah has said that al-Husayn ibn Hashim has mentioned that he asked ibn Bukayr who gave this answer and he then asked, 'Have you heard anything about it?' He replied, 'No, it is what Allah, most Majestic, most Glorious, has granted in the form of opinion.' Ibn Sama'ah has said, 'We do not accept the words of ibn Bukayr; in fact *Hadith* says, 'If there is a husband between them.'"

H 10553, Ch. 18, h 4

Muhammad ibn abu 'Abd Allah has narrated from Mu'awiyah ibn Hakam from 'Abd Allah ibn al-Mughirah who has said the following:

"I once asked abu 'Abd Allah, *'Alayhi al-Salam,* about the case of a man who divorces his wife and leaves until she becomes stranger to him, then marries her. He (the Imam) said, 'She can live with him just as she did with marriage.' I then said, *'Hadith* of Rifa'ah says, "If there is a husband in between."' Then 'Abd Allah said to me, 'This is husband and it is what Allah has granted of opinion. Whenever he divorces once and then she becomes stranger to him, then another man marries her then her husband divorces, then she marries the first husband, she can live with him accepted as she was.' I then asked 'Abd Allah, 'According to whose *Hadith* is this?' He replied, 'It is what Allah has granted.' Mu'awiyah ibn Hukaym has said that our people have narrated from Rifa'ah ibn Musa that husband destroys the first divorce and if he marries her she lives with him accepted.' Abu 'Abd Allah, *'Alayhi al-Salam,* then said, 'Three divorces destroy but not one and two.' *Hadith* of Rifa'ah from abu 'Abd Allah, *'Alayhi al-Salam,* is the one on the basis of which ibn Bukayr has argued.'"

Chapter 19 - An Absent Man Returns and Divorces at that Time that Divorce Does not Take Place until She Experiences Hayd (menses)

H 10554, Ch. 19, h 1
Muhammad ibn Yahya has narrated from Ahmad ibn Muhammad from ibn Faddal from *al-Hajj*aj al-Khashshab who has said the following:
"I once asked abu 'Abd Allah, *'Alayhi al-Salam,* about the case of a man who is on a journey and when he enters the city he brings two witnesses, and when his wife comes to the door he asks them to bear witness to the divorce. He (the Imam) said, 'Divorce does not take place in this way.'"

H 10555, Ch. 19, h 2
Muhammad ibn Yahya ibn al-Husayn has narrated from Hakam ibn Miskin from Mu'awiyah ibn 'Ammar who has said the following:
"Abu 'Abd Allah, *'Alayhi al-Salam,* has said, 'When a man is absent from his wife for one year or two years or more, then comes and wants to divorce her when she is experiencing *Hayd* (menses), he must leave her until she becomes clean, then divorce her.'"

Chapter 20 - Women who Can be Divorced in all Conditions

H 10556, Ch. 20, h 1
A number of our people have narrated from Sahl ibn Ziyad from Ahmad ibn Muhammad from ibn abu Nasr from Jamil ibn Darraj from 'Isma'il al-Ju'fiy who has said the following:
"Abu Ja'far, *'Alayhi al-Salam,* has said, 'A man can divorce five kinds of women in all conditions: They are pregnant women, women with whom one has not gone to bed, those whose husbands are absent, those who do not experience *Hayd* (menses) and those in their menopause.'"

H 10557, Ch. 20, h 2
Ali ibn Ibrahim has narrated from his father from ibn abu 'Umayr from Hammad from al-Halabiy who has said the following:
"Abu 'Abd Allah, *'Alayhi al-Salam,* has said, 'It is not unlawful to divorce five kinds of women in all conditions. They are those whose husbands are absent, those who do not experience *Hayd* (menses), women with whom one has not gone to bed, pregnant women, and those in their menopause.'"

H 10558, Ch. 20, h 3
Humayd ibn Ziyad has narrated from ibn Sama'ah from 'Abd Allah ibn Jabalah and Ja'far ibn Sama'ah from Jamil from 'Isma'il al-Ju'fiy who has said the following:
"Abu Ja'far, *'Alayhi al-Salam,* has said, 'Five kinds of women can be divorced in all conditions. They are pregnant women, those whose husbands are absent, those who do not experience *Hayd* (menses), those in their menopause and women with whom one has not gone to bed.'"

Ali ibn Ibrahim has narrated from his father from ibn abu 'Umayr from Jamil from `Isma'il al-Ju'fiy a similar *Hadith.*

Chapter 21 - Divorce by an Absent Husband

H 10559, Ch. 21, h 1
Ali ibn Ibrahim has narrated from his father from ibn abu 'Umayr from ibn 'Udhaynah from Zurarah from ibn Bukayr who has said the following:

"I can testify that I heard abu Ja'far, *'Alayhi al-Salam,* saying, 'A man absent from his wife can divorce her by counting new moons and months.'"

H 10560, Ch. 21, h 2
Muhammad ibn Yahya has narrated from Ahmad ibn Muhammad from Ali ibn al-Hakam from al-Husayn ibn 'Uthman from Ishaq ibn 'Ammar who has said the following:

"Abu 'Abd Allah, *'Alayhi al-Salam,* has said, 'If a man who is absent from his wife wants to divorce her, he can do so and he must leave her for one month.'"

H 10561, Ch. 21, h 3
Ali has narrated from his father from ibn abu 'Umayr from Muhammad ibn abu Hamzah and al-Husayn ibn 'Uthman from Ishaq ibn 'Ammar who has said the following:

"Abu 'Abd Allah, *'Alayhi al-Salam,* has said, 'If a man who is absent from his wife wants to divorce her, he can do so and he must leave her for one month.'"

H 10562, Ch. 21, h 4
Muhammad ibn Yahya has narrated from Ahmad ibn Muhammad from ibn Mahbub from al-Hassan ibn Salih who has said the following:

"I once asked abu Ja'far, *'Alayhi al-Salam,* about the case of a man who divorces his wife when he is absent from her. He is in another city and has two men as witness about his divorce; then he goes back to her without witness. After expiration of waiting period he comes and finds out that she has married another man. He sends a message to her informing her about his revoking the divorce before the expiration of waiting period without witnesses. He (the narrator) has said that he (the Imam) said, 'He has no way to her because he has confirmed divorce and has claimed revocation without witness, thus, he has no way to her. It is proper for one who divorces or revokes divorce to have witness about revocation like divorce. Had he been there before her marriage he could have been one of those who proposes to her for marriage.'"

H 10563, Ch. 21, h 5
Ali ibn Ibrahim has narrated from his father from `Isma'il ibn Marrar from Yunus from ibn Muskan from Sulayman ibn Khalid who has said the following:

"I once asked abu 'Abd Allah, *'Alayhi al-Salam,* about the case of a man who divorces his wife when he is absent from her. He arranges witnesses about his divorce; then he comes home and stays with her for months without informing her of divorce and the woman claims to have become pregnant but the man says. 'I had divorced you in the presence of witnesses. He (the Imam) said, 'He is responsible for the child and his words are not accepted.'"

H 10564, Ch. 21, h 6

Ali has narrated from his father from Ahmad ibn Muhammad from Hammad ibn 'Uthaman who has said the following:

"I once asked abu 'Abd Allah, *'Alayhi al-Salam,* about the case of a man who has four wives, of whom he divorces one when he is absent from them. When is it permissible for him to marry? He (the Imam) said, 'He can do so after nine months because there are two appointed times, the irregularity of *Hayd* (menses) and the irregularity of pregnancy.'"

H 10565, Ch. 21, h 7

Muhammad ibn Yahya has narrated from Ahmad ibn Muhammad from Ali ibn al-Hakam from al-'Ala' ibn Razin from Muhammad ibn Muslim who has said the following:

"I once asked one of the two Imam, (abu Ja'far or abu 'Abd Allah), *'Alayhim al-Salam,* about the case of a man who divorces his wife when he is absent from her. He (the Imam) said, 'His divorce is permissible in all conditions and his wife commences waiting period from the day of divorce.'"

H 10566, Ch. 21, h 8

Humayd ibn Ziyad has narrated from ibn Sama'ah who has said the following:

"I once asked Muhammad ibn abu Hamzah about when a man absent from his wife can divorce. He said that Ishaq ibn 'Ammar narrated to him from abu 'Abd Allah, *'Alayhi al-Salam,* or abu al-Hassan, *'Alayhi al-Salam,* who said that he can do so after one month."

H 10567, Ch. 21, h 9

A number of our people have narrated from Sahl ibn Ziyad and Muhammad ibn Yahya has narrated from Ahmad ibn Muhammad from Ali ibn Mahziyar from Muhammad ibn al-Hassan al-Ash'ariy who has said the following:

"A certain one of our Mawali once wrote to abu Ja'far, *'Alayhi al-Salam,* asking, 'With me there is a woman who is knowledgeable, whose husband created something unpopular and ran away from the land. A certain one of the people of the woman followed him and told him to divorce or that he returns him back. He then divorced and himself went his own way. What is your instruction for the woman?' He (the Imam) wrote in his handwriting, 'You can marry, may Allah be kind to you.'"

Chapter 22 - Divorce of a Pregnant Woman

H 10568, Ch. 22, h 2

Muhammad ibn Yahya has narrated from Ahmad ibn Muhammad from ibn Faddal from ibn Bukayr from abu Basir who has said the following:

"Abu 'Abd Allah, *'Alayhi al-Salam,* has said, 'A pregnant woman is divorced once.'"

H 10569, Ch. 22, h 2

Muhammad ibn Yahya has narrated from Ahmad ibn Muhammad ibn 'Isma'il ibn Bazi' from Muhammad ibn al-Fudayl from abu al-Sabbah al-Kinaniy who has said the following:

"Abu 'Abd Allah, *'Alayhi al-Salam,* has said, 'Divorce of a pregnant woman is once and her waiting period is the closest of the two periods, (that is, childbirth or three months).'"

H 10570, Ch. 22, h 3

Humayd ibn Ziyad has narrated from al-Hassan ibn Muhammad ibn Sama'ah from 'Abd Allah ibn Jabalah and Ja'far ibn Sama'ah from Jamil from 'Isma'il al-Ju'fiy 'Isma'il who has said the following:

"Abu Ja'far, *'Alayhi al-Salam*, has said, 'Divorce of a pregnant woman is one and when she gives birth to what is inside her, she becomes stranger to him.'"

H 10571, Ch. 22, h 4

It is narrated from the narrator of the previous *Hadith* from 'Abd Allah ibn Jabalah and from Safwan ibn Yahya from ibn Bukayr from abu Basir who has said the following:

"Abu 'Abd Allah, *'Alayhi al-Salam*, has said, 'A pregnant woman is divorced once.'"

H 10572, Ch. 22, h 5

A number of our people have narrated from Sahl ibn Ziyad from ibn abu Nasr from Jamil from 'Isma'il al-Ju'fiy who has said the following:

"Abu Ja'far, *'Alayhi al-Salam*, has said, 'Divorce of a pregnant woman is one and when she gives birth she become stranger to him.'"

H 10573, Ch. 22, h 6

Abu Ali al-Ash'ariy has narrated from Muhammad ibn 'Abd al-Jabbar and abu al-'Abbas al-Razzaz from Ayyub ibn Nuh all from Safwan from ibn Muskan from abu Basir who has said the following:

"Abu 'Abd Allah, *'Alayhi al-Salam*, has said, 'Divorce of a pregnant woman is one and her waiting period is childbirth, if it is the nearer of the two.'"

H 10574, Ch. 22, h 7

A number of our people have narrated from Ahmad ibn Muhammad from ibn Khalid and Ali ibn Ibrahim has narrated from his father from all from 'Uthman ibn 'Isa from Sama'ah who has said the following:

"I once asked him (the Imam), *'Alayhi al-Salam*, about the divorce of a pregnant woman. He (the Imam) said, 'It is one and her waiting period is childbirth.'"

H 10575, Ch. 22, h 8

Ali ibn Ibrahim has narrated from his father from ibn abu 'Umayr from Hammad from al-Halabiy who has said the following:

"Abu 'Abd Allah, *'Alayhi al-Salam*, has said, 'Divorce of a pregnant woman is one and her waiting period ends with childbirth if it is the nearer of the two.'"

H 10576, Ch. 22, h 9

Humayd ibn Ziyad has narrated from ibn Sama'ah from al-Husayn ibn al-Hashim and Muhammad ibn Ziyad from 'Abd al-Rahman ibn *al-Hajj*aj who has said the following:

"I once asked abu al-Hassan, *'Alayhi al-Salam*, about the case of a woman who is pregnant: if her husband divorces her and she gives birth prematurely or by abortion or it is just a lump. He (the Imam) said, 'Whatever she gives birth to shows that she was pregnant, complete or not. Her waiting period is complete even if it is a lump.'"

H 10577, Ch. 22, h 10

It is narrated from the narrator of the previous *Hadith* from Ja'far ibn Sama'ah from Ali 'Imran al-Shifa' from Rib'iy ibn 'Abd Allah from 'Abd al-Rahman ibn abu 'Abd Allah al-Basriy who has said the following:

"I once asked abu 'Abd Allah, *'Alayhi al-Salam,* about the case of a man who divorces his pregnant wife with two children in her womb. She gives birth to one and one remains. He (the Imam) said, 'She becomes stranger with the birth of one child and she is not lawful for marriage until the birth of the other child.'"*

H 10578, Ch. 22, h 11

It is narrated from the narrator of the previous *Hadith* from Safwan from Musa ibn Bakr from Zurarah who has said the following:

"Abu Ja'far, *'Alayhi al-Salam,* has said, 'If a woman is divorced when she is pregnant her waiting period is childbirth even if she gives birth in the same hour.'"

H 10579, Ch. 22, h 12

Muhammad ibn Yahya has narrated from Ahmad ibn Muhammad and Ali ibn Ibrahim has narrated from his father from ibn Mahbub from abu Ayyub al-Khazzaz from Yazid al-Kunasiy who has said the following:

"I once asked abu Ja'far, *'Alayhi al-Salam,* about the divorce of a pregnant woman. He (the Imam) said, 'She is divorced once for waiting period by months and in the presence of witnesses.' I then asked, 'Can he go back to her?' He (the Imam) said, 'Yes, she is his wife.' (I then asked,) 'What happens if he revokes the divorce, then decides to divorce once more?' He (the Imam) said, 'He cannot divorce until a month passes after he has touched her.' I then asked, 'What happens if he divorces for the second time and arranges for witness about his revoking the divorce and touches her? Then he divorces for the third time in the presence of witnesses for waiting period of every month; if she becomes stranger like the woman who is divorced with waiting period because of which she is not lawful for her husband until she marries another man?' He (the Imam) said, 'Yes, it can happen.' I then asked, 'What is her waiting period?' He (the Imam) said, 'Her waiting period is giving birth to what is in her womb; then she becomes lawful for whoever wants to marry her.'"

Chapter 23 - Divorce of a Woman whose Marriage is not Consummated

H 10580, Ch. 23, h 1

A number of our people have narrated from Sahl ibn Ziyad and Ali ibn Ibrahim has narrated from his father from ibn abu Nasr from 'Abd al-Karim from abu Basir who has said the following:

"I once asked abu 'Abd Allah, *'Alayhi al-Salam,* about the case of a man who divorces his wife with whom he has not gone to bed. He (the Imam) said, 'She becomes stranger to him and she can marry in the same hour after divorce.'"

H 10581, Ch. 23, h 2

Ali ibn Ibrahim has narrated from his father from ibn abu 'Umayr from Jamil ibn Darraj from certain persons of our people who has said the following:

"One of the two Imam, (abu Ja'far or abu 'Abd Allah), *'Alayhim al-Salam,* has said, 'If a woman with whom her husband has not gone to bed is divorced, she becomes stranger to him by one divorce.'"

H 10582, Ch. 23, h 3

Ali ibn Ibrahim has narrated from his father from ibn abu 'Umayr from Hammad from al-Halabiy who has said the following:

"Abu 'Abd Allah, *'Alayhi al-Salam,* has said, 'If a man divorces his wife before going to bed with her, she does not need to wait for a waiting period. She can marry in the same hour after divorce if she wants. With one divorce she becomes stranger to him and if mahr (dower) is set for her, she deserves half of such mahr (dower).'"

H 10583, Ch. 23, h 4

Muhammad ibn Yahya has narrated from Ahmad ibn Muhammad from ibn Mahbub from abu Ayyub and ibn Ri'ab from Zurarah who has said the following:

"There is the case of a man who marries a virgin woman, then divorces her before going to bed with three divorces, one divorce every month. One of the two Imam, (abu Ja'far or abu 'Abd Allah), *'Alayhim al-Salam,* has said, 'With the first divorce she becomes stranger to him and the other two are extra. He is one of those who may propose marriage when he wants with new mahr (dower).' It then was asked from him (the Imam), 'Can he go back to her before the passing of three months?' He (the Imam) said, 'No, he cannot do so. He could have done so if he were to go to bed with her before, but with a divorce without going to bed with her he cannot revoke and she becomes stranger to him in the same hour of his divorcing.'"

H 10584, Ch. 23, h 5

Abu Ali al-Ash'ariy has narrated from al-Hassan ibn Ali ibn 'Abd Allah from 'Ubays ibn Hisham from Thabit ibn Shurayh from abu Basir who has said the following:

"Abu 'Abd Allah, *'Alayhi al-Salam,* has said, 'If a man marries a woman, then divorces before going to bed with her, she then does not need to count her waiting period. She can marry whomever she wants in the same hour after divorce and she becomes stranger to him by one divorce.'"

Humayd ibn Ziyad has narrated from ibn Sama'ah from Salih ibn Khalid and 'Ubays ibn Hisham from Thabit ibn Shurayh from abu Basir from abu 'Abd Allah, *'Alayhi al-Salam,* a similar *Hadith* .

H 10585, Ch. 23, h 6

Abu al-'Abbas al-Razzaz has narrated from Ayyub ibn Nuh and Humayd ibn Ziyad from ibn Sama'ah from Safwan from ibn Muskan from abu Basir who has said the following:

"Abu 'Abd Allah, *'Alayhi al-Salam,* has said, 'If a man divorces his wife before going to bed with her with one divorce, she becomes stranger to him in the same hour after divorce. She can marry someone if she wants.'"

H 10586, Ch. 23, h 7

Muhammad ibn Yahya has narrated from Ahmad ibn Muhammad, from ibn Muskan from al-'Ala' ibn Razin from Muhammad ibn Muslim who has said the following:

"One of the two Imam, (abu Ja'far or abu 'Abd Allah), *'Alayhim al-Salam,* has said, 'Waiting period is because of water (seed, semen).'"

Chapter 24 - Divorce of One who is not Mature yet and Divorce of One after Menopause

H 10587, Ch. 24, h 1

Ali ibn Ibrahim has narrated from his father from ibn abu 'Umayr from Jamil ibn Darraj from certain persons of our people who has said the following:

"There is the case of a man who divorces a girl who is not mature yet and the like of whom cannot become pregnant, but he has gone to bed with her and a woman after menopause when women of her condition cannot give birth. One of the two Imam, (abu Ja'far or abu 'Abd Allah), *'Alayhim al-Salam,* has said, 'There is no waiting period for them.'"

Muhammad ibn Yahya has narrated from Ahmad ibn Muhammad from Ali ibn Hadid from Jamil ibn Darraj from certain persons of our people a similar *Hadith.*

H 10588, Ch. 24, h 2

Ali ibn Ibrahim has narrated from his father from ibn Mahbub from Hammad ibn 'Uthman from the one who narrated to him who has said the following:

"About the case of a girl whose likes do not experience *Hayd* (menses) and a woman after menopause abu 'Abd Allah, *'Alayhi al-Salam,* has said, 'They do not need to count waiting period even if he has gone to bed with them.'"

H 10589, Ch. 24, h 3

Abu Ali al-Ash'ariy has narrated from Muhammad ibn 'Abd al-Jabbar and al-Razzaz from Ayyub ibn Nuh and Humayd ibn Ziyad from ibn Sama'ah all from Safwan from Muhammad ibn Hakim from Muhammad ibn Muslim who has said the following:

"Abu Ja'far, *'Alayhi al-Salam,* has said, 'A woman the like of whom cannot become pregnant does not need to count a waiting period.'"

H 10590, Ch. 24, h 4

A number of our people have narrated from Sahl ibn Ziyad from ibn abu Najran from Safwan from 'Abd al-Rahman ibn *al-Hajj*aj who has said the following:

"Abu 'Abd Allah, *'Alayhi al-Salam,* has said, 'Three kinds of women can marry in all conditions: a woman who does not experience *Hayd* (menses) and alike whom women do not experience *Hayd* (menses).' He (the narrator) has said that I then asked, 'What is her limit?' He (the Imam) said, 'One who is less than nine years, one with whom he has not gone to bed and one after menopause and whose like do not experience *Hayd* (menses).' I then asked, 'What is the limit?' He (the Imam) said, 'It is when she becomes fifty years old.'"

H 10591, Ch. 24, h 5

Certain persons of our people have narrated from Ahmad ibn Muhammad, from Safwan from Muhammad ibn Hakim from Muhammad ibn Muslim who has said the following:

"I once heard abu Ja'far, *'Alayhi al-Salam,* saying, 'A woman after menopause if divorced becomes stranger to him and she does not need to count a waiting period.'"

It is also narrated that if sexual intercourse has taken place with them there is a waiting period for them.

H 10592, Ch. 24, h 6
Humayd ibn Ziyad has narrated from ibn Sama'ah from 'Abd Allah ibn Jabalah from Ali ibn abu Hamzah from abu Basir who has said the following:

"Waiting period of those who do not experience *Hayd* (menses) and after menopause is three months and ibn Sama'ah would follow it. He would say it is about slave-girls. They do not need Istibra' (quarantine) if they have not become mature. The rules for free women are in the Quran as Allah, most Majestic, most Glorious, says, '. . . after menopause if you have doubts their waiting period is three months and those who do not experience *Hayd* (menses).' Mu'awiyah ibn Hukaym would say, 'They do not need to count waiting period and ibn Sama'ah's argument is based on '*if you doubt*' which is only when there is doubt about menopause. When she passes this limit and doubt is removed and that the girl has not reached the limit then waiting period does not apply to their case.'"

Chapter 25 - Women Whose Hayd (menses) is Confusing

H 10593, Ch. 25, h 1
Muhammad ibn Yahya has narrated from Ahmad ibn Muhammad and Ali ibn Ibrahim has narrated from his father all from ibn Mahbub from 'Abd al-Rahman ibn *al-Hajj*aj who has said the following:

"I once asked abu al-Hassan, *'Alayhi al-Salam,* about the case of a man who marries a woman secretly in the house of her family. He wants to divorce her but cannot reach her to know about her *Hayd* (menses) and does not know when she becomes clean of *Hayd* (menses). He (the Imam) said, 'This is like the case of a husband who is absent who divorces by counting new moon and months.' I then asked, 'What happens if he is able to reach her at certain times to find out about her *Hayd* (menses): how he should divorce her?' He (the Imam) said, 'When a month, during which he is not able to reach her, passes he can divorce her when he finds himself in the beginning of the next month. He must write down about the month in which he has divorced and arrange for two men as witnesses. When three months pass she becomes stranger to him and he becomes one of those who can propose marriage. He, however, must pay her expenses for the three months in which she counted the waiting period.'"

Chapter 26 - The Time when a Divorced Woman in the Manner of Divorce with Waiting Period and Revocable Form Becomes Stranger to him

H 10594, Ch. 26, h 1
Ali ibn Ibrahim has narrated from his father from ibn abu 'Umayr from ibn 'Udhaynah from Zurarah who has said the following:

"I once said to abu Ja'far, *'Alayhi al-Salam,* 'I pray to Allah to keep you well, a man has divorced his wife in *Hayd* (menses)-free period, in the presence of two just witnesses before going to bed with her. He (the Imam) said, 'When she experiences *Hayd* (menses) for the third time her waiting period is complete and she is lawful for marriage.' I then said, 'I pray to Allah to keep you well, people of Iraq narrate from Ali, *'Alayhi al-Salam,* who has said that he has the right to go back to her before she takes Ghusl (bath) for the third *Hayd* (menses). He (the Imam) said, 'They have spoken a lie.'"

H 10595, Ch. 26, h 2

Ali has narrated from his father from ibn abu 'Umayr and A number of our people have narrated from Sahl ibn Ziyad from ibn abu Nasr all from Jamil ibn Darraj from Zurarah who has said the following:

"Abu Ja'far, *'Alayhi al-Salam,* has said, 'When a divorced woman experiences blood discharge of the third *Hayd* (menses) she becomes stranger to him.'"

H 10596, Ch. 26, h 3

Ali has narrated from his father from ibn Bukayr and Jamil ibn Darraj and 'Umar ibn 'Udhaynah from Zurarah who has said the following:

"Abu 'Abd Allah, *'Alayhi al-Salam,* has said, 'A woman divorced becomes stranger to her husband at the time of her experiencing the first drop of blood of *Hayd* (menses) for the third time (after divorce).' I then said that Rabi'ah al-Rai'y also is of the opinion that she becomes stranger as soon as she experiences the first drop of blood.' He (the Imam) said, 'It is not true. It is not his opinion but is something that has reached him from Ali, *'Alayhi al-Salam.*'"

H 10597, Ch. 26, h 4

Abu Ali al-Ash'ariy has narrated from Muhammad ibn 'Abd al-Jabbar from Safwan from Ishaq ibn 'Ammar from 'Isma'il al-Ju'fiy who has said the following:

"I once said to abu Ja'far, *'Alayhi al-Salam,* that a man has divorced his wife. He (the Imam) said, 'He has the right to go back to her as long as she has not seen blood discharge because of *Hayd* (menses) for the third time (after divorce).'"

H 10598, Ch. 26, h 5

It is narrated from the narrator of the previous *Hadith* from Safwan from ibn Muskan from Zurarah who has said the following:

"About the case of a woman who is divorced, one of the two Imam, (abu Ja'far or abu 'Abd Allah), *'Alayhim al-Salam,* has said, 'She inherits and is inherited until she sees blood of *Hayd* (menses) for the third time after divorce and when that happens it (such relation) is cut off.'"

H 10599, Ch. 26, h 6

Humayd ibn Ziyad has narrated from ibn Sama'ah from 'Abd Allah ibn Jabalah from Jamil ibn Darraj and Safwan ibn Yahya from ibn Bukayr and Ja'far ibn Sama'ah from ibn Bukayr and Jamil all of them from Zurarah who has said the following:

"Abu Ja'far, *'Alayhi al-Salam,* has said, 'With the first blood that she sees because of *Hayd* (menses) for the third time after divorce she becomes stranger to him.'"

Humayd ibn Ziyad has narrated from ibn Sama'ah from Safwan from ibn Muskan from Zurarah a similar *Hadith*.

H 10600, Ch. 26, h 7

Safwan has narrated from ibn Bukayr from Zurarah who has said the following:

"I once heard abu Ja'far, *'Alayhi al-Salam,* saying, 'A woman divorced becomes stranger to him with the first drop of blood because of *Hayd* (menses) during the last *Hayd* (menses)-free period.'"

H 10601, Ch. 26, h 8

Humayd ibn Ziyad has narrated from ibn Sama'ah from 'Abd Allah ibn Jabalah from Ishaq ibn 'Ammar from 'Isma'il al-Ju'fiy who has said the following:

"About the case of a man who divorces his wife, abu Ja'far, *'Alayhi al-Salam,* has said, 'He has the right to go back to her until she experiences *Hayd* (menses) for the third time after divorce.'"

H 10602, Ch. 26, h 9

It is narrated from the narrator of the previous *Hadith* from Safwan from Musa ibn Bakr from Zurarah who has said the following:

"I once asked abu Ja'far, *'Alayhi al-Salam,* 'I have heard that Rabi'ah al-Ra'iy says, "When a divorced woman experiences *Hayd* (menses) for the third time after divorce she becomes stranger to him and that the *Hayd* (menses)-free period is between the two *Hayd* (menses)" and he thinks that it is his own opinion.' Abu Ja'far, *'Alayhi al-Salam,* said, 'What he has said, by my life is not true because he has taken it from Ali, *'Alayhi al-Salam.*' I then asked, 'What Ali, *'Alayhi al-Salam,* has said about it?' He (the Imam) said that he (Imam Ali) would say, 'When she sees blood of the third *Hayd* (menses) (after divorce) her waiting period expires and he has no way to her and that *Hayd* (menses)-free period is between two *Hayd* (menses). She cannot marry before taking Ghusl (bath) for the third *Hayd* (menses) (after divorce).'

"Al-Hassan ibn Muhammad ibn Sama'ah has said that Ja'far ibn Sama'ah would say, 'A divorced woman becomes stranger to him with the first drop of blood of *Hayd* (menses) for the third time after divorce. It is not lawful for her to marry until she takes Ghusl (bath) because of *Hayd* (menses) for the third time after divorce.' Al-Hassan ibn Muhammad ibn Sama'ah has said that she becomes stranger with the first drop of blood because of *Hayd* (menses) for the third time after divorce and thereafter if she wants to marry she can do so or not to do so. Ali ibn Ibrahim has said that she can marry if so she wants or not to do so but if she marries he must not go to bed with her before Ghusl (bath).'"

H 10603, Ch. 26, h 10

Al-Husayn from Muhammad has narrated from Mu'alla' ibn Muhammad from al-Hassan ibn Ali from Aban ibn 'Uthman from 'Abd al-Rahman ibn abu 'Abd Allah who has said the following:

"I once asked abu 'Abd Allah, *'Alayhi al-Salam,* about the case of a woman who is divorced; when can she get the control of her affairs? He (the Imam) said, 'It happens when she sees *Hayd* (menses) for the third time after divorce.' I then asked, 'What happens if blood discharge begins earlier in her *Hayd* (menses)-free period?' He (the Imam) said, 'If blood discharge is before ten days it is part of the previous *Hayd* (menses), thus he has the control of the affairs but if it is after ten days then it is of the third *Hayd* (menses) and she gets control of her affairs.'"

H 10604, Ch. 26, h 11
Muhammad ibn Yahya has narrated from Muhammad ibn al-Husayn from certain persons of his people, I think he is Muhammad ibn 'Abd Allah ibn Hilal or Ali ibn al-Hakam from al-'Ala' ibn Razin from Muhammad ibn Muslim who has said the following:
"I once asked abu Ja'far, *'Alayhi al-Salam,* about the case of a man who divorces his wife and about when she becomes stranger to him. He (the Imam) said, 'It is when blood of the third *Hayd* (menses) appears. She gets control of her own affairs.' I then asked, 'Can she marry in that condition?' He (the Imam) said, 'Yes, but she must not allow him to approach her before she is clean of blood of *Hayd* (menses).'"

Chapter 27 - Meaning of al-'Iqra' (Hayd-free period)

H 10605, Ch. 27, h 1
Ali ibn Ibrahim has narrated from his father from ibn abu 'Umayr from 'Umar ibn 'Udhaynah from Zurarah who has said the following:
"I heard Rabi' al-Ra'iy saying, 'It is my opinion that *al-'Iqra'* which Allah, most Majestic, most Glorious, has mentioned in the Quran is nothing but *Hayd* (menses)-free period between the two *Hayd* (menses).' He (the Imam) said, 'He has spoken a lie. It is not his opinion. In fact it has reached him from Ali, *'Alayhi al-Salam.'* I then said, 'I pray to Allah to keep you well, did Ali, *'Alayhi al-Salam,* say so?' He (the Imam) said, *'Al-Qur'* means clean. Blood stops coming out and accumulates. During *Hayd* (menses) it is pushed out.'" (Al-Qur' means accumulates and *Hayd* means flows).

H 10606, Ch. 27, h 2
Ali ibn Ibrahim has narrated from his father from ibn abu 'Umayr and A number of our people have narrated from Sahl ibn Ziyad from ibn abu Nasr all from Jamil ibn Darraj from Zurarah who has said the following:
"Abu Ja'far, *'Alayhi al-Salam,* has said, *'Al-Qur'* is the period between two *Hayd* (menses).'"

H 10607, Ch. 27, h 3
Ali has narrated from his father from ibn abu 'Umayr from Jamil from Muhammad ibn Muslim who has said the following:
"Abu Ja'far, *'Alayhi al-Salam,* has said, *'Al-Qur'* is the period between two *Hayd* (menses).'"

H 10608, Ch. 27, h 4
Muhammad ibn Yahya has narrated from Ahmad ibn Muhammad from *al-Hajj*al from Tha'labah from Zurarah who has said the following:
"Abu Ja'far, *'Alayhi al-Salam,* has said, *'Al-Qur'* is being clean (*Hayd* (menses)-free).'"

Chapter 28 - Waiting Period for a Divorced Woman and Where She must have it

H 10609, Ch. 28, h 1

Ali ibn Ibrahim has narrated from his father from ibn abu 'Umayr from Hammad from al-Halabiy who has said the following:

"Abu 'Abd Allah, *'Alayhi al-Salam,* has said, 'A divorced woman must not go out without the permission of her husband until her waiting period is complete after three *Hayd* (menses)-free periods or three months, if she does not experience *Hayd* (menses).'"

H 10610, Ch. 28, h 2

A number of our people have narrated from Sahl ibn Ziyad from ibn abu Nasr from Dawud ibn Sarhan who has said the following:

"Abu 'Abd Allah, *'Alayhi al-Salam,* has said, 'Waiting period for a divorced woman is three *Hayd* (menses)-free periods or three months if she does not experience *Hayd* (menses).'" Humayd has narrated from ibn Sama'ah from Ja'far ibn Sama'ah from Dawud ibn Sarhan from abu 'Abd Allah, *'Alayhi al-Salam,* a similar *Hadith*.

H 10611, Ch. 28, h 3

Ali ibn Ibrahim has narrated from his father from 'Uthman ibn 'Isa from Sama'ah ibn Mehran who has said the following:

"I once asked him (the Imam), *'Alayhi al-Salam,* about the case of a woman who is divorced and about where she must complete her waiting period. He (the Imam) said, 'She completes her waiting period in her house and must not go out. If she wants to visit she must go after midnight but not during the day. She does not have the right to perform *al-Hajj* until her waiting period is complete.' I asked about one whose husband dies; if her case is the same. He (the Imam) said, 'Yes, it is the same but she can perform *al-Hajj* if she wants.'"

H 10612, Ch. 28, h 4

Ali has narrated from his father from ibn abu Najran from 'Asem ibn Hamid from Muhammad ibn Qays who has said the following:

"Abu Ja'far, *'Alayhi al-Salam,* has said, 'A woman divorced must complete her waiting period in her home and it is not proper for her to go out until her waiting period is complete. Her waiting period is three *Hayd*-(menses)-free periods or three months except if she experiences *Hayd* (menses).'"

H 10613, Ch. 28, h 5

Muhammad ibn Yahya has narrated from Ahmad ibn Muhammad from ibn Mahbub from Sa'd ibn abu Khalaf who has said the following:

"I once asked abu al-Hassan, Musa ibn Ja'far, *'Alayhim al-Salam,* something about divorce. He (the Imam) said, 'When a man divorces his wife in a manner because of which he cannot go back to her, she becomes stranger to him in the hour divorce is pronounced and she takes control of her affairs and he has no way to her. She can complete her waiting period where she wants. He does not owe her maintenance.' He (the narrator) has said that I then said, 'Does Allah, most Majestic, most Glorious, not say, '. . . do not send them out of their houses and they must not go out'? He (the Imam) said, 'It means she is divorced after being divorced. She is the one who must not be sent out of her house and must not go out of her house until the third divorce. When the third divorce is pronounced she becomes stranger to him and he does not owe her maintenance. A woman whom a man divorces once then leaves so that her waiting period is complete is the kind of woman who must stay in the house of her husband and she must be paid maintenance and lodging until waiting period is complete.'"

H 10614, Ch. 28, h 6

Muhammad ibn Yahya has narrated from Ahmad ibn Muhammad from Muhammad ibn 'Isma'il from Muhammad ibn al-Fudayl from abu al-Sabbah al-Kinaniy who has said the following:

"Abu 'Abd Allah, *'Alayhi al-Salam,* has said, 'A divorced woman completes her waiting period in her home and it is not proper for her husband to send her out and she also must not go out.'"

H 10615, Ch. 28, h 7

A number of our people have narrated from Sahl ibn Ziyad from ibn abu Nasr from 'Asem ibn Hamid from Muhammad ibn Qays who has said the following:

"Abu Ja'far, *'Alayhi al-Salam,* has said, 'A woman who is divorced and her husband has the right to go back to her, can beautify herself before her husband and he does not need to ask permission to go to her.'"

H 10616, Ch. 28, h 8

Humayd ibn Ziyad has narrated from ibn Sama'ah from ibn Ribat from Ishaq ibn 'Ammar who has said the following:

"I once asked abu al-Hassan, *'Alayhi al-Salam,* about the divorced woman; where she completes her waiting period. He (the Imam) said, 'She completes it in the house of her husband.'"

H 10617, Ch. 28, h 9

It is narrated from the narrator of the previous *Hadith* from Wuhayb ibn Hafs from abu Basir who has said the following:

"I once asked one of the two Imam, (abu Ja'far or abu 'Abd Allah), *'Alayhim al-Salam,* about the case of a woman who is divorced and about where she counts her waiting period. He (the Imam) said, 'She completes it in her home if divorce is in a manner where he has the right to go back to her. He cannot send her out and it is not for her to go out until waiting period is complete.'"

It is narrated from the narrator of the previous *Hadith* from 'Abd Allah ibn Jabalah from Ali ibn abu Hamzah and Muhammad ibn Yahya has narrated from Ahmad ibn Muhammad from Ali ibn al-Hakam from Ali ibn abu Hamzah from abu Basir a similar *Hadith.*

H 10618, Ch. 28, h 10

Humayd ibn Ziyad has narrated from ibn Sama'ah from Wuhayb ibn Hafs from abu Basir who has said the following:

"About the case of a divorced woman, one of the two Imam, (abu Ja'far or abu 'Abd Allah), *'Alayhim al-Salam,* has said that she completes her waiting period in her house and she can beautify herself; perhaps Allah brings about something thereafter.'"

H 10619, Ch. 28, h 11
Muhammad ibn Yahya has narrated from Ahmad ibn Muhammad [from Muhammad ibn Khalid] and al-Husayn ibn Sa'id from al-Qasim ibn 'Urwah from al-'Abbas who has said the following:

"He (the Imam), *'Alayhi al-Salam,* has said, that it is not proper for a divorced woman to go out without the permission of her husband until waiting period is complete with three *Hayd* (menses)-free periods or three months if she does not experience *Hayd* (menses).'"

H 10620, Ch. 28, h 12
Humayd ibn Ziyad has narrated from ibn Sama'ah from Muhammad ibn Ziyad from Mu'awiyah ibn 'Ammar who has said the following:

"I once heard abu 'Abd Allah, *'Alayhi al-Salam,* saying, 'A divorced woman can perform *al-Hajj* if her husband agrees.'"

H 10621, Ch. 28, h 13
Muhammad ibn 'Isma'il has narrated from al-Fadl ibn Shadhan and Abu Ali al-Ash'ariy has narrated from Muhammad ibn 'Abd al-Jabbar from Safwan from al-'Ala' from Muhammad ibn Muslim who has said the following:

"He (the Imam), *'Alayhi al-Salam,* has said, 'A divorced woman can perform *al-Hajj* and testify about rights.'"

H 10622, Ch. 28, h 14
Muhammad ibn Yahya has narrated from Ahmad ibn Muhammad from Muhammad ibn Khalid from al-Qasim ibn 'Urwah from Zurarah who has said the following:

"Abu 'Abd Allah, *'Alayhi al-Salam,* has said, 'A divorced woman can use kohl, dyes, perfumes and wear whatever she likes because Allah, most Majestic, most Glorious, says, '. . .perhaps Allah may bring about something thereafter.' Perhaps something happens in his mind and he goes back to her.'"

Chapter 29 - The Difference between one Divorced in Non-Sunnah manner and the One who Goes out in her Waiting Period or is Sent out by the Husband

H 10623, Ch. 29, h 1
Al-Husayn ibn Muhammad has said that narrated to me Hamdan al-Qalanisiy that 'Umar ibn Shihab al-'Abdiy asked me, 'On what basis your people say that divorce pronounced three times does not make it three divorces?' I said to him, 'They believe that divorce is based on the book and al-*Sunnah* and whatever is against them is returned to them.' He then asked, 'What do you say about one who has divorced according to the book and *Sunnah* and his wife goes out or he sends her out and she counts the waiting period somewhere other than her house? Allah, most Majestic, most Glorious, has said, "Do not send them out of their house and they must not go out."' I replied him with an answer, which was not from me. I met Ayyub ibn Nuh, asked him about it and informed him of the words of 'Umar (ibn Shihab). He said, 'We do not accept analogy. We only say what texts say.' I then met Ali ibn Rashid and asked him about it and about the

words of 'Umar (ibn Shihab). He said, 'He has used analogy against you to bind you. If divorce is not permissible without the book and *Sunnah*, waiting period also is not accepted without the book and *Sunnah*.' I then asked Mu'awiyah ibn al-Hukaym about it and informed him of the words of 'Umar (ibn Shihab). Mu'awiyah said, 'Waiting period is not like divorce. There is a difference between them. Divorce is the act of divorcee. If he does against the book and against what he is commanded to do we can say to him to return to the book, otherwise, divorce is not valid. The waiting period is not the act of the man or woman. The days pass. *Hayd* (menses) takes place and it is not her act or his act. It is the act of Allah, most Blessed, most High. The act of Allah, most Majestic, most Glorious, cannot be analogized with his acts or her acts. If she acts against the law, the waiting period passes, and she has committed a sin in acting against the law. Had the waiting period been her act we would not make it to take place on her like divorce is invalid if it is against the law.

"Al-Fadl ibn Shadhan has said, in answer presented by abu 'Ubayd in the book of divorce that certain people of al-Kalam (theology) has said, 'When Allah, the most Blessed, the most High, sanctioned divorce with waiting period He did not inform us that whoever divorces without waiting period his divorce is invalid. It is something that men and women obey and do not go out of the house as long as waiting period is not complete. We are only informed about sin. Allah has said, '. . . such is the limits set by Allah so do not transgress against them and those who transgress against the limits of Allah has done injustice to himself .' Is disobedience in divorce like disobedience in waiting period by going out of her house? Do you not say that the nation collectively says that if a divorced woman goes out of her house for days, such days are counted as part of her waiting period even if she has disobeyed Allah? In addition, divorce during *Hayd* (menses) is counted against divorcee even though he has disobeyed Allah.

[Translator's Note: The words of al-Fadl ibn Shadhan are not translated but the Arabic text is preserved in applicable editions of this book.]

Chapter 30 - Explanation of the words of Allah, most, High, 'You must not send them out of their homes and they must not go out. . .'

H 10624, Ch. 30, h 1
Ali ibn Ibrahim has narrated from his father from certain persons of his people who has said the following:
"About the words of Allah, most Majestic, most Glorious, '. . . you must not send them out of their homes and they must not go out except if they commit an open indecent act', abu al-Hassan, al-Rida', *'Alayhi al-Salam,* has said, 'It is a reference to her troubling the family of the man and her bad moral behavior.'"

H 10625, Ch. 30, h 2
Certain persons of our people have narrated from Ali ibn al-Hassan al-Taymuliy from Ali ibn Asbat from Muhammad ibn Ali ibn Ja'far who has said the following:
"Once al-Ma'mun asked al-Rida', *'Alayhi al-Salam,* about the words of Allah,

most Majestic, most Glorious, '. . . you must not send them out of their homes and they must not go out except if they commit an open indecent act' He (the Imam) said, '. . . 'open indecent act', is a reference to her troubling the family of the man. If she did he can send her out, if he wants, before the end of her waiting period.'"

Chapter 31 - Divorce of a Woman whose Hayd (menses) is Confusing

H 10626, Ch. 31, h 1

A number of our people have narrated from Ahmad ibn Muhammad from al-Barqiy from Dawud ibn abu Yazid al-'Attar from certain persons of our people who have said the following:

"I once asked abu 'Abd Allah, *'Alayhi al-Salam,* about the case of a woman whose *Hayd* (menses) is confusing, when women like her become pregnant and also women like her do not become pregnant and do not experience *Hayd* (menses). Her husband has gone to bed with her and about how can he divorce her if he so wants. He (the Imam) said, 'He must hold back from her for three months then divorce her.'"

Chapter 32 - Divorce of Women Who Hide Their Experiencing Hayd (menses)

H 10627, Ch. 32, h 1

Muhammad ibn Yahya has narrated from 'Abd Allah ibn Ja'far from al-Hassan ibn Ali ibn Kaysan who has said the following:

"I once wrote to the man, *'Alayhi al-Salam,* and asked about the case of a man who has a wife who is of *'Ammah* (the general population). He wants to divorce her but she hides her *Hayd* (menses) and *Hayd* (menses)-free period for fear of divorce. He (the Imam), *'Alayhi al-Salam,* wrote, 'He can hold back from her for three months, then divorce her.'"

Chapter 33 - The Case of a Woman who Experiences Hayd (menses) after Every Two or Three Months

H 10628, Ch. 33, h 1

Ali ibn Ibrahim has narrated from his father from al-Hassan ibn Mahbub from Hisham ibn Salim from 'Ammar al-Sabatiy who has said the following:

"Once abu 'Abd Allah, *'Alayhi al-Salam,* was asked about the case of a man who has a young wife who experiences *Hayd* (menses) every two or three months after once and about how he can divorce her. He (the Imam) said, 'Her case is difficult. He can divorce her according to *Sunnah* once in a *Hayd* (menses)-free period in the presence of witnesses and without going to bed; then leave her until she experiences *Hayd* (menses) three times whenever she experiences *Hayd* (menses). When she experiences three *Hayd* (menses) her waiting period is complete.' It then was asked, 'What happens if one year passes and she does not experience *Hayd* (menses)?' He (the Imam) said, 'If one year passes and she does not experience three *Hayd* (menses) he waits three months after that (one year) time then her waiting period expires.' It then asked, 'What happens if he or she dies?' He (the Imam) said, 'Whoever dies, the living one inherits the deceased one from that day up to fifteen months.'"

Chapter 34 - Waiting Period of a Woman whose Hayd (menses) is Confused

H 10629, Ch. 34, h 1

Ali ibn Ibrahim has narrated from his father from ibn abu 'Umayr from Jamil ibn Darraj from Zurarah who has said the following:

"Abu Ja'far, *'Alayhi al-Salam,* has stated this *Hadith.* 'In the case of a woman whose *Hayd* (menses) is confusing, of the two issues whichever comes first marks a woman's becoming stranger to her husband. One is passing of three months without any blood discharge and taking place of three *Hayd* (menses) the two of which are not three months apart from each other.'"

According to ibn abu 'Umayr Jamil has made this statement. 'It can be explained as follows: If three months one day less pass and she experiences *Hayd* (menses) then three months one day less pass and she experiences *Hayd* (menses) then three months one day less pass and she experiences *Hayd* (menses), she counts waiting period with *Hayd* (menses) in this way. She does not count by months. If three months pass without blood discharge for three months and she does not experience *Hayd* (menses) she then becomes stranger to her husband.'

H 10630, Ch. 34, h 2

A number of our people have narrated from Sahl ibn Ziyad from Ahmad ibn Muhammad from ibn abu Nasr al-Bazantiy from 'Abd al-Karim from Muhammad ibn Hakim who has said the following:

"I once asked the virtuous servant of Allah about the case of a young girl who does not experience *Hayd* (menses) when girls like her become pregnant and her husband has divorced her. He (the Imam) said, 'Her waiting period is three months.'"

H 10631, Ch. 34, h 3

Sahl ibn Ziyad has narrated from Ahmad from 'Abd al-Karim from abu Basir who has said the following:

"Abu 'Abd Allah, *'Alayhi al-Salam,* has said, 'Waiting period of a woman who does not experience *Hayd* (menses) and the one who experiences Istihadah who does not be become clean is three months. Waiting period of one whose *Hayd* (menses) is straight is three *Quru'* (*Hayd* free periods). Al-Quru' (*Hayd* free period) is the time of accumulation of blood between two *Hayd* (menses).'"

H 10632, Ch. 34, h 4

Muhammad ibn Yahya has narrated from Ahmad ibn Muhammad from Muhammad ibn `Isma'il from Muhammad ibn al-Fudayl from abu al-Sabbah al-Kinaniy who has said the following:

"I once asked abu 'Abd Allah, *'Alayhi al-Salam,* about the case of a woman who experiences *Hayd* (menses) once every three months: if she needs to count a waiting period. He (the Imam) said, 'She must wait for a period of time equal to that when she experienced *Hayd* normally; thus she counts her waiting period for three *Hayd-free* periods. Thereafter she can marry if she so wants.'"

H 10633, Ch. 34, h 5

Muhammad ibn Yahya has narrated from Ahmad ibn Muhammad from Ali ibn al-Hakam from al-'Ala' from Muhammad ibn Muslim who has said the following:

"One of the two Imam, (abu Ja'far or abu 'Abd Allah), *'Alayhim al-Salam*, has said that the waiting period for women of the following condition is three months. Of such women is one who experiences *Hayd* (menses) once every three, six or seven months. Another is one who experiences Istihadah and has not reach the age of experiencing *Hayd* (menses) also one who experiences *Hayd* (menses) in one month but not in the other month as well as one who has no hope to have a child. Another is one in her menopause who thinks that she is not of such age and the one who sees a yellowish discharge whose *Hayd* (menses) is not straight'"

H 10634, Ch. 34, h 6

Muhammad ibn Yahya has narrated from Ahmad ibn Muhammad from al-Husayn ibn Sa'id from Hammad ibn 'Isa from Shu'ayb from abu Basir who has said the following:

"About the case of a woman who is divorced and experiences *Hayd* (menses) once every three months, abu 'Abd Allah, *'Alayhi al-Salam*, has said, 'When three months are over her waiting period is complete. For every month he counts for her one *Hayd* (menses).'"

H 10635, Ch. 34, h 7

Ali ibn Ibrahim has narrated from his father from ibn abu Nasr, from Dawud ibn al-Husayn, from abu al-'Abbas who has said the following:

"I once asked abu 'Abd Allah, *'Alayhi al-Salam*, about the case of a man who divorces his wife after childbirth and her becoming clean and she is a woman who does not experience *Hayd* (menses) as long as she breastfeeds and about how much is her waiting period. He (the Imam) said, 'It is three months.'"

H 10636, Ch. 34, h 8

Ali has narrated from his father from ibn abu 'Umayr from Hammad ibn 'Uthaman from al-Halabiy who has said the following:

"Abu 'Abd Allah, *'Alayhi al-Salam*, has said, 'The waiting period of a woman who does not experience *Hayd* (menses) and one who experiences Istihadah which does not become clean for three months, their waiting period is three months. Waiting period of a woman whose *Hayd* is straight is three *Hayd-free* periods.' I then asked about the meaning of the words of Allah, most Majestic, most Glorious, '. . . if you have doubt.' He (the Imam) said, 'This 'doubt' is about what is more than one month, thus, she counts her waiting period for three months and ignores *Hayd*. Whatever of *Hayd* is in a month which does not increase in *Hayd* her waiting period is three cycles of *Hayd*.'"

H 10637, Ch. 34, h 9

Muhammad ibn Yahya has narrated from Ahmad ibn Muhammad from al-Hassan ibn Ali ibn Faddal from ibn Bukayr from Zurarah who has said the following:

"One of the two Imam, (abu Ja'far or abu 'Abd Allah), *'Alayhim al-Salam*, has stated this *Hadith*. 'Of the two issues whichever comes first, it marks the end of her waiting period: one is passing of three months in which she does not see *Hayd* (menses), thus her waiting period ends. If three *Hayd-free* periods pass this also marks the end of her waiting period.'"

H 10638, Ch. 34, h 10
Muhammad has narrated from Ahmad from Ali ibn al-Hakam from Musa ibn Bakr from Zurarah who has said the following:

"He (the Imam), *'Alayhi al-Salam,* has said, 'If she waits and does not find the *Hayd* (menses)-free period except three months then if her *Hayd* (menses) is not straight. If she experiences *Hayd* in a month several times such woman's waiting period is like the waiting period of one who experiences Istihadah, whose 'Iddah (waiting period) is three months. If she experiences *Hayd* straightly, thus, in every month is one *Hayd* and between two *Hayd* (menses) one month of time it is the *Hayd-free* period.'"

H 10639, Ch. 34, h 11
Muhammad ibn Yahya has narrated from Muhammad ibn al-Husayn from Yazid ibn Ishaq Sha'ir from Harun ibn Hamzah who has said the following:

"About the case of a woman who is divorced and is old but experiences *Hayd* (menses) once then her *Hayd* stops, abu 'Abd Allah, *'Alayhi al-Salam,* has said, 'She must count her waiting period for one *Hayd* and two months in future because she has reached menopause.'"

Chapter 35 - The Word of Women are Accepted in Matters of Hayd (menses)

H 10640, Ch. 35, h 1
Ali ibn Ibrahim has narrated from his father from ibn abu 'Umayr from Jamil from Zurarah who has said the following:

"Abu Ja'far, *'Alayhi al-Salam,* has said, 'Waiting period and *Hayd* (menses) are for women. If they say something about it their words are accepted.'"

Chapter 36 - A Woman Confused about Pregnancy

H 10641, Ch. 36, h 1
Ali ibn Ibrahim has narrated from his father and Muhammad ibn 'Isma'il has narrated from al-Fadl ibn Shadhan from all from ibn abu 'Umayr from 'Abd al-Rahman ibn *al-Hajj*aj who has said the following:

"I once heard abu Ibrahim, *'Alayhi al-Salam,* saying, 'If one divorces his wife and she claims to be pregnant, he must wait for nine months if she gives birth, otherwise, she counts a waiting period of three months.'"

H 10642, Ch. 36, h 2
Humayd ibn Ziyad has narrated from ibn Sama'ah from Muhammad ibn abu Hamzah from Muhammad ibn Hakim who has said the following:

"I once asked abu al-Hassan, *'Alayhi al-Salam,* about the case of a woman who is young and other women like her experience *Hayd* (menses). She is divorced: then her *Hayd* stops. How long is her waiting period? He (the Imam) said, 'It is three months.' I then asked that she has claimed to be pregnant after three months. He (the Imam) said, 'Her waiting period is nine months.' I then said that after nine months she has claimed to be pregnant. He (the Imam) said, 'Pregnancy is for nine months.' I then asked, 'Can she marry?' He (the Imam) said, 'She must observe precaution for three months.' I then said that after three months she has claimed. He (the Imam) said, 'There is no doubt about her, so she can marry if she wants.'"

H 10643, Ch. 36, h 3

Al-Husayn ibn Muhammad has narrated from Mu'alla' ibn Muhammad from al-Hassan ibn Ali from Aban ibn Hakim who has said the following:

"About the case of a woman who is divorced and she claims to be pregnant; so she waits for one year, abu Ibrahim or his father, '*Alayhi al-Salam,* has said, 'If she comes up with such claim after a year it is not accepted even if it is one hour more.'"

H 10644, Ch. 36, h 4

Humayd ibn Ziyad has narrated from ibn Sama'ah and Abu Ali al-Ash'ariy has narrated from Muhammad ibn 'Abd al-Jabbar from Safwan from Muhammad ibn Hakim who has said the following:

"I once asked the virtuous servant, '*Alayhi al-Salam,* about the case of a woman who is young and women like her experience *Hayd* (menses). Her husband divorces her and her *Hayd* stops. How long is her waiting period? He (the Imam) said, 'It is three months.' I then said that she after three months became married and after going with her husband it was found that she is pregnant. He (the Imam) said, 'This cannot happen, O ibn Hakim. Stoppage of *Hayd* is because of two reasons; it is because of disorder in *Hayd* in which case husbands were lawful for her, but she was not pregnant or that she is pregnant in which case it becomes apparent in three months because Allah, most Majestic, most Glorious, has set a time for it in which time pregnancy becomes apparent.' I then asked, 'What happens if she has doubts?' He (the Imam) said, 'Her 'Iddah (waiting period) is nine months.' I then said that she after nine months has doubts. He (the Imam) said, 'Pregnancy is for nine months only.' I then asked if she could marry. He (the Imam) said, 'She must observe precaution for three months.' I then said that she has doubts after three months.' He (the Imam) said, 'There is no doubt in her case, so she can marry if she wants.'"

H 10645, Ch. 36, h 5

A number of our people have narrated from Sahl ibn Ziyad from Muhammad ibn 'Isa from Yunus from Muhammad ibn Hakim who has said the following:

"I once asked abu 'Abd Allah, or abu al-Hassan, '*Alayhi al-Salam,* about the case of a man who divorces his wife and after three months she claims to be pregnant. He (the Imam) said, 'There is a waiting for her for nine months.' I then said, 'She has claimed to be pregnant after that. He (the Imam) said, 'This is far from reality. *Hayd* (menses) stops for two reasons, because of a clear pregnancy or disorder in *Hayd*. However, she can remain cautious for three months thereafter.'

"He (the narrator) also asked about a woman who experienced *Hayd* and then it stopped after one year and about how she is divorced. He (the Imam) said, 'She is divorced in the presence of witnesses.'"

(The following paragraph does not seem to be part of *Hadith*)

Certain ones have said that if he wants to divorce her, she does not experience *Hayd* (menses) and he has gone to bed with her; he can place her in quarantine. He must hold back from her for three months from the time a divorced woman becomes stranger to her husband, a woman whose *Hayd* (menses) is straight if pregnancy becomes clear, otherwise, he can divorce her once in the presence of two witnesses. If he leaves her for three months she becomes stranger by one divorce. If he wants to divorce her three times, he can leave her for one month, then go back to her, then divorce her for the second time, then hold back from her three months to place her in quarantine; if pregnancy becomes clear thereafter he only has to divorce her once."

Chapter 37 - Maintenance of Pregnant Divorced Women

H 10646, Ch. 37, h 1
Ali ibn Ibrahim has narrated from his father from ibn abu Najran from 'Asem ibn Hamid from Muhammad ibn Qays who has said the following:
"Abu Ja'far, *'Alayhi al-Salam,* has said, 'Waiting period of a pregnant divorcee expires at childbirth and he must pay for her maintenance in fairness until childbirth.'"

H 10647, Ch. 37, h 2
Muhammad ibn Yahya has narrated from Ahmad ibn Muhammad ibn 'Isma'il from Muhammad ibn al-Fudayl from abu al-Sabbah al-Kinaniy who has said the following:
"Abu 'Abd Allah, *'Alayhi al-Salam,* has said, 'If a man divorces his pregnant wife he must pay for her maintenance until childbirth. When she gives birth, he must pay her wages without causing any harm to her, unless he finds someone who breastfeeds for less. If she also agrees for less then she has the priority to have her son until weaning.'"

H 10648, Ch. 37, h 3
Ali has narrated from his father from ibn abu 'Umayr from Hammad from al-Halabiy who has said the following:
"A pregnant divorcee must receive her maintenance until childbirth, and she has the priority to breastfeed the child for wages equal to what another woman asks. Allah, most Majestic, most Glorious, has said, 'A mother must not be harmed because of her child or the father because of the child and the heirs also bear such responsibility.' (2:232) He (the Imam) said, 'A woman (from us) would raise her hand before her husband, when he wanted to go to bed with her, and say, 'I do not want to allow you because I fear of becoming pregnant with my child.' The man would say, 'I do not want to go to bed with you for my fear of suspending you, thus killing my child.' Allah prohibited a woman's harming a man or a man's harming a woman' and His words '. . . the heirs also bear the

same responsibility' is a prohibition against harming the child or his mother in breastfeeding. She must not charge for breastfeeding for more than two complete years. If they with mutual agreement wean the child before such time, it is fine.'"

H 10649, Ch. 37, h 4
Muhammad ibn Yahya has narrated from Ahmad ibn Muhammad from al-Husayn ibn Sa'id from Hammad ibn 'Isa from 'Abd Allah ibn al-Mughirah from 'Abd Allah ibn Sinan who has said the following:

"About the case of a woman who is pregnant and is divorced, abu 'Abd Allah, *'Alayhi al-Salam,* has said, 'Her waiting period ends with childbirth and he must pay for her maintenance until she gives birth.'"

Chapter 38 - A Woman Divorcee Three Times Does not have the Right for Lodging or Maintenance

H 10650, Ch. 38, h 1
Al-'Abbas al-Razzaz from Ayyub ibn Nuh and Abu Ali al-Ash'ariy has narrated from Muhammad ibn 'Abd al-Jabbar and Muhammad ibn 'Isma'il has narrated from al-Fadl ibn Shadhan from and Humayd ibn Ziyad from ibn Sama'ah all from Safwan ibn Yahya from Musa ibn Bakr from Zurarah who has said the following:

"Abu Ja'far, *'Alayhi al-Salam,* has said, 'A woman divorced three times does not have the right to ask for her maintenance from her husband. Such right becomes due on a husband who has the right to go back to her.'"

H 10651, Ch. 38, h 2
Humayd ibn Ziyad has narrated from ibn Sama'ah from Muhammad ibn Ziyad from 'Abd Allah ibn Sinan who has said the following:

"I once asked abu 'Abd Allah, *'Alayhi al-Salam,* about the case of a woman who is divorced three times according to *Sunnah;* if she deserves maintenance and accommodation. He (the Imam) said, 'No, it does not apply to her case.'"

H 10652, Ch. 38, h 3
Ali ibn Ibrahim has narrated from his father from Hammad ibn 'Isa or a man from Hammad from Shu'ayb from abu Basir who has said the following:

"Once abu 'Abd Allah, *'Alayhi al-Salam,* was asked about the case of a woman who is divorced three times; if she deserves maintenance and accommodation. He (the Imam) asked, 'Is she pregnant?' I replied, 'No, she is not pregnant.' He (the Imam) said, 'No, she does not deserve it.'"

H 10653, Ch. 38, h 4
Muhammad ibn Yahya has narrated from Ahmad ibn Muhammad from Ali ibn al-Hakam from Musa ibn Bakr from Zurarah who has said the following:

"Abu Ja'far, *'Alayhi al-Salam,* has said, 'A woman who is divorced three times does not deserve maintenance from her husband; it is for the one whose husband has the right to go back to her.'"

H 10654, Ch. 38, h 5
A number of our people have narrated from Ahmad ibn Muhammad ibn Khalid and Ali ibn Ibrahim has narrated from his father from 'Uthman ibn 'Isa from Sama'ah who has said the following:

"I once asked him (the Imam), *'Alayhi al-Salam,* about the case of a woman who is divorced three times: if she deserves maintenance and accommodation. He (the Imam) asked, 'Is she pregnant?' I replied, 'No, she is not pregnant.' He (the Imam) said, 'No, she does not deserve it.'"

Chapter 39 - Benefits for a Divorced Woman

H 10655, Ch. 39, h 1

Ali ibn Ibrahim has narrated from his father from ibn abu 'Umayr from Hafs ibn al-Bakhtariy who has said the following:

"I once asked abu 'Abd Allah, *'Alayhi al-Salam,* about the case of a man who divorces his wife; if he can benefit her. He (the Imam) said, 'Yes, does he not want to be of the people of good deeds, does he not want to be of the pious people?'"

H 10656, Ch. 39, h 2

Ali ibn Ibrahim has narrated from his father and a number of our people have narrated from Sahl ibn Ziyad from al-Bazantiy who has said the following:

"Certain persons of our people have mentioned that benefiting a divorced woman is obligatory.'"

H 10657, Ch. 39, h 3

Ahmad ibn Muhammad from ibn abu Nasr has narrated from al-Bazantiy from 'Abd al-Karim from al-Halabiy who has said the following:

"About the words of Allah, most Majestic, most Glorious, '. . . divorced women have rights on the pious ones,' (2:241) abu 'Abd Allah, *'Alayhi al-Salam,* has said, 'It is benefiting her after her waiting period ends. An affluent man or one who is not affluent, each must benefit according to their abilities. During the waiting period, however, why he should not benefit her when she is in her waiting period and hopes for him as well as he hopes for her that Allah, most Majestic, most Glorious, as He wills, may make something happen for them?' He (the Imam) said, 'If a man is affluent he benefits his wife with servants and a not-so-affluent one benefits with wheat [and barley], raisins, clothes and dirham. Al-Hassan, ibn Ali, *'Alayhi al-Salam,* benefited his wife with a slave-girl. He, *'Alayhi al-Salam,* benefited all the women that he divorced.'"

H 10658, Ch. 39, h 4

Humayd ibn Ziyad has narrated from Sama'ah from Muhammad ibn Ziyad from 'Abd Allah ibn Sinan and Ali ibn Ibrahim has narrated from his father from 'Uthman ibn 'Isa from Sama'ah all abu 'Abd Allah, *'Alayhi al-Salam,* who has said the following:

"About the words of Allah, most Majestic, most Glorious, '. . . divorced women must be benefited with fairness; it is a right on the pious ones', abu 'Abd Allah, *'Alayhi al-Salam,* has stated this *Hadith.* 'It is after the end of waiting period, and about, 'an affluent man and one not-so-affluent each according to their abilities', he (the Imam) said, 'Why should he not benefit her during her waiting period when she hopes and he hopes that Allah by His will may make something good to happen for them? An affluent man must benefits his woman with servant and one not affluent, benefit with wheat, (dates), raisins, clothes and dirham. Al-Hassan ibn Ali, *'Alayhi al-Salam,* benefited the woman he divorced with a slave-girl. He (the Imam) benefited all the women he divorced.'"

Humayd ibn Ziyad has narrated from ibn Sama'ah from Muhammad ibn Ziyad from Mu'awiyah ibn 'Ammar from abu 'Abd Allah, *'Alayhi al-Salam,* a similar *Hadith* except that he has said, 'Al-Hassan ibn Ali, *'Alayhi al-Salam,* would benefit his women with slave-girls.'"

H 10659, Ch. 39, h 5

A number of our people have narrated from Sahl ibn Ziyad from ibn abu Nasr from 'Abd al-Karim from abu Nasr who has said the following:

"I once asked abu Ja'far, *'Alayhi al-Salam,* about the words of Allah, most Majestic, most Glorious, '. . . divorced women must be benefited with fairness. It is a right on the pious ones,' and about what is the minimum of such benefits if one is not affluent. He (the Imam) said, 'It is a scarf or similar things.'"

Chapter 40 - The Rights of a Divorced Woman of mahr (dower) with Whom He has not Gone to Bed

H 10660, Ch. 40, h 1

Abu Ali al-Ash'ariy has narrated from Muhammad ibn 'Abd al-Jabbar and al-'Abbas Muhammad ibn Ja'far al-Razzaz from Ayyub ibn Nuh and Humayd ibn Ziyad has narrated from ibn Sama'ah all from Safwan from ibn Muskan from abu Basir who has said the following:

"Abu 'Abd Allah, *'Alayhi al-Salam,* has said, 'If a man divorces his wife before going to bed with her, she becomes stranger to him and she can marry if she wants in the same hour after divorce. If mahr (dower) is set, she deserves one-half of it but if mahr (dower) is not set he must benefit her.'"

H 10661, Ch. 40, h 2

Safwan has narrated from in from abu Basir and Ali has narrated from his father and A number of our people have narrated from Ahmad ibn Muhammad from ibn Khalid f, 'Uthman ibn 'Isa from Sama'ah all from abu 'Abd Allah, *'Alayhi al-Salam,* who has said the following:

"The following are the words of Allah, most Majestic, most Glorious. 'If you divorce them before you touch them and if you have set mahr (dower) for them that must be paid them one-half of it is payable unless it is waved or one who has authority in the matter of marriage waves it.' (2:237) Abu 'Abd Allah, *'Alayhi al-Salam,* has said, 'Of people with such authority is the father, or brother or the executor of the will and those whose command in the assets of the woman is effective to buy certain things and she authorizes, if such person waves, then it is permissible.'"

H 10662, Ch. 40, h 3

Ali has narrated from his father from ibn abu 'Umayr from Hammad from al-Halabiy who has said the following:

"About the case of a man who divorces his wife before going to bed with her, abu 'Abd Allah, *'Alayhi al-Salam,* has stated this *Hadith.* 'He owes to her one-half of mahr (dower) if he has set something for her; but if he has not set anything for her he must benefit her like the benefits that similar women receive.' The words of Allah, most Majestic, most Glorious, say, '. . . or it is waived by the one who has authority in the matters of marriage. . .' He (the

Imam) said, 'Of such people is father, or a brother or the executor of the will or a man who is authorized in dealing with the assets of the woman to buy for her and he buys if he waves, it then is effective.'"

H 10663, Ch. 40, h 4
Ali has narrated from his father from ibn abu 'Umayr from ibn Bukayr from 'Ubayd ibn Zurarah who has said the following:

"I once asked abu 'Abd Allah, *'Alayhi al-Salam,* about the case of a man who marries a woman and sets a mahr (dower) of one hundred sheep. He then delivers them to her, then divorces her before going to bed with her and the sheep have given birth to their young. He (the Imam) said, 'If the sheep had become pregnant with him she must return one-half of them and one-half of the young ones; but if they did not become pregnant with him she must return one-half of the sheep but not the young ones.'"

Muhammad ibn Yahya has narrated from Ahmad ibn Muhammad from ibn Faddal from ibn Bukayr from 'Ubayd ibn Zurarah who has narrated the following:

"He has narrated a similar *Hadith* from abu 'Abd Allah, *'Alayhi al-Salam,* except that he has said, 'He delivered sheep and slaves, then sheep and slaves gave birth.'"

H 10664, Ch. 40, h 5
Muhammad has narrated from Ahmad from ibn Mahbub, from ibn Bukayr from ibn Ri'ab from Zurarah who has said the following:

"About the case of a man who marries a non-virgin woman or a virgin one and divorces her in the hour that she enters his house, abu Ja'far, *'Alayhi al-Salam,* has stated this *Hadith.* 'Trustworthy women must examine them and if they find such woman with the condition before she came to him then she deserves one-half of the mahr (dower) which is set for her and she does not need to count any waiting period.'"

H 10665, Ch. 40, h 6
Muhammad ibn Ahmad has narrated from ibn Mahbub from Jamil ibn Salih from al-Fudayl ibn Yasar who has said the following:

"I once asked abu 'Abd Allah, *'Alayhi al-Salam,* about the case of a man who marries a woman and sets a mahr (dower) of one thousand dirham and gives her a runaway slave and a gown of Hibr for the one thousand set as mahr (dower). He (the Imam) said, 'If she knows about the slave and has agreed, then it is not unlawful if she has taken delivery of the cloths and has agreed about the slave.' I then asked, 'What happens if he divorces her before going to bed with her? He (the Imam) said, 'She has no mahr (dower) and she must return five hundred dirham and the slave is for her.'"

H 10666, Ch. 40, h 7
Humayd ibn Ziyad has narrated from ibn Sama'ah from more than one person from Aban ibn 'Uthman from ibn abu Ya'fur who has said the following:

"I once asked abu 'Abd Allah, *'Alayhi al-Salam,* about the case of a man who marries a woman and has set her father as her mahr (dower) and that she must return one thousand dirham to him. He then divorces her before going to bed with her. What must she return to him when she deserves only one-half of the mahr (dower)? Her father is an old man who is worth only five hundred dirham and he says, 'Were it not because of you I would not sell him for three thousand dirham. He (the Imam) said, 'His words are not considered and nothing is returned to him.'"

H 10667, Ch. 40, h 8

Muhammad ibn Yahya has narrated from Ahmad ibn Muhammad from ibn Mahbub from Salih ibn Razin from Shihab who has said the following:

"I once asked abu 'Abd Allah, *'Alayhi al-Salam,* about the case of a man who marries a woman for one thousand dirham and pays to her; but she gives it as a gift to him and says, 'I am interested in you.' He then divorces her before going to bed with her.' He (the Imam) said, 'He must return to her five hundred dirham.'"

H 10668, Ch. 40, h 9

Muhammad has narrated from Ahmad from Muhammad ibn 'Isma'il from Mansur ibn Yunus from ibn 'Udhaynah fm mm who has said the following:

"I once asked abu 'Abd Allah, *'Alayhi al-Salam,* about the case of a man who marries a woman and sets a mahr (dower) of one thousand dirham and pays it to her. She then keeps five hundred and returns five hundred to him as gift. He then divorces before going to bed with her. He (the Imam) said, 'She must return the other five hundred because five hundred belonged to her. Her giving as gift to him or others is the same.'"

H 10669, Ch. 40, h 10

Muhammad has narrated from Ahmad from al-Husayn ibn Sa'id from al-Nadr ibn Suwayd from al-Qasim ibn Sulayman from 'Ubayd ibn Zurarah who has said the following:

"I once asked abu 'Abd Allah, *'Alayhi al-Salam,* about the case of a man who marries a woman and sets her (slave) father as her mahr (dower). His price is five hundred dirham; then he divorces before going to bed with her.' He (the Imam) said, 'She does not owe anything to him.'"

H 10670, Ch. 40, h 11

Muhammad ibn Yahya has narrated from Ahmad ibn Muhammad from Ali ibn al-Hakam from Ali ibn abu Hamzah from abu Basir who has said the following:

"I once asked abu 'Abd Allah, *'Alayhi al-Salam,* about the case of a man who divorces his wife before going to bed with her. He (the Imam) said, 'He owes to her one-half of the mahr (dower) if he has set mahr (dower) for her, but if he has not set anything for her then he must benefit her in a fair manner as it is done with women similar to her.'"

H 10671, Ch. 40, h 12

Muhammad ibn Yahya in a *marfu'* manner has narrated from Ishaq ibn 'Ammar who has said the following:

"This is the case of a man who marries a woman for a slave with his wife. He delivers them to her then the wife of the slave dies in the possession of the woman; then he divorces her before going to bed with her. Abu al-Hassan, al-Awwal, *'Alayhi al-Salam,* has said, 'If he had appraised her for her on the day of marriage he then appraises the slave. He then counts the difference of the day of marriage which she must return to him, then he gives her one-half of what he has received back.'"

H 10672, Ch. 40, h 13
Ali ibn Ibrahim has narrated from his father from al-Nawfaliy from al-Sakuniy who has said the following:

"Abu 'Abd Allah, 'Alayhi al-Salam, has said that 'Amir al-Mu'minin has said this. 'If a woman marries for a woman as mahr (dower) who grows with her whereby her price increases or reduces, then he divorces her before going to bed with her. She must give back half of the price of the day it was given to her regardless of any increase or decrease.'"

H 10673, Ch. 40, h 14
Through the same chain of narrators as that of the previous *Hadith* the following is narrated:

"About the case of a man who sets his slave-girl free then sets her freedom as her mahr (dower) then divorces before going to bed with her. He (the Imam) said, 'She must return one-half of her price and must work to pay the rest.'"

Chapter 41(a) - The Issue that Completes Mahr (dower)

H 10674, Ch. 41a, h 1
Ali ibn Ibrahim has narrated from his father from ibn abu 'Umayr from Hammad from al-Halabiy who has said the following:

"I once asked abu 'Abd Allah, 'Alayhi al-Salam, about the case of a man who has married a woman and has gone to bed with her. He (the Imam) said, 'When the two organs meet mahr (dower) become obligatory.'"

H 10675, Ch. 41a, h 2
Ali has narrated from his father from ibn abu 'Umayr from Hafs ibn al-Bakhtariy who has said the following:

"Abu 'Abd Allah, 'Alayhi al-Salam, has said, 'When the two organs meet, mahr (dower), waiting period and Ghusl (bath) become obligatory.'"

H 10676, Ch. 41a, h 3
A number of our people have narrated from Sahl ibn Ziyad and Ali ibn Ibrahim has narrated from his father from all ibn abu Nasr from Dawud ibn Sarhan who has said the following:

"Abu 'Abd Allah, 'Alayhi al-Salam, has said, 'If he makes it penetrate, Ghusl (bath), whipping, stoning and mahr (dower) become obligatory.'"

H 10677, Ch. 41a, h 4
Muhammad ibn Yahya has narrated from Ahmad ibn Muhammad from ibn Mahbub from 'Abd Allah ibn Sinan who has said the following:

"Abu 'Abd Allah, 'Alayhi al-Salam, has said, 'Touching women is falling upon them (going to bed with them).'"

H 10678, Ch. 41a, h 5
Muhammad ibn Yahya has narrated from Ahmad ibn Muhammad from ibn Faddal from Yunus ibn Ya'qub who has said the following:

"I once asked abu 'Abd Allah, 'Alayhi al-Salam, about the case of a man who marries a woman, closes the door, pulls the curtains, touches and kisses her; then divorces; if mahr (dower) becomes obligatory. He (the Imam) said, 'Mahr (dower) becomes obligatory only after sexual intercourse.'"

H 10679, Ch. 41a, h 6

Muhammad ibn Yahya has narrated from Ahmad ibn Muhammad from ibn Mahbub from 'Abd Allah ibn Sinan who has said the following:

"Abu Basir once asked abu 'Abd Allah, *'Alayhi al-Salam,* when I was also there, about a man who marries a woman, goes to her but does not touch or approach her before divorcing if she needs to count the waiting period. He (the Imam) said, 'Waiting period is because of fluid discharge.' It was asked, 'What happens if there is sexual intercourse without semen discharge?' He (the Imam) said, 'If he inserts it, Ghusl (bath), mahr (dower) and waiting period become obligatory.'"

H 10680, Ch. 41a, h 7

Ali ibn Ibrahim has narrated from his father from ibn abu 'Umayr from Hammad from al-Halabiy who has said the following:

"I once asked abu 'Abd Allah, *'Alayhi al-Salam,* about the case of a man who divorces a woman whom he has touched without sexual intercourse if waiting period is obligatory. He (the Imam) said, 'Abu Ja'far, *'Alayhi al-Salam,* had faced such a condition and his father, Ali ibn al-Husayn, *'Alayhi al-Salam,* said, 'When doors are closed and curtains are pulled down mahr (dower) and waiting period become necessary.'"

Ibn abu 'Umayr has said that *Ahadith* are not the same about this issue if mahr (dower) is complete or not. Certain ones have said that it is one-half of mahr (dower) and it means that a judge rules according to apparent condition of a case. When the doors are closed and curtains are pulled down mahr (dower) becomes obligatory. It is up to her when she knows before Allah that he has not touched then she deserves only half of mahr (dower).'"

H 10681, Ch. 41a, h 8

A number of our people have narrated from Sahl ibn Ziyad from ibn Ri'ab from abu Basir who has said the following:

"I once asked abu 'Abd Allah, *'Alayhi al-Salam,* about the case of a man who marries a woman; then pulls the curtains down upon himself and on her and closes the door; then divorces her and the woman is asked, 'Did he come to you? She says, 'No, he did not come to me.' He then is asked, 'Did you go to her?' He says, 'No, I did go to her.' He (the Imam) said, 'Their words are not accepted because she wants to avoid waiting period from herself and he wants to avoid mahr (dower), meaning when they are accused.'"

H 10682, Ch. 41a, h 9

Abu Ali al-Ash'ariy has narrated from Muhammad ibn 'Abd al-Jabbar from Safwan from Ishaq ibn 'Ammar who has said the following:

"I once asked abu al-Hassan, *'Alayhi al-Salam,* about the case of a man who marries a woman then goes to her, closes the door, pulls down the curtain on her and thinks that he has not touched her and she also confirms his words; if she must count waiting period. He (the Imam) said, 'No, it is not necessary.' I then asked, 'One thing is near the thing.' He (the Imam) said, 'If fluid is discharged she must count the waiting period but if they are trusted then their words are accepted.'"

Chapter 41(b) - The Divorced Woman Whose Husband is Absent Commences Her 'Iddah (waiting period) from the Day She is Divorced

H 10683, Ch. 41b, h 1
Ali ibn Ibrahim has narrated from his father from ibn abu 'Umayr from Hammad who has narrated the following:
"I once asked abu 'Abd Allah, *'Alayhi al-Salam*, about the case of a man who divorces his wife when he is absent. When must his wife commence her 'Iddah (waiting period)? He (the Imam) said, 'If just testimony is established for his divorcing her on a known day which gives her certainty, she must commence her 'Iddah (waiting period) from the day she is divorced; but if she is not certain then she must commence her 'Iddah from the day she is informed.'"

H 10684, Ch. 41b, h 2
Ali ibn Ibrahim has narrated from his father from ibn abu 'Umayr, from 'Umar ibn 'Udhaynah, from Zurarah and Muhammad ibn Muslim and Burayd ibn Mu'awiyah ibn 'Ammar who has narrated the following:
"About the case of one who is absent if he divorces his wife abu Ja'far, *'Alayhi al-Salam,* has said, 'She must commence her 'Iddah (waiting period) from the day he has divorced her.'"

H 10685, Ch. 41b, h 3
A number of our people have narrated from Sahl ibn Ziyad from ibn abu Nasr from al-Muthanna' from Zurarah who has narrated the following:
"I once asked abu 'Abd Allah, *'Alayhi al-Salam,* about the case of a man who divorces his wife when he is absent. When must she commence her 'Iddah (waiting period)? He (the Imam) said, 'If testimony is established that he has divorced on a known day, of a known month, she must commence her 'Iddah (waiting period) from that day; but if she cannot ascertain the date, then she must commence her 'Iddah (waiting period) from the day she is informed.'"

H 10686, Ch. 41b, h 4
Muhammad ibn Yahya has narrated from Ahmad ibn Muhammad from al-Husayn ibn Sa'id from Hammad ibn 'Isa from Shu'ayb ibn Ya'qub from abu Basir who has narrated the following:
"Once, abu 'Abd Allah, *'Alayhi al-Salam,* was asked about the case of a man who divorces his wife. He informs her about it only after one year. He (the Imam) said, 'If two just witness testify to prove it, she does not need to complete any 'Iddah (waiting period), otherwise, she must commence her 'Iddah (waiting period) from the day she is informed.'"

H 10687, Ch. 41b, h 5
Muhammad ibn Ahmad has narrated from Ali ibn al-Hakam from al-'Ala' ibn Razin from Muhammad ibn Muslim who has narrated the following:

"Abu Ja'far, recipient of divine supreme covenant, has said, 'If a man divorces his wife when he is absent he must appoint witnesses. When three *Hayd* (menses)-free periods pass from that time her 'Iddah (waiting period) is complete.'"

H 10688, Ch. 41b, h 6

Ali ibn Ibrahim has narrated from his father from ibn abu Nasr who has narrated the following:

"Abu al-Hassan al-Rida', *'Alayhi al-Salam,* has said, 'If proof is established that she was divorced on such and such date which proves the expiration of her 'Iddah (waiting period) she becomes a stranger for him.'"

H 10689, Ch. 41b, h 7

Muhammad ibn Yahya has narrated from Ahmad ibn Muhammad from Ali ibn al-Hakam from Musa ibn Bakr al-Wasitiy from Zurarah who has narrated the following:

"Abu Ja'far, *'Alayhi al-Salam,* has said, 'If one divorces his wife when he is absent and proof is established to prove such divorce, her 'Iddah (waiting period) commences from the day he has divorced her.'"

H 10690, Ch. 41b, h 8

Muhammad ibn Yahya has narrated from Ahmad ibn Muhammad from Muhammad ibn 'Isma'il from Muhammad ibn al-Fudayl from abu al-Sabbah al-Kinaniy who has narrated the following:

"Abu 'Abd Allah, *'Alayhi al-Salam,* has stated this *Hadith.* 'If a man divorces his wife when he is absent and testimony is established to prove the date of such divorce, she can commence her 'Iddah (waiting period) from the day her husband had divorced her. If it is not proved then she must commence her 'Iddah (waiting period) from the time she is informed.'"

Chapter 42 - Waiting period of a Widow whose Husband is Absent

H 10691, Ch. 42, h 1

Muhammad ibn Yahya has narrated from Ahmad ibn Muhammad from Ali ibn al-Hakam from al-'Ala' ibn Razin from Muhammad ibn Muslim who has said the following:

"About the case of a man who dies and leaves behind a widow and he is absent, one of the two Imam, (abu Ja'far or abu 'Abd Allah), *'Alayhim al-Salam,* has said, 'She must commence her 'Iddah (waiting period) from the day she receives the news of his death.'"

H 10692, Ch. 42, h 2

Muhammad ibn Yahya has narrated from Ahmad ibn Muhammad from Muhammad ibn `Isma'il from Muhammad ibn al-Fudayl abu al-Sabbah al-Kinaniy who has said the following:

"About the case of a woman whose husband dies and who is absent, abu 'Abd Allah, *'Alayhi al-Salam,* has said, 'Her waiting period begins from the day she is informed, regardless, there is proving evidence or not.'"

H 10693, Ch. 42, h 3

Ali ibn Ibrahim has narrated from his father from ibn abu 'Umayr from 'Umar ibn 'Udhaynah from Zurarah Ahmad ibn Muhammad from Muhammad ibn Muslim and Burayd who has said the following:

"About the case of a woman whose husband is absent when he dies, abu Ja'far, *'Alayhi al-Salam,* has said, 'She must count her waiting period from the day the news reaches her because she commences mourning for him.'"

H 10694, Ch. 42, h 4

Abu Ali al-Ash'ariy has narrated from Muhammad ibn 'Abd al-Jabbar and abu al-'Abbas al-Razzaz from Ayyub ibn Nuh all from Safwan from ibn Muskan from al-Hassan ibn Ziyad who has said the following:

"Abu 'Abd Allah, *'Alayhi al-Salam,* has said, 'When a woman receives the news of the death of her husband, she must begin counting her waiting period and mourning for him.'"

H 10695, Ch. 42, h 5

A number of our people have narrated from Sahl ibn Ziyad from ibn abu Nasr from Rifa'ah who has said the following:

"I once asked abu 'Abd Allah, *'Alayhi al-Salam,* about the case of a woman whose husband dies and he is absent and about when she must begin counting her waiting period. He (the Imam) said, 'It is from the day the news reaches her. The Messenger of Allah, *O Allah, grant compensation to Muhammad and his family worthy of their services to Your cause,* said to women, "One of you would wait for one year, when her husband died and he was absent, hold back her carnal desires and throw it behind her."'"

H 10696, Ch. 42, h 6

Muhammad ibn Yahya has narrated from Ahmad ibn Muhammad Ali ibn al-Hakam from Musa ibn Bakr from Zurarah who has said the following:

"Abu Ja'far, *'Alayhi al-Salam,* has stated this *Hadith.* 'When a woman's husband who is absent dies and evidence is established about it, then her waiting period is counted from the day the news reaches her up to four months and ten days. She must begin mourning for him for four months and ten days, thus, she must stay away from musk, kohl, perfumes and dyes.'"

H 10697, Ch. 42, h 7

Ali ibn Ibrahim has narrated from his father from ibn abu Nasr who has said the following:

"Abu al-Hassan, al-Rida', *'Alayhi al-Salam,* has said, 'A woman whose husband dies must begin counting her waiting period from the day the news reaches her as well as mourning for him.'"

Chapter 43 - Reason for Difference about Waiting Period and Waiting Period of a Widow

H 10698, Ch. 43, h 1

Ali ibn Ibrahim has narrated from his father from al-Husayn ibn Sayf from Muhammad ibn Sulayman who has said the following:

"I once asked abu Ja'far, al-Thaniy, *'Alayhi al-Salam,* saying, 'I pray to Allah to keep my soul in service for your cause, why is it that waiting period for a woman divorced three times, is three cycles of *Hayd* (menses) or three months, and the waiting period of a widow is four months and ten days? He (the Imam) said, 'Waiting period for a woman divorced three times is passing of three *Hayd* (menses)-free periods. It is to ascertain a womb is free of child and pregnancy. About the waiting period of a widow Allah, most Majestic, most Glorious, has set a condition for and a condition against women. In the condition for them He does not hold them accountable and in the condition against them He has not done injustice to them. In the case of *'Ila'* (swearing not to go to bed with one's wife) it is four months as Allah, most Majestic, most Glorious, says, '. . . for those who swear there is a four month waiting period.' (2:226) He has not made it permissible for anyone in the case of 'Ila' to wait more than four months because He, most Blessed, most High, knows how long women can wait without going to bed and without men. The condition against women is in the case of the death of their husband in which case they must wait for four months and ten days. Thus He has taken from her when he dies as much as He has takes for her from him during his life time in the case of 'Ila' as Allah, most Blessed, most High, says, '. . . they must wait for four months and ten days.' He has not mentioned the ten days in waiting period except with four months. He knows that women can wait without men only for four months and without going to bed. For this reason He has set conditions for and against them.'"

Chapter 44 - Waiting Period of a Pregnant Widow and Her Expenses

H 10699, Ch. 44, h 1

A number of our people have narrated from Ahmad ibn Muhammad from ibn Khalid and Ali ibn Ibrahim has narrated from his father from 'Uthman ibn 'Isa from Sama'ah who has said the following:

"He (the Imam), *'Alayhi al-Salam,* has said, 'The waiting period for a pregnant widow is the one which ends last. If she is pregnant when four months end but her child is not yet born, then her waiting period ends when the child is born. If she gives birth before the end of four months and ten days, she must wait until the four months and ten days are complete and this is the longer of the two time periods.'"

H 10700, Ch. 44, h 2

Ali has narrated from his father from ibn abu 'Umayr from Hammad from al-Halabiy who has said the following:

"Abu 'Abd Allah, *'Alayhi al-Salam,* has said, 'The waiting period of a widow ends with the end of the longer of the two time periods.'"

H 10701, Ch. 44, h 3

Ali ibn Ibrahim has narrated from his father from ibn abu 'Umayr from Hammad from al-Halabiy who has said the following:

"Abu 'Abd Allah, *'Alayhi al-Salam,* has said, 'A pregnant widow does not have any right for maintenance.'"

H 10702, Ch. 44, h 4

Muhammad ibn Yahya has narrated from Ahmad ibn Muhammad from Ali ibn al-Hakam from Musa ibn Bukayr from Zurarah who has said the following:

"Abu Ja'far, *'Alayhi al-Salam,* has said, 'The waiting period of a widow ends with the end of one of the two which ends last because she must sit in mourning for four months and ten days, while in divorce there is no mourning.'"

H 10703, Ch. 44, h 5
Ali ibn Ibrahim has narrated from his father and a number of our people have narrated from Sahl ibn Ziyad from ibn abu Najran from 'Asem ibn Hamid from Muhammad ibn Qays who has said the following:
"Abu Ja'far, *'Alayhi al-Salam,* has said that 'Amir al-Mu'minin issued a judgment in the case of a pregnant widow who gave birth before the end of four months and ten days and married. The judgment said that she must be left alone and no one must propose to her for marriage until the longer of the two periods of time ends; and thereafter if her family wants they can give her in marriage or keep her, but if they choose to keep her they must return his (one who had married her) assets.'"

H 10704, Ch. 44, h 6
Humayd ibn Ziyad has narrated from ibn Sama'ah from Muhammad ibn Ziyad from 'Abd Allah ibn Sinan who has said the following:
"Abu 'Abd Allah, *'Alayhi al-Salam,* has said, 'Waiting period of a pregnant widow ends with the end of the longer of the two time periods.'"

H 10705, Ch. 44, h 7
It is narrated from the narrator of the previous *Hadith* from Safwan ibn Yahya from ibn Muskan from Muhammad ibn Muslim who has said the following:
"I once asked abu 'Abd Allah, *'Alayhi al-Salam,* about the case of a pregnant widow who after childbirth marries before the end of four months and ten days. He (the Imam) said, 'If the new husband has gone to bed with her he must stay away from her and she must complete the remaining time of the first waiting period and another waiting period for the later (separation). If he has not gone to bed with her they must separate from each other and she must complete the remaining of the first waiting period and he is then one of those who may propose for marriage.'"

It is narrated from the narrator of the previous *Hadith* from Ja'far ibn Sama'ah and Ali ibn Khalid al-'Aquliy from Karram from Muhammad ibn Muslim from abu Ja'far, *'Alayhi al-Salam,* a similar *Hadith.*

H 10706, Ch. 44, h 8
Muhammad ibn Yahya has narrated from Ahmad ibn Muhammad from Muhammad ibn 'Isma'il from Muhammad ibn al-Fudayl from abu al-Sabbah al-Kinaniy who has said the following:
"I once asked abu 'Abd Allah, *'Alayhi al-Salam,* about the case of a pregnant widow if she has the right for maintenance. He (the Imam) said, 'No, she does not have such right.'"

H 10707, Ch. 44, h 9
A number of our people have narrated from Sahl ibn Ziyad from ibn abu Nasr from Muthanna' al-Hannat from Zurarah who has said the following:
"About the case of a pregnant widow abu 'Abd Allah, *'Alayhi al-Salam,* has said that she does not have the right to receive maintenance.'"

It is also narrated that her maintenance is from the assets of the child in her womb. [So he has narrated].

H 10708, Ch. 44, h 10

Muhammad ibn Yahya has narrated from Ahmad ibn Muhammad from Muhammad ibn 'Isma'il ibn Bazi' from Muhammad ibn al-Fudayl from abu al-Sabbah al-Kinaniy who has said the following:

"Abu 'Abd Allah, *'Alayhi al-Salam,* has said that the maintenance of a pregnant widow is paid from the assets of the child in her womb.'"

Chapter 45 - Waiting Period of a Widow with whom he has Gone to Bed and where she must Complete her Waiting Period and Her Obligations

H 10709, Ch. 45, h 1

Humayd ibn Ziyad has narrated from ibn Sama'ah from Muhammad ibn Ziyad from 'Abd Allah ibn Sinan and Mu'awiyah ibn 'Ammar who has said the following:

"I once asked abu 'Abd Allah, *'Alayhi al-Salam,* about the case of a widow; if she must complete her waiting period in her home or wherever she wants. He (the Imam) said, 'It is wherever she wants; Ali, *'Alayhi al-Salam,* brought 'Umm Kulthum to his home when 'Umar died.'"

H 10710, Ch. 45, h 2

Muhammad ibn Yahya and others have narrated from Ahmad ibn Muhammad ibn 'Isa from al-Husayn ibn Sa'id from al-Nadr ibn Suwayd from Hisham ibn Salim from Sulayman ibn Khalid who has said the following:

"I once asked abu Ibrahim, *'Alayhi al-Salam,* about the case of a widow and about where she must complete her waiting period; if it is the house of her husband or wherever she wants. He (the Imam) said, 'She can complete wherever she likes. Ali, *'Alayhi al-Salam,* held the hand of 'Umm Kulthum and brought her to his home, when 'Umar died.'"

H 10711, Ch. 45, h 3

Al-Husayn from Muhammad has narrated from Mu'alla' ibn Muhammad from al-Hassan ibn Ali or others from Aban ibn 'Uthman from 'Abd Allah ibn Sulayman who has said the following:

"I once asked abu 'Abd Allah, *'Alayhi al-Salam,* about the case of a widow if she can go out to the house of her father and mother from her house, if she so chooses, to complete her waiting period. He (the Imam) said, 'If she wants to complete her waiting period in the house of her husband, she can do so. If she wants to complete it in the house of her family she must not use kohl or wear ornaments.'"

H 10712, Ch. 45, h 4

Abu Ali al-Ash'ariy has narrated from Muhammad ibn 'Abd al-Jabbar from Muhammad ibn 'Isma'il from Aban from ibn abu Ya'fur who has said the following:

"I once asked abu Ibrahim, *'Alayhi al-Salam,* about the case of a woman whose husband dies. He (the Imam) said, 'She must not use kohl for beautification or perfume and must not wear colorful dress, spend the night somewhere else. She can pay off rights, use hair clip and go for *al-Hajj* even though she is in her waiting period.'"

H 10713, Ch. 45, h 5

Humayd ibn Ziyad has narrated from ibn Sama'ah from 'Abd Allah ibn Jabalah from ibn Bukayr from 'Ubayd ibn Zurarah who has said the following:

"I once asked abu 'Abd Allah, *'Alayhi al-Salam,* about the case of a woman whose husband dies if she can perform *al-Hajj* and bear witness for rights. He (the Imam) said, 'Yes, she can do so.'"

H 10714, Ch. 45, h 6

Humayd has narrated from ibn Sama'ah from ibn Ribat from ibn Muskan from abu al-'Abbas who has said the following:

"I once asked abu Ibrahim, *'Alayhi al-Salam,* about the case of a woman whose husband dies. He (the Imam) said, 'She must not use kohl for beautification, perfume or colorful dresses. She must not go out of her house during the day or spend the night somewhere other than her house.' I then asked, 'Can she go out to bear witness for a right? He (the Imam) said, 'She can do so after midnight and return in *al-'Isha'* (darkness).'"

H 10715, Ch. 45, h 7

Humayd has narrated from ibn Sama'ah from 'Abd Allah ibn Jabalah from ibn Bukayr from 'Ubayd ibn Zurarah who has said the following:

"I once asked abu Ibrahim, *'Alayhi al-Salam,* about the case of a woman whose husband dies; if she can go out of the house of her husband. He (the Imam) said, 'She can go out of the house of her husband, travel for *al-Hajj* or move from one house to another house.'"

H 10716, Ch. 45, h 8

Muhammad ibn Yahya has narrated from Ahmad ibn Muhammad from Ali ibn al-Hakam from al-'Ala' ibn Razin from Muhammad ibn Muslim who has said the following:

"I once asked one of the two Imam, (abu Ja'far or abu 'Abd Allah), *'Alayhim al-Salam,* about the case of a woman whose husband dies and about where she can complete her waiting period. He (the Imam) said, 'She can do so wherever she likes but she must not pass a night in a place other than her house.'"

H 10717, Ch. 45, h 9

Muhammad ibn Ahmad has narrated from Muhammad ibn al-Husayn from Muhammad ibn 'Isa from Yunus from a man who has said the following:

"I once asked abu Ibrahim, *'Alayhi al-Salam,* about the case of a woman who is widowed; if she can count her waiting period in a house for a month or less or more then move to another house and stay there as she did in the other house and so on until her waiting period is complete. He (the Imam) said, 'It is permissible and it is not harmful.'"

H 10718, Ch. 45, h 10

Humayd has narrated from ibn Sama'ah from Muhammad ibn abu Hamzah from abu Ayyub from Muhammad ibn Muslim who has said the following:

"A woman came to abu 'Abd Allah, *'Alayhi al-Salam,* to ask for a fatwa about spending the night in another house; her husband had died. He (the Imam) said, 'In the time of ignorance widows had to sit in mourning for twelve months. When Muhammad, *O Allah, grant compensation to Muhammad and his family worthy of their services to Your cause,* was sent he felt sympathy for their weakness and reduced it (mourning) to four months and ten days but you do not bear it patiently.'"

H 10719, Ch. 45, h 11
Ali ibn Ibrahim has narrated from his father from ibn abu 'Umayr from Hammad from al-Halabiy who has said the following:
"Once abu 'Abd Allah, *'Alayhi al-Salam,* was asked about the case of a woman whose husband dies; if it is proper for her to perform *al-Hajj* and visit the sick people. He (the Imam) said, 'Yes, she can do so for the sake of Allah, but must not use kohl and perfume.'"

H 10720, Ch. 45, h 12
Muhammad ibn Yahya has narrated from Ahmad ibn Muhammad from Muhammad ibn Khalid from al-Qasim ibn 'Urwah from Zurarah who has said the following:
"Abu 'Abd Allah, *'Alayhi al-Salam,* has said, 'A widow whose husband has died must not use perfumes and beautify herself until her 'Iddah (waiting period) of four months and ten days is complete.'"

H 10721, Ch. 45, h 13
Ali ibn Ibrahim has narrated from his father from ibn Mahbub from ibn Ri'ab from abu Basir who has said the following:
"I once asked abu 'Abd Allah, *'Alayhi al-Salam,* about the case of a woman whose husband dies; if she during her waiting period can go out for a right. He (the Imam) said, 'Certain ones of the wives of the Holy Prophet, *O Allah, grant compensation to Muhammad and his family worthy of their services to Your cause,* asked saying, 'Husband of so and so has died; if she can go out for a right which affects her.' The Messenger of Allah said, 'Woe upon you! Before I commenced my mission a woman among you whose husband would die needed to hold back carnal desires and throw it behind her.' She then would say, 'I will not use comb, kohl, or dyes for one complete year.' I have only commanded you to wait for four months and ten days; even then you do not remain patient not to use comb, kohl, dyes not to go out during the day and not to spend the night somewhere other than your home.' She then asked, 'O Messenger of Allah, what must she do? There is a right that affects her.' He (the Messenger of Allah) said, 'She can go only after midnight and return when it is dark after sunset so that she is not spending the night somewhere other than her house.' I then asked him (the Imam) if she could perform *al-Hajj.* He (the Imam) said, 'Yes, she can do so.'"

H 10722, Ch. 45, h 14
Muhammad ibn Yahya has narrated from Ahmad ibn Muhammad from ibn Faddal from ibn Bukayr who has said the following:
"I once asked abu Ibrahim, *'Alayhi al-Salam,* about the case of a woman whose husband dies; if she can perform *al-Hajj.* He (the Imam) said, 'Yes, she can do so and she can move from one house to another house.'"

Chapter 46 - The Case of a Woman whose Husband Dies before Going to Bed with her and that there is no Waiting Period and Mahr (dower) for her

H 10723, Ch. 46, h 1

Muhammad ibn Yahya has narrated from Ahmad ibn Muhammad from Ali ibn al-Hakam from al-'Ala' ibn Razin from Muhammad ibn Muslim who has said the following:

"I once asked one of the two Imam, (abu Ja'far or abu 'Abd Allah), *'Alayhim al-Salam,* about the case of a woman whose husband dies before going to bed with her. He (the Imam) said, 'She deserves one-half of mahr (dower) and complete inheritance but she must count a complete waiting period.'"

H 10724, Ch. 46, h 2

Muhammad ibn Yahya has narrated from Ahmad ibn Muhammad from ibn Faddal from ibn Bukayr from 'Ubayd ibn Zurarah who has said the following:

"I once asked abu 'Abd Allah, *'Alayhi al-Salam,* about the case of a man who marries a woman but has not gone to bed with her. He (the Imam) said, 'If he or she dies or he divorces her, she deserves one-half of the mahr (dower), complete inheritance and must count complete waiting period.'"

H 10725, Ch. 46, h 3

Ali ibn Ibrahim has narrated from his father and Muhammad ibn 'Isma'il has narrated from al-Fadl ibn Shadhan from all from ibn abu 'Umayr from 'Abd al-Rahman ibn *al-Hajj*aj from a man who has said the following:

"About the case of a woman whose husband dies before going to bed with her, Ali ibn al-Husayn, *'Alayhi al-Salam,* has said, 'She deserves one-half of mahr (dower), complete inheritance and must count complete waiting period.'"

H 10726, Ch. 46, h 4

Ali ibn Ibrahim has narrated from his father from ibn abu 'Umayr from Hammad from al-Halabiy who has said the following:

"Abu 'Abd Allah, *'Alayhi al-Salam,* has said, 'If one has not gone to bed with his wife but has set up mahr (dower), she deserves one-half of the mahr (dower) that is set for her and complete inheritance. She must count complete waiting period.'"

H 10727, Ch. 46, h 5

Ali has narrated from his father and a number of our people have narrated from Sahl ibn Ziyad from ibn Mahbub from ibn Ri'ab from Zurarah who has said the following:

"I once asked him (the Imam), *'Alayhi al-Salam,* about the case of a woman who dies before his going to bed with her or her husband dies before going to bed with her. He (the Imam) said, 'Whoever of them dies she deserves one-half of mahr (dower) which is set for her, but if it is not set for her then mahr (dower) is not payable to her.'"

H 10728, Ch. 46, h 6

Al-Husayn from Muhammad has narrated from Mu'alla' ibn Muhammad from al-Washsha' from Aban from ibn abu Ya'fur who has said the following:

"About the case of a woman who dies before his going to bed with her, about her mahr (dower) and her inheritance, abu 'Abd Allah, *'Alayhi al-Salam,* has said, 'If mahr (dower) is set for her, she deserves one-half of it and he inherits her legacy. If mahr (dower) is not set then mahr (dower) is not payable to her.' About the case of a man who dies before going to bed with his wife, he (the Imam) said, 'If he has set mahr (dower) for her she deserves one-half of it and she inherits him, but if mahr (dower) is not set she then does not have the right to demand any mahr (dower).'"

H 10729, Ch. 46, h 7
Through the same chain of narrators as that of the previous *Hadith* the following is narrated from Aban ibn 'Uthman from 'Ubayd ibn Zurarah and Fadl ibn al-'Abbas who have said the following:

"Once we asked abu 'Abd Allah, *'Alayhi al-Salam,* about the case of a man who marries a woman and then dies. He has set mahr (dower) for her. He (the Imam) said, 'She deserve one-half of the mahr (dower) and complete inheritance. If she dies the same rule applies in her favor.'"

H 10730, Ch. 46, h 8
Humayd ibn Ziyad has narrated from ibn Sama'ah from Muhammad ibn Ziyad from 'Abd Allah ibn Sinan who has said the following:

"Abu 'Abd Allah, *'Alayhi al-Salam,* has said that `Amir al-Mu'minin issued a judgment about one whose husband had died before going to bed with her, that said, 'She must not marry until her waiting period of four months and ten days is complete, which is the waiting period for one whose husband dies.'"

H 10731, Ch. 46, h 9
Humayd has narrated from ibn Sama'ah from Ahmad ibn al-Hassan from Mu'awiyah ibn Wahab from 'Ubayd ibn Zurarah who has said the following:

"About the case of a woman whose husband dies before going to bed with her, abu 'Abd Allah, *'Alayhi al-Salam,* has said, 'She is like a divorced woman with whom he has not gone to bed. If mahr (dower) is set for her she deserves one-half of it, otherwise, she does not have the right to demand mahr (dower) but she has the right to inherit.' I asked about waiting period. He (the Imam) said, 'Do not ask about it.'"

H 10732, Ch. 46, h 10
Humayd has narrated from ibn Sama'ah and abu al-'Abbas al-Razzaz from Ayyub ibn Nuh and Muhammad ibn `Isma'il has narrated from al-Fadl ibn Shadhan from all from Safwan ibn Yahya from ibn Muskan from al-Hassan al-Sayqal and abu Abbas who has said the following:

"About the case of a woman whose husband dies before going to bed with her, abu 'Abd Allah, *'Alayhi al-Salam,* has said, 'She deserves one-half of mahr (dower), complete inheritance and she must count the waiting period.'"

H 10733, Ch. 46, h 11
Muhammad ibn Yahya has narrated from Ahmad ibn Muhammad from ibn Faddal from ibn Bukayr from 'Ubayd ibn Zurarah who has said the following:

"I once asked abu Ibrahim, *'Alayhi al-Salam,* about the case of a woman whose husband dies before going to bed with her. He (the Imam) said, 'She inherits and must count the waiting period, if mahr (dower) was set for her she deserved one-half of it, otherwise, she does not have the right to demand mahr (dower).'"

Chapter 47 - The Case of a Man who Divorces his Wife and Dies before her Waiting period Ends

H 10734, Ch. 47, h 1

Ali ibn Ibrahim has narrated from his father from ibn abu 'Umayr from Jamil ibn Darraj from certain persons of our people who has said the following:

"This is about the case of a man who divorces his wife in a manner that gives him the right to go back to her, then he dies. One of the two Imam, (abu Ja'far or abu 'Abd Allah), 'Alayhi al-Salam, has said, 'She must count her waiting period in the form of the longer period of time, which is four months and ten days.'"

H 10735, Ch. 47, h 2

It is narrated from the narrator of the previous Hadith from certain persons of our people who has said the following:

"About the case of a woman divorced irrevocably if her husband dies, he (the Imam), 'Alayhim al-Salam, has said, 'She must count her waiting period according to the longer of the two forms of waiting periods.'"

H 10736, Ch. 47, h 3

Humayd ibn Ziyad has narrated from ibn Sama'ah from Muhammad ibn Ziyad from 'Abd Allah ibn Sinan who has said the following:

"Abu 'Abd Allah, 'Alayhi al-Salam, has stated this Hadith. 'Amir al-Mu'minin issued a judgment in the case of a man who divorced his wife; then died; when she counted her waiting period, that said, 'She inherits his legacy, and if she dies during her waiting period he inherits her legacy, each one inherits from the wergild of the other, if one of them does not kill the other.'"

Muhammad ibn abu Hamzah has added, 'She counts her waiting period for a woman whoes husband has died.' Al-Hassan ibn Sama'ah has said that this much is missing from the book of ibn Ziyad and I do not think except that he has narrated it.

H 10737, Ch. 47, h 4

Muhammad ibn Yahya has narrated from Ahmad ibn Muhammad from Ali ibn al-Hakam from al-'Ala' from Muhammad ibn Muslim who has said the following:

"About the case of a woman whose husband has died, one of the two Imam, (abu Ja'far or abu 'Abd Allah), 'Alayhim al-Salam, has said that her maintenance must be paid from her husband's assets.'"

H 10738, Ch. 47, h 5

Muhammad ibn Yahya has narrated from 'Abd Allah ibn Muhammad ibn 'Isa from ibn abu 'Umayr from Hisham ibn Salim who has said the following:

"I once asked abu 'Abd Allah, 'Alayhi al-Salam, about the case of a man who divorces his wife and dies before the end of her waiting period. He (the Imam) said, 'She must count her waiting period according to the longer of the two periods of time.'"

H 10739, Ch. 47, h 6

Ali ibn Ibrahim has narrated from his father from ibn abu Najran and Ahmad ibn Muhammad from ibn abu Nasr from 'Asem ibn Hamid from Muhammad ibn Qays who has said the following:

"I once heard abu Ja'far, *'Alayhi al-Salam,* saying, 'If a woman is divorced and her husband dies before her waiting period ends, when she has not become stranger to him, she inherits his legacy and must complete a waiting period for a widow. If she dies before the end of her waiting period when she has not become stranger to him, he inherits her legacy.'"

Chapter 48 - Divorce and Marriage during one's Illness

H 10740, Ch. 48, h 1

Muhammad ibn Yahya has narrated from Ahmad ibn Muhammad from ibn Mahbub from ibn Bukayr from 'Ubayd ibn Zurarah who has said the following:

"I once asked abu 'Abd Allah, *'Alayhi al-Salam,* about the case of a man who is ill; if he can divorce his wife in such condition. He (the Imam) said, 'No, he cannot divorce, however, he can marry if he wants and if he goes to bed with her, she inherits his legacy but if he did not go to bed with her his marriage is invalid.'"

H 10741, Ch. 48, h 2

Through the same chain of narrators as that of the previous *Hadith* the following is narrated from ibn Mahbub from Rabi' al-Asamm from abu 'Ubaydah al-Hadhdha' and Malik ibn 'Atiyyah from abu al-Ward who both have said the following:

"About the case of a man who divorces his wife once during his illness and waits until her waiting period ends she inherits him as long as she does not marry; but if she marries after her waiting period she then does not inherit his legacy.'"

H 10742, Ch. 48, h 3

Abu Ali al-Ash'ariy has narrated from Muhammad ibn 'Abd al-Jabbar and al-Razzaz from Ayyub ibn Nuh and Muhammad ibn 'Isma'il has narrated from al-Fadl ibn Shadhan and Humayd ibn Ziyad from ibn Sama'ah all from Safwan from 'Abd al-Rahman ibn *al-Hajj*aj from those who narrated to him who has said the following:

"About the case of a man who divorces his wife during his illness, abu 'Abd Allah, *'Alayhi al-Salam,* has said, 'If he dies from his illness and she has not married, she inherits his legacy. If she has married then she has agreed with what she has done, thus, she does have the right to inherit.'"

H 10743, Ch. 48, h 4

Humayd ibn Ziyad has narrated from ibn Sama'ah from 'Abd Allah ibn Jabalah from ibn Bukayr from 'Ubayd ibn Zurarah who has said the following:

"Abu 'Abd Allah, *'Alayhi al-Salam,* has said, 'One's divorcing during his illness is not permissible, however, his marriage is permissible.'"

H 10744, Ch. 48, h 5

It is narrated from the narrator of the previous *Hadith* from Ahmad ibn Muhammad from Muhsin from Mu'awiyah ibn Wahab from 'Ubayd ibn Zurarah who has said the following:

"I once asked abu 'Abd Allah, *'Alayhi al-Salam,* about the case of a man who divorces his wife during his illness and one year passes. He (the Imam) said,

'She inherits if it is during his illness in which he divorced her, but not in between (she does not inherit if divorce takes place between two illnesses).'"

H 10745, Ch. 48, h 6
It is narrated from the narrator of the previous *Hadith* from al-Hassan ibn Muhammad from ibn Sama'ah from ibn Ribat from ibn Muskan from abu al-'Abbas who has said the following:

"I once asked abu 'Abd Allah, *'Alayhi al-Salam,* about the case of a man who divorces his wife once when he is ill and he had divorced her twice before. He (the Imam) said, 'She inherits his legacy if it was during his illness.' I then asked, 'What is the limit of illness?' He (the Imam) said, 'The illness which continues until he dies even if it prolongs for one year.'"

H 10746, Ch. 48, h 7
Ali ibn Ibrahim has narrated from his father from ibn abu 'Umayr from Jamil ibn Darraj from abu al-'Abbas who has said the following:

"Abu 'Abd Allah, *'Alayhi al-Salam,* has said, 'If a man divorces his wife during his illness she inherits his legacy as long as it is in his illness even if her waiting period ends unless he gets well from that illness.' I then asked, 'What happens if the illness prolongs?' He (the Imam) said, 'It is up to one year.'"

H 10747, Ch. 48, h 8
Muhammad ibn Yahya has narrated from Ahmad ibn Muhammad from ibn Faddal from ibn Bukayr from Zurarah who has said the following:

"Abu 'Abd Allah, *'Alayhi al-Salam,* has said, 'One cannot divorce his wife in his illness but his marriage is permissible.'"

H 10748, Ch. 48, h 9
Muhammad has narrated from Ahmad from al-Husayn ibn Sa'id from his brother al-Hassan from Zur'ah ibn Muhammad from Sama'ah who has said the following:

"I once asked abu 'Abd Allah, *'Alayhi al-Salam,* about the case of a man who divorces his wife when he is ill. He (the Imam) said that she inherits his legacy. She inherits him as long as she is in her waiting period. If he has divorced her in a condition that harms her, she inherits him up to one year; and if it is more than one year even by one day, then she does not inherit and she counts a waiting period for four months and ten days like the waiting period for a widow.'"

H 10749, Ch. 48, h 10
Ali ibn Ibrahim has narrated from his father from ibn abu 'Umayr from Aban ibn 'Uthman from a man who has said the following:

"About the case of a man who divorces his wife twice when he is not ill and the third divorce is in his illness, abu 'Abd Allah, *'Alayhi al-Salam,* has said, 'She inherits him as long as he is ill even if it prolongs for one year.'"

H 10750, Ch. 48, h 11
Ali has narrated from his father from ibn abu 'Umayr from Hammad from al-Halabiy who has said the following:

"Once abu 'Abd Allah, *'Alayhi al-Salam,* was asked about the case of a man who is about to die, and he divorces his wife; if such divorce is permissible. He (the Imam) said, 'Yes, it is permissible and if he dies she inherits his legacy but if she dies he does not inherit her legacy.'"

H 10751, Ch. 48, h 12

Ali has narrated from his father from ibn Mahbub from ibn Ri'ab from Zurarah who has said the following:

"One of the two Imam, (abu Ja'far or abu 'Abd Allah), *'Alayhim al-Salam,* has said, 'A man in his illness must not divorce his wife; but he can marry a woman. If he marries and goes to bed with her, it is permissible; and if he did not go to bed with her until he dies from that illness, his marriage is invalid and she does not have mahr (dower) or inheritance.'"

Chapter 49 - About words of Allah, most Majestic, most Glorious, '. . . do not harm them (women) to make it Difficult for them

H 10752, Ch. 49, h 1

Ali ibn Ibrahim has narrated from his father from ibn abu 'Umayr from Hammad from al-Halabiy who has said the following:

"Abu 'Abd Allah, *'Alayhi al-Salam,* has said, 'A man must not harm his wife when he divorces her to make it difficult for her so she is forced to move away before the end of her waiting period. Allah, most Majestic, most Glorious, has prohibited it, saying, '. . . you must not harm them (women) to make it difficult for them.'" (65:6)

Muhammad ibn Yahya has narrated from Ahmad ibn Muhammad, from Ali ibn al-Hakam, from Ali ibn abu Hamzah from abu Basir from abu 'Abd Allah, *'Alayhi al-Salam,* a similar *Hadith.*

Chapter 50 - Divorce of Children

H 10753, Ch. 50, h 1

A number of our people have narrated from Ahmad ibn Muhammad from ibn Khalid and Ali ibn Ibrahim has narrated from his father from all from 'Uthman ibn 'Isa from Sama'ah who has said the following:

"I once asked him (the Imam), *'Alayhi al-Salam,* about the divorce of a boy who is not mature yet, and his charity. He (the Imam) said, 'If he divorces according to *Sunnah* and places charity in the proper place where it rightly belongs, it is not unlawful and it is permissible.'"

H 10754, Ch. 50, h 2

Muhammad ibn Yahya has narrated from Ahmad ibn Muhammad from Muhammad ibn 'Isma'il from Muhammad ibn al-Fudayl from abu al-Sabbah al-Kinaniy who has said the following:

"Abu 'Abd Allah, *'Alayhi al-Salam,* has said that divorce of a child does not have any valid effect.'"

H 10755, Ch. 50, h 3

Humayd ibn Ziyad has narrated from ibn Sama'ah 'Abd Allah ibn Jabalah from Ali ibn abu Hamzah from abu Basir who has said the following:

"Abu 'Abd Allah, *'Alayhi al-Salam,* has said, 'Divorce by a child and one who is drunk do not have any valid effect.'"

H 10756, Ch. 50, h 4

A number of our people have narrated from Sahl ibn Ziyad from Muhammad ibn al-Husayn from a number of his people from ibn Bukayr who has said the following:

"Abu 'Abd Allah, *'Alayhi al-Salam,* has said, 'Divorce by a child is [not] permissible if he understands as well as his will and charity and even if he does not experience wet dream.'"

Muhammad ibn Yahya has narrated from Ahmad ibn Muhammad Ahmad ibn Muhammad from Muhammad ibn al-Husayn all from ibn Faddal from ibn Bukayr from 'Abd Allah *'Alayhi al-Salam,* a similar *Hadith.*

H 10757, Ch. 50, h 5

Ali ibn Ibrahim has narrated from his father from ibn abu 'Umayr from certain persons of his people who has said the following:

"Abu 'Abd Allah, *'Alayhi al-Salam,* has said that divorce by a child is [not] permissible when he becomes ten years old."

Chapter 51 - Divorce of People with Mental Condition and Insane Ones and their Guardian

H 10758, Ch. 51, h 1

Muhammad ibn Yahya has narrated from Ahmad ibn Muhammad from al-Husayn ibn Sa'id, from al-Nadr ibn Suwayd, from Muhammad ibn abu Hamzah from abu Khalid al-Qammat who has said the following:

"I once asked abu 'Abd Allah, *'Alayhi al-Salam,* about the case of a man who has a mental condition and his reason is gone; if divorce by his guardian is permissible. He (the Imam) said, 'Why does he not divorce?' I replied, 'He does not feel safe because tomorrow he may say that he did not divorce or he does not know how to do it.' He (the Imam) said, 'I do not see his guardian except like a sultan (king, authority).'"

H 10759, Ch. 51, h 2

Abu Ali al-Ash'ariy has narrated from Muhammad ibn 'Abd al-Jabbar and abu al-'Abbas al-Razzaz from Ayyub ibn Nuh and Humayd ibn Ziyad has narrated from ibn Sama'ah Ahmad ibn Muhammad from Muhammad ibn 'Isma'il has narrated from al-Fadl ibn Shadhan from 'Abd Allah from Safwan from abu Khalid al-Qammat who has said the following:

"I once asked abu 'Abd Allah, *'Alayhi al-Salam,* about the case of a man who sometime understands and sometimes does not understand: if his divorce by his guardian is permissible. He (the Imam) asked, 'What is the matter with him, why does he not divorce?' I replied, 'He does not know the rules of divorce and does not feel safe. Perhaps tomorrow he will say that he did not divorce.' He (the Imam) said, 'I do not see him (guardian) except like an Imam (in his case).'"

H 10760, Ch. 51, h 3

Ali ibn Ibrahim has narrated from his father from Hammad ibn 'Isa from 'Umar ibn 'Udhaynah from Zurarah and Bukayr and Muhammad ibn Muslim and Burayd and Fudayl ibn Yasar Ahmad ibn abu 'Abd Allah 'Isma'il ibn al-Azraq and Mu'ammar ibn Yahya who has said the following:

"Abu Ja'far, and abu 'Abd Allah, *'Alayhi al-Salam,* have said, 'Divorce by al-Muwallah (confused, excited, awestruck); one's divorce and setting free of slaves is not valid.'"

H 10761, Ch. 51, h 4

A number of our people have narrated from Sahl ibn Ziyad ibn abu Nasr from 'Abd al-Karim from al-Halabiy who has said the following:

"I once asked abu 'Abd Allah, *'Alayhi al-Salam,* about the case of a man who has a mental condition whose reason has gone; if his divorce is permissible. He (the Imam) said, 'No, it is not permissible.' About a woman of the same condition if her selling and charity is permissible, he (the Imam) said, 'It is not permissible.'"

H 10762, Ch. 51, h 5

Ali ibn Ibrahim has narrated from his father from and Muhammad ibn Yahya has narrated from Ahmad ibn Muhammad from ibn Mahbub from al-Hassan ibn Salih from Shihab ibn 'Abd Rabbihi who has said the following:

"Abu 'Abd Allah, *'Alayhi al-Salam,* has said, 'If a man because of a mental condition cannot divorce properly, his guardian must do it for him according to *Sunnah.*' I then asked, 'What happens if because of ignorance he divorced her three times at the same place and time?' He (the Imam) said, 'It is returned to the *Sunnah* and when three months pass or three *Hayd* (menses)-free periods, she becomes stranger to him with one divorce.'"

H 10763, Ch. 51, h 6

Ali ibn Ibrahim has narrated from his father from al-Nawfaliy from al-Sakuniy who has said the following:

"Abu 'Abd Allah, *'Alayhi al-Salam,* has said, 'Divorce is permissible except divorce by a man with mental condition, a child or *Mubarsam*, (suffering from a disease of diaphragm), an insane or a coerced one.'"

H 10764, Ch. 51, h 7

A number of our people have narrated from Sahl ibn Ziyad from Muhammad ibn al-Husayn from Muhammad ibn Sinan from abu Khalid al-Qammat who has said the following:

"About the case of a man suffering from a mental condition, abu 'Abd Allah, *'Alayhi al-Salam,* has said, 'His guardian divorces for him because I see him like the Imam (for him).'"

Chapter 52 - Divorce by a Drunk Man

H 10765, Ch. 52, h 1

Ali ibn Ibrahim has narrated from his father from ibn abu 'Umayr from Hammad from al-Halabiy who has said the following:

"I once asked abu 'Abd Allah, *'Alayhi al-Salam,* about the divorce of a drunken man. He (the Imam) said, 'It is not permissible and it is not an honorable thing.'"

H 10766, Ch. 52, h 2

Muhammad ibn Yahya has narrated from Ahmad ibn Muhammad from Muhammad ibn 'Isma'il has narrated from al-Fadl ibn Shadhan from abu al-Sabbah al-Kinaniy who has said the following:

"Abu 'Abd Allah, *'Alayhi al-Salam,* has said, 'Divorce of a drunken man does not have any valid effect.'"

H 10767, Ch. 52, h 3

Muhammad has narrated from Ahmad ibn Muhammad from Muhammad ibn Sinan from ibn Muskan from al-Halabiy who has said the following:

"I once asked abu 'Abd Allah, *'Alayhi al-Salam,* about the divorce of a drunken man. He (the Imam) said, 'It is not permissible and it is not an honorable thing.'"

H 10768, Ch. 52, h 4

Humayd ibn Ziyad has narrated from ibn Sama'ah from ibn Ribat and al-Husayn ibn Hashim from Safwan all from ibn Muskan from al-Halabiy who has said the following:

"I once asked abu 'Abd Allah, *'Alayhi al-Salam,* about the divorce of a drunken man. He (the Imam) said, 'It is not permissible as well as his setting free of slaves.'"

Chapter 53 - Divorce of One Compelled and Coerced

H 10769, Ch. 53, h 1

Ali ibn Ibrahim has narrated from his father from certain persons of his people from ibn abu 'Umayr or others from 'Abd Allah ibn Sinan who has said the following:

"I once heard abu 'Abd Allah, *'Alayhi al-Salam,* saying, 'If a Muslim man passes by a people who do have not any valid authority and they force him, he fears for his life, to set free a slave or divorce and he complies, it does not have any valid effect against him.'"

H 10770, Ch. 53, h 2

Ali ibn Ibrahim has narrated from his father from ibn abu 'Umayr from 'Umar ibn 'Udhaynah from Zurarah who has said the following:

"I once asked abu Ja'far, *'Alayhi al-Salam,* about the divorce of a man who is coerced and about his setting free slaves. He (the Imam) said, 'His divorce is not a divorce and his setting free slaves is not valid freedom.' I then said, 'I am a merchant and I pass by a one-tenth tax collector, with certain amount of assets with me.' He (the Imam) said, 'Keep it concealed as much as you can in their proper place.' I then asked, 'What must I do if they ask me to swear about divorce and setting free slaves?' He (the Imam) said, 'You can swear for him.' He (the Imam) then took a piece of date and immersed it in butter in front of him (the Imam).' He (the Imam) then said, 'I do not mind about your swearing for divorce and setting free slaves or eating this.'"

H 10771, Ch. 53, h 3

Humayd ibn Ziyad has narrated from ibn Sama'ah from 'Ubays ibn Hisham and Salih ibn Khalid from Mansur ibn Yunus who has said the following:

"I once asked Allah's virtuous servant, *'Alayhi al-Salam,* when he was in al-'Arid, (name of a place) saying, 'I pray to Allah to keep my soul in service for your cause, I married a woman who loved me. I then married the daughter of my maternal uncle and from the woman I had a son. I returned to Baghdad and divorced her once, then I went back to her, then divorced her for the second time, then I went back to her and then left for this journey. I arrived in al-Kufah to see the daughter of my maternal uncle, and my sister and maternal aunt told me that, by Allah, I could never look at her until I divorced so and so. I then told them: 'Fie on you; I have no way to divorce her.' He said, 'It is up to you and it is your problem.' I then said, 'I pray to Allah to keep my soul in service for your cause. From her I had a daughter who lived in Baghdad and this is in al-Kufah; I had left her before four and they refused to allow me to see her unless I divorced her three times. No, by Allah, I pray to Allah to keep my soul in service for your cause, I did not want to do so except that I wanted to keep them away from myself, and my heart has become full (of disappointment with them). I pray to Allah to keep my soul in service for your cause.' He (the Imam) then bent down his head for a long time, then raised his head, smiling and said, 'Between you and Allah, most Majestic, most Glorious, there is no problem, however, if they take their case against you before the Sultan (ruling authorities) they can make her to become stranger to you.'"

H 10772, Ch. 53, h 4
Muhammad ibn Yahya has narrated from Ahmad ibn Muhammad from ibn Mahbub from Yahya ibn 'Abd Allah ibn al-Hassan who has said the following:
"I once heard abu 'Abd Allah, *'Alayhi al-Salam,* saying, 'Divorce under coercion is not permissible or setting free of a slave. It is not permissible to swear for cutting off good relations with relatives or for a sinful act in disobedience to Allah. Thus, whoever swears or is made to swear about something of this kind, it does not have any valid effect on him. Divorce is what is meant to be divorce, and without coercion or harming in a divorce in the manner of waiting period, according to the *Sunnah,* in a *Hayd* (menses)-free period, without sexual intercourse and is pronounced in the presence of two witnesses. If one opposes this, his divorce and oath do not have any valid effect and it is returned to the book of Allah, most Majestic, most Glorious.'"

H 10773, Ch. 53, h 5
Muhammad ibn Yahya has narrated from Ahmad ibn Muhammad from Ali ibn al-Hakam from Mu'awiyah ibn Wahab from 'Isma'il al-Ju'fiy who has said the following:
"I pass by one-tenth tax collector for trading with a certain amount of assets with me and the party (tax collector) asks me to swear. If I swear he allows me to go, but if I do not swear he searches my assets and does injustice to me. He (the Imam) said, 'You can swear for him.' I then said, 'He asks me to swear in the issue of divorce. He (the Imam) said, 'You can swear for him.' I said, 'The asset does not belong to me.' He (the Imam) said, 'Do it for the assets of your brother. The Messenger of Allah, *O Allah, grant compensation to Muhammad and his family worthy of their services to Your cause,* reversed the divorce of ibn 'Umar, who had divorced his wife three times during her *Hayd* (menses) and the Messenger of Allah considered it invalid and devoid of valid effect.'"

Chapter 54 - Divorce by a Speechless Man

H 10774, Ch. 54, h 1
Ali ibn Ibrahim has narrated from his father from Ahmad ibn Muhammad from ibn abu Nasr who has said the following:
"I once asked abu al-Hassan, *'Alayhi al-Salam,* about the case of a man who is mute, does not speak and has a wife. He (the Imam) asked, 'Is he speechless?' I

replied, 'Yes, he is speechless and it is seen that he hates his wife and dislikes her. Is it permissible for his guardian to divorce on his behalf?' He (the Imam) said, 'No, it is not permissible, however, he can write and arrange for witnesses for it.' I then said. 'He cannot write or speak, how can he divorce?' He (the Imam) said, 'It then is done by what is understood from him in the form of his deeds like what you mentioned that he hates and dislikes his wife.'"

H 10775, Ch. 54, h 2
Ali ibn Ibrahim has narrated from his father from Salih ibn al-Sindiy from Ja'far ibn Bashir from Aban ibn 'Uthman who has said the following:

"I once asked abu 'Abd Allah, *'Alayhi al-Salam,* about the case of a man who is speechless. He (the Imam) said, 'He must wrap her scarf around her head, then pull it away.'"

H 10776, Ch. 54, h 3
Ali ibn Ibrahim has narrated from his father from al-Nawfaliy from al-Sakuniy who has said the following:

"Abu 'Abd Allah, *'Alayhi al-Salam,* has said, 'Divorce by a speechless man can happen by his placing her headscarf on her head and then taking it away from her head.'"

H 10777, Ch. 54, h 4
Ali has narrated from his father from 'Isma'il ibn Marrar from Yunus from a speechless man who wrote on the ground the divorce for his wife.

He (the Imam), *'Alayhi al-Salam,* said, 'If he has done so during a *Hayd* (menses)-free period in the presence of witnesses and it is understood from him as it is understood from people like him who decide to divorce, his divorce is permissible according to *Sunnah.*

Chapter 55 - Appointing an Attorney for Divorce

H 10778, Ch. 55, h 1
Abu Ali al-Ash'ariy has narrated from Muhammad ibn 'Abd al-Jabbar and al-Razzaz from Ayyub ibn Nuh Ahmad ibn Muhammad from Humayd ibn Ziyad has narrated from ibn Sama'ah all from Safwan ibn Yahya from Sa'id al-A'raj who has said the following:

"I once asked abu 'Abd Allah, *'Alayhi al-Salam,* about the case of a man who has left the affair of his wife to another man saying, 'Bear witness that I have left the affairs of so and so, to so and so; if it is permissible for the man. He (the Imam) said, 'Yes, it is permissible.'"

H 10779, Ch. 55, h 2
Muhammad ibn Yahya has narrated from Ahmad ibn Muhammad from al-Husayn ibn Sa'id and Abu Ali al-Ash'ariy has narrated from Muhammad ibn 'Abd al-Jabbar from Muhammad ibn 'Isma'il all from Ali ibn al-Nu'man from Sa'id al-'A'raj who has said the following:

"About the case of a man who leaves the affairs of his wife to a man to deal with saying, 'Bear witness that I have left the affairs of so and so, to so and so to deal with; if it is permissible. He (the Imam) said, 'Yes, it is permissible.'"

H 10780, Ch. 55, h 3

Ali ibn Ibrahim has narrated from his father from al-Nawfaliy from al-Sakuniy who has said the following:

"Abu 'Abd Allah, *'Alayhi al-Salam,* has said that about the case of a man who had left the affairs of his wife to two men to deal with; of whom one divorced her but the other one refused, 'Amir al-Mu'minin also refused to approve it unless both agreed to divorce her.'"

H 10781, Ch. 55, h 4

Muhammad has narrated from Ahmad ibn Muhammad from ibn Faddal from ibn Muskan from abu Hilal al-Raziy who has said the following:

"I once asked abu 'Abd Allah, *'Alayhi al-Salam,* about the case of a man who appoints a man to divorce his wife after she experiences *Hayd* (menses) and becomes clean and he himself goes away; but he changes his mind and arranges witnesses that he has changed his mind. He (the Imam) said, 'He must inform his wife and his attorney about it.'"

H 10782, Ch. 55, h 5

A number of our people have narrated from Sahl ibn Ziyad from Muhammad ibn al-Hassan ibn Shammun from 'Abd Allah ibn 'Abd al-Rahman from Misma' who has said the following:

"About the case of a man who leaves the matters about the divorce of his wife to two men, of whom one divorces and the other refuses, abu 'Abd Allah, *'Alayhi al-Salam,* has said, 'The other man should also agree about divorce to have the agreement of both people.'"

It is also narrated that attorney in divorce is not permissible.'"

H 10783, Ch. 55, h 6

Al-Husayn from Muhammad has narrated from Mu'alla' ibn Muhammad from al-Hassan ibn Ali Ahmad ibn Muhammad from Humayd ibn Ziyad has narrated from ibn Sama'ah from Ja'far ibn Sama'ah al from Hammad ibn 'Uthaman from Zurarah who has said the following:

"Abu 'Abd Allah, *'Alayhi al-Salam,* has said, 'It is not permissible to appoint an attorney in divorce.'"

Al-Hassan ibn Sama'ah has narrated that this is the *Hadith* which we follow.

Chapter 56 - Swearing and Taking an Oath

H 10784, Ch. 56, h 1

Ali ibn Ibrahim has narrated from his father from ibn abu 'Umayr from 'Umar ibn 'Udhaynah from Burayd ibn Mu'awiyah who has said the following:

"I once heard abu 'Abd Allah, *'Alayhi al-Salam,* state this *Hadith.* 'If a man swears not to go to bed with his wife, not to touch her and not to place his head next to her head, he then has the choice before passing of four months. When four months pass he then must be taken in custody to reach a settlement and go to bed with her, or decide to divorce, thus, he must leave her until she experiences *Hayd* (menses) and becomes clean from *Hayd* (menses), then divorce her once before going to bed with her and in the presence of two just witnesses. Thereafter he has the right to go back to her until her passing three cycles of *Hayd* (menses)-free periods.'"

H 10785, Ch. 56, h 2

Ali has narrated from his father from ibn abu 'Umayr from Hammad from al-Halabiy who has said the following:

"I once asked abu 'Abd Allah, *'Alayhi al-Salam,* about the case of a man who separates from his wife without divorce and swearing. He does not go near her bed for one year. He (the Imam) said, 'He must go to his wife.' He (the Imam) then said, 'If one swears about his wife, it takes place by one's saying, "No, by Allah, I will not have sexual intercourse with you so and so, and say, by Allah I must reduce you" and then become angry with her. He can wait for four months. After four months, he must be taken in custody, so that he may reach reconciliation with his wife; Allah is forgiving and merciful. If he does not reach a settlement, he then is made to divorce. Divorce cannot take place until he is placed under custody. If it is after four months, still he is made to reach a settlement or divorce.'"

H 10786, Ch. 56, h 3

Muhammad ibn Yahya has narrated from Ahmad ibn Muhammad from Ali ibn al-Hakam from Ali ibn abu Hamzah from abu Basir who has said the following:

"I once heard abu 'Abd Allah, *'Alayhi al-Salam,* saying, 'If one swears about his wife and it takes place by one's saying, "By Allah, I will not have sexual intercourse with you so and so," and says, "By Allah I must reduce you" and then become angry with her. He can wait for four months. After four months, he must be taken in custody so that he pays expiation, which is reconciliation with his wife or divorce. Divorce cannot take place until he is placed under custody. If it is after four months, still he is made to expiate (find remedy) or divorce.'"

H 10787, Ch. 56, h 4

Ali has narrated from his father from Hammad ibn 'Isa from 'Umar ibn 'Udhaynah from Bukayr ibn A'yan and Burayd ibn Mu'awiyah who has said the following:

"Abu Ja'far, and abu 'Abd Allah, *'Alayhim al-Salam,* have said, 'If a man swears not to go near his wife, then he has no say and no right for four months; and it is not a sin on him to stay away from her for four months. When four months pass if he agrees to touch her and she remains silent and agrees, then it is fine. He is within the law and his choices; but if she takes her case to the court he then will be told to expiate (find a remedy), then he can touch her or divorce her. Divorce becomes final when he leaves her until she experience *Hayd* (menses) and becomes clean, then he divorces her and he has the right to go back to her until three *Hayd* (menses)-free periods pass. This is the *'Ila'* (swearing) that Allah, most Blessed, most High, has revealed in His book and in the *Sunnah* of His prophet, *O Allah, grant compensation to Muhammad and his family worthy of their services to Your cause.'"

H 10788, Ch. 56, h 5

Ali ibn Ibrahim has narrated from his father from ibn abu 'Umayr from Jamil ibn Darraj from Mansur ibn Hazim who has said:

"One who swears is made to divorce in the form of a final divorce which makes the spouses strangers to each other. People other than Mansur have narrated that he divorces once but has the right to go back to her; and certain persons of his people have said to him that this is deleted. He replied that it is true if she complains and says that he compels her, harms her and prevents her from getting married. In such case he is made to divorce her in the form of a final divorce which makes them to become strangers to each other; but the one who remains silent and does not complain then if he wants he can divorce her once with the choice to go back to her.

H 10789, Ch. 56, h 6

Ali has narrated from his father from al-Nawfaliy from al-Sakuniy who has said the following:

"Abu 'Abd Allah, *'Alayhi al-Salam,* has said that once a man came to `Amir al-Mu'minin and said, 'O `Amir al-Mu'minin, my wife breastfed a boy and I said, "By Allah, I will not go to bed with you until you wean him."'" He (the Imam) said, ' *'Ila'* (swearing) does not take place in constructive and virtuous deeds.'"

H 10790, Ch. 56, h 7

Muhammad ibn Yahya has narrated from Ahmad ibn Muhammad from Muhammad ibn `Isma'il from Muhammad ibn al-Fudayl from abu al-Sabbah al-Kinaniy who has said the following:

"I once asked abu 'Abd Allah, *'Alayhi al-Salam,* about the case of a man who after going to bed with his wife swears not to go to bed with his wife. He (the Imam) said, 'When four months pass he is taken in custody even after a while. If he expiates (finds a remedy), then it is fine and she is his wife. If he decides to divorce he can do so.' He (the Imam) said, ' *'Ila'* (swearing) takes place when one says to his wife, 'By Allah, I will reduce you to make you look bad.' Thereafter, separates from her and does not go to bed with her up to four months. When four months pass then swearing becomes effective and the Imam must make him to expiate or divorce. If he expiates (finds remedy), Allah is Forgiving and Merciful but if he decides to divorce, Allah is hearing and knowing and that is the word of Allah, most Majestic, most Glorious, in His book.'"

H 10791, Ch. 56, h 8

Al-Husayn from Muhammad has narrated from Mu'alla' ibn Muhammad from al-Hassan ibn Ali from Aban from abu Maryam who has said the following:

"Abu Ja'far, *'Alayhi al-Salam,* has said, 'One who swears not to go to bed with his wife is taken in custody after four months. He may keep her in a fair manner or leave her in the same way. If he decides to divorce it then is once and he has the right to go back to her.'"

H 10792, Ch. 56, h 9

Abu Ali al-Ash'ariy has narrated from Muhammad ibn 'Abd al-Jabbar. Abu al-'Abbas has narrated from Muhammad ibn Ja'far from Ayyub ibn Nuh. Ahmad ibn Muhammad has narrated from Muhammad ibn `Isma'il from al-Fadl ibn Shadhan, from Ahmad ibn Muhammad. Humayd ibn Ziyad has narrated from ibn Sama'ah all from Safwan from ibn Muskan from abu Basir who has said the following:

"I once asked abu 'Abd Allah, *'Alayhi al-Salam,* about *'Ila'* (swearing) and what it is. He (the Imam) said, 'It takes place when a man says to his wife, 'By Allah, I will not go to bed with you so and so, and says, 'By Allah I will reduce you and then waits for four months. Thereafter he is taken in custody, if he expiates

123

and reconciles with his wife, Allah is Forgiving and Merciful and if he did not expiate he then is made to divorce. Divorce cannot take place if it is after four months until it is taken before the Imam.'"

H 10793, Ch. 56, h 10

Al-Husayn from Muhammad has narrated from Mu'alla' ibn Muhammad from al-Hassan ibn Ali from Hammad ibn 'Uthaman who has said the following:

About the case of a man's *'Ila'* (swearing) abu 'Abd Allah, *'Alayhi al-Salam,* has said that if he refuses to divorce 'Amir al-Mu'minin has said, that an enclosure of reeds must be made for him and to keep him there without food and drink until he agrees to divorce.'"

H 10794, Ch. 56, h 11

Muhammad ibn Yahya has narrated from Ahmad ibn Muhammad from Muhammad ibn Khalid from Khalaf ibn Hammad in a *marfu'* manner who has said the following:

"About the case of a man's *'Ila'* (swearing), abu 'Abd Allah, *'Alayhi al-Salam,* has said, 'He either expiates or divorces or is beheaded.'"

H 10795, Ch. 56, h 12

Ali ibn Ibrahim has narrated from his father from ibn abu 'Umayr from Hafs ibn al-Bakhtariy who has said the following:

"Abu 'Abd Allah, *'Alayhi al-Salam,* has said, 'If a man angers his wife and does not go to bed with her without swearing for four months and she complains against him, he then must expiate or divorce her. If he leaves her without anger or swearing, then the rules of *'Ila'* (swearing) do not apply.'"

H 10796, Ch. 56, h 13

Al-Husayn from Muhammad has narrated from Hamdan al-Qalanisiy from Ishaq ibn Bunan ibn Baqqah from Ghiyath ibn Ibrahim who has said the following:

"Abu 'Abd Allah, *'Alayhi al-Salam,* has said that when a man because of *'Ila'* (swearing) refused to divorce 'Amir al-Mu'minin placed him inside an enclosure and gave him one-fourth of his food and drink until he agreed to divorce."

Chapter 57 - `Ila' (swearing) does not Take Place except after Going to Bed with one's Wife

H 10797, Ch. 57, h 1

Muhammad ibn Yahya has narrated from Ahmad ibn Muhammad from Muhammad ibn 'Isma'il from Muhammad ibn al-Fudayl from abu al-Sabbah al-Kinaniy who has said the following:

"Abu 'Abd Allah, *'Alayhi al-Salam,* has said, ''Ila' (swearing) does not take place unless one has gone to bed with his wife.'"

H 10798, Ch. 57, h 2

A number of our people have narrated from Sahl ibn Ziyad from Ahmad ibn Muhammad from ibn abu Nasr from 'Abd al-Karim from abu Basir who has said the following:

"I once asked abu 'Abd Allah, *'Alayhi al-Salam,* about the case of a man's *'Ila'* (swearing) against his wife before going to bed with her. He (the Imam) said, ''Ila' (swearing) does not take place until one goes to bed with his wife.'"

H 10799, Ch. 57, h 3

Ali ibn Ibrahim has narrated from his father from ibn abu 'Umayr from ibn 'Udhaynah who has said that I do not know this *Hadith* except from Zurarah who has said the following:

"Abu 'Abd Allah, *'Alayhi al-Salam,* has said, 'One can only be in *'Ila'* (swearing) against his wife when he goes to bed with her.'"

H 10800, Ch. 57, h 4

Muhammad ibn Yahya has narrated from Ahmad ibn Muhammad from Muhammad ibn 'Isma'il from Muhammad ibn al-Fudayl from abu al-Sabbah al-Kinaniy who has said the following:

"Abu 'Abd Allah, *'Alayhi al-Salam,* has said that once a man who was involved in *'Ila'* (swearing) against his wife before going to bed with her, asked 'Amir al-Mu'minin. He (the Imam) said, ' *'Ila'* (swearing) does not place until one goes to bed with his wife,' He (the Imam) then said, 'If a man swears not to go to bed with his wife for two years or more, can this be *'Ila'* (swearing)?'"

Chapter 58 - If a Man Says to his Wife, 'You are Unlawful for me"

H 10801, Ch. 58, h 1

A number of our people have narrated from Sahl ibn abu Nasr from Muhammad ibn Sama'ah from Zurarah who has said the following:

"I once asked abu Ja'far, *'Alayhi al-Salam,* about the case of a man who says to his wife, 'You are unlawful for me.' He (the Imam) said to me, 'Had I the control over him I would give him a headache. You should have said to him that Allah has made her lawful for you then what has made her unlawful for you? In fact it (saying, 'You are unlawful for me') is nothing more than a lie. He thus has thought that what Allah has made lawful for him has become unlawful and there is no divorce or expiation on him.' I then asked about the meaning of the words of Allah, most Majestic, most Glorious, 'O Prophet, why do you make unlawful what Allah has made lawful for you' (65:2) then expiation is made necessary.' He (the Imam) said, 'He only made unlawful for him his slave-girl, Maria and swore not to go near her. He, in the case of swearing, made expiation necessary not in the case of making something unlawful.'"

H 10802, Ch. 58, h 2

Ali ibn Ibrahim has narrated from his father from ibn abu 'Umayr from 'Umar ibn 'Udhaynah from Zurarah who has said the following:

"I once asked abu Ja'far, *'Alayhi al-Salam,* about the case of a man who says to his wife, 'You are unlawful for me.' We in Iraq narrate that Ali, *'Alayhi al-Salam,* made it three times (divorce). He (the Imam) said, 'They have spoken a lie. He (the Imam) did not make it (one's saying, 'You are unlawful for me') a divorce. Had I the control over him I would have given him a headache. I then say to him that Allah, most Majestic, most Glorious, has made it lawful for you. You have done nothing other than speaking a lie by saying unlawful what Allah has made lawful.'"

H 10803, Ch. 58, h 3

Humayd ibn Ziyad has narrated from ibn Sama'ah from Ribat from abu Mukhallad al-Sarraj who has said the following:

"Abu 'Abd Allah, *'Alayhi al-Salam,* has said that Shabbah ibn 'Aqqal once said to me, 'You think that if one says, "What Allah has made lawful is unlawful for me" (as you believe) does not have any valid effect.' I said, 'About your word 'lawful is unlawful for me' you can consider what 'Amir al-Mu'minin, al-Walid decided about the issue of Salamah and his wife when he sent for a fatwa from people of Iraq and people of al-Sham who had differences over the issue. He then decided according to the words of the people of al-Hijjaz who say that it does not have any valid effect.'"

H 10804, Ch. 58, h 4

Humayd ibn Ziyad has narrated from ibn Sama'ah from Safwan from Hariz from Muhammad ibn Muslim who has said the following:

"I once asked abu 'Abd Allah, *'Alayhi al-Salam,* about the case of a man who says to his wife, 'You are unlawful for me.' He (the Imam) said, 'There is no expiation on him and it is not a divorce.'"

Chapter 59 - The Free, Cleared and Severed Woman

H 10805, Ch. 59, h 1

Ali ibn Ibrahim has narrated from his father from ibn abu 'Umayr from Jamil ibn Darraj from Muhammad ibn Muslim who has said the following:

"I once asked abu Ja'far, *'Alayhi al-Salam,* about the case of a man who says to his wife, 'You from my side are free, cleared and severed' or 'you are unlawful.' He (the Imam) said, 'It does not have any valid effect.'"

H 10806, Ch. 59, h 2

A number of our people have narrated from Ahmad ibn Muhammad from ibn Khalid and Ali ibn Ibrahim has narrated from his father all from 'Uthman ibn 'Isa from Sama'ah who has said the following:

"I once asked him (the Imam), *'Alayhi al-Salam,* about the case of a man who says to his wife, 'You from my side are free and cleared.' He (the Imam) said, 'It does not have any valid effect.'"

H 10807, Ch. 59, h 3

Ali ibn Ibrahim has narrated from his father from ibn abu 'Umayr from Hammad from al-Halabiy who has said the following:

"I once asked abu 'Abd Allah, *'Alayhi al-Salam,* about the case of a man who says to his wife, 'You from my side are free, cleared and severed' or 'you are unlawful.' He (the Imam) said, 'It does not have any valid effect.'"

Chapter 60 - The Choices

H 10808, Ch. 60, h 1

Muhammad ibn abu 'Abd Allah has narrated from Mu'awiyah ibn Hakam from Safwan and Ali ibn al-Husayn ibn Ribat from abu Ayyub al-Khazzaz from Muhammad ibn Muslim who has said the following:

"I once asked abu Ja'far, *'Alayhi al-Salam,* about choices. He (the Imam) said, 'Who is he and what is that; it was something only for the Messenger of Allah, *O Allah, grant compensation to Muhammad and his family worthy of their services to Your cause.'"*

H 10809, Ch. 60, h 2
Humayd ibn Ziyad has narrated from ibn Sama'ah from Muhammad ibn Ziyad and ibn Ribat from abu Ayyub al-Khazzaz from Muhammad ibn Muslim who has said the following:

"I once said to abu 'Abd Allah, *'Alayhi al-Salam,* that I once heard your father saying, 'The Messenger of Allah, *O Allah, grant compensation to Muhammad and his family worthy of their services to Your cause,* offered his wives the choice and they chose Allah and His Messenger. He did not keep them for divorce. Had they chosen themselves they would become strangers.' He (the Imam) said, 'This is a *Hadith* that my father would narrate from 'A'ishah. What people have to do with choice! It was something with which Allah, most Majestic, most Glorious, specially treated His Messenger.'"

H 10810, Ch. 60, h 3
Humayd has narrated from ibn Sama'ah from ibn Ribat from 'Es ibn al-Qasim who has said the following:

"I once asked abu 'Abd Allah, *'Alayhi al-Salam,* about the case of a man who gives his wife the choice; if she becomes stranger for him. He (the Imam) said, 'No, this was something especially for the Messenger of Allah, *O Allah, grant compensation to Muhammad and his family worthy of their services to Your cause.* He (the Messenger of Allah) was commanded to do so and if they were to choose themselves he would divorce them. This is in the words of Allah, most Majestic, most Glorious, 'Say to your wives, "If you want the worldly life and its beauty, then be prepared, so he (the Messenger of Allah) benefits you and allows you to be free with fairness." (33:28)'"

H 10811, Ch. 60, h 4
Muhammad ibn Yahya has narrated from Ahmad ibn Muhammad from ibn Faddal from Harun ibn Muslim from certain persons of our people who have said the following:

"I once asked abu 'Abd Allah, *'Alayhi al-Salam,* about the case of a man who leaves the affairs of his wife in her own hands. He (the Imam) said, 'He has given the matter in the hands of someone who is not proper for it, thus, he has opposed the *Sunnah* and has not made marriage permissible.'"

Chapter 61 - How the Choice originally was

H 10812, Ch. 61, h 1
Muhammad ibn Yahya has narrated from Ahmad ibn Muhammad from ibn Faddal from ibn Bukayr from Zurarah who has said the following:

"I once heard abu Ja'far, *'Alayhi al-Salam,* saying, 'Allah, most Majestic, most Glorious, disdained and rejected the words of certain ones of his wives against the Messenger of Allah, *O Allah, grant compensation to Muhammad and his family worthy of their services to Your cause,* and sent revelation about choice. The Messenger of Allah stayed away from his wives for twenty-nine days in the *mashrabah* (a place for water containers) of 'Umm Ibrahim. He then called them and gave them the choice. They chose him (the Messenger of Allah) then nothing happened. Had they chosen themselves it would have been one final divorce which made them all become strangers to him (the Messenger of

Allah).' I then asked him (the Imam) about the word of the woman and who she was?' He (the narrator) has said that he (the Imam) said, 'She said, "Muhammad thinks that if he divorces us no one of our match from our tribes will marry us."'"

H 10813, Ch. 61, h 2

Muhammad ibn Yahya has narrated from Ahmad ibn Muhammad from Muhammad ibn `Isma'il has narrated from al-Fadl ibn Shadhan from Muhammad ibn al-Fudayl from abu al-Sabbah al-Kinaniy who has said the following:

"Abu 'Abd Allah, *'Alayhi al-Salam,* has said that Zaynab said, 'You are not fair and you are the Messenger of Allah.' Hafsah said, 'If you divorce us we will find our match in our people.' Revelation stopped coming to the Messenger of Allah for twenty days. He (the Imam) said that Allah, most Majestic, most Glorious, disdained and rejected the words of these women against His Messenger and sent revelation that said, 'O Prophet, say to your wives, "If you want the worldly life and its beauty become prepared . . . great reward."' He (the Imam) said that they chose the Messenger of Allah. Had they chosen themselves they would have become stranger to him (the Messenger of Allah) and they chose the Messenger of Allah, then not anything else happened.'"

H 10814, Ch. 61, h 3

A number of our people have narrated from Sahl ibn Ziyad from ibn abu Nasr from Hammad ibn 'Uthaman from 'Abd al-'Ala' ibn `A'yan who has said the following:

"I once heard abu 'Abd Allah, *'Alayhi al-Salam,* saying, 'Certain ones of the wives of the Holy Prophet, had said, 'Does Muhammad think that if he divorces us, no one from our people will marry us?' He (the Imam) said that Allah, most Majestic, most Glorious, became angry from above the seven heavens and commanded him (the Messenger of Allah) and he gave them the choice until it was the turn of Zaynab bint Jahash. She stood and kissed him (the Messenger of Allah) and accepted, saying, "I choose Allah and His Messenger."'"

H 10815, Ch. 61, h 4

Humayd ibn Ziyad has narrated from ibn Sama'ah from Ja'far ibn Sama'ah from Dawud ibn Sarhan who has said the following:

"Abu 'Abd Allah, *'Alayhi al-Salam,* has said that Zaynab bint Jahash once said, 'Does the Messenger of Allah think that if he divorces us we will not find anyone other than him to marry us?' He had stayed away from his wives for twenty-nine days. When Zaynab said this Allah, most Majestic, most Glorious, sent Jibril to Muhammad, *O Allah, grant compensation to Muhammad and his family worthy of their services to Your cause.* He said, 'Say to your wives, "If you want the worldly life and its beauty, then be prepared he will benefit you . . ." They said, 'We choose Allah and His Messenger and the house in the hereafter.'"

H 10816, Ch. 61, h 5

It is narrated from the narrator of the previous *Hadith* from al-Husayn ibn Sama'ah from Wuhayb ibn Hafs from abu Basir who has said the following:

"Abu Ja'far, *'Alayhi al-Salam,* has said that once Zaynab bint Jahash said to the Messenger of Allah, *O Allah, grant compensation to Muhammad and his family worthy of their services to Your cause,* 'You are not fair and you are the Prophet.' He (the Messenger of Allah) replied, 'May your hands become soiled, 'If I am not fair then who is fair?' She then asked, 'O Messenger of Allah, did you pray that my hands get cut off?' He (the Messenger of Allah) replied, 'No, but they become soiled.' She then said, 'If you divorce us we will find in our people men as our match who will marry us.' Revelation stopped coming for twenty-nine nights.' Abu Ja'far, *'Alayhi al-Salam,* then said, 'Allah, most Majestic, most Glorious, disdained and rejected her words and sent revelation that said, 'O Prophet, say to your wives, "If you want the worldly life and its beauty . . ." to the end of the two verses. They chose Allah and His Messenger then further things did not happen. Had they chosen themselves they would have become stranger to him (the Messenger of Allah).'" ('Your hands become soiled' may mean poverty and it may also mean wealth)

H 10817, Ch. 61, h 6
Through the same chain of narrators as that of the previous *Hadith* the following is narrated from Ya'qub ibn Salim from Muhammad ibn Muslim who has said the following:

"About the case of a man who gives his wife the choice abu 'Abd Allah, *'Alayhi al-Salam,* has said, 'The choice is only for us and not for anyone else. The Messenger of Allah, *O Allah, grant compensation to Muhammad and his family worthy of their services to Your cause,* gave the choice because of the words of 'A'ishah. They then chose Allah and His Messenger and they must not have chosen anyone other than the Messenger of Allah, *O Allah, grant compensation to Muhammad and his family worthy of their services to Your cause.'"

Chapter 62 - Al-Khul' (Divorce for Payment)

H 10818, Ch. 62, h 1
Ali ibn Ibrahim has narrated from his father from ibn abu 'Umayr from Hammad from al-Halabiy who has said the following:

"Abu 'Abd Allah, *'Alayhi al-Salam,* has stated this *Hadith.* 'Al-Khul' (divorce for payment) is not lawful until she says to her husband, "By Allah, I will not honor your turn, will not obey your order, will not take Ghusl (bath) for you because of sexual intercourse, will not sit on your furnishing and I will give permission without your permission." People applied *Khul'* for less than that. The woman's saying that to her husband makes it lawful for him to receive payment from her. She remains for him for two more divorces and *al-Khul'* is one divorce.' He (the Imam) said, 'The statements come from her.' He (the Imam) said, 'Had the matter been in our hands we would not allow divorce except with waiting period.'"

H 10819, Ch. 62, h 2
It is narrated from the narrator of the previous *Hadith* from his father and A number of our people have narrated from Ahmad ibn Muhammad from ibn Khalid all from 'Uthman ibn 'Isa from Sama'ah who has said the following:

"I once asked him (the Imam), *'Alayhi al-Salam,* about the case of a woman divorced by means of *al-Khul'.* He (the Imam) said, 'It is not lawful for him until she says, 'I will not honor your turn, follow any of the laws of Allah about you, will not take Ghusl (bath) for you because of sexual intercourse, will not step on your furnishings, will allow to enter your house, without your knowledge, such people whom you dislike. They do not speak to her and she is the one who makes such statements. When she finalizes *al-Khul'* she becomes stranger and he can take from her assets as much as he can. He does not have the right to take all that the contesting and denouncing wife gives.'"

H 10820, Ch. 62, h 3

Ali ibn Ibrahim has narrated from his father from ibn abu 'Umayr from abu Ayyub from Muhammad ibn Muslim who has said the following:

"Abu 'Abd Allah, *'Alayhi al-Salam,* has said, 'The woman who is divorced by means of *al-Khul'*, who says to her husband, 'Divorce me and I pay what I have received from you.' He (the Imam) said, 'It is not lawful for him to receive such payment until she says, 'By Allah, I will not honor your turn, will not obey any of your orders, will allow people to enter your house without your permission and will allow others to sleep in your bed.' When she does this without informing him, then receiving payment from her is lawful, she is divorced once without any other divorce to follow, and she becomes a stranger. He is then one of those who can propose marriage with her.'"

H 10821, Ch. 62, h 4

Muhammad ibn Yahya has narrated from Ahmad ibn Muhammad from Muhammad ibn 'Isma'il has narrated from al-Fadl ibn Shadhan from abu al-Sabbah al-Kinaniy who has said the following:

"Abu 'Abd Allah, *'Alayhi al-Salam,* has said, 'If a man divorces his wife in the manner of *al-Khul'*, it then is one divorce with which she becomes stranger to him and he then is one of those who may propose marriage. Al-Khul' is not lawful for him unless she is the one who demands for divorce from him without being beaten by her husband. That she says, 'I will not honor your turn, will not take Ghusl (bath) for you because of sexual intercourse, I will allow people whom you dislike to enter your house, allow your bed to be used by others and will not obey any of the laws of Allah about you.' When this happens from her side, then it is fine for him to receive the payment from her.'"

H 10822, Ch. 62, h 5

A number of our people have narrated from Sahl ibn Ziyad from Ahmad ibn Muhammad from ibn abu Nasr from 'Abd al-Karim from abu Basir who has said the following:

"Abu 'Abd Allah, *'Alayhi al-Salam,* has said that *al-Khul'* is not permissible until she says to her husband . . . he (the Imam) then mentioned what his people mention. Abu 'Abd Allah, *'Alayhi al-Salam,* then said, 'Less than such expressions was permitted for women and when she said such things to her husband then *al-Khul'* became lawful for her husband for whatever payment he received. She is then for two more divorces and *al-Khul'* is one divorce. The expressions must come from her side.' He (the Imam) then said, 'Had the matter been in our hands divorce could only take place in the manner with the waiting period.'"

H 10823, Ch. 62, h 6

Ali ibn Ibrahim has narrated from his father from ibn abu 'Umayr from Jamil from Muhammad ibn Muslim who has said the following:

"Abu Ja'far, *'Alayhi al-Salam,* has said that if a woman says to her husband in general, 'I will not obey any of your orders with or without explanation, then it is lawful for him to receive payment and he cannot do ruju' (go back to her).'"

H 10824, Ch. 62, h 7

Through the same chain of narrators as that of the previous *Hadith* the following is narrated:

"Abu 'Abd Allah, *'Alayhi al-Salam,* has said, *'Al -Khul'* and *al-Mubarat* (denouncing) is of the kind of divorce which makes the parties become strangers to each other and he becomes one of those who may propose marriage.'"

H 10825, Ch. 62, h 8

Humayd has narrated from ibn Sama'ah from 'Abd Allah ibn Jabalah from Jamil from Muhammad ibn Muslim who has said the following:

"Abu Ja'far, *'Alayhi al-Salam,* has said that when a woman says, 'By Allah I will not obey any of your commands with or without explanation', then whatever payment he receives from her becomes lawful for him and he cannot do ruju' (go back to her).'"

H 10826, Ch. 62, h 9

Humayd ibn Ziyad has narrated from al-Hassan ibn Muhammad ibn Sama'ah from Ja'far ibn Sama'ah that Jamil wanted *al-Khul'* for his daughter from a certain persons of our people; that Jamil said to that man, 'What do you say, do you agree with what you have received and leave her free?' He replied, 'Yes, I agree.' Jamil then said to them, 'You can get up and go.' They asked, 'O abu Ali, do you not want that divorce follows it?' He replied, 'No, I do not need it.' Ja'far ibn Sama'ah would say that it must be followed by divorce in the manner with waiting period. He presented narration of Musa ibn Bakr from the virtuous servant of Allah as proof. He (the Imam), *'Alayhi al-Salam,* has said that Ali, *'Alayhi al-Salam,* has said, 'When a woman divorced in the manner of *al-Khul'* it must be followed by divorce as long as she is in waiting period.'"

H 10827, Ch. 62, h 10

Ali ibn Ibrahim has narrated from his father from ibn abu 'Umayr from certain persons of his people who has said the following:

"Abu 'Abd Allah, *'Alayhi al-Salam,* has said that a woman involved in *al-Khul'* cannot become lawful for him until she repents because of her statements that she has expressed when proceeding for *al-Khul'.*'"

Chapter 63 - Al-Mubarat (disavowing) or Divorce for Payment

H 10828, Ch. 63, h 1

Ali ibn Ibrahim has narrated from his father from and A number of our people have narrated from Ahmad ibn Muhammad from ibn Khalid all from 'Uthman ibn 'Isa from Sama'ah who has said the following:

"I once asked him (the Imam), *'Alayhi al-Salam,* about al-Mubarat and about how it takes place. He (the Imam) said, 'It happens when a man owes something to his wife like mahr (dower) or so, of which a certain amount is paid to her, then they dislike each other. The woman says to her husband, 'Whatever I have received from you is for me and whatever remains on you will be for you and I want to be free (from the bond of marriage).' The man then says to her, 'If you will demand from me whatever you have waved, I will be more rightful to have you as my wife.'"

(In al-Khul' dislike is from the woman only but in al-Mubarat the dislike is from both wife and husband).

H 10829, Ch. 63, h 2
Ali ibn Ibrahim has narrated from his father from ibn abu 'Umayr from Jamil from Zurarah who has said the following:

"Abu Ja'far, *'Alayhi al-Salam,* has said that in al-Mubarat (disavowing) he can receive an amount which is less than mahr (dower) but in *al-Khul'* he can receive whatever he wants or on what both parties agree, like the amount of mahr (dower) or more. In al-Mubarat (disavowing) she pays less than mahr (dower) and in *al-Khul'* he can receive whatever he likes, it is because of her transgressing in her statements of what is not lawful for her to say.'"

H 10830, Ch. 63, h 3
Muhammad ibn Yahya has narrated from Ahmad ibn Muhammad from Muhammad ibn 'Isma'il has narrated from al-Fadl ibn Shadhan from abu al-Sabbah al-Kinaniy who has said the following:

"Abu 'Abd Allah, *'Alayhi al-Salam,* has said that if a woman demands for divorce in the manner of al-Mubarat (disavowing) it is a divorce only once, because of which he becomes one of those who can propose marriage with her.'"

H 10831, Ch. 63, h 4
Ali ibn Ibrahim has narrated from his father from Hammad, from Hariz from Muhammad ibn Muslim who has said the following:

"I once asked abu 'Abd Allah, *'Alayhi al-Salam,* about the case of a woman who says to her husband, 'So and so amount is for you to set me free (from the bonds of marriage). He (the Imam) said, 'This is al-Mubarat (disavowing).'"

H 10832, Ch. 63, h 5
Abu Ali al-Ash'ariy has narrated from Muhammad ibn 'Abd al-Jabbar and Muhammad ibn 'Isma'il has narrated from al-Fadl ibn Shadhan from and abu al-'Abbas from Muhammad ibn Ja'far from Ayyub ibn Nuh and Humayd ibn Ziyad has narrated from ibn Sama'ah all from Sufyan from ibn Muskan from abu Basir who has said the following:

"Abu 'Abd Allah, *'Alayhi al-Salam,* has said that al-Mubarat (disavowing) takes place when a woman says to her husband, 'Whatever you owe to me is for you and set me free (from the bond of marriage).' Or she pays extra from her side so he sets her free, except that he can say that if she goes back in anything, then he will be more rightful to have her as his wife. It is not lawful for her husband to take more than what is equal to her mahr (dower) or less.'"

H 10833, Ch. 63, h 6
Humayd ibn Ziyad has narrated from ibn Sama'ah from Muhammad ibn Ziyad from 'Abd Allah ibn Sinan who has said the following:

"Abu 'Abd Allah, *'Alayhi al-Salam,* has said that in al-Mubarat (disavowing) a woman says to her husband, 'You can have whatever you owe to me and free me (from the bonds of marriage). He then sets her free (from the bonds of marriage).' I (the narrator) then asked, 'Will he then say to her, "If you demand anything back then I will have more right than anyone else to have you as my wife"?' He (the Imam) said, 'Yes, he can say so.'"

H 10834, Ch. 63, h 7

Muhammad ibn Yahya has narrated from Ahmad ibn Muhammad from Muhammad ibn 'Isma'il who has said the following:

"I once asked al-Rida', *'Alayhi al-Salam,* about the case of a woman who arranges al-Mubarat (disavowing) or *al-Khul'* in the presence of two witnesses, in a *Hayd* (menses)-free period and without sexual intercourse; if she becomes stranger to him. He (the Imam) said, 'Yes, if it happens as you said has happened.' I then said, 'It is narrated to us that it does not make them to become stranger until it is followed by divorce.' He (the Imam) said, 'It then is not *al-Khul'*.' I then asked, 'Does it make her to become stranger to him?' He said, 'Yes, that is what it does.'"

H 10835, Ch. 63, h 8

Muhammad ibn 'Isma'il has narrated from al-Fadl ibn Shadhan and Abu Ali al-Ash'ariy has narrated from Muhammad ibn 'Abd al-Jabbar all from Safwan from 'Abd al-Rahman ibn *al-Hajj*aj who has said the following:

"I once asked abu 'Abd Allah, *'Alayhi al-Salam,* if al-Mubarat (disavowing) or *al-Khul'* can take place without *Hayd* (menses)-free period. He (the Imam) said, 'It cannot take place without *Hayd* (menses)-free period.'"

H 10836, Ch. 63, h 9

Safwan has narrated from 'Abd Allah ibn Muskan from Muhammad ibn Muslim from abu Ja'far, *'Alayhi al-Salam,* and Safwan from 'Anbasah ibn Mus'ab from Sama'ah who has said the following:

"Abu 'Abd Allah, *'Alayhi al-Salam,* has said that no divorce, choice or al-Mubarat (disavowing) can take place without *Hayd* (menses)-free period, free from sexual intercourse and without the presence of witnesses.'"

H 10837, Ch. 63, h 10

Muhammad ibn Yahya Ahmad ibn Muhammad from Ali ibn al-Hakam from al-'Ala' from Muhammad ibn Muslim who has said the following:

"Abu Ja'far, *'Alayhi al-Salam,* has said, 'Divorce, *al-Khul'* , al-Mubarat (disavowing) and choice are only valid during a *Hayd* (menses)-free period in which sexual intercourse has not happened.'"

Chapter 64 - Waiting Period for al-Khul' and al-Mubarat (disavowing), the Maintenance and Housing for such Women

H 10838, Ch. 64, h 1

A number of our people have narrated from Sahl ibn Ziyad from Ahmad ibn Muhammad from ibn abu Nasr from 'Abd al-Karim from ibn abu Nasr who has said the following:

"Abu 'Abd Allah, *'Alayhi al-Salam,* has said that waiting period for *al-Khul'* is like the waiting period for divorced woman and *al-Khul'* is her divorce.'"

H 10839, Ch. 64, h 2

Through the same chain of narrators as that of the previous *Hadith* the following is narrated Ahmad ibn Muhammad from 'Abd al-Karim from al-Halabiy who has said the following:

"Abu 'Abd Allah, *'Alayhi al-Salam,* has said that a woman because of *al-Khul'* does not receive any benefit.'"

H 10840, Ch. 64, h 3

Ali ibn Ibrahim has narrated from his father from ibn abu 'Umayr from Hammad from al-Halabiy who has said the following:

"He (the Imam) *'Alayhi al-Salam,* has said that woman of *al-Khul'* does not receive any benefits.'"

H 10841, Ch. 64, h 4

Al-Husayn from Muhammad has narrated from Mu'alla' ibn Muhammad from al-Hassan ibn Ali al-Washsha' from Aban from Zurarah who has said the following:

"I once asked abu Ja'far, *'Alayhi al-Salam,* about the waiting period of a woman in *al-Khul'*. He (the Imam) said, 'It is like the waiting period of a divorced woman and she must complete her waiting period in her home and a woman in al-Mubarat (disavowing) is the same as the one in *al-Khul'*.'"

H 10842, Ch. 64, h 5

Humayd ibn Ziyad has narrated from ibn Sama'ah from Muhammad ibn Ziyad from 'Abd Allah ibn Sinan who has said the following:

"Abu 'Abd Allah, *'Alayhi al-Salam,* has said that waiting period for a woman in *al-Khul'* is like that of a divorced woman and her *al-Khul'* is her divorce.' He (the narrator) has said that he then asked if she receives any benefits. He (the Imam) said, 'No, she does not receive any benefits.'"

H 10843, Ch. 64, h 6

Humayd has narrated from al-Hassan from Ja'far ibn Sama'ah from Dawud ibn Sarhan who has said the following:

"About the case of a woman in *al-Khul'* abu 'Abd Allah, *'Alayhi al-Salam,* has said, 'Her waiting period is like the waiting period of a divorced woman. She must count her waiting period in her home and a woman of *al-Khul'* is like the woman in al-Mubarat (disavowing).'"

H 10844, Ch. 64, h 7

Humayd ibn Ziyad has narrated from al-Hassan from Muhammad ibn Ziyad and Safwan from Rifa'ah who has said the following:

"Abu 'Abd Allah, *'Alayhi al-Salam,* has said that women in *al-Khul'* do not have the right for maintenance and housing.'"

H 10845, Ch. 64, h 8

Muhammad ibn Yahya has narrated from Ahmad ibn Muhammad from al-Barqiy from abu al-Bakhtariy who has said the following:

"Abu 'Abd Allah, *'Alayhi al-Salam,* has said that 'Amir al-Mu'minin has said, 'Every divorced woman has the right to receive benefits except women in *al-Khul'* who purchase themselves.'"

H 10846, Ch. 64, h 9

Muhammad ibn Yahya has narrated from Ahmad ibn Muhammad from ibn Mahbub from ibn Ri'ab from abu Basir who has said the following:

"I once asked abu 'Abd Allah, *'Alayhi al-Salam,* about the case of a man whose wife has arranged *al-Khul'*: if it is permissible for him to propose marriage to her sister before waiting period because of *al-Khul'* is complete. He (the Imam) said, 'Yes, because she has freed herself from the bonds of his marriage and he does not have the right to go back to her.'"

Chapter 65 - Disharmony Between Wife and Husband

H 10847, Ch. 65, h 1
Muhammad ibn Yahya has narrated from Ahmad ibn Muhammad from Ali ibn al-Hakam from Ali ibn abu Hamzah who has said the following:
"I once asked abu al-Hassan, *'Alayhi al-Salam,* about the words of Allah, most Majestic, most Glorious, 'If a woman is afraid of disharmony from her husband or his disregarding her. . . .' (4:128) He (the Imam) has stated this *Hadith.* 'If he intends to divorce her and she says to him, 'Keep me; I will leave for you something of what you owe to me and wave my day and night.' It is lawful for him and it is not a sin on anyone of them.'"

H 10848, Ch. 65, h 2
Ali ibn Ibrahim has narrated from his father from ibn abu 'Umayr from Hammad from al-Halabiy who has said the following:
"I once asked abu 'Abd Allah, *'Alayhi al-Salam,* about the words of Allah, most Majestic, most Glorious. 'If a woman is afraid of disharmony from her husband or his disregarding her. . . .' (4:128). He (the Imam) said, 'She is a woman who is married and he dislikes her and tells her that he wants to divorce her. She then says, 'Do not do so because I am afraid people will reproach me but I wave for you my turn of night with which you can do what you like, and besides, this if there is anything it is for you to leave me in my condition. This is mentioned in the words of Allah, most Blessed, most High, '. . . it is not an offense for both of them to reach a settlement among themselves,' and it is a reference to that settlement.'"

H 10849, Ch. 65, h 3
Humayd ibn Ziyad has narrated from ibn Sama'ah from al-Husayn ibn Hashim from abu Basir who has said the following:
"I once asked abu 'Abd Allah, *'Alayhi al-Salam,* about the words of Allah, most Majestic, most Glorious, 'If a woman is afraid of disharmony from her husband or his disregarding her. . . .' (4:128) He (the Imam) said, 'This is a man who has a wife whom he does not like. He wants to divorce her, thus, she says to him, "Keep me and do not divorce me. I will leave for you what you owe to me and pay you from my assets, wave in your favor my day and night," all such offers are acceptable for him.'"

Chapter 66 - The Two Arbitrators in the case of Discord

H 10850, Ch. 66, h 1
Muhammad ibn Yahya has narrated from Ahmad ibn Muhammad from Ali ibn al-Hakam from Ali ibn abu Hamzah who has said the following:
"I once asked the virtuous servant of Allah, *'Alayhi al-Salam,* about the words

of Allah, most Majestic, most Glorious, 'If you are afraid of discord between them then send one arbitrator from his people and another from her people.' (4:35) He (the Imam) then said, 'The two arbitrators stipulate upon them that their decision to separate or bring them together must be treated binding and on that basis if they separate or bring them together it is permissible.'"

H 10851, Ch. 66, h 2

Ali ibn Ibrahim has narrated from his father from ibn abu 'Umayr from Hammad from al-Halabiy who has said the following:

"I once asked abu 'Abd Allah, *'Alayhi al-Salam,* about the words of Allah, most Majestic, most Glorious, 'If you are afraid of discord between them then send one arbitrators from his people and another from her people.' (4:35) He (the Imam) said, 'The arbitrator cannot separate or unite them without first getting approval from the man and woman and a stipulation that their decision of separating or uniting them must be treated binding. Thus, if they decided for separation or unification it is permissible.'"

H 10852, Ch. 66, h 3

Humayd ibn Ziyad has narrated from ibn Sama'ah from 'Abd Allah ibn Jabalah from Ali ibn abu Hamzah from abu Basir who has said the following:

"I once asked abu 'Abd Allah, *'Alayhi al-Salam,* about the words of Allah, most Majestic, most Glorious, 'If you are afraid of discord between them then send one arbitrators from his people and another from her people.' (4:35) He (the Imam) said, 'The two arbitrators stipulate upon them that their decision to separate or to bring them together must be treated binding and on that basis if they separate or bring them together it is permissible.'"

H 10853, Ch. 66, h 4

Muhammad ibn Yahya has narrated from Ahmad ibn Muhammad from ibn Mahbub from abu Ayyub from Sama'ah who has said the following:

"I once asked abu 'Abd Allah, *'Alayhi al-Salam,* about the words of Allah, most Majestic, most Glorious, '. . . an arbitrator from his people and an arbitrator from her people' who then by the permission of both parties and with their stipulation that their decision must be accepted as binding. They then agree in the presence of witnesses; if the decision of the arbitrators to separate them is permissible. He (the Imam) said, 'Yes, it is permissible, however, it must take place in a *Hayd* (menses)-free period and without sexual intercourse by the husband.' It then was asked, 'What happens if one of the arbitrators decides to separate them and the other disagrees?' He (the Imam) said, 'It cannot take place unless they both agree for separation. If they both agreed then separation is permissible.'"

H 10854, Ch. 66, h 5

It is narrated from the narrator of the previous *Hadith* from 'Abd Allah ibn Jabalah and others from al-'Ala' from Muhammad ibn Muslim who has said the following:

"I once asked abu 'Abd Allah, *'Alayhi al-Salam,* about, 'If you are afraid of discord between them then send one arbitrator from his people and another from her people.' (4:35) He (the Imam) said, 'They cannot decide to separate them without previous authorization of their decision by the parties (the wife and husband).'"

Chapter 67 - The Absent and Missing

H 10855, Ch. 67, h 1
Ali ibn Ibrahim has narrated from his father from ibn abu 'Umayr from Hammad from al-Halabiy who has said the following:

"Once abu 'Abd Allah, *'Alayhi al-Salam,* was asked about the case of a man who is absent and missing. He (the Imam) said, 'If one is absent and missing for four years the authorities must send in writing to the area where he has disappeared, and if no trace of him is found the authority then commands his guardian to provide maintenance for her and she is his woman.' I (the narrator) then said, 'She may say, "I want what women want."' He (the Imam) said, 'She cannot do so and it is not honorable. If his guardian did not provide maintenance or his attorney, then he (the authority) commands to divorce her and it then is obligatory divorce for her.'"

H 10856, Ch. 67, h 2
Ali ibn Ibrahim has narrated from his father from ibn abu 'Umayr from 'Umar ibn 'Udhaynah from Burayd ibn Mu'awiyah who has said the following:

"I once asked abu 'Abd Allah, *'Alayhi al-Salam,* about the case of a man who is absent and missing and about how to deal with the issue of his wife. He (the Imam) said, 'If she is silent and has exercised patience, she is not disturbed, but if she brings her case before the authorities she will be told to wait for four years. Thereafter they write to the area where he has disappeared to find out about him. If information is achieved that he is alive, she then must wait; but if no information is found until four years the guardian of the husband is summoned and asked if any assets belonging to the missing man exist. If such assets exist then her maintenance must be paid therefrom until it is found out if he is alive or not. If no asset belonging to him exists his guardian is told to provide her maintenance. If his guardian provides her maintenance she has no way to marry; but if he did not provide her maintenance the authority then compels him to divorce her one divorce before her commencing waiting period when she is in a *Hayd* (menses)-free period. Divorce by the guardian is treated like the divorce of the husband. If the husband comes before the end of her waiting period from the day divorce has taken place and he decides to go back to her, she is his wife. She is for him for two more divorces, but if he comes after her waiting period ends then she becomes lawful for marriage to whoever she likes and the first husband has no way to her.'"

H 10857, Ch. 67, h 3
Muhammad ibn Yahya has narrated from Ahmad ibn Muhammad ibn 'Isa from Muhammad ibn 'Isma'il has narrated from al-Fadl ibn Shadhan from abu al-Sabbah al-Kinaniy who has said the following:

"About the case of a woman whose husband is missing and absent for four years, has not provided her maintenance and it is not known if he is alive or not, if his guardian is compelled to divorce her. He (the Imam) said, 'Yes, he is compelled to do so. If he does not have any guardian, the authority and al-Sultan divorces her.' I then asked what happens if the guardian says, 'I can provide her maintenance?' He (the Imam) said, 'He is not then forced to divorce her.' I then asked what happens if she says, 'I want what women want, I do not want to wait patiently as I am.' He (the Imam) said, 'She does not have such right and it is not honorable to say so when he provides maintenance.'"

H 10858, Ch. 67, h 4

A number of our people have narrated from Ahmad ibn Muhammad from ibn Khalid and Ali ibn Ibrahim has narrated from his father all from 'Uthman ibn 'Isa from Sama'ah who has said the following:

"I once asked him (the Imam), *'Alayhi al-Salam,* about the case of a man who is absent and missing. He (the Imam) said, 'If it is known that he is in a certain location she waits for ever until the news of his death comes or her divorce. If it is not known where he is and no letter comes from him or any news, she then comes to the Imam who commands her to wait for four years and search for him in the land. If no trace of him is found until four years pass, she then is commanded to count her waiting period for four months and ten days and then she becomes lawful for men. If she marries after the end of her waiting period, he cannot go back to her and if he comes before the end of her waiting period he has the right to go back to her as her husband.'"

Chapter 68 - A Woman Receives News of the Death of her Husband or her Divorce, Counts her Waiting Period then Marries and her Previous Husband Comes

H 10859, Ch. 68, h 1

Muhammad ibn Yahya has narrated from Ahmad ibn Muhammad from Ali ibn al-Hakam from Musa ibn Bakr from Zurarah who has said the following:

"Abu Ja'far, *'Alayhi al-Salam,* has said, 'If a woman receives news of the death of her husband or she is informed about her being divorced by her husband and she counts her waiting period. Thereafter marries then her previous husband comes. The first one is more rightful than the second one, regardless, he (the second) has gone to bed with her or not, but she can demand mahr (dower) from the second one because of his going to bed with her and the second one can thereafter never lawfully marry her again.'"

Abu al-'Abbas al-Razzaz, Muhammad ibn Ja'far has narrated from abu Ayyub ibn Nuh. Abu Ali al-Ash'ariy has narrated from Muhammad ibn 'Abd al-Jabbar Ahmad ibn Muhammad from Muhammad ibn 'Isma'il has narrated from al-Fadl ibn Shadhan from all from Safwan from Musa ibn Bakr from Zurarah from abu Ja'far, *'Alayhi al-Salam,* a similar *Hadith.*

H 10860, Ch. 68, h 2

Muhammad has narrated from Ahmad ibn Muhammad from ibn Mahbub from 'Ila' (swearing) and abu Ayyub from Muhammad ibn Muslim who has said the following:

"I once asked abu Ja'far, *'Alayhi al-Salam,* about the case of a woman before whom two men testify that her absent husband has divorced her and she counts waiting period then marries; then the absent husband comes. He says that he has not divorced her and one of the two testifying people says that he has lied. He (the Imam) said, 'The second has no way to her and the one who testified must pay the mahr (dower) to the second man and she must count her waiting period because of the second marriage. The first husband must not go near her until her waiting period is complete.'"

H 10861, Ch. 68, h 3
Ali ibn Ibrahim has narrated from his father and A number of our people have narrated from Sahl ibn Ziyad all from ibn abu Najran from 'Asem ibn Hamid ibn Qays who has said the following:

"I once asked abu Ja'far, *'Alayhi al-Salam,* about the case of a man whose wife thinks that he has died or is killed; thus she marries as well as his slave-girl and both give birth to their husband; then the first husband comes and the master of the slave-girl. He (the Imam) said, 'He takes back his wife because he has the right to do so. He also takes back his slave-girl and her child or the cost of the child's value.'"

H 10862, Ch. 68, h 4
Muhammad ibn 'Isma'il has narrated from al-Fadl ibn Shadhan from and Ali ibn Ibrahim has narrated from his father all from ibn abu 'Umayr from Ibrahim ibn 'Abd al-Hamid from abu Basir and others who has said the following:

"About the case of two witnesses who testify that a woman's husband has divorced her or that he has died, thus, she marries, then the husband comes, abu 'Abd Allah, *'Alayhi al-Salam,* has stated this *Hadith.* 'They are whipped for their crime. They are held responsible for the mahr (dower) to be paid to the husband for deceit; then she counts waiting period and returns to her first husband.'"

H 10863, Ch. 68, h 5
A number of our people have narrated from Sahl ibn Ziyad and Ali ibn Ibrahim has narrated from his father all from ibn abu Nasr from 'Abd al-Karim from Zurarah who has said the following:

"Abu Ja'far, *'Alayhi al-Salam,* has said, 'If a woman receives news of the death of her husband or she is informed about her being divorced by her husband and she counts her waiting period and thereafter marries, then her previous husband comes. The first one is more rightful than the second one, regardless, he (the second) has gone to bed with her or not; but she can demand mahr (dower) from the second one because of his going to bed with her and the second one can thereafter never lawfully marry her again.'"

Chapter 69 - A Woman's Receiving News of being Divorced by her husband thus She Marries then her first Husband Comes then She is Separated from Both

H 10864(a), Ch. 69, h 1
Muhammad ibn Yahya has narrated from Ahmad ibn Muhammad from Ali ibn al-Hakam from Musa ibn Bakr from Zurarah who has said the following:

"I once asked abu Ja'far, *'Alayhi al-Salam,* about the case of a woman who receives news of the death of her husband and she counts her waiting period; then marries. Then her first husband comes. She then separates from him and he from her and about how long is her waiting period. He (the Imam) said, 'It is three *Hayd* (menses)-free periods. She only needs to place her womb in quarantine for three *Hayd* (menses)-free periods and thereafter she becomes lawful for anyone of all people.' Zurarah has said that it is because people said she needs two waiting periods, one waiting period because of each one. Abu Ja'far, *'Alayhi al-Salam,* rejected it and said, 'She must count three *Hayd* (menses)-free periods and thereafter she becomes lawful for men for marriage.'"

H 10864(b), Ch. 69, h 2
Ali ibn Ibrahim has narrated from his father from 'Isma'il ibn Marrar from Yunus from certain persons of his people who has said the following:
"About the case of a woman who receives news of the death of her husband, then she marries; then her first husband comes who divorces her and also the second husband divorces. Ibrahim al-Nakha'iy has said that she must count two waiting periods. Zurarah then took the question to abu Ja'far, *'Alayhi al-Salam,* who said that she has only one waiting period.'"

Chapter 70 - A Woman Waiting Period from a Castrated Husband

H 10865, Ch. 70, h 1
Muhammad ibn Yahya has narrated from Ahmad ibn Muhammad and Ali ibn Ibrahim has narrated from his father all from ibn Mahbub from Jamil ibn Salih from abu 'Ubaydah who has said the following:
"Once abu Ja'far, *'Alayhi al-Salam,* was asked about the case of a castrated man who marries a woman, assigns mahr (dower) for her and she knows that he is castrated. He (the Imam) said, 'It is permissible.' It then was said that he lives with her as long as Allah wills, then divorces her; if she has any waiting period. He (the Imam) said, 'Yes, because he has enjoyed her and she from him.' It then was asked, 'For whatever they may have done is there Ghusl (bath) on them because of it?' He (the Imam) said, 'If there has been enjoyment and because of him she has ejaculated, then Ghusl (bath) is obligatory on her.' It then was asked, 'Can he ask for refund of mahr (dower) in case he divorces her?' He (the Imam) said, 'No, he cannot do so.'"

Chapter 71 - One Who Becomes ill Mentally after Marriage

H 10866, Ch. 71, h 1
Muhammad ibn Yahya has narrated from Ahmad ibn Muhammad from Ali ibn al-Hakam from Ali ibn abu Hamzah who has said the following:
"Once, abu Ibrahim, *'Alayhi al-Salam,* was asked about the case of a woman whose husband becomes mentally ill after marriage or becomes insane. He (the Imam) said, 'If she wants to pull herself away from him she can do so if so she wishes.'"

Chapter 72 - Al-Zihar

H 10867, Ch. 72, h 1

Ali ibn Ibrahim has narrated from his father from ibn Mahbub from abu Wallad al-Hannat from Humran who has said the following:

"Abu Ja'far, *'Alayhi al-Salam,* has said that 'Amir al-Mu'minin has stated this *Hadith.* 'Once a Muslim woman came to the Messenger of Allah, *O Allah, grant compensation to Muhammad and his family worthy of their services to Your cause,* and said, "O Messenger (of Allah) so and so married me. I gave birth to many children for him. I helped him in his world and religion and he has not seen any dislikeable things from me. I complain against him before Allah, most Majestic, most Glorious, and before you." He (the Messenger of Allah) asked, "What is your complaint against him?" She replied, "Today he said to me, 'You are unlawful for me like the back of my mother is.' He expelled me from my house, please look into my affairs." The Messenger of Allah said, "Allah has not sent down any book by which I can decide between you and your husband and I do not like to take the trouble on myself." She began to weep and complain before Allah and His Messenger and returned. Allah, most Majestic, most Glorious, heard her conversations with His Messenger, *O Allah, grant compensation to Muhammad and his family worthy of their services to Your cause,* about her husband and what she complained about. Allah, most Majestic, most Glorious, sent a reading about it:

"In the Name of Allah, the Beneficent, the Merciful. Allah has certainly heard the words of the woman who argued with you about her husband and who (after not having received a favorable response from you) complained to Allah. Allah was listening to your argument [meaning the statements of the Messenger of Allah about her husband]. Allah is All hearing and All aware. (58:1)

"Those who renounce their wives by calling them to be as their mothers should know that their wives could never become their mothers. Their mothers are those who have given birth to them. The words that they speak are certainly detestable and sinful. However, Allah is Pardoning and All forgiving." (58:2)'

"The Messenger of Allah, *O Allah, grant compensation to Muhammad and his family worthy of their services to Your cause,* sent for her and she came. He (the Messenger of Allah) said to bring her husband before him. She brought her husband. He (the Messenger of Allah) asked, 'Have you said this to your wife, 'you are unlawful to me like the back of my mother is?' He replied, 'I have said so to her.' The Messenger of Allah, *O Allah, grant compensation to Muhammad and his family worthy of their services to Your cause,* said, 'Allah, most Majestic, most Glorious, has sent verses of al-Quran about you and your wife.' He (the Messenger of Allah) read for him what Allah had revealed, 'Allah has heard the words of the woman . . . Allah is Pardoning and All-forgiving.' (58:2) Hold your wife to yourself because you have said evil and sinful words. Allah has forgiven you and has pardoned you. You must not do such thing again.' The man returned and he was regretful because of what he had said to his wife. Allah

141

disliked it for the believers thereafter and then He revealed, 'Those who involve themselves in *Zihar* against their women then return from what they have said. . .' meaning when the first man said to his wife, 'You are unlawful to me like the back of my mother.' He (the Imam) said, 'Whoever says it after Allah pardoned and forgave the first man, "must set free a slave before touching (going to bed with) his wife. This is how Allah gives advice and Allah is well aware of what you do. If one cannot set free a slave he must fast for two consecutive months before touching each other. If one cannot do this also then he must feed sixty destitute people." Allah has sanctioned this penalty after He prohibited *Zihar* and said, "This is done so that you believe in Allah and His Messenger and such are the laws of Allah." Allah, most Majestic, most Glorious, has sanctioned this penalty because of *Zihar*.'"

Humran has said that abu Ja'far, *'Alayhi al-Salam,* has said, '*Zihar* does not take place by swearing, harming and in anger. *Zihar* can only take place during a *Hayd* (menses)-free period and without sexual intercourse and in the presence of two Muslim witnesses.'"

H 10868, Ch. 72, h 2
Ali ibn Ibrahim has narrated from his father from ibn abu 'Umayr from ibn Bukayr from 'Ubayd ibn Zurarah who has said the following:
"Abu 'Abd Allah, *'Alayhi al-Salam,* has said, 'Divorce is not a divorce unless it is intended to be a divorce, and *Zihar* is not *Zihar* unless it is intended to be so.'"

H 10869, Ch. 72, h 3
Ali has narrated from his father from ibn Mahbub from ibn Ri'ab from Zurarah who has said the following:
"I once asked abu Ja'far, *'Alayhi al-Salam,* about *al-Zihar*. He (the Imam) said, 'It applies to all relatives (Dhi Mahram) like mother, sister, paternal or maternal aunts. Al-*Zihar* is not by swearing.' I then asked, 'How does it take place?' He (the Imam) said, 'It happens by a man's saying to his wife when she is clean of *Hayd* (menses) and sexual intercourse, 'You are unlawful to me like the back of my mother or sister', and he thereby intends *al-Zihar*.'"

H 10870, Ch. 72, h 4
Muhammad ibn Yahya has narrated from Ahmad ibn Muhammad from ibn Faddal from ibn Bukayr from a man of our people from a man who has said the following:
"I once asked abu al-Hassan, *'Alayhi al-Salam,* about my saying to my wife, 'You are like the back of my mother if you went out of the room' and she went out of the room. He (the Imam) said, 'There it does not have any valid effect on you.' I then said, 'I am strong to expiate.' He (the Imam) said, 'You do not owe anything because of it.' I said, 'I am strong to set free one or two slaves.' He (the Imam) said, 'You do not owe anything because of it, regardless you are strong or not strong.'"

H 10871, Ch. 72, h 5
Ibn Faddal has narrated from the one who narrated to him who has said the following:

"Abu 'Abd Allah, *'Alayhi al-Salam,* has said, *'Al-Zihar* can take place only in the environment of divorce.'"

H 10872, Ch. 72, h 6

Muhammad ibn Yahya has narrated from Ahmad ibn Muhammad from ibn abu Najran from ibn abu 'Umayr from 'Abd Allah ibn al-Mughirah and others who has said the following:

"Hamzah ibn Humran married the daughter of Bukayr. In the night that she was to be brought to him women said to him that divorce does not matter to you much and it is not important for you. 'We will not bring her (the bride) to you until you form *al-Zihar* about the mothers of your children.' He (the narrator) has said that he agreed to do so and mentioned it to abu 'Abd Allah, *'Alayhi al-Salam.* He (the Imam) commanded him to settle (keep) them.'"

H 10873, Ch. 72, h 7

Abu Ali al-Ash'ariy has narrated from Muhammad ibn 'Abd al-Jabbar and abu al-'Abbas al-Razzaz from Ayyub ibn Nuh all from Safwan from ibn abu 'Umayr from 'Abd Allah ibn al-Mughirah who has said the following:

"Hamzah ibn Humran married daughter of Bukayr. In the night that she was to be brought to him women said to him, 'We would not bring her to you until you swear. We will not agree to your swearing about setting free slaves because you do not consider it anything important; but you must swear about *al-Zihar* and form *al-Zihar* about the mothers of your children and slave-girls.' He formed *al-Zihar* about them, then he mentioned it to abu 'Abd Allah, *'Alayhi al-Salam.* He (the Imam) said, 'You do not owe anything because of it and you can go back to them.'"

H 10874, Ch. 72, h 8

Abu Ali al-Ash'ariy has narrated from Muhammad ibn 'Abd al-Jabbar from Safwan who has said the following:

"I once asked abu 'Abd Allah, *'Alayhi al-Salam,* about the case of a man who doubts a great deal in his wudu. He then says, 'If I repeat my *Salat* (prayer) or wudu (because of doubts), then my wife will be like the back of my mother and swears for it about divorce.' He (the Imam) said, 'It is of the misdeeds of Satan. He does not owe anything because of it.'"

H 10875, Ch. 72, h 9

Ali ibn Ibrahim has narrated from his father and A number of our people have narrated from Ahmad ibn Muhammad from 'Uthman ibn 'Isa from Sama'ah from abu Basir who has said the following:

"I once heard abu 'Abd Allah, *'Alayhi al-Salam,* saying that once a man came to the Messenger of Allah, *O Allah, grant compensation to Muhammad and his family worthy of their services to Your cause,* and said, 'O Messenger of Allah, I have formed *al-Zihar* with my wife'. He (the Messenger of Allah) said, 'Go and set free a slave.' He said, 'I do not have anything.' He (the Messenger of Allah) said, 'Go and fast for two consecutive months.' He said, 'I cannot do so.' He (the Messenger of Allah) said, 'Go and feed sixty destitute people.' He said, 'I do not have that much food.' He (the Imam) has said that the Messenger of Allah then said, 'I will do it for you.' He (the Messenger of Allah) gave him dates to feed sixty destitute people and told him to give to them.' He then said, 'I swear by the One who has sent you with truth, I do not know of anyone between the two mountains on both sides of this city needier to this date than myself and my family.' He (the Messenger of Allah) said, 'Go, eat thereof and feed to your family.'"

H 10876, Ch. 72, h 10
Ali ibn Ibrahim has narrated from his father from ibn abu 'Umayr from Jamil ibn Darraj who has said the following:

"I once said to abu 'Abd Allah, *'Alayhi al-Salam,* that a man says to his wife that she is like the back of his paternal or maternal aunt. He (the Imam) said, 'It is *al-Zihar.*' He (the narrator) has said that we asked him (the Imam) about *al-Zihar* and about when expiation becomes due on such man. He (the Imam) said, 'It is when he wants to go to bed with his wife.' I then asked, 'Will there be expiation if he divorces her before going to bed with her?' He (the Imam) said, 'Expiation does not fall off of him.' I then asked, 'If he fasts a part of fasting, then he falls ill and he discontinues his fast, must he start it all over again or continue from where he had left to complete what he owes?' He (the Imam) said, 'If he has fasted one month, then has fallen ill, he must start all over again, but if he has done more than one month by one day or two days he can continue from there onward to complete the rest.' He (the narrator) has said that he (the Imam) said, 'Free and slaves are the same except that slaves owe one-half of expiation on a free person. He (a slave) does not owe setting free of slaves or charity. He must only fast for one month.'"

H 10877, Ch. 72, h 11
Abu Ali al-Ash'ariy has narrated from Muhammad ibn 'Abd al-Jabbar and al-Razzaz from Ayyub ibn Nuh from Safwan ibn Yahya from Ishaq ibn 'Ammar who has said the following:

"I once asked abu Ibrahim, *'Alayhi al-Salam,* about the case of a man who forms *al-Zihar* about his slave-girl. He (the Imam) said, 'Free and slaves are the same in *al-Zihar.*'"

H 10878, Ch. 72, h 12
Muhammad ibn Yahya has narrated from Ahmad ibn Muhammad from Ali ibn al-Hakam from al-'Ala' from Muhammad ibn Muslim who has said the following:

"I once asked one of the two Imam, (abu Ja'far or abu 'Abd Allah), *'Alayhim al-Salam,* about the case of a man who forms *al-Zihar* about his wife five times or more. He (the Imam) said, 'For every time there is expiation.' He (the narrator) has said, 'I asked him (the Imam) about a man who forms *al-Zihar* about his wife, then divorces her before going to bed with her; if there is expiation on him. He (the Imam) said, 'No, there is no expiation on him.' He (the narrator) has said, 'I asked him (the Imam) about *al-Zihar* of free and a slave-girl. He (the Imam) said, 'Yes, it can happen.' It was asked, 'If it takes place in the month of Sha'ban and he cannot find a slave to free.' He (the Imam) said, 'He must wait until he completes fasting of the month of Ramadan, then fast for two consecutive months; and if he forms *al-Zihar* on a journey he must wait until he comes home. If he fasts then finds assets, he continues with what he has started.'"

H 10879, Ch. 72, h 13

Muhammad ibn Ahmad has narrated from ibn abu Najran from Muhammad ibn Humran who has said the following:

"I once asked abu 'Abd Allah, *'Alayhi al-Salam,* about the case of a slave if there is *al-Zihar* on him. He (the Imam) said, 'He owes one-half of what becomes due on free people. He owes only to fast one month and setting free of slaves does not apply to him as well as charity.'"

H 10880, Ch. 72, h 14

Ali ibn Ibrahim has narrated from his father from ibn abu 'Umayr from Hammad from al-Halabiy who has said the following:

"I once asked abu 'Abd Allah, *'Alayhi al-Salam,* about the case of a man who forms *al-Zihar* about his wife three times. He (the Imam) said, 'He must pay expiation three times.' I then asked about if he goes to bed with her before paying expiation. He (the Imam) said, 'He must ask forgiveness from Allah and abstain until he pays expiation.'"

H 10881, Ch. 72, h 15

A number of our people have narrated from Sahl ibn Ziyad from ibn Mahbub from abu Hamzah al-Thumaliy who has said the following:

"I once asked abu Ja'far, *'Alayhi al-Salam,* about a slave if there is expiation for *al-Zihar* on him. He (the Imam) said, 'He owes one-half of what is due on a free person of fasting, and setting free of slaves as expiation does not apply in his case as well as paying charity.'"

H 10882, Ch. 72, h 16

Ali ibn Ibrahim has narrated from his father from ibn abu 'Umayr from Hafs ibn al-Bakhtariy who has said the following:

"About the case of a man who had ten slave-girls and formed *al-Zihar* about all of them by one statement, abu 'Abd Allah, or abu al-Hassan, *'Alayhi al-Salam,* has said that he must pay ten expiations.'"

H 10883, Ch. 72, h 17

Ali ibn Ibrahim has narrated from his father from ibn abu 'Umayr from 'Umar ibn 'Udhaynah from Zurarah and from more than one person from abu Basir who has said the following:

"He (the Imam) has said, 'If one goes to bed with the woman for the second time before paying expiation he must pay another expiation' He (the narrator) has said that there is no differences in this issue.'"

H 10884, Ch. 72, h 18
Abu Ali al-Ash'ariy has narrated from Muhammad ibn 'Abd al-Jabbar from Safwan from Sayf al-Tammar who has said the following:

"I once asked abu 'Abd Allah, *'Alayhi al-Salam,* about the case of a man who says to his wife, 'You are like the back of my sister, maternal or paternal aunt.' He (the Imam) said, 'Allah has mentioned the mothers, this certainly is unlawful.'"

H 10885, Ch. 72, h 19
Muhammad ibn Yahya has narrated from Ahmad ibn Muhammad from Ali ibn Mahziyar from who has said the following:

"'Abd Allah ibn Muhammad once wrote to abu al-Hassan, *'Alayhi al-Salam,* saying, 'I pray to Allah to keep my soul in service for your cause, certain ones of your followers think that if a man speaks the statement of *al-Zihar,* then expiation becomes due, violating the swearing or not. They say that its sinfulness and violation is in the very statement of *al-Zihar* and expiation is as penalty for such statement. Certain others think that expiation is not due unless swearing is violated in something about which he swears, and if he violates then expiation is due on him, otherwise, there is no expiation. He (the Imam), *'Alayhi al-Salam,* signed the answer in his own handwriting that said, 'Expiation does not become obligatory until violation of oath occurs.'"

H 10886, Ch. 72, h 20
Abu Ali al-Ash'ariy has narrated from Muhammad ibn 'Abd al-Jabbar from Safwan who has said the following:

"Once, al-Husayn ibn Mehran asked abu al-Hassan al-Rida', *'Alayhi al-Salam,* about a man who formed *al-Zihar* about four women. He (the Imam) said, 'He owes expiation for each one.' He asked him (the Imam) about a man who formed *al-Zihar* about his wife and his slave-girl and what must he pay. He (the Imam) said, 'For each one he must pay expiation in the form of freeing a slave or fasting two consecutive months or feeding sixty destitute people.'"

H 10887, Ch. 72, h 21
Muhammad ibn Yahya has narrated from Ahmad ibn Muhammad Ahmad ibn Muhammad and Ali ibn Ibrahim has narrated from his father from all from ibn Mahbub from Jamil ibn Salih from al-Fudayl ibn Yasar who has said the following:

"I once asked abu 'Abd Allah, *'Alayhi al-Salam,* about a Mumlak (a man owned as offspring of slaves) who expresses *al-Zihar* (calling one's wife as one's mother) about his wife. He (the Imam) said to me, 'It is not *al-Zihar* (calling one's wife as one's mother) or swearing before going to bed with her.'"

H 10888, Ch. 72, h 22
Muhammad ibn Yahya has narrated from Ahmad ibn Muhammad from Ali ibn al-Hakam from Mu'awiyah ibn Wahab who has said the following:

"I once asked abu 'Abd Allah, *'Alayhi al-Salam,* about the case of a man who says to his wife that she is like the back of his mother to him. He (the Imam) said, 'The expiation for it is setting free of a slave or fasting for two consecutive months or feeding sixty destitute people. For freeing a slave, a child born in Islam is sufficient.'"

H 10889, Ch. 72, h 23

Ali ibn Ibrahim has narrated from his father from ibn abu 'Umayr from Jamil an ibn Bukayr and Hammad ibn 'Uthaman who has said the following:

"Abu 'Abd Allah, *'Alayhi al-Salam,* has said, 'If one who has expressed *al-Zihar* (calling one's wife as one's mother) about his wife, divorces her then expiation cancels out and it no more is applicable to his case.'"

Ali ibn Ibrahim has said that if a man divorces his wife or takes his slave-girl out of his possession he then does not owe expiation of *al-Zihar* unless he goes back to his wife and returns his slave-girl into his possession. When he does so then it is not proper for him to go near them without paying the expiation.

H 10890, Ch. 72, h 24

A number of our people have narrated from Sahl ibn Ziyad from al-Qasim ibn Muhammad al-Zayyat who has said the following:

"I once said to abu 'Abd Allah, *'Alayhi al-Salam,* 'I have expressed the statement of *al-Zihar* about my wife.' He (the Imam) asked, 'How did you say it?' I replied that it was, 'You are like the back of my mother to me if you did so and so.' He (the Imam) said, 'It does not have any valid effect but you must not repeat it again.'"

H 10891, Ch. 72, h 25

Muhammad ibn Yahya has narrated from Ahmad ibn Muhammad from ibn abu Nasr who has said the following:

"Al-Rida', *'Alayhi al-Salam,* has said, 'Al-*Zihar* (calling one's wife as one's mother) does not take place upon anger (if expressed because of anger).'"

H 10892, Ch. 72, h 26

Muhammad ibn Yahya has narrated from Ahmad ibn Muhammad from Ahmad ibn al-Hassan from ''Amr ibn Sa'id from Musaddiq ibn Sadaqah from 'Ammar ibn Musa who has said the following:

"I once asked abu 'Abd Allah, *'Alayhi al-Salam,* about *al-Zihar* (calling one's wife as one's mother) which brings about the obligation. He (the Imam) said, 'It is exactly that whereby a man wants *al-Zihar.*'"

H 10893, Ch. 72, h 27

Ali ibn Ibrahim has narrated from his father from al-Nawfaliy from al-Sakuniy who has said the following:

"Abu 'Abd Allah, *'Alayhi al-Salam,* has said that `Amir al-Mu'minin has said, 'When a woman says, "My husband is unlawful like the back of my mother" expiation does not become due on her thereby.' He (the Imam) said that once a man from al-Ansar (people of al-Madinah) from Banu al-Najjar came to the Messenger of Allah, *O Allah, grant compensation to Muhammad and his family worthy of their services to Your cause,* and said, 'I have expressed the statement of *al-Zihar* about my wife, then went to bed with her before paying the expiation.' He (the Messenger of Allah) asked, 'What made you do so?' He replied, 'When I expressed the statement of *al-Zihar* about her I then saw her shining anklet in the moonlight and the whiteness of her leg, then I went to bed with her before paying the expiation.' He (the Messenger of Allah) said, 'Stay away from her until you pay the expiation.' He (the Messenger of Allah) commanded him to pay the expiation once and ask forgiveness from Allah.'"

H 10894, Ch. 72, h 28

Abu Ali al-Ash'ariy has narrated from Muhammad ibn 'Abd al-Jabbar or others from al-Hassan ibn Ali from Ali ibn 'Uqbah, from Musa ibn 'Ukayl al-Numayriy, from certain persons of our people who has said the following:

"About the case of a man who expresses the statement of *al-Zihar* about his wife then divorces her, abu 'Abd Allah, *'Alayhi al-Salam,* has said, 'Expiation does not apply to his case when he divorces before going to bed with her.' It was then asked, 'What happens if he goes back to her?' He (the Imam) said, 'If he has divorced her to escape from expiation, then goes back to her, expiation is obligatory for whenever he goes to bed with her, but if he divorced without such intention then it is not unlawful to go back to her and expiation is not due on him.'"

H 10895, Ch. 72, h 29

Abu Ali al-Ash'ariy, has narrated from Muhammad ibn 'Abd al-Jabbar and al-Razzaz from Ayyub ibn Nuh all from Safwan who has said that abu 'Uyaynah narrated from Zurarah who has said the following:

"I once said to abu Ja'far, *'Alayhi al-Salam,* 'I have expressed the statement of *al-Zihar* about the mother of my children, then went to bed with her, then paid the expiation. He (the Imam) said, 'This is how a faqih (scholar of law) man does; when he goes to bed he pays expiation.'"

H 10896, Ch. 72, h 30

Ali ibn Ibrahim has narrated from his father from ibn abu 'Umayr from 'Umar ibn 'Udhaynah from Zurarah who has said the following:

"I once asked abu 'Abd Allah, *'Alayhi al-Salam,* about the case of a man who expresses the statement of *al-Zihar* about his wife, then goes to bed with her before paying expiation. He (the Imam) said, 'Is it not the way a faqih (scholar of law) man does?'"

H 10897, Ch. 72, h 31

Al-Husayn from Muhammad has narrated from Mu'alla' ibn Muhammad from al-Hassan ibn Ali from Aban from al-Hassan al-Sayqal who has said the following:

"I once asked abu 'Abd Allah, *'Alayhi al-Salam,* about the case of a man who expressed the statement of *al-Zihar* about his wife. He (the Imam) said, 'He must pay expiation.' I then said, 'He has gone to bed with her before paying the expiation.' He (the Imam) said, 'He has come across a law of laws of Allah, most Majestic, most Glorious, and he must ask forgiveness from Allah and stay away until he pays expiation.'"

H 10898, Ch. 72, h 32

Ali ibn Ibrahim has narrated from his father and Muhammad ibn 'Isma'il has narrated from al-Fadl ibn Shadhan from ibn abu 'Umayr from 'Abd al-Rahman ibn *al-Hajj*aj who has said the following:

"Abu 'Abd Allah, *'Alayhi al-Salam,* has said, 'Al-*Zihar* is of two kinds. One kind is that because of which expiation becomes obligatory before going to bed with her, and the other kind is that for which expiation becomes obligatory after going to bed with her. The first kind is that in which one says, 'For me you are like the back of my mother' without saying, "If I did so and so with you." The other kind is that for which expiation becomes obligatory after going to bed with her and it is that in which he says, 'For me you are like the back of my mother if I come near you (for sexual intercourse).'"

H 10899, Ch. 72, h 33

Muhammad ibn abu 'Abd Allah al-Kufiy has narrated from Mu'awiyah ibn al-Hakim from Safwan from 'Abd al-Rahman ibn *al-Hajj*aj who has said the following:

"I once heard abu 'Abd Allah, *'Alayhi al-Salam,* saying, 'If one swear to express *al-Zihar* then violates it, expiation becomes obligatory on him before going to bed with her, but if he has expressed the statement of *al-Zihar* without swearing, then expiation becomes due on him after going to bed with her.'"

Mu'awiyah has said that this is not correct from thinking point of view. *Hadith* has come and our people have narrated that swearing can only take place 'by Allah' and that is about which Quran has come.'"

H 10900, Ch. 72, h 34

Muhammad ibn Yahya has narrated from Ahmad ibn Muhammad and Ali ibn Ibrahim has narrated from his father all from ibn Mahbub from abu Ayyub al-Khazzaz from Yazid al-Kunasiy who has said the following:

"I once asked abu Ja'far, *'Alayhi al-Salam,* about the case of a man who expresses the statement of *al-Zihar* about his wife, then divorces her once. He (the Imam) said, 'If he has divorced her once *al-Zihar* becomes void and divorce abolishes *al-Zihar*.' I then asked, 'What happens if he goes back to her?' He (the Imam) said, 'Yes, he can do so. She is his wife and if he went back to her he will owe what a man who has expressed the statement of *al-Zihar* owes before they touch each other.' I then asked, 'What happens if he allows until her waiting period ends and she becomes free of the bonds of marriage, and he then marries her; if there is expiation for *al-Zihar* before they touch each other. He (the Imam) said, 'No, there is no expiation because she became stranger to him and was free of the bonds of marriage.' I then asked, 'What happens if he expresses the statement of *al-Zihar* about his wife, then leaves her without touching except that he sees her naked without touching; if expiation becomes obligatory. He (the Imam) said, 'She is his wife, his going to bed with her is not unlawful, however, what is obligatory on him is what is obligatory on those who expressed the statement of *al-Zihar* about their wives before going to bed with her who is his wife.' I then asked, 'What happens if she brings him before the Sultan and says, 'This is my husband who has expressed the statement of *al-Zihar* about me and he has withheld me. He does not touch me for fear of expiation which is obligatory on those who express the statement of *al-Zihar*.' He (the Imam) said, 'He (the sultan) cannot force him about the expiation of setting free of a slave or fasting for two consecutive months or feeding sixty destitute people if he is not able to set free a slave, fast for two consecutive months or feed sixty destitute people.' He (the Imam) said, 'If he is able in setting free of a slave or fasting for two consecutive months or feeding sixty destitute people, then the Imam must make him ready for setting free a slave and charity before he touches her or after he touches her.'"

H 10901, Ch. 72, h 35
Ibn Mahbub has narrated from al-'Ala' from Muhammad ibn Muslim who has said the following:
"I once asked abu Ja'far, *'Alayhi al-Salam,* about the case of a man who expresses the statement of *al-Zihar* about his wife, then divorces her before going to bed with her until she becomes stranger to him: if he owes expiation. He (the Imam) said, 'No, expiation is not obligatory on him.'"

H 10902, Ch. 72, h 36
Ali ibn Ibrahim has narrated from his father from Salih ibn Sa'id from Yunus from certain persons of his people who has said the following:
"I once asked abu 'Abd Allah, *'Alayhi al-Salam,* about the case of a man, who expresses the statement of *al-Zihar* about his wife. He says, 'For me you are like the back of my mother or like her hand, or like her belly, or like her vagina, or like her soul, or like her feet'; if this is *al-Zihar* and if he owes what one who expressed the statement of *al-Zihar* owes. He (the Imam) said, 'If one expresses the statement of *al-Zihar* about his wife and says that she is like the back of his mother to him, or like her hand, like her leg, her hairs or something of her with the intention for it to be unlawful, then expiation becomes obligatory in a little or more of it. So also is the case if he says that she is like his relatives and expiation becomes obligatory on him.'"

Chapter 73 - Al-Li 'an (Condemnation)

H 10903, Ch. 73, h 1
A number of our people have narrated from Sahl ibn Ziyad and Ali ibn Ibrahim has narrated from his father from ibn abu Nasr from 'Abd al-Karim from abu Basir who has said the following:
"Abu 'Abd Allah, *'Alayhi al-Salam,* has said, *'Al-Li'an* (condemnation) does not take place until one goes to bed with his wife.'"

H 10904, Ch. 73, h 2
Al-Husayn from Muhammad has narrated from Mu'alla' ibn Muhammad from al-Hassan ibn Ali from Aban from Muhammad ibn Muslim who has said the following:
"Abu Ja'far, *'Alayhi al-Salam,* has said, 'Condemnation and swearing take place only after going to bed with her.'"

H 10905, Ch. 73, h 3
A number of our people have narrated from Sahl ibn Ziyad from Ahmad ibn Muhammad from ibn abu Nasr from al-Muthanna' from Zurarah who has said the following:
"Once abu 'Abd Allah, *'Alayhi al-Salam,* was asked about the words of Allah, most Majestic, most Glorious, 'Those who accuse their wives and do not have witnesses except themselves. . . .' (24:4) He (the Imam) said, 'He is one who accuses his wife. If he accuses then confesses that he has lied against her, the punishment for him is whipping and his wife is returned to him. If he refuses and goes ahead he must testify four times against her, by Allah, that he is

truthful. For the fifth time he must condemn himself if he is of the lying people. If she wanted to defend herself against suffering (punishment and penalty), which is to be stoned, she must testify four times, by Allah, that he is of the lying people and for the fifth time must condemn herself by saying that she must be subjected to the anger of Allah if he has spoken the truth. If she did not do it she then is stoned but if she defended herself, penalty is diverted from her and thereafter she will never become lawful for him in marriage until the day of Day of Judgment.' I then asked, 'What happens if they are separated and she has a child who dies? He (the Imam) said, 'His mother inherits him and if his mother dies his maternal uncles inherit him. Those who say that he is born out of wedlock must be punished by whipping.' I then asked, 'Is the child returned to him if he confesses that he has lied?' He (the Imam) said, 'No, it is not honorable. He does not inherit the son but the son inherits him.'"

H 10906, Ch. 73, h 4
Ali ibn Ibrahim has narrated from his father from ibn Mahbub from 'Abd al-Rahman ibn *al-Hajj*aj who has said the following:

"Once 'Abbad al-Basriy asked abu 'Abd Allah, *'Alayhi al-Salam,* when I was present, 'How does a man go through the process of *Mula'inah* (condemnation) against the woman?' Abu 'Abd Allah, *'Alayhi al-Salam,* explained a judgment of the Messenger of Allah. He (the Imam) said, 'Once a man of the Muslims came to the Messenger of Allah, *O Allah, grant compensation to Muhammad and his family worthy of their services to Your cause.* He asked, "O Messenger of Allah, what happens if a man enters his house and finds a man with his wife involved in sexual intercourse? What must he do?"' He (the Imam) said that the Messenger of Allah turned away from him and that man left. That man was the one who had faced that issue from his woman. He (the Imam) said that revelation from Allah, most Majestic, most Glorious, came with the commandment about them and the Messenger of Allah sent to summon that man. When he came, he (the Messenger of Allah) asked, 'Did you see a man with your woman?' He replied, 'Yes, that it is true.' He (the Messenger of Allah) then said, 'You must go back and bring your woman because Allah, most Majestic, most Glorious, has sent a commandment about you and about her.' He (the Imam) said that her husband then brought her and the Messenger of Allah held them in custody. He (the Messenger of Allah) said to the man, 'Testify four times by Allah that you are truthful (of the truthful ones) in your accusing her of what you accuse her.' He (the Imam) said that he testified; then he (the Messenger of Allah) said, 'You must wait.' He (the Messenger of Allah) preached to him and gave him advice then said, 'Be pious and have fear of Allah; condemnation of Allah is severe.' He (the Messenger of Allah) then told him to testify for the fifth time and say, 'Condemnation of Allah will be upon me if I am of the liars.' He (the Imam) said that the man testified and he (the Messenger of Allah) commanded him and he moved away. Then he (the Messenger of Allah) said to the woman, 'Do you testify four times that your husband is of the lying people in what he has accused you of?' He (the Imam) said that she then testified. Then he (the Messenger of Allah) told her to wait. He (the Messenger of Allah) preached to her, gave her good advice and told her

151

to have fear of Allah; the condemnation of Allah is severe. He (the Messenger of Allah) then told her to testify for the fifth time saying that she will be subjected to the anger of Allah if her husband is of the truthful people in what he has accused her of.' He (the Imam) said that she testified. He (the Imam) said that he (the Messenger of Allah) separated them from each other and told them that they can never come together in marriage after lodging condemnation upon each other.'"

H 10907, Ch. 73, h 5
Al-Hassan ibn Mahbub has narrated from 'Abbad ibn Suhayb who has said the following:
"A man is placed under arrest by the Imam in the case of *al-Li'an* (condemnation). He testifies twice, then refuses and confesses that he has lied before completing *al-Li'an* (condemnation). Abu 'Abd Allah, *'Alayhi al-Salam,* has said that he is whipped as the penalty for accusing the woman of committing fornication. He is not separated from his woman.'"

H 10908, Ch. 73, h 6
Ali ibn Ibrahim has narrated from his father from ibn abu 'Umayr from Hammad from al-Halabiy who has said the following:
"Abu 'Abd Allah, *'Alayhi al-Salam,* has said, 'If a man accuses his wife he cannot condemn her unless he can say that he has seen a man between her legs fornicating.' He (the narrator) has said that he (the Imam) was asked about the man who accuses. He (the Imam) said, 'He condemns her and then they are separated from each other. She will never be lawful for him in marriage. However, if he confesses against himself before *al-Li'an* (condemnation) he is whipped as the penalty and she remains his woman.'"

"He (the narrator) has said, 'I asked him (the Imam) about a free person with a slave-girl in his control and about his accusing her. He (the Imam) said, 'He can deal with it by the process of *al-Li'an* (condemnation).'

"He (the narrator) has said, 'I asked him (the Imam) about *al-Li'an* (condemnation) in which the husband accuses her, denies her child and goes through the process of *al-Li'an* (condemnation), separates from her and thereafter says, 'The child is my child' and calls himself a liar. He (the Imam) said, 'The woman cannot return to him forever, however, I return the child if he claims him as his child but do not call him his child. He (the man) cannot inherit the child but he inherits the father and the father does not inherit the son. The legacy of the son goes to his maternal uncles. If his father did not claim him his maternal uncles inherit his legacy but he does not inherit them. If anyone calls him the son of fornication such person is whipped as punishment for such crime.'"

H 10909, Ch. 73, h 7
Ali ibn Ibrahim has narrated from his father from ibn abu 'Umayr from Jamil ibn Darraj who has said the following:
"I once asked abu 'Abd Allah, *'Alayhi al-Salam,* if *al-Li'an* (condemnation) can take place between a free man and a slave-girl. He (the Imam) said, 'Yes, it can

take place between a slave and a free woman, between a slave and a slave-girl, between a Muslim and a Jewish woman or a Christian woman but they do not inherit each other and there is no inheritance between a free and a slave-girl.'"

H 10910, Ch. 73, h 8

A number of our people have narrated from Sahl ibn Ziyad and Ali ibn Ibrahim has narrated from his father from ibn abu Nasr from 'Abd al-Karim from al-Halabiy who has said the following:

"About the case of a man who goes through the process of al-Li'an (condemnation) against his wife who is pregnant, then claims her child to be his child after childbirth thinking that the child is his. He (the Imam) said, 'The child can be given to him without whipping because al-Li'an (condemnation) has become a matter of the past in the case.'"

H 10911, Ch. 73, h 9

Ali ibn Ibrahim has narrated from his father from ibn abu 'Umayr from Hammad from al-Halabiy from Muhammad ibn Muslim who has said the following:

"About the case of a man who goes through the process of al-Li'an (condemnation) against his wife who is speechless, abu 'Abd Allah, 'Alayhi al-Salam, has said, 'They must be separated from each other.'"

H 10912, Ch. 73, h 10

Ali has narrated from his father from ibn abu Nasr from Jamil from Muhammad ibn Muslim who has said the following:

"I once asked abu Ja'far, 'Alayhi al-Salam, about the case of a man and woman who are involved in al-Li'an (condemnation) and about how they do it. He (the Imam) said, 'The Imam sits with his back to al-Qiblah (al-Ka'bah) and they stand in front of him facing al-Qiblah (al-Ka'bah) before him and he begins with the man, then the woman. The woman on whom stoning is obligatory, is stoned from her backside and not from her front side; beating and stoning must not affect the face. Other parts of the body can be targeted in both, beating and stoning.'" [Note: Such cases are only applicable after due Islamic judicial process]

H 10913, Ch. 73, h 11

Ahmad ibn Muhammad from ibn abu Nasr has said the following:

"I once asked al-Rida', 'Alayhi al-Salam, saying, 'I pray to Allah to keep you well, how is al-Li'an (condemnation) completed?' He (the Imam) said, 'The Imam sits down with his back to the al-Qiblah (al-Ka'bah) and keeps the man on his right and the woman on his left.'"

H 10914, Ch. 73, h 12

Muhammad ibn Yahya has narrated from al-'Amrakiy ibn Ali from Ali ibn Ja'far from his brother abu al-Hassan, 'Alayhi al-Salam, who has said the following:

"I once asked him (the Imam), 'Alayhi al-Salam, about the case of a man who goes through the process of al-Li'an (condemnation) against his woman and testifies swearing by Allah four times but declines the fifth time. He (the Imam) said, 'If he declines the fifth time she is his woman but he is whipped. If the woman declines when swearing is on her, she is subjected to the same process as he was.' I then asked if al-Li'an (condemnation) is completed in a sitting or standing position. He (the Imam) said, 'Al-Li'an (condemnation) and similar things are done in a standing position.'

"I then asked about a man who has divorced his wife before going to bed with her and then claims that she is pregnant. He (the Imam) said, 'If he presents proof that he has uncovered a secret then denies the child to be his child, he can go through the process of al-Li'an (condemnation) and she becomes stranger to him, but he must pay the mahr (dower).'"

H 10915, Ch. 73, h 13

A number of our people have narrated from Sahl ibn Ziyad, Ali ibn Ibrahim has narrated from his father, and Muhammad ibn Yahya has narrated from Ahmad ibn Muhammad from ibn Mahbub from ibn Ri'ab from al-Halabiy who has said the following:

"I once asked abu 'Abd Allah, *'Alayhi al-Salam,* about the case of a man who has gone through the process of *al-Li'an* (condemnation) against his wife who is pregnant and her pregnancy has become clear but denies what is in her womb. When the child is born, he claims the child, keeps him close, and thinks that the child is his child. He (the Imam) said, 'The child is given to him and he inherits him but he is not whipped; *al-Li'an* (condemnation) has become a matter of the past in the case.'"

H 10916, Ch. 73, h 14

Muhammad ibn Yahya has narrated from Ahmad ibn Muhammad from Ali ibn al-Hakam from al-'Ala' from Muhammad ibn Muslim who has said the following:

"I once asked one of the two Imam, (abu Ja'far or abu 'Abd Allah), *'Alayhim al-Salam,* about the case of a slave who accuses his woman. He (the Imam) said, 'They can go through the process of *al-Li'an* (condemnation) against each other like free people do.'"

H 10917, Ch. 73, h 15

Ali ibn Ibrahim has narrated from his father, from Hammad from Hariz from Muhammad ibn Muslim who has said the following:

"I once asked him (the Imam), *'Alayhi al-Salam,* about the case of a man who falsely accuses his wife. He (the Imam) said, 'He is whipped, then they are left alone. He does not go through the process of *al-Li'an* (condemnation) who then is made to say, 'I testify that I saw you doing so and so.'"

H 10918, Ch. 73, h 16

Muhammad ibn Yahya has narrated from Ahmad ibn Muhammad, from Ali ibn Hadid from Jamil ibn Darraj from Muhammad ibn Muslim who has said the following:

"One of the two Imam, (abu Ja'far or abu 'Abd Allah), *'Alayhim al-Salam,* has said, '*al-Li'an* (condemnation) does not take place without denying the child.' He (the Imam) said, 'When a man accuses his woman he can go through the process of *al-Li'an* (condemnation) against her.'"

H 10919, Ch. 73, h 17

Muhammad ibn Ahmad has narrated from ibn Mahbub from al-'Ala' ibn Razin from ibn abu Ya'fur who has said the following:

"Abu 'Abd Allah, *'Alayhi al-Salam,* has said, 'A man cannot go through the process of *al-Li'an* (condemnation) against his wife in the manner of Mut'ah (advantageous marriage).'"

H 10920, Ch. 73, h 18
Muhammad has narrated from Ahmad ibn Muhammad from ibn Mahbub from Hisham ibn Salim from abu Basir who has said the following:

"Once abu 'Abd Allah, *'Alayhi al-Salam,* was asked about the case of a man who accuses his wife of committing fornication and she is speechless, deaf and cannot hear. He (the Imam) said, 'If she has witnesses who testify before the Imam in her favor, he is whipped as punishment and they are separated from each other. Thereafter she will not be lawful for him in marriage forever. If she does not have witnesses she becomes unlawful for him as long as he stays with her and there is no sin on her because of it.'"

H 10921, Ch. 73, h 19
It is narrated from the narrator of the previous *Hadith* from al-Hassan from certain persons of his people who has said the following:

"About the case of a woman who accuses her husband who is speechless, abu 'Abd Allah, *'Alayhi al-Salam,* has said, 'They are separated from each other and he is not lawful for her forever.'"

H 10922, Ch. 73, h 20
Ali ibn Ibrahim has narrated from his father from ibn abu Nasr from abu Jamilah from Muhammad ibn Marwan who has said the following:

"About the case of a woman who is speechless and about how can he go through the process of *al-Li'an* (condemnation) against her, abu 'Abd Allah, *'Alayhi al-Salam,* has said, 'They must be separated from each other and she is not lawful for him in marriage forever.'"

H 10923, Ch. 73, h 21
Al-Husayn from Muhammad has narrated from Mu'alla' ibn Muhammad from al-Hassan ibn Ali al-Washsha' from Aban from a man who has said the following:

"Abu 'Abd Allah, *'Alayhi al-Salam,* has said, 'Al-Li'an (condemnation) does not take place unless one believes that he has seen it.'"

(The remaining chapters of this section, which deal with slaves and slave-girls are not translated due to the absence of any practical benefit at this time)

Part Three:
The Book of Hunting

Chapter 1 - Hunting Dog and Cheetah

H 10924, Ch. 1, h 1

Narrated to us abu Muhammad Harun ibn Musa al-Tal'akbariy, who has said that narrated to us abu Ja'far Muhammad ibn Ya'qub al-Kulayniy, who has said that narrated to him Ali ibn Ibrahim, from his father and Muhammad ibn Yahya has narrated from Ahmad ibn Muhammad ibn 'Isa. All of them have narrated from ibn abu 'Umayr from Hammad ibn 'Uthaman from al-Halabiy who has narrated the following:

"Abu 'Abd Allah, *'Alayhi al-Salam*, has said, 'It is in the book of Ali, *'Alayhi al-Salam*, about the meaning of the words of Allah, most Majestic, most Glorious, '. . . and whatever of the hunting beasts you may train. . . .' He (the Imam) has said, 'It is a reference to (hunting) dogs.'"

H 10925, Ch. 1, h 2

Ali ibn Ibrahim has narrated from his father from ibn abu 'Umayr from 'Umar ibn 'Udhaynah from Muhammad ibn Muslim and from more than one person who has said the following:

"About the case of a man who sends a hunting dog with the mention of the name of Allah, the two Imam, *'Alayhim al-Salam*, have stated this *Hadith*. 'If the dog catches the prey and you arrive to slaughter it properly, then you must do so; but if you arrive when it has already killed the prey and has eaten thereof you can also eat what is left, however, you must not apply to other hunting animals what you apply to hunting dogs.'"

H 10926, Ch. 1, h 3

Muhammad ibn Yahya has narrated from Ahmad ibn Muhammad from al-Hassan ibn Ali from ibn Faddal from 'Abd Allah ibn Bukayr from Salim al-Ashal who has said the following:

"I once asked abu 'Abd Allah, *'Alayhi al-Salam*, about the case of a dog which catches the prey, holds it in place and has eaten a part thereof. He (the Imam) said, 'Dog's eating is not harmful and it is lawful for you to use it for food.'"

H 10927, Ch. 1, h 4

A number of our people have narrated from Sahl ibn Ziyad from [Salim] and Ali ibn Ibrahim has narrated from his father and Muhammad ibn Yahya has narrated from Ahmad ibn Muhammad all from ibn Mahbub from ibn Ri'ab from abu 'Ubaydah al-Hadhdha who has said the following:

"I once asked abu 'Abd Allah, *'Alayhi al-Salam*, about the case of a man who sends his trained dog to catch a prey and mentions the name of Allah. He (the Imam) said, 'He can use for food what the dog has caught and he must slaughter it properly, if he arrives at the site before the dog kills the prey. He must not use the catch for food if he finds a non-hunting dog with it.' I asked about Cheetah. He (the Imam) said, 'If you arrive in time to slaughter it properly then you can use it for food, otherwise, you cannot use it for food.' I then asked, 'Is not Cheetah like dog?' He (the Imam) said, 'No other animals are called *Mukallab* (dogged, trained dogs) except dogs.'"

H 10928, Ch. 1, h 5

Ali ibn Ibrahim has narrated from his father from 'Abd al-Rahman ibn abu Najran from 'Asem ibn Hamid from Muhammad ibn Qays who has said the following:

"Abu Ja'far, *'Alayhi al-Salam,* has said, 'What is killed by dogs trained for hunting and the name of Allah is mentioned, you can use it for food, and what is killed by dogs not trained before and before you arrive to slaughter properly, then do not use it for food.'"

H 10929, Ch. 1, h 6

Muhammad ibn Yahya has narrated from Ahmad ibn Muhammad from Muhammad ibn Yahya from Jamil ibn Darraj al-Marwah has said that narrated to me Hakam ibn Hakim al-Sayrafiy who has said the following:

"I once asked abu 'Abd Allah, *'Alayhi al-Salam,* about the hunting dog which hunts and kills the prey. He (the Imam) said, 'It is not unlawful and you can use it for food.' I then said, 'They say that if the dog kills the prey it has caught it for itself, thus, you must not use it for food.' He (the Imam) said, 'You can use it for food. Do they not all agree with you that its kill is proper slaughtering?' I replied, 'Yes, it is true.' He (the Imam) then asked, 'What do they say about a sheep slaughtered by a man? Is his slaughtering proper?' I replied, 'Yes, he has done so.' He (the Imam) said, 'If a beast comes and after his slaughtering eats something from the slaughtered sheep can the rest be used for food?' I replied, 'Yes, it can be used for food.' He (the Imam) said that if they answer you in this way ask them this question. 'How is it that even though what is slaughtered properly (the catch of the trained hunting dog) and the dog ate thereof, you do not use the rest for food, but you use for food the sheep slaughtered by a man and a beast eats thereof?'"

H 10930, Ch. 1, h 7

Ahmad ibn Muhammad has narrated from Muhsin ibn Ahmad from Yunus ibn Ya'qub who has said the following:

"I once asked abu 'Abd Allah, *'Alayhi al-Salam,* about the case of a man who sends his dog and he arrives at the site when the dog has killed the prey. He (the Imam) said, 'You can use it for food even if the dog has eaten thereof.'"

H 10931, Ch. 1, h 8

A number of our people have narrated from Sahl ibn Ziyad, Ali ibn Ibrahim has narrated from his father, and Muhammad ibn Yahya has narrated from Ahmad ibn Muhammad all from Ahmad ibn Muhammad from ibn abu Nasr from Jamil ibn Darraj who has said the following:

"I once asked abu 'Abd Allah, *'Alayhi al-Salam,* about the case of a man who sends his dog to catch a prey which the dog catches; but he does not have a knife to slaughter it and about if he can leave it alone for the dog to kill and eat thereof. He (the Imam) said, 'It is not unlawful because Allah, most Majestic, most Glorious, has said, 'Eat what they catch for you', but it is not proper to eat what a cheetah has killed.'"

H 10932, Ch. 1, h 9

Muhammad ibn Yahya has narrated from Ahmad ibn Muhammad from Ali ibn al-Hakam from Sayf ibn 'Amirah from abu Bakr al-Hadramiy who has said the following:

"I once asked abu 'Abd Allah, *'Alayhi al-Salam,* about the hunting of Falcons, hawks, dogs and leopards. He (the Imam) said, 'Do not use for food what is hunted by any of these unless you slaughter it properly, except dogs trained for hunting.' I then asked, 'What happens if the dog kills it?' He (the Imam) said, 'You can use it for food; Allah, most Majestic, most Glorious, says, ". . . and what you train of dogs for hunting, eat of what they catch for you and mention the name of Allah on it." (5:4)'"

H 10933, Ch. 1, h 10

It is narrated from the narrator of the previous *Hadith* from Ali ibn al-Hakam from Sayf ibn 'Amirah from Aban ibn Taghlib from Sa'id ibn Musayyib who has said the following:

"I heard Salman saying, 'You can use for food the prey that dogs catch for you even if the dog has eaten two-thirds of it.'"

H 10934, Ch. 1, h 11

Ali ibn Ibrahim has narrated from his father from al-Nawfaliy from al-Sakuniy who has said the following:

"Abu 'Abd Allah, *'Alayhi al-Salam,* has said, 'The dogs of al-Kurdiyah (Kurdish people), when you train them, are like the dogs of al-Saluqiyyah (name of town in Yemen).'"

H 10935, Ch. 1, h 12

It is narrated from the narrator of the previous *Hadith* from Sayf ibn 'Amirah from Mansur ibn Hazim from Salim al-Ashal who has said the following:

"I once asked abu 'Abd Allah, *'Alayhi al-Salam,* about dog trained for hunting which has eaten of the prey. He (the Imam) said, 'You can use it (the prey) for food.'"

H 10936, Ch. 1, h 13

Al-Husayn from Muhammad has narrated from Mu'alla' ibn Muhammad from al-Hassan ibn Ali from Aban ibn 'Uthman from 'Abd al-Rahman ibn abu 'Abd Allah who has said the following:

"I once asked abu 'Abd Allah, *'Alayhi al-Salam,* about the case of a man who sends his dog, it catches a prey and eats thereof: if one can use the remaining for food. He (the Imam) said, 'You can use for food what a dog has killed when you mention the name of Allah on it. If you forget to do so you still can use it for food as well as the remaining of what the dog has eaten.'"

H 10937, Ch. 1, h 14

Muhammad ibn Yahya has narrated from Ahmad ibn Muhammad from Ali ibn al-Hakam from Musa ibn Bakr from Zurarah who has said the following:

"About the case of a man's sending a hunting dog, with the mention of the name of Allah, to catch a prey, abu 'Abd Allah, *'Alayhi al-Salam,* has stated this *Hadith.* 'He can use it (the catch) for food even if the dog kills it and has eaten thereof. If the dog is not trained already for hunting, but is trained at that hour, then is sent to catch and it did and ate thereof, the dog is still a trained dog. On the other hand different from hunting dogs is what leopards, hawks and similar animals hunt. You must not use it for food unless you arrive in time to slaughter it properly; Allah, most Majestic, most Glorious, says, 'Mukallabin' (dogged, trained dogs), thus, what is different from dogs its hunting is not edible unless you arrive in time to slaughter it.'"

H 10938, Ch. 1, h 15

Ali ibn Ibrahim has narrated from his father from ibn abu 'Umayr from Hammad from al-Halabiy who has said the following:

"Once abu 'Abd Allah, *'Alayhi al-Salam,* was asked about the hunting of falcons and dogs that kill the prey and eat thereof; if the remaining can be used for food. He (the Imam) said, 'Do not use for food what birds like falcons kill, unless you slaughter it properly; but if it is killed by dog when you have mentioned the name of Allah, most Majestic, most Glorious, you can use it for food even if the dog has eaten thereof.'"

H 10939, Ch. 1, h 16

Muhammad ibn Yahya has narrated from Ahmad ibn Muhammad from al-Husayn ibn Sa'id from al-Nadr ibn Suwayd from al-Qasim ibn Sulayman who has said the following:

"I once asked abu 'Abd Allah, *'Alayhi al-Salam,* about a dog that slips away without his owner's sending to hunt but it hunts and the owner arrives when it has killed the prey; if he can use it for food. He (the Imam) said, 'No, it is not lawful for food.' He (the Imam) said, 'If it hunts and the name of Allah is mentioned he can use it for food but if the name of Allah is not mentioned he must not use it for food and that is the meaning of '. . .and what you train of dogs for hunting.'"

H 10940, Ch. 1, h 17

Muhammad ibn Yahya has narrated from Ahmad ibn Muhammad from Mu'awiyah ibn Hakim from abu Malik al-Hadramiy from Jamil ibn Darraj who has said the following:

"I once asked abu 'Abd Allah, *'Alayhi al-Salam,* about my sending a dog to hunt and after mentioning the name of Allah, when I have nothing with me to slaughter the prey. He (the Imam) said, 'Allow the dog to kill the prey, then you can use it for food.'"

H 10941, Ch. 1, h 18

Ahmad ibn Muhammad has narrated from Ali ibn al-Hakam from Musa ibn Bakr from Zurarah who has said the following:

"Abu 'Abd Allah, *'Alayhi al-Salam,* has said, 'If a man sends a dog but forgets to mention the name of Allah, it then is like slaughtering and forgetting to mention the name of Allah and so also is the case of shooting the prey with an arrow and forgetting to mention the name of Allah.'"

H 10942, Ch. 1, h 19

Muhammad ibn Yahya has narrated from Ahmad ibn Muhammad from certain persons of our people from al-Hassan ibn Ali from Ali ibn abu Hamzah from his father from abu Basir who has said the following:

"I once asked abu 'Abd Allah, *'Alayhi al-Salam,* about the case of a people who send their trained dogs to hunt and who mention the name of Allah. When the dogs go, a stray dog joins them and the dogs jointly hunt. He (the Imam) said, 'Do not use it for food because you do not know if the trained ones have hunted it or the one without training.'"

H 10943, Ch. 1, h 20

Ali ibn Ibrahim has narrated from his father from al-Nawfaliy from al-Sakuniy who has said the following:

"Abu 'Abd Allah, *'Alayhi al-Salam,* has said that `Amir al-Mu'minin has said, 'What a very black colored dog hunts is not edible because the Messenger of Allah, *O Allah, grant compensation to Muhammad and his family worthy of their services to Your cause,* commanded to kill it.'"

Chapter 2 - Hunting of Falcons, Hawks and Others

H 10944, Ch. 2, h 1

Abu Ali al-Ash'ariy has narrated from Muhammad ibn 'Abd al-Jabbar and Muhammad ibn `Isma'il has narrated from al-Fadl ibn Shadhan from all from Safwan ibn Yahya from ibn Muskan from al-Halabiy who has said the following:

"Abu 'Abd Allah, *'Alayhi al-Salam,* has said, 'My father would give fatwa but he was afraid, so he was cautious. We were afraid about hunting by falcons and hawks but now we are not afraid, and we say that it is not lawful, unless one arrives in time to slaughter it properly. It is in the book of Ali, *'Alayhi al-Salam,* that Allah, most Majestic, most Glorious, says, '. . . and what you train of dogs for hunting' is about dogs only.'"

H 10945, Ch. 2, h 2

Muhammad ibn Yahya has narrated from Ahmad ibn Muhammad from Ali ibn al-Hakam from Ali ibn abu Hamzah from abu Basir who has said the following:

"Abu 'Abd Allah, *'Alayhi al-Salam,* has said, 'If you send a falcon, a hawk or an eagle to catch a prey, do not use it for food unless you arrive in time to slaughter it properly, and if it has already killed the prey then do not use it for food.'"

H 10946, Ch. 2, h 3

Muhammad ibn Yahya has narrated from Ahmad ibn Muhammad from Ali ibn al-Hakam from Aban ibn 'Uthman from 'Abd Allah ibn Sulayman who has said the following:

"I once asked abu 'Abd Allah, *'Alayhi al-Salam,* about the case of a man who sends his dog and hawk to hunt. He (the Imam) said, 'Do not use for food what the hawk hunts, unless you arrive in time to slaughter it properly. You can use for food what the dog hunts if you have mentioned the name of Allah on it, regardless, the dog has eaten anything or has not eaten.'"

H 10947, Ch. 2, h 4

Ali ibn Ibrahim has narrated from his father from Hammad ibn 'Isa from Hariz from Muhammad ibn Muslim who has said the following:

"Abu Ja'far, *'Alayhi al-Salam,* disliked what a falcon hunted unless one arrived in time to slaughter it properly.'"

H 10948, Ch. 2, h 5

Al-Husayn from Muhammad has narrated from Mu'alla' ibn Muhammad from al-Hassan ibn Ali from Aban ibn 'Uthman from 'Abd al-Rahman ibn abu 'Abd Allah who has said the following:

"I once asked abu 'Abd Allah, *'Alayhi al-Salam,* about the case of a man who sends his falcon or dog to catch a prey which then catches a prey and eats thereof; if he can use the remaining for food. He (the Imam) said, 'No, do not use for food what the falcon kills, unless you slaughter it properly.'"

H 10949, Ch. 2, h 6

Aban has narrated from abu al-'Abbas who has said the following:

"I once asked him (the Imam), *'Alayhi al-Salam,* about the hunting of falcons and hawks. He (the Imam) said, 'Do not use for food what falcons and hawks kill as well as what the predator birds kill.'"

H 10950, Ch. 2, h 7

A number of our people have narrated from Sahl ibn Ziyad and Ali ibn Ibrahim has narrated from his father all from ibn Mahbub from ibn Ri'ab from abu 'Ubaydah al-Hadhdha' who has said the following:

"I once said to abu 'Abd Allah, *'Alayhi al-Salam,* 'What do you say about falcons, hawks and eagle?' He (the Imam) said, 'If you arrive in time to slaughter it properly, then you can use it for food but if you do not arrive in time then do not use it for food.'"

H 10951, Ch. 2, h 8

A number of our people have narrated from Sahl ibn Ziyad from Ahmad ibn Muhammad from ibn abu Nasr from al-Mufaddal ibn Salih from Aban ibn Taghlib who has said the following:

"I once heard abu 'Abd Allah, *'Alayhi al-Salam,* saying, 'In the time of banu 'Umayyah my father, *'Alayhi al-Salam,* would give fatwa that what falcons and hawks kill is lawful for food. He (the Imam) was afraid but I am not afraid and I say that it (what is hunted by falcons and hawks) is not lawful to use for food.'"

H 10952, Ch. 2, h 9

Ali ibn Ibrahim has narrated from his father from 'Isma'il ibn Marrar from Yunus from 'Abd Allah ibn Sinan who has said the following:

"I once asked abu 'Abd Allah, *'Alayhi al-Salam,* about the hunting of falcons which it catches and eats thereof; if the remaining can be used for food. He (the Imam) said, 'Whatever birds eat do not use it for food unless you slaughter it properly.'"

H 10953, Ch. 2, h 10

Abu Ali al-Ash'ariy has narrated from Muhammad ibn 'Abd al-Jabbar from ibn Faddal from Mufaddal ibn Salih from Layth al-Muradiy who has said the following:

"I once asked abu 'Abd Allah, *'Alayhi al-Salam,* about falcons and hawks and their hunting. He (the Imam) said, 'Whatever they have not killed and you have slaughtered properly, is lawful and the last time for slaughtering is when the eyes move, legs run and the tails move.' He (the Imam) then said, 'Hawks and falcons are not mentioned in the Quran.'"

H 10954, Ch. 2, h 11

Ahmad ibn Muhammad has narrated from Muhammad ibn Ahmad al-Nahdiy from Muhammad ibn al-Walid from Aban from al-Fadl ibn 'Abd al-Malik who has said the following:

"He (the Imam), *'Alayhi al-Salam,* has said, 'Do not eat what predator birds kill.'"

Chapter 3 - Hunting of Zoroastrian and Taxpayer's Dogs

H 10955, Ch. 3, h 1

Ali ibn Ibrahim has narrated from his father from ibn abu 'Umayr from Hisham ibn Salim from Sulayman ibn Khalid who has said the following:

"I once asked abu 'Abd Allah, *'Alayhi al-Salam,* about the dog that belongs to a

Zoroastrian person; if a Muslim person can take and send it to catch a prey and mentions the name of Allah and if he can use the hunt for food. He (the Imam) said, 'Yes, because it is trained and he has mentioned the name of Allah.'"

H 10956, Ch. 3, h 2
Muhammad ibn Yahya has narrated from Ahmad ibn Muhammad from Ali ibn al-Hakam from Mansur ibn Yunus from 'Abd al-Rahman ibn Siyabah who has said the following:
"I once asked abu 'Abd Allah, *'Alayhi al-Salam,* about my borrowing the dog of a Zoroastrian person for hunting. He (the Imam) said, 'Do not use it for food unless a Muslim has trained it and it has learned.'"

H 10957, Ch. 3, h 3
Ali ibn Ibrahim has narrated from his father from al-Nawfaliy from al-Sakuniy who has said the following:
"Abu 'Abd Allah, *'Alayhi al-Salam,* has said, 'Do not use for food what the dog of a Zoroastrian person hunts, unless a Muslim has taken it to train and sends it to hunt. This applies to what the dogs of taxpayers and their falcons hunt, thus, it is lawful for the Muslims to use for food.'"

Chapter 4 - Hunting with Weapons

H 10958, Ch. 4, h 1
Muhammad ibn Yahya has narrated from Ahmad ibn Muhammad from ibn Faddal from Tha'labah ibn Maymun from Burayd ibn Mu'awiyah al-'Ijliy from Muhammad ibn Muslim who has said the following:
"Abu Ja'far, *'Alayhi al-Salam,* has said, 'Whatever is hunted by swords, arrows and spears are lawful to use for food.' He (the Imam) was asked about the prey, which is assigned to several people in portions before it dies. He (the Imam) said, 'It is not unlawful.'"

H 10959, Ch. 4, h 2
It is narrated from the narrator of the previous *Hadith* from Ahmad ibn Muhammad from 'Abd al-Rahman ibn abu Najran from 'Asem ibn Humayd ibn Ziyad has narrated from Muhammad ibn Qays who has said the following:
"Abu Ja'far, *'Alayhi al-Salam,* has stated this *Hadith.* 'If one causes injuries to a prey and mentions the name of Allah, most Majestic, most Glorious, then it remains for one or two nights without being eaten by the beasts; and he knows that his weapon is that which has caused its death, he can use it for food if he wants.' About a mountain goat hunted by a man but people intercept him and the man follows it; if you consider it a plunder. He (the Imam) said, 'It is not plundering and it is not unlawful.'"

H 10960, Ch. 4, h 3
Ali ibn Ibrahim has narrated from his father from Hammad from Hariz who has said the following:
"Once abu 'Abd Allah, *'Alayhi al-Salam,* was asked about the prey which his owner finds the next day; if he can use it for food. He (the Imam) said, 'If he knows that it is the prey which he had killed, he can use it for food if he had mentioned the name of Allah.'"

H 10961, Ch. 4, h 4

A number of our people have narrated from Ahmad ibn Muhammad from ibn Khalid from 'Uthman ibn 'Isa from Sama'ah who has said the following:

"I once asked him (the Imam), *'Alayhi al-Salam,* about the case of a man who shoots a wild donkey or a deer which is shot and he searches for it but finds it the next day with his arrow in it. He (the Imam) said, 'If he knows that his shot had hit it and the arrow is his arrow which has killed it, he then can use it for food, otherwise, he cannot use it for food.'"

H 10962, Ch. 4, h 5

Muhammad ibn Yahya has narrated from 'Abd Allah ibn Muhammad from Ali ibn al-Hakam from Aban ibn 'Uthman from 'Isa al-Qummiy who has said the following:

"I once said to abu 'Abd Allah, *'Alayhi al-Salam,* 'I shoot my arrow but I am not certain if I mentioned the name of Allah or not.' He (the Imam) said, 'You can use it for food and it is not unlawful.' I then asked, 'What happens if I shoot and the prey disappears, then I find it with my arrow in it. He (the Imam) said, 'You can use for food if it is not eaten yet, but if something has eaten thereof then do not use it for food.'"

H 10963, Ch. 4, h 6

Abu Ali al-Ash'ariy has narrated from Muhammad ibn 'Abd al-Jabbar and Muhammad ibn 'Isma'il has narrated from al-Fadl ibn Shadhan from all from Safwan from ibn Muskan from al-Halabiy who has said the following:

"I once asked abu 'Abd Allah, *'Alayhi al-Salam,* about a prey that a man hits with a sword or with a spear or shoots with an arrow and kills, and he has mentioned the name of Allah when shooting. He (the Imam) said, 'You can use it for food and it is not unlawful.'"

H 10964, Ch. 4, h 7

Muhammad ibn Yahya has narrated from Ahmad ibn Muhammad from al-Husayn ibn Sa'id from al-Nadr ibn Suwayd from Hisham ibn Salim from Sulayman ibn Khalid who has said the following:

"I once asked abu 'Abd Allah, *'Alayhi al-Salam,* about a prey that its owner finds; if he can use it for food. He (the Imam) said, 'If he knows that it is his shot that has killed it, he can use it for food.'"

H 10965, Ch. 4, h 8

Muhammad ibn Yahya has narrated from Ahmad ibn Muhammad ibn abu Najran from 'Asem ibn Hamid from Muhammad ibn Qays who has said the following:

"Abu Ja'far, *'Alayhi al-Salam,* has said that 'Amir al-Mu'minin, about a prey that is found dead with an arrow in it and it is not known who has killed it, said, 'Do not use it for food.'"

H 10966, Ch. 4, h 9

Muhammad ibn Yahya has narrated from 'Abd Allah ibn Muhammad from Ali ibn al-Hakam from Aban ibn 'Uthman from Muhammad al-Halabiy who has said the following:

"I once asked him (the Imam), *'Alayhi al-Salam,* about the case of a man who shoots a prey and hits it. People before him come and interrupt him. He (the Imam) said, 'He can use it for food.'"

H 10967, Ch. 4, h 10

Abu Ali al-Ash'ariy has narrated from Muhammad ibn 'Abd al-Jabbar from Safwan from Musa ibn Bakr from Zurarah who has said the following:

"Abu 'Abd Allah, *'Alayhi al-Salam,* has said, 'If you shoot a prey then find it without any other marks except your arrow and you know that nothing other than your arrow has killed it, you can use it for food, regardless, it had disappeared from you or not.'"

H 10968, Ch. 4, h 11

Muhammad ibn Yahya has narrated from Ahmad ibn Muhammad ibn 'Isa from ibn Mahbub from Hisham ibn Salim from Sama'ah ibn Mehran who has said the following:

"I once asked abu 'Abd Allah, *'Alayhi al-Salam,* about the case of a man who shoots a prey from the mountain and the arrow pierces through and comes out from the other side. He (the Imam) said, 'He can use it for food. 'He (the Imam) said, 'If it falls in water or rolls down the mountain and dies then do not use it for food.'"

H 10969, Ch. 4, h 12

Muhammad ibn Yahya has narrated from a man in a *marfu'* manner who has said the following:

"Abu 'Abd Allah, *'Alayhi al-Salam,* has said, 'A prey must not be hit with something bigger than the prey.'"

(It is because the cause of death becomes confused with the weight and force of the hunter).

Chapter 5 - Al-Mi'rad (Featherless Arrows)

H 10970, Ch. 5, h 1

Muhammad ibn Yahya has narrated from 'Abd Allah ibn Muhammad from Ali ibn al-Hakam from Aban from Zurarah and 'Isma'il al-Ju'fiy who has said the following:

"Zurarah and 'Isma'il al-Ju'fiy had asked abu Ja'far, *'Alayhi al-Salam,* about the prey which is killed by a featherless arrow. He (the Imam) said, 'It is not unlawful if it is what you have shot and it is what you have made for it.'"

H 10971, Ch. 5, h 2

Ali ibn Ibrahim has narrated from his father from ibn abu 'Umayr from Hammad from al-Halabiy who has said the following:

"Once abu 'Abd Allah, *'Alayhi al-Salam,* was asked about the prey that falls because of a featherless arrow. He (the Imam) said, 'If he does not have any other arrow and has mentioned the name of Allah, most Majestic, most Glorious, he can use it for food. If he has other arrows then he cannot use it for food.'"

H 10972, Ch. 5, h 3

A number of our people have narrated from Sahl ibn Ziyad and Muhammad ibn Yahya has narrated from Ahmad ibn Muhammad all from ibn Mahbub from ibn Ri'ab from abu 'Ubaydah who has said the following:

"Abu 'Abd Allah, *'Alayhi al-Salam,* has said, 'If you shoot the prey with a featherless arrow and if it pierces into the prey you can use it for food; but if it does not pierce into the prey and hits it widthwise, then do not use it for food.'"

H 10973, Ch. 5, h 4

Abu Ali al-Ash'ariy has narrated from Muhammad ibn 'Abd al-Jabbar and Muhammad ibn 'Isma'il has narrated from al-Fadl ibn Shadhan from all from Safwan ibn Yahya from ibn Muskan from al-Halabiy who has said the following:

"I once asked abu 'Abd Allah, *'Alayhi al-Salam,* about a prey that is shot by a man with an arrow and it hits widthwise and kills it. He had mentioned the name of Allah when shooting but no iron has hit the prey. He (the Imam) said, 'If the arrow that has hit is the one that has caused its death and he has seen it, he can use it for food.'"

H 10974, Ch. 5, h 5

Muhammad ibn Yahya has narrated from Ahmad ibn Muhammad from Ali ibn al-Hakam from abu al-Mighra' from al-Halabiy who has said the following:

"I once asked abu 'Abd Allah, *'Alayhi al-Salam,* about a prey which is hit by an arrow widthwise and no iron part has hit it. He had mentioned the name of Allah when shooting. He (the Imam) said, 'He can use it for food if it hits and he sees it hitting.' I asked him (the Imam) about hunting with featherless arrows. He (the Imam) said, 'If he has no other arrow and he has mentioned the name of Allah when shooting, he can use it for food; but if he had other arrows then he cannot use it for food.'"

Chapter 6 - Hunting with Stone and Clay-ball

H 10975, Ch. 6, h 1

Ali ibn Ibrahim has narrated from his father from ibn abu 'Umayr from Hammad from al-Halabiy who has said the following:

"Once, abu 'Abd Allah, *'Alayhi al-Salam,* was asked about a prey killed by stone or clay-ball; if it is edible. He (the Imam) said, 'No, it cannot be used for food.'"

H 10976, Ch. 6, h 2

Abu Ali al-Ash'ariy has narrated from Muhammad ibn 'Abd al-Jabbar from Safwan from al-'Ala' from Muhammad ibn Muslim who has said the following:

"I once asked one of the two Imam, (abu Ja'far or abu 'Abd Allah), *'Alayhim al-Salam,* about a prey killed with a stone or clay-ball; if it can be used for food. He (the Imam) said, 'No, it is not edible.'"

H 10977, Ch. 6, h 3

Muhammad ibn Yahya has narrated from Ahmad ibn Muhammad from al-Husayn ibn Sa'id from al-Nadr ibn Suwayd from Hisham ibn Salim from Sulayman ibn Khalid who has said the following:

"I once asked abu 'Abd Allah, *'Alayhi al-Salam,* about a prey killed with a stone or clay-ball; if it can be used for food. He (the Imam) said, 'No, it is not edible.'"

H 10978, Ch. 6, h 4

Ali ibn Ibrahim has narrated from his father from Hammad ibn 'Isa from Hariz who has said the following:

"Once abu 'Abd Allah, *'Alayhi al-Salam,* was asked about the prey killed with a stone or a clay-ball if it is edible. He (the Imam) said, 'No, it is not edible.'"

H 10979, Ch. 6, h 5

A number of our people have narrated from Sahl ibn Ziyad, from Ahmad ibn Muhammad, from ibn abu Nasr from al-'Ala' ibn Razin, from Muhammad ibn Muslim who has said the following:

"Once, I asked one of the two Imam, (abu Ja'far or abu 'Abd Allah), *'Alayhi al-Salam,* about a prey. A stone or clay-ball kills it if it is edible. He (the Imam) said, 'No, it is not edible.'"

H 10980, Ch. 6, h 6

Muhammad ibn Yahya has narrated from Ahmad ibn Muhammad from Muhammad ibn Yahya from Ghiyath ibn Ibrahim who has narrated the following:

"Abu 'Abd Allah, *'Alayhi al-Salam,* disliked *al-Julahiq* (a kind of clay-ball)."

H 10981, Ch. 6, h 7

Abu Ali al-Ash'ariy has narrated from Muhammad ibn 'Abd al-Jabbar from ibn Faddal from Ahmad ibn 'Umar from 'Abd Allah ibn Sinan who has said the following:

"About the case of a man who hits a prey with a stone or clay-ball and kills it; if he can use it for food, he (the Imam) said, 'Do not eat it.'"

Chapter 7 - Hunting with a Snare

H 10982, Ch. 7, h 1

Ali ibn Ibrahim has narrated from his father from ibn abu 'Umayr and ibn abu Najran from 'Asem ibn Hamid from Muhammad ibn Qays who has said the following:

"Abu Ja'far, *'Alayhi al-Salam,* has said that 'Amir al-Mu'minin has said, 'If a prey is caught by a snare, whatever is cut off like a leg or so, must be thrown away; it is dead. You can use the rest that you find alive and the name of Allah was mentioned on it.'"

H 10983, Ch. 7, h 2

Humayd ibn Ziyad has narrated from al-Hassan ibn Muhammad ibn Sama'ah from more than one person from Aban ibn 'Uthman from 'Abd al-Rahman ibn abu 'Abd Allah who has said the following:

"Abu 'Abd Allah, *'Alayhi al-Salam,* has said, 'If a prey is caught in a snare and certain part of it is cut off, it is dead, but what you find alive of the rest of the body you can slaughter it properly and use it for food.'"

H 10984, Ch. 7, h 3

Al-Husayn from Muhammad has narrated from Mu'alla' ibn Muhammad from al-Washsha' from 'Abd al-Rahman ibn abu 'Abd Allah who has said the following:

"Abu 'Abd Allah, *'Alayhi al-Salam,* has said, 'Whatever of a prey is caught in the snare is dead and whatever of the rest of the body you find alive, slaughter it properly; then you can use it for food.'"

H 10985, Ch. 7, h 4

Aban has narrated from 'Abd Allah ibn Sulayman who has said the following:

"Abu 'Abd Allah, *'Alayhi al-Salam,* has said, 'Whatever of the prey is caught in the snare which is cut off or has died is dead.'"

H 10986, Ch. 7, h 5

Aban has narrated from Zurarah who has said the following:

"Abu Ja'far, *'Alayhi al-Salam,* has said, 'Whatever of a prey is caught in the snare and is cutoff, it is dead, but what you find alive of the rest of the body, you can slaughter it properly and use it for food.'"

Chapter 8 - A Man Shoots a Prey, Hits it and it Falls in Water or Rolls Down the Mountain

H 10987, Ch. 8, h 1

Muhammad ibn Yahya has narrated from Ahmad ibn 'Isa from Muhammad ibn 'Isa from Hajjaj from Khalid ibn *al-Hajj*aj who has said the following:

"Abu al-Hassan, *'Alayhi al-Salam,* has said, 'Do not eat the prey that falls in water and dies.'"

H 10988, Ch. 8, h 2

A number of our people have narrated from Ahmad ibn Muhammad ibn Khalid from 'Uthman ibn 'Isa from Sama'ah who has said the following:

"Once abu 'Abd Allah, *'Alayhi al-Salam,* was asked about the case of a man who shoots a prey on a mountain or wall. The arrow pierces into it and it dies. He (the Imam) said, 'You can use it for food; but if it falls in water and dies, then do not eat it.'"

Ali ibn Ibrahim has narrated from his father from ibn abu 'Umayr from Hammad from al-Halabiy from 'Abd Allah *'Alayhi al-Salam,* has narrated a similar *Hadith.*

Muhammad ibn Yahya has narrated from Ahmad ibn Muhammad from certain persons of our people from Hisham ibn Salim from Sama'ah from 'Abd Allah, *'Alayhi al-Salam,* has narrated a similar *Hadith.*

Chapter 9 - A Man Shoots a Prey, Misses it but Hits another

H 10989, Ch. 9, h 1

Muhammad ibn Yahya has narrated from Ahmad ibn Muhammad from ibn Mahbub from 'Abbad ibn Suhayb who has said the following:

"I once asked abu 'Abd Allah, *'Alayhi al-Salam,* about the case of a man who shoots a prey and mentions the name of Allah, but misses it and hits another one. He (the Imam) said, 'He can use it for food.'"

Chapter 10 - Hunting During the Night

H 10990, Ch. 10, h 1

Muhammad ibn Yahya has narrated from Ahmad ibn Muhammad ibn 'Isa from Ahmad ibn Muhammad from ibn abu Nasr who has said the following:

"I once asked al-Rida', *'Alayhi al-Salam,* about hunting birds at night in their nests. He (the Imam) said, 'It is not unlawful.'"

Ahmad ibn Muhammad ibn 'Isa has narrated from Ahmad ibn 'Ushaym from Safwan ibn Yahya from abu al-Hassan al-Rida; *'Alayhi al-Salam,* has narrated a similar *Hadith.*

H 10991, Ch. 10, h 2

A number of our people have narrated from Ahmad ibn abu 'Abd Allah, from al-Hassan ibn Ali from Muhammad ibn al-Fudayl, from Muhammad ibn 'Abd al-Rahman who has said the following:

"Abu 'Abd Allah, *'Alayhi al-Salam,* has said that the Messenger of Allah, *O Allah, grant compensation to Muhammad and his family worthy of their services to Your cause,* has said, 'Do not go to the baby birds in their nests at night or to the birds during their sleep [until the morning].' A man then asked, 'What is during their sleep, O Messenger of Allah?' He (the Messenger of Allah) said, 'Night is their sleep, so do not enter in its sleep until the morning. Do not go to the baby birds in their nests until its feathers grow to fly. When it flies then aim your bow at it and fix for it your net.'"

H 10992, Ch. 10, h 3

A number of our people have narrated from Sahl ibn Ziyad from Muhammad ibn al-Hassan ibn Shammun from 'Abd Allah ibn 'Abd al-Rahman from Misma' who has said the following:

"Abu 'Abd Allah, *'Alayhi al-Salam,* has said that the Messenger of Allah, *O Allah, grant compensation to Muhammad and his family worthy of their services to Your cause,* prohibited hunting birds during the night, saying that the night is sanctuary for them.'"

Chapter 11 - Fishing

H 10993, Ch. 11, h 1

Ali ibn Ibrahim has narrated from his father from ibn abu 'Umayr from Hammad from al-Halabiy who has said the following:

"I once asked abu 'Abd Allah, *'Alayhi al-Salam,* about catching fish without a mention of the name of Allah. He (the Imam) said, 'It is not unlawful.'"

H 10994, Ch. 11, h 2

Ali ibn Ibrahim has narrated from his father from 'Amr ibn 'Uthman from al-Mufaddal ibn Salih from Zayd al-Shahham who has said the following:

"Once abu 'Abd Allah, *'Alayhi al-Salam,* was asked about catching fish without a mention of the name of Allah. He (the Imam) said, 'It is not unlawful if it is alive when he catches it.'"

H 10995, Ch. 11, h 3

Muhammad ibn Yahya has narrated from 'Abd Allah ibn Muhammad from Ali ibn al-Hakam from Aban from 'Abd al-Rahman ibn Sayabah who has said the following:

"I once asked abu 'Abd Allah, *'Alayhi al-Salam,* about fish which is caught, then placed in something but it returns into the water and dies in it. He (the Imam) said, 'Do not use it for food.'"

H 10996, Ch. 11, h 4

Ali ibn Ibrahim has narrated from his father from ibn abu 'Umayr from abu Ayyub who has said the following:

"I once asked abu 'Abd Allah, *'Alayhi al-Salam,* about the case of a man who catches fish, then ties it to a string, then sends it in the water where it dies; if he can use it for food. He (the Imam) said, 'No, he must not use it for food.'"

H 10997, Ch. 11, h 5

A number of our people have narrated from Ahmad ibn Muhammad ibn Khalid from 'Uthman ibn 'Isa from abu Basir who has said the following:

"I once asked abu 'Abd Allah, *'Alayhi al-Salam,* about fishing by Zoroastrian and Jews by means of fishing nets without a mention of the name of Allah. He (the Imam) said, 'It is not unlawful, fishing is to catch it alive.'"

H 10998, Ch. 11, h 6

Ali ibn Ibrahim has narrated from his father from ibn abu 'Umayr from Hisham ibn Salim from Sulayman ibn Khalid who has said the following:

"I once asked abu 'Abd Allah, *'Alayhi al-Salam,* about the fish caught by Zoroastrians. He (the Imam) said that Ali, *'Alayhi al-Salam,* would say, 'Fish and locusts are clean (slaughtered properly).'"

H 10999, Ch. 11, h 7

Muhammad ibn Yahya has narrated from 'Abd Allah ibn Muhammad from Ali ibn al-Hakam from Aban from Salmah abu Hafs who has said the following:

"Abu 'Abd Allah, *'Alayhi al-Salam,* has said that Ali, *'Alayhi al-Salam,* about catching fish would say, 'When a man catches fish and it struggles, hits with its fins, moves its back fins and looks with its eyes, this is its properly slaughtering.'"

H 11000, Ch. 11, h 8

Aban has narrated from 'Isa ibn 'Abd Allah who has said the following:

"I once asked abu 'Abd Allah, *'Alayhi al-Salam,* about the hunting by Zoroastrians. He (the Imam) said, 'It is not unlawful, if he gives it to you alive as well as the fish also, otherwise, their testimony is not acceptable unless you witness its being fished alive.'"

H 11001, Ch. 11, h 9

Ali ibn Ibrahim has narrated from his father from ibn abu 'Umayr from Hammad from al-Halabiy who has said the following:

"Once abu 'Abd Allah, *'Alayhi al-Salam,* was asked about the fishing by Zoroastrian by means of fishing nets and with a mention of the pagan consecration expressions. He (the Imam) said, 'Their fishing is not unlawful; fishing is catching them (alive).' I then asked about a barricade of reeds with water in it for fish. Fish enters it and certain ones of them die in it. He (the Imam) said, 'It is not unlawful; the barricade is set for fishing.'"

H 11002, Ch. 11, h 10

Muhammad ibn Yahya has narrated from Ahmad ibn Muhammad from al-Husayn ibn Sa'id from fadalah from al-Qasim ibn Burayd from Muhammad ibn Muslim who has said the following:

"It is the case of a man who sets a fishing net in water, then returns home leaving the net in water when thereafter he comes back he finds fish caught in it but they are dead. Abu Ja'far, *'Alayhi al-Salam,* has said, 'It is what his hands have done. It is not unlawful and he can use what is in it for food.'"

H 11003, Ch. 11, h 11

Muhammad ibn Yahya has narrated from al-'Amrakiy ibn Ali from Ali ibn Ja'far from his brother, Musa ibn Ja'far, *'Alayhi al-Salam,* who has said the following:

"I once asked him (the Imam), *'Alayhi al-Salam,* about a fish that jumps out of the canal and lands on the side and it then dies: if it can be used for food. He (the Imam) said, 'If you pick it up before it dies you can use it for food but if it dies before you pick it up, then do not use it for food.'"

H 11004, Ch. 11, h 12

Ali ibn Ibrahim has narrated from his father from al-Nawfaliy from al-Sakuniy who has said the following:

"Abu 'Abd Allah, *'Alayhi al-Salam,* has said that Ali, *'Alayhi al-Salam,* was asked about fish inside which another fish is found. He (the Imam) said, 'You can use both of them for food.'"

H 11005, Ch. 11, h 13

Al-Husayn from Muhammad has narrated from Mu'alla' ibn Muhammad from al-Washsha' from 'Abd Allah ibn Sinan who has said the following:

"I once heard abu 'Abd Allah, *'Alayhi al-Salam,* saying, 'It is not unlawful to use for food the fish which is caught by Zoroastrians.'"

H 11006, Ch. 11, h 14

Abu Ali al-Ash'ariy has narrated from al-Hassan ibn Ali al-Kufiy from al-'Abbas ibn 'Amir from Aban from certain persons of our people who has said the following:

"I once asked abu 'Abd Allah, *'Alayhi al-Salam,* about the case of a man who catches a fish and finds another fish inside it. He (the Imam) said, 'He can use both of them for food.'"

H 11007, Ch. 11, h 15

Ali ibn Ibrahim has narrated from Harun ibn Muslim from Mas'adah ibn Sadaqah who has said the following:

"Abu 'Abd Allah, *'Alayhi al-Salam,* has said, 'I heard my father saying, "If a man sets a fishing net whatever is caught in it dead or alive is lawful for food, except that which does not have scales and the dead fish floating on the water."'"

H 11008, Ch. 11, h 16

Muhammad ibn Yahya has narrated, from Ahmad ibn Muhammad, from Ya'qub ibn Yazid from Ahmad ibn al-Mubarak, from Salih ibn 'A'yan from al-Washsha' from Ayyub ibn 'A'yan who has said the following:

"I once said to abu 'Abd Allah, *'Alayhi al-Salam,* I pray to Allah to keep my soul in service for your cause. What do you say about a snake that has swallowed a fish then has thrown it out and it still is alive and struggling; if it can be used for food. He (the Imam) said, 'If its scales are peeled off then do not use it for food; but if it is not peeled off you can use it for food.'"

H 11009, Ch. 11, h 17

Muhammad ibn Yahya has narrated from Muhammad ibn Musa from al-'Abbas ibn Ma'ruf from Marwak ibn 'Ubayd from Sama'ah ibn Mehran who has said the following:

"Abu 'Abd Allah, *'Alayhi al-Salam,* has said that 'Amir al-Mu'minin prohibited a man's fishing on Fridays before *Salat* (prayer). He, *'Alayhi al-Salam,* would go to the fish market on Fridays and prohibit them from fishing on Fridays before Friday *Salat* (prayer).'"

H 11010, Ch. 11, h 18

Ali ibn Ibrahim has narrated from his father from 'Abd Allah ibn al-Mughirah from those whom he has mentioned who has said the following:

"Once, abu 'Abd Allah, *'Alayhi al-Salam,* mentioned fish which floats on water and what people dislike. He (the Imam) said, 'The fish floating on the water are disliked because their smell has changed.'"

Chapter 12 - Another Chapter on the Same Topic

H 11011, Ch. 12, h 1

A number of our people have narrated from Sahl ibn Ziyad and Muhammad ibn Yahya has narrated from Ahmad ibn Muhammad all from ibn Mahbub and Ahmad ibn Muhammad from ibn abu Nasr all from al-'Ala' from Muhammad ibn Muslim who has said the following:

"Once abu Ja'far, *'Alayhi al-Salam,* made me read something from the books of Ali, *'Alayhi al-Salam.* Therein I found this: 'I prohibit you from using eel for food, *al-Zimir,* (a certain kind of fish), *Mar mahi* (something like fish), snake fish, dead fish floating on water and the spleen.' I then asked, 'O child of the Messenger of Allah, may Allah grant you kindness, 'People bring to us a kind of fish that has no scales.' He (the Imam) said, 'You can use for food of fish that which has scales and do not use for food the kind of fish which has no scales.'"

H 11012, Ch. 12, h 2

Al-Husayn from Muhammad has narrated from Mu'alla' ibn Muhammad from al-Hassan ibn Ali from Hammad ibn 'Uthman who has said the following:

"I once asked abu 'Abd Allah, *'Alayhi al-Salam,* saying, 'I pray to Allah to keep my soul in service for your cause, of fish which kind is edible?' He (the Imam) said, 'The kind of fish that has scales is edible.' I then asked, 'I pray to Allah to keep my soul in service for your cause, what do you say about al-Kan'at (a kind of fish with very little scales). He (the Imam) said, 'It is not unlawful to use it for food.' I then said, 'It does not have scales?' He (the Imam) said, 'Yes, it has scales but it is a bad mannered fish and it sticks to everything. If you look at the base of its ears you can find scales.'"

H 11013, Ch. 12, h 3

Ali ibn Ibrahim has narrated from his father from Hammad from Hariz from those whom he has mentioned who has said the following:

"One of the two Imam, (abu Ja'far or abu 'Abd Allah), *'Alayhim al-Salam,* has said that 'Amir al-Mu'minin, *'Alayhi al-Salam,* disliked eel. He (the Imam) had said, 'Do not use for food the kind of fish which has no scales' and he (the Imam) disliked al-Mar Mahi (catfish).'"

H 11014, Ch. 12, h 4

A number of our people have narrated from Ahmad ibn Muhammad from 'Uthman ibn 'Isa from Sama'ah who has said the following:

"Abu 'Abd Allah, *'Alayhi al-Salam,* has said, 'Do not use for food eel, al-Mar Mahi, the dead fish floating on water and the spleen because it is the home of blood and a morsel of Satan.'"

H 11015, Ch. 12, h 5

Ali ibn Ibrahim has narrated from his father from ibn abu 'Umayr from Hisham ibn Salim from 'Umar ibn Hanzalah who has said the following:

"Dried up rabitha (shrimp) was sent to me in a sack and I visited abu 'Abd Allah, *'Alayhi al-Salam,* and asked him (the Imam) about it. He (the Imam) said, 'You can use it for food; it has scales.'"

H 11016, Ch. 12, h 6

Ali ibn Ibrahim has narrated from his father from 'Abd Allah ibn al-Mughirah from 'Abd Allah ibn Sinan who has said the following:

"Abu 'Abd Allah, *'Alayhi al-Salam,* has stated this *Hadith.* `Amir al-Mu'minin, Ali ibn abu Talib in al-Kufah would ride the mule of the Messenger of Allah, *O Allah, grant compensation to Muhammad and his family worthy of their services to Your cause,* then pass by the fish market and say, 'Do not use for food and do not sell of fish whatever has no scales.'"

H 11017, Ch. 12, h 7

Ali ibn Ibrahim has narrated from his father from Hanan ibn Sadir who has said the following:

"Al-'Ala' ibn Kamil asked abu 'Abd Allah, *'Alayhi al-Salam,* when I was present, about eel. He (the Imam) said, 'We have found in the book of Ali, *'Alayhi al-Salam,* of fish certain varities are unlawful for food so do not go close to them.' Abu 'Abd Allah, *'Alayhi al-Salam,* then said, 'Of fish those which have no scales, do not go close to them.'"

H 11018, Ch. 12, h 8

Hanan ibn Sadir has the following:

"Once, al-Fayd ibn al-Mukhtar sent rabitha as gift to abu 'Abd Allah, *'Alayhi al-Salam.* It was brought for him when I was present. He (the Imam) looked at it and said, 'This has scales.' He (the Imam) ate thereof and we saw him eating.'"

H 11019, Ch. 12, h 9

Ali ibn Ibrahim has narrated [from his father] from Harun ibn Muslim from Mas'adah ibn Sadaqah who has said the following:

"Abu 'Abd Allah, *'Alayhi al-Salam,* has stated this *Hadith.* `Amir al-Mu'minin would ride the mule of the Messenger of Allah, *O Allah, grant compensation to Muhammad and his family worthy of their services to Your cause.* He (the Imam) then would pass by the fish market and say, 'You must not use for food and must not sell whatever does not have scales.'"

H 11020, Ch. 12, h 10

Abu Ali al-Ash'ariy has narrated from al-Hassan ibn Ali from his uncle Muhammad ibn Sulayman ibn Ja'far who has said the following:

"Ishaq, fisherman, narrated to me the following, 'Once we went out with fish to meet abu al-Hassan, al-Rida', *'Alayhi al-Salam.* We went out of al-Madinah and he (the Imam) was coming from his journey and he (the Imam) said, 'Fie upon, you O so and so, perhaps you have fish with you.' I replied, 'Yes, O my master, I pray to Allah to keep my soul in service for your cause.' He (the Imam) said, 'Bring them down.' He (the Imam) then said, 'Perhaps it is *Zahw.*' I replied, 'Yes, it is and I showed him (the Imam) *Zahw*' He (the Imam) said, 'Ride your stumpers; we cannot use them for food.' *Al-Zahw* is a fish that has no scales.'"

H 11021, Ch. 12, h 11
Muhammad ibn Yahya has narrated from al-'Amrakiy from Ali ibn Ja'far from his brother abu al-Hassan, *'Alayhi al-Salam,* who has said the following:

"Abu al-Hassan, *'Alayhi al-Salam,* has said, 'It is not lawful to use eel, turtle and crab for food.' I then asked him (the Imam) about the shellfish of the ocean and al-Furat: if they could be used for food. He (the Imam) said, 'That is the flesh of frogs and it is not lawful to use it for food.'"

H 11022, Ch. 12, h 12
Al-Husayn from Muhammad has narrated from Mu'alla' ibn Muhammad from Muhammad ibn Ali al-Hamadaniy from Sama'ah ibn Mehran from al-Kalbiy al-Nassabah who has said the following:

"I once asked abu 'Abd Allah, *'Alayhi al-Salam,* about eel. He (the Imam) said, 'Allah, most Majestic, most Glorious, metamorphosed a group of banu Israelites, those of them who went to the sea are eels, *al-Zimir* and *al-Mar Mahi* and others, and those who remained on land are apes, pigs, wild cats and lizards and others.'"

H 11023, Ch. 12, h 13
Ali ibn Ibrahim has narrated from his father from Salih al-Sindiy from Yunus who has said the following:

"I once wrote to abu al-Hassan, al-Rida', *'Alayhi al-Salam,* and asked if fish which has no scales can be used for food. He (the Imam) said, 'Of fish there are those which have bad manners and they rub against everything and its scales go away, but if its two ends are different, its tail and head, then you can use it for food.'"

Chapter 13 - Locusts

H 11024, Ch. 13, h 1
Ali ibn Ibrahim has narrated (from his father) from Harun ibn Muslim from Mas'adah ibn Sadaqah who has said the following:

"Once abu 'Abd Allah, *'Alayhi al-Salam,* was asked about using locusts for food. He (the Imam) said, 'It is not unlawful.' He (the Imam) then said, 'Locusts are of the small pieces of fish in the ocean.' He (the Imam) then said that Ali, *'Alayhi al-Salam,* has said, 'Locust and fish on being taken out of the water are clean and slaughtered properly. The land is the hunting place of locusts and it can happen in the case of fish also.'"

H 11025, Ch. 13, h 2
A number of our people have narrated from Ahmad ibn abu 'Abd Allah, from his father from 'Awn ibn Jarir, from 'Amr ibn Harun al-Thaqafiy who has said the following:

"Abu 'Abd Allah, *'Alayhi al-Salam,* has stated this *Hadith.* 'Amir al-Mu'minin has said, '*Al-Jarad* (locust) is clean and slaughtered, you can use it for food, however, do not use for food whatever dies in water.'"

H 11026, Ch. 13, h 3
Muhammad ibn Yahya has narrated from al-'Amrakiy from Ali ibn Ja'far from his brother, (abu al-Hassan, *'Alayhi al-Salam*) who has said the following:

"I once asked abu al-Hassan, *'Alayhi al-Salam,* about *al-Jarad* (locust) that we find dead in the wilderness or in water; if it can be used for food. He (the Imam) said, 'Do not use them for food.' I then asked him (the Imam) about *al-Daba',* which is a kind of *al-Jarad,* if it can be used for food.' He (the Imam) said, 'No, until it is independent in flying.'"

Chapter 14 - Hunting Domestic Birds

H 11027, Ch. 14, h 1
A number of our people have narrated from Ahmad ibn abu 'Abd Allah from Ahmad ibn Muhammad from ibn abu Nasr who has said the following:
"I once asked al-Rida', *'Alayhi al-Salam,* about the case of a man who hunts a bird which is worth a large amount of dirham and it has leveled wings. He knows the owner of the bird or that he comes to ask about the bird but does not accuse him. He (the Imam) said, 'It is not lawful for him to keep. He must return it to him.' I then asked, 'What happens if he hunts that which has control over its wings and no one asking for it is known?' He (the Imam) said, 'It becomes his property.'"

H 11028, Ch. 14, h 2
It is narrated from the narrator of the previous *Hadith* from ibn Faddal from ibn Bukayr from those who narrated to him who has said the following:
"Abu 'Abd Allah, *'Alayhi al-Salam,* has said, 'If a bird has full control over its wings (is able to fly) it then belongs to whoever catches it.'"

H 11029, Ch. 14, h 3
It is narrated from the narrator of the previous *Hadith* from ibn Faddal from Muhammad ibn al-Fudayl who has said the following:
"I once asked abu al-Hassan, *'Alayhi al-Salam,* about hunting pigeons worth one-half of a dirham or one dirham. He (the Imam) said, 'If you know its owner return it to him; but if you do not know its owner and its wings are complete with both of which it can fly then it is yours.'"

H 11030, Ch. 14, h 4
It is narrated from the narrator of the previous *Hadith* from ibn Faddal from 'Ubayd ibn Hafs ibn al-Qurt from `Isma'il ibn Jabir who has said the following:
"I once said to abu 'Abd Allah, *'Alayhi al-Salam,* I pray to Allah to keep my soul in service for your cause, if a bird is trapped in the house and it is taken, is taking it lawful or unlawful. He (the Imam) asked, 'O `Isma'il is it healthy or it is not healthy and free?' I then asked, 'I pray to Allah to keep my soul in service for your cause, what is healthy?' He (the Imam) said, 'It is one with complete wings with full control on them and is able to fly wherever it wants.' He (the Imam) said, 'Such ones belong to whoever catches them.'"

H 11031, Ch. 14, h 5
Ali ibn Ibrahim has narrated from his father from al-Nawfaliy from al-Sakuniy who has said the following:
"Abu 'Abd Allah, *'Alayhi al-Salam,* has said that `Amir al-Mu'minin has said, 'The birds which have full control over their wings, belong to whoever catches

them and they are lawful for them.'"

H 11032, Ch. 14, h 6
Through the same chain of narrators as that of the previous *Hadith* the following is narrated:
"About a man who sees a bird and follows it until it sits on a tree and another man comes and takes it, 'Amir al-Mu'minin, *'Alayhi al-Salam,* has said, 'For an eye is what it has seen and for hands is what they catch'"

Chapter 15 - Al-Khuttaf the Bird of Black Color, a kind of Crow

H 11033, Ch. 15, h 1
Ali ibn Muhammad ibn Bandar has narrated from Ibrahim ibn Ishaq from Ali ibn Muhammad in a *marfu'* manner from Dawud al-Riqqiy or others who has said the following:
"As we were sitting with abu 'Abd Allah, *'Alayhi al-Salam,* a man passed by with a slaughtered *khuttaf* in his hand. Abu 'Abd Allah, *'Alayhi al-Salam,* quickly got up, took it from his hand and threw it away saying, 'Has your scholar or your faqih commanded you to kill it? My father narrated to me from my grandfather that the Messenger of Allah, *O Allah, grant compensation to Muhammad and his family worthy of their services to Your cause,* prohibited killing of six things of which one is al-khuttaf. Its roaming in the sky is in regret for what is done to the family of Muhammad, *O Allah, grant compensation to Muhammad and his family worthy of their services to Your cause,* and its reading Tasbih (Allah is free of all defects) is its reciting, "All praise belongs to Allah, Cherisher of the worlds." Have you not noticed that it says, "*Waladdallin* (and who are not straying)?" (the last word in Chapter 1 of the Quran)'

H 11034, Ch. 15, h 2
A number of our people have narrated from Sahl ibn Ziyad and Ahmad ibn abu 'Abd Allah all from al-Jamuraniy from al-Hassan ibn Ali ibn abu Hamzah from Muhammad ibn Yusuf al-Tamimiy from Muhammad ibn Ja'far from his father who has said the following:
"Abu 'Abd Allah, *'Alayhi al-Salam,* has said that the Messenger of Allah, *O Allah, grant compensation to Muhammad and his family worthy of their services to Your cause,* recommended to be good to al-Sininat (the crows). They among the birds are the ones that feel comfortable with people and he (the Messenger of Allah) then said, 'Do you know what al-Sininah says when it passes by or sings? It says, "In the name of Allah, the Beneficent, the Merciful, All praise belongs to Allah, Cherisher of the worlds . . ." until it reads 'Umm al-Kitab (the first chapter of al-Quran) and in the end it sings, "*Waladdallin*".' He (the Messenger of Allah) prolonged his voice saying, '*waladdallin*'."

H 11035, Ch. 15, h 3
Ali ibn Ibrahim has narrated from his father from ibn abu 'Umayr from Jamil ibn Darraj who has said the following:
"I once asked abu 'Abd Allah, *'Alayhi al-Salam,* about killing crows and disquieting them in *al-Haram* (the sacred area). He (the Imam) said, 'You must not kill them. I was with Ali ibn al-Husayn, *'Alayhi al-Salam,* and he saw me troubling them. He (the Imam) said to me, 'Do not kill them or trouble them;

they do not trouble anything.'"

Chapter 16 - Hoopoe and Shrike

H 11036, Ch. 16, h 1

A number of our people have narrated from Ahmad ibn abu 'Abd Allah al-Barqiy from Ali ibn Muhammad ibn Sulayman from abu Ayyub al-Madiniy from Sulayman ibn Ja'far al-Ja'fariy who has said the following:

"Abu al-Hassan, al-Rida', *'Alayhi al-Salam,* has said, 'On each wing of the Hoopoe in Assyrian language it is written, 'Family of Muhammad are the best of creatures.'"

H 11037, Ch. 16, h 2

It is narrated from the narrator of the previous *Hadith* from Ya'qub ibn Yazid from Ali ibn Ja'far who has said the following:

"I once asked my brother, abu al-Hassan, *'Alayhi al-Salam,* about Hoopoe, killing and slaughtering it. He (the Imam) said, 'It must not be troubled or slaughtered, it is a very good bird.'"

H 11038, Ch. 16, h 3

It is narrated from the narrator of the previous *Hadith* from Ali ibn Muhammad from abu Ayyub al-Madiniy from Sulayman Ja'fariy who has said the following:

"Abu al-Hassan, al-Rida', *'Alayhi al-Salam,* has said, that the Messenger of Allah, *O Allah, grant compensation to Muhammad and his family worthy of their services to Your cause,* prohibited killing hoopoes, shrike, *al-Suwwam* (a certain bird) and honey bees.'"

Chapter 17 - The Lark

H 11039, Ch. 17, h 1

A number of our people have narrated from Ahmad ibn abu 'Abd Allah from Ali ibn Muhammad ibn Sulayman from abu Ayyub al-Madiniy from Sulayman al-Ja'fariy who has said the following:

"Abu al-Hassan, al-Rida', *'Alayhi al-Salam,* has narrated from his father this *Hadith.* 'Do not use lark for food, do not abuse it and do not give it to children to play with; it says Tasbih a great deal and it is, 'O Allah, condemn those who hate Muhammad and his family, *O Allah, grant compensation to Muhammad and his family worthy of their services to Your cause.*'"

H 11040, Ch. 17, h 2

Through the same chain of narrators as that of the previous *Hadith* the following is narrated:

"Ali ibn al-Husayn, *'Alayhi al-Salam,* has said, 'I do not work in plantation for gains except that I want this gain for the destitute, the needy and especially for the lark among birds.'"

H 11041, Ch. 17, h 3

A number of our people have narrated from Sahl ibn Ziyad from abu 'Abd Allah, al-Jamuraniy from Sulayman al-Ja'fariy who has said the following:

"I once heard abu al-Hassan, al-Rida', *'Alayhi al-Salam,* saying, 'Do not kill the lark and do not use its flesh for food, because it says a great deal of Tasbih (Allah is free of all defects) and at the end it says, 'May Allah condemn those who hate the family of Muhammad, *'Alayhim al-Salam.'*"

H 11042, Ch. 17, h 4

Muhammad ibn al-Hassan and Ali ibn Ibrahim al-Hashimiy have narrated from certain persons of our people from Sulayman al-Ja'fariy who has said the following:

"Abu al-Hassan, al-Rida', *'Alayhi al-Salam,* has said that Ali ibn al-Husayn, has said, 'The crest on the head of lark is because of wiping of Solomon ibn David, *'Alayhi al-Salam.* It happened when the male lark wanted to mount the female (and) she refused. The male said, 'Do not refuse because I want that Allah, most Majestic, most Glorious, to give us the offspring because of which you will be remembered.' The female then agreed. When it was to lay eggs the male asked, 'Where do you want to lay eggs?' The female replied, 'I do not know. Can I lay the eggs away from the road?' The male said, 'I am afraid of bypassers, however, I think you should lay eggs near the road and those who see you may think that you are picking grains from the road.' The female agreed and laid the eggs; then sat on them to hatch until they were about to hatch that Solomon son of David, *'Alayhi al-Salam,* with his army, while birds forming shadow on him, appeared. The female said, 'This is Solomon coming to us with his army and I do not feel safe for my eggs being crushed under their feet.' The male said, 'Solomon is a kind man. Do you have anything which you may have saved for your baby larks when they are hatched to offer him as present?' The female replied, 'Yes, it is a locust that I had hidden from you for the baby larks when they are hatched; but do you have anything for a present?' The male replied, 'Yes, it is a date that I had hidden from you for the bay larks.' The female said, 'You take your date and I take my locust to present them to Solomon *'Alayhi al-Salam,* he is a man who loves presents. The male took the date in its beak and the female took the locust in its paws and appeared before Solomon. When he saw them he was on his throne. He extended his hands for them. The male sat on his right hand and the female on his left hand. He asked how they were doing and they informed him. He accepted their gift and asked his army to be careful about their eggs. He wiped their heads and prayed for them for blessing. The crest on their head is because of the wiping of Solomon, *'Alayhi al-Salam.'*"

End of the Book of Hunting of the book of al-Kafi followed by the Book of Slaughtering. All praise belongs to Allah, cherisher of the worlds.

Part Four:
The Book of Slaughtering
Animals for Food

Chapter 1: Tools for Slaughtering

H 11043, Ch. 1, h 1

Ali ibn Ibrahim has narrated from his father from ibn abu 'Umayr from 'Umar ibn 'Udhaynah from Muhammad ibn Muslim who has said the following:

"I once asked abu Ja'far, *'Alayhi al-Salam,* if an animal can be slaughtered with a piece of sharp wood or stone. He (the Imam) said, 'Without iron it is not a proper slaughtering.'"

H 11044, Ch. 1, h 2

Ali ibn Ibrahim has narrated from his father from ibn abu 'Umayr from Hammad from al-Halabiy who has said the following:

"I once asked abu 'Abd Allah, *'Alayhi al-Salam,* about slaughtering with (sharp) piece of wood, reeds and stone. He (the Imam) said that Ali ibn abu Talib, *'Alayhi al-Salam,* has said, 'Without iron slaughtering is not proper.'"

H 11045, Ch. 1, h 3

Muhammad ibn Yahya has narrated from Ahmad ibn Muhammad from Ali ibn al-Hakam from Sayf ibn 'Amirah from abu Bakr al-Hadramiy who has said the following:

"Abu 'Abd Allah, *'Alayhi al-Salam,* has said, 'Animals that are not slaughtered with iron cannot be used for food.'"

H 11046, Ch. 1, h 4

A number of our people have narrated from Ahmad ibn Muhammad from ibn Khalid from 'Uthman ibn 'Isa from Sama'ah ibn Mehran who has said the following:

"I once asked him (the Imam), *'Alayhi al-Salam,* about slaughtering. He (the Imam) said, 'Slaughtering cannot properly be done without iron and `Amir al-Mu'minin, *'Alayhi al-Salam,* prohibited slaughtering without it.'"

Chapter 2 - Another Chapter on the above Subject in an Emergency

H 11047, Ch. 2, h 1

Muhammad ibn Yahya has narrated from 'Abd Allah ibn Muhammad from Ali ibn al-Hakam from Aban from Muhammad ibn Muslim who has said the following:

"About the case of slaughtering without iron, abu Ja'far, *'Alayhi al-Salam,* has said, 'In an emergency when you cannot find iron you can slaughter with stone.'"

H 11048, Ch. 2, h 2

Ali ibn Ibrahim has narrated from his father from ibn abu 'Umayr from 'Abd al-Rahman ibn *al-Hajj*aj who has said the following:

"I once asked abu Ibrahim, *'Alayhi al-Salam,* if slaughtering with stone, sharp reeds, and wood when a knife cannot be found is acceptable. He (the Imam) said, 'If they can cut the jugular veins it is not unlawful.'"

Abu Ali al-Ash'ariy has narrated from Muhammad ibn 'Abd al-Jabbar from Safwan ibn Yahya from 'Abd al-Rahman ibn *al-Hajj*aj from abu Ibrahim, *'Alayhi al-Salam,* a similar *Hadith.*

H 11049, Ch. 2, h 3
Muhammad ibn Yahya has narrated from Ahmad ibn Muhammad from ibn Mahbub from Zayd al-Shahham who has said the following:
"I once asked abu 'Abd Allah, *'Alayhi al-Salam,* about the case of a man who does not have a knife; if he can slaughter with a piece of reed. He (the Imam) said, 'You can use reeds, stones, bones or wood for slaughtering when you cannot find iron, if such things cut the throat and blood comes out; then it is not unlawful.'"

Chapter 3 - The Manner of Slaughtering and al-Nahr

H 11050, Ch. 3, h 1
Ali ibn Ibrahim has narrated from his father from ibn abu 'Umayr from Mu'awiyah ibn 'Ammar who has said the following:
"Abu 'Abd Allah, *'Alayhi al-Salam,* has said, 'For *al-Nahr* the cut must be made in the upper part of the chest and in slaughtering the throat must be cut.'"

H 11051, Ch. 3, h 2
Ali has narrated from his father from Safwan who has said the following:
"I once asked abu 'Abd Allah, *'Alayhi al-Salam,* about slaughtering of cows in the upper part of the chest. He (the Imam) said, 'Cows are slaughtered by cutting the throat; and if it is Nahr (a cut in the upper part of the chest) in the case of cows, it is not lawfully slaughtered.'"

H 11052, Ch. 3, h 3
A number of our people have narrated from Sahl ibn Ziyad and Ali ibn Ibrahim has narrated from his father from and Ali ibn Muhammad from Ahmad ibn Muhammad from ibn abu Nasr from Yunus ibn Ya'qub who has said the following:
"I once said to abu al-Hassan, *'Alayhi al-Salam,* that people of Makkah in the case of cows do Nahr (make a cut in the upper part of the chest); so what do you say about using it for food? He (the Imam) said, 'They slaughtered it but they almost failed to do so thus, you must not eat unless it is slaughtered and it is not killed by means of Nahr.'"

H 11053, Ch. 3, h 4
Ali ibn Ibrahim has narrated from his father from abu Hashim al-Ja'fariy from his father from Humran ibn 'A'yan who has said the following:
"Abu 'Abd Allah, *'Alayhi al-Salam,* has said, 'When you slaughter an animal, do not tie down all the legs, do not push the knife under the throat and veins then turn it to cut upward. You must allow the bird to remain loose especially, but if it falls in a well or a hole, then do not use it for food or feed; you do not know if the fall has killed it or slaughtering. If it is a sheep, then hold it by its fur or wool

and do not hold its legs. In the case of cows tie down the front legs and leave the tail. In the case of camels tie down its hoofs to its armpit and leave its legs. If a bird turns loose when you want to slaughter it and escapes and flies away, you can shoot it down with your arrow, if it falls down it then is like hunting.'"

H 11054, Ch. 3, h 5

Muhammad ibn Yahya has narrated from Ahmad ibn Muhammad from al-Hassan ibn Mahbub from al-'Ala' ibn Razin from Muhammad ibn Muslim who has said the following:

"I once asked abu Ja'far, *'Alayhi al-Salam,* about slaughtering. He (the Imam) said, 'You must turn the animal to be slaughtered toward al-Qiblah (al-Ka'bah) and do not cut its spinal cord before it dies. You must not use for food what is not properly slaughtered from the proper place.'"

H 11055, Ch. 3, h 6

Abu Ali al-Ash'ariy has narrated from Muhammad ibn 'Abd al-Jabbar from Safwan from ibn Muskan from Muhammad al-Halabiy who has said the following:

"Abu 'Abd Allah, *'Alayhi al-Salam,* has said, 'Do not cut off the spinal cord of the animal you slaughter before it dies; and when it dies, then you can cut off its spinal cord.'"

H 11056, Ch. 3, h 7

Muhammad ibn Yahya has narrated from Ahmad ibn Muhammad from Muhammad ibn Yahya from Ghiyath ibn Ibrahim who has said the following:

"Abu 'Abd Allah, *'Alayhi al-Salam,* has said that 'Amir al-Mu'minin has said, 'Do not slaughter a sheep near another sheep or a camel near another camel when it is looking to the one being slaughtered.'"

H 11057, Ch. 3, h 8

Muhammad ibn Yahya has narrated from in a *marfu'* manner the following:

"Abu al-Hassan, al-Rida', *'Alayhi al-Salam,* has said, 'When you slaughter a sheep and remove its skin or a certain part of its skin before it dies, it then is not lawful to use it for food.'"

Chapter 4 - The Case of a Man who Wants to Slaughter an Animal and the Knife by Mistake Cuts off the Head

H 11058, Ch. 4, h 1

Ali ibn Ibrahim has narrated from his father from ibn abu 'Umayr from 'Umar ibn 'Udhaynah from al-Fudayl ibn Yasar who has said the following:

"I once asked abu Ja'far, *'Alayhi al-Salam,* about the case of a man who slaughters an animal but by mistake the knife cuts off its head before it dies. He (the Imam) said, 'It is a fast slaughtering and it is not unlawful to use it for food.'"

H 11059, Ch. 4, h 2

Ali ibn Ibrahim has narrated from his father from Hammad ibn 'Isa from Hariz from Muhammad ibn Muslim who has said the following:

"I once asked abu Ja'far, *'Alayhi al-Salam,* about the case of a Muslim man who slaughters a sheep and mentions the name of Allah but because of sharpness of the knife he cuts off the head. He (the Imam) said, 'If blood has come out you can use it for food.'"

H, Ch. 4, h 3

Ali ibn Ibrahim has narrated from (his father from) Harun ibn Muslim from Mas'adah ibn Sadaqah who has said the following:

"I once heard abu 'Abd Allah, *'Alayhi al-Salam,* saying, when a man asked him about slaughtering an animal but the knife moves fast and the head is cutoff, 'It is a fast slaughtering, it is not unlawful to use it for food if it is not intentional.'"

Chapter 5 - The Camel and Bull Resist Slaughtering

H, Ch. 5, h 1

Muhammad ibn Yahya has narrated from Ahmad ibn Muhammad from al-Husayn ibn Sa'id, from al-Qasim ibn Muhammad from Ali ibn abu Hamzah from abu Basir who has said the following:

"Abu 'Abd Allah, *'Alayhi al-Salam,* has stated this *Hadith.* 'A camel may resist slaughtering when you want Nahr (manner of slaughtering camels) it. If it turns loose and you are afraid of its acting faster than you and you hit it with a sword or spear after mentioning the name of Allah, you can use it for food, unless you can control it while still alive, in which case you must slaughter it properly.'"

H 11060, Ch. 5, h 2

Ali ibn Ibrahim has narrated from his father from Safwan from 'Is ibn al-Qasim who has said the following:

"Abu 'Abd Allah, *'Alayhi al-Salam,* has said that once in al-Kufah a bull revolted and broke loose. People rushed with their swords and beat it down. They asked `Amir al-Mu'minin, *'Alayhi al-Salam,* about it and he (the Imam) said, 'It is a fast slaughtering but its flesh is lawful for food.'"

H 11061, Ch. 5, h 3

Abu Ali al-Ash'ariy has narrated from Muhammad ibn 'Abd al-Jabbar and Muhammad ibn `Isma'il has narrated from al-Fadl ibn Shadhan from ibn Muskan from Muhammad al-Halabiy who has said the following:

"About the case of a bull that broke loose and people rushed with their swords and beat it down, abu 'Abd Allah, *'Alayhi al-Salam,* has said, 'They asked `Amir al-Mu'minin, *'Alayhi al-Salam,* about it and he (the Imam) said, 'It is a fast slaughtering but its flesh is lawful for food.'"

H 11062, Ch. 5, h 4

Muhammad ibn Yahya has narrated from 'Abd Allah ibn Muhammad from Ali ibn al-Hakam from Aban 'Uthman from Ali has narrated from his father from-Fadl ibn 'Abd al-Malik and 'Abd al-Rahman ibn abu 'Abd Allah who has said the following:

"Abu 'Abd Allah, *'Alayhi al-Salam,* has said that certain people once came to the Holy Prophet, *O Allah, grant compensation to Muhammad and his family worthy of their services to Your cause,* and said that their cow became difficult with them and they had only to subdue it with their sword. He (the Messenger of Allah) commanded them to use it for food.'"

H 11063, Ch. 5, h 5

Humayd ibn Ziyad has narrated from al-Hassan ibn Muhammad ibn Sama'ah from Ahmad ibn al-Hassan al-Mithamiy from Aban from 'Isma'il al-Ju'fiy who has said the following:

"I once asked abu 'Abd Allah, *'Alayhi al-Salam,* about the case of a camel that falls in a well and about how to Nahr (manner of slaughtering camels) it. He (the Imam) said, 'You can use weapons for Nahr and mention the name of Allah; then you can use it for food.'"

Chapter 6 - The Case of an Animal Slaughtered from a Part other than the Proper Place

H 11064, Ch. 6, h 1

Ali ibn Ibrahim has narrated from his father from ibn abu 'Umayr from Hammad from al-Halabiy who has said the following:

"It is the case of a man who hits a camel or sheep with his sword, with a mention of the name of Allah, in a part which is not for slaughtering. Abu 'Abd Allah, *'Alayhi al-Salam,* has said, 'The flesh of an animal slaughtered from a part which is not for slaughtering is not useable for food if it is done intentionally, and it is not a case of emergency. However, if it is an emergency and it becomes difficult to slaughter him then it is not unlawful.'"

Chapter 7 - How Proper Slaughtering is Achieved

H 11065, Ch. 7, h 1

Muhammad ibn Yahya has narrated from 'Abd Allah ibn Muhammad ibn 'Isa from Ali ibn al-Hakam from Aban 'Uthman from 'Abd Allah ibn Sulayman who has said the following:

"Abu 'Abd Allah, *'Alayhi al-Salam,* has said that it is in the book of Ali, *'Alayhi al-Salam,* that if the eyes move or the leg runs or the tail moves and you can achieve such opportunity, you then must slaughter it.'"

H 11066, Ch. 7, h 2

Muhammad ibn Yahya has narrated from Ahmad ibn Muhammad from Ali ibn al-Hakam from Salim al-Farra' from al-Hassan ibn Muslim who has said the following:

"Once I was with abu 'Abd Allah, *'Alayhi al-Salam,* when Muhammad ibn 'Abd al-Salam came. I said, 'I pray to Allah to keep my soul in service for your cause. My grandfather asks you about the case of a man who has hit a cow with a hammer and it has fallen down, then he has slaughtered it.' He (the Imam) did not send the answer but he (the Imam) called Sa'idah, a slave-girl of 'Umm Farwah and said to her, 'Muhammad came to me with a letter from you but I disliked to send the answer with him. In the case of the man who has slaughtered the cow, when slaughtering if blood has come out normally you can use it for food and feed, but if its coming is heavy, then do not go close to it.'"

H 11067, Ch. 7, h 3

Al-Husayn from Muhammad has narrated from Mu'alla' ibn Muhammad from Aban from 'Abd al-Rahman ibn abu 'Abd Allah who has said the following:

"Abu 'Abd Allah, *'Alayhi al-Salam,* has said that it is in the book of Ali, *'Alayhi al-Salam,* that if the eye turns or the leg runs or the tail moves, then slaughtering properly is achieved.'"

H 11068, Ch. 7, h 4

A number of our people have narrated from Sahl ibn Ziyad ibn abu Najran from Muthanna' al-Hannat from Aban ibn Taghlib who has said the following:

"Abu 'Abd Allah, *'Alayhi al-Salam,* has said that in a doubtful condition about a sheep being alive or dead, see if its eyes turn, or its ears move or its tail moves, then slaughter it, it is lawful for food.'"

H 11069, Ch. 7, h 5

Abu Ali al-Ash'ariy has narrated from Muhammad ibn 'Abd al-Jabbar from Safwan ibn Yahya from ibn Muskan from Muhammad al-Halabiy who has said the following:

"I once asked abu 'Abd Allah, *'Alayhi al-Salam,* about slaughtering. He (the Imam) said, 'If the animal moves its tail or turns its eyes or moves its ears, it then is clean and properly slaughtered.'"

H 11070, Ch. 7, h 6

A number of our people have narrated from Sahl ibn Ziyad from ibn abu Nasr from Rifa'ah who has said the following:

"Abu 'Abd Allah, *'Alayhi al-Salam,* has said, 'If a sheep turns its eyes or moves its tail, it then is clean and properly slaughtered.'"

Chapter 8 - The Case of an Animal Slaughtered without Facing al-Qiblah (al-Ka'bah), Mentioning the name of Allah or one after Sexual Intercourse Slaughters

H 11071, Ch. 8, h 1

Ali ibn Ibrahim has narrated from his father from ibn abu 'Umayr from 'Umar ibn 'Udhaynah from Muhammad ibn Muslim who has said the following:

"I once asked abu Ja'far, *'Alayhi al-Salam,* about the case of a man who slaughters an animal but does not know about making it to face al-Qiblah (al-Ka'bah). He (the Imam) said, 'You can use it for food.' I then said, 'He has not made it to face al-Qiblah (al-Ka'bah).' He (the Imam) said, 'Do not use it for food and so also is the case with that on which the name of Allah, most Majestic, most Glorious, is not mentioned.' He (the Imam) said, 'When you want to slaughter make it (the animal) to face al-Qiblah (al-Ka'bah).'"

H 11072, Ch. 8, h 2

Muhammad ibn Yahya has narrated from Ahmad ibn Muhammad from al-Hassan ibn Mahbub from al-'Ala' ibn Razin from Muhammad ibn Muslim who has said the following:

"I once asked abu Ja'far, *'Alayhi al-Salam,* about the case of a man who slaughters but does not mention the name of Allah. He (the Imam) said, 'If it is because of forgetfulness, it is not unlawful if he is a Muslim, knows slaughtering properly, and does not cut off the spinal cord and the neck after slaughtering.'"

H 11073, Ch. 8, h 3

Ali ibn Ibrahim has narrated from his father from ibn abu 'Umayr from Hammad from al-Halabiy who has said the following:

"Once abu 'Abd Allah, *'Alayhi al-Salam,* was asked about an animal which is slaughtered facing a direction other than al-Qiblah (al-Ka'bah). He (the Imam) said, 'It is not unlawful if it is not intentional.' He (the Imam) was asked about a man who forgets to mention the name of Allah; if it can be used for food. He (the Imam) said, 'Yes, it can be used for food if he is not accused of (unreliability), who before was able to slaughter properly, does not cutoff the spinal cord and does not break the neck until the animal slaughtered becomes cold.'"

H 11074, Ch. 8, h 4

Ali ibn Ibrahim has narrated from his father from Hammad ibn 'Isa from Hariz from Muhammad ibn Muslim who has said the following:

"I once asked abu 'Abd Allah, *'Alayhi al-Salam,* about an animal which is slaughtered facing a direction other than al-Qiblah (al-Ka'bah). He (the Imam) said, 'It is not unlawful if it is not intentional.' I then asked about a man who slaughters an animal without mentioning the name of Allah. He (the Imam) said, 'If it is because of forgetfulness, he can mention the name of Allah when he remembers and say, 'I begin with the name of Allah at the beginning and at the end.'"

H 11075, Ch. 8, h 5

Muhammad ibn Yahya has narrated from Ahmad ibn Muhammad from al-Hassan ibn Mahbub from al-'Ala' ibn Razin from Muhammad ibn Muslim who has said the following:

"I once asked him (the Imam), *'Alayhi al-Salam,* about the case of a man who slaughters an animal but he says Tasbih (Allah is free of all defects) or Takbir (Allah is great beyond description) or Tahlil, (no one deserves worship except Allah) or Tahmid, (all praise belongs to Allah). He (the Imam) said, 'All these are names of Allah, most Majestic, most Glorious, and are not harmful.'"

H 11076, Ch. , h 6

Ali ibn Ibrahim has narrated from his father from ibn abu 'Umayr from certain persons of his people who has said the following:

"Abu 'Abd Allah, *'Alayhi al-Salam,* has said, 'It is not unlawful if a person after sexual intercourse and before Ghusl (bath) slaughters an animal.'"

Chapter 9 - The Unborn Young that is Found inside the Animal Slaughtered

H 11077, Ch. 9, h 1

Ali ibn Ibrahim has narrated from his father from ibn abu 'Umayr from 'Umar ibn 'Udhaynah from Muhammad ibn Muslim who has said the following:

"I once asked one of the two Imam, (abu Ja'far or abu 'Abd Allah), *'Alayhim al-Salam,* about the words of Allah, most Majestic, most Glorious, 'He has made lawful for you the pitch-black animals for food.' (5:2) He (the Imam) said, 'It means the young in the womb of the mother when it grows hair or wool, thus, proper slaughtering for it is the proper slaughtering of the mother and that is to which the words of Allah refer.'"

H 11078, Ch. 9, h 2

Ali ibn Ibrahim has narrated from his father from ibn abu 'Umayr from Hammad from al-Halabiy who has said the following:

"Abu 'Abd Allah, *'Alayhi al-Salam,* has said, 'If you slaughter an animal and find inside its young in a complete form, you can use it for food but if it is not complete then do not use it for food.'"

H 11079, Ch. 9, h 3
Abu Ali al-Ash'ariy has narrated from Muhammad ibn 'Abd al-Jabbar from Muhammad ibn 'Isma'il from Ali ibn al-Nu'man from Ya'qub ibn who has said the following:
"I once asked abu 'Abd Allah, *'Alayhi al-Salam*, about the young of camel when the mother is slaughtered; if it can also be used for food because its mother is slaughtered. He (the Imam) said, 'If it is formed completely and hairs or its fur has grown, then you can use it for food.'"

A number of our people have narrated from Sahl ibn Ziyad from Ahmad ibn Muhammad ibn abu Nasr from Dawud ibn al-Haseen from Ya'qub ibn Shu'ayb from abu 'Abd Allah, *'Alayhi al-Salam*, a similar *Hadith*.

H 11080, Ch. 9, h 4
A number of our people have narrated from Ahmad ibn Muhammad ibn Khalid from 'Uthman ibn 'Isa from Sama'ah who has said the following:
"I once asked him (the Imam), *'Alayhi al-Salam*, about a sheep which is slaughtered and its young, which has grown its wool, is found inside. He (the Imam) said, 'Slaughtering for it is the slaughtering of its mother.'"

H 11081, Ch. 9, h 5
Ali ibn Ibrahim has narrated from (his father) from Harun ibn Muslim from Mas'adah ibn Sadaqah who has said the following:
"About the case of a young found inside an animal which is slaughtered, abu 'Abd Allah, *'Alayhi al-Salam*, has said, 'You can use it for food if it has grown hairs, otherwise, do not use it for food, that is, if it has not grown any hairs.'"

Chapter 10 - Slaughtering of Animals butted by other Animals Fall or Eaten by Predators

H 11082, Ch. 10, h 1
Al-Husayn from Muhammad has narrated from Mu'alla' ibn Muhammad from al-Washsha' who has said the following:
"Abu al-Hassan, *'Alayhi al-Salam*, would say, 'If you arrive in time (when it still is alive) to slaughter an animal butted by other animals, fallen from height or eaten by predators, you can use it for food.'"

H 11083, Ch. 10, h 2
Muhammad ibn Yahya has narrated from Ahmad ibn Muhammad from Ali ibn al-Hakam from Ali ibn abu Hamzah from abu Basir who has said the following:
"Abu 'Abd Allah, *'Alayhi al-Salam*, has said, 'Do not use for food an animal eaten by predator, injured because of fall of something on it or fallen from height, unless you arrive in time (when it is still alive) to slaughter it properly.'"

Chapter 11 - Blood that Falls in the Cooking Pot

H 11084, Ch. 11, h 1

Abu Ali al-Ash'ariy has narrated from Muhammad ibn 'Abd al-Jabbar from Muhammad ibn 'Isma'il from Ali ibn al-Nu'man from Sa'id al-A'raj who has said the following:

"I once asked abu 'Abd Allah, *'Alayhi al-Salam,* about a cooking pot with camel's meat in it being cooked and an amount of blood equal to an Awqiyah (one ounce) falls; if the content of the pot can be used for food. He (the Imam) said, 'Yes, because fire eats the blood.'"

Chapter 12 - The Time in which Slaughtering is not Desirable

H 11085, Ch. 12, h 1

Muhammad ibn Yahya has narrated from Muhammad ibn Musa from al-'Abbas ibn Ma'ruf from Marwak ibn 'Ubayd from certain persons of our people from 'Abd Allah ibn Muskan from Muhammad al-Halabiy who has said the following:

"Abu 'Abd Allah, *'Alayhi al-Salam,* has said that the Messenger of Allah, *O Allah, grant compensation to Muhammad and his family worthy of their services to Your cause,* disliked slaughtering (animals) and spilling blood on Fridays before *Salat* (prayer) except in the case of an emergency.'"

H 11086, Ch. 12, h 2

A number of our people have narrated from Sahl ibn Ziyad from Muhammad ibn Ali from Muhammad ibn 'Amr from Jamil ibn Darraj from Aban ibn Taghlib who has said the following:

Abu 'Abd Allah, *'Alayhi al-Salam,* has said that Ali ibn al-Husayn, would command his servants not to slaughter any animal before dawn on Friday. This *Hadith* is of rare Ahadith about Fridays.'"

H 11087, Ch. 12, h 3

Ali ibn 'Isma'il has narrated from m ibn 'Amr from Jamil ibn Darraj from Aban ibn Taghlib who has said the following:

"I once heard Ali ibn al-Husayn, *'Alayhim al-Salam,* saying to his servants (slaves), 'Do not slaughter any animal before it is dawn because Allah has made the night for everything to rest.' I then asked him (the Imam) saying, 'I pray to Allah to keep my soul in service for your cause, what happens if we are afraid?' He (the Imam) then said, 'If you are afraid of death then you can slaughter.'"

Chapter 13 - Another Chapter on the above Issue

H 11088, Ch. 13, h 1

Ali ibn Ibrahim has narrated from his father from ibn abu 'Umayr from Hammad from al-Halabiy who has said the following:

"I once asked abu 'Abd Allah, *'Alayhi al-Salam,* about an animal slaughtered by a person of al-Murji'ah people or al-Harawriy people. He (the Imam) said, 'You can use it for food, remain determined and firm until it happens what has to happen (reappearance of al-Mahdi with divine authority and power).'"

H 11089, Ch. 13, h 2

Ali ibn Ibrahim has narrated from his father from ibn abu 'Umayr from 'Umar ibn 'Udhaynah from al-Fudayl, Zurarah, and Muhammad ibn Muslim who have said the following:

"They had asked abu Ja'far, *'Alayhi al-Salam,* about the meat from the market place about which one does not know what the butchers do. He (the Imam), *'Alayhi al-Salam,* said, 'You can use it for food if it is in the market place of Muslims and do not ask about it.'"

Chapter 14 - The Case of Animal Slaughtered by Children, Women and a Blind Person

H 11090, Ch. 14, h 1

Ali ibn Ibrahim has narrated from his father from Hammad from al-Halabiy, from Hariz from Muhammad ibn Muslim who has said the following:

"I once asked abu 'Abd Allah, *'Alayhi al-Salam,* about an animal slaughtered by a child. He (the Imam) said, 'It is acceptable if the child is intelligent, five shibr (a certain unit of measurement) in height and able to use the knife.' About women he (the Imam) said, 'If they are all women and no men among them, then the one most intelligent must slaughter and mention the name of Allah on the animal to be slaughtered.'"

H 11091, Ch. 14, h 2

Ali ibn Ibrahim has narrated Harun ibn Muslim from Mas'adah ibn Sadaqah who has said the following:

"Once abu 'Abd Allah, *'Alayhi al-Salam,* was asked about the animal slaughtered by a boy. He (the Imam) said, 'If he is strong enough, slaughters properly and mentions the name of Allah on it, you can use it for food.' He (the Imam) was asked about women's slaughtering. He (the Imam) said, 'If she is Muslimah and has mentioned the name of Allah, you can use it for food.'"

H 11092, Ch. 14, h 3

Ali ibn Ibrahim has narrated from his father from ibn abu 'Umayr from Hisham ibn Salim from Sulayman ibn Khalid who has said the following:

"I once asked abu 'Abd Allah, *'Alayhi al-Salam,* about the slaughtering by a boy and women if it can be used for food. He (the Imam) said, 'If she is Muslimah and has mentioned the name of Allah, most Majestic, most Glorious, on the animal to be slaughtered, then what she has slaughtered is lawful and so also is the boy if he is strong enough, has mentioned the name of Allah, most Majestic, most Glorious, on the animal he has slaughtered. This is when there is fear for losing the animal to be slaughtered and there is no one else other then these people.'"

H 11093, Ch. 14, h 4

Muhammad ibn Yahya has narrated from Ahmad ibn Muhammad from certain persons of his people who have said the following:

"Once, al-Marzuban asked al-Rida', *'Alayhi al-Salam,* about animal slaughtered by a child who is not mature yet, and the slaughtering by women. He (the Imam) said, 'It is not unlawful to use for food what is slaughtered by castrated people, a child and a woman if they slaughter it properly and mention the name of Allah, if they are compelled to do so in an emergency.'"

H 11094, Ch. 14, h 5

Ali ibn Ibrahim has narrated from his father from ibn abu 'Umayr from 'Umar ibn 'Udhaynah from more than one person who has said the following:

"One of the two Imam, (abu Ja'far or abu 'Abd Allah), *'Alayhi al-Salam,* has said, 'If a woman slaughters an animal properly and mentions the name of Allah, then it is not unlawful to use it for food and so also is slaughtering by a blind person if he is helped in what he needs.'"

H 11095, Ch. 14, h 6

Muhammad ibn Yahya has narrated from Ahmad ibn Muhammad from al-Husayn ibn Sa'id from Ibrahim ibn abu al-Balad who has said the following:

"I once asked abu 'Abd Allah, *'Alayhi al-Salam,* about an animal slaughtered by a castrated person. He (the Imam) said, 'It is not unlawful to use it for food.'"

H 11096, Ch. 14, h 7

Ali ibn Ibrahim has narrated from his father from ibn abu 'Umayr from Hammad from al-Halabiy who has said the following:

"Abu 'Abd Allah, *'Alayhi al-Salam,* has said that Ali ibn al-Husayn, *'Alayhi al-Salam,* had a slave-girl who would slaughter animals if he (the Imam) wanted.'"

H 11097, Ch. 14, h 8

Al-Husayn from Muhammad has narrated from Mu'alla' ibn Muhammad from al-Washsha' from Aban ibn 'Uthman from 'Abd al-Rahman ibn abu 'Abd Allah who has said the following:

"Abu 'Abd Allah, *'Alayhi al-Salam,* has said, 'When a child grows five Ashbar (span of the hand) it is not unlawful to use for food what he has slaughtered.'"

Chapter 15 - Slaughtering by the People of the Book

H 11098, Ch. 15, h 1

Ali ibn Ibrahim has narrated from his father from 'Amr ibn 'Uthman from Mufaddal ibn Salih from Zayd al-Shahham who has said the following:

"Once abu 'Abd Allah, *'Alayhi al-Salam,* was asked about the slaughtering of the taxpayers (who are non-Muslims). He (the Imam) said, 'Do not use it for food even if he has mentioned the name of Allah or not.'"

H 11099, Ch. 15, h 2

Muhammad ibn Yahya has narrated from Ahmad ibn Muhammad from Muhammad ibn 'Isma'il from Hanan ibn Sadir from al--Husayn ibn al--Mundhir who has said the following:

"I once said to abu 'Abd Allah, *'Alayhi al-Salam,* that we often meet a people from the mountains, the distance between us is quite far to the mountains by many Farsakh (a certain unit of measurement for distance). We buy one, two or three flocks and every flock numbers one thousand five hundred, one thousand six hundred or one thousand seven hundred sheep. Then two or three sheep are cut (killed) and we ask the shepherd about their religion. They say that they are Christians. What do you say about the slaughtering by Jews and Christians? He (the Imam) said, 'O al-Husayn, 'Slaughtering is by name and no one can be trusted in this matter except people who believe in the Oneness of Allah.'"

H 11100, Ch. 15, h 3

It is narrated from the narrator of the previous *Hadith* from Hanan who has said the following:

"I once said to abu 'Abd Allah, *'Alayhi al-Salam,* 'Al-Husayn ibn al-Mundhir has narrated from you that you have said, "Slaughtering is by name and you cannot trust for it in (slaughtering) except the people of the name."' He (the Imam) said, 'They have invented in it something that I do not like.' Hanan has said, 'I asked a Christian about what they say when slaughtering.' He said, 'We say, "In the name of al-Masih."'"

H 11101, Ch. 15, h 4

A number of our people have narrated from Sahl ibn Ziyad from Ahmad ibn abu Nasr from al-'Ala' ibn Razin from Muhammad ibn Muslim who has said the following:

"I once asked abu Ja'far, *'Alayhi al-Salam,* if animal slaughtered by the Christian Arabs can be used for food. He (the Imam) said, 'Ali ibn al-Husayn, *'Alayhi al-Salam,* would prohibit using what they slaughtered for food, as well as their hunting and marriage with them.'"

H 11102, Ch. 15, h 5

Muhammad ibn Yahya has narrated from Ahmad ibn Muhammad from Ali ibn al-Hakam from abu al-Mighra' from Sama'ah who has said the following:

"I once asked abu Ibrahim, *'Alayhi al-Salam,* about the animals slaughtered by the Jews and Christians. He (the Imam) said, 'Do not go close to such slaughtered animals.'"

H 11103, Ch. 15, h 6

Muhammad ibn Yahya has narrated from Ahmad ibn Muhammad from al-Husayn ibn Sa'id from Hammad ibn 'Isa from al-Husayn ibn al-Mukhtar from al-Husayn ibn 'Abd Allah who has said the following:

"I once said to abu 'Abd Allah, *'Alayhi al-Salam,* 'We go to the mountains and send the shepherds to look after the sheep. Perhaps a sheep becomes injured and they slaughter it; if we can use it for food. He (the Imam) said, 'It is a matter of proper slaughtering, thus, no one can be trusted in it except a Muslim.'"

H 11104, Ch. 15, h 7

It is narrated from the narrator of the previous *Hadith* from Hammad ibn 'Isa from al-Husayn ibn al-Mukhtar from al-Husayn ibn 'Abd Allah who has said the following:

"At one time I travelled with al-Mu'alla' ibn Khunays and ibn abu Ya'fur. One of them used the flesh of the animal slaughtered by Jews and Christians and the other abstained. They both went to visit abu 'Abd Allah, *'Alayhi al-Salam,* and informed him of their story. He (the Imam) asked, 'Which one of you abstained?' He (one of them) said, 'I abstained.' He (the Imam) said, 'You have done the right thing.'"

H 11105, Ch. 15, h 8

Ali ibn Ibrahim has narrated from his father from ibn abu 'Umayr from al-Husayn al-Ahmasiy who has said the following:

"Once a man said to 'Abd Allah, *'Alayhi al-Salam,* 'I pray to Allah to keep you well, we have a neighbor who is a butcher and he brings Jews who slaughter for him so that Jews can buy from him.' He (the Imam) said, 'Do not use for food what he sells and do not buy from him.'"

H 11106, Ch. 15, h 9

Ibn abu 'Umayr has narrated from al-Husayn al-Ahmasiy who has said the following:

"Abu 'Abd Allah, *'Alayhi al-Salam,* has said, 'It is a matter of the name (mentioning the name of Allah), thus, no one can be trusted in it except a Muslim.'"

H 11107, Ch. 15, h 10

Abu Ali al-Ash'ariy has narrated from Muhammad ibn 'Abd al-Jabbar from Muhammad ibn 'Isma'il from Ali ibn al-Nu'man from ibn Muskan from Qutaybah al-A'sha' who has said the following:

"A man once asked abu 'Abd Allah, *'Alayhi al-Salam,* when I was with him (the Imam) and said, 'Sheep are sent to Jews and Christian for maintenance and something happens and it is slaughtered; if I can use it for food. Abu 'Abd Allah, *'Alayhi al-Salam,* has said, 'Do not mix the price you receive for it with your other assets and do not use it for food. It is a matter of name (mentioning the name of Allah) and no one can be trusted in it except a Muslim.' A man then said, 'Allah, most High, says, 'Today We have made the good things lawful for you and the food of the people of the book is lawful for you.' (5:5) Abu 'Abd Allah, *'Alayhi al-Salam,* then said to him, 'My father, *'Alayhi al-Salam,* would say that it is about grains and similar things.'"

H 11108, Ch. 15, h 11

A number of our people have narrated from Sahl ibn Ziyad from Ya'qub ibn Yazid from Muhammad ibn Sinan from 'Isma'il ibn Jabir and 'Abd Allah ibn Talhah. Ibn Sinan has said that 'Isma'il ibn Jabir has said, the following:

"Abu 'Abd Allah, *'Alayhi al-Salam,* has said, 'Do not use for food what is slaughtered by Jews and Christians and do not eat in their utensils.'"

H 11109, Ch. 15, h 12

It is narrated from the narrator of the previous *Hadith* from ibn Sinan from Qutaybah al-A'sha' who has said the following:

"I once asked abu 'Abd Allah, *'Alayhi al-Salam,* about the animals slaughtered by Jews and Christians. He (the Imam) said, 'Slaughtering is a matter of name (mentioning the name of Allah); no one can be trusted in it except a Muslim.'"

H 11110, Ch. 15, h 13

Muhammad ibn Yahya has narrated from Ahmad ibn Muhammad from Muhammad ibn Sinan from 'Isma'il from Jabir who has said the following:

"Abu 'Abd Allah, *'Alayhi al-Salam,* has said, 'Do not use for food the animals they slaughter, do not eat in their utensils, meaning thereby people of the book.'"

H 11111, Ch. 15, h 14

Ali ibn Ibrahim has narrated from his father from 'Isma'il ibn Marrar from Yunus from Mu'awiyah ibn Wahab who has said the following:

"I once asked abu 'Abd Allah, *'Alayhi al-Salam,* about the animals slaughtered by the people of the book. He (the Imam) said, 'It is not unlawful if they mention the name of Allah, most Majestic, most Glorious, and I mean those of them who are on the command of Moses and Jesus.'"

H 11112, Ch. 15, h 15

Ali ibn Ibrahim has narrated from his father from Hanan ibn Sadir who has said the following:

"Once my father and I visited abu 'Abd Allah, *'Alayhi al-Salam,* and said, 'We pray to Allah to keep our souls in service for your cause, we have Christian associates and they slaughter for us chickens and goats; if we can eat thereof. He (the Imam) said, 'Do not eat and do not get close to it; what they say on it is something because of which I do not like if you to eat thereof.' He (the narrator) has said, when we arrived in al-Kufah certain ones of them invited us and we declined their invitation. He asked about the reason saying, 'You were coming to us and now you have refused.' We replied, 'Our scholar, *'Alayhi al-Salam,* prohibited and he thinks that you say something on what you slaughter because of which he does not like that we eat thereof.' He then asked, 'Who is your scholar? He by Allah, is the most knowledgeable of all people and more knowledgeable than what Allah has created. He has spoken the truth by Allah. We say, 'In the name of al-Masih, *'Alayhi al-Salam.*'"

H 11113, Ch. 15, h 16

Ali ibn Ibrahim has narrated from his father from ibn abu 'Umayr from certain persons of his people who has said the following:

"I once asked abu 'Abd Allah, *'Alayhi al-Salam,* about the animals the people of the book slaughter. He (the Imam) said, 'By Allah they do not eat what you slaughter; then how can you consider what they slaughter as lawful? It is a matter of name (mentioning the name of Allah), and no one can be trusted in it except a Muslim.'"

H 11114, Ch. 15, h 17

Certain persons of our people have narrated from Mansur ibn al-'Abbas from 'Amr ibn 'Uthman from Qutaybah al-A'sha' who has said the following:

"I once saw a man with abu 'Abd Allah, *'Alayhi al-Salam,* who asked, 'I have a brother in the mountains who exchanges things for other things. He (the Imam) asked, 'Is it because of mutual agreement?' he replied, 'Yes, that is true.' He (the Imam) said, 'It then is not unlawful.' He then said, 'He may have an agent who is a Jew or Christians who comes across something that sells slaughtered and brings its price, or salt it then brings it salted.' He (the Imam) said, 'He must not eat it. It is a matter of name (mentioning the name of Allah) in which no one can be trusted except a Muslim.' A certain person present said, 'What about the words of Allah, most Majestic, most Glorious, ". . . the food of the people of the book is lawful for you and your food is lawful for them.' He (the Imam) said, 'My father, *'Alayhi al-Salam,* would say that it is grains and similar things.'"

End of the Book of Slaughtering followed by the Book of Food. All praise belongs to Allah, Cherisher of the worlds.

Part Five:
The Book of Food

Chapter 1 - Reason for Unlawfulness

H 11115, Ch. 1, h 1

A number of our people have narrated from Sahl ibn Ziyad, Ali ibn Ibrahim has narrated from his father all, from 'Amr ibn 'Uthman from Muhammad ibn 'Abd Allah, from certain persons of our people from abu 'Abd Allah, *'Alayhi al-Salam.* A number of our people have narrated from Ahmad ibn Muhammad ibn Khalid from Muhammad ibn Aslam from 'Abd al-Rahman ibn Salim from Mufaddal ibn 'Umar who has said the following:

"I once asked abu 'Abd Allah, *'Alayhi al-Salam,* saying, 'I pray to Allah to keep my soul in service for your cause, why has Allah, most Blessed, most High, made wine, dead animals, blood and the flesh of pigs unlawful?' He (the Imam) said, 'Allah, who is free of all defects, the most High has not made such things unlawful for His servants and made certain things lawful for them because of His interest in what He has made unlawful and His dislike of what He has made lawful for them. In fact He created the creatures and He, most Majestic, most Glorious, knew what their bodies needed and what was beneficial for them; so He made such things lawful for them as a favor to them from Him, most Blessed, most High, for their well being. He knew what was harmful to them, so He prohibited them and made it unlawful to them but then He made lawful for those compelled and in the times when their bodies could not survive without it so He commanded to use it for the bare necessities and not more.'

"He (the Imam) said, 'The dead animals are unlawful; no one must use it every now and then because it weakens their bodies, makes it thin and his power goes away, his offspring become cutoff and those who eat dead bodies die suddenly.

"Blood is unlawful because eating it causes yellow fluid, bad breath, foul smell, bad moral behavior and causes an illness similar to madness, hardheartedness, lack of kindness and sympathy so much so that one may murder his children, and parents, and he cannot be trusted about his best friends and his companions.

"The flesh of pigs is unlawful because Allah, most Blessed, most High, metamorphosed certain people in different shapes such as pigs, apes and bears and others. He then prohibited eating such things, it is a kind of cannibalism, so people must not take advantage of such things and must not take consequent suffering lightly.

"Wine is made unlawful because of its bad effects and damages it may cause. He (the Imam) then said, 'One who often uses wine is like a worshipper of idols, it causes tremors, takes away the light (beauty), abolishes kindness, carries him to excessive boldness against the relatives like bloodshed and fornication. He, when drunk cannot be trusted and he may disregard his sanctity when failing to understand. Drinking wine does not increase anything to one except what is worse and evil.'"

Chapter 2 - Comprehensive Chapter on Animals that are not Edible

H 11116, Ch. 2, h 1

Al-Husayn from Muhammad has narrated from Mu'alla' ibn Muhammad from Bistam ibn Murrah from Ishaq ibn Hassan from Haytham ibn Waqid from Ali ibn al-Hassan al-'Abdiy from abu Harun from abu Sa'id al-Khudriy who was asked about the following:

"Abu Harun once asked abu Sa'id al-Khudriy, 'What do you say about this fish that our brothers in al-Kufah use for food, is it unlawful?' Abu Sa'id said, 'I heard the Messenger of Allah, *O Allah, grant compensation to Muhammad and his family worthy of their services to Your cause,* saying, "Al-Kufah is the skull and the spear of Allah, most Blessed, most High, and the mine of faith, thus you must accept from them. I can inform you that the Messenger of Allah stayed in Makkah one day and one night hungry. Then he went out and I went with him (the Messenger of Allah). We passed by a group of friends who were eating lunch. They said, 'O Messenger of Allah, join us for lunch.' He (the Messenger of Allah) said, 'Yes, make room for your Prophet.' He (the Messenger of Allah) sat between two men and I also sat down. He (the Messenger of Allah) took a loaf and made it into two portions, then he (the Messenger of Allah) looked at their curry and asked, 'What your curry is made of?' They replied, 'It is made of eel, O Messenger of Allah.' He (the Messenger of Allah) threw the piece of bread from his hand and left. Abu Sa'id has said, 'I stayed behind to find out people's opinion. People differed. One group said that the Messenger of Allah has made it (eel) unlawful. The other group said, 'He (the Messenger of Allah) did not make it unlawful but just left, had he made it unlawful he would have prohibitted eating it.' He (abu Sa'id) has said, 'I memorized what they had said and followed running to join the Messenger of Allah, then we met a group of friends eating lunch; and they asked, 'O Messenger of Allah, join us for lunch.' He (the Messenger of Allah) said, 'Yes, make room for your Prophet.' He (the Messenger of Allah) sat between two men and I also sat with him. When he took a piece of bread and looked at their curry, then asked, 'What your curry is made of?' They replied, 'It is made of lizard, O Messenger of Allah.' He (the Messenger of Allah) threw the piece of bread from his hand and left. Abu Sa'id has said, 'I stayed behind and people differed. They were two groups. One group said, 'The Messenger of Allah has made it unlawful and for this reason, he (the Messenger of Allah) did not eat.' The other group said, 'He (the Messenger of Allah) just left. Had he made it unlawful he would have prohibited us from eating.' I then followed the Messenger of Allah until I joined him and we passed by the foot of al-Safa' where cooking pots were boiling. They said, 'O Messenger of Allah if you can wait until our cooking pots are ready.' He (the Messenger of Allah) asked them, 'What is in your cooking pots?' They replied, 'Our donkeys that we used to ride, have failed to move so we slaughtered them.' The Messenger of Allah went close and turned the cooking pots with his foot, then he (the Messenger of Allah) left fast. I stayed behind and certain ones of them said, 'The Messenger of Allah has made the flesh of donkeys unlawful' and others said, 'No, he did not do so. He only emptied out your cooking pots so that you never slaughter your stumpers.' Abu Sa'id has said that the Messenger of Allah sent for me and when I arrived in his presence he (the Messenger of Allah) said. 'Call for me Bilal.' When I brought Bilal in, he (the Messenger of Allah) said, 'O Bilal climb on abu Qubays hill and announce that the Messenger of Allah has declared, eel, lizard and domestic donkeys unlawful for food. So have fear of Allah, most Majestic, most Glorious, and do not eat of fish except what has peels and the peels have scales, because Allah, most Blessed, most High, has metamorphosed seven hundred nations who had disobeyed the executors of wills after the messengers. Four hundred of them remained on land and three hundred of them went in the sea', then he read this verse. '. . . We turned their existence into ancient tales by making them disintegrate totally.' (34:19)"

(The above *Hadith* is from 'Ammah narrators and its style is very different from those of the Khassah narrators).

H 11117, Ch. 2, h 2
Ali ibn Ibrahim has narrated from his father from ibn Mahbub from Dawud ibn Farqad who has said the following:
"Abu 'Abd Allah, *'Alayhi al-Salam,* has said, 'Of the beasts that which have canine teeth and of birds those which have claws are not lawful for food.'"

H 11118, Ch. 2, h 3
Ali ibn Ibrahim has narrated from his father from ibn abu 'Umayr from Hammad from al-Halabiy who has said the following:
"Abu 'Abd Allah, *'Alayhi al-Salam,* has said that the Messenger of Allah, *O Allah, grant compensation to Muhammad and his family worthy of their services to Your cause,* has said, 'Of the beasts that which have canine teeth and of birds that which have claws are not lawful for food.' He (the Imam) has said, 'Do not use any of the beasts for food.'"

H 11119, Ch. 2, h 4
Ali ibn Ibrahim has narrated from his father from 'Amr ibn 'Uthman from al-Husayn ibn Khalid who has said the following:
"I once asked abu al-Hassan, Musa ibn Ja'far, *'Alayhi al-Salam,* about the flesh of elephants. He (the Imam) said, 'No, it is not lawful for food.' I then asked, 'Why is it so?' He (the Imam) said, 'It has deformities and Allah, most Majestic, most Glorious, has made what is metamorphosed unlawful for food as well as the flesh of what is deformed in its shape.'"

H 11120, Ch. 2, h 5
Ali ibn Ibrahim has narrated from his father from ibn abu 'Umayr from Hammad from al-Halabiy who has said the following:
"I once asked abu 'Abd Allah, *'Alayhi al-Salam,* about eating lizards. He (the Imam) said, 'Lizards, rats, apes and pigs are metamorphosed.'"

H 11121, Ch. 2, h 6
A number of our people have narrated from Sahl ibn Ziyad from ibn abu Najran from 'Asem ibn Hamid from abu Sahl al-Qarashiy who has said the following:
"I once asked abu 'Abd Allah, *'Alayhi al-Salam,* about the flesh of dogs. He (the

Imam) said, 'It is metamorphosed.' I asked, 'Is it unlawful for food?' He (the Imam) said, 'It is *Najis* (unclean). I repeat it three times for you and each one says it is Najis (unclean).'"

H 11122, Ch. 2, h 7

Muhammad ibn Yahya has narrated from Ahmad ibn Muhammad from Muhammad ibn Yahya from Ghiyath ibn Ibrahim who has said the following:

"Abu 'Abd Allah, *'Alayhi al-Salam,* disliked using poisonous things for food.'"

H 11123, Ch. 2, h 8

Muhammad ibn Yahya has narrated from al-'Amrakiy ibn Ali from Ali ibn Ja'far from his brother abu al-Hassan, *'Alayhi al-Salam,* who has said the following:

"I once asked abu al-Hassan, *'Alayhi al-Salam,* about using crows of several colors and black ones, for food. He (the Imam) said, 'None of the crows are lawful for food, *zagh* or others.'"

H 11124, Ch. 2, h 9

A number of our people have narrated from Ahmad ibn Muhammad ibn Khalid from Bakr ibn Salih from Sulayman ibn Ja'far who has said the following:

"I once asked abu al-Hassan, al-Rida', *'Alayhi al-Salam,* about peacock. He (the Imam) said, 'It is not lawful to use it or its eggs for food.'"

H 11125, Ch. 2, h 10

Ali ibn Ibrahim has narrated from his father from ibn abu 'Umayr from 'Umar ibn 'Udhaynah from Muhammad ibn Muslim and Zurarah who have said the following:

"We once asked abu Ja'far, *'Alayhi al-Salam,* about using domestic donkeys for food. He (the Imam) said, 'The Messenger of Allah, *O Allah, grant compensation to Muhammad and his family worthy of their services to Your cause,* prohibited it on the day of Khaybar. He (the Messenger of Allah) did so on that day because people used it for transportation. Unlawful is what Allah, most Majestic, most Glorious, has made unlawful in the Quran.'"

H 11126, Ch. 2, h 11

Muhammad ibn Yahya has narrated from Ahmad ibn Muhammad from Muhammad ibn Sinan from abu al-Jarud who has said the following:

"I once heard abu Ja'far, *'Alayhi al-Salam,* saying, 'Muslims during the days of Khaybar faced difficulties and they rushed their stumpers. The Messenger of Allah, *O Allah, grant compensation to Muhammad and his family worthy of their services to Your cause,* commanded that the cooking pots must be emptied (of cooking donkey flesh) and did not say it is unlawful for food. It was to preserve stumpers.'"

H 11127, Ch. 2, h 12

Muhammad ibn Yahya has narrated from Ahmad ibn Muhammad from Ali ibn al-Hakam from Aban Taghlib from the one who narrated to him who has said the following:

"I once asked abu 'Abd Allah, *'Alayhi al-Salam,* about the flesh of horses. He (the Imam) said, 'Do not use it for food unless it is a matter of necessity, as well as the flesh of the domestic donkeys. He (the Imam) said, 'It is in the book of Ali, *'Alayhi al-Salam,* that he (the Imam) prohibited using it for food.'"

H 11128, Ch. 2, h 13

Abu Ali al-Ash'ariy has narrated from Muhammad ibn 'Abd al-Jabbar from Safwan from ibn Muskan who has said the following:

"I once asked abu 'Abd Allah, *'Alayhi al-Salam,* about the flesh of donkeys. He (the Imam) said, 'The Messenger of Allah, *O Allah, grant compensation to Muhammad and his family worthy of their services to Your cause,* prohibited using it for food on the day of Khaybar.' I asked him (the Imam) about using horses and mules for food. He (the Imam) said, 'The Messenger of Allah has prohibited using them for food, so do not use them for food unless it is due to necessity and you are compelled.'"

H 11129, Ch. 2, h 14

Muhammad ibn Yahya has narrated from Ahmad ibn Muhammad from Muhammad ibn al-Hassan al-Ash'ariy who has said the following:

"Abu al-Hassan, al-Rida', *'Alayhi al-Salam,* has said, 'The Elephant is metamorphosed, he was a king who fornicated. The wolf is metamorphosed. He was an A'rabi and a pimp. The Fox is metamorphosed. She was a woman who cheated her husband and would not take Ghusl (bath) because of her *Hayd* (menses). The Bat is metamorphosed. He stole people's dates. The apes and pigs were from people of banu Israel who transgressed on *Sabat.* Eel and lizard are from a group of banu Israel who did not believe in the table sent for Jesus, son of Mary *'Alayhi al-Salam.* They strayed, one group fell in the sea and one group remained on land. The Rat is metamorphosed; it is the indecent woman. The scorpion is metamorphosed. It was a taleteller. The bear is metamorphosed and the wasp was a butcher who stole from the balance.'"

H 11130, Ch. 2, h 15

Muhammad ibn Yahya has narrated from Ahmad ibn Muhammad from Muhammad ibn Muslim from abu Yahya al-Wasitiy who has said the following:

"Al-Rida', *'Alayhi al-Salam,* was asked about the crow of several colors; if it can be use for food. He (the Imam) said, 'Who is he that has made the black lawful for you for food?'"

H 11131, Ch. 2, h 16

A number of our people have narrated from Ahmad ibn Muhammad from Bakr ibn Salih from Sulayman al-Ja'fariy who has said the following:

"Abu al-Hassan, al-Rida', *'Alayhi al-Salam,* has said, 'The Peacock is metamorphosed. He was a beautiful man. He treated with disregard the woman of a believing man. The woman loved him and he fell on her, then continued and was metamorphosed by Allah, most Majestic, most Glorious, in the form of male and female. It is not edible, in the form of flesh or its eggs.'"

Chapter 3 - Another Chapter; Signs of Edible and Inedible Birds

H 11132, Ch. 3, h 1

Ali ibn Ibrahim has narrated from his father from ibn Mahbub from Sama'ah ibn Mehran who has said the following:

"I once asked abu 'Abd Allah, *'Alayhi al-Salam,* about edible birds and beasts (animals). He (the Imam) said, 'The Messenger of Allah, *O Allah, grant compensation to Muhammad and his family worthy of their services to Your cause,* prohibited using for food of every bird that has claws and beast that has canine teeth.' He (the Imam) said, 'O Sama'ah, all beasts are inedible; even if it is a beast that does not have canine teeth. The Messenger of Allah has mentioned canine teeth for explanation. Allah, most Majestic, most Glorious, and His Messenger prohibited all metamorphosed animals. From the birds on land you can use for food that which has craw, and from the sea birds that which has gizzard like the gizzard of pigeons; not stomach like the stomach of human beings. Every bird which flies straight and has claws is not edible, and so also are the straight fliers like falcons and hawks and *al-Hida'ah* (a bird that hunts rats) and similar birds that flap their wings in flight and have craws or gizzard which defines every edible bird that cannot be distinguished from its flight and the unknown ones.'"

H 11133, Ch. 3, h 2

Muhammad ibn Yahya has narrated from Ahmad ibn Muhammad from ibn abu Ibn abu Najran from 'Abd Allah ibn Sinan who has said the following:

"I once asked abu 'Abd Allah, *'Alayhi al-Salam,* about what is edible of birds. He (the Imam) said, 'None of them is edible unless it has a craw.'"

H 11134, Ch. 3, h 3

Ali ibn Ibrahim has narrated from his father from ibn abu 'Umayr from Ali al-Zayyat (Ali ibn Ri'ab) from Zurarah who has said the following:

"I swear by Allah that I have never seen anyone like abu Ja'far, *'Alayhi al-Salam.* I once, said to him (the Imam), 'I pray to Allah to keep you well, what is edible of birds?' He (the Imam) said, 'You can use for food all that flap their wings in flight, and do not eat what keeps its wings straight in flight.' I then asked about eggs. He (the Imam) said, 'All eggs with ends of similar shapes are not edible and those that have their ends of different shapes are edible.' I then asked about the birds of water. He (the Imam) said, 'All that have gizzards are edible and that which have no gizzard are not edible.'"

H 11135, Ch. 3, h 4

Ali ibn Ibrahim has narrated from his father from Harun ibn Muslim from Mas'adah ibn Sadaqah who has said the following:

"Abu 'Abd Allah, *'Alayhi al-Salam,* has said, 'Of birds you can eat that which has gizzard and no claws.' I then asked about birds in water and he (the Imam) said a similar thing.'"

H 11136, Ch. 3, h 5

A number of our people have narrated from Sahl ibn Ziyad from ibn Faddal from ibn Bukayr who has said the following:

"Abu 'Abd Allah, *'Alayhi al-Salam,* has said, 'Of birds you can eat whatever has gizzard or spur of the rooster or craws.'"

H 11137, Ch. 3, h 6

Certain persons of our people have narrated from ibn Jumhur from Muhammad ibn al-Qasim from 'Abd Allah ibn abu Ya'fur who has said the following:

"I once asked abu 'Abd Allah, *'Alayhi al-Salam,* about birds that I find in wilderness and about which is edible. He (the Imam) said, 'All birds that flap their wings in flight are edible and all birds that keep their wings straight in flight are not edible.' 'What happens if they are brought to me already slaughtered?' He (the Imam) said, 'Eat whatever has craws.'"

Chapter 4 - Signs of Edible and Inedible Eggs

H 11138, Ch. 4, h 1

A number of our people have narrated from Sahl ibn Ziyad from Ahmad ibn Muhammad from ibn abu Nasr from al-'Ala' from Muhammad ibn Muslim who has said the following:

"I once asked one of the two Imam, (abu Ja'far or abu 'Abd Allah), *'Alayhim al-Salam,* about the eggs that I may find in the wilderness. He (the Imam) said, 'Do not eat unless the shape of its both ends is different.'"

H 11139, Ch. 4, h 2

Ali ibn Ibrahim has narrated from his father from ibn abu 'Umayr from Ali ibn al-Zayyat (Ali ibn Ri'ab) from Zurarah who has said the following:

"I once asked abu Ja'far, *'Alayhi al-Salam,* about the eggs that I may find in the wilderness. He (the Imam) said, 'Do not eat whatever has its both ends of the same shape and eat that which has the ends of different shapes.'"

H 11140, Ch. 4, h 3

It is narrated from the narrator of the previous *Hadith* from his father from ibn abu 'Umayr from 'Umar ibn 'Udhaynah Zurarah from abu al-Khattab who has said the following:

"I once asked abu 'Abd Allah, *'Alayhi al-Salam,* about the case of a man who enters the wilderness and finds different eggs which he does not know from what kind of birds they are; if it is of birds that are undesirable or of the desirable ones. He (the Imam) said, 'There is knowledge in it which is not unclear. If you look at each egg you can find which end is the head and which end is the bottom in which case you can eat; but if you cannot distinguish the shape of one end from the other, then leave it.'"

H 11141, Ch. 4, h 4

Ali ibn Ibrahim has narrated from Harun ibn Muslim from Mas'adah ibn Sadaqah who has said the following:

"I once heard abu 'Abd Allah, *'Alayhi al-Salam,* saying, 'If both ends of an egg are not of the same shape you then can use it for food.' He (the Imam) said, 'If it is of the eggs of the birds of water like the eggs of chicken with one end wider, otherwise, do not use it for food.'"

H 11142, Ch. 4, h 5

Certain persons of our people have narrated from Ahmad ibn Jumhur from Muhammad ibn al-Qasim from ibn abu Ya'fur who has said the following:

"I once asked abu 'Abd Allah, *'Alayhi al-Salam,* about the eggs that I may find in the wilderness and about which ones are edible. He (the Imam) said, 'Eat whatever is of different shapes at both ends.'"

Chapter 5 - Lamb and Young Goats Fed with the Milk of Pigs

H 11143, Ch. 5, h 1
Ali ibn Ibrahim has narrated from his father from Hanan ibn Sadir who has said the following:
"Once abu 'Abd Allah, *'Alayhi al-Salam,* was asked, when I was with him (the Imam) about the young goat fed with milk from pigs until it grew up and became of strong bones; then a man used it for impregnating the flock of his sheep and young were produced. He (the Imam) said, 'If you can find out its offspring exactly, then do not get close to it; but you can use for food those that you cannot recognize because it is like cheese; and do not ask about it.'"

H 11144, Ch. 5, h 2
Humayd ibn Ziyad has narrated from 'Abd Allah ibn Ahmad al-Nuhaykiy from ibn abu 'Umayr from Bishr ibn Muslimah who has said the following:
"About the case of a young goat that is fed with the milk of a pig and it is used to impregnate the flock of sheep, abu al-Hassan, al-Rida', *'Alayhi al-Salam,* has said, 'It is like cheese. If you recognize its offspring exactly, then do not eat; but you can eat if you cannot recognize it.'"

H 11145, Ch. 5, h 3
Muhammad ibn Yahya has narrated from Ahmad ibn Muhammad from al-Washsha' from 'Abd Allah ibn Sinan from abu Hamzah in a *marfu'* manner has said the following:
"He (the Imam), *'Alayhi al-Salam,* do not use for food the flesh of a lamb which is fed with the milk of a pig.'"

H 11146, Ch. 5, h 4
A number of our people have narrated from Ahmad ibn Muhammad from who has said the following:
"I once wrote to him (the Imam), *'Alayhi al-Salam,* saying, 'I pray to Allah to keep my soul in service for your cause against all evil, a woman has breastfed a young she-goat and weaned it. It grew up and gave birth. Is it permissible to use its milk and flesh for food?' He (the Imam) wrote back saying, 'It is an undesirable act but it is not unlawful.'"

H 11147, Ch. 5, h 5
Ali ibn Ibrahim has narrated from his father from al-Nawfaliy from al-Sakuniy who has said the following:
"Abu 'Abd Allah, *'Alayhi al-Salam,* has said that 'Amir al-Mu'minin was asked about a lamb that was fed with the milk of a pig. He (the Imam) said, 'You must quarantine it and feed it animal feed, oil residue, nuts, barley and bread, if it is independent of milk; but if it is not independent of milk then feed it with milk of a sheep for seven days, then it can be used for food.'"

Chapter 6 - Flesh of Animals that Feed on Human Feces, their Eggs and the Sheep that Drinks Wine

H 11148, Ch. 6, h 1
Muhammad ibn Yahya has narrated from Ahmad ibn Muhammad from Ali ibn al-Hakam from Hisham ibn Salim from abu Hamzah who has said the following:

"Abu 'Abd Allah, *'Alayhi al-Salam,* has said, 'Do not eat the flesh of animals that feed on human feces, and if their perspiration comes in contact with you, wash it clean."

H 11149, Ch. 6, h 2

Ali ibn Ibrahim has narrated from his father from ibn abu 'Umayr from Hafs ibn al-Bakhtariy who has said the following:

"Abu 'Abd Allah, *'Alayhi al-Salam,* has said, 'Do not drink the milk of camels that feed on human feces; and if their perspiration comes in contact with you, wash it clean.'"

H 11150, Ch. 6, h 3

Ali ibn Ibrahim has narrated from his father from al-Nawfaliy from al-Sakuniy who has said the following:

"Abu 'Abd Allah, *'Alayhi al-Salam,* has stated this *Hadith.* `Amir al-Mu'minin has said, "If a chicken feeds on human feces, it cannot be used for food until it is quarantined for three days. 'If it is a duck, quarantine time is five days, for a sheep for ten days, for a cow twenty days and for a camel it is forty days.'"

H 11151, Ch. 6, h 4

Muhammad ibn Yahya has narrated from Ahmad ibn Muhammad from ibn Faddal from abu Jamilah from Zayd al-Shahham who has said the following:

"Abu 'Abd Allah, *'Alayhi al-Salam,* has said, 'If a sheep drinks wine until it is drunk, then is slaughtered in that condition, the contents of its inside are not edible.'"

H 11152, Ch. 6, h 5

Muhammad ibn Yahya has narrated from Muhammad ibn Ahmad from certain persons of our people from Ali ibn Hassa'n from Ali ibn 'Uqbah from Musa ibn 'Ukayl from certain persons of our people who has said the following:

"About the case of a sheep that drinks urine, then is slaughtered, abu Ja'far, *'Alayhi al-Salam,* has said, 'The contents of its inside must be washed clean, then it is not unlawful, and also if it eats feces but is not a *Jallal,* which is an animal that has feces as its only feed.'"

H 11153, Ch. 6, h 6

A number of our people have narrated from Sahl ibn Ziyad al-Adamiy from Ya'qub ibn Yazid in a marfu' manner has said the following:

"Abu 'Abd Allah, *'Alayhi al-Salam,* has said, 'A camel that feeds on feces; if you want to *Nahr* (slaughter) it, then keep it in quarantine for forty days; such a cow for thirty days and keep such a sheep for ten days.'"

H 11154, Ch. 6, h 7

Muhammad ibn Yahya has narrated from Ahmad ibn Muhammad from al-Khashshab from Ali ibn Asbat from the one who narrated to him who has narrated the following:

"About animals that feed on feces he (the Imam), *'Alayhi al-Salam,* has said, 'If the feed of an animal is mixed with other feed besides feces, then it is not unlawful to use it for food.'"

201

H 11155, Ch. 6, h 8

Muhammad ibn Yahya has narrated from Ahmad ibn Muhammad from al-Barqiy from Sa'd ibn Sa'd al-Ash'ariy who has said the following:

"I once asked al-Rida', *'Alayhi al-Salam,* about the chickens in a village which move around unrestricted. They may pass by feces freely and eat thereof and about their eggs. He (the Imam) said, 'It is not unlawful.'"

H 11156, Ch. 6, h 9

Al-Husayn from Muhammad al-Sayyariy has narrated from Ahmad ibn al-Fudayl from Yunus who has said the following:

"I once asked al-Rida', *'Alayhi al-Salam,* about the fish that feeds on feces. He (the Imam) said, 'It must be kept in quarantine for a day and a night, such a chicken for three days, such a duck for seven days, a sheep for fourteen days, a cow thirty days and such a camel must be kept in quarantine for forty days before being slaughtered.'"

H 11157, Ch. 6, h 10

Muhammad ibn Yahya has narrated from 'Abd Allah ibn Muhammad from Ali ibn al-Hakam from abu 'Isma'il who has said the following:

"I once asked al-Rida', *'Alayhi al-Salam,* about the eggs of crows. He (the Imam) said, 'Do not eat them.'"

H 11158, Ch. 6, h 11

Humayd ibn Ziyad has narrated from al-Hassan ibn Muhammad ibn Sama'ah from Ahmad ibn al-Hassan al-Mithamiy from Aban ibn 'Uthman from Bassam al=Sayrafiy who has said the following:

"About the case of a camel that feeds on feces, abu Ja'far, *'Alayhi al-Salam,* has said, 'It cannot be used for food or riding for forty days.'"

H 11159, Ch. 6, h 12

A number of our people have narrated from Sahl ibn Ziyad from Muhammad ibn al-Hassan al-Shammun from 'Abd Allah ibn 'Abd al-Rahman from Misma' who has said the following:

"Abu 'Abd Allah, *'Alayhi al-Salam,* has stated this *Hadith.* 'Amir al-Mu'minin has said, 'The milk and flesh of a camel that feeds on feces are not edible until it feeds on clean feed for forty days, such a cow for thirty days, such a sheep for ten days, such a duck for five days and such a chicken must be kept in quarantine for three days.'"

Chapter 7 - Things Inedible in Sheep and other Animals

H 11160, Ch. 7, h 1

Muhammad ibn Yahya has narrated from Muhammad ibn Ahmad from Muhammad ibn 'Isa from 'Ubayd Allah al-Dihqan from Durust from Ibrahim ibn 'Abd al-Hamid who has said the following:

"Abu al-Hassan, al-Rida', *'Alayhi al-Salam,* has said, 'Seven things in sheep are unlawful for food. Of such things is blood, testicles, penis, bladder, glands, spleen and gallbladder.'"

H 11161, Ch. 7, h 2

Muhammad ibn Yahya has narrated from Ahmad ibn Muhammad from abu Yahya al-Wasitiy in a *marfu'* manner has the following:

"'Amir al-Mu'minin, *'Alayhi al-Salam,* once passed by the butchers' market and prohibited the selling of seven items in a sheep. He (the Imam) prohibited the selling of blood, glands, ears of the heart, the spleen, spinal cord, testicles and penis. Certain one of the butchers said, 'O `Amir al-Mu'minin, liver and spleen' are not different. They are the same thing.' 'You suffer from a lack of understanding and what you say is not true' `Amir al-Mu'minin, *'Alayhi al-Salam,* explained and then asked, 'Bring two bowls of water. I will show the difference between the liver and spleen.' Two bowls of water were brought and he (the Imam) said, 'Cut the middle of the liver and cut the middle of the spleen. He (the Imam) then commanded to rub them in the water. After being rubbed in water the liver turned (a little) white but it remained the same and nothing was reduced thereof. The spleen in this process did not turn white but all of its contents came out and turned into blood, all that was left was its skin and its vein. He (the Imam) said, 'This is the difference between the two. This is flesh and this is blood.'"

H 11162, Ch. 7, h 3
A number of our people have narrated from Sahl ibn Ziyad from Ya'qub ibn Yazid from ibn abu 'Umayr from certain persons of our people who has said the following:
"Abu 'Abd Allah, *'Alayhi al-Salam,* has said, 'Ten items in a sheep are not edible. Of such items is dung, blood, spleen, spinal cord, al-'Ilba'(thyroid glands), penis, testicles, al-Haya (female genitals) and gallbladder.'"

H 11163, Ch. 7, h 4
Ali ibn Ibrahim has narrated from his father from `Isma'il ibn Marrar from *'A'immah,* 'Alayhim al-Salam, who has said the following:
"He (the Imam), *'Alayhi al-Salam,* has said, 'In the edible animals like camels, cows, sheep and others certain items are not edible. Of such items are genitals, the apparent and unapparent parts, the penis and testicles, the womb which is the place of the development of the young, the spleen because it is blood, the glands with veins and marrow and that which is in the back, the gallbladder, the eyeball, the gland which is situated near the brain, and blood.'"

H 11164, Ch. 7, h 5
A number of our people have narrated from Sahl ibn Ziyad Muhammad ibn al-Hassan ibn al-Shammun from al-Asamm from Misma' who has said the following:
"Abu 'Abd Allah, *'Alayhi al-Salam,* has said that `Amir al-Mu'minin, *'Alayhi al-Salam,* has said, 'If anyone of you buys meat, he must take out the glands because it accelerates the vein of leprosy.'"

H 11165, Ch. 7, h 6
Sahl ibn Ziyad has narrated from certain persons of our people who have said the following:
"He (the Imam), *'Alayhi al-Salam,* disliked the kidneys and said that they are the collectors of urine.'"

Chapter 8 - The Case of the Tails of Sheep Cut off into two and the Animal Hunted

H 11166, Ch. 8, h 1
A number of our people have narrated from Sahl ibn Ziyad from Ahmad ibn Muhammad from ibn abu Nasr from al-Kahiliy who has said the following:

"Once a man asked abu 'Abd Allah, *'Alayhi al-Salam,* when I was with him (the Imam), about the tails of sheep being cut off. He (the Imam) said, 'It is not unlawful if it serves your interest.' He (the Imam) then said, 'It is in the book of Ali, *'Alayhi al-Salam,* that whatever is cut off from sheep, is dead and must not be used to benefit thereby.'"

H 11167, Ch. 8, h 2
Muhammad ibn Yahya has narrated from Ahmad ibn Muhammad from Ali ibn al-Hakam from Ali ibn abu Hamzah from abu Basir who has said the following:

"Abu 'Abd Allah, *'Alayhi al-Salam,* has said, 'If the tails of sheep are cut off when the sheep is alive, the tail is dead like being slaughtered improperly.'"

H 11168, Ch. 8, h 3
Al-Husayn from Muhammad has narrated from Mu'alla' ibn Muhammad from al-Hassan ibn Ali who has said the following:

"I once asked abu al-Hassan, *'Alayhi al-Salam,* saying, 'I pray to Allah to keep my soul in service for your cause, people who live in the mountains cut off the tails of their sheep because they become very large.' He (the Imam) said, 'It is not lawful (inedible).' I then asked, saying, 'I pray to Allah to keep my soul in service for your cause, can it be used in lamps for lighting during the night? He (the Imam) said, 'You must take notice that it can come in contact with your hand and clothes and it is unlawful.'"

H 11169, Ch. 8, h 4
Muhammad ibn Yahya has narrated from Ahmad ibn Muhammad from Ya'qub ibn Yazid and Yahya ibn Mubarak from 'Abd Allah ibn Jabalah from Ishaq ibn 'Ammar who has said the following:

"About the case of a man who strikes a deer with his sword until it is cut into two: if he can use it for food. He (the Imam) said, 'Yes, he can use it for food, only the piece with the head and leave the tail.'"

H 11170, Ch. 8, h 5
A number of our people have narrated from Ahmad ibn abu 'Abd Allah from his father from 'Abd Allah ibn al-Fadl al-Nawfaliy from his father from certain persons of our people who has said the following:

"I once asked abu 'Abd Allah, *'Alayhi al-Salam,* about my hunting with a flareless arrow and it kills. He (the Imam) said, 'If it is cut into two pieces then throw away the smaller piece and use the larger one for food. If both are equal then use both.'"

H 11171, Ch. 8, h 6
Muhammad ibn Yahya has narrated from Ahmad ibn Muhammad ibn 'Isa from al-Nadr ibn Suwayd from certain persons of our people in a *marfu'* manner the following is narrated:

"About the case of a deer or wild donkey hunted with sword; if it is cut in pieces, he (the Imam) said, 'It is not unlawful to use both pieces for food if one of them is not still moving, but if one piece moves, the other piece then is not edible because it is dead.'"

H 11172, Ch. 8, h 7
Muhammad ibn Yahya has narrated from Ahmad ibn Muhammad from Muhammad ibn Yahya from Ghiyath ibn Ibrahim who has said the following:

"About the case of a man who hunts a prey and cuts it into two pieces, abu 'Abd Allah, *'Alayhi al-Salam,* has said, 'He can use both of them for food but if he cuts a part only he then must not eat what is cut off but he can eat the rest.'"

Chapter 9 - Things that can be Used from a Dead Animal and things that Cannot be Used

H 11173, Ch. 9, h 1
A number of our people have narrated from Ahmad ibn Muhammad, from ibn Khalid from Muhammad ibn Ali from Muhammad ibn al-Fudayl from abu Hamzah al-Thumaliy who has said the following:

"Once I was in the Masjid of the Messenger of Allah, *O Allah, grant compensation to Muhammad and his family worthy of their services to Your cause,* when a man came and offered Salam (the phrase of offering greeting of peace) and asked, 'Who are you, O servant of Allah?' I replied, 'I am a man from al-Kufah.' I then asked, 'What do you need?' He asked, 'Do you know abu Ja'far, Muhammad ibn Ali, *'Alayhi al-Salam?'* I replied, 'Yes, I know him (the Imam). What do you need from him?' He said, 'I have prepared forty questions to ask from him for answers and then what is right and true I will accept, and what is false, leave them alone.' Abu Hamzah has said, 'I then asked him if he was able to distinguish between truth and falsehood.' He replied, 'Yes, I can do so.' I then asked him, 'Why do you need him when you are able to distinguish between truth and falsehood?' He said, 'People of al-Kufah, you are such that one cannot talk to you. If you see abu Ja'far then inform me.' Our conversation was not yet complete that abu Ja'far, *'Alayhi al-Salam,* came with people of Khurasan around him as well as other people asking him questions about the rules of *al-Hajj.* He (the Imam) went to his place and sat down and the man (Qatadah) sat near him (the Imam). Abu Hamzah has said, 'I then sat where I could hear (people) speaking. Around him (the Imam) there was a world (large group) of people. When he (the Imam) completed what the people needed and they left, he (the Imam) turned to the man and asked, 'Who are you?' He replied, 'I am Qatadah ibn al-Da'amah al-Basriy.' Abu Ja'far, *'Alayhi al-Salam,* asked, 'Are you faqih of people of al-Basrah?' He replied, 'Yes, I am their faqih.' Abu Ja'far, *'Alayhi al-Salam,* then said, 'Fie upon you, O Qatadah. You must notice that Allah, most Majestic, most Glorious, has created creatures in His creation and has made them a barrier over His creation, and they are the pillars on His earth, protectors of His commandments, the noble ones in His knowledge whom He had chosen before His creation, while as shadows on the right of His throne.' He (the narrator) has said that Qatadah remained silent for a long time, then said, 'I pray to Allah to keep you well, I have sat before scholars of fiqh and before ibn 'Abbas but my heart did not become nervous before anyone of them as it has become nervous before you.' Abu Ja'far, *'Alayhi al-Salam,* said, 'Fie upon you, do you realize where are sitting? You are before the houses for which Allah has declared to be raised and therein Allah is spoken of. (It happens there) in the mornings and evenings, by men who are not distracted by trade or other forms of business from speaking about Allah, performing *Salat* (prayer) and paying Zakat. You are in such house and we are the people therein.' Qatadah said, 'You have spoken the truth by Allah, I pray to Allah to keep my soul in service for your cause, by Allah they are not houses of stones and clay.' Qatadah then asked, 'Tell me about cheese.' Abu Ja'far, *'Alayhi al-Salam,* smiled then said, 'Have all of your questions ended up to this?' He replied, 'They have become mixed and confusing.' He (the Imam) said, 'It is not unlawful.' He said, 'What happens if perhaps rennet from a dead animal is placed in it?' He (the Imam) said, 'It is not unlawful because rennet does not have any veins and blood or bones. It only comes out of a dead animal from the middle of dung and blood.' He (the Imam) then said, 'Rennet is like an egg that comes out of a dead chicken. Is that egg edible?' Qatadah said, 'No, it is not edible and I do not command anyone to eat it.' Abu Ja'far, *'Alayhi al-Salam,* asked, 'Why do you not eat it?' He replied, 'Because it is dead.' He (the Imam) then asked, 'If that egg is hatched and it becomes a chicken will you eat the chicken?' Qatadah replied, 'Yes, I will do so.' He (the Imam) then asked, 'What is it that makes you to eat the chicken but not the egg from which it has come out?' He (the Imam) then said, 'The same rule applies to rennet which is like the egg. You can buy cheese from the market of Muslims from the hands of those who perform *Salat* (prayer) and do not ask about it, unless someone comes and informs you about it.'"

H 11174, Ch. 9, h 2

Ali ibn Ibrahim has narrated from his father from 'Isma'il ibn Marrar from Yunus from *'A'immah,* 'Alayhim al-Salam, who has said the following:

"'A'immah, *'Alayhim al-Salam,* have said, 'Five advantageous things to people are clean. Of such things, one is rennet, eggs, wool, hairs, and fur and it is not unlawful to eat cheese. All of such things must come from the hands of Muslims or non-Muslims. It is only undesirable to eat them, except rennet, which is in the utensils of Zoroastrian and people of the book, because they do not pay attention to dead animals and wine.'"

H 11175, Ch. 9, h 3

Muhammad ibn Yahya has narrated from Ahmad ibn Muhammad from ibn Faddal from ibn Bukayr from al-Husayn ibn Zurarah who has said the following:

"Once I was with abu 'Abd Allah, *'Alayhi al-Salam,* and my father was asking him (the Imam) questions about milk from a dead animal, eggs from dead chickens and rennet from dead animals. He (the Imam) said, 'All of these things are clean.' He (the narrator) has said, 'I then asked him (the Imam) about the hairs of pigs from which ropes are made and are used to draw water from wells for drinking or wudu.' He (the Imam) said, 'It is not unlawful.' Ali ibn 'Uqbah and Ali ibn al-Husayn ibn Ribat have added saying, 'Hairs and wool, all of it is clean.'

In the *Hadith* of Safwan from al-Husayn ibn Zurarah from abu 'Abd Allah, *'Alayhi al-Salam,* it says that hairs, wool, fur and feathers and all growing things (on the body of animals which is slaughtered properly) but are not dead. He (the narrator) has said, 'I then asked about the egg that comes from a dead chicken. He (the Imam) said, 'You can eat it.'"

H 11176, Ch. 9, h 4

Ali ibn Ibrahim has narrated from his father from Hammad from Hariz who has said the following:

"Abu 'Abd Allah, *'Alayhi al-Salam,* once said to Zurarah and Muhammad ibn Muslim has stated this *Hadith*. 'The milk, that kind of milk which is drawn first, eggs, hairs, wool, horns, teeth, hooves and everything separated from sheep and the stumper is clean but if you take such things after the animal dies then wash it and perform *Salat* (prayer) with it.'"

H 11177, Ch. 9, h 5

Muhammad ibn Yahya has narrated from Ahmad ibn Muhammad from Muhammad ibn Yahya from Ghiyath ibn Ibrahim who has said the following:

"About the case of an egg which comes out of the bottom of a dead chicken, abu 'Abd Allah, *'Alayhi al-Salam,* has said, 'If the egg is covered with its thick crust , then it is not unlawful.'"

H 11178, Ch. 9, h 6

Ali ibn Ibrahim has narrated from al-Mukhtar ibn Muhammad ibn al-Mukhtar and Muhammad ibn al-Hassan from 'Abd Allah ibn al-Hassan al-'Alawiy all from al-Fath ibn Yazid al-Jurjaniy who has said the following:

"I once wrote to abu al-Hassan, *'Alayhi al-Salam,* asking about the skins of dead animals which are of the edible kind if slaughtered properly. He (the Imam) wrote in answer, 'It is not permissible to benefit from the skins of dead animals or sinew (but you can benefit) from items from lambs, like wool even if they are pulled out, hairs, fur and rennet and nothing besides these by the will of Allah.'"

H 11179, Ch. 9, h 7

Muhammad ibn Yahya has narrated from Ahmad ibn Muhammad from ibn Mahbub from 'Asem ibn Hamid from Ali ibn al-Mughirah who has said the following:

"I once said to abu 'Abd Allah, *'Alayhi al-Salam,* 'I pray to Allah to keep my soul in service for your cause, is it permissible to benefit from dead animals?' He (the Imam) said, 'No, it is not permissible.' I then said, 'It is narrated to us from the Messenger of Allah, *O Allah, grant compensation to Muhammad and his family worthy of their services to Your cause,* that he (the Messenger of Allah) passed by a dead sheep and said, "What was wrong with the owners of this sheep? If they could not benefit from its flesh why did they not benefit from its skin?"' He (the Imam) said, 'That sheep belonged to Sawdah daughter of Zam'ah, wife of the Holy Prophet. The sheep was very skinny and weak and its flesh was not useful; so they left it until it died. The Messenger of Allah then said, "What was wrong with the owners of this sheep. If they could not benefit from its flesh why did they not benefit from its skin?"'

Chapter 10 - Unlawful to use for Food the Flesh of Animals Sexually Molested by Human Beings

H 11180, Ch. 10, h 1

A number of our people have narrated from Sahl ibn Ziyad from Muhammad ibn al-Hassan ibn Shammun from 'Abd Allah ibn 'Abd al-Rahman from Misma' who has said the following:

"Abu 'Abd Allah, *'Alayhi al-Salam,* has said that 'Amir al-Mu'minin, *'Alayhi al-Salam,* was asked about an animal sexually molested. 'Amir al-Mu'minin, *'Alayhi al-Salam,* said, 'Its flesh is unlawful for food as well as its milk.'"

Chapter 11 - About the Flesh of a Sexually Active Ram

H 11181, Ch. 11, h 1

Ali ibn Ibrahim has narrated from his father from al-Nawfaliy from al-Sakuniy who has said the following:

"Abu 'Abd Allah, *'Alayhi al-Salam,* has said that the Messenger of Allah, *O Allah, grant compensation to Muhammad and his family worthy of their services to Your cause,* prohibited to use for food the flesh of a sexually active ram.'"

Chapter 12 - Mixing of Dead Animals with Slaughtered Clean

H 11182a, Ch. 12, h 1

Ali ibn Ibrahim has narrated from his father from ibn abu 'Umayr from Hammad from al-Halabiy who has said the following:

"Once abu 'Abd Allah, *'Alayhi al-Salam,* was asked about the case of a man who had sheep and cows and he separated the clean and the dead then they became mixed and about what he should do. He (the Imam) said, 'He can sell it to one who considers dead animals lawful then use what he receives as payment; it is not unlawful.'"

H 11182b, Ch. 12, h 2

Muhammad ibn Yahya has narrated from Ahmad ibn Muhammad from Ali ibn al-Hakam from abu al-Mighra' from al-Halabiy who has said the following:

"I once heard abu 'Abd Allah, *'Alayhi al-Salam,* saying, 'If clean (properly slaughtered) become mixed with the dead ones, one can sell them to one who considers dead animals as lawful and use the payment that one receives.'"

Chapter 13 - Another Chapter on the Above Issue

H 11183, Ch. 13, h 1

Muhammad ibn Yahya has narrated from Ahmad ibn Muhammad ibn 'Isa from Ahmad ibn Muhammad from ibn abu Nasr from 'Isma'il ibn 'Umar from Shu'ayb who has said the following:

"It is about the case of a man who enters a town where he finds a certain amount of meat, but does not know if it is clean (properly slaughtered) or from dead animals. He (the Imam) said, 'He can throw it on fire. If it shrinks it is clean (properly slaughtered) but if expands it is from dead animals.'"

Chapter 14 - The Rat that Dies in Food or Drinks

H 11184, Ch. 14, h 1

Ali ibn Ibrahim has narrated from his father from ibn abu 'Umayr from 'Umar ibn 'Udhaynah from Zurarah who has said the following:

"Abu Ja'far, *'Alayhi al-Salam,* has stated this *Hadith.* 'If a rat falls in ghee and dies in it, if it is solid, it (the rat) then must be thrown away as well as whatever has come in contact with it. If it is fluid you must not use it for food but you can use it for lighting during the night and so also is the case about oil.'"

H 11185, Ch. 14, h 2

Muhammad ibn Yahya has narrated from Ahmad ibn Muhammad from Ali ibn al-Hakam from Mu'awiyah ibn Wahab who has said the following:

"I once asked abu 'Abd Allah, *'Alayhi al-Salam,* about the mouse that dies in ghee or oil or honey. He (the Imam) said, 'In the case of ghee and honey the mouse and whatever has come in contact with it can be taken out; but oil can be used only for lighting during the night.'"

H 11186, Ch. 14, h 3

Abu Ali al-Ash'ariy has narrated from Muhammad ibn 'Abd al-Jabbar from Muhammad ibn `Isma'il from Ali ibn al-Nu'man from Sa'id al-A'raj who has said the following:

"I once asked abu 'Abd Allah, *'Alayhi al-Salam,* about rat or dog that falls in ghee and oil, then it is taken out alive. He (the Imam) said, 'It is not unlawful to use it for food.'"

(In al-Tahdhib by Shaykh there is no mention of dog. It perhaps is a mistake by scribes).

Chapter 15 - Mixing of Lawful Things with others in Something

H 11187, Ch. 15, h 1

Muhammad ibn Yahya has narrated from Ahmad ibn Muhammad from Ahmad ibn al-Hassan ibn Ali from 'Amr ibn Sa'id from Musaddiq ibn Sadaqah from 'Ammar ibn Musa who has said the following:

"Abu 'Abd Allah, *'Alayhi al-Salam,* has said that he was asked about eel and fish on roasting bars on fire. He (the Imam) said, 'Whatever is above the eel can be used for food but not what is below; and if anything has dropped from eel, it must be thrown away.' He (the Imam) said that he was asked about a spleen on roasting bars with meat and underneath there is bread with *al-Judha'b* (a kind of sandwich); if what is below can be used for food. He (the Imam) said, 'Yes, the meat and sandwich can be used for food but the spleen must be thrown away because it has a barrier and nothing drips out of it unless a hole is made in it or a cut, in which case you must not eat the items on which drops have fallen from the spleen.'"

H 11188, Ch. 15, h 2

Ali ibn Ibrahim has narrated from his father from `Isma'il ibn Marrar from Yunus from *'A'immah,* 'Alayhim al-Salam, who have said the following:

"'A'immah, 'Alayhim al-Salam, were asked about a certain amount of wheat on which the fat of pigs has melted. He (the Imam) said, 'If they can wash it they must do so and use it for food;but if they cannot wash it then they can use it as seed to grow a plantation.'"

Chapter 16 - The Food of Taxpayers' Eating with them and their Utensils

H 11189, Ch. 16, h 1

A number of our people have narrated from Ahmad ibn Muhammad from ibn Khalid from 'Uthman ibn 'Isa from Sama'ah who has said the following:

"I once asked abu 'Abd Allah, 'Alayhi al-Salam, about the food of the people of the book and what is lawful for food thereof. He (the Imam) said, 'It is grains.'"

H 11190, Ch. 16, h 2

Muhammad ibn Yahya has narrated from Ahmad ibn Muhammad ibn 'Isa from Muhammad ibn Sinan from 'Ammar ibn Marwan from Sama'ah who has said the following:

"I once asked abu 'Abd Allah, 'Alayhi al-Salam, about the food of the people of the book and what is lawful for food thereof. He (the Imam) said, 'It is grains.'"

H 11191, Ch. 16, h 3

Abu Ali al-Ash'ariy has narrated from Muhammad ibn 'Abd al-Jabbar from Safwan from 'Is ibn al-Qasim who has said the following:

"I once asked abu 'Abd Allah, 'Alayhi al-Salam, about eating with the Jews, Christians and Zoroastrians. He (the Imam) said, 'If the food belongs to you then make wudu (wash) and eat with them; it is not unlawful.'"

H 11192, Ch. 16, h 4

Muhammad ibn Yahya has narrated from Ahmad ibn Muhammad from Ali ibn al-Hakam from 'Abd Allah ibn Yahya al-Kahiliy who has said the following:

"I once asked abu 'Abd Allah, 'Alayhi al-Salam, about the case of a Muslim people who take food and a Zoroastrian man comes to them; if they can invite him for food. He (the Imam) said, 'I do not eat food with Zoroastrians and I dislike making unlawful for you what you do in your lands.'"

H 11193, Ch. 16, h 5

Muhammad ibn Yahya has narrated from Ahmad ibn Muhammad from ibn Mahbub, from al-'Ala' ibn Razin from Muhammad ibn Muslim who has said the following:

"I once asked abu Ja'far, 'Alayhi al-Salam, about the utensils of the non-Muslim taxpayer and Zoroastrians. He (the Imam) said, 'Do not eat in their utensils or from their food which they cook or in the utensils that they use for drinking wine.'"

H 11194, Ch. 16, h 6

Muhammad ibn Yahya has narrated from Ahmad ibn Muhammad from Muhammad ibn Sinan from abu al-Jarud who has said the following:

"I once asked abu 'Abd Allah, 'Alayhi al-Salam, about the words of Allah, most Majestic, most Glorious, 'The food of the people to whom the book was given is lawful for you and your food is lawful for them.' (5:5) He (the Imam) said, 'It is grains and vegetables.'"

H 11195, Ch. 16, h 7
A number of our people have narrated from Ahmad ibn Muhammad from ibn Khalid from Ya'qub ibn Yazid from Ali ibn Ja'far from his brother abu al-Hassan, Musa, *'Alayhi al-Salam,* who has said the following:

"I once asked abu al-Hassan, *'Alayhi al-Salam,* about eating with a Zoroastrian in a bowl and sleeping with him on one furnishing and shaking hands with him. He (the Imam) said, 'No.'"

H 11196, Ch. 16, h 8
It is narrated from the narrator of the previous *Hadith* from 'Isma'il ibn Mehran from Muhammad ibn Ziyad from Harun ibn Kharijah who has said the following:

"I once asked abu 'Abd Allah, *'Alayhi al-Salam,* if I can associate with Zoroastrians and eat from their food. He (the Imam) said, 'No.'"

H 11197, Ch. 16, h 9
Abu Ali al-Ash'ariy has narrated from Muhammad ibn 'Abd al-Jabbar from Safwan ibn Yahya from 'Isma'il ibn Jabir who has said the following:

"I once asked abu 'Abd Allah, *'Alayhi al-Salam,* about the people of the book and what he (the Imam) says about their food. He (the Imam) said, 'Do not eat it.' He (the Imam) then remained quiet then said, 'Do not eat it' He (the Imam) then remained quiet then said, 'Do not eat it and do not leave it. Say that it is unlawful, however, you can leave to abstain thereof because in their utensils there is wine and flesh of pigs.'"

H 11198, Ch. 16, h 10
Muhammad ibn Yahya has narrated from Ahmad ibn Muhammad from Ali ibn al-Hakam from Mu'awiyah ibn Wahab from Zakariya ibn Ibrahim who has said the following:

"I was a Christian, then became a Muslim and said to abu 'Abd Allah, *'Alayhi al-Salam,* 'People of my family are Christians. I live with them in one house and eat in their utensils. He (the Imam) asked, 'Do they eat pork?' I replied, 'No, they do not eat pork.' He (the Imam) said, 'It is not unlawful.'"

Chapter 17 - A Mention of Transgressors and Rebels

H 11199, Ch. 17, h 1
A number of our people have narrated from Sahl ibn Ziyad from Ahmad ibn Muhammad from ibn abu Nasr from those whom he has mentioned who has said the following:

"I once asked abu 'Abd Allah, *'Alayhi al-Salam,* about the words of Allah, most Blessed, most High, 'Those who are compelled without being rebels or transgressors . . .' (2:172) He (the Imam) said, 'A rebel is one who rises against the Imam and a transgressor is one who cuts off the road and dead animals are not lawful for him.'"

Chapter 18 - Eating Clay

H 11200, Ch. 18, h 1
Muhammad ibn Yahya has narrated from Ahmad ibn Muhammad from abu Yahya al-Wasitiy from a man who has said the following:

"Abu 'Abd Allah, *'Alayhi al-Salam,* has said, 'Eating clay is unlawful in its entirety, like the flesh of pork. If one eats it and dies, I will not perform *Salat* (prayer) for him except the clay from the grave (of al-Husayn, *'Alayhi al-Salam*) in which there is cure for all kinds of illnesses but if one eats it because of strong desire, then there is no cure in it.'"

H 11201, Ch. 18, h 2

A number of our people have narrated from Ahmad ibn Muhammad from ibn Khalid from 'Uthman ibn 'Isa from Talhah ibn Zayd who has said the following:

"Abu 'Abd Allah, *'Alayhi al-Salam,* has said, 'Eating clay is of the sources of hypocrisy.'"

H 11202, Ch. 18, h 3

A number of our people have narrated from Sahl ibn Ziyad ibn Mahbub from Ibrahim ibn Mehzam from Talhah ibn Zayd who has said the following:

"Abu 'Abd Allah, *'Alayhi al-Salam,* has said that `Amir al-Mu'minin has said, 'One who continues eating clay has a share in his own murder.'"

H 11203, Ch. 18, h 4

A number of our people have narrated from Ahmad ibn Muhammad from al-Hassan ibn Ali from Hisham ibn Salim who has said the following:

"Abu 'Abd Allah, *'Alayhi al-Salam,* has said that Allah, most Majestic, most Glorious, created Adam from clay and has made it unlawful for his offspring to eat clay.'"

H 11204, Ch. 18, h 5

A number of our people have narrated from Sahl ibn Ziyad from ibn Faddal from ibn al-Qaddah who has said the following:

"About the case of a man who ate clay `Amir al-Mu'minin, *'Alayhi al-Salam,* prohibited and said, 'Do not eat clay; if you eat clay and die, you have helped to murder yourself.'"

H 11205, Ch. 18, h 6

Muhammad ibn Yahya has narrated from Ahmad ibn Muhammad from Ali ibn al-Hakam from `Isma'il ibn Muhammad from his grandfather Ziyad ibn abu Ziyad who has said the following:

"Abu Ja'far, *'Alayhi al-Salam,* has said, 'Wishing and longing is an act of Satan. Eating clay is of the greater part of the hunting devices of Satan. It causes illness in the body and accelerates pain. If one because of eating clay loses his power that he had before eating clay and fails to work as he did before eating clay he will be made to suffer proportionate to the amount of power that he had lost because of eating clay.'"

H 11206, Ch. 18, h 7

Ahmad ibn Muhammad has narrated from Mu'ammar ibn Khallad who has said the following:

"I once asked abu al-Hassan, *'Alayhi al-Salam,* about what people narrate as regards eating clay and that it is undesirable. He (the Imam) said, 'It is clay and chunks of dirt.'"

H 11207, Ch. 18, h 8
Ali ibn Ibrahim has narrated from his father from al-Nawfaliy from al-Sakuniy who has said the following:
"Abu 'Abd Allah, *'Alayhi al-Salam,* has said that the Messenger of Allah, *O Allah, grant compensation to Muhammad and his family worthy of their services to Your cause,* has said, 'If one eats clay and dies he has helped to kill himself.'"

H 11208, Ch. 18, h 9
Ali ibn Muhammad has narrated from certain persons of our people from Ja'far ibn Ibrahim al-Hadramiy from Sa'd ibn Sa'd who has said the following:
"I once asked abu al-Hassan, *'Alayhi al-Salam,* about clay. He (the Imam) said, ' It is unlawful like dead animals, blood, flesh of pigs except the clay from the grave of al-Husayn, *'Alayhi al-Salam,* in which there is cure for all kinds of illness and security from all kinds of fear.'"

Chapter 19 - Eating and drinking in Gold and Silver Utensils

H 11209, Ch. 19, h 1
Al-Husayn from Muhammad has narrated from Mu'alla' ibn Muhammad from al-Washsha' from Dawud ibn Sarhan who has said the following:
"Abu 'Abd Allah, *'Alayhi al-Salam,* has said, 'Do not eat from the utensils of gold and silver.'"

H 11210, Ch. 19, h 2
Muhammad ibn Yahya has narrated from Ahmad ibn Muhammad from Muhammad ibn `Isma'il ibn Bazi' who has said the following:
"I once asked abu al-Hassan, al-Rida', *'Alayhi al-Salam,* about the utensils of gold and silver which he disliked and I then said, 'It is narrated from certain persons of our people that abu al-Hassan, *'Alayhi al-Salam,* had a mirror that had a silver covering.' He (the Imam) said, 'No, all praise belongs to Allah. It had only a ring of silver and it is with me.' He then said, 'When al-'Abbas was circumcised a stick with a silver covering was made for him like things that are made for children. It had about ten dirham of silver and abu al-Hassan, commanded to break it.'"

H 11211, Ch. 19, h 3
Ali ibn Ibrahim has narrated from his father from ibn abu 'Umayr from Hammad from al-Halabiy who has said the following:
"Abu 'Abd Allah, *'Alayhi al-Salam,* has said, 'Do not eat from the utensils of silver or that which is silver-coated.'"

H 11212, Ch. 19, h 4
A number of our people have narrated from Sahl ibn Ziyad, from ibn Mahbub from al-'Ala' ibn Razin from Muhammad ibn Muslim who has said the following:
"Abu Ja'far, *'Alayhi al-Salam,* prohibited the use of utensils of gold and silver.'"

H 11213, Ch. 19, h 5
Muhammad ibn Yahya has narrated from Ahmad ibn Muhammad from ibn Faddal from Tha'labah from Burayd who has said the following:
"Abu 'Abd Allah, *'Alayhi al-Salam,* disliked drinking from silver and silver-

coated utensils as well as silver coated containers of perfumes and combs.'"

H 11214, Ch. 19, h 6
Ali ibn Ibrahim has narrated from Salih ibn al-Sindiy from Ja'far ibn Bashir from 'Amr ibn abu Miqdam who has said the following:
"I saw abu 'Abd Allah, *'Alayhi al-Salam,* when a bowl of water was brought to him (the Imam) in which there was a patch of silver, removing it with his teeth.'"

H 11215, Ch. 19, h 7
A number of our people have narrated from Sahl ibn Ziyad from Ali ibn Hassan from Musa ibn Bakr who has said the following:
"Abu al-Hassan, Musa, *'Alayhi al-Salam,* has said, 'Utensils of gold and silver are of the assets of those who do not have certainty (in the laws of Allah).'"

Chapter 20 - Undesirability of Eating and Drinking on the Table where Wine is Served

H 11216, Ch. 20, h 1
A number of our people have narrated from Ahmad ibn abu 'Abd Allah from Harun ibn al-Jahm who has said the following:
"We were with abu 'Abd Allah, *'Alayhi al-Salam,* in al-Hirah when he (the Imam) visited abu Ja'far, al-Mansur, and one of his commanders had a circumcision feast for his child. Food was prepared and people were invited. Abu 'Abd Allah, *'Alayhi al-Salam,* was one of the people invited. When he was on the table to have food from a group of people near by, a man asked for water but a bowl of wine was brought for him. When the bowl reached the hand of the man abu 'Abd Allah, *'Alayhi al-Salam,* stood up to leave the table. He (the Imam) was asked about the reason for getting up and he (the Imam) said, 'The Messenger of Allah, *O Allah, grant compensation to Muhammad and his family worthy of their services to Your cause,* has said, 'Condemned is one who sits on a table where wine is served.' In another *Hadith* it is said, 'Condemned is he, condemned is he who sits on a table voluntarily where wine is served.'"

H 11217, Ch. 20, h 2
Muhammad ibn Yahya has narrated from Ahmad ibn Muhammad ibn 'Isa, from al-Husayn ibn Sa'id from al-Nadr ibn Suwayd from al-Qasim ibn Sulayman from Jarrah al-Mad'iniy who has said the following:
"Abu 'Abd Allah, *'Alayhi al-Salam,* has said that the Messenger of Allah, *O Allah, grant compensation to Muhammad and his family worthy of their services to Your cause,* has said, 'Whoever believes in Allah and the Day of Judgment, must not eat at a table where wine exists.'"

Chapter 21 - Undesirability of Over-Eating

H 11218, Ch. 21, h 1
Abu Ali al-Ash'ariy has narrated from Muhammad ibn 'Abd al-Jabbar from Muhammad ibn Salim from Ahmad ibn al-Nadr from 'Amr ibn Shamir in a *marfu'* manner has said the following:
"The Messenger of Allah, *O Allah, grant compensation to Muhammad and his*

family worthy of their services to Your cause, once in one of his speeches said, 'After me there will come a year when the believing person will eat (an amount needed) for one stomach and the unbelievers will eat (as if needed) for seven stomachs.'"

H 11219, Ch. 21, h 2
A number of our people have narrated from Sahl ibn Ziyad Muhammad ibn Sinan from ibn Muskan from abu Basir who has said the following:

"Abu 'Abd Allah, *'Alayhi al-Salam,* has said, 'Overeating is undesirable.'"

H 11220, Ch. 21, h 3
Ali ibn Ibrahim has narrated from his father from al-Nawfaliy from al-Sakuniy who has said the following:

"Abu 'Abd Allah, *'Alayhi al-Salam,* has said that the Messenger of Allah, *O Allah, grant compensation to Muhammad and his family worthy of their services to Your cause,* has said, 'The most evil companion for religion is a coward heart, very spacious stomach and intense sexual desire.'"

H 11221, Ch. 21, h 4
Humayd ibn Ziyad has narrated from al-Hassan ibn Muhammad ibn Sama'ah from Wuhayb ibn Hafs from abu Basir who has said the following:

"Abu 'Abd Allah, *'Alayhi al-Salam,* once said to me, 'O abu Muhammad, the stomach becomes excessive in its eating. A servant is nearest to Allah, most Majestic, most Glorious, when his stomach is empty and light. The most hated condition of a servant to Allah, most Majestic, most Glorious, is when his stomach is full.'"

H 11222, Ch. 21, h 5
Ali ibn Ibrahim has narrated from his father from al-Nawfaliy from al-Sakuniy who has said the following:

"Abu 'Abd Allah, *'Alayhi al-Salam,* has stated this *Hadith.* Abu Dharr, *may Allah grant him mercy,* has said, that the Messenger of Allah, *O Allah, grant compensation to Muhammad and his family worthy of their services to Your cause,* has said, 'The one among you with the longest belching will be hungry for the longest time on the Day of Judgment.'"

H 11223, Ch. 21, h 6
Through the same chain of narrators as that of the previous *Hadith* the following is narrated:

'Abu 'Abd Allah, *'Alayhi al-Salam,* has said that the Messenger of Allah, *O Allah, grant compensation to Muhammad and his family worthy of their services to Your cause,* has said, 'When you belch then do not make it loud.'"

H 11224, Ch. 21, h 7
Through the same chain of narrators as that of the previous *Hadith* the following is narrated from A number of our people from Ahmad ibn abu 'Abd Allah from Muhammad ibn 'Isa al-Yaqtiniy from 'Ubayd Allah al-Dihqan from Durust from 'Abd Allah ibn Sinan who has said the following:

"Abu 'Abd Allah, *'Alayhi al-Salam,* has said, 'Eating on a full stomach can cause leprosy (vitiligo).'"

H 11225, Ch. 21, h 8

It is narrated from the narrator of the previous *Hadith* from Muhammad ibn Ali from ibn Sinan from those whom he has mentioned who has said the following:

"Abu 'Abd Allah, *'Alayhi al-Salam,* has said, 'Every illness is because of overeating except, fever (infection) which enters the body.'"

H 11226, Ch. 21, h 9

Muhammad ibn Yahya has narrated from Ahmad ibn Muhammad from ibn Sinan from Salih al-Niliy who has said the following:

"Abu 'Abd Allah, *'Alayhi al-Salam,* has said, 'Allah, most Majestic, most Glorious, hates overeating.' Abu 'Abd Allah, *'Alayhi al-Salam,* has said, 'Children of Adam must eat to keep their backs straight. When one of you eats keep one-third of your stomach for food one-third for water and one-third for breathing and never become fat like pigs to be slaughtered.'"

H 11227, Ch. 21, h 10

Muhammad ibn Yahya has narrated from Ahmad ibn Muhammad from ibn Faddal from ibn Bukayr from certain persons of his people from abu 'Ubaydah who has said the following:

"Abu Ja'far, *'Alayhi al-Salam,* has said, 'When the stomach is full it rebels.'"

H 11228, Ch. 21, h 11

It is narrated from the narrator of the previous *Hadith* from Muhammad ibn Sinan from abu al-Jarud who has said the following:

"Abu Ja'far, *'Alayhi al-Salam,* has said, 'Nothing walks as hated in the sight of Allah, most Majestic, most Glorious, as a full stomach.'"

Chapter 22 - Walking to a Feast without Being Invited

H 11229, Ch. 22, h 1

Ali ibn Ibrahim has narrated from his father from al-Nawfaliy from al-Sakuniy who has said the following:

"Abu 'Abd Allah, *'Alayhi al-Salam,* has said, 'When one of you is invited for food do not allow your children to follow you, because in doing so he eats unlawfully and enters (the house of host) as a usurper.'"

H 11230, Ch. 22, h 2

Muhammad ibn Yahya has narrated from Ahmad ibn Muhammad from ibn abu 'Umayr from al-Husayn ibn Ahmad al-Minqariy from his maternal uncle who has said the following:

"I once heard abu 'Abd Allah, *'Alayhi al-Salam,* saying, 'If one eats a food to which he is not invited he eats a piece of fire.'"

Chapter 23 - Eating when Leaning Against Something

H 11231, Ch. 23, h 1

Al-Husayn from Muhammad has narrated from Mu'alla' ibn Muhammad from al-Washsha' from Aban ibn 'Uthman from Zayd al-Shahham who has said the following:

"Abu 'Abd Allah, *'Alayhi al-Salam,* has said that the Messenger of Allah, *O Allah, grant compensation to Muhammad and his family worthy of their services to Your cause,* never ate while leaning against something from the day Allah, most Majestic, most Glorious, sent him as the Messenger of Allah to the day he passed away. He (the Messenger of Allah) ate like a servant and sat like a servant.' I then asked, 'Why did he do so?' He (the Imam) said, 'He did so to show humbleness before Allah, most Majestic, most Glorious.'"

H 11232, Ch. 23, h 2

Ali ibn Ibrahim has narrated from his father from Safwan from ibn Muskan from al-Hassan al-Sayqal who has said the following:

"I once heard abu 'Abd Allah, *'Alayhi al-Salam*, saying, 'Once an indecent woman passed by the Messenger of Allah, *O Allah, grant compensation to Muhammad and his family worthy of their services to Your cause*, when he was eating while sitting on the ground. She said, 'O Muhammad, you eat like a slave and sit like one.' He (the Messenger of Allah) said to her, 'I am a slave and where is that slave who is a better slave than I am.' She then said, 'Give me a morsel from you food.' He (the Messenger of Allah) gave her a morsel but she said, 'No, by Allah, (I will not accept) until you give from what is in your mouth.' The Messenger of Allah then took the morsel out of his mouth and gave it to her and she ate it.' Abu 'Abd Allah, *'Alayhi al-Salam*, has said that she thereafter was never affected by indecency until she left this world.'"

H 11233, Ch. 23, h 3

Muhammad ibn Yahya has narrated from Ahmad ibn Muhammad from Ali ibn al-Hakam from abu al-Mighra' from Harun ibn Kharijah who has said the following:

"Abu 'Abd Allah, *'Alayhi al-Salam*, has said that the Messenger of Allah, *O Allah, grant compensation to Muhammad and his family worthy of their services to Your cause*, would eat like a slave, sit like one and knew that he was a slave (of Allah).'"

H 11234, Ch. 23, h 4

A number of our people have narrated from Ahmad ibn abu 'Abd Allah from 'Uthman ibn 'Isa from Sama'ah who has said the following:

"I once asked abu 'Abd Allah, *'Alayhi al-Salam*, about the case of a man who eats leaning backward. Abu 'Abd Allah, *'Alayhi al-Salam*, has said, 'No, one must not lean forward also.'"

H 11235, Ch. 23, h 5

Ali ibn Ibrahim has narrated from his father from ibn abu 'Umayr from abu 'Isma'il al-Basriy from al-Fudayl ibn Yasar who has said the following:

"'Abbad al-Basriy was once with abu 'Abd Allah, *'Alayhi al-Salam*, while eating, abu 'Abd Allah, *'Alayhi al-Salam*, placed his hand on the ground. 'Abbad said, 'I pray to Allah to keep you well. Do you not know that the Messenger of Allah prohibited this (manner of sitting).' He (the Imam) raised his hand, ate, and placed his hand on the ground again. 'Abbad said what he had said before. He (the Imam) raised his hand, then ate and placed his hand on the ground again and 'Abbad said what he had said before. Abu 'Abd Allah, *'Alayhi al-Salam*, then said, 'No, by Allah, the Messenger of Allah never prohibited it.'"

H 11236, Ch. 23, h 6

Abu Ali al-Ash'ariy has narrated from Muhammad ibn 'Abd al-Jabbar from Muhammad ibn Salim from Ahmad ibn al-Nadr from 'Amr ibn Shamir from Jabir who has said the following:

"Abu Ja'far, *'Alayhi al-Salam,* has said that the Messenger of Allah, *O Allah, grant compensation to Muhammad and his family worthy of their services to Your cause,* would eat like a slave and sit like one. The Messenger of Allah would eat while sitting on the ground and sleep on the ground.'"

H 11237, Ch. 23, h 7

Al-Husayn from Muhammad has narrated from Mu'alla' ibn Muhammad from al-Hassan ibn Ali from Ahmad ibn 'A'idh from abu Khadijah who has said the following:

"Once Bashir al-Dahhan asked abu 'Abd Allah, *'Alayhi al-Salam,* when I was present, saying, 'Did the Messenger of Allah eat while leaning against something to his right or left?' He (the Imam) said, 'The Messenger of Allah never ate while leaning against something on his right or left, he (the Messenger of Allah) however, sat like slaves.' I then asked, 'Why did he do so?' He (the Imam) said, 'He did so to express humbleness before Allah.'"

H 11238, Ch. 23, h 8

Abu Ali al-Ash'ariy has narrated from Muhammad ibn 'Abd al-Jabbar, from Safwan from Mu'alla' ibn 'Uthman from Mu'alla' ibn Khunayth who has said the following:

"Abu 'Abd Allah, *'Alayhi al-Salam,* has said that the Holy Prophet never ate while leaning against something, from the time Allah, most Majestic, most Glorious, sent him as His Messenger. He (the Messenger of Allah) disliked sitting as kings, but we are not able to do so.'"

H 11239, Ch. 23, h 9

Ali ibn Ibrahim has narrated from his father from ibn abu 'Umayr from Hammad from al-Halabiy ibn abu Sha'bah who has said the following:

"Ibn abu Ayyub informed me that abu 'Abd Allah, *'Alayhi al-Salam,* would eat while sitting in a cross-legged manner. He (the narrator) has said that he saw abu 'Abd Allah, *'Alayhi al-Salam,* ate while leaning. He has said, that he has said, 'The Messenger of Allah never ate while leaning against something.'" [Note: This account appears to be the words of narrators and not the words of the Imam]

H 11240, Ch. 23, h 10

Muhammad ibn Yahya has narrated from Ahmad ibn Muhammad from al-Qasim ibn Yahya from his grandfather al-Hassan ibn Rashid from abu Basir who has said the following:

"Abu 'Abd Allah, *'Alayhi al-Salam,* has stated this *Hadith.* ''Amir al-Mu'minin, *'Alayhi al-Salam,* has said, 'When one of you sits for food, he must sit like slaves and must not place one leg over the other or sit in a cross-legged manner; it is the kind of sitting for which Allah, most Majestic, most Glorious, hates and abhors one who sits in such manner.'"

Chapter 24 - Eating with the Right Hand

H 11241, Ch. 24, h 1

Muhammad ibn Yahya has narrated from Ahmad ibn Muhammad from al-Husayn ibn Sa'id from al-Nadr ibn Suwayd from al-Qasim ibn Sulayman from Jarrah al-Mada'iniy who has said the following:

"Abu 'Abd Allah, *'Alayhi al-Salam,* has said that he dislikes for a man to eat with his left hand or drink with it and take something with it.'"

H 11242, Ch. 24, h 2
Ahmad ibn Muhammad has narrated from al-Husayn, from al-Qasim ibn Muhammad from Ali ibn abu Hamzah from abu Basir who has said the following:
"Abu 'Abd Allah, *'Alayhi al-Salam,* has said, 'Do not eat with your left hand if you can.'"

H 11243, Ch. 24, h 3
A number of our people have narrated from Ahmad ibn abu 'Abd Allah from 'Uthman ibn 'Isa from Sama'ah who has said the following:
"I once asked abu 'Abd Allah, *'Alayhi al-Salam,* about the case of a man who eats or drinks with his left hand. He (the Imam) said, 'He must not eat with his left hand and must not drink with his left hand or lift up anything with it.'"

Chapter 25 - Eating while Walking

H 11244, Ch. 25, h 1
Ali ibn Ibrahim has narrated from his father from al-Nawfaliy from al-Sakuniy who has said the following:
"Abu 'Abd Allah, *'Alayhi al-Salam,* has said that once the Messenger of Allah, *O Allah, grant compensation to Muhammad and his family worthy of their services to Your cause,* came out in the morning with a piece of bread in his hand which he had immersed in milk. He (the Messenger of Allah) walked while eating and Bilal said 'Iqamah for *Salat* (prayer). He (the Messenger of Allah) then performed *Salat* (prayer) with people.'"

H 11245, Ch. 25, h 2
A number of our people have narrated from Ahmad ibn abu 'Abd Allah from his father from the one who narrated to him from 'Abd al-Rahman al-'Arzamiy who has said the following:
"Abu 'Abd Allah, 'Alayhi al-Salam, has said that 'Amir al-Mu'minin has said, 'It is not unlawful if a man eats while walking. The Messenger of Allah, O Allah, grant compensation to Muhammad and his family worthy of their services to Your cause, ate while walking.'"

Chapter 26 - Several Hands Should Come Together for Food

H 11246, Ch. 26, h 1
Muhammad ibn Yahya has narrated from Ahmad ibn Muhammad from Muhammad ibn Yahya from Ghiyath ibn Ibrahim who has said the following:
"Abu 'Abd Allah, *'Alayhi al-Salam,* has said that the Messenger of Allah, *O Allah, grant compensation to Muhammad and his family worthy of their services to Your cause,* has said, 'Food for one is sufficient for two, food for two is sufficient for three and food for three is sufficient for four people.'"

H 11247, Ch. 26, h 2
Ali ibn Ibrahim has narrated from his father from al-Nawfaliy from al-Sakuniy who has said the following:
"Abu 'Abd Allah, *'Alayhi al-Salam,* has stated this *Hadith.* 'The Messenger of Allah, *O Allah, grant compensation to Muhammad and his family worthy of*

their services to Your cause, has said, 'A food with four characteristics is complete, that it is lawful, numerousness of hands on it, mention of the name of Allah on it, and praise of Allah, most Majestic, most Glorious, at its end.'"

Chapter 27 - The Inviolability of Food

H 11248, Ch. 27, h 1

Ali ibn Ibrahim has narrated from his father from ibn Faddal from certain persons of our people who has said the following:

"Abu 'Abd Allah, *'Alayhi al-Salam,* has said, 'Allah, most Majestic, most Glorious, has never made a people to undergo suffering while eating food. Allah, most Majestic, most Glorious, is honorable. He does not give people sustenance, then make them to undergo suffering before they finish eating their food.'"

Chapter 28 - Accepting the Invitation of a Muslim

H 11249, Ch. 28, h 1

Muhammad ibn Yahya has narrated from Ahmad ibn Muhammad from ibn Mahbub from Ibrahim al-Karkhiy who has said the following:

"Abu 'Abd Allah, *'Alayhi al-Salam,* has said that the Messenger of Allah, *O Allah, grant compensation to Muhammad and his family worthy of their services to Your cause,* has said, 'If a believing man invites me for food that consists of only a hand of sheep, I accept it and that is of religion. If an idolater or hypocrite invites me for food that consists of a whole camel, I do not accept and that is of religion. Allah, most Majestic, most Glorious, disdains one's receiving gifts from pagans and hypocrites and their food.'"

H 11250, Ch. 28, h 2

Ahmad ibn Muhammad has narrated from Ali ibn al-Hakam from Muthanna' al-Hannat from Ishaq ibn Yazid who has said the following:

"Abu 'Abd Allah, *'Alayhi al-Salam,* has said, 'It is of the rights of a Muslim on a Muslim to accept his invitation.'"

H 11251, Ch. 28, h 3

Ali ibn Ibrahim has narrated from his father from Hammad ibn 'Isa from Ibrahim ibn 'Umar from Mu'alla' ibn Khunayth who has said the following:

"Abu 'Abd Allah, *'Alayhi al-Salam,* has said, 'It is of obligatory rights of a believer that you accept his invitation.'"

H 11252, Ch. 28, h 4

Muhammad ibn Yahya has narrated from Ahmad ibn Muhammad from al-Hassan ibn Mahbub from ''Amr ibn abu al-Miqdam from Jabir who has said the following:

"Abu Ja'far, *'Alayhi al-Salam,* has said that the Messenger of Allah, *O Allah, grant compensation to Muhammad and his family worthy of their services to Your cause,* advised, 'Those of my followers present must inform those absent to accept the invitation of a Muslim even if it is five miles away, because it is of religion.'"

H 11253, Ch. 28, h 5

Abu Ali al-Ash'ariy has narrated from Muhammad ibn 'Abd al-Jabbar from ibn Faddal from Tha'labah ibn Maymun from 'Abd al-'A'la' Mawla Ale Sam from Mu'alla' ibn Khunayth who has said the following:

"Abu 'Abd Allah, *'Alayhi al-Salam,* has said, 'It is of the obligatory rights of a Muslim on his brother (in faith) to accept his invitation.'"

H 11254, Ch. 28, h 6

Ali ibn Ibrahim has narrated from his father from al-Nawfaliy from al-Sakuniy who has said the following:

"Abu 'Abd Allah, *'Alayhi al-Salam,* has said, 'Accept an invitation for a wedding and circumcision; but do not accept for *Khafd* (lowering) girls.'"

Chapter 29 - Offering Food and Showing Courtesy

H 11255, Ch. 29, h 1

A number of our people have narrated from Ahmad ibn Muhammad from ibn Khalid from Ali ibn Muhammad al-Qashaniy from abu Ayyub Sulayman ibn Muqatil al-Madiniy from Dawud ibn 'Abd Allah ibn Muhammad al-Ja'fariy from his father who has said the following:

"During one of his expeditions, the Messenger of Allah, *O Allah, grant compensation to Muhammad and his family worthy of their services to Your cause,* was performing *Salat* (prayer) when a caravan passed by. They stopped by the companions of the Messenger of Allah and asked them about him (the Messenger of Allah), prayed, praised and said, 'Were we not in a hurry we would have waited for the Messenger of Allah, so convey our Salam (the phrase of offering greeting of peace) to him (the Messenger of Allah); and they left. The Messenger of Allah became angry and said to them, 'A caravan stops by and asks you about me. They ask you to convey their Salam (the phrase of offering greeting of peace) to me but you do not show any courtesy and invite them for food. Had beloved Ja'far been present, he would not send the people away without inviting them for food.'"

H 11256, Ch. 29, h 2

Muhammad ibn Yahya has narrated from Ahmad ibn Muhammad ibn 'Isa from a number of our people who have narrated in a marfu' manner the following:

"Abu 'Abd Allah, *'Alayhi al-Salam,* has said, 'When your brother (in belief) comes to your house, offer him food, if he did not want, then offer him water and if he did not want water offer him wudu (to wash his face or perfume).'"

Chapter 30 - A Man's Finding Comfort in the House of His Brother (in belief)

H 11257, Ch. 30, h 1

Ali ibn Ibrahim has narrated from his father from al-Nawfaliy from al-Sakuniy who has said the following:

"Abu 'Abd Allah, *'Alayhi al-Salam,* has said that the Messenger of Allah, *O Allah, grant compensation to Muhammad and his family worthy of their services to Your cause,* has said, 'Of a man's honoring his brother (in belief) is to accept his gift and present him a gift of what he has and should not overburden himself.' The Messenger of Allah has said, 'I do not like those who overburden and strain themselves.'"

H 11258, Ch. 30, h 2

Ali ibn Ibrahim has narrated from his father from ibn abu 'Umayr from Jamil ibn Darraj who has said the following:

"Abu 'Abd Allah, *'Alayhi al-Salam,* has said, 'A believing man should not behave formally toward his brother (in belief). One will not know which is stranger; the one who overburdens his brother to be formal or the one who behaves unnecessarily formal with his brother (in belief).'"

H 11259, Ch. 30, h 3

Muhammad ibn Yahya has narrated from Muhammad ibn 'Isma'il has narrated from al-Fadl ibn Shadhan from Safwan ibn Yahya who has said the following:

"Once 'Abd Allah ibn Sinan came to me and asked, 'Do you have anything?' I replied, 'Yes, I have something.' I then sent my son and gave him two dirham to buy meat and eggs. He asked, 'Where did you send your son?' I then informed him about it. He said, 'Call him back. Do you have any oil?' I replied, 'Yes, we have oil.' He then said, 'Bring it; I heard abu 'Abd Allah, *'Alayhi al-Salam,* saying, "A man who looks down on what his brother (in belief) brings for him is ruined and so also is one who looks down on what he brings for his brother (in belief)."'"

H 11260, Ch. 30, h 4

Muhammad ibn Yahya has narrated from Ahmad ibn Muhammad from Ali ibn Hadid from Murazim ibn Hakim from the one who has narrated it in a marfu' manner saying the following:

"Harith al-A'war once came to 'Amir al-Mu'minin, *'Alayhi al-Salam,* and said, 'O 'Amir al-Mu'minin, I wish you grant me the honor of having food with me. 'Amir al-Mu'minin, *'Alayhi al-Salam,* said, 'I accept your invitation, provided, that you do not overburden yourself by acting formally'. He (the Imam) went to his house. Harith brought a piece of bread and 'Amir al-Mu'minin began to eat. Al-Harith said, 'I have a few dirham' and he showed them. They were in his sleeves. 'If you give permission I like to buy something for you besides these pieces of bread.' 'Amir al-Mu'minin, *'Alayhi al-Salam,* said, 'This is what is in your house (so it is sufficient).'"

H 11261, Ch. 30, h 5

Muhammad ibn Yahya has narrated from Ahmad ibn Muhammad from ibn Mahbub from 'Abd Allah ibn Sinan who has said the following:

"Abu 'Abd Allah, *'Alayhi al-Salam,* has said, 'A man who looks down on what he has for the guest is ruined.'"

H 11262, Ch. 30, h 6

Ali ibn Ibrahim has narrated from his father from ibn abu 'Umayr from Hisham ibn Salim who has said the following:

"Abu 'Abd Allah, *'Alayhi al-Salam,* has said, 'If your brother (in belief) comes to you, then serve him with whatever you have, but if you invite him then you can act formally (as you like).'"

Chapter 31 - A Man's Eating in the House of his Brother (in belief) without his Permission

H 11263, Ch. 31, h 1
Abu Ali al-Ash'ariy has narrated from Muhammad ibn 'Abd al-Jabbar from Safwan ibn Yahya from 'Abd Allah ibn Muskan from Muhammad al-Halabiy who has said the following:
"I once asked abu 'Abd Allah, *'Alayhi al-Salam,* about this verse, 'It is not unlawful for you to eat in your houses, in the houses of your fathers. . . .' (24:61) and I asked what is the meaning of, 'or your friend'?' He (the Imam) said, 'That by Allah is the house of his friend where he can eat without his permission.'"

H 11264, Ch. 31, h 2
A number of our people have narrated from Ahmad ibn Muhammad from ibn Khalid from his father from Safwan from Musa ibn Bakr from Zurarah who has said the following:
"About the words of Allah, most Majestic, most Glorious, '. . . or the house to which you have the keys or your friend', abu 'Abd Allah, *'Alayhi al-Salam,* has stated this *Hadith.* 'The people Allah, most Majestic, most Glorious, has mentioned in this verse can eat without the permission of the owner of the house, things such as dates and curries and so also can a woman eat from the house of her husband without his permission. However, it is not permissible for them to eat other items of food besides the ones mentioned above.'"

H 11265, Ch. 31, h 3
A number of our people have narrated from Sahl ibn Ziyad from Ahmad ibn Muhammad from ibn abu Nasr from Jamil ibn Darraj who has said the following:
"Abu 'Abd Allah, *'Alayhi al-Salam,* has said, 'A woman can eat and give charity and a friend can eat and give charity from the house of his brother.'"

H 11266, Ch. 31, h 4
Muhammad ibn Yahya has narrated from Ahmad ibn Muhammad from ibn Khalid from al-Qasim ibn Muhammad ibn 'Urwah from 'Abd Allah ibn Bukayr from Zurarah who has narrated the following:
"I once asked one of the two Imam, (abu Ja'far or abu 'Abd Allah), *'Alayhim al-Salam,* about the meaning of the words of Allah. '. . . it is not an offense on your part if you eat from your homes or the homes of your fathers or the homes of your mothers. . . .' He (the Imam) said, 'It is not an offense on your part if you eat or consume from the homes for which you have the keys as long as you do not destroy it.'"

H 11267, Ch. 31, h 5
Ali ibn Ibrahim has narrated from his father from ibn abu 'Umayr from those whom he has mentioned who has said the following:
"About the words of Allah, most Majestic, most Glorious, '. . . and that to which you have the keys' Abu 'Abd Allah, *'Alayhi al-Salam,* has said, 'A man can be an agent who is being made the incharge person to look after certain assets, he can eat without the permission of the owner.'"

Chapter 32 - Without Title

H 11268, Ch. 32, h 1

Ali ibn Ibrahim has narrated from his father from ibn abu 'Umayr from Hisham ibn Salim who has said the following:

"Once we along with ibn abu Ya'fur visited abu 'Abd Allah, *'Alayhi al-Salam,* and we were a group. Food was prepared and we had lunch. He (the Imam) also took lunch with us. I was the youngest in the group and I made it shorter in my eating. He (the Imam) then said, 'Eat. Did you not know that one's love for his brother (in belief) comes to light when he eats from his food?'"

H 11269, Ch. 32, h 2

Muhammad ibn Yahya has narrated from Ahmad ibn Muhammad ibn 'Isa from 'Umar ibn 'Abd al-'Aziz from a man from 'Abd al-Rahman ibn *al-Hajj*aj who has said the following:

"Once we were having food with abu 'Abd Allah, *'Alayhi al-Salam,* and a bowl of rice was brought but we just left it untouched. He (the Imam), *'Alayhi al-Salam,* said, 'You did not eat anything thereof. You must take notice that the one among you with intense love for us is the one who eats our food well.' 'Abd al-Rahman said, 'I then ate even the pieces that had fallen on the table-spread.' He (the Imam) said, 'Now this is good' and he (the Imam) kept speaking that the Messenger of Allah, *O Allah, grant compensation to Muhammad and his family worthy of their services to Your cause,* was presented with a gift of a bowl of rice from the side of al-Ansar (people of al-Madinah). He (the Messenger of Allah) called Salman, al-Miqdad and abu Dharr, may Allah be happy with them, but they did not eat thereof. He (the Messenger of Allah) said, 'You did not eat anything thereof. The one among you of intense love for us is the one who eats our food well.'"

H 11270, Ch. 32, h 3

Muhammad ibn Yahya Ahmad ibn Muhammad from al-Hassan ibn Mahbub from Yunus ibn Ya'qub from 'Isa ibn abu Mansur who has said the following:

"I once was having food with abu 'Abd Allah, *'Alayhi al-Salam,* and he (the Imam) kept placing *Kabab* before me. He (the Imam) then said, 'O 'Isa, it is said that if you like to find out how much one loves his brother (in belief), see how much he eats from the food of his brother.'"

H 11271, Ch. 32, h 4

Ali ibn Muhammad ibn Bandar has narrated from Ahmad ibn abu 'Abd Allah from a number of his people from Yunus ibn Ya'qub from 'Abd Allah ibn Sulayman al-Sayrafiy who has said the following:

"I once was with abu 'Abd Allah, *'Alayhi al-Salam,* and food was brought for us with kabab and other things in it, then a bowl of rice was brought. I ate with him (the Imam). He (the Imam) said, 'Eat.' I said, 'I ate.' He (the Imam) said, 'Eat because the love of a brother (in belief) is proportionate with how much he eats from his food.' He (the Imam) then marked with his finger in the bowl and said to me, 'You must eat that after you have eaten.' I then ate it.'"

H 11272, Ch. 32, h 5

Ali ibn Muhammad ibn abu 'Abd Allah has narrated from 'Isma'il ibn Mehran from Sayf ibn 'Amirah from abu al-Mighra' al-'Ijliy who has said that narrated to me 'Anbasah ibn Mus'ab saying the following:

"We once visited abu 'Abd Allah, *'Alayhi al-Salam,* when he (the Imam) was about to leave for Makkah. He (the Imam) ordered a package of food and it was placed before us. He (the Imam) said, 'Eat.' We ate. He (the Imam) said, 'You have proved it, you have proved it, because it is said to find out a people's love for you by means of the manner of their eating your food.' We ate and there was no formality.'"

H 11273, Ch. 32, h 6

Al-Husayn from Muhammad has narrated from Mu'alla' ibn Muhammad from al-Hassan ibn Ali from Yunus from abu al-Rabi' who has said the following:

"Abu 'Abd Allah, *'Alayhi al-Salam,* asked for food. Mashed grain and meat was brought for us. He (the Imam) said, 'Come near and eat.' He (the narrator) has said, 'The people went close but made the eating short. He (the Imam) said, 'Eat because it shows one's love for his brother (in belief).' We then ate in large morsels like hungry camels do.'"

Chapter 33 - Another Chapter about Measurement and that there is no Accounting for Food

H 11274, Ch. 33, h 1

Muhammad ibn Yahya has narrated from Ahmad ibn Muhammad ibn 'Isa from ibn Faddal from ibn Bukayr from certain persons of our people who has said the following:

"Abu 'Abd Allah, *'Alayhi al-Salam,* would feed us milk with sugar or a mixture of dates and bread, then give us bread and oil. It was then said to him (the Imam), 'We wish you organize and plan your affairs to balance them out.' He (the Imam) said, 'We do so by the command of Allah, most Majestic, most Glorious. When He expands sustenance for us, we also expand spending; and when He gives us in measures, we also spend in measures.'"

H 11275, Ch. 33, h 2

A number of our people have narrated from Sahl ibn Ziyad from ibn Mahbub from ibn Ri'ab from al-Halabiy who has said the following:

"Abu 'Abd Allah, *'Alayhi al-Salam,* has said, 'There are three things for which Allah does not ask a believing person for accounting. One of such item is the food that he eats, the clothes that he wears and a virtuous wife who cooperates and with her he protects his chastity.'"

H 11276, Ch. 33, h 3

A number of our people have narrated from Ahmad ibn Muhammad from ibn Khalid from 'Uthman ibn 'Isa from abu Sa'id from abu Hamzah who has said the following:

"Once we were in a group with abu 'Abd Allah, *'Alayhi al-Salam.* He (the Imam) ordered such a food the like of which in good taste and elegance we had never seen. Thereafter dates were brought, in which we could see the reflection of our faces because of their clarity and goodness. A man then said, 'We will be held accountable for these bounties that we have received in the house of the child of the Messenger of Allah, *O Allah, grant compensation to Muhammad and his family worthy of their services to Your cause.* Abu 'Abd Allah, *'Alayhi al-Salam,* then said, 'Allah, most Majestic, most Glorious, is honorable and glorious. Once He gives you food and makes it delicious, He then does not hold you accountable for it. However, He will ask you about what He has granted through Muhammad and Ale (of) Muhammad, *O Allah, grant compensation to Muhammad and his family worthy of their services to Your cause.'"

H 11277, Ch. 33, h 4

Ali ibn Ibrahim has narrated from his father from ibn abu 'Umayr from Hisham ibn al-Hakam from Shihab ibn 'Abde Rabbihi who has said the following:

"Abu 'Abd Allah, *'Alayhi al-Salam,* has said, 'Extragance (overspending) is not applicable in food.'"

H 11278, Ch. 33, h 5

A number of our people have narrated from Ahmad ibn abu 'Abd Allah, from his father from al-Qasim ibn Muhammad al-Jawhariy from al-Harith ibn Hariz from Sadir al-Sayrafiy from abu Khalid al-Kabuliy who has said the following:

"I once visited abu Ja'far, *'Alayhi al-Salam.* He (the Imam) ordered food. I ate a food with him the like of which I never before had seen in cleanness and elegance. When we finished our food he (the Imam) asked, 'O abu Khalid, how was your food' or that he (the Imam) said, 'Our food?' I said, 'I pray to Allah to keep my soul in service for your cause, I had never seen such a food in delicacy and cleanness ever before; but I remembered the verse which is in the book of Allah, most Majestic, most Glorious, '. . . on that day you will be asked about the bounties.' (108:8) Abu Ja'far, *'Alayhi al-Salam,* said, 'No, you will be asked only about the truth in which you are, (belief in the divine authority of *'A'immah).'"

H 11279, Ch. 33, h 6

Ali ibn Ibrahim has narrated from his father from ibn abu 'Umayr from Hisham ibn al-Hakam from Shihab ibn 'Abd Rabbibi who has said the following:

"Abu 'Abd Allah, *'Alayhi al-Salam,* has said, 'Prepare food and make it unique; then invite your friends for it.'"

Chapter 34 - Preparation of Food for a Ceremony, like Wedding and so forth

H 11280, Ch. 34, h 1

Muhammad ibn Yahya has narrated from Ahmad ibn Muhammad from Ali ibn al-Hakam from certain persons of our people who has said the following:

"Abu al-Hassan, Musa, *'Alayhi al-Salam,* ordered to prepare food for the ceremony of a certain one of his children and fed people of al-Madinah with Faludhat (a certain kind of sweet) in large cooking pots for three days in Masjids and streets. Certain people of al-Madinah criticized him (the Imam) about it. The information reached him (the Imam) and he (the Imam) said, 'Everything that Allah, most Majestic, most Glorious, gave to any Prophet, He gave such things to Muhammad, *O Allah, grant compensation to Muhammad and his family worthy of their services to Your cause,* and more which He did not give to the

Prophets. To Sulayman, *'Alayhi al-Salam* He said, "This is our gift. You can give to others or keep it without being questioned." He said to Muhammad, "What the messenger brings you must take and what he prohibits, you must stay away from it."' (Deeds of *'A'immah* are of the *Sunnah* like the deeds of the Holy Prophet)"

H 11281, Ch. 34, h 2

Ahmad ibn Muhammad has narrated from al-Haytham ibn abu Masruq from Hisham ibn Salim who has said the following:

"Inviting (people for food) is not obligatory except for four occasions. Such occasions are: weddings, the birth of a child, circumcisions, and returning from a journey.'"

H 11282, Ch. 34, h 3

Ali ibn Ibrahim has narrated from his father from al-Nawfaliy from al-Sakuniy who has said the following:

"Abu 'Abd Allah, *'Alayhi al-Salam,* has said that the Messenger of Allah, *O Allah, grant compensation to Muhammad and his family worthy of their services to Your cause,* has said, 'Food can be prepared for four kinds of ceremonies. It is for a wedding, birth of a child for whom *'Aqiqah* is offered and fed to deserving people, circumcision of a male child, and returning of a man from a journey, for which he invites his brothers (in belief) after his absence.' In another *Hadith* it is said that it is for a new home and others.'"

H 11283, Ch. 34, h 4

Al-Husayn from Muhammad has narrated from Mu'alla' ibn Muhammad from those whom he has mentioned who has said the following:

"Abu Ibrahim, *'Alayhi al-Salam,* has said that the Messenger of Allah, *O Allah, grant compensation to Muhammad and his family worthy of their services to Your cause,* prohibited feeding during a ceremony, only the rich and not the poor.'"

H 11284, Ch. 34, h 5

Ali ibn Ibrahim has narrated from his father from ibn Mahbub from Mu'awiyah ibn 'Ammar who has said the following:

"A man once asked abu 'Abd Allah, *'Alayhi al-Salam,* 'Why do we find the aroma in a food for wedding which is not found in other food?' He (the Imam) said, 'In every wedding for which a camel or sheep or a cow is slaughtered Allah, most Blessed, most High, sends an angel with a carat (carafe) of musk from paradise which he soaks in water in their food and that is the aroma which is felt because of it.'"

H 11285, Ch. 34, h 6

Ali ibn Muhammad ibn Bandar has narrated from Ahmad ibn abu 'Abd Allah from certain persons of Iraq from Ibrahim ibn 'Uqbah from Ja'far al-Qalanisiy who has said the following:

"I once said to abu 'Abd Allah, *'Alayhi al-Salam,* 'Why is it that we prepare good food and make it unique but we do not find the fragrance like that of the food for wedding in it?' He (the Imam) said, 'It is because in the food for wedding, air from paradise blows; it is a food that is prepared for a lawful matter

227

(marriage).'"

Chapter 35 - When a Man Enters a Town he is a Guest of his Brothers (in belief) who Live there

H 11286, Ch. 35, h 12

Ali ibn Ibrahim has narrated from his father from 'Abd al-Rahman ibn Ishaq al-Ahmar through the chain of his narrators from those whom he has mentioned from al-Fudayl ibn Yasar who has said the following:

"Abu Ja'far, *'Alayhi al-Salam*, has stated this *Hadith*. 'The Messenger of Allah, *O Allah, grant compensation to Muhammad and his family worthy of their services to Your cause*, has said, "When a man enters a town he then is a guest of his brothers (in belief) who live there and the people of his religion until he leaves that town."'"

H 11287, Ch. 35, h 2

Abu Ali al-Ash'ariy has narrated from al-Sayyariy from Muhammad ibn 'Abd Allah al-Karkhiy from a man who has said the following:

"I once heard abu 'Abd Allah, *'Alayhi al-Salam*, saying, 'The Messenger of Allah, *O Allah, grant compensation to Muhammad and his family worthy of their services to Your cause*, has said, "When a man enters a town he is the guest of those who live there of the people of his religion until he leaves that town."'"

Chapter 36 - Guest is for Three Days Only

H 11288, Ch. 36, h 1

Ali ibn Ibrahim has narrated from his father from al-Hassan ibn al-Husayn al-Farsi from Sulayman ibn Hafs al-Basriy who has said the following:

"Abu 'Abd Allah, *'Alayhi al-Salam*, has stated this *Hadith*. 'The Messenger of Allah, *O Allah, grant compensation to Muhammad and his family worthy of their services to Your cause*, has said, "Special treatment should be offered to a guest for the two nights; but in the third night he is of the people of the family, and he eats what he receives."'"

H 11289, Ch. 36, h 2

Al-Husayn ibn Muhammad has narrated from Mu'alla' ibn Muhammad, from Wasil, from 'Abd Allah ibn Sinan who has said the following:

"Abu 'Abd Allah, *'Alayhi al-Salam*, has said that the Messenger of Allah, *O Allah, grant compensation to Muhammad and his family worthy of their services to Your cause*, has said, 'Special treatment for a guest is in the first day, in the second day and on the third day. Anything beyond this is charity that you give to him.' He (the Messenger of Allah) then said, 'One of you must not stay with his brother (in belief) to cause him difficulties.' It was asked, 'O Messenger of Allah, how can he cause difficulties?' He (the Messenger of Allah) said, 'He stays with him until he (the host) has nothing else to spend for him.'"

Chapter 37 - Undesirability of Making the Guest Work

H 11290, Ch. 37, h 1

Muhammad ibn Yahya has narrated from Ahmad ibn Musa from Dhubyan ibn Hakim from Musa al-Numayriy from ibn abu Ya'fur who has said the following:

"I once saw a guest with abu 'Abd Allah, *'Alayhi al-Salam,* who stood up one day to work for him (the Imam). He (the Imam) prohibited him. He (the Imam) himself stood up to do that work. He (the Imam), *'Alayhi al-Salam,* said, 'The Messenger of Allah, *O Allah, grant compensation to Muhammad and his family worthy of their services to Your cause,* prohibited making the guest to work.'"

H 11291, Ch. 37, h 2

Al-Husayn from Muhammad has narrated from al-Sayyariy from 'Ubayd ibn abu 'Abd Allah al-Baghdadiy from those who narrated to him who has said the following:

"Once abu al-Hassan, al-Rida' *'Alayhi al-Salam,* had a guest who was sitting with him (the Imam) and speaking during the night. The lamp began to become dim and the man stretched his hand to repair it. Abu al-Hassan, stopped him seriously and he (the Imam) himself repaired the lamp saying, 'We are a people who do not make the guests work.'"

H 11292, Ch. 37, h 3

Muhammad ibn Yahya has narrated from Ahmad ibn Musa from Dhubyan ibn Hakim from Musa ibn 'Ukayl al-Numayriy from Maysarah who has said the following:

"Abu Ja'far, *'Alayhi al-Salam,* has said, 'Ignoring to counter-balance a favor that one receives is one of the reasons to weaken one; and it is of injustice to make a guest to work. When a guest comes to you help him. When he leaves do not help him to leave, it is of lowliness. You must provide him supplies and make his supplies good; it is an act of generosity.'"

Chapter 38 - The Sustenance of a Guest Comes with Him

H 11293, Ch. 38, h 1

Ali ibn Ibrahim has narrated from his father from al-Hassan ibn al-Husayn al-Farsiy from Sulayman ibn Hafs ibn al-Basriy who has said the following:

"Abu 'Abd Allah, *'Alayhi al-Salam,* has stated this *Hadith.* 'The Messenger of Allah, *O Allah, grant compensation to Muhammad and his family worthy of their services to Your cause,* has said, "When a guest comes and disembarks with a people, he comes with his sustenance from the sky. When he eats Allah forgives them because of his staying with them.'"

H 11294, Ch. 38, h 2

Muhammad ibn Yahya has narrated from Ahmad ibn Muhammad from Muhammad ibn Sinan from Musa ibn Bukayr who has said the following:

"Abu al-Hassan, al-Awwal, *'Alayhi al-Salam,* has said, 'Help descends on a people proportionate to their needs. A guest comes to a people but he comes with his sustenance in his lap.'"

H 11295, Ch. 38, h 3

Ali ibn Ibrahim has narrated from his father from al-Nawfaliy from al-Sakuniy who has said the following:

"Abu 'Abd Allah, *'Alayhi al-Salam,* has said that the Messenger of Allah, *O Allah, grant compensation to Muhammad and his family worthy of their services to Your cause,* has said, 'There is no guest who comes to a people without his sustenance in his lap.'"

H 11296, Ch. 38, h 4

Ali ibn Ibrahim has narrated from his father from ibn abu 'Umayr from Muhammad ibn Qays who has said the following:

"Our people once mentioned a people and I said, 'By Allah, I do not take lunch or dinner without one two or three of them or more or less with me.' Abu 'Abd Allah, *'Alayhi al-Salam,* then said, 'Their favor to you is more than your favor to them.' I then said, 'I pray to Allah to keep my soul in service for your cause, how does that happen? I feed them my food, spend on them from my assets and my servants serve them.' He (the Imam) said, 'When they come to you they come with sustenance from Allah, most Majestic, most Glorious, and when they leave they leave forgiveness for you.'"

Chapter 39 - The Right of Guest and Honoring Him

H 11297, Ch. 39, h 1

Muhammad ibn Yahya has narrated from Ahmad ibn Muhammad ibn 'Isa from 'Umar ibn 'Abd al-'Aziz from Ishaq ibn 'Abd al-'Aziz and Jamil and Zurarah who have said the following:

"Abu 'Abd Allah, *'Alayhi al-Salam,* has stated this *Hadith.* 'Of the matters that the Messenger of Allah, *O Allah, grant compensation to Muhammad and his family worthy of their services to Your cause,* taught to Fatimah, *'Alayha al-Salam,* was his saying, "O Fatimah, whoever believes in Allah and in the Day of Judgment, he must honor his guest."'"

H 11298, Ch. 39, h 2

Ali ibn Ibrahim has narrated from his father from ibn abu 'Umayr from Ishaq ibn 'Abd al-'Aziz from Zurarah who has said the following:

"Abu Ja'far, *'Alayhi al-Salam,* has said, 'Of the matters that the Messenger of Allah, *O Allah, grant compensation to Muhammad and his family worthy of their services to Your cause,* taught to Ali, *'Alayhi al-Salam,* was his saying, "Whoever believes in Allah and in the Day of Judgment, he must honor his guest."'"

H 11299, Ch. 39, h 3

Ali ibn Ibrahim has narrated from his father from al-Hassan ibn al-Husayn al-Farsiy from Sulayman ibn Hafs who has said the following:

"Abu 'Abd Allah, *'Alayhi al-Salam,* has said that the Messenger of Allah, *O Allah, grant compensation to Muhammad and his family worthy of their services to Your cause,* has said, 'It is of the rights of the guest to be honored and to prepare for him toothpicks [restroom according to another script of al-Kafi].'"

Chapter 40 - Eating with the Guest

H 11300, Ch. 40, h 1
A number of our people have narrated from Sahl ibn Ziyad from Ja'far ibn Muhammad al-Ash'ariy from ibn al-Qaddah who has said the following:
"Abu 'Abd Allah, *'Alayhi al-Salam,* has said that the Messenger of Allah, *O Allah, grant compensation to Muhammad and his family worthy of their services to Your cause,* when eating food with a people would, as the first one, begin eating and the be last to stop it, so that the people complete eating.'"

H 11301, Ch. 40, h 2
Muhammad ibn Yahya has narrated from Ahmad ibn Muhammad from ibn Faddal f, ibn al-Qaddah who has said the following:
"Abu 'Abd Allah, *'Alayhi al-Salam,* has said that the Messenger of Allah, *O Allah, grant compensation to Muhammad and his family worthy of their services to Your cause,* when eating food with a people would, as the first one, begin eating and be the last to stop it, so that the people complete eating.'"

H 11302, Ch. 40, h 3
It is narrated from the narrator of the previous *Hadith* from Ahmad ibn Muhammad from 'Umar ibn 'Abd al-'Aziz from Jamil ibn Darraj who has said the following:
"I once heard abu 'Abd Allah, *'Alayhi al-Salam,* saying, 'When a visitor visits someone and eats with him, formality comes down, and when he eats with him (the visitor) feels constraint a little.'"

H 11303, Ch. 40, h 4
It is narrated from the narrator of the previous *Hadith* from Sulayman ibn Hafs from Ali ibn Ja'far from his brother, Musa, *'Alayhi al-Salam,* has said the following:
"Abu al-Hassan, Musa, *'Alayhi al-Salam,* has said, that when a guest would come to the Messenger of Allah, *O Allah, grant compensation to Muhammad and his family worthy of their services to Your cause,* he (the Messenger of Allah) would eat with him and would not stop eating before the guest did.'"

Chapter 41 - The Child of Adam is Hollow; thus He must Eat Food

H 11304, Ch. 41, h 1
Ali ibn Ibrahim has narrated from his father from ibn abu 'Umayr from (from Sulayman ibn Ja'far) from Hisham ibn Salim from Zurarah who has said the following:
"Al-Abrash al-Kalbiy once asked abu Ja'far, *'Alayhi al-Salam,* about the meaning of the words of Allah, most Majestic, most Glorious, 'On the day when the earth will be replaced with another earth.' (14:48) He (the Imam) said, 'It means that there will be purified bread for people to eat until Allah will clear the accounts.' Al-Abrash has said, 'I then said, "People on that day will already have other things to worry about instead of eating."' Abu Ja'far, *'Alayhi al-Salam,* said, 'If they in the fire will be eating *al-Dari'* (a terrible kind of food for those in hell) and drinking hot, filthy water in suffering instead of worrying about other things; they can also eat purified bread during the time their accounts are cleared.'"

H 11305, Ch. 41, h 2

Ali ibn Ibrahim has narrated from his father from ibn abu 'Umayr from Hisham from Zurarah who has said the following:

"Abu Ja'far, *'Alayhi al-Salam,* has said, 'Allah, most Majestic, most Glorious, has created the child of Adam hollow.'"

H 11306, Ch. 41, h 3

Muhammad ibn Yahya has narrated from Ali ibn al-Hassan al-Tamimiy from Ja'far ibn Muhammad Hakim from Ibrahim ibn 'Abd al-Hamid from al-Walid ibn Sabih who has said the following:

"Abu 'Abd Allah, *'Alayhi al-Salam,* has said, 'The body is made out of bread (food).'"

H 11307, Ch. 41, h 4

A number of our people have narrated from Ahmad ibn abu 'Abd Allah from al-Qasim ibn al-'Urwah from 'Abd Allah ibn Bukayr from Zurarah who has said the following:

"I once asked abu Ja'far, *'Alayhi al-Salam,* about the meaning of the words of Allah, most Majestic, most Glorious, 'On the day when the earth will be replaced with another earth.' (14:48) He (the Imam) said, 'It will be replaced with purified bread from which people will eat until their accounting is complete.' Someone then said to him (the Imam), 'People on that day will already have other things to worry about instead of eating.' He (the Imam) said, 'Allah, most Majestic, most Glorious, has created the child of Adam hollow. He must have food and drink. Will they be more seriously preoccupied on that day or those in hellfire who plead? And Allah, most Majestic, most Glorious, says, "If they plead their pleading will be responded with water like al-Muhl that roasts the faces and it is the worst kind of drink." (18:29)'"

H 11308, Ch. 41, h 5

Ali ibn Ibrahim has narrated from his father from ibn abu 'Umayr from those whom he has mentioned who has said the following:

"About the meaning of the words of Allah, most Majestic, most Glorious, quoting Musa, *'Alayhi al-Salam,* 'My Lord, I am in great need of the good things You have sent to me...' (27:24) Abu 'Abd Allah, *'Alayhi al-Salam,* has said, 'He (Moses) asked for food.'"

H 11309, Ch. 41, h 6

A number of our people have narrated from Ahmad ibn abu 'Abd Allah from his father from abu al-Bakhtariy in a marfu' manner has said the following:

"The Messenger of Allah, *O Allah, grant compensation to Muhammad and his family worthy of their services to Your cause,* has said, 'O Lord, grant us blessings in bread and do not separate it from us. If bread had not been available, we could not fast or perform *Salat* (prayer) or fulfill any of our obligation toward our Lord, most Majestic, most Glorious.'"

H 11310, Ch. 41, h 7

Muhammad ibn Yahya has narrated from Muhammad ibn 'Isma'il has narrated from al-Fadl ibn Shadhan from and Ali ibn Ibrahim has narrated from his father all from ibn abu 'Umayr from Ibrahim ibn 'Abd al-Hamid from al-Walid ibn Sabih who has said the following:

"Abu 'Abd Allah, *'Alayhi al-Salam,* has said, 'The body is built on bread only.'"

Chapter 42 - Lunch and Dinner

H 11311, Ch. 42, h 1
A number of our people have narrated from Ahmad ibn Muhammad from ibn Khalid from Muhammad ibn Ali from Ali ibn Asbat from Ya'qub ibn Salim from al-Muthanna' who has said the following:
"Abu 'Abd Allah, *'Alayhi al-Salam,* has said Ya'qub, *'Alayhi al-Salam,* had an announcer who every morning announced from his house to three miles, 'Those who want lunch can come to the house of Ya'qub.' In the evening the announcement said, 'Those who want dinner can come to the house of Ya'qub.'"

H 11312, Ch. 42, h 2
Muhammad ibn Yahya has narrated from Ahmad ibn Muhammad from al-Husayn ibn Sa'id from al-Nadr ibn Suwayd from Ali ibn al-Salt from the son of brother of Shihab ibn 'Abd Rabbihi who has said the following:
"I once complained before abu 'Abd Allah, *'Alayhi al-Salam,* against pain and an upset stomach that I (often) experienced . He (the Imam) said to me, 'Take lunch and dinner and do not eat anything in between because it harms the body. Have you not heard Allah, most Majestic, most Glorious, saying, "For them there is their sustenance in the early morning and evening?"(19:62)'

Chapter 43 - Excellence of Dinner and Undesirability of Ignoring it

H 11313, Ch. 43, h 1
A number of our people have narrated from Ahmad ibn Muhammad from al-Qasim ibn Yahya from his grandfather al-Hassan ibn Rashid from Muhammad ibn Muslim who has said the following:
"Abu 'Abd Allah, *'Alayhi al-Salam,* has said that `Amir al-Mu'minin has said, 'Dinner of the Prophets is after al-'Atmah (the time of late evening *Salat* (prayer)); so you must not ignore dinner because ignoring it leads to neglecting the body.'"

H 11314, Ch. 43, h 2
Ali ibn Ibrahim has narrated from his father from ibn abu 'Umayr from Hisham ibn al-Hakam who has said the following:
"Abu 'Abd Allah, *'Alayhi al-Salam,* has said, 'The origin of the ruination of body is in ignoring dinner.'"

H 11315, Ch. 43, h 3
Ali ibn Ibrahim has narrated from his father from ibn abu 'Umayr from Jamil ibn Salih who has said the following:
"Abu 'Abd Allah, *'Alayhi al-Salam,* has said, 'Neglecting dinner is senility, thus it is necessary for an aged man to go to sleep when his stomach is full of food.'"

H 11316, Ch. 43, h 4
Muhammad ibn Yahya has narrated from Ahmad ibn Muhammad from Sa'id ibn Junah who has said the following:
"Abu al-Hassan, al-Rida', *'Alayhi al-Salam,* has said, 'When a man becomes old he must not neglect eating something during the night; it brings peaceful sleep

and nicer breath.'"

H 11317, Ch. 43, h 5
Ali ibn Muhammad ibn Bandar has narrated from Ahmad ibn abu 'Abd Allah from his father from Sulayman ibn Ja'far al-Ja'fariy who has said the following:

"Abu al-Hassan, *'Alayhi al-Salam,* would not neglect dinner even if it was one cookie; and he (the Imam) would say, 'Neglecting dinner is ruination of the body.' He (the narrator) has said, 'I am not certain perhaps he (the Imam) said that it is helpful in going to bed with one's wife.'"

H 11318, Ch. 43, h 6
A number of our people have narrated from Sahl ibn Ziyad Ahmad ibn Muhammad from ibn abu Nasr from Hammad ibn 'Uthaman from al-Walid ibn Sabih who has said the following:

"I once heard abu 'Abd Allah, *'Alayhi al-Salam,* saying, 'It is not good for one of old age to spend the night very light, instead it is better for him to pass the night with full stomach.'"

H 11319, Ch. 43, h 7
Muhammad ibn Yahya has narrated from Ahmad ibn Muhammad from Muhammad ibn Sinan from Ziyad ibn abu al-Hallal who has said the following:

"I once took dinner with abu 'Abd Allah, *'Alayhi al-Salam,* and he said, 'Dinner after *'Isha' al-Akhirah* (time of late evening *Salat* (prayer)) is like the dinner of the prophets, *'Alayhim al-Salam.'*"

H 11320, Ch. 43, h 8
Ali ibn Muhammad ibn Bandar has narrated from Ahmad ibn abu 'Abd Allah, from abu Sulayman, from Ahmad ibn al-Hassan al-Jabaliy (al-Halabiy), from his father, from Jamil ibn Darraj who has said the following:

"I once heard abu 'Abd Allah, *'Alayhi al-Salam,* saying, 'If one does not take dinner one Saturday and Sunday nights consecutively, his strength will go away and will not come back until forty days later.'"

H 11321, Ch. 43, h 9
Ali ibn Ibrahim has narrated from his father from ibn abu 'Umayr from certain persons of his people from Dharih who has said the following:

"Abu 'Abd Allah, *'Alayhi al-Salam,* has said, 'An old man must not neglect dinner even if it is one morsel.'"

H 11322, Ch. 43, h 10
A number of our people have narrated from Sahl ibn Ziyad from Bakr ibn Salih from ibn Faddal from 'Abd Allah ibn Ibrahim from Ali ibn abu Ali al-Lahbiy who has said the following:

"Abu 'Abd Allah, *'Alayhi al-Salam,* once asked me, 'What do your physicians say about dinner?' I replied, 'They prohibit taking dinner.' He (the Imam) said, 'I however, command you to take dinner.'"

H 11323, Ch. 43, h 11
Muhammad ibn Yahya has narrated from Muhammad ibn al-Husayn from *al-Hajj*al from Tha'labah from a man whom he has mentioned who has said the following:

"Abu 'Abd Allah, *'Alayhi al-Salam,* has said, 'Food during the night is more useful than food during the day.'"

H 11324, Ch. 43, h 12

A number of our people have narrated from Sahl ibn Ziyad from certain persons of Ahwaz who has said the following:

"Al-Rida', *'Alayhi al-Salam,* has said, 'In the body there is a vein called *'Isha'.* If one does not take dinner, it continues praying against him until morning; and it says, 'May Allah make you hungry just as you kept me hungry, and may Allah make you thirsty just as you kept me thirsty.' No one of you must neglect taking dinner, even if it is one morsel of bread or a sip of water.'"

Chapter 44 - Wudu (washing hands clean) before and after Food

H 11325, Ch. 44, h 1

A number of our people have narrated from Sahl ibn Ziyad from Ja'far ibn Muhammad al-Ash'ariy from ibn al-Qaddah who has said the following:

"Abu 'Abd Allah, *'Alayhi al-Salam,* has said, 'One who washes his hand before and after food, lives a rich life and remains safe from troubles in his body.'"

H 11326, Ch. 44, h 2

Ali ibn Ibrahim has narrated from his father from Ahmad ibn Muhammad from ibn abu Nasr from Safwan al-Jammal from abu Hamzah al-Thumaliy who has said the following:

"Abu 'Abd Allah, *'Alayhi al-Salam,* once said, 'O abu Hamzah, Wudu (washing) before and after eating food removes poverty.' I then said, I pray to Allah to keep my soul in service for your cause, does it remove poverty?' He (the Imam) said, 'Yes, it removes poverty.'"

H 11327, Ch. 44, h 3

Muhammad ibn Yahya has narrated from Ahmad ibn Muhammad from al-Qasim ibn Yahya from his grandfather Hisham ibn Salim ibn Rashid from abu Basir who has said the following:

"Abu 'Abd Allah, *'Alayhi al-Salam,* has said that `Amir al-Mu'minin has said, 'Washing hands before and after eating food removes stains from clothes and clears eyesight.'"

H 11328, Ch. 44, h 4

Ali ibn Ibrahim has narrated from his father from al-Nawfaliy from al-Sakuniy who has said the following:

"Abu 'Abd Allah, *'Alayhi al-Salam,* has said, 'If one likes to see blessings in his house to increase, he must take wudu for taking food.'"

H 11329, Ch. 44, h 5

Ali ibn Ibrahim has narrated from his father from ibn abu 'Umayr from abu 'Awf al-Bajaliy who has said the following:

"I once heard abu 'Abd Allah, *'Alayhi al-Salam,* saying, 'Wudu before and after eating food increases one's sustenance.' It is narrated that the Messenger of Allah has said, 'Wudu before eating food removes poverty and that which is after food removes depression.'"

Chapter 45 - Description of Wudu before Eating Food

H 11330, Ch. 45, h 1

A number of our people have narrated from Ahmad ibn Muhammad from ibn Khalid from 'Uthman ibn 'Isa from Muhammad ibn 'Ajlan who has said the following:

"Abu 'Abd Allah, *'Alayhi al-Salam,* has said, 'The host must begin wudu so that no one feels shy. After eating food the person on the right of the host begins it, regardless of being a free or a slave.' He (the narrator) has said that in another *Hadith* it says, 'The first before food and the last after food to wash should be the owner of the house, because he can remain patient with food stains.'"

H 11331, Ch. 45, h 2

Muhammad ibn Yahya has narrated from Ahmad ibn Muhammad from Muhammad ibn Khalid from Khalaf ibn Hammad from 'Amr ibn Thabit who has said the following:

"Abu 'Abd Allah, *'Alayhi al-Salam,* has said, 'Wash your hands in one utensil; it is good for the betterment of your moral behavior.'"

H 11332, Ch. 45, h 3

Ali ibn Muhammad has narrated from Ahmad ibn Muhammad from al-Fadl ibn al-Mubarak from al-Fadl ibn Yunus who has said the following:

"When abu al-Hassan, *'Alayhi al-Salam,* had lunch and the hand-basin was brought, he (the Imam) was the first to wash his hand while he (the Imam) was sitting in the middle of the assembly room, and he (the Imam) said, 'Begin with one who is on your right side.' When one made wudu the servant wanted to remove the hand-basin, but abu al-Hassan, *'Alayhi al-Salam,* said to him, 'Leave it so that you can wash your hands in it.'"

Chapter 46 - Using a Towel to Wipe one's Face after Wudu (Washing)

H 11333, Ch. 46, h 1

Ali ibn Muhammad has narrated from Muhammad ibn Ahmad from abu Mahmud from his father from a man who has said the following:

"Abu 'Abd Allah, *'Alayhi al-Salam,* has said, 'When you wash your hand for food do not wipe it with a towel because blessings continue in the food as long as hands have moisture in them.'"

H 11334, Ch. 46, h 2

Ali ibn Ibrahim has narrated from his father from ibn abu 'Umayr from Murazim who has said the following:

"I saw abu al-Hassan, *'Alayhi al-Salam,* when making wudu (washing his hands) before food did not wipe his hands with a towel, but he wiped them when he (the Imam) made wudu after food.'"

H 11335, Ch. 46, h 3

A number of our people have narrated from Ahmad ibn Muhammad from ibn Faddal from abu al-Mighra' from Zayd al-Shahham who has said the following:

"Abu 'Abd Allah, *'Alayhi al-Salam,* disliked wiping his hands with a towel because of food stains due to sanctity of food, until he (the Imam) absorbed them or a child next to him (the Imam) did so.'"

H 11336, Ch. 46, h 4

Al-Husayn from Muhammad has narrated from Mu'alla' ibn Muhammad from Ahmad ibn abu 'Abd Allah from certain persons of his people from Ibrahim ibn 'Uqbah in a *marfu'* manner has said the following:

"Abu 'Abd Allah, *'Alayhi al-Salam,* has said, 'Wiping one's hands with a towel after wudu (washing) removes troubles and increases sustenance.'"

H 11337, Ch. 46, h 5

Ali ibn Muhammad in a marfu' manner has narrated from al-Mufaddal who has said the following:

"I once visited abu 'Abd Allah, *'Alayhi al-Salam,* and complained before him (the Imam) about eye ache. He (the Imam) said, 'Do you want something unique?' He (the Imam) then said to me, 'When you wash your hands after eating food, wipe your eye brows and say three times, "All praise belongs to Allah, the Benefactor, the Graceful, the Munificent, the Pre-eminent."' He (the narrator) has said, 'I followed the instruction and thereafter my eyes did not experience any pain and ache, all praise belongs to Allah, Cherisher of the worlds.'"

Chapter 47 - Mentioning the name of Allah and Tahmid (All Praise Belongs to Allah) over the Food

H 11338, Ch. 47, h 1

Ali ibn Ibrahim has narrated from his father from al-Nawfaliy from al-Sakuniy who has said the following:

"Abu 'Abd Allah, *'Alayhi al-Salam,* has stated this *Hadith.* 'The Messenger of Allah, *O Allah, grant compensation to Muhammad and his family worthy of their services to Your cause,* has said, "When the table is spread four thousand angels surround it and when a servant of Allah says, 'In the name of Allah' the angels say, 'May Allah grant you blessings in your food.' Then they (angels) say to Satan, 'Move away, O disobedient, you have no authority over them.' When they complete eating their food and say, 'All praise belongs to Allah' the angels say, 'They are a people to whom Allah has granted blessings and they have expressed their thanks to their Lord.' If they do not mention the name of Allah, the angels say to Satan, 'Come close, O disobedient and eat with them.' When the table is removed and if they did not mention the name of Allah on it the angels say, 'They are a people to whom Allah has granted favors but they forgot their Lord, most Majestic, most Glorious.'"'"

H 11339, Ch. 47, h 2

Ali ibn Ibrahim has narrated from his father from ibn abu 'Umayr from Ali ibn abu Hamzah from abu Basir who has said the following:

"Abu 'Abd Allah, *'Alayhi al-Salam,* has said, 'When the table is prepared say, 'In the name of Allah.' When your eating is complete say, 'In the name of Allah at its beginning and at its end.' When it is removed say, 'All praise belongs to Allah.'"

H 11340, Ch. 47, h 3

Ali ibn Muhammad has narrated from Salih abu Hammad from al-Washsha' from Ahmad ibn 'A'idh from abu Khadijah who has said the following:

"Abu 'Abd Allah, *'Alayhi al-Salam,* has said, 'Once the brother of my father, *'Alayhi al-Salam,* 'Abd Allah ibn Ali came to ask permission for 'Amr ibn 'Ubayd, Wasil and Bashir al-Rahhahl and he granted them permission. They sat down. He (the Imam) said, 'For everything there is a limit where it ends.' They brought food and it was made available. They said to each other, 'We have achieved the chance we wanted.' They said, 'O abu Ja'far, is this table of food something?' He (the Imam) said, 'Yes, that is true.' They asked, 'What are its limits?' He (the Imam) said, 'Of its limits is that when it is made ready one must say, 'In the name of Allah', and when it is taken away one must say, 'All praise belongs to Allah,' that every human being must eat from what is nearest to him, and must not take from what is before the others.'"

H 11341, Ch. 47, h 4

Abu Ali al-Ash'ariy has narrated from Muhammad ibn 'Abd al-Jabbar from abu Jamilah from Muhammad ibn Marwan who has said the following:

"Abu 'Abd Allah, *'Alayhi al-Salam,* has said, 'When food for lunch or dinner is made ready, say, 'In the name of Allah,' because Satan, may Allah condemn him says to his friends, 'Go out there is no dinner here or a place to spend the night.' When one forgets saying, 'In the name of Allah', Satan says to his friends, 'Come; there is dinner and a place here for you to spend the night.'"

H 11342, Ch. 47, h 5

Muhammad ibn Yahya has narrated from Ahmad ibn Muhammad from Muhammad ibn Yahya from Ghiyath ibn Ibrahim who has said the following:

"Abu 'Abd Allah, *'Alayhi al-Salam,* has said that `Amir al-Mu'minin has said, 'One who eats food must mention the name of Allah, most Majestic, most Glorious on it; but if one forgets and remembers later, Satan, may Allah condemn him, throws up what he has eaten and one feels as if the food is not sufficient.'"

H 11343, Ch. 47, h 6

Through the same chain of narrators as that of the previous *Hadith* the following is narrated:

"He (the Imam), *'Alayhi al-Salam,* has said, 'One who mentions the name of Allah, most Majestic, most Glorious, on food, he will never be asked any questions about that blessing.'"

H 11344, Ch. 47, h 7

Abu Ali al-Ash'ariy has narrated from Muhammad ibn 'Abd al-Jabbar from Safwan from Kulayb al-Asadiy who has said the following:

"Abu 'Abd Allah, *'Alayhi al-Salam,* has said, 'When a Muslim man wants to eat food and extends his hand saying, 'In the name of Allah' and 'All praise belongs to Allah, Lord of the worlds' Allah, most Majestic, most Glorious, forgives him before a morsel reaches his mouth.'"

H 11345, Ch. 47, h 8

A number of our people have narrated from Sahl ibn Ziyad from Ya'qub ibn Yazid from Ahmad ibn al-Hassan al-Mithamiy in a marfu' manner has said, the following:

"The Messenger of Allah, *O Allah, grant compensation to Muhammad and his family worthy of their services to Your cause,* when food was made available for him said, 'O Lord, You are free of all defects, how good is Your trial for us. O Lord, You are free of all defects, and how great is what You have granted us, O Lord, You are free of all defects, how often it is that You give us good health, O Lord, expand our sustenance and for the poor believers, male and female and Muslims.'"

H 11346, Ch. 47, h 9

Muhammad ibn Yahya has narrated from Ahmad ibn Muhammad from ibn Mahbub from 'Abd al-Rahman ibn *al-Hajj*aj who has said the following:

"I once heard abu 'Abd Allah, *'Alayhi al-Salam,* saying, 'When the table of food is made available and a man among them says, 'In the name of Allah', it is sufficient for all of them.'"

H 11347, Ch. 47, h 10

Ali ibn Ibrahim has narrated from his father from al-Nawfaliy from al-Sakuniy who has said the following:

"Abu 'Abd Allah, *'Alayhi al-Salam,* has stated this *Hadith.* 'The Messenger of Allah, *O Allah, grant compensation to Muhammad and his family worthy of their services to Your cause,* when eating food with a family would say to them, "Fasting people have received food with you, virtuous people have eaten food with you and chosen angels have prayed for you."'"

H 11348, Ch. 47, h 11

Ali ibn Ibrahim has narrated from his father from ibn abu 'Umayr from al-Husayn ibn 'Uthman from a man who has said the following:

"Abu 'Abd Allah, *'Alayhi al-Salam,* has said, 'When you eat food say, 'In the name of Allah' at its beginning and at its end'; when a servant says it before he eats, Satan cannot eat with him; but if he did not mention the name of Allah, Satan eats with him. If he then says, 'In the name of Allah' after he begins and Satan had been eating with him, Satan then throws up what he had eaten.'"

H 11349, Ch. 47, h 12

A number of our people have narrated from Ahmad ibn abu 'Abd Allah from Muhammad ibn 'Abd Allah from 'Amr al-Mutatabbib from abu Yahya al-San'aniy who has said the following:

"Abu 'Abd Allah, *'Alayhi al-Salam,* has said that Ali ibn al-Husayn, *'Alayhim al-Salam*, when finding food placed before him said, 'O Lord, this is from You, from Your favor, generosity and gift. Make it a blessing for us and make it delicious for us, grant us favors in future when we finish it. Many are those who need it and You have made it available for them. O Lord, make us of those who appreciate favors.' When the table had been taken away he (the Imam) said, 'All praise belongs to Allah, who moves us on land and in the sea, has granted us fine sustenance and has given us preference over many of His creatures, a good preference.'"

H 11350, Ch. 47, h 13

It is narrated from the narrator of the previous *Hadith* from al-Nadr ibn Suwayd from al-Qasim ibn Sulayman from Jarrah al-Mada'iniy who has said the following:

"Abu 'Abd Allah, *'Alayhi al-Salam,* has said, 'Mention the name of Allah, most Majestic, most Glorious, on food and when you complete eating say, 'All praise belongs to Allah who feeds and is not fed.'"

H 11351, Ch. 47, h 14

It is narrated from the narrator of the previous *Hadith* from his father from those who narrated to him from 'Abd al-Rahman al-'Arzamiy who has said the following:

"Abu 'Abd Allah, *'Alayhi al-Salam,* has said that 'Amir al-Mu'minin has said, 'One who mentions the name of Allah on food or drink at the beginning and 'All praise belongs to Allah' at the end, he will never be asked about the blessings of the food.'"

H 11352, Ch. 47, h 15

Ali ibn Ibrahim has narrated from his father from Ahmad ibn al-Hassan al-Mithamiy from Ibrahim ibn Mehzam from a man who has said the following:

"Abu 'Abd Allah, *'Alayhi al-Salam,* has stated this *Hadith.* 'The Messenger of Allah, *O Allah, grant compensation to Muhammad and his family worthy of their services to Your cause,* when the table was moved would say, "O Lord, you have granted a great deal, have made it very good, blessed it, made us satisfied and quenched. All praise belongs to Allah who feeds and is not fed."'"

H 11353, Ch. 47, h 16

Ali ibn Ibrahim has narrated from his father from ibn abu 'Umayr from Hisham ibn Salim who has said the following:

"Abu 'Abd Allah, *'Alayhi al-Salam,* has stated this *Hadith.* 'My father would say, "All praise belongs to Allah who has made us satisfied with food among the hungry ones, quenched our thirst among the thirsty people. He has given us shelter among the homeless ones, given us means of transport among those who move without means of transportation, has granted us safety among the frightened ones and has serviced us among the toiling ones."'"

H 11354, Ch. 47, h 17

Muhammad ibn Yahya has narrated from Ahmad ibn Muhammad from ibn Faddal from ibn Bukayr from 'Ubayd ibn Zurarah who has said the following:

"I ate food with abu 'Abd Allah, *'Alayhi al-Salam,* and I do not know how many times he (the Imam) said, 'All praise belongs to Allah who has made me to have the appetite for food.'"

H 11355, Ch. 47, h 18

Ahmad ibn Muhammad has narrated from ibn Faddal from Dawud ibn Farqad who has said the following:

"Abu 'Abd Allah, *'Alayhi al-Salam,* has said that 'Amir al-Mu'minin guaranteed those who mention the name of Allah on food that it will not harm them. Ibn al-Kawwa, said to 'Amir al-Mu'minin, 'O 'Amir al-Mu'minin last night I ate a meal and I mentioned the name of Allah on it but it has given me trouble.' He (the Imam) said, 'Perhaps you ate several kinds. On certain ones of them you mentioned the name of Allah and not on others, O *Luka'* (suffering from weak understanding).'"

H 11356, Ch. 47, h 19
Ahmad ibn Muhammad has narrated from abu 'Abd Allah, al-Barqiy from abu Talib from Misma'
who has said the following:
"I once complained before abu 'Abd Allah, *'Alayhi al-Salam,* about the trouble I
face from food. He (the Imam) said, 'You may have eaten without mentioning
the name of Allah.' I said, 'I had mentioned the name of Allah but it gives me
trouble.' He (the Imam) said, 'When you discontinue mentioning the name of
Allah by speaking, then return to eat, do you mention the name of Allah?' I
replied, 'No, I do not do so.' He (the Imam) said, 'This is why it gives you
trouble. Were you to return to eating if you mention the name of Allah, it would
not harm you.'"

H 11357, Ch. 47, h 20
Abu Ali al-Ash'ariy has narrated from Muhammad ibn 'Abd al-Jabbar from Safwan from Dawud ibn
Farqad who has said the following:
"I once asked abu 'Abd Allah, *'Alayhi al-Salam,* about how I should mention
the name of Allah on food. He (the Imam) said, 'If the dishes are more than one,
then you should mention the name of Allah on each one.' I then asked, 'What
happens if I forget mentioning the name of Allah?' He (the Imam) told me to
say, 'In the name of Allah at its beginning and at its end.'"

H 11358, Ch. 47, h 21
It is narrated from the narrator of the previous *Hadith* from al-Hassan ibn Ali al-Kufiy from 'Ubays
ibn Hisham from al-Husayn ibn Ahmad al-Minqariy from Yunus ibn Zabyan who has said the
following:
"Once I was with abu 'Abd Allah, *'Alayhi al-Salam,* and it became the time of
al-'Isha' *Salat* (prayer). I went to say Iqamah. He (the Imam) said, 'Sit down, O
abu 'Abd Allah.' I then sat down until food was made available. He (the Imam)
mentioned the name of Allah when food was placed for eating. When he (the
Imam) finished he (the Imam) said, 'All praise belongs to Allah. This is from
You and from Muhammad, *O Allah, grant compensation to Muhammad and his
family worthy of their services to Your cause.*'"

H 11359, Ch. 47, h 22
Muhammad ibn Yahya has narrated from Ahmad ibn Muhammad from al-Qasim ibn Yahya from his
grandfather al-Hassan ibn Rashid from ibn Bukayr who has said the following:
"Once we were with abu 'Abd Allah, *'Alayhi al-Salam,* and he (the Imam) fed
us food then we stopped eating and said, 'All praise belongs to Allah.' Abu
'Abd Allah, *'Alayhi al-Salam,* then said, 'O Lord, this is from You and from
Muhammad, Your messenger, *O Lord, all praise belongs to you, O Allah, grant
compensation to Muhammad and his family worthy of their services to Your
cause.*'"

H 11360, Ch. 47, h 23
Muhammad ibn Yahya has narrated from Ahmad ibn Muhammad from al-Qasim ibn Yahya from his
grandfather al-Hassan ibn Rashid from Muhammad ibn Muslim who has said the following:
"Abu 'Abd Allah, *'Alayhi al-Salam,* has stated this *Hadith.* ``Amir al-Mu'minin

has said, "You must mention the name of Allah, most Majestic, most Glorious, on your food and do not speak nonsense, because it is a bounty of the bounties of Allah, and it is obligatory on those to whom He grants it to thank Him, speak of Him and praise Him.'"

H 11361, Ch. 47, h 24
A number of our people have narrated from Sahl ibn Ziyad from Ya'qub ibn Yazid from `Isma'il al-Mada'iniy from 'Abd Allah ibn Bukayr from a man who has said the following:

"Abu 'Abd Allah, *'Alayhi al-Salam,* commanded to bring meat but it became cold and later it was brought. He (the Imam) said, 'All praise belongs to Allah who made me to have the appetite for it.' He (the Imam) then said, 'Bounty in good health is better than the bounty with constraints.'"

H 11362, Ch. 47, h 25
Sahl ibn Ziyad has narrated from Muhammad ibn al-Hassan ibn Shammun from al-Asamm from Misma' who has said the following:

"Abu 'Abd Allah, *'Alayhi al-Salam,* has stated this *Hadith.* 'The Messenger of Allah, *O Allah, grant compensation to Muhammad and his family worthy of their services to Your cause,* has said, "Allah forgives a family who come together, prepare the table of food, they all mention the name of Allah at the beginning of food and praise Allah, most Majestic, most Glorious, at the end of food.'"

Chapter 48 - The Rare Ahadith

H 11363, Ch. 48, h 1
Muhammad ibn Yahya has narrated from Ahmad ibn Muhammad from Muhammad ibn Yahya from Ghiyath ibn Ibrahim who has said the following:

"Abu 'Abd Allah, *'Alayhi al-Salam,* has said that `Amir al-Mu'minin has said, 'Do not eat from the top of Tharid but eat from its sides because blessing is on its top.'" (Tharid is loaf of bread broken in pieces in broth.)

H 11364, Ch. 48, h 2
Ali ibn Ibrahim has narrated from his father from al-Nawfaliy from al-Sakuniy who has said the following:

"Abu 'Abd Allah, *'Alayhi al-Salam,* has said that `Amir al-Mu'minin was asked about a package of food which is found having been left on the road, in which there is a large amount of meat, bread, eggs and cheese and there is a knife in it. `Amir al-Mu'minin said, 'It must be evaluated and its contents used for food because it is perishable; and if someone claims it, the evaluated price must be paid to him.' It was said, 'O `Amir al-Mu'minin, it is not known if it belongs to a Muslim or it is a package of a Zoroastrian.' He (the Imam) said, 'They are free to use it until they know.'"

H 11365, Ch. 48, h 3
A number of our people have narrated from Sahl ibn Ziyad from Ja'far ibn Muhammad al-Ash'ariy from ibn al-Qaddah who has said the following:

"Abu 'Abd Allah, *'Alayhi al-Salam,* has said that the Messenger of Allah, *O Allah, grant compensation to Muhammad and his family worthy of their services*

to Your cause, has said, 'When you eat you must eat from what is nearest to you.'"

H 11366, Ch. 48, h 4
Humayd ibn Ziyad has narrated from al-Khashshab from ibn Baqqah from 'Amr ibn Jami' who has said the following:

"Abu 'Abd Allah, *'Alayhi al-Salam,* has said, 'The Messenger of Allah, when eating would wipe the dish clean and say, "Whoever, wipes the dish clean is as if has given charity as much.""

H 11367, Ch. 48, h 5
Ali ibn Muhammad in a marfu' manner has said the following:

"'Amir al-Mu'minin, *'Alayhi al-Salam,* would brush his teeth widthwise and eat using all of his fingers.'"

H 11368, Ch. 48, h 6
Muhammad ibn Yahya has narrated from Muhammad ibn al-Hassan from 'Abd al-Rahman ibn abu Hashim from abu Khadijah who has said the following:

"Abu 'Abd Allah, *'Alayhi al-Salam,* would sit like slaves, place his hand on the ground and eat with his three fingers. The Messenger of Allah, *O Allah, grant compensation to Muhammad and his family worthy of their services to Your cause,* would also eat in the same way and not the way a tyrant one eats with his two fingers.'"

H 11369, Ch. 48, h 7
Muhammad ibn Yahya has narrated from Ahmad ibn Muhammad from al-Qasim ibn Yahya from his grandfather al-Hassan ibn Rashid from abu Basir who has said the following:

"Abu 'Abd Allah, *'Alayhi al-Salam,* has stated this *Hadith.* 'The Messenger of Allah, *O Allah, grant compensation to Muhammad and his family worthy of their services to Your cause,* has said, "When one of you eats food he should wipe (lick) his fingers, clean with which he has eaten; Allah, most Majestic, most Glorious, says, 'Allah grants you blessings.'""

H 11370, Ch. 48, h 8
Ali ibn Muhammad ibn Bandar has narrated from Ahmad ibn abu 'Abd Allah from Nuh ibn Shu'ayb from Yasir al-Khadim who has said the following:

"One day boys ate fruit but they did not eat them all and threw them away. Abu al-Hassan, *'Alayhi al-Salam,* said to them, 'Allah is free of all defects, if you did not need them, there are people who need them. You must feed those who are needy.'"

H 11371, Ch. 48, h 9
Ahmad ibn Muhammad has narrated from 'Uthman ibn 'Isa from Sama'ah ibn Mehran who has said the following:

"I once asked abu 'Abd Allah, *'Alayhi al-Salam,* about *Salat* (prayer) for which the time has begun and food is made available. He (the Imam) said, 'If it is the beginning of the time for *Salat* (prayer), then first begin with food; but if the time has passed and you are afraid of missing *Salat* (prayer) for which you then must do Qada' (the compensatory *Salat*), then begin with *Salat* (prayer) first.'"

H 11372, Ch. 48, h 10

It is narrated from the narrator of the previous *Hadith* from Nuh ibn Shu'ayb from Yasar al-Khadim and Nadir who both have said the following:

"Abu al-Hassan, *'Alayhi al-Salam,* said to us, 'If I stand up above you when you are eating, do not stand up until you complete eating.' Perhaps he called a certain one of us and it was said that they are eating; he (the Imam) would say, 'Leave them until they finish.'"

H 11373, Ch. 48, h 11

It is narrated from Nadir al-Khadim who has said the following:

"Abu al-Hassan, *'Alayhi al-Salam,* would not ask us to work when we were eating until we finished eating.'"

H 11374, Ch. 48, h 12

It is narrated from Nadir al-Khadim who has said the following

"Abu al-Hassan, *'Alayhi al-Salam,* would place *Jawzinajah* (a type of sweet) one on top of the other, and then give them to me.'"

H 11375, Ch. 48, h 13

Ahmad has narrated from his father from Sulayman al-Ja'fariy who has said the following:

"Abu al-Hassan, *'Alayhi al-Salam,* when food was made available and certain people had not washed their hands, would say, 'Those whose hands are clean can eat without washing their hands.'"

H 11376, Ch. 48, h 14

Ahmad has narrated from Yahya ibn Ibrahim from Muhammad ibn Yahya from ibn abu al-Balad from his father from Bazi' ibn 'Umar ibn Bazi' who has said the following:

"I once visited abu Ja'far, *'Alayhi al-Salam,* when he was eating vinegar with oil in a black bowl, in the middle of which it was written, 'Say Allah is one'. He (the Imam) said to me, 'Come close, O Bazi''. I went close and ate with him (the Imam). He (the Imam) sipped water three times when bread was finished; then he gave it to me and I drank the rest of the water.'"

H 11377, Ch. 48, h 15

Muhammad ibn Yahya has narrated from Ahmad ibn Muhammad ibn 'Isa from Mu'ammar ibn Khallad who has said the following:

"I once heard al-Rida', *'Alayhi al-Salam,* saying, 'If one eats food in his house and pieces fall, he must pick them up; but if one eats in wilderness or out of the house he can leave such pieces for the birds and beasts.'"

H 11378, Ch. 48, h 16

Ali ibn Ibrahim has narrated from his father from ibn abu 'Umayr from Hammad ibn 'Uthaman who has said the following:

"'Isma'il prepared food for a ceremony and abu 'Abd Allah, *'Alayhi al-Salam,* said to him, 'You must pay attention to the destitute to satisfy their hunger. Allah, most Majestic, most Glorious, says, "Falsehood is not served first or revisited for service." (34:49)'"

H 11379, Ch. 48, h 17

Muhammad ibn Yahya has narrated from Ali ibn Ibrahim al-Ja'fariy from Muhammad ibn al-Fudayl in a marfu' manner has said, the following:

"'*A'immah, 'Alayhi al-Salam,* have said that the Holy Prophet, when eating would eat from what was in front of (nearest to) him, and when drinking would offer water to one on his right side.'"

H 11380, Ch. 48, h 18

A number of our people have narrated from Ahmad ibn abu 'Abd Allah from a number of our people have narrated from Ali ibn Asbat from Ya'qub ibn Salim in a marfu' manner has said the following:

"'Amir al-Mu'minin, *'Alayhi al-Salam,* has said that the Messenger of Allah has said, 'Do not leave a food-stained towel at home without its being washed; it becomes plaything for Satan.'"

H 11381, Ch. 48, h 19

Ali ibn Ibrahim has narrated from his father from al-Nawfaliy from al-Sakuniy who has said the following:

"Abu 'Abd Allah, *'Alayhi al-Salam,* has said that the Messenger of Allah, *O Allah, grant compensation to Muhammad and his family worthy of their services to Your cause,* has said, 'Every Friday present fruits to your family or meat, so that they become happy because of Friday.'"

H 11382, Ch. 48, h 20

Ali ibn Ibrahim has narrated from his father from al-Nawfaliy from al-Sakuniy who has said the following:

"Abu 'Abd Allah, *'Alayhi al-Salam,* has said that the Messenger of Allah, *O Allah, grant compensation to Muhammad and his family worthy of their services to Your cause,* has said, 'Whoever builds a house should slaughter a healthy ram and feed its meat to the destitute. He then should say, 'O Lord, drive away from me defiant ones of Jinn and men and Shayatin and bless for us our homes,' whatever he asks will be granted.'"

H 11383, Ch. 48, h 21

A number of our people have narrated from Sahl ibn Ziyad from Ahmad ibn Muhammad from ibn abu Nasr who has said the following:

"Abu al-Hassan, al-Rida', *'Alayhi al-Salam,* has said, 'When you eat [something], then lie down on your back, then place your right leg on your left leg.'"

Chapter 49 - Eating Pieces of Food that Fall on the Table-spread

H 11384, Ch. 49, h 1

Muhammad ibn Yahya has narrated from Ahmad ibn Muhammad from al-Qasim ibn Yahya from his grandfather al-Hassan ibn Rashid from abu Basir who has said the following:

"Abu 'Abd Allah, *'Alayhi al-Salam,* has said that 'Amir al-Mu'minin has said, 'Eat what falls off of food, because in it is cure for all kinds of illness by the permission of Allah, most Majestic, most Glorious, for those who seek cures.'"

H 11385, Ch. 49, h 2

Ali ibn Ibrahim has narrated from Salih ibn al-Sindiy from Ja'far ibn Bashir from Aban 'Uthman from Dawud ibn Kathir who has said the following:

"Once I had dinner with abu 'Abd Allah, *'Alayhi al-Salam,* at 'Atmah (time of late evening *Salat* (prayer)). When he (the Imam) ended his dinner, he praised Allah, most Majestic, most Glorious, and said, 'This is my (manner of having) dinner and the dinner of my ancestors. When the table-spread was pulled out, he (the Imam) picked pieces of food fallen on it and ate them.'"

H 11386, Ch. 49, h 3

Ali ibn Ibrahim has narrated from his father from ibn abu 'Umayr from Ibrahim ibn 'Abd al-Hamid from 'Abd Allah ibn Salih al-Khath'amiy who has said the following:

"I once complained before abu 'Abd Allah, *'Alayhi al-Salam,* against lower back pain. He (the Imam) said, 'You must eat pieces of food that fall on the table-spread.' I (the narrator) followed the instruction and the pain went away. Ibrahim has said, 'I then found it on the left and the right side; I did the same thing again and benefited thereby.'"

H 11387, Ch. 49, h 4

A number of our people have narrated from Sahl ibn Ziyad from Mansur ibn al-'Abbas from al-Hassan ibn Wahab from his father who has said the following:

"Once we ate food with abu 'Abd Allah, *'Alayhi al-Salam.* When the table-spread was collected, he (the Imam) picked up the pieces that had fallen on it and ate them then said to us, 'This removes poverty and increases the number of children.'"

H 11388, Ch. 49, h 5

Humayd ibn Ziyad has narrated from al-Khashshab from ibn Baqqah from 'Amr ibn Jami' who has said the following:

"He (the Imam), *'Alayhi al-Salam,* has stated this *Hadith.* 'The Messenger of Allah, *O Allah, grant compensation to Muhammad and his family worthy of their services to Your cause,* has said, "If one finds pieces of food and eats them it is one good deed, and if one finds them in unclean places, then washes them, then picks them up, he will have seventy good deeds recorded for him."'"

H 11389, Ch. 49, h 6

Through the same chain of narrators as that of the previous *Hadith* the following is narrated: from 'Amr ibn Jami' who has said the following:

"Abu 'Abd Allah, *'Alayhi al-Salam,* has said that the Messenger of Allah, *O Allah, grant compensation to Muhammad and his family worthy of their services to Your cause,* once entered 'A'ishah's home and saw pieces of food on which he was about to step. He (the Messenger of Allah) picked them up and said, 'O Humayra' you must honor the company of the bounties of Allah, most Majestic, most Glorious, with you; from whoever they get farther away they never then return to them.'"

H 11390, Ch. 49, h 7

A number of our people have narrated from Ahmad ibn Muhammad, from ibn Khalid from Muhammad ibn Ali from Ibrahim ibn Mehzam who has said the following:

"Abu al-Hassan, *'Alayhi al-Salam,* has said that once a man complained before abu 'Abd Allah, *'Alayhi al-Salam,* against his lower back pain. He (the Imam) said, 'Why do you not eat pieces of food that fall on the table-spread.'"

H 11391, Ch. 49, h 8
Muhammad ibn Yahya has narrated from Ahmad ibn Muhammad from Mu'ammar ibn Khallad who has said the following:

"I once heard abu al-Hassan, *'Alayhi al-Salam,* saying, 'If one eats food in his house and pieces of food fall off, he must pick them up and eat; but if one eats food in the wilderness or outdoors he should leave such pieces for the birds and beasts.'" (See also Ch. 48, h 15)

H 11392, Ch. 49, h 9
A number of our people have narrated from Ahmad ibn Muhammad from ibn Khalid from certain persons of his people from al-Asamm from 'Abd Allah al-Arjaniy who has said the following:

"Once I was with abu 'Abd Allah, *'Alayhi al-Salam,* and he was eating. I saw him searching for pieces of food fallen on the table-spread of the size of sesame seed. I then said, 'I pray to Allah to keep my soul in service for your cause, are you looking for such pieces?' He (the Imam) said, 'O 'Abd Allah, it is your sustenance; do not leave them, and besides there is cure in them for all kinds of illness.'"

Chapter 50 - The Excellence of Bread

H 11393, Ch. 50, h 1
Ali ibn Ibrahim has narrated from his father from 'Abd Allah ibn al-Mughirah 'Amr ibn Shamir who has said the following:

"I once heard abu 'Abd Allah, *'Alayhi al-Salam,* saying, 'I lick food from my fingers but I fear my servants' seeing me and their thinking that I am greedy. That is not true. A people upon whom bounties were poured owned a very large canal. They bleached the wheat for bread for food and used it to wipe their children with it until the dumpsite became like a huge mountain. A virtuous man passed by and saw a woman wipe her child with it. He said to them, 'Fie upon you, have fear of Allah, most Majestic, most Glorious, and do not change the bounty you enjoy.' She said, 'Are you frightening us of hunger? As long as we have our great canal flowing we will not be afraid of hunger.' It angered Allah, most Majestic, most Glorious, and He made their canal to weaken, stopped the sky to rain on them and the earth to grow (anything). He (the Imam) said, 'They became needy of that dumpsite and divided it among them by means of balance.'"

H 11394, Ch. 50, h 2
Ali ibn Ibrahim has narrated from his father from Harun ibn Muslim from Mas'adah ibn Sadaqah who has said the following:

"It is a narration of abu 'Abd Allah, *'Alayhi al-Salam,* from the Messenger of Allah, *O Allah, grant compensation to Muhammad and his family worthy of their services to Your cause.* He (the Messenger of Allah) once said, 'You must treat bread with reverence because from the throne to earth and what is in it, a large number of His creatures have worked for it (to make it ready).' He (the

Messenger of Allah) then said, 'Will you like if I tell you something?' They replied, 'Yes, O Messenger of Allah, we pray to Allah to keep the fathers and mothers in service for your cause.' He (the Messenger of Allah) said, 'Among the Prophets before you there was a Prophet called Daniel. He once gave one loaf of bread to the owner of the crossing (means) to help for crossing. He threw the bread away saying, 'It is of no use for me. We crush bread under our foot.' When Daniel saw it, he raised his hands to the sky and said, 'O Lord, make bread revered because I saw what this servant just did to it and what he said.' Allah, most Majestic, most Glorious, sent revelation to the sky and told it to withhold rain and the earth to turn into a piece of pottery.' It did not rain and they ended up eating each other. When their condition reached the point which Allah, most Majestic, most Glorious, wanted, one woman said to the other, who each had a child, to one day eat the child of one of them. The other woman agreed and they ate the child. When they became hungry again the other woman demanded to eat the child of the other woman but she refused saying, 'Between us there is the Prophet of Allah.' They went to Daniel, *'Alayhi al-Salam,* for judgment. He said to them, 'I can see to what degree the condition has reached.' They said, 'Yes, O Prophet of Allah and it is more difficult.' He raised his hands to the sky and said, 'O Lord, return to us with Your generosity, and the extra of Your mercy and do not make the children to suffer because of the sins of the owner of the crossing and his disrespecting Your bounties.' Allah, most Majestic, most Glorious, commanded the sky to send rain and earth to grow produce for His creatures what they had lost of the goodness because He had turned to them with kindness through the small child.'"

H 11395, Ch. 50, h 3
A number of our people have narrated from Ahmad ibn Muhammad from al-Washsha' from al-Mithamiy from Aban ibn Taghlib who has said the following:

"Abu 'Abd Allah, *'Alayhi al-Salam,* has said, 'A loaf of bread must not be placed under the dish."

H 11396, Ch. 50, h 4
Al-Husayn from Muhammad has narrated from al-Sayyariy from Ali ibn Asbat from certain persons of his people who has said the following:

"Abu 'Abd Allah, *'Alayhi al-Salam,* has said, 'You must treat bread with reverence.' It was asked, 'What is treating it with reverence?' He (the Imam) said, 'When it is made available one must not wait for others.'"

H 11397, Ch. 50, h 5
Ali ibn Ibrahim has narrated from his father from 'Abd Allah ibn al-Mughirah from Talhah ibn Zayd from certain persons of our people who has said the following:

"He (the Imam) has said that the Messenger of Allah, once said, 'You must treat bread with reverence.' It was asked, 'What is its reverence?' He (the Messenger of Allah) said, 'When it is made available one must not wait for others.' The Messenger of Allah has said that of treating it with reverence is not to step on it or cut it.'"

H 11398, Ch. 50, h 6

Ali ibn Ibrahim has narrated from his father from al-Nawfaliy from al-Sakuniy who has said the following:

"Abu 'Abd Allah, *'Alayhi al-Salam,* has said that the Messenger of Allah, *O Allah, grant compensation to Muhammad and his family worthy of their services to Your cause,* has said, 'You must never smell bread like the beasts do. Bread is blessed and Allah, most Majestic, most Glorious, has sent the sky with rain and because of it He has grown the pastures. By means of bread you perform *Salat* (prayer), observe fast and perform *al-Hajj* of the House of your Lord.'"

H 11399, Ch. 50, h 7

Through the same chain of narrators as that of the previous *Hadith* the following is narrated:

"He (the Imam) has said that the Messenger of Allah has said, 'When bread and meat is brought for you, eat bread first to stop the emptiness of hunger, then eat the meat.'"

H 11400, Ch. 50, h 8

Muhammad ibn Yahya has narrated from Ahmad ibn Muhammad ibn 'Isa from Ya'qub ibn Yaqtin who has said the following:

"Abu al-Hassan, al-Rida' *'Alayhi al-Salam,* has said that the Messenger of Allah, *O Allah, grant compensation to Muhammad and his family worthy of their services to Your cause,* has said, 'Make your bread of small loaves because there is blessing with each loaf.' Ya'qub ibn Yaqtin has said, 'I saw abu al-Hassan, *'Alayhi al-Salam,* break the bread upward.'"

H 11401, Ch. 50, h 9

Muhammad ibn Yahya has narrated from Ahmad ibn Muhammad from al-Sayyariy from abu Ali ibn Rashid in a *marfu'* manner has said the following:

"Abu 'Abd Allah, *'Alayhi al-Salam,* has said that when `Amir al-Mu'minin did not have curry; he would cut the bread with a knife.'"

H 11402, Ch. 50, h 10

Al-Sayyariy in a marfu' manner has said the following:

"Abu 'Abd Allah, *'Alayhi al-Salam,* has said that the least of curry is to cut the bread with a knife.'"

H 11403, Ch. 50, h 11

Ali ibn Muhammad Bandar and others have narrated from Ahmad ibn abu 'Abd Allah from his father from 'Abd Allah ibn al-Fadl al-Nawfaliy from al-Fadl ibn Yunus who has said the following:

"I once had lunch with abu al-Hassan, *'Alayhi al-Salam,* and the dish was brought with bread underneath the dish. He (the Imam) said, 'You must revere bread and do not allow it to be placed under the dish.' He (the Imam) then said to me to command the slave to take the bread from underneath the dish.'"

H 11404, Ch. 50, h 12

Ahmad has narrated from ibn Faddal from al-Mithamiy from abu Basir who has said the following:

"Abu 'Abd Allah, *'Alayhi al-Salam,* disliked placing of the loaf of bread under the dish.'"

H 11405, Ch. 50, h 13
Ahmad ibn Muhammad has narrated from Ya'qub ibn Yazid from Muhammad ibn Jumhur from Idris ibn Yusuf who has said the following:
"Abu 'Abd Allah, *'Alayhi al-Salam,* has said that the Messenger of Allah, *O Allah, grant compensation to Muhammad and his family worthy of their services to Your cause,* has said, 'Do not cut bread with knife but break it with your hand and others must break it for you. You must do the opposite of al-'Ajam (non-Arabs).'"

H 11406, Ch. 50, h 14
Ali ibn Ibrahim has narrated from Muhammad ibn 'Isa from Yunus who has said the following:
"Abu al-Hassan, al-Rida', *'Alayhi al-Salam,* has said, 'Do not cut bread with knife, instead break it with the hands and do the opposite of *al-'Ajam* (non-Arabs).'"

Chapter 51 - Barley Bread

H 11407, Ch. 51, h 1
Ali ibn Ibrahim has narrated from Muhammad ibn 'Isa from Yunus who has said the following:
"Abu al-Hassan, al-Rida', *'Alayhi al-Salam,* has said, 'The excellence of barley bread over wheat bread is like our excellence over the people. There had not been any Prophet, who did not ask to eat barley bread and blessed it. In whichever stomach it enters, it removes every illness thereof. It is the sustenance of the Prophets and the food of the virtuous ones. Allah, most High, disdained to make the food of His Prophets in anything other than barley.'"

Chapter 52 - Bread of Rice

H 11408, Ch. 52, h 1
Ali ibn Ibrahim has narrated from Muhammad ibn 'Isa from Yunus who has said the following:
"Abu al-Hassan, al-Rida', *'Alayhi al-Salam,* has said, 'Nothing more useful enters the stomach of one suffering from Tuberculosis than bread of rice.'"

H 11409, Ch. 52, h 2
Muhammad ibn Yahya has narrated from Muhammad ibn Musa from al-Khashshab from Ali ibn Hassan from certain persons of our people who has said the following:
"Abu 'Abd Allah, *'Alayhi al-Salam,* has said, 'Feed bread of rice to a person suffering from diarrhea; nothing else is more useful for such a sufferer than this, it also tans (treats) the stomach and dispels the pain sufficiently.'"

H 11410, Ch. 52, h 3
Muhammad ibn Yahya has narrated from Ahmad ibn Muhammad from al-Sayyariy from Yahya ibn abu Rafi' and other in a marfu' manner has said the following:
"Abu 'Abd Allah, *'Alayhi al-Salam,* has said, 'No other food from lunch remains inside until night except bread of rice.'"

Chapter 53 - Kinds of *Sawiq* (roasted flour) and the Excellence of *Sawiq* of Wheat

H 11411, Ch. 53, h 1
Muhammad ibn Yahya has narrated from Ahmad ibn Muhammad ibn 'Isa from abu Hammam from Sulayman al-Ja'fariy who has said the following:

"Abu al-Hassan, al-Rida', *'Alayhi al-Salam,* has said, *sawiq* is a very good food. If you are hungry, it holds you. If you are full it digests your food.'"

H 11412, Ch. 53, h 2
Muhammad ibn Yahya has narrated from Ahmad ibn Muhammad from ibn Faddal from 'Abd Allah ibn Jundab from certain persons of his people who has said the following:

"Once, *sawiq* was mentioned before abu 'Abd Allah, *'Alayhi al-Salam,* and he (the Imam) said, 'It was prepared by the instruction of divine revelation.'"

H 11413, Ch. 53, h 3
Al-Husayn from Muhammad has narrated from Ahmad ibn Ishaq from Bakr ibn Muhammad who has said the following:

"Abu 'Abd Allah, *'Alayhi al-Salam,* has said, *sawiq* grows flesh and strengthens the bones .'"

H 11414, Ch. 53, h 4
Ali ibn Muhammad ibn Bandar has narrated from Ahmad ibn abu 'Abd Allah from 'Uthman ibn 'Isa Khalid ibn Najih who has said the following:

"Abu 'Abd Allah, *'Alayhi al-Salam,* has said, *sawiq* is the food of the messengers' or he (the Imam) said, 'the food of the Prophets.'"

H 11415, Ch. 53, h 5
It is narrated from the narrator of the previous *Hadith* from A number of our people have narrated from Ali ibn Asbat from Muhammad ibn 'Abd Allah ibn Sayabah from Jundab ibn 'Abd Allah who has said the following:

"I once heard abu al-Hassan, Musa, *'Alayhi al-Salam,* saying, *sawiq* was made by the instruction from the heavens.'"

H 11416, Ch. 53, h 6
A number of our people have narrated from Sahl ibn Ziyad from Yahya ibn al-Mubarak from 'Abd Allah ibn Jabalah from Ishaq ibn 'Ammar who has said the following:

"Abu 'Abd Allah, *'Alayhi al-Salam,* has said, 'Dry *sawiq* removes whiteness (vitiligo).'"

H 11417, Ch. 53, h 7
Ali ibn Muhammad ibn Bandar and others have narrated from Ahmad ibn abu 'Abd Allah from Muhammad ibn 'Isa from 'Ubayd Allah ibn Muskan who has said the following:

"I once heard abu 'Abd Allah, *'Alayhi al-Salam,* saying, 'Drinking *sawiq* with oil grows flesh, strengthens the bones, softens the skin and increases *al-Bah* (sexual desire).'"

H 11418, Ch. 53, h 8
A number of our people have narrated from Ahmad ibn Muhammad from Ali ibn al-Hakam from Qutaybah al-'A'sha' who has said the following:

"Abu 'Abd Allah, *'Alayhi al-Salam,* has said, 'Three handfuls of dry *sawiq* before breakfast absorbs phlegm and bile and it almost does not leave anything behind.'"

H 11419, Ch. 53, h 9
It is narrated from the narrator of the previous *Hadith* from Ali ibn al-Hakam from al-Nadr ibn Qarwash who has said the following:
"Abu al-Hassan, al-Awwal, *'Alayhi al-Salam,* has said, 'If you turn *sawiq* seven times upside down and change its place from one pot into the other it then can remove fever and send power to the legs and feet.'"

H 11420, Ch. 53, h 10
It is narrated from the narrator of the previous *Hadith* from Ahmad ibn Muhammad from ibn abu Nasr from Hammad ibn 'Uthaman and Muhammad ibn Sawqah who has said the following:
"Abu 'Abd Allah, *'Alayhi al-Salam,* has said, *sawiq* digests heads (hard to digest food).'" (See also *Hadith* 1 above).

H 11421, Ch. 53, h 11
Ali ibn Muhammad ibn Bandar has narrated from Ahmad ibn abu 'Abd Allah from Musa ibn al-Qasim from Yahya ibn Musawir who has said the following:
"Abu 'Abd Allah, *'Alayhi al-Salam,* has said, *sawiq* removes bitterness (bile) and phlegm from the stomach and dispels seventy kinds of illness.'"

H 11422, Ch. 53, h 12
It is narrated from the narrator of the previous *Hadith* from his father from abu 'Abd Allah, al-Barqiy from Bakr ibn Muhammad from Khaythamah who has said the following:
"If one drinks sawiq for forty mornings his shoulder will fill up with strength.'"

H 11423, Ch. 53, h 13
Muhammad ibn Yahya has narrated from Musa ibn al-Hassan from al-Sayyariy from 'Ubayd Allah ibn abu 'Abd Allah who has said the following:
"Abu al-Hassan, *'Alayhi al-Salam,* wrote from Khurasan to al-Madinah, 'Do not make abu Ja'far al-Thaniy to drink *sawiq* with sugar because it is bad for man.'

"Al-Sayyariy has explained it from 'Ubayd Allah that it is undesirable for men because it weakens manhood desire due to its cold nature with sugar."

H 11424, Ch. 53, h 14
Muhammad ibn Yahya has narrated from 'Abd Allah ibn Ja'far from Muhammad ibn Khalid from Sayf al-Tammar who has said the following:
"One of our friends became ill in Makkah and began to hallucinate. I went to see abu 'Abd Allah, *'Alayhi al-Salam,* and informed him (the Imam) about him. He (the Imam) said, 'Make him drink *sawiq* of barley; it will cure him by the will of Allah and it is the food for the stomach of patients.' He (the narrator) has said, 'We made him drink it for two days or he said, 'twice' our friend was cured.'"

Chapter 54 - *Sawiq* of Lintels

H 11425, Ch. 54, h 1
Muhammad ibn Yahya has narrated from Muhammad ibn Musa in a marfu' manner has said, the following:

"Abu 'Abd Allah, *'Alayhi al-Salam*, has said, *sawiq* of lintels calms down thirst, makes the stomach strong and there is cure for seventy illnesses in it. It abolishes yellowish fluid and gives coolness to the stomach. He (the Imam) would not travel without it. He (the Imam) said that when blood becomes excited with any of one's associates, he (the Imam) said, 'Drink *sawiq* of lintels because it calms down the excitement of blood and extinguishes the heat.'"*\

H 11426, Ch. 54, h 2
It is narrated from the narrator of the previous *Hadith* from Muhammad ibn 'Isa from Ali ibn Mahziyar from who has said the following:
"We had a girl whose *Hayd* (menses) would not stop and she was about to die. Abu Ja'far, *'Alayhi al-Salam*, instructed to make her drink *sawiq* of lintels. She used the drink, bleeding stop and she was cured.'"

H 11427, Ch. , h 3
A number of our people have narrated from Sahl ibn Ziyad from al-Sayyariy from Ibrahim ibn Bitam from a man of the people of Marv who has said the following:
"Abu al-Hassan, al-Rida', *'Alayhi al-Salam*, once sent to us someone asking for *sawiq* and we sent to him (the Imam) *sawiq* mixed with ghee or oil. He (the Imam) returned it saying, 'If one takes dry *sawiq* before breakfast it dispels temperature, calms down bitterness but when it is mixed it then does not have that effect.'"

Chapter 55 - Excellence of Meat

H 11428, Ch. 55, h 1
Muhammad ibn Yahya has narrated from Ahmad ibn Muhammad from al-Washsha' from 'Abd Allah ibn Sinan who has said the following:
"I once asked abu 'Abd Allah, *'Alayhi al-Salam*, about the master curries in this world and in the next life. He (the Imam) said, 'It is meat. Have you not heard the words of Allah, most Majestic, most Glorious, '. . . meat of bird from that which they desire.' (56:21)"

H 11429, Ch. 55, h 2
Ali ibn Muhammad ibn Bandar has narrated from Ahmad ibn abu 'Abd Allah from Muhammad ibn Ali from 'Isa ibn 'Abd Allah al-'Alawiy from his father from his grandfather who has said the following:
"Ali, *'Alayhi al-Salam*, has said that the Messenger of Allah, *O Allah, grant compensation to Muhammad and his family worthy of their services to Your cause*, has said, 'Meat is the master food in this world and in the next life.'"

H 11430, Ch. 55, h 3
It is narrated from the narrator of the previous *Hadith* from Ali ibn al-Rayyan in a marfu' manner has said, the following:
"Abu 'Abd Allah, *'Alayhi al-Salam*, has said that the Messenger of Allah, *O Allah, grant compensation to Muhammad and his family worthy of their services to Your cause*, has said, 'The master food in paradise is meat.'"

H 11431, Ch. 55, h 4

Muhammad ibn Yahya has narrated from Ahmad ibn Muhammad from Ali ibn al-Hakam from certain persons of our people who has said the following:

"Abu Ja'far, *'Alayhi al-Salam,* has said, 'The master food is meat.'"

H 11432, Ch. 55, h 5

Ali ibn Muhammad ibn Bandar and others have narrated from Ahmad ibn abu 'Abd Allah from Muhammad ibn Ali from al-Hassan ibn Ali ibn Yusuf from Zakariya ibn Muhammad al-Azdiy from 'Abd al-'A'la' Mawla' Ale Sam who has said the following:

"I once said to abu 'Abd Allah, *'Alayhi al-Salam,* 'We narrate among us that the Messenger of Allah, *O Allah, grant compensation to Muhammad and his family worthy of their services to Your cause,* has said, 'Allah, most Blessed, most High, disliked the house of meat.' He (the Imam) said, 'They have lied. The Messenger of Allah spoke only about the house in which people backbite and eat people's meat. My father, *'Alayhi al-Salam,* liked meat and on the day he passed away, there was thirty dirham in the sleeve of the mother of his child to buy meat.'"

H 11433, Ch. 55, h 6

It is narrated from the narrator of the previous *Hadith* from 'Uthman ibn 'Isa from Misma' abu Sayyar who has said the following:

"Once, a man said to abu 'Abd Allah, *'Alayhi al-Salam,* 'People before us narrate that Allah, most Majestic, most Glorious, dislikes the house of meat.' He (the Imam) said, 'They have spoken the truth, but not as they think it is. It is in the sense that Allah, most Majestic, most Glorious, dislikes the house in which people eat other peoples' meat (backbite them).'"

H 11434, Ch. 55, h 7

Muhammad ibn Yahya has narrated from Ahmad ibn Muhammad from Ali ibn al-Hakam from al-Husayn ibn abu al-'Ala' who has said the following:

"Abu 'Abd Allah, *'Alayhi al-Salam,* has said that the Messenger of Allah, *O Allah, grant compensation to Muhammad and his family worthy of their services to Your cause,* 'Liked meat a great deal.'"

H 11435, Ch. 55, h 8

Ahmad ibn Muhammad has narrated from Ali ibn al-Hakam from Sayf ibn 'Amirah from al-Hassan ibn Harun who has said the following:

"Abu 'Abd Allah, *'Alayhi al-Salam,* has said, 'Abu Ja'far, *'Alayhi al-Salam,* on the day he passed away, left thirty dirham to buy meat, because he was a man who liked meat.'"

H 11436, Ch. 55, h 9

A number of our people have narrated from Sahl ibn Ziyad from Ja'far ibn Muhammad al-Ash'ariy from ibn al-Qaddah who has said the following:

"Abu 'Abd Allah, *'Alayhi al-Salam,* has said that the Messenger of Allah, *O Allah, grant compensation to Muhammad and his family worthy of their services to Your cause,* has said, 'We members of Quraysh people like meat a great deal.'"

Chapter 56 - One who Does not Eat Meat for Forty Days his Manners Change

H 11437, Ch. 56, h 1
Ali ibn Ibrahim has narrated from his father from ibn abu 'Umayr from Hisham ibn Salim who has said the following:
"Abu 'Abd Allah, *'Alayhi al-Salam,* has said, 'Meat grows meat and one who does not eat meat for forty days his manners change to worse, you must say Adhan in the ears of one whose manners change to worse.'"

H 11438, Ch. 56, h 2
A number of our people have narrated from Ahmad ibn Muhammad from Ahmad ibn Muhammad from ibn abu Nasr from al-Husayn ibn Khalid who has said the following:
"I once said to abu al-Hassan, al-Rida', *'Alayhi al-Salam,* 'People say that if one does not eat meat for three days his manners change to worse.' He (the Imam) said, 'They have spoken lies. However, one who does not eat meat for forty days his manners change and it is because the seed (sperm) transfers (from one stage of development to another) within the duration of forty days.'"

H 11439, Ch. 56, h 3
Ali ibn Muhammad ibn Bandar and others from Ahmad ibn abu 'Abd Allah, from Muhammad ibn Ali from ibn Baqqah from al-Hakam ibn Ayman from abu 'Usamah Zayd al-Shahham who has said the following:
"Abu 'Abd Allah, *'Alayhi al-Salam,* has said that the Messenger of Allah, *O Allah, grant compensation to Muhammad and his family worthy of their services to Your cause,* has said, 'One with whom forty days pass and has not eaten meat should borrow, on the credit of Allah, most Majestic, most Glorious, to buy meat to eat.'"

Chapter 57 - The Excellence of the Meat of Sheep Over Goats

H 11440, Ch. 57, h 1
Ali ibn Muhammad has narrated from Sahl ibn Ziyad from certain persons of his people, I think Muhammad ibn 'Isma'il who has said the following:
"Certain ones among us mentioned two kinds of meat before abu al-Hassan, al-Rida', *'Alayhi al-Salam.* He said, 'No other meat is better than the meat of goat.' Abu al-Hassan, *'Alayhi al-Salam,* looked at him and said, 'Had Allah, most Majestic, most Glorious, created any chunk of meat finer than that of sheep He would have presented that instead (of the ram) as ransom for 'Isma'il, *'Alayhi al-Salam.'"

H 11441, Ch. 57, h 2
Muhammad ibn Yahya has narrated from Ahmad ibn Muhammad ibn Khalid from Sa'd ibn Sa'd who has said the following:
"I once said to abu al-Hassan, *'Alayhi al-Salam,* 'My family does not like the meat of sheep.' He (the Imam) then asked, 'Why do they not like it?' I replied, 'They say that it accelerates bitterness, headache and pains.' He (the Imam) said, 'O Sa'd.' I replied, 'Yes, my Imam.' He (the Imam) said, 'Had Allah, most Majestic, most Glorious, considered anything more revered than sheep He

would have presented it instead (of the ram) as ransom for 'Isma'il, *'Alayhi al-Salam.'"*

H 11442, Ch. 57, h 3
Certain persons of our people have narrated from Ja'far ibn Ibrahim al-Hadramiy from Sa'd ibn Sa'd
who has said the following:
"I once said to abu al-Hassan, al-Rida', *'Alayhi al-Salam,* 'My family eats the meat of goats but not that of sheep.' He (the Imam) asked, 'Why they do so?' I replied, 'They say that it excites bitterness (stomach acid).' He (the Imam) said, 'Had Allah, most Majestic, most Glorious, known anything better than sheep He would have presented it as ransom for Ishaq.'" This is how it has come in *Hadith.*

Chapter 58 - The Meat of Cows and their Fat

H 11443, Ch. 58, h 1
Muhammad ibn Yahya Ali ibn al-Hassan al-Mithamiy, from Sulayman ibn 'Abbad, from 'Isa ibn
abu al-Ward from Muhammad ibn Qays who has said the following:
"Abu Ja'far, *'Alayhi al-Salam,* has said that the Israelites complained before Musa, *'Alayhi al-Salam,* against illness of whiteness (vitiligo) and he (Moses) complained before Allah, most Majestic, most Glorious, and Allah, most Majestic, most Glorious, sent him revelation that said, 'Command them to eat cow meat with (white) beets.'"

H 11444, Ch. 58, h 2
A number of our people have narrated from Sahl ibn Ziyad from Yahya ibn al-Mubarak saw it to be
from 'Abd Allah ibn Jabalah from abu al-Sabbah al-Kinaniy who has said the following:
"Abu 'Abd Allah, *'Alayhi al-Salam,* has said, 'Broth of cow meat expels whiteness (Vitiligo) illness.'"

H 11445, Ch. 58, h 3
Muhammad ibn Yahya has narrated from Ahmad ibn Muhammad from Muhammad ibn Khalid from
'Abd Allah ibn al-Mughirah from 'Isma'il ibn abu Ziyad who has said the following:
"Abu 'Abd Allah, *'Alayhi al-Salam,* has said, 'Cow milk and ghee (or fat) are cures but their meat is illness.'"

H 11446, Ch. 58, h 4
A number of our people have narrated from Sahl ibn Ziyad from Ali ibn Hassan from Musa ibn Bakr
who has said the following:
"I once heard abu al-Hassan, *'Alayhi al-Salam,* saying, 'Meat grows meat, but if one sends a morsel of *shahm* (fat) inside it expels the same amount of illness out.'"

H 11447, Ch. 58, h 5
Ali ibn Ibrahim has narrated from his father from Ahmad ibn Muhammad from ibn abu Nasr from
Hammad ibn 'Uthaman from Muhammad ibn Sawqah who has said the following:
"Abu 'Abd Allah, *'Alayhi al-Salam,* has said, 'If one eats a morsel of *shahm* (fat) it expels the same amount of illness out.'"

H 11448, Ch. 58, h 6

A number of our people have narrated from Ahmad ibn 'Abd Allah from certain persons of his people (and) brought by Zurarah who has said the following:

"I once said to abu 'Abd Allah, *'Alayhi al-Salam,* 'I pray to Allah to keep my soul in service for your cause, *'Al-Shahmah* (the fat) that expels the same amount of illness, which *shahmah* is it?' He (the Imam) said, 'It is *shahmah* of *al-Baqar* (cow) and no one before you has asked me about it.'"

H 11449, Ch. 58, h 7

A number of our people have narrated from Sahl ibn Ziyad from Muhammad ibn 'Isma'il ibn Bazi' from Yahya ibn Musawir who has said the following:

"Abu Ibrahim, *'Alayhi al-Salam,* has said, *sawiq* and broth of cow meat remove *al-Bars* (Vitiligo) illness.'"

Chapter 59 - Meat of Camels and Camels of Khurasan

H 11450, Ch. 59, h 1

Muhammad ibn Yahya has narrated from Ahmad ibn Muhammad ibn 'Isa from Ali ibn al-Hakam from Dawud al-Riqqiy who has said the following:

"I once wrote to abu al-Hassan, *'Alayhi al-Salam,* and ask about the meat of camels of Khurasan and their milk. He (the Imam) said, 'It is not unlawful.'"

H 11451, Ch. 59, h 2

Muhammad ibn Yahya has narrated from Ahmad ibn Muhammad from al-Hassan ibn Ali from Dawud al-Riqqiy who has said the following:

"I once said to abu 'Abd Allah, *'Alayhi al-Salam,* 'I pray to Allah to keep my soul in service for your cause, a man from the companions of abu al-Khattab prohibited eating the meat of camels of Khurasan and the meat of al-Musarwal (pigeons that have feathers on their legs).

He (the Imam) said, 'It is not unlawful to ride camel of Khurasan, drink their milk and eat the meat of al-Musarwal pigeons.'"

Chapter 60 - The Meat of Birds

H 11452, Ch. 60, h 1

A number of our people have narrated from Ahmad ibn Muhammad from ibn Khalid from 'Amr ibn 'Uthman in a marfu' manner has said the following:

"'Amir al-Mu'minin has said, 'Duck is the buffalo of birds, a hen is like the pig in birds and black partridge is the turkey in birds. You should not miss the two fledgling that were brought up by the woman of Rabi'ah with the leftover of her sustenance.'"

H 11453, Ch. 60, h 2

It is narrated from the narrator of the previous *Hadith* from al-Sayyariy in a marfu' manner who has said the following:

"Two kinds of meat were mentioned before 'Umar and 'Umar said, 'The better of the two kinds of meat is the meat of hen. 'Amir al-Mu'minin, *'Alayhi al-Salam,* said, 'No, it is like pigs in birds and the better of the two kinds of meat is the meat of the chick that has just risen or is about to rise.'"

H 11454, Ch. 60, h 3
Al-Sayyariy has narrated from those who narrated to him who has said the following:
"Abu 'Abd Allah, *'Alayhi al-Salam,* has said that the Messenger of Allah, *O Allah, grant compensation to Muhammad and his family worthy of their services to Your cause,* has said, 'If reducing one's anger makes him happy he should eat partridge meat.'"

H 11455, Ch. 60, h 4
Muhammad ibn Yahya has narrated from Muhammad ibn Musa who has said that narrated to me Ali ibn Sulayman from ibn abu 'Umayr from Muhammad ibn Hakim who has said the following:
"Abu al-Hassan, al-Awwal, *'Alayhi al-Salam,* has said, 'Feed one who is suffering from fever with the meat of *al-Qabaj* (a kind of partridge) because it strengthens the legs and dispels fever completely.'"

H 11456, Ch. 60, h 5
It is narrated from the narrator of the previous *Hadith* from Muhammad ibn 'Isa from Ali ibn Mahziyar from who has said the following:
"I once had lunch with abu Ja'far, *'Alayhi al-Salam,* and sand grouse was brought. He (the Imam) said, 'It is blessed; my father liked it and would instruct to feed roasted to one who suffers from jaundice; it benefits him.'"

H 11457, Ch. 60, h 6
It is narrated from the narrator of the previous *Hadith* from Ali ibn Sulayman from Marwak ibn 'Ubayd from Nashit ibn Salih who has said the following:
"I once heard abu al-Hassan, *'Alayhi al-Salam,* saying, 'It is not unlawful to eat the meat of *al-Habara'* (bustard). It is good for hemorrhoids and back-pain and it helps increase the ability to go to bed with one's wife.'"

Chapter 61 - The Meat of Deer and Wild Donkeys

H 11458, Ch. 61, h 1
A number of our people have narrated from Sahl ibn Ziyad from Nasr ibn Muhammad who has said the following:
"I once wrote to abu al-Hassan, *'Alayhi al-Salam,* and asked about the meat of the wild donkeys. He (the Imam) wrote the answer that said, 'It is not unlawful because of its being wild but not to eat is better to me.'"

Chapter 62 - The Meat of Buffalo

H 11459, Ch. 62, h 1
Ali ibn Ibrahim has narrated from his father from and Ali ibn Muhammad all from Ali ibn al-Husayn al-Tamimiy from Ayyub ibn Nuh from Safwan ibn Yahya from 'Abd Allah ibn Jundab who has said the following:
"I once heard abu al-Hassan, *'Alayhi al-Salam,* saying, 'It is not unlawful to eat buffalo meat and the use of its milk and ghee for food.'"

H 11460, Ch. 62, h 2
Muhammad ibn Yahya has narrated from Muhammad ibn abu al-Hassan from Safwan from 'Abd Allah ibn Jundab who has said the following:
"I once asked abu al-Hassan, *'Alayhi al-Salam,* about the meat of a buffalos and

its milk. He (the Imam) said, 'It is not unlawful to use such items for food.'"

Chapter 63 - Undesirability of Eating Fresh (Raw)Meat

H 11461, Ch. 63, h 1
Ali ibn Ibrahim has narrated from his father from Hammad ibn 'Isa from Hariz from Zurarah who has said the following:
"Abu Ja'far, *'Alayhi al-Salam,* has said that the Messenger of Allah, *O Allah, grant compensation to Muhammad and his family worthy of their services to Your cause,* prohibited eating fresh (raw) meat and said that beasts eat fresh meat, thus it must be used for food only after it is changed by sun or fire.'"

H 11462, Ch. 63, h 2
Muhammad ibn Yahya has narrated from Ahmad ibn Muhammad from Ali ibn al-Hakam from Hisham ibn Salim who has said the following:
"I once asked abu 'Abd Allah, *'Alayhi al-Salam,* about eating fresh (raw) meat. He (the Imam) said, 'It is the food of beasts.'"

Chapter 64 - About Qadid (Dried Meat)

H 11463, Ch. 64, h 1
Muhammad ibn Yahya has narrated from Ahmad ibn Muhammad ibn 'Isa from al-Hassan ibn Ali from 'Abd al-Samad ibn Bashir from 'Atiyyah brother of al-Mighra' who has said the following:
"I once said to abu 'Abd Allah, *'Alayhi al-Salam,* that companions of al-Mughirah prohibit eating of meat which is dried up in the sun and fire has not touched it. He (the Imam) said, 'It is not unlawful to eat it.'"

H 11464, Ch. 64, h 2
It is narrated from the narrator of the previous *Hadith* in a marfu' manner who has said the following:
"I once asked abu 'Abd Allah, *'Alayhi al-Salam,* if meat can be dried up by salting and leaving in the shade. He (the Imam) said, 'It is not unlawful to eat it because salt has changed it.'"

H 11465, Ch. 64, h 3
Muhammad ibn Yahya has narrated from Musa ibn al-Hassan from Muhammad ibn 'Isa who has said the following:
"Abu al-Hassan, al-Thalith, *'Alayhi al-Salam,* would say, 'I have not used anything for food more inducing illnesses than dried up meat, that is, *al-Qadid.*'"

H 11466, Ch. 64, h 4
It is narrated from the narrator of the previous *Hadith* who has said the following:
"Abu al-Hassan, *'Alayhi al-Salam,* would say, '*Al-Qadid* (dried up meat) is a bad kind of meat because it softens in the stomach and induces every kind of illness and it does not benefit anything, instead it harms.'"

H 11467, Ch. 64, h 5
A number of our people have narrated from Ahmad ibn Muhammad from ibn Khalid from certain persons of his people in a *marfu'* manner who has said the following:

"Abu 'Abd Allah, *'Alayhi al-Salam*, has said, 'There are two good things that never enter a bad stomach which they do not repair, and there are two bad things which never enter a good stomach which they do not damage. The two good things are pomegranate and warm water, and the two bad things are cheese and *al-Qadid* (dried up meat).'"

H 11468, Ch. 64, h 6

He has said that Abu 'Abd Allah, *'Alayhi al-Salam*, has said, 'Three things destroy the body; perhaps kill a person. One is eating of rotten meat, going to the bath with a full stomach and going to bed with old women. He has said that abu Ishaq al-Nahawandiy has added, going to bed with women when one's stomach is full.'"

H 11469, Ch. 64, h 7

It is narrated from the narrator of the previous *Hadith* from certain persons of his people in a marfu' manner who has said the following:

"Abu 'Abd Allah, *'Alayhi al-Salam*, has said, 'Use of three things forms fat in one's body, another three things cause weight loss. Two things benefit harmlessly and two things do all kinds of harm without any benefit. The three that can cause fatness are use of linen, perfume and lime. The ones that can cause weight loss are eating dried meat, cheese and spadix (al-Tal'). In another *Hadith* it is meat of the back of the camel and residue of oil.' The two that benefit without harm are warm water and pomegranate, and the two that harm without any benefit are dried meat and cheese.' I then said, 'I pray to Allah to keep my soul in service for your cause, 'Are the ones that cause weight loss harmful?' He (the Imam) said, 'Have you not heard that losing weight is harmful?'"

Chapter 65 - The Excellence of Shoulder Over other Parts

H 11470, Ch. 65, h 1

A number of our people have narrated from Ahmad ibn Muhammad from Ali ibn al-Rayyan in a marfu' manner who has said the following:

"I once asked abu 'Abd Allah, *'Alayhi al-Salam*, 'Why did the Messenger of Allah, *O Allah, grant compensation to Muhammad and his family worthy of their services to Your cause*, like shoulder meat more than meat from other parts of a sheep? He (the Imam) said, 'It is because Adam offered a sacrifice for Prophets of his offspring and he for everyone named a part. The shoulder was assigned to the Messenger of Allah. For this reason he liked it, desired and preferred over the other parts.'"

H 11471, Ch. 65, h 2

Muhammad ibn Yahya has narrated from Ahmad ibn Muhammad from ibn Faddal from ibn Bukayr from Zurarah who has said the following:

"Abu Ja'far, *'Alayhi al-Salam*, has said that the Messenger of Allah, *O Allah, grant compensation to Muhammad and his family worthy of their services to Your cause*, liked shoulder meat greatly.'"

H 11472, Ch. 65, h 3

A number of our people have narrated from Sahl ibn Ziyad from Ja'far ibn Muhammad al-Ash'ariy from ibn al-Qaddah who has said the following:

"I once heard abu 'Abd Allah, *'Alayhi al-Salam,* saying, 'The Jewish woman poisoned the Holy Prophet with shoulder meat and the Holy Prophet, liked it greatly but he disliked meat from the hip area because it is close to the urinating part.'"

Chapter 66 - Mixed Dish

H 11473, Ch. 66, h 1

Ali ibn Ibrahim has narrated from his father from ibn abu 'Umayr from Hisham ibn Salim who has said the following:

"Abu 'Abd Allah, *'Alayhi al-Salam,* has said, 'Meat with milk is the sauce of Prophets, *'Alayhim al-Salam.* '"

H 11474, Ch. 66, h 2

Muhammad ibn Yahya has narrated from Ahmad ibn Muhammad ibn 'Isa from al-Qasim ibn Yahya from his grandfather al-Hassan ibn Rashid from Muhammad ibn Muslim who has said the following:

"Abu 'Abd Allah, *'Alayhi al-Salam,* has said that 'Amir al-Mu'minin has said, 'When a Muslim becomes weak, he should eat meat with milk.'"

H 11475, Ch. 66, h 3

Ahmad ibn Muhammad from Muhammad ibn Sinan from Ziyad ibn abu al-Hallal who has said the following:

"I once had dinner with abu 'Abd Allah, *'Alayhi al-Salam,* and it was meat with milk. He (the Imam) said, 'It is the sauce of the Prophets, *'Alayhim al-Salam.*'"

H 11476, Ch. 66, h 4

A number of our people have narrated from Ahmad ibn abu 'Abd Allah from Muhammad ibn 'Isa from 'Ubayd Allah ibn 'Abd Allah al-Dihqan from Durust from 'Abd Allah ibn Sinan who has said the following:

"Abu 'Abd Allah, *'Alayhi al-Salam,* has said, 'One of the prophets complained before Allah, most Majestic, most Glorious, against weakness and it was said to him, 'Cook meat with milk; they strengthen the body.' He (the narrator) has said that I then asked if it is al-Mudayrah (butter milk).' He (the Imam) said, 'No, it is meat with yogurt of milk.'"

H 11477, Ch. 66, h 5

A number of our people have narrated from Sahl ibn Ziyad from Muhammad ibn al-Walid from Yunus ibn Ya'qub who has said the following:

"He (the Imam) has said, 'The most desirable food to the Messenger of Allah, *O Allah, grant compensation to Muhammad and his family worthy of their services to Your cause,* was al-Nar Bajah (broth made of pomegranate).'"

H 11478, Ch. 66, h 6

Muhammad ibn al-Walid has narrated from Yunus ibn Ya'qub who has said the following:

"I once sent for abu 'Abd Allah, *'Alayhi al-Salam,* a cooking pot with al-Nar Bajah in it (broth made of pomegranate). He (the Imam) ate from it and told to save the rest for him to have it twice or three times. The slave then added water in it and brought it to him. He (the Imam) said, 'Fie upon you. You have destroyed it.'"

H 11479, Ch. 66, h 7
A number of our people have narrated from Ahmad ibn Muhammad from Muhammad ibn Khalid al-Nadr ibn Suwayd from abu Basir who has said the following:

"Abu 'Abd Allah, *'Alayhi al-Salam,* liked *Zabibiyah* (a dish with raisins) quite well.'"

H 11480, Ch. 66, h 8
Ali ibn Ibrahim has narrated from his father from al-Nawfaliy from al-Sakuniy who has said the following:

'Amir al-Mu'minin, *'Alayhi al-Salam,* has said, 'Eating many kinds of foods at the same time enlarges the belly and numbs the buttocks.'"

Chapter 67 - Tharid (Pieces of Bread in Broth)

H 11481, Ch. 67, h 1
Ali ibn Muhammad ibn Bandar has narrated from Ahmad ibn Muhammad from Mansur ibn al-'Abbas from Sulayman ibn Rashid from his father from al-Mufaddal ibn 'Umar who has said the following:

"I once ate food with abu 'Abd Allah, *'Alayhi al-Salam,* and the food was of one kind. He (the Imam) said, 'You can have this food but to me any other food is not as desirable as Tharid. I would have liked if al-Asfanajat was prohibited.'" (Al-Asfananjat is either spinach or something presented before the main course of food, which reduces one's appetite.)

H 11482, Ch. 67, h 2
Ali ibn Ibrahim has narrated from his father from al-Nawfaliy from al-Sakuniy who has said the following:

"Abu 'Abd Allah, *'Alayhi al-Salam,* has said that the Holy Prophet has said, 'The first one who made food of several kinds was Ibrahim, and the first who made Tharid was Hashim.'"

H 11483, Ch. 67, h 3
A number of our people have narrated from Sahl ibn Ziyad from Ja'far ibn Muhammad al-Ash'ariy from ibn al-Qaddah who has said the following:

"Abu 'Abd Allah, *'Alayhi al-Salam,* has said that the Messenger of Allah, *O Allah, grant compensation to Muhammad and his family worthy of their services to Your cause,* has said, 'O Lord, bless for my followers al-Thard and *al-Tharid.'* Ja'far has said, that al-Thard is whatever is small and *al-Tharid* is whatever is large."

H 11484, Ch. 67, h 4
Ali ibn Ibrahim has narrated from his father from al-Nawfaliy from al-Sakuniy who has said the following:

"Abu 'Abd Allah, *'Alayhi al-Salam,* has said, 'Tharid is the food of Arabs.'"

H 11485, Ch. 67, h 5

Ali ibn Ibrahim has narrated from his father from ibn abu 'Umayr from Hisham ibn Salim from Salmah ibn Muhriz who has said the following:

"Abu 'Abd Allah, *'Alayhi al-Salam,* once said to me, 'You should eat Tharid because I do not find anything more agreeable than Tharid.'"

H 11486, Ch. 67, h 6

Muhammad ibn Yahya has narrated from Ahmad ibn Muhammad from Ali ibn al-Hakam from Mu'awiyah ibn Wahab from abu 'Usamah Zayd al-Shahham who has said the following:

"I once went to visit my master abu 'Abd Allah, *'Alayhi al-Salam,* when he (the Imam) was having sikbajah (broth with vinegar) of cow meat.'"

H 11487, Ch. 67, h 7

Ali ibn Muhammad ibn Bandar has narrated from Ahmad ibn abu 'Abd Allah from his father from Sa'dan ibn Muslim from 'Isma'il ibn Jabir who has said the following:

"Once I was with 'Abd Allah *'Alayhi al-Salam,* and he (the Imam) asked for table-spread with food. Tharid and meat was brought and he (the Imam) asked for oil which he (the Imam) poured on the meat and I ate with him (the Imam).'"

H 11488, Ch. 67, h 8

Zurarah has narrated from certain persons of his people in a marfu' manner the following:

"He (the Imam) said that the Holy Prophet, *O Allah, grant compensation to Muhammad and his family worthy of their services to Your cause,* has said, 'Tharid is a blessing.'"

H 11489, Ch. 67, h 9

Muhammad ibn Yahya has narrated from Ahmad ibn Muhammad from Muhammad ibn Yahya from Ghiyath ibn Ibrahim who has said the following:

"Abu 'Abd Allah, *'Alayhi al-Salam,* has said that 'Amir al-Mu'minin has said, 'Do not eat from the top of Tharid but eat from its sides because blessing is in its top.'"

H 11490, Ch. 67, h 10

A number of our people have narrated from Sahl ibn Ziyad Muhammad ibn 'Isa from 'Umayyah ibn 'Amr from al-Shu'ayriy who has said the following:

"Abu 'Abd Allah, *'Alayhi al-Salam,* has said, 'You must extinguish the flame of malice with meat and Tharid (bread in broth).'"

Chapter 68 - Roast, al-Kabab and Heads

H 11491, Ch. 68, h 1

Muhammad ibn Yahya has narrated from Muhammad ibn al-Hassan from Musa ibn 'Umar from Ja'far ibn Bashir from Ibrahim ibn Mehzam from abu Maryam from al-Asbagh ibn Nabatah who has said the following:

"I once went to visit 'Amir al-Mu'minin and before him (the Imam) there was roasted meat. He (the Imam) said to me, 'Come close and eat.' I said, 'O 'Amir al-Mu'minin, this thing is harmful for me.' He (the Imam) said, 'Come close. I will teach you certain words with which not even one thing will harm you of which you are afraid. Say, 'In the name of Allah, the best of names, to the fill of the earth and sky, the Beneficent, the Merciful, the one with whose name not even one thing and illness harms.' Now you can have lunch with us.'"

H 11492, Ch. 68, h 2

A number of our people have narrated from Sahl ibn Ziyad from Ali ibn Hassan from Musa ibn Bakr who has said the following:

"I once in al-Madinah became very weak and visited abu al-Hassan, *'Alayhi al-Salam*. He (the Imam) said, 'I can see you are very weak.' I replied, 'Yes, I feel weak.' He (the Imam) said, 'Eat *kabab*.' I then ate *kabab* and I was cured.'"

H 11493, Ch. 68, h 3

Muhammad ibn Yahya has narrated from Ahmad ibn Muhammad ibn 'Isa from Muhammad ibn Sinan from Musa ibn Bakr who has said the following:

"Once abu al-Hassan, al- Awwal asked me, 'Why do you look pale?' I replied, 'I suffer from a certain pain.' He (the Imam) said, 'Eat meat.' I ate meat and the next Friday he (the Imam) saw me as pale as before and said, 'Did I not tell you to eat meat?' I replied, 'Yes, I have not eaten anything other than meat from the day you instructed me.' He (the Imam) then asked, 'How did you eat?' I replied, 'I ate as mixed with other items.' He (the Imam) said, 'No, eat as kabab.' I then ate kabab and he (the Imam) sent for me next Friday when my blood level had come back in my face, and he (the Imam) said to me, 'Now it is good, you are fine.'"

H 11494, Ch. 68, h 4

Ali ibn Ibrahim has narrated from his father from Ahmad ibn Muhammad from ibn abu Nasr from 'Abd Allah ibn Muhammad al-Shamiy from al-Husayn ibn Hanzalah who has said the following:

"One of the two Imam, (abu Ja'far or abu 'Abd Allah), *'Alayhim al-Salam,* has said, eating kabab dispels fever.'"

H 11495, Ch. 68, h 5

A number of our people have narrated from Ahmad ibn abu 'Abd Allah from Ali ibn al-Rayyan ibn al-Salt from 'Ubayd Allah ibn 'Abd Allah al-Wasitiy from Wasil ibn Sulayman from Durust who has said the following:

"We once mentioned heads of sheep before abu 'Abd Allah, *'Alayhi al-Salam,* and he (the Imam) said, 'The head is the place of slaughtering (intelligence), close to means for grazing and far from harms.'"

Chapter 69 - Al-Harisah (Mashed Grains and Meat)

H 11496, Ch. 69, h 1

Al-Husayn from Muhammad has narrated from Mu'alla' ibn Muhammad from Bistam ibn Murrah al-Farsiy who has said that narrated to us 'Abd al-Rahman ibn Yazid al-Farsiy from Muhammad ibn Ma'ruf from Salih ibn Razin who has said the following:

"Abu 'Abd Allah, *'Alayhi al-Salam,* has said that 'Amir al-Mu'minin has said, 'You must eat al-Harisah (mashed grains and meat) because it energizes you for worshipping for forty days. It was of the items in the table-spread with food that was revealed to the Messenger of Allah, *O Allah, grant compensation to Muhammad and his family worthy of their services to Your cause.*'"

H 11497, Ch. 69, h 2

A number of our people have narrated from Ahmad ibn Khalid from Muhammad ibn 'Isa from al-Dihqan from Durust ibn abu Mansur from 'Abd Allah ibn Sinan who has said the following:

"Abu 'Abd Allah, *'Alayhi al-Salam,* has said, 'A Prophet of the Prophets of Allah, most Majestic, most Glorious, complained against deficiency in going to bed with one's wife and he was commanded to eat al-Harisah (mashed grains and meat).'"

H 11498, Ch. 69, h 3

In another *Hadith* in a marfu' manner the following is narrated:

"Abu 'Abd Allah, *'Alayhi al-Salam,* has said that the Messenger of Allah, *O Allah, grant compensation to Muhammad and his family worthy of their services to Your cause,* complained before Allah, most Majestic, most Glorious, against back pain and He commanded him to eat grains with meat, that is, al-Harisah.'"

H 11499, Ch. 69, h 4

Muhammad ibn Yahya has narrated from Ahmad ibn Muhammad ibn 'Isa from Muhammad ibn Sinan from Mansur al-Sayqal from his father from abu Basir who has said the following:

"Abu 'Abd Allah, *'Alayhi al-Salam,* has said that Allah, most Blessed, most High, sent to His Messenger, *O Allah, grant compensation to Muhammad and his family worthy of their services to Your cause,* al-Harisah. It was of the kind planted in gardens of paradise, which is stirred by *al-Hur al-'iyn* as a gift and the Messenger of Allah ate it. It increased his power equal to forty men. This was something with which Allah, most Majestic, most Glorious, wanted to make His Prophet, Muhammad, happy.'"

Chapter 70 - Al-Muthallathah (Preparation of three Kinds of Grains) Al-Hasa' Flour Cooked with Oil Sweet or without

H 11500, Ch. 70, h 1

A number of our people have narrated from Ahmad ibn Muhammad ibn Khalid from Yahya ibn Ibrahim ibn abu al-Balad from his father from al-Walid ibn Sabih who has said the following:

"Abu 'Abd Allah, *'Alayhi al-Salam,* once asked, 'What do you feed your family in winter?' I replied, 'I feed them meat, if there is no meat then it is oil and ghee.' He (the Imam) said, 'What prevents you from using for food this *al-Kar kur* which is the most palatable for the body, that is, the tri-mixture.' Certain persons of our people informed me that this mixture consists of one-third rice, one-third beans and one-third kidney beans or other grains, which then are mixed together and cooked.'"

H 11501, Ch. 70, h 2

Muhammad ibn Yahya has narrated from Ahmad ibn Muhammad ibn 'Isa from Ali ibn Hadid from certain persons of our people who has said the following:

"Abu 'Abd Allah, *'Alayhi al-Salam,* has said, *'al-Talbiyn* (white flour cooked with oil that looks like milk) clears the sad heart, just as fingers wipe perspiration from the forehead.'"

H 11502, Ch. 70, h 3

It is narrated from abu 'Abd Allah, *'Alayhi al-Salam,* who has said that the Messenger of Allah, *O Allah, grant compensation to Muhammad and his family worthy of their services to Your cause,* has said, 'If anything can help one against death it can only be al-Talbinah.' It was asked, 'O Messenger of Allah, what is al-Talbinah?' 'It is *al-Hasa'* (flour cooked with oil, sweet or without sweet) with milk, it is al-Hasa' with milk,' he (the Messenger of Allah) repeated it three times.'

"Sahl ibn Ziyad has narrated from Muhammad ibn al-Hassan ibn Shammun from al-Asamm from Misma' ibn 'Abd al-Malik from abu 'Abd Allah, *'Alayhi al-Salam,* a similar *Hadith.*"

Chapter 71 - Al-Halwa' (Sweet)

H 11503, Ch. 71, h 1

A number of our people have narrated from Sahl ibn Ziyad from Ahmad ibn Harun ibn Muwaffaq al-Madiniy from his father who has said the following:

"Once al-Madiy (the previous) abu al-Hassan *'Alayhi al-Salam,* called me for food and I ate food with him. He (the Imam) ate quite a bit of al-Halwa' (sweet) and I said, 'This is quite a bit of al-Halwa'.' He (the Imam) said, 'I and our followers are created from sweetness; thus we like sweet.'"

H 11504, Ch. 71, h 2

Muhammad ibn Yahya has narrated from Ahmad ibn Muhammad from Ali ibn abu Hamzah from abu Basir who has said the following:

"If one of us does not want al-Halwa' he wants drink (which is sweet).'"

H 11505, Ch. 71, h 3

Ahmad ibn Muhammad has narrated from ibn Faddal from Yunus ibn Ya'qub from 'Abd-al-'A'la' who has said the following:

"I once ate with abu 'Abd Allah, *'Alayhi al-Salam,* a chicken filled with Khabis (a sweet made of bread and dates). We opened and ate it."

"Ibn Faddal has narrated from Yunus ibn Ya'qub from 'Abd al-'A'la' who has said that he ate with abu 'Abd Allah, *'Alayhi al-Salam,* like what is mentioned in the previous *Hadith.*"

H 11506, Ch. 71, h 4

Ibn Faddal has narrated from Yunus ibn Ya'qub who has said the following:

"We were in al-Madinah and abu 'Abd Allah, *'Alayhi al-Salam,* sent a message to us to make for him (the Imam) *Faludah* (a kind of sweet) of a little quantity . We then sent it to him (the Imam) in a small bowl.'"

Chapter 72 - Hot Food

H 11507, Ch. 72, h 1

Muhammad ibn Yahya has narrated from Ahmad ibn Muhammad from al-Qasim ibn Yahya from his grandfather al-Hassan ibn Rashid from Muhammad ibn Muslim who has said the following:

"Abu 'Abd Allah, *'Alayhi al-Salam,* has said that `Amir al-Mu'minin has said, 'Leave the hot (food) until it becomes cold. The Messenger of Allah, *O Allah, grant compensation to Muhammad and his family worthy of their services to Your cause,* once was given hot food and he (the Messenger of Allah) said,

"Leave it until it becomes cold. Allah, most Majestic, most Glorious, is not the one to feed us fire; the blessing is in the cold.""""

H 11508, Ch. 72, h 2

Ali ibn Ibrahim has narrated from his father from al-Nawfaliy from al-Sakuniy who has said the following:

"Abu 'Abd Allah, *'Alayhi al-Salam,* has said that once very hot food was brought to the Messenger of Allah, *O Allah, grant compensation to Muhammad and his family worthy of their services to Your cause,* who said, 'Allah, most Majestic, most Glorious, is not to feed us fire. Leave it until it becomes cold and possible to eat it. Hot food is without blessing and Satan has a share in it.'"

H 11509, Ch. 72, h 3

Ali ibn Ibrahim has narrated from his father from ibn abu 'Umayr from Muhammad ibn Hakim who has said the following:

"Abu 'Abd Allah, *'Alayhi al-Salam,* has said that hot food is devoid of blessings.'"

H 11510, Ch. 72, h 4

Muhammad ibn Yahya has narrated from Ahmad ibn Muhammad from ibn Faddal from ibn al-Qaddah who has said the following:

"Abu 'Abd Allah, *'Alayhi al-Salam,* has stated this *Hadith.* 'Once, hot food was brought to the Messenger of Allah, *O Allah, grant compensation to Muhammad and his family worthy of their services to Your cause.* He (the Messenger of Allah) said, 'Allah, most Majestic, most Glorious, is not the one to feed us what is similar to fire. Wait, until it becomes cold', thus, it was left to become cold.'"

H 11511, Ch. 72, h 5

Ahmad ibn Muhammad has narrated from ibn Mahbub from Yunus ibn Ya'qub from Sulayman ibn Khalid who has said the following:

"I once attended dinner with abu 'Abd Allah, *'Alayhi al-Salam,* in the summer and they brought a table-spread with bread inside it and a bowl of *Tharid* (bread made in pieces in broth) and meat. He (the Imam) said, 'Come for food.' I went close. He (the Imam) placed his hand in it and pulled back saying, 'I seek refuge with Allah against fire, I seek protection with Allah against fire, I seek protection with Allah against fire. We cannot bear this, how the fire will be, we cannot bear with this, how the fire will be, we cannot bear with this, how the fire will be.' He (the Imam) kept repeating it until it became possible to eat the food. He (the Imam) ate and we ate with him.'"

Chapter 73 - Making the Bones Bare

H 11512, Ch. 73, h 1

A number of our people have narrated from Ahmad ibn abu 'Abd Allah from Muhammad ibn Ali from Muhammad ibn al-Haytham from his father who has narrated the following:

"Abu Hamzah once made food for us and we were in a group and when we were all present, a man made a bone bare and took out its marrow. He (the Imam) said to him aloud, 'Do not do so because I heard Ali ibn al-Husayn, *'Alayhim al-Salam,* saying, "Do not remove bone marrows and make bare; in it there is a share for al-Jinn. If you remove it things better than this will go away from the house.'"

Chapter 74 - About Fish

H 11513, Ch. 74, h 1
Muhammad ibn Yahya has narrated from Ahmad ibn Muhammad ibn 'Isa from Sa'id ibn Janah from a Mawla of abu 'Abd Allah, *'Alayhi al-Salam,* who has said the following:

"Abu 'Abd Allah, *'Alayhi al-Salam,* once asked for dates and ate it; then said, 'I have no appetite for it but it is because I just ate fish. He (the Imam) then said, 'If one goes to sleep for the night and there is fish in his stomach after which he has not made a few dates or honey to follow it the vein of paralysis continues to beat on him until the morning.'"

H 11514, Ch. 74, h 2
A number of our people have narrated from Ahmad ibn abu 'Abd Allah from Nuh ibn Shu'ayb from certain persons of our people who has said the following:

"Abu 'Abd Allah, *'Alayhi al-Salam,* has said that the Messenger of Allah, *O Allah, grant compensation to Muhammad and his family worthy of their services to Your cause,* when eating fish would say, 'O Lord, make it a blessing for us and change it for us with what is better.'"

H 11515, Ch. 74, h 3
Al-Husayn from Muhammad has narrated from Mu'alla' ibn Muhammad from Muhammad ibn Ali al-Hamadaniy from Mu'attib who has said the following:

"Abu 'Abd Allah, or abu al-Hassan, *'Alayhim al-Salam,* once said, 'O Mu'attib, order for us fresh fish; I want to apply cupping.' I ordered fish and brought them. He (the Imam) said to me to cook for him (the Imam) a part of it and roast another part. He (the Imam) had lunch with it and abu al-Hassan had dinner with it.'"

Ali ibn Ibrahim has narrated from (his father) and Ali ibn Muhammad ibn Bandar from his father and Ahmad ibn abu 'Abd Allah all from Muhammad ibn Ali al-Hamadaniy has narrated a similar *Hadith.*"

H 11516, Ch. 74, h 4
Ali ibn Ibrahim has narrated from his father from ibn abu 'Umayr from Ibrahim ibn 'Abd al-Hamid who has said the following:

I once heard abu al-Hassan, *'Alayhi al-Salam,* saying, 'You must eat fish; if you eat it without bread it is sufficient; and if you eat with bread it becomes more palatable for you.'"

H 11517, Ch. 74, h 5
Ali ibn Ibrahim has narrated from Harun ibn Muslim from Mas'adah ibn Sadaqah from ibn al-Yasa' who has said the following:

"Abu 'Abd Allah, *'Alayhi al-Salam,* has said that 'Amir al-Mu'minin has said, 'Do not eat fish very often; it melts the body.'"

H 11518, Ch. 74, h 6

Ali ibn Muhammad ibn Bandar has narrated from Muhammad ibn 'Isa from Yunus from 'Abd Allah ibn Sinan who has said the following:

"Abu 'Abd Allah, *'Alayhi al-Salam,* has said, 'Eating fish melts the body.'"

H 11519, Ch. 74, h 7

Sahl ibn Ziyad from Ali ibn Hassan from Musa ibn Bakr who has said the following:

"Abu al-Hassan, *'Alayhi al-Salam,* has said, 'Eating fresh fish melts the body.'"

H 11520, Ch. 74, h 8

A number of our people have narrated from Ahmad ibn Muhammad from 'Uthman ibn 'Isa in a marfu' manner has said the following:

"He (the Imam), *'Alayhi al-Salam,* has said, 'Fresh fish melts the fat of the eye.'"

H 11521, Ch. 74, h 9

Sahl ibn Ziyad has narrated from Ali ibn Hassan from Musa ibn Bakr who has said the following:

"Abu al-Hassan, *'Alayhi al-Salam,* has said, 'Fresh fish melts the fat of the eyes.'"

H 11522, Ch. 74, h 10

Muhammad ibn Yahya has narrated the following:

"Certain persons of our people once wrote to abu Muhammad, *'Alayhi al-Salam,* complaining about blood and yellowness, saying, 'If I apply cupping, yellowness stirs up, when I delay it blood harms me, so what would you advise me in such case?' He (the Imam), *'Alayhi al-Salam,* wrote, 'Apply cupping and after cupping eat fresh fish as kabab.' He (the narrator) has said, 'I repeated exactly the same question to him (the Imam). He (the Imam) wrote, 'Apply cupping and after cupping eat fresh fish as kabab with water and salt.' He (the narrator) has said, 'I followed the instruction and I lived in good health and it became my food.'"

Chapter 75 - Eggs and Chicken

H 11523, Ch. 75, h 1

A number of our people have narrated from Ahmad ibn Muhammad ibn Khalid from Ja'far ibn Muhammad Hakim from Yunus from Murazim who has said the following:

"Abu 'Abd Allah, *'Alayhi al-Salam,* once mentioned eggs and said, 'It is light and it reduces the desire for meat.'

"He (the narrator) has said, 'Muhammad ibn 'Isma'il ibn Bazi' has narrated from Ja'far ibn Muhammad ibn Hakim from Murazim with an addition of, 'it does not have the harmfulness of meat.'"

H 11524, Ch. 75, h 2

Abu Ali al-Ash'ariy has narrated from Muhammad ibn Salim from Ahmad ibn al-Nadr from 'Umar ibn abu Hasnah al-Jammal who has said the following:

"I once complained before abu al-Hassan, *'Alayhi al-Salam,* about not having any children. He (the Imam) said, 'Ask forgiveness from Allah and eat eggs with onion.'"

H 11525, Ch. 75, h 3

A number of our people have narrated from Ahmad ibn abu 'Abd Allah from Muhammad ibn 'Isa from 'Ubayd Allah ibn 'Abd Allah al-Dihqan from Durust from 'Abd Allah ibn Sinan who has said the following:

"Abu 'Abd Allah, *'Alayhi al-Salam,* has said, 'One of the prophets complained before Allah, most Majestic, most Glorious, about not having any children. He (Allah) told him to eat meat with egg.'"

H 11526, Ch. 75, h 4

A number of our people have narrated from Sahl ibn Ziyad from Ali ibn Hassan from Musa ibn Bakr who has said the following:

"I once heard abu al-Hassan, *'Alayhi al-Salam,* saying, 'Eating egg often increases the number of one's children.'"

H 11527, Ch. 75, h 5

A number of our people have narrated from Ahmad ibn abu 'Abd Allah from Muhammad ibn 'Isa from his father from his grandfather and Qays ibn 'Abd al-'Aziz who has said the following:

"Abu 'Abd Allah, *'Alayhi al-Salam,* has said, 'The egg yoke is light and its white is heavy.'"

H 11528, Ch. 75, h 6

Muhammad ibn Yahya has narrated from Muhammad ibn Musa from Ya'qub ibn Yazid from ibn Faddal from certain persons of our people from ibn abu Ya'fur who has said the following:

"I once said to abu 'Abd Allah, *'Alayhi al-Salam,* that a domestic hen without a roster feeds on dump site and so on and gives eggs without mating with a rooster. 'What do you say about such an egg and if such egg is edible? He (the Imam) said to me, 'If such egg is from an edible bird it is not unlawful and eating it is permissible.'"

H 11529, Ch. 75, h 7

Abu Ali al-Ash'ariy has narrated from certain persons of our people from ibn abu Najran from Dawud ibn Farqad who has said the following:

"I once asked abu 'Abd Allah, *'Alayhi al-Salam,* about sheep and cows from which I may draw milk without their mating and the eggs of a hen without mating with a rooster . He (the Imam) said, 'All of such things are lawful and fine for you if they are from edible animals. Milk, eggs, rennet all of such things are lawful and fine. Mating with a male may have taken place but is delayed and all of such things are lawful.'"

Chapter 76 - Excellence of Salt

H 11530, Ch. 76, h 1

Muhammad ibn Yahya has narrated from Ahmad ibn Muhammad ibn 'Isa from Ali ibn al-Hakam from ibn Bukayr from Zurarah who has said the following:

"Abu 'Abd Allah, *'Alayhi al-Salam,* has said that the Messenger of Allah, *O Allah, grant compensation to Muhammad and his family worthy of their services to Your cause,* said to 'Amir al-Mu'minin, 'O Ali, begin taking food with salt and end it with salt. It dispels seventy kinds of troubles of which the least serious is leprosy.'"

H 11531, Ch. 76, h 2
Ali ibn Ibrahim has narrated from his father from ibn abu 'Umayr from Hisham ibn Salim who has said the following:

"Abu 'Abd Allah, *'Alayhi al-Salam,* has said that the Messenger of Allah, *O Allah, grant compensation to Muhammad and his family worthy of their services to Your cause,* said to `Amir al-Mu'minin, 'O Ali, begin taking your food with salt and end it with salt. One who begins taking his food with salt and ends it with salt remains safe from seventy-two kinds of troubles of which is leprosy, insanity and vitiligo.'"

H 11532, Ch. 76, h 3
Ali ibn Ibrahim has narrated from his father from `Isma'il ibn Marrar from Yunus from a man from Sa'd al-Iskaf who has said the following:

"Abu Ja'far, *'Alayhi al-Salam,* has said, 'In salt there is cure for seventy kinds of pains.' He (the Imam) then said, 'Had people known that which is in salt they would not seek treatment for an illness with anything other than salt.'"

H 11533, Ch. 76, h 4
Muhammad ibn Yahya has narrated from Ahmad ibn Muhammad from al-Qasim ibn Yahya from his grandfather al-Hassan ibn Rashid from Muhammad ibn Muslim who has said the following:

"Abu 'Abd Allah, *'Alayhi al-Salam,* has said that `Amir al-Mu'minin has said, 'You must begin your food with salt. Had people known that which is in salt they would choose it before using the experimented antidote.'"

H 11534, Ch. 76, h 5
Muhammad ibn Yahya has narrated from Ahmad ibn Muhammad from Bakr ibn Salih from al-Ja'fariy who has said the following:

"Abu al-Hassan, *'Alayhi al-Salam,* has said, 'A table-spread with food in it has no blessings without salt. For good health of the body one must begin his food with salt.'"

H 11535, Ch. 76, h 6
Humayd ibn Ziyad has narrated from al-Hassan ibn Muhammad ibn Sama'ah from Ahmad ibn al-Hassan al-Mithamiy from Sukayn ibn 'Ammar from Fudayl al-Rassan from Farwah who has said the following:

"Abu Ja'far, *'Alayhi al-Salam,* has said that Allah, most Majestic, most Glorious, sent revelation to Moses son of 'Imran, *'Alayhi al-Salam* to command his people to begin their food with salt and end it with salt, otherwise, they must not blame anyone other than their ownselves.'"

H 11536, Ch. 76, h 7
Muhammad ibn Yahya has narrated from Ahmad ibn Muhammad ibn 'Isa from Ibrahim ibn abu Mahmud who has said the following:

"Al-Rida', *'Alayhi al-Salam,* once asked us, 'Which food is of greater preference?' Certain ones among us said that it is meat, others said that it is oil, yet others said it is milk. He (the Imam) said, 'No, it is salt.' We then went outside for freshness and a certain one of servants forgot salt. They slaughtered a sheep for us which was the most fat one and we could not benefit thereof anything until we returned back.'"

H 11537, Ch. 76, h 8

It is narrated from the narrator of the previous *Hadith* from Ya'qub ibn Yazid in a marfu' manner who has said the following:

"Abu 'Abd Allah, *'Alayhi al-Salam,* has said, 'If one spreads salt on the first morsel of his food, blemish of skin goes away from his face.'"

H 11538, Ch. 76, h 9

Ali ibn Ibrahim has narrated from his father from ibn abu 'Umayr from abu Ayyub al-Khazzaz from Muhammad ibn Muslim who has said the following:

"He (the Imam), *'Alayhi al-Salam,* has said that once scorpion bit the Messenger of Allah, *O Allah, grant compensation to Muhammad and his family worthy of their services to Your cause,* and he (the Messenger of Allah) said, 'May Allah condemn you. You do not distinguish between a believer and unbeliever and do not know whom you can hurt'. He (the Messenger of Allah) then asked for salt and rubbed it on the bitten place and it calmed down. Abu Ja'far, *'Alayhi al-Salam,* then said, 'Had people known that which is in salt they would not seek another antidote.'"

H 11539, Ch. 76, h 10

A number of our people have narrated from Ahmad ibn abu 'Abd Allah from his father and 'Amr ibn Ibrahim all from Khalaf ibn Hammad from Ya'qub ibn Shu'ayb who has said the following:

"Once, scorpion bit the Messenger of Allah, *O Allah, grant compensation to Muhammad and his family worthy of their services to Your cause.* He (the Messenger of Allah) then threw it away, saying, 'May Allah condemn you, both believers and unbelievers are not safe from you.' He (the Messenger of Allah) then asked for salt, placed it on the bitten place and squeezed it with his thumb until it melted and then said, 'Had people known that which is in salt, they would not need to seek any other antidote.'"

Chapter 77 - The Vinegar and Oil

H 11540, Ch. 77, h 1

A number of our people have narrated from Ahmad ibn Muhammad ibn Khalid from 'Uthman ibn 'Isa from Khalid ibn Najih who has said the following:

"I would break my fast with abu 'Abd Allah, and abu al-Hassan al-Awwal, *'Alayhim al-Salam,* in the month of Ramadan. First they would bring a bowl of Tharid (bread made in pieces in broth) with vinegar and oil, and at first he (the Imam) would take three morsels, then afterward a big bowl would come.'"

H 11541, Ch. 77, h 2

It is narrated from the narrator of the previous *Hadith* from 'Uthman ibn 'Isa from Hammad ibn 'Isa from Salamah al-Qalanisiy who has said the following:

"I once visited abu 'Abd Allah, *'Alayhi al-Salam,* and when I spoke to him he (the Imam) asked, 'Why do I hear your voice as weak?' I replied, 'Because my mouth has fallen (perhaps a tooth).' As if it seemed to grieve him (the Imam); and then he asked, 'What do you eat?' I replied, 'I eat whatever is at home.' He (the Imam) said, 'You must eat Tharid (bread made in pieces in broth) because there is blessing in it and if it does not have meat then vinegar and oil are fine.'"

H 11542, Ch. 77, h 3

It is narrated from the narrator of the previous *Hadith* from 'Isma'il ibn Mehran from Hammad ibn 'Uthman from Zayd ibn al-Hassan who has said the following:

"I once heard abu 'Abd Allah, *'Alayhi al-Salam,* saying, ''Amir al-Mu'minin was very similar to the Messenger of Allah in eating. He would eat bread with vinegar and oil and feed people bread and meat.'"

H 11543, Ch. 77, h 4

Ali ibn Ibrahim has narrated from his father from ibn abu 'Umayr from 'Ubaydah al-Wasitiy from 'Ajlan who has said the following:

"I once had dinner with abu 'Abd Allah, *'Alayhi al-Salam,* after *Salat* (prayer) of *al-'Isha'.* He (the Imam) would take dinner after *Salat* (prayer) of *al-'Isha'.* Vinegar, oil and cold meat were brought. He began to pull pieces of meat and give them to me but himself eat vinegar and oil and left the meat. He (the Imam) said, 'This is our food and the food of the prophets *'Alayhim al-Salam.*'"

H 11544, Ch. 77, h 5

Muhammad ibn Yahya has narrated from Ahmad ibn Muhammad ibn 'Isa from ibn Faddal from Yunus ibn Ya'qub from 'Abd al-'A'la' who has said the following:

"I once ate with abu 'Abd Allah, *'Alayhi al-Salam,* and he (the Imam) said, 'O Jariyah (female servant), bring for us our popular food.' She then brought a bowl with vinegar and oil in it and we ate.'"

H 11545, Ch. 77, h 6

Ali ibn Ibrahim has narrated from his father from al-Nawfaliy from al-Sakuniy who has said the following:

"Abu 'Abd Allah, *'Alayhi al-Salam,* has said, 'The best of dishes to the Messenger of Allah was vinegar and oil and he would say it was the food of the Prophets *'Alayhim al-Salam.*'"

H 11546, Ch. 77, h 7

Through the same chain of narrators as that of the previous *Hadith* the following is narrated:

"'Amir al-Mu'minin has said, 'A family that uses vinegar and oil as their sauce, never becomes needy; it is the sauce of the Prophets, *'Alayhim al-Salam.*'"

H 11547, Ch. 77, h 8

A number of our people have narrated from Ahmad ibn Muhammad al-Barqiy from his father from certain persons of his people from Ayyub ibn al-Hurr from Muhammad ibn Ali al-Halabiy who has said the following:

"I once asked abu 'Abd Allah, *'Alayhi al-Salam,* about food. He (the Imam) said, 'You must use vinegar and oil for food; it is palatable and Ali, *'Alayhi al-Salam,* ate it very often. I eat it very often and it is palatable.'"

H 11548, Ch. 77, h 9

A number of our people have narrated from Sahl ibn Ziyad from Ali ibn Asbat from his uncle Ya'qub ibn Salim who has said the following:

"I once heard abu 'Abd Allah, *'Alayhi al-Salam,* saying, ''Amir al-Mu'minin, would eat vinegar with oil and keep his expenses under the carpet.'"

Chapter 78 - The Khall (Wine Turned to Vinegar)

H 11549, Ch. 78, h 1
Al-Husayn from Muhammad has narrated from Mu'alla' ibn Muhammad from al-Hassan ibn Ali al-Washsha' from 'Abd Allah ibn Sinan who has said the following:
"Abu 'Abd Allah, *'Alayhi al-Salam,* has said that once the Messenger of Allah went to the house of 'Umm Salamah, may Allah be pleased with her, and she brought pieces of bread. He (the Messenger of Allah) asked, 'Do you have any sauce?' She replied, 'No, O Messenger of Allah except vinegar.' He (the Messenger of Allah) said, 'Yes, vinegar is the best sauce; a house which has vinegar does not become poor.'"

H 11550, Ch. 78, h 2
Ali ibn Ibrahim has narrated from his father from ibn abu 'Umayr from Hisham ibn Salim from Sulayman ibn Khalid who has said the following:
"Abu 'Abd Allah, *'Alayhi al-Salam,* has said, 'Vinegar strengthens the power of understanding.'"

H 11551, Ch. 78, h 3
Ali ibn Ibrahim has narrated from his father from ibn abu 'Umayr from Ali ibn abu Hamzah who has said the following:
"I once heard abu 'Abd Allah, *'Alayhi al-Salam,* saying, 'A house in which there is vinegar does not become needy, and the Messenger of Allah, *O Allah, grant compensation to Muhammad and his family worthy of their services to Your cause,* has already said it.'"

H 11552, Ch. 78, h 4
Ali ibn Muhammad ibn Bandar has narrated from his father from Muhammad ibn Ali al-Hamadaniy who has said the following:
"A man in Khurasan once was with al-Rida', *'Alayhi al-Salam,* and the table-spread with food inside, vinegar and salt, was brought to him. He (the Imam) began with vinegar and the man said, 'I pray to Allah to keep my soul in service for your cause, have you commanded us to begin with salt?' He (the Imam) said, 'This is like that', meaning vinegar, 'and that vinegar strengthens the mind and increases the ability to understand.'"

H 11553, Ch. 78, h 5
Ali ibn Muhammad has narrated from Ahmad ibn abu 'Abd Allah from Aban ibn 'Abd al-Malik from 'Isma'il ibn Jabir who has said the following:
"Abu 'Abd Allah, *'Alayhi al-Salam,* has said, 'We begin with vinegar which is with us as you begin with salt which is with you, and vinegar strengthens the ability to understand better.'"

H 11554, Ch. 78, h 6
Ali ibn Ibrahim has narrated from his father from al-Nawfaliy from al-Sakuniy who has said the following:
"Abu 'Abd Allah, *'Alayhi al-Salam,* has said that the best sauce to the Messenger of Allah, *O Allah, grant compensation to Muhammad and his family worthy of their services to Your cause,* was vinegar.'"

H 11555, Ch. 78, h 7

Ali ibn Ibrahim has narrated from certain persons of our people from 'Abd Allah ibn 'Abd al-Rahman al-Asamm from Shu'ayb from abu Basir who have said the following:

"Abu 'Abd Allah, *'Alayhi al-Salam,* has said that `Amir al-Mu'minin has said, 'The best sauce is vinegar, it breaks bitterness, (bile) extinguishes yellowness (gall) and brings the heart to life.'"

H 11556, Ch. 78, h 8

Ali has narrated from his father from Hanan ibn Sadir from his father who has said the following:

"Once, vinegar of wine (clean grape juice with vinegar in it placed in the sun to turn the whole thing into vinegar) was mentioned before abu 'Abd Allah, *'Alayhi al-Salam.* He (the Imam) said, 'It kills *dawab* (the insects) in the belly and strengthens the mouth (the teeth).'"

H 11557, Ch. 78, h 9

Muhammad ibn Yahya has narrated from Ahmad ibn Muhammad from Ali ibn al-Hakam from Sama'ah who has said the following:

"Abu 'Abd Allah, *'Alayhi al-Salam,* has said, 'Vinegar of wine strengthens tooth gum, kills dawab in the belly and strengthens the ability to understand.'"

H 11558, Ch. 78, h 10

Muhammad ibn Yahya has narrated from Ibrahim al-Ja'fariy from Muhammad and Ahmad sons of 'Umar ibn Musa from their father in a marfu' manner who has said the following:

"Abu 'Abd Allah, *'Alayhi al-Salam,* has said, 'Using vinegar as sauce cuts down the desire of fornication.'"

H 11559, Ch. 78, h 11

Ahmad ibn Muhammad has narrated from Ali ibn al-Hakam from Rabi' al-Musliy from Ahmad ibn Razin from Sufyan al-Simt who has said the following:

"Abu 'Abd Allah, *'Alayhi al-Salam,* has said, 'You must eat vinegar of wine and immerse (the morsel or use it very often) in it, because it does not leave any *dawab* (insects) animal in your belly without killing them.'"

H 11560, Ch. 78, h 12

Muhammad ibn Yahya has narrated from certain persons of our people from Ali ibn Sulayman ibn Rashid from Muhammad ibn 'Abd Allah from Sulayman al-Daylamiy who has said the following:

"Abu 'Abd Allah, *'Alayhi al-Salam,* has said, 'Banu Israel would begin their food with vinegar and end with it but we begin with salt and end with vinegar.'"

Chapter 79 - Al-Mury (a certain sauce)

H 11561, Ch. 79, h 1

Muhammad ibn Yahya has narrated from Musa ibn al-Hassan from Muhammad ibn Ahmad ibn abu Mahmud f his father in a marfu' manner who has said the following:

"Abu 'Abd Allah, *'Alayhi al-Salam,* has said that when Yusuf (Joseph) was in jail, he complained before his Lord, most Majestic, most Glorious, about eating bread alone and asked for sauce and there were a great deal of pieces of dry bread with him. He commanded him to place the bread in a pot, pour water on it with salt and it became *Mury.* He, *'Alayhi al-Salam* used it as sauce.'"

Chapter 80 - Oil and the Olive

H 11562, Ch. 80, h 1
A number of our people have narrated from Sahl ibn Ziyad from Ja'far ibn Muhammad al-Ash'ariy from ibn al-Qaddah who has said the following:

"Abu 'Abd Allah, *'Alayhi al-Salam,* has said that the Messenger of Allah, *O Allah, grant compensation to Muhammad and his family worthy of their services to Your cause,* has said, 'Use Olive oil for food and rubbing; it is from the blessed tree.'

Muhammad ibn Yahya has narrated from Ahmad ibn Muhammad from ibn Faddal from ibn al-Qaddah from abu 'Abd Allah, *'Alayhi al-Salam,* has narrated from a similar *Hadith.*"

H 11563, Ch. 80, h 2
Abu Ali al-Ash'ariy has narrated from Muhammad ibn 'Abd al-Jabbar from 'Ubayd Allah al-Dihqan from Durust from Ibrahim ibn 'Abd al-Hamid who has said the following:

"Abu al-Hassan, *'Alayhi al-Salam,* has said, 'Of the matters that Adam said in his will to Hibbahtu Allah, his son was this: 'You must eat olives because they are from the blessed tree.'"

H 11564, Ch. 80, h 3
A number of our people have narrated from Ahmad ibn abu 'Abd Allah from Ya'qub ibn Yazid from Yahya ibn al-Mubarak from 'Abd Allah ibn Jabalah from Ishaq ibn 'Ammar and others who has said the following:

"I once said to abu 'Abd Allah, *'Alayhi al-Salam,* that they say, 'Olives stir up gas. He (the Imam) said, 'Olives dispel gas.'"

H 11565, Ch. 80, h 4
It is narrated from the narrator of the previous *Hadith* from Mansur ibn al-'Abbas from Muhammad ibn 'Abd Allah ibn Wasi' from Ishaq ibn 'Isma'il from Muhammad ibn Yazid from abu Dawud al-Nakha'iy who has said the following:

"'Amir al-Mu'minin, *'Alayhi al-Salam,* has said, 'Use olives for rubbing and as sauce; it is the rubbing oil of the virtuous people and the sauce of the chosen ones. It was touched with holiness twice and it was blessed when coming and returning (plentiful or scarce) and with it illness does not harm.'"

H 11566, Ch. 80, h 5
Mansur ibn al-'Abbas has narrated from Ibrahim ibn Muhammad al-Zari' al-Basriy from a man who has said the following:

"We mentioned olives before abu 'Abd Allah, *'Alayhi al-Salam,* and a man said it stirs up gas. He (the Imam) said, 'No, it dispels gas.'"

H 11567, Ch. 80, h 6
A number of our people have narrated from Sahl ibn Ziyad from al-Nawfaliy al-Jaririy from 'Abd al-Mu'min al-Ansariy who has said the following:

"Abu Ja'far, *'Alayhi al-Salam,* has said that the Messenger of Allah, has said, 'Olives are the rubbing oil of the virtuous ones and the sauce of the selected ones. It was blessed when coming as well as returning (plentiful or scarce) and immersed in holiness twice.'"

H 11568, Ch. 80, h 7

Muhammad ibn Yahya has narrated from 'Abd Allah ibn Ja'far in a marfu' manner who has said the following:

"Abu 'Abd Allah, *'Alayhi al-Salam,* has said, 'Olives increase in water.'"

Chapter 81 - Honey

H 11569, Ch. 81, h 1

A number of our people have narrated from Sahl ibn Ziyad from Ahmad ibn Muhammad from ibn abu Nasr from Hammad ibn 'Uthaman from Muhammad ibn Sawqah who has said the following:

"Abu 'Abd Allah, *'Alayhi al-Salam,* has said, 'People are not cured as good as with honey.'"

H 11570, Ch. 81, h 2

Muhammad ibn Yahya has narrated from Ahmad ibn Muhammad from al-Qasim ibn Yahya from his grandfather al-Hassan ibn Rashid from Muhammad ibn Muslim who has said the following:

"Abu 'Abd Allah, *'Alayhi al-Salam,* has said that 'Amir al-Mu'minin has said, 'Licking honey is cure for all illnesses. Allah, most Majestic, most Glorious, has said, "From its belly, drink of many colors come out. In it there is cure for people." Honey with reading Quran and chewing frankincense dissolves phlegm.'"

H 11571, Ch. 81, h 3

Ali ibn Ibrahim has narrated from his father from ibn abu 'Umayr from Hisham ibn Salim who has said the following:

"Abu 'Abd Allah, *'Alayhi al-Salam,* has said that the Messenger of Allah, *O Allah, grant compensation to Muhammad and his family worthy of their services to Your cause,* liked honey a great deal.'"

H 11572, Ch. 81, h 4

Muhammad ibn Yahya has narrated from 'Abd Allah ibn Ja'far from Muhammad ibn 'Isa from Ibrahim from 'Abd Allah al-Hamid from Sukayn who has said the following:

"Abu 'Abd Allah, *'Alayhi al-Salam,* has said that the Messenger of Allah, *O Allah, grant compensation to Muhammad and his family worthy of their services to Your cause,* would (say) eating honey, reciting verses of Quran and chewing frankincense dissolve phlegm.'"

H 11573, Ch. 81, h 5

A number of our people have narrated from Sahl ibn Ziyad from Ali ibn Hassan from Musa ibn Bakr who has said the following:

"A patient does not receive a cure as he can with honey.'"

Chapter 82 - Sugar

H 11574, Ch. 82, h 1

A number of our people have narrated from Sahl ibn Ziyad from Ali ibn Hassan from Musa ibn Bakr who has said the following:

"Abu al-Hassan, al-Awwal would eat sugar very often when going to sleep.'"

H 11575, Ch. 82, h 2

Muhammad ibn Yahya has narrated from Ahmad ibn Muhammad from ibn Mahbub from 'Abd al-'Aziz al-'Abdiy who has said the following:

"Abu 'Abd Allah, *'Alayhi al-Salam,* has said, 'If cheese is harmful in all things and does not benefit in anything, sugar on the other hand benefits in all things and does not harm in anything.'"

H 11576, Ch. 82, h 3

Muhammad ibn Yahya has narrated from Ahmad ibn Muhammad from Muhammad ibn Ahmad al-Azdiy from certain persons of our people in a *marfu'* manner who has said the following:

"Once, a man complained before abu 'Abd Allah, *'Alayhi al-Salam,* saying, 'I am a complaining man.' He (the Imam) said, 'What he needs is al-Mubarak.' I then asked, 'I pray to Allah to keep my soul in service for your cause, what is al-Mubarak?' He (the Imam) said, 'It is sugar.' I then asked, 'What kind of sugar.' He (the Imam) said, 'It is your Sulaymaniy, this one.'"

H 11577, Ch. 82, h 4

Ahmad ibn Muhammad has narrated from Muhammad ibn Sahl from al-Rida', *'Alayhi al-Salam,* or certain persons of our people from al-Rida' who has said the following:

"Al-Rida', *'Alayhi al-Salam,* has said, the sugar which is chipped with a hammer eats away (abolishes) phlegm entirely.'"

H 11578, Ch. 82, h 5

Ahmad ibn Muhammad has narrated from al-Hassan ibn Ali ibn al-Nu'man from certain persons of our people who has said the following:

"I once complained before abu 'Abd Allah, *'Alayhi al-Salam,* against pain and he (the Imam) said, 'When you lie down in your bed eat two pieces of sugar.' He (the narrator) has said, 'I followed the instruction and I became well. I told a physician about it, which was the best in our town. He asked me, 'How has abu 'Abd Allah, *'Alayhi al-Salam,* learned about it? It is of our secret knowledge. However he owns books, so he may have found it in his books.'"

H 11579, Ch. 82, h 6

A number of our people have narrated from Ahmad ibn abu 'Abd Allah from his father from Sa'dan ibn Muslim from Mu'attib who has said the following:

"After abu 'Abd Allah, *'Alayhi al-Salam,* took his dinner, he said, 'When you go in the storage look for two pieces of sugar for me.' I said, 'I pray to Allah to keep my soul in service for your cause, there is nothing there.' He (the Imam) said, 'Go there, fie upon you.' He has said, 'I went there and found two pieces of sugar and brought them to him (the Imam).'"

H 11580, Ch. 82, h 7

Ali ibn Ibrahim has narrated from his father from ibn abu 'Umayr from in a marfu' manner who has said the following:

"Once, a man complained before abu 'Abd Allah, *'Alayhi al-Salam,* about plague. He (the Imam) said, 'What you need is the fine and blessed.' I then asked, 'What is the fine and blessed?' He (the Imam) said, 'It is your Sulaymaniy, this one.' He (the narrator) has said that abu 'Abd Allah, *'Alayhi al-Salam,* then said, 'The first one who found sugar was Sulayman ibn Dawud, *'Alayhim al-Salam.'"

H 11581, Ch. 82, h 8

Muhammad ibn Yahya has narrated from Musa ibn al-Hassan from 'Ubayd al-Khayyat from 'Abd 'Abd al-'Aziz from ibn Sinan from a man who has said the following:

"Abu 'Abd Allah, *'Alayhi al-Salam,* has said, 'If a man has one thousand dirham and he does not have anything else with him but he buys sugar with it, he is not considered a spendthrift.'"

H 11582, Ch. 82, h 9

A number of our people have narrated from Ahmad ibn abu 'Abd Allah from a number of his people from Ali ibn Asbat from Yahya ibn Bashir al-Nabbal who has said the following:

"Abu 'Abd Allah, *'Alayhi al-Salam,* once said to my father, 'O Bashir, with what do you treat your people for illnesses?' he replied, 'It is those bitter medicines.' He (the Imam) said, 'When any of you becomes ill take white sugar, make it into powder, pour cold water on it and make him drink it. The One who has made cure in bitter things has the power to make it in the sweet things also.'"

H 11583, Ch. 82, h 10

A number of our people have narrated from Sahl ibn Ziyad from Yasar who has said the following:

"Al-Rida', *'Alayhi al-Salam,* has said, 'The sugar chipped with a small hammer dissolves phlegm entirely.'"

H 11584, Ch. 82, h 11

Muhammad ibn Yahya has narrated from Ahmad ibn Muhammad from Ali ibn Ahmad ibn 'Ushaym from certain persons of his people who has said the following:

"Someone in our family had a fever and physicians had prescribed al-ghafith (a certain herb) and we made the patient to drink it, but it did not benefit him I then complained against it before abu 'Abd Allah, *'Alayhi al-Salam,* and he (the Imam) said, 'Allah has not placed cure in anything which is bitter (only). Take one or one and a half piece of sugar in a bowl and pour water on it. Rub it with your hand and make the patient drink it. In the second night make it two and a half pieces of sugar, dissolve it and make the patient to drink. In the third night make it three and a half pieces and dissolve it as before.' He (the narrator) has said, 'I followed the instruction and Allah, most Majestic, most Glorious, granted cure to our patient.'"

Chapter 83 - The Ghee

H 11585, Ch. 83, h 1

Ali ibn Ibrahim has narrated from his father from al-Nawfaliy from al-Sakuniy who has said the following:

"Abu 'Abd Allah, *'Alayhi al-Salam,* has said that `Amir al-Mu'minin has said, 'In ghee from cows there is a cure.'"

H 11586, Ch. 83, h 2

It is narrated from the narrator of the previous *Hadith* from his father from al-Nawfaliy from al-Sakuniy who has said the following:

"Abu 'Abd Allah, *'Alayhi al-Salam,* has said that `Amir al-Mu'minin has said, 'In ghee there is a cure. It is better in summer than it is in winter and no other thing like it enters inside (the stomach).'"

H 11587, Ch. 83, h 3
A number of our people have narrated from Ahmad ibn abu 'Abd Allah from his father from al-Muttalib ibn Ziyad who has said the following:
"Abu 'Abd Allah, *'Alayhi al-Salam,* has said, 'Ghee is a very fine sauce.'"

H 11588, Ch. 83, h 4
Ali ibn Ibrahim has narrated from his father from ibn abu 'Umayr from Hammad ibn 'Uthaman who has said the following:
"Abu 'Abd Allah, *'Alayhi al-Salam,* has said, 'When a man becomes fifty years old he must not go to sleep with an amount of ghee in his stomach.'"

H 11589, Ch. 83, h 5
A number of our people have narrated from Ahmad ibn Muhammad from al-Washsha' from Hammad ibn 'Uthaman who has said the following:
"Once I was with abu 'Abd Allah, *'Alayhi al-Salam,* and an old man from Iraq spoke to him (the Imam) who asked the man, 'Why has your voice changed?' The man replied, 'It is because my front teeth have gone, so there is defect in my speaking.' Abu 'Abd Allah, *'Alayhi al-Salam,* said to him, 'Certain ones of my teeth have also gone. Satan presents the temptation that what will happen if your other teeth go, how will then you eat? I say that there is no means and no power without Allah.' He (the Imam) then said, 'You must eat Tharid (bread made in pieces in broth), it is suitable, and stay away from ghee because it is not suitable for an old man.'"

H 11590, Ch. 83, h 6
Ali ibn Muhammad ibn Bandar has narrated from Ahmad ibn abu 'Abd Allah from his father from those whom he has mentioned from abu Hafs al-Abbar who has said the following:
"Abu 'Abd Allah, *'Alayhi al-Salam,* has said, 'Nothing entering inside is (as good) as ghee but I dislike it for an old man.'"

Chapter 84 - The Milk Products

H 11591, Ch. 84, h 1
A number of our people have narrated from Ahmad ibn Muhammad from Ali ibn al-Hakam from al-Rabi' ibn Muhammad al-Musliy from 'Abd Allah ibn Sulayman who has said the following:
"Abu Ja'far, *'Alayhi al-Salam,* has stated this *Hadith.* 'Whenever the Messenger of Allah, *O Allah, grant compensation to Muhammad and his family worthy of their services to Your cause,* ate food or drank a drink, he said, "O Lord, grant us blessing in it and better to replace it." However when drinking milk he (the Messenger of Allah) would say, 'O Lord, grant us blessing in it and increase it for us.'"

H 11592, Ch. 84, h 2
Muhammad ibn Yahya has narrated from Salmah ibn al-Khattab from 'Abbad ibn Ya'qub from 'Ubayd ibn Muhammad from Muhammad ibn Qays who has said the following:
"Abu Ja'far, *'Alayhi al-Salam,* has said, 'The milk of black sheep is better than that of the red ones; and the milk of red cows is better than that of the black ones.'"

H 11593, Ch. 84, h 3

A number of our people have narrated from Sahl ibn Ziyad from Ja'far ibn Muhammad al-Ash'ariy from ibn al-Qaddah who has said the following:

"Abu 'Abd Allah, *'Alayhi al-Salam,* has said that the Messenger of Allah, *O Allah, grant compensation to Muhammad and his family worthy of their services to Your cause,* when drinking milk would say, 'O Lord, make it a blessing for us and increase it for us.'"

H 11594, Ch. 84, h 4

Al-Husayn from Muhammad has narrated from al-Sayyariy from 'Ubayd Allah ibn abu 'Abd Allah al-Farsiy from those whom he has mentioned who has said the following:

"Once, a man said to abu 'Abd Allah, *'Alayhi al-Salam,* 'I eat milk products and they harm me.' Abu 'Abd Allah, *'Alayhi al-Salam,* said to him, 'No, by Allah, milk never harms; but you may have eaten something else with it which has harmed you, but you thought it is milk.'"

H 11595, Ch. 84, h 5

Ali ibn Ibrahim has narrated from his father from al-Nawfaliy from al-Sakuniy who has said the following:

"Abu 'Abd Allah, *'Alayhi al-Salam,* has said that the Messenger of Allah, *O Allah, grant compensation to Muhammad and his family worthy of their services to Your cause,* has said, 'There is no one who is choked when drinking milk; Allah, most Majestic, most Glorious, says, ' . . .pure milk which is suitable for those who drink.'"*

H 11596, Ch. 84, h 6

A number of our people have narrated from Ahmad ibn Muhammad from 'Uthman ibn 'Isa from Khalid ibn Najih who has said the following:

"Abu 'Abd Allah, *'Alayhi al-Salam,* has said, 'Milk is the food of the Messenger (of Allah).'"

H 11597, Ch. 84, h 7

Ali ibn Muhammad ibn Bandar and others have narrated from Ahmad ibn abu 'Abd Allah from his father from al-Qasim ibn Muhammad al-Jawhariy from abu al-Hassan al-Asbahaniy who has said the following:

"I once was with abu 'Abd Allah *'Alayhi al-Salam,* and a man said to him (the Imam), when I was hearing, 'I pray to Allah to keep my soul in service for your cause, I feel weakness in my body.' He (the Imam) said, 'You must drink milk, it grows flesh and strengthens the bones.'"

H 11598, Ch. 84, h 8

It is narrated from the narrator of the previous *Hadith* from Nuh ibn Shu'ayb from those whom he has mentioned who has said the following:

"Abu al-Hassan, *'Alayhi al-Salam,* has said, 'For one on whom water of the back (sexual desire) has changed milk and honey are beneficial.'"

H 11599, Ch. 84, h 9

It is narrated from the narrator of the previous *Hadith* from Muhammad ibn Ali from 'Abd al-Rahman ibn abu Hashim from Muhammad ibn Ali ibn abu Hamzah from abu Basir who has said the following:

"We ate with abu 'Abd Allah, *'Alayhi al-Salam*. There was meat of camel (or sheep) and I thought it was from his house. We ate, and then bowls of milk were brought. He (the Imam) drank from it and said to me, 'O abu Muhammad drink.' I tasted it and asked, 'I pray to Allah to keep my soul in service for your cause, is it milk?' He (the Imam) said, 'It is *al- Fitrah* (nature, seed).' Then dates were brought and we ate.'"

Chapter 85 - The Milk Products from Cows

H 11600, Ch. 85, h 1
Ali ibn Ibrahim has narrated from his father from al-Nawfaliy from al-Sakuniy who has said the following:
"Abu 'Abd Allah, *'Alayhi al-Salam,* has said that `Amir al-Mu'minin has said, 'Milk products from cows are medicine.'"

H 11601, Ch. 85, h 2
A number of our people have narrated from Ahmad ibn Muhammad ibn Khalid, from Yahya ibn Ibrahim ibn abu al-Balad, from his father from his grandfather who has said the following:
"I once complained before abu Ja'far, *'Alayhi al-Salam,* about stomach trouble and he (the Imam) said, 'What prevents you from drinking cow milk, have you ever drank it before?' I replied, 'Yes, many times.' He (the Imam) asked, 'How did you find it?' I replied, 'It tans the stomach, covers the kidneys with fat and increases one's appetite for food.' He (the Imam) then said, 'Had it been the right time, you and I could have gone to Yanba' so we could drink milk.'"

H 11602, Ch. 85, h 3
Muhammad ibn Yahya has narrated from Ahmad ibn Muhammad from Ahmad ibn Muhammad from ibn abu Nasr from Aban 'Uthman from Zurarah who has said the following:
"One of the two Imam, (abu Ja'far or abu 'Abd Allah), *'Alayhim al-Salam,* has said that the Messenger of Allah, *O Allah, grant compensation to Muhammad and his family worthy of their services to Your cause,* has said, 'You must drink cow milk; it mixes with every tree.'"

Chapter 86 - Yogurt

H 11603, Ch. 86, h 1
Muhammad ibn Yahya in a marfu' manner has narrated the following:
"Once abu al-Hassan, *'Alayhi al-Salam,* said, 'If one wants to eat yogurt without harming him, he should pour *al-Hadum* on it.' I then asked, 'What is *al-Hadum?'* He (the Imam) said, 'It is *al-Nankhowah.'"

Chapter 87 - The Milk Products from Camels

H 11604, Ch. 87, h 1
Muhammad ibn Yahya has narrated from Ahmad ibn Muhammad ibn 'Isa from Bakr ibn Salih from al-Ja'fariy who has said the following:
"I once heard abu al-Hassan, Musa, *'Alayhi al-Salam,* saying, 'Urine of camels is better than their milk, and Allah, most Majestic, most Glorious, has placed cure in their milk products.'"

H 11605, Ch. 87, h 2

A number of our people have narrated from Ahmad ibn abu 'Abd Allah from Nuh ibn Shu'ayb from certain persons of our people from Musa ibn 'Abd Allah ibn al-Hassan who has said the following:

"I have heard my shaykh's saying, 'The milk of camels is a cure for all kinds of illness and defects, and for one's stomach trouble it is their urine.'"

Chapter 88 - Yogurt Water

H 11606, Ch. 88, h 1

Muhammad ibn Yahya has narrated from Ahmad ibn Muhammad ibn 'Isa from 'Abd al-Rahman ibn abu ibn abu Najran from Safwan ibn Yahya from al-'Is ibn al-Qasim who has said the following:

"I once had lunch with abu 'Abd Allah, *'Alayhi al-Salam,* and he (the Imam) said to me, 'Do you know what this is?' I replied, 'No, I do not know.' He (the Imam) said, 'This is Shiraz al-'Utun (yogurt-water) that we have extracted for one of our patients. If you like to eat you can eat it.'"

H 11607, Ch. 88, h 2

Ahmad ibn Muhammad has narrated from Muhammad ibn Khalid from Khalaf ibn Hammad from Yahya ibn 'Abd Allah who has said the following:

"I once was with abu 'Abd Allah, *'Alayhi al-Salam,* that small bowls were brought and he (the Imam) pointed with his hand toward one of them saying, 'This is Shiraz al-'Utun which we have extracted for a patient with us. Whoever wants to eat he can eat and whoever does not want can leave it.'"

H 11608, Ch. 88, h 3

Ali ibn Ibrahim has narrated from his father from Safwan ibn Yahya from 'Is ibn al-Qasim who has said the following

'I once asked abu 'Abd Allah, *'Alayhi al-Salam,* about drinking yogurt water. He (the Imam) said, 'You can drink it.'"

H 11609, Ch. 88, h 4

A number of our people have narrated from Ahmad ibn abu 'Abd Allah from his father from al-Husayn ibn al-Mubarak from abu Maryam al-Ansariy who has said the following:

"I once asked abu Ja'far, *'Alayhi al-Salam,* about drinking yogurt water. He (the Imam) said, 'It is not unlawful.'"

Chapter 89 - Cheese

H 11610, Ch. 89, h 1

Muhammad ibn Yahya has narrated from Ahmad ibn Muhammad ibn 'Isa from ibn Mahbub from 'Abd Allah ibn Sinan from 'Abd Allah ibn Sulayman who has said the following:

"I once asked abu Ja'far, *'Alayhi al-Salam,* about cheese. He (the Imam) said, 'You have asked me about a food that is attractive to me.' He (the Imam) then gave a dirham to the boy and asked him to bring cheese. He (the Imam) asked for lunch which was brought. He (the Imam) ate and we ate with him (the Imam). When we finished lunch I asked, 'What do you say about cheese?' He (the Imam) asked me, 'Did you not see me eating it with you?' I replied, 'Yes, I saw you but I like to hear it from you.' He (the Imam) said, 'I will tell you about cheese and other things. Whatever has lawful in it as well as unlawful is lawful for you, until you learn that it particularly is unlawful, then you must leave it.'"

H 11611, Ch. 89, h 2

Ahmad ibn Muhammad al-Kufiy has narrated from Muhammad ibn Ahmad al-Nahdiy from Muhammad ibn al-Walid from Aban ibn 'Abd al-Rahman from 'Abd Allah ibn Sulayman who has said the following:

"About cheese abu 'Abd Allah, *'Alayhi al-Salam,* has said, 'Everything is lawful for you until two witnesses testify before you that it is dead animal.'"

H 11612, Ch. 89, h 3

Muhammad ibn Yahya has narrated from Ali ibn Ibrahim al-Hashimiy, from his father from Muhammad ibn al- Fadl al-Naysaburiy from certain persons of our people who has said the following:

"A man once asked abu 'Abd Allah, *'Alayhi al-Salam,* about cheese. He (the Imam) said, 'It is an illness for which there is no cure.' When it was al-'Isha' (evening) the man came to abu 'Abd Allah, *'Alayhi al-Salam,* and looked at cheese on the table-spread and said, 'I pray to Allah to keep my soul in service for your cause. At lunchtime, I asked you about cheese. You said to me that it is an illness for which there is no cure and now I see it on the table-spread.' He (the Imam) said, 'It is harmful at lunch and useful in dinner and it increases the water of one's back.' It is narrated that harmfulness of cheese is in its crust."

Chapter 90 - Cheese with Walnut

H 11613, Ch. 90, h 1

Ali ibn Ibrahim has narrated from his father from al-Nawfaliy from al-Sakuniy who has said the following:

"Abu 'Abd Allah, *'Alayhi al-Salam,* has said that 'Amir al-Mu'minin has said, 'Eating walnut in hot weather stirs heat inside and blisters on the body; but eating it in winter warms up the kidneys and repels cold.'"

H 11614, Ch. 90, h 2

Muhammad ibn Yahya has narrated from Ahmad ibn Muhammad from ibn Mahbub from 'Abd 'Abd al-'Aziz al-'Abdiy who has said the following:

"Abu 'Abd Allah, *'Alayhi al-Salam,* has said, 'When cheese and walnut come together in each of them there is a cure but separately each one has an illness with it.'"

H 11615, Ch. 90, h 3

Muhammad ibn Yahya has narrated from Ahmad ibn Muhammad from Idris ibn al-Hassan from 'Ubayd ibn Zurarah who has said the following:

"He (the Imam), *'Alayhi al-Salam,* has said, 'Walnut and cheese together are medicine but separately they are ailments and diseases.'"

Chapters on Grains
Chapter 1 - Rice

H 11616, Ch. 1, h 1

Muhammad ibn Yahya has narrated from Ahmad ibn Muhammad from Ali ibn al-Hakam from and al-Hassan ibn Ali ibn Faddal from Yunus ibn Ya'qub who has said the following:

"Abu 'Abd Allah, *'Alayhi al-Salam,* has said, 'From your area no other thing comes more desirable to me than rice and viola. I had intense pain and I was inspired to eat rice. I ordered to wash it, dry it, and pick up to grind it, then in a powder form with oil and a mixture, I drank it. Allah, most Majestic, most Glorious, removed with it that pain.'"

H 11617, Ch. 1, h 2

Ali ibn Ibrahim has narrated from his father from 'Isma'il ibn Marrar and others from Yunus from Hisham ibn al-Hakam from Zurarah who has said the following:

"I once saw the nurse of abu al-Hassan, Musa, *'Alayhi al-Salam,* feed him rice with morsels and threw it on him. It made me upset and I went to see abu 'Abd Allah, *'Alayhi al-Salam,* who said to me, 'I think what you have seen from the nurse of abu al-Hassan, Musa, *'Alayhi al-Salam,* has made you upset.' I replied, 'Yes, I pray to Allah to keep my soul in service for your cause.' He (the Imam) said, 'Yes, food from rice expands the intestine and cuts down hemorrhoids. We deem people of Iraq as fortunate for their eating rice and fresh dates because they expand the intestine and cut down hemorrhoids.'"

H 11618, Ch. 1, h 3

A number of our people have narrated from Ahmad ibn abu 'Abd Allah from abu Sulayman al-Hadhddha' from Muhammad ibn al-Fayd who has said the following:

"I once was with abu 'Abd Allah, *'Alayhi al-Salam,* that a man came to him (the Imam) and said, 'My daughter has become weak and she is pregnant.' He (the Imam) said, 'What prevents you from feeding her rice with fat? Take four pieces of stone or five and place them near the fire. Cook the rice in a pot until it is cooked. Take the fresh fat of a kidney. When rice is cooked then place the fat in a pot with the stones, then cover it with another pot and stir it fairly well. Fix the pots so that no steam comes out. When the fat melts; then place it in the rice, then she can eat it (ingest it).'"

H 11619, Ch. 1, h 4

A number of our people have narrated from Ahmad ibn Muhammad ibn Khalid from 'Uthman ibn 'Isa from those who narrated to him who has said the following:

"Abu 'Abd Allah, *'Alayhi al-Salam,* has said, 'Rice is very good food and we preserve it for our people who suffer from illnesses.'"

H 11620, Ch. 1, h 5

It is narrated from the narrator of the previous *Hadith* from Yahya ibn 'Isa from those who narrated to him who has said the following:

"Abu 'Abd Allah, *'Alayhi al-Salam,* has said, 'Rice is very good and we use it as medicine to cure our people from illness.'"

H 11621, Ch. 1, h 6

It is narrated from the narrator of the previous *Hadith* from 'Uthman ibn 'Isa from Khalid ibn Najih who has said the following:

"I once complained before abu 'Abd Allah, *'Alayhi al-Salam,* about pain in my belly. He (the Imam) said, 'Take rice, wash it, then dry it in the shadow, crush it; then take one fill of your palm every morning.' Ishaq al-Jaririy has added that it should be fried a little and taken one *awqiyah* to drink."

H 11622, Ch. 1, h 7

A number of our people have narrated from Sahl ibn Ziyad from ibn Faddal from Tha'labah ibn Maymun from Humran who has said the following:

"Abu 'Abd Allah, *'Alayhi al-Salam,* once experienced pain in his belly and he ordered to cook rice for him (the Imam) with sumac on it, and after eating it the pain went away from him (the Imam).'"

Chapter 2 - The Chickpea (Garbanzo Bean)

H 11623, Ch. 2, h 1

Muhammad ibn Yahya has narrated from Ahmad ibn Muhammad ibn 'Isa from al-Husayn ibn Sa'id from Nadir al-Khadim who has said the following:

"Abu al-Hassan, al-Rida', *'Alayhi al-Salam,* would eat cooked chickpeas before and after food.'"

H 11624, Ch. 2, h 2

Ali ibn Ibrahim has narrated from his father from ibn abu 'Umayr from Mu'awiyah ibn 'Ammar who has said the following:

"I once said to abu 'Abd Allah, *'Alayhi al-Salam,* 'People narrate that the Holy Prophet has said, "Seventy Prophets have blessed chickpeas."' He (the Imam) said, 'This is what you call chickpeas but we call it lintels.'"

H 11625, Ch. 2, h 3

A number of our people have narrated from Ahmad ibn Muhammad ibn Khalid from his father from fadalah from Rifa'ah who has said the following:

"I once heard abu 'Abd Allah, *'Alayhi al-Salam,* saying, 'When Allah, most Blessed, most High, granted good health to Ayyub, *'Alayhi al-Salam*, he looked to the Israelites who had their plantations. He raised his eyes to the sky and said, 'O Lord, my Master, this is Your slave Ayyub who was in suffering and You granted him good health but he does not have any plantation. These are people of banu Israel who have their plantations.' Allah, most Majestic, most Glorious, sent him revelation that said, 'Take a handful from you rosary beads and use it as seed .' His rosary beads had salt in it, Ayyub, *'Alayhi al-Salam,* took a handful from it and used it as seed and what grew was this lintel. You call it chickpeas and we call it lintels.'"

H 11626, Ch. 2, h 4

It is narrated from the narrator of the previous *Hadith* from Ahmad ibn Muhammad from ibn abu Nasr who has said the following:

"Abu al-Hassan, al-Rida', *'Alayhi al-Salam,* has said, 'Chickpeas are good cures for back pain and he (the Imam) would ask for it before and after food.'"

Chapter 3 - The Lintels

H 11627, Ch. 3, h 1

Ali ibn Ibrahim has narrated from his father from al-Nawfaliy from al-Sakuniy who has said the following:

"Abu 'Abd Allah, *'Alayhi al-Salam,* has said that `Amir al-Mu'minin has said, 'Eating lintels softens the heart and increases tears.'"

H 11628, Ch. 3, h 2

A number of our people have narrated from Ahmad ibn Muhammad ibn Khalid from Furat ibn Ahnaf (in a *Maqtu'* manner) who has said the following:

"A certain person of the Israelites complained before Allah, most Majestic, most Glorious, about hardheartedness and lack of tears. Allah, most Majestic, most Glorious, revealed to him to eat lintels. He followed the instruction and his tears began to flow.'"

H 11629, Ch. 3, h 3

It is narrated from the narrator of the previous *Hadith* from Muhammad ibn Ali from Muhammad ibn al-Fudayl from 'Abd al-Rahman ibn Zayd who has said the following:

"Abu 'Abd Allah, *'Alayhi al-Salam,* has said that once a man complained before the Holy Prophet, about hardheartedness. He (the Messenger of Allah) told him to eat lintels; it softens the heart and makes tears to flow quicker.'"

H 11630, Ch. 3, h 4

It is narrated from the narrator of the previous *Hadith* from Dawud ibn Ishaq al-Hadhdha' from Muhammad ibn al-Fayd who has said the following:

"I once ate with abu 'Abd Allah, *'Alayhi al-Salam,* broth with lintels and I said, 'I pray to Allah to keep my soul in service for your cause, these people say that lintels are blessed by seventy Prophets.' He (the Imam) said, 'They have spoken a lie, no, by Allah not even twenty Prophets have done so.' It is narrated that it softens the heart and makes the tears to flow quicker."

Chapter 4 - The Broad Beans and the Kidney Beans

H 11631, Ch. 4, h 1

Muhammad ibn Yahya has narrated from Muhammad ibn Ahmad from Musa ibn Ja'far from Muhammad ibn al-Hassan from 'Umar ibn Salmah from Muhammad ibn 'Abd Allah who has said the following:

"Abu 'Abd Allah, *'Alayhi al-Salam,* has said, 'Eating broad beans grows bone marrows of the legs, adds in the brain and produces fresh blood.'"

H 11632, Ch. 4, h 2

It is narrated from the narrator of the previous *Hadith* from Ahmad ibn Muhammad ibn 'Isa from Ahmad ibn Muhammad from ibn abu Nasr who has said the following:

"Abu al-Hassan, al-Rida', *'Alayhi al-Salam,* has said, 'Eating broad beans grows the bone marrow of the legs and produces fresh blood.'"

H 11633, Ch. 4, h 3

A number of our people have narrated from Ahmad ibn abu 'Abd Allah from certain persons of his people from Salih ibn 'Uqbah who has said the following:

"I once, heard abu 'Abd Allah, *'Alayhi al-Salam,* saying, 'Eat broad beans with its peels. It cleanses (tans) the stomach.'"

H 11634, Ch. 4, h 4

Ali ibn Muhammad from Sahl ibn Ziyad from ibn abu Najran from those whom he has mentioned who has said the following:

"Abu 'Abd Allah, *'Alayhi al-Salam,* has said, 'Kidney beans dispel gases from the belly.'"

Chapter 5 - Al-Mash (Peeled Black beans)

H 11635, Ch. 5, h 1
Muhammad ibn Yahya has narrated from Muhammad ibn Musa from Ahmad ibn al-Hassan al-Jallab certain persons of our people who have said the following:
"Once a man complained before abu al-Hassan, *'Alayhi al-Salam,* about vitiligo (white spots on one's skin) and he (the Imam) commanded him to cook *al-Mash* then drink it and make it a part of his food."

Chapter 6 - *Al-Jawars*

H 11636, Ch. 6, h 1
A number of our people have narrated from Sahl ibn Ziyad from Ayyub ibn Nuh who has said the following:
"I once ate *Harisah* (mashed meat and grains) with *al-Jawars* with abu 'Abd Allah, *'Alayhi al-Salam,* and he (the Imam) said, 'It is a kind of food which is not heavy or troublesome. I like it so I ordered to use it with my food, however, with milk it is more beneficial and soft on stomach.'"

H 11637, Ch. 6, h 2
Muhammad ibn Yahya has narrated from certain persons of our people from Ali ibn Hassan from 'Abd al-Rahman ibn al-Kathir who has said the following:
"I once became ill in al-Madinah because of diarrhea and abu 'Abd Allah, *'Alayhi al-Salam,* described for me how to prepare a *sawiq* (fried flour) of *al-Jawars* and commanded me to use *sawiq* of *al-Jawars* and drink it with water of *al-Kamun* (cumin). I followed the instruction and the diarrhea stopped.'"

Chapter 7 - The Dates

H 11638, Ch. 7, h 1
A number of our people have narrated from Ahmad ibn Muhammad ibn Khalid from Ibrahim ibn 'Uqbah from Muyassir from Muhammad ibn 'Abd 'Abd al-'Aziz from his father who has said the following:
"About the meaning of the words of Allah, most Majestic, most Glorious, '. . . he must find clean and pure food and must bring thereof for you for your sustenance' (18:9) abu Ja'far, or abu 'Abd Allah, *'Alayhim al-Salam,* has said, 'Dates are the most pure food.'"

H 11639, Ch. 7, h 2
It is narrated from the narrator of the previous *Hadith* from his father from ibn Sinan from Ibrahim ibn Mehzam from 'Anbasah ibn Bijad who has said the following:
"Abu 'Abd Allah, *'Alayhi al-Salam,* has said, 'Whenever food was brought to the Messenger of Allah in which there were dates, he began with dates.'"

H 11640, Ch. 7, h 3
Ali ibn Ibrahim has narrated from his father from Hanan ibn Sadir from his father who has said the following:
"Ali ibn al-Husayn, *'Alayhim al-Salam,* loved to see a man who liked (worked with) dates because of the love of the Messenger for Allah for dates.'"

H 11641, Ch. 7, h 4

Ali ibn Ibrahim has narrated from his father from ibn abu 'Umayr from abu al-Mighra' from certain persons of his people from 'Uqbah ibn Bashir who has said the following:

"Once we visited abu Ja'far, *'Alayhi al-Salam,* and he (the Imam) asked for dates which we then ate with him (the Imam), but quite a lot of it. The Imam then said that the Messenger of Allah has said, 'I like a man who is a man of dates (likes dates).'"

H 11642, Ch. 7, h 5

Ali ibn Ibrahim has narrated from his father from 'Amr ibn 'Uthman from abu 'Amr from a man who has said the following:

"Abu 'Abd Allah, *'Alayhi al-Salam,* has said, 'The best of your dates is al-*Barniy* (a certain kind of date) which removes illnesses and there is no illness in it. It takes away fatigue, there is no harm in it, and it dissolves phlegm. With every date there is one good deed.' In another *Hadith* it is said that dates give one delight, palatability, take away fatigue and satisfy one's hunger.'"

H 11643, Ch. 7, h 6

A number of our people have narrated from Sahl ibn Ziyad from Muhammad ibn 'Isma'il al-Raziy from Sulayman ibn Ja'far al-Ja'fariy who has said the following:

"Once I visited abu al-Hassan, al-Rida', *'Alayhi al-Salam,* and there were *barniy* dates in front of him. He (the Imam) seemed assiduous in eating it with zest. He (the Imam) said, 'O Sulayman come close and eat.' I then went close and ate thereof saying, 'I pray to Allah to keep my soul in service for your cause, I see you eat it with great zest.' He (the Imam) said, 'Yes, because I love it.' He (the narrator) has said, that I asked, 'Why is it so?' He (the Imam) said, 'It is because the Messenger of Allah liked dates. Ali, *'Alayhi al-Salam,* liked dates. Al-Hassan liked dates, abu 'Abd Allah, al-Husayn liked dates, Zayn al-'Abidin liked dates, Abu Ja'far, liked dates, abu 'Abd Allah, liked dates, my father liked dates, I like dates and our followers like dates because they are created from our clay; and our enemies, O Sulayman like intoxicants because they are created from smokeless fire.'"

H 11644, Ch. 7, h 7

Ali ibn Ibrahim has narrated from his father from 'Isma'il ibn Marrar from Yunus from Hisham ibn al-Hakam from Zurarah who has said the following:

"Abu 'Abd Allah, *'Alayhi al-Salam,* has said, 'Al-Barniy dates give one delight, and palatability. It is a medicine without illness. It takes away fatigue and with every date there is one good deed.'"

H 11645, Ch. 7, h 8

A number of our people have narrated from Ahmad ibn abu 'Abd Allah from Muhammad ibn Ali from Ali ibn Khattab al-Hallal from al-'Ala' ibn Razin who has said the following:

"Abu 'Abd Allah, *'Alayhi al-Salam,* once said to me, 'O 'Ala', do you know what was the first tree that grew on earth?' I replied, 'Allah, His Messenger and the child of His Messenger know best. He (the Imam) said, 'It was *al-'Ajwah.* What is pure is *al-'Ajwah* (a certain kind of date) and whatever is other than this they are only of the similar one's.'"

H 11646, Ch. 7, h 9

It is narrated from the narrator of the previous *Hadith* from his father from Hammad ibn 'Isa from Rib'iy from 'Abd Allah ibn al-Fudayl who has said the following:

"Abu Ja'far, *'Alayhi al-Salam,* has said, 'Allah, most Majestic, most Glorious, sent al-'Ajwah and *al-'Atiq* from the sky.' I then asked, 'What is *al-'Atiq?*' He (the Imam) said, 'It is the male.'"

H 11647, Ch. 7, h 10

Muhammad ibn Yahya One Hundred and Twenty Muhammad ibn al-Husayn from 'Abd al-Rahman ibn abu Hashim from abu Khadijah who has said the following:

"Abu 'Abd Allah, *'Alayhi al-Salam,* has said, *'al-'Ajwah* is the mother of dates which Allah, most Majestic, most Glorious, sent for Adam from paradise.'"

H 11648, Ch. 7, h 11

Al-Husayn from Muhammad has narrated from Mu'alla' ibn Muhammad from al-Washsha' from Ahmad ibn 'A'idh from abu Khadijah who has said the following:

"Abu 'Abd Allah, *'Alayhi al-Salam,* has said, *'al-'Ajwah* is the mother of dates. It is the date that Allah, most Majestic, most Glorious, sent from paradise for Adam, *'Alayhi al-Salam,* as mentioned in His words, '. . . whatever you cut down of palm trees and left standing on their trunks' is a reference to al-'Ajwah.'"

H 11649, Ch. 7, h 12

Muhammad ibn Yahya has narrated from Ahmad ibn Muhammad from Mu'ammar ibn Khallad who has said the following:

"Abu al-Hassan, al-Rida', *'Alayhi al-Salam,* has said, 'The palm tree of Mary was *al-'Ajwah* which was sent in the month of Kanun (one of the months of winter). With Adam *al-'Atiq* and *al-'Ajwah* were sent, from these other kinds of palm trees spread.'"

H 11650, Ch. 7, h 13

Muhammad ibn Yahya has narrated from Muhammad ibn al-Husayn from 'Abd al-Rahman ibn abu Hashim from abu Khadijah who has said the following:

"Once we took date-stones of *al-'Ajwah* from al-Madinah and a friend of us planted them in a garden. What grew thereof was *al-Sukkar, al-Hirun, al-Shahriz* and *al-Sarfan* (names of certain kinds of dates) and all kinds of dates.'"

H 11651, Ch. 7, h 14

Ali ibn Ibrahim has narrated from his father from ibn abu 'Umayr from Hisham ibn al-Hakam who has said the following:

"Abu 'Abd Allah, *'Alayhi al-Salam,* has said, *'Al-Sarfan* is the master of your dates.'"

H 11652, Ch. 7, h 15

Al-Husayn ibn Muhammad has narrated from Ahmad ibn Ishaq and Muhammad ibn Yahya has narrated from Ahmad ibn Muhammad ibn 'Isa from Muhammad ibn 'Isma'il all from Sa'dan ibn Muslim from certain persons of our people who has said the following:

"When abu 'Abd Allah, *'Alayhi al-Salam,* went to al-Hirah, he (the Imam) rode a stumper and with him (the Imam) was a black slave. A man from al-Kufah who had bought a garden of palm trees saw him (the Imam). The man asked the slave, 'Who is he?' He replied, 'He is Ja'far ibn Muhammad, *'Alayhi al-Salam.*' He then brought a large tray and placed it before him (the Imam). He (the Imam) asked, 'What is this?' He replied, 'It is *al-Barniy.*' He (the Imam) said, 'In it there is a cure.' He (the Imam) then looked at *al-Saberiy* and asked, 'What is this?' He replied, 'It is *al-Saberiy.*' He (the Imam) said, 'We call it *al-Biyd.*' About al-Mushan he (the Imam) asked, 'What is this?' He replied, 'It is *al-Mushan.*' He (the Imam) said, 'We call it *'Umm Jirdhan.*' He (the Imam) looked at *al-Sarfan* and asked, 'What is this?' He replied, 'It is *al-Sarfan.*' He (the Imam) said, 'We call it *al-'Ajwah* and in it there is a cure.'"

H 11653, Ch. 7, h 16

Ali ibn Ibrahim has narrated from his father from ibn abu 'Umayr from Hisham ibn al-Hakam who has said the following:

"Once dates were mentioned before abu 'Abd Allah, *'Alayhi al-Salam,* and he said, 'One with you is better than one with us and all which are with us are better than all that are with you.'"

H 11654, Ch. 7, h 17

Muhammad ibn Yahya has narrated from Ahmad ibn Muhammad from 'Abd Allah ibn Muhammad al-Hajjal from abu Sulayman al-Hammar who has said the following:

"Once we were with abu 'Abd Allah, *'Alayhi al-Salam,* and Mudayrah (a certain sauce) was brought then food, then a basket of dates of several colors was brought. He (the Imam) then picked up one by one and asked, 'What do you call it?' and we said that we call it so and so, until he (the Imam) picked up one more and asked, 'What do you call this?' We replied, 'We call it *al-Mushan.*' He (the Imam) said, 'We call it *'Umm Jirdhan.* A certain amount of it was brought to the Messenger of Allah, *O Allah, grant compensation to Muhammad and his family worthy of their services to Your cause,* and he ate a few from it and prayed because of it; therefore, no other palm tree bears as much dates as this.'"

H 11655, Ch. 7, h 18

Abu Ali al-Ash'ariy has narrated from Muhammad ibn 'Abd al-Jabbar from ibn Faddal from Tha'labah ibn Maymun from 'Ammar al-Sabatiy who has said the following:

"I once was with abu 'Abd Allah, *'Alayhi al-Salam,* when fresh dates were brought. He (the Imam) began to eat, drink water and gave to me the bowl of water and I disliked to decline. Therefore, I drank until he (the Imam) did it several times. I then said, 'I experience increased phlegm, and I complained about it before Ahran, the physician of *al-Hajjaj* and he asked me, "Do you have palm trees in the garden?" I replied, "Yes, there are." He asked me to name them and I named until I mentioned *al-Hirun* (a certain tree) and he said, "Eat seven dates thereof when going to bed and do not drink water." I followed his instruction and I did not have any moisture in my mouth to spit. I complained before him and he said drink a small amount of water and hold back from drinking more until your condition is balanced.' Abu 'Abd Allah, *'Alayhi al-Salam,* said, 'I without water do not even mind if I did not taste it.'"

H 11656, Ch. 7, h 19

A number of our people have narrated from Ahmad ibn abu 'Abd Allah from Muhammad ibn 'Isa from al-Dihqan from Durust ibn abu Mansur from 'Abd Allah ibn Sinan who has said the following:

"Abu 'Abd Allah, *'Alayhi al-Salam,* has said, 'If one eats seven dates everyday of al-'Ajwah of al-'Aliyah (name of a place in al-Madinah), poison, magic and Satan do not harm him.'"

H 11657, Ch. 7, h 20
It is narrated from the narrator of the previous *Hadith* from Ya'qub ibn from Ziyad ibn Marwan al-Qandiy from 'Abd Allah ibn Sinan who has said the following:
"Abu 'Abd Allah, *'Alayhi al-Salam,* has said, 'Eating seven dates of al-'Ajwah at bed time kill the worms in one's belly.'"

Chapters on Fruits
Chapter 1

H 11658, Ch. 1, h 1
A number of our people have narrated from Ahmad ibn abu 'Abd Allah from his father from Ahmad ibn Sulayman from Ahmad ibn Yahya al-Tahhan from those who narrated to him who has said the following:
Abu 'Abd Allah, *'Alayhi al-Salam,* has said, 'Five kinds of fruit are from paradise: Pomegranates of 'Imlisiy, apples of al-Shaysaqan, quince, grapes of al-Raziqiy and fresh dates of al-Mushan.'"

H 11659, Ch. 1, h 2
Muhammad ibn Yahya has narrated from 'Abd Allah ibn Ja'far from 'Abd 'Abd al-'Aziz ibn Zakariya al-Lu'lu'iy from Sulayman ibn al-Mufaddal who has said the following:
"I heard abu al-Jarud narrate from abu Ja'far, *'Alayhi al-Salam,* saying, 'Four kinds of fruit came from paradise: There were grapes of al-Raziqiy, fresh dates of al-Mushan, pomegranates of al-'Imlisiy and apples of al-Shaysaqan.'"

H 11660, Ch. 1, h 3
A number of our people have narrated from Sahl ibn Ziyad from Ja'far ibn Muhammad from ibn al-Qaddah who has said the following:
"Abu 'Abd Allah, *'Alayhi al-Salam,* disliked the peeling of fruits.'"

H 11661, Ch. 1, h 4
A number of our people have narrated from Ahmad ibn abu 'Abd Allah from al-Husayn al-Mundhir from those whom he has mentioned from Furat ibn Ahnaf who has said the following:
"Abu 'Abd Allah, *'Alayhi al-Salam,* has said, 'Every fruit has poison. When you get them make them touch the water or immerse them in water, that is, wash them.'"

Chapter 2 - Grapes

H 11662, Ch. 2, h 1
A number of our people have narrated from Ahmad ibn Muhammad from Ali ibn al-Hakam from al-Rabi ' al-Musliy from Ma'ruf ibn Kharrabudh from those who had seen 'Amir al-Mu'minin, *'Alayhi al-Salam,* eating bread with grapes."

H 11663, Ch. 2, h 2

It is narrated from the narrator of the previous *Hadith* from al-Qasim al-Zayyat from Aban ibn 'Uthman from Musa ibn al-'Ala' who has said the following:

"Abu 'Abd Allah, *'Alayhi al-Salam,* has said, 'When water dried up and bones of the dead bodies were unveiled, Nuh, *'Alayhi al-Salam,* became extremely unhappy and sad. Allah, most Majestic, most Glorious, sent him revelation that said, 'This is your own act. It was you who prayed against them.' Nuh said, 'My Lord, I ask You to forgive me and I turn to You (for kindness).' Allah, most Majestic, most Glorious, sent him revelation to eat black grapes.'"

H 11664, Ch. 2, h 3

Ali ibn Ibrahim has narrated from his father from ibn abu 'Umayr from Hisham ibn Salim who has said the following:

"Ali ibn al-Husayn, *'Alayhim al-Salam*, liked grapes. One day he fasted and when it was the time to break his fast, the first thing that was brought to him was grapes. A mother of his child brought a bunch of grapes and placed before him. A beggar came and he (the Imam) give it to him. The mother of his child managed to buy it secretly from the beggar. She then placed it before him (the Imam). Another beggar came and he (the Imam) give it to the beggar. The mother of his child again secretly bought it from the beggar. She placed it before him (the Imam). Another beggar came and he (the Imam) give it to the beggar and she again secretly bought and placed it before him (the Imam). In the fourth time he (the Imam), *'Alayhi al-Salam,* was able to eat it.'"

H 11665, Ch. 2, h 4

A number of our people have narrated from Ahmad ibn Muhammad from Bakr ibn Salih in a *marfu'* manner who has said the following:

"Abu 'Abd Allah, *'Alayhi al-Salam,* has said, 'One of the Prophets complained before Allah, most Majestic, most Glorious, about sadness and Allah, most Majestic, most Glorious, commanded him to eat grapes.'"

H 11666, Ch. 2, h 5

Muhammad ibn Yahya has narrated from Musa ibn al-Husayn from certain persons of his people from ibn al-Qaddah from Harun ibn al-Khattab from abu al-Hassan al-Rassan who has said the following:

"I once was grazing my camels on the road of al-Khawarnaq (name of a place) and I saw a group of people coming. I then asked a man among them, 'Who are these people?' He replied, 'They are Ja'far ibn Muhammad, *'Alayhi al-Salam,* and 'Abd Allah ibn al-Hassan who are summoned by al-Mansur.' Afterward I asked about them and it was said that they are in al-Hirah.' The next morning I went to offer them greeting of peace. When I was there, I saw baskets before them with fresh dates given to them as gift from al-Kufah. The baskets were opened before them. Ja'far ibn Muhammad, *'Alayhim al-Salam,* extended his hand and ate, then said to me, 'Eat.' He (the Imam) then said to 'Abd Allah ibn al-Hassan, 'O abu Muhammad, what do you say about these fine fresh dates?' Ja'far ibn Muhammad, *'Alayhi al-Salam,* then turned to me and said, 'O people of al-Kufah, you have been given preference over other people in matters of food by three things: Your fish, al-Bunaniy, your grapes, this al-Raziqiy and your fresh dates, this al-Mushan.'"

H 11667, Ch. 2, h 6

Al-Husayn from Muhammad has narrated from Mu'alla' ibn Muhammad, from Ali ibn al-Sindiy who has said, that narrated to me 'Isa ibn Ibrahim from his father from his grandfather who has said the following:

"Once abu 'Ukashah ibn Mihsan al-Asadiy visited abu Ja'far, *'Alayhi al-Salam,* then grapes were brought for him and he (the Imam) said to him, 'An old man and small children eat one piece after one piece. Three and three pieces or four pieces at a time eating is the manner of a person who thinks that he cannot become satisfied but you can eat two pieces at a time because it is preferable.'"

Chapter 3 - The Raisins

H 11668, Ch. 3, h 1

Ali ibn Ibrahim has narrated from his father from al-Nawfaliy from al-Sakuniy who has said the following:

"Abu 'Abd Allah, *'Alayhi al-Salam,* has said that `Amir al-Mu'minin has said, 'One who eats twenty-one pieces of red raisins every morning before breakfast will not become ill except the illness to die, by the will of Allah.'"

H 11669, Ch. 3, h 2

Muhammad ibn Yahya has narrated from Ahmad ibn Muhammad from al-Qasim ibn Yahya from his grandfather al-Hassan ibn Rashid from abu Basir who has said the following:

"Abu 'Abd Allah, *'Alayhi al-Salam,* has said that `Amir al-Mu'minin has said, 'Eating twenty-one pieces of red raisins every day before breakfast dispels all kinds of illnesses except the illness of death.'"

H 11670, Ch. 3, h 3

A number of our people have narrated from Ahmad ibn abu 'Abd Allah from Ahmad ibn Muhammad from ibn abu Nasr who has said the following:

"A man from Egypt narrated to me that abu 'Abd Allah, *'Alayhi al-Salam,* has said, 'Raisins strengthen nerves, dispels illness and make one's breathe pleasant.'"

H 11671, Ch. 3, h 4

A number of our people have narrated from Sahl ibn Ziyad from Ya'qub Yazid from Ahmad ibn Muhammad from ibn abu Nasr from Fulan al-Misriy who has said the following:

"Abu 'Abd Allah, *'Alayhi al-Salam,* has said, 'Raisin of Taef strengthens nerves, removes troubles and makes one's breath pleasant.'"

Chapter 4 - The Pomegranate

H 11672, Ch. 4, h 1

Ali ibn Ibrahim has narrated from his father from and Muhammad ibn `Isma'il has narrated from al-Fadl ibn Shadhan from ibn abu 'Umayr from Ibrahim ibn 'Abd al-Hamid who has said the following:

"I once heard abu 'Abd Allah, *'Alayhi al-Salam,* saying, 'You must eat pomegranate; it suffices the hungry person and it is pleasant to satisfied ones'"

H 11673, Ch. 4, h 2

Ali ibn Ibrahim has narrated from his Harun ibn Muslim from Mas'adah ibn Ziyad who has said the following:

"Abu 'Abd Allah, *'Alayhi al-Salam,* has said, 'Fruits are of one hundred twenty colors and the pomegranate is its master.'"

H 11674, Ch. 4, h 3

A number of our people have narrated from Ahmad ibn abu 'Abd Allah from his father from Fadalah ibn from 'Umar ibn Aban al-Kalbiy who has said the following:

"I once heard abu Ja'far, and abu 'Abd Allah, *'Alayhim al-Salam,* saying, 'No other fruit on earth was as much desirable to the Messenger of Allah, *O Allah, grant compensation to Muhammad and his family worthy of their services to Your cause,* as pomegranate. He (the Messenger of Allah) liked not to share it with anyone.'"

H 11675, Ch. 4, h 4

It is narrated from the narrator of the previous *Hadith* from Muhammad ibn 'Isa from al-Dihqan from Durust from Ibrahim ibn 'Abd al-Hamid who has said the following:

"Abu al-Hassan, *'Alayhi al-Salam,* has said, 'Of the matters that Adam said in his will to Hibbatu Allah was his saying, 'You must eat pomegranate; if you eat it when you are hungry, it is sufficient; and if you eat when satisfied it is pleasant to you.'"

H 11676, Ch. 4, h 5

Ali ibn Ibrahim has narrated from his father from ibn abu 'Umayr from Hammad ibn 'Uthaman who has said the following:

"Abu 'Abd Allah, *'Alayhi al-Salam,* has said, 'Sharing of other things is not more hateful to me than sharing one pomegranate. In every pomegranate there is one grain from paradise, thus when an unbeliever eats it, Allah, most Majestic, most Glorious, sends an angel to remove it thereof.'"

H 11677, Ch. 4, h 6

Abu Ali al-Ash'ariy has narrated from Muhammad ibn 'Abd al-Jabbar, from Muhammad ibn Salim, from Ahmad ibn al-Nadr from Mufaddal who has said the following:

"I once heard abu 'Abd Allah, *'Alayhi al-Salam,* state this *Hadith.* 'I like to share with someone every food that I eat,' or that he (the Imam) said, 'A human being shares with me except pomegranate. In every pomegranate there is a grain from paradise.'"

H 11678, Ch. 4, h 7

A number of our people have narrated from Ahmad ibn Muhammad from 'Uthman ibn 'Isa from Sama'ah who has said the following:

"Abu 'Abd Allah, *'Alayhi al-Salam,* has said that 'Amir al-Mu'minin when eating pomegranate would spread a handkerchief. He was asked about it and he replied, 'There is a grain from paradise in it.' It was said that Jews, Christians and others eat it. He (the Imam) said, 'When that happens Allah, most Majestic, most Glorious, sends an angel to remove it thereof so he will not eat it.'"

H 11679, Ch. 4, h 8

Abu Ali al-Ash'ariy has narrated from Muhammad ibn 'Abd al-Jabbar from Safwan ibn Yahya from Mansur ibn Hazim who has said the following:

"Abu 'Abd Allah, *'Alayhi al-Salam,* has said, 'If one eats a grain of pomegranate it makes the Satan of temptation sick for forty days.'"

H 11680, Ch. 4, h 9

Muhammad ibn Yahya has narrated from Ahmad ibn Muhammad ibn 'Isa Ahmad ibn Muhammad from Muhammad ibn al-Hassan all from Muhammad ibn 'Isma'il ibn Bazi' from Salih ibn 'Uqbah from Yazid ibn 'Abd al-Malik al-Nawfaliy who has said the following:

"I once visited abu 'Abd Allah, *'Alayhi al-Salam,* and there was a pomegranate in his hand. He (the Imam) said, 'O Mu'attib give him a pomegranate; sharing of no other thing is more hateful to me than sharing a pomegranate.' He (the Imam) then applied cupping and I also applied cupping. He (the Imam) then asked for another pomegranate. He (the Imam) then said, 'O Yazid, if any believing person eats a pomegranate completely, Allah, most Majestic, most Glorious, dispels Satan from the brightness of his heart for forty days. If one eats two pieces completely Allah, most Majestic, most Glorious, dispels Satan from the bright part of his heart for one hundred days. If one eats three pomegranates completely, Allah, most Majestic, most Glorious, removes Satan from the brightness of his heart for one year. One from the brightness of whose heart Allah, most Majestic, most Glorious, removes Satan, he does not commit sins and one who does not commit sins enters paradise.'"*

H 11681, Ch. 4, h 10

Muhammad ibn Yahya has narrated from Ahmad ibn Muhammad from ibn Mahbub from 'Abd Allah ibn Sinan who has said the following:

"I once heard abu 'Abd Allah, *'Alayhi al-Salam,* saying, 'You must eat sweet pomegranate. Every grain that reaches the stomach of a believing person; it abolishes the illnesses and extinguishes the temptation of Satan thereof.'"

H 11682, Ch. 4, h 11

Ali ibn Ibrahim has narrated from his father from ibn abu 'Umayr from Hisham ibn Salim who has said the following:

"I once heard abu 'Abd Allah, *'Alayhi al-Salam,* saying, 'If one eats a pomegranate before breakfast his heart remains bright for forty days.'"

H 11683, Ch. 4, h 12

Ali ibn Muhammad ibn Bandar has narrated from his father from Muhammad ibn Ali al-Hamadaniy from Sa'id al-Raqqam from Salih ibn 'Uqbah who has said the following:

"I once heard abu 'Abd Allah, *'Alayhi al-Salam,* saying, 'Eat pomegranate with its flesh; it tans (cleans) the stomach and increases the brain's ability.'"

H 11684, Ch. 4, h 13

A number of our people have narrated from Sahl ibn Ziyad from Ja'far ibn Muhammad al-Ash'ariy from ibn al-Qaddah who has said the following:

"Abu 'Abd Allah, *'Alayhi al-Salam,* has said, 'Eat sour-sweet pomegranate with its flesh; it tans (cleanses) the stomach.'"

H 11685, Ch. 4, h 14

Ali ibn Ibrahim has narrated from his father from ibn abu 'Umayr from Ibrahim ibn 'Abd al-Hamid from al-Walid ibn Sabih who has said the following:

"Once sweet pomegranate was mentioned and abu 'Abd Allah, *'Alayhi al-Salam,* said, 'Sour-sweet pomegranate is more suitable for the stomach.'"

Muhammad ibn 'Isma'il has narrated from al-Fadl ibn Shadhan from ibn abu 'Umayr from Ibrahim ibn 'Abd al-Hamid from al-Walid ibn Sabih from abu 'Abd Allah, *'Alayhi al-Salam,* has narrated from a similar *Hadith.*"

H 11686, Ch. 4, h 15

A number of our people have narrated from Ahmad ibn Muhammad ibn Khalid from ibn Baqqah from Salih ibn 'Uqbah al-Khayyat or al-Qammat from Yazid ibn 'Abd al-Malik who has said the following:

"I once heard abu 'Abd Allah, *'Alayhi al-Salam,* saying, 'If one eats pomegranate his heart becomes bright and whosoever's heart Allah brightens Satan is kept away from him.' I then asked, 'What kind of pomegranate is this? I pray to Allah to keep my soul in service for your cause.' He (the Imam) said, 'It is the one from Sur (name of a place near Baghdad), this one.'"

H 11687, Ch. 4, h 16

It is narrated from the narrator of the previous *Hadith* from al-Nuhaykiy from 'Ubayd Allah ibn Ahmad from Ziyad ibn Marwan al-Qandiy who has said the following:

"I once heard abu al-Hassan, al-Awwal, *'Alayhi al-Salam,* saying, 'If one eats pomegranate on Friday before breakfast his heart becomes bright for forty mornings. If one eats two pomegranates, it then is eighty days, if one eats three pomegranates, it then is three hundred and twenty days and temptation of Satan is kept away from him. One from whom temptation of Satan is kept away he does not disobey Allah, most Majestic, most Glorious, and one who does not disobey Allah is admitted in paradise.'"

H 11688, Ch. 4, h 17

It is narrated from the narrator of the previous *Hadith* from al-Husayn ibn Sa'id from 'Amr ibn Ibrahim from al-Khurasaniy who has said the following:

"He (the Imam), *'Alayhi al-Salam,* has said, 'Eating sweet pomegranate increases one's seed and forms the child well.'"

H 11689, Ch. 4, h 18

A number of our people have narrated from Sahl ibn Ziyad from Ibrahim ibn 'Abd al-Rahman from Ziyad who has said the following:

"Abu al-Hassan, *'Alayhi al-Salam,* has said, 'Smoke from the tree of pomegranate dispels vermin.'"

Chapter 5 - The Apple

H 11690, Ch. 5, h 1

Muhammad ibn Yahya has narrated from Ahmad ibn Muhammad ibn 'Isa from Muhammad ibn Sinan from 'Isma'il ibn Jabir who has said the following:

"I once heard abu 'Abd Allah, *'Alayhi al-Salam,* saying, 'The apple is a stomach cleanser.'"

H 11691, Ch. 5, h 2

Ahmad ibn Muhammad has narrated from Bakr ibn Salih from al-Ja'fariy who has said the following:

"I once heard abu al-Hassan, Musa, *'Alayhi al-Salam,* saying, 'The apple has several benefits. It is beneficial against poison, magic and slight mental derangement, which is caused (spread) from the people of the earth and increased phlegm. No other thing is so quickly beneficial.'"

H 11692, Ch. 5, h 3

Ali ibn Muhammad ibn Bandar has narrated from his father from Muhammad ibn Ali al-Hamadaniy from 'Abd Allah ibn Sinan from Durust ibn abu Mansur who has said the following:

"Al-Mufaddal ibn 'Umar once sent me to abu 'Abd Allah, *'Alayhi al-Salam,* for a favor (from the Imam). I went to him (the Imam) on a summer day and before him there was a tray with green apples in it and I by Allah could hardly wait until I asked saying, 'I pray to Allah to keep my soul in service for your cause, do you eat this while people dislike it?' He (the Imam) said, as if he still remembered me, 'Last night I had a fever so I sent for it and it was brought for me. I ate it and it cuts down the fever and calms down high temperature.' I returned and found my family with fever. I fed them (such apples) and fever was cut off from them."

H 11693, Ch. 5, h 4

A number of our people have narrated from Sahl ibn Ziyad from Ya'qub ibn Yazid from Ziyad al-Qandiy who has said the following:

"I once entered al-Madinah with my brother Sayf. People suffered from nasal hemorrhage because of which a man after two days died. I returned to my lodging and found Sayf with nasal hemorrhage severely. I went to abu al-Hassan, *'Alayhi al-Salam.* He (the Imam) said, 'O Ziyad feed Sayf apples.' I fed him apples and he got well.'"

H 11694, Ch. 5, h 5

Muhammad ibn Yahya has narrated from Ahmad ibn Muhammad from Ali ibn al-Hakam from Ziyad ibn Marwan who has said the following:

"People in Makkah suffered plague. I wrote to abu al-Hassan, *'Alayhi al-Salam,* about it and he (the Imam) wrote to me and said to eat apples."

H 11695, Ch. 5, h 6

Abu Ali al-Ash'ariy has narrated from Muhammad ibn 'Abd al-Jabbar from ibn Faddal from ibn Bukayr who has said the following:

"I one year suffered nasal hemorrhage in al-Madinah and our people asked abu 'Abd Allah, *'Alayhi al-Salam,* about something that can stop nose bleeding. He (the Imam) said, 'Make him drink sawiq of apples (soup of apples).' They followed the instruction and my nose bleeding stopped.'"

H 11696, Ch. 5, h 7

Muhammad ibn Yahya has narrated from Muhammad ibn Musa from certain persons of our people in a marfu' manner who has said the following:

"Abu 'Abd Allah, *'Alayhi al-Salam,* has said, 'I do not know of anything more beneficial against poisoning than sawiq of apples.'"

H 11697, Ch. 5, h 8

It is narrated from the narrator of the previous *Hadith* from Ahmad ibn Muhammad from al-Husayn ibn Sa'id from Ahmad ibn Muhammad ibn Yazid who has said the following:

"Whenever a poisonous thing like snake or scorpion would bite anyone in the family he (the Imam) would say, 'Make him drink sawiq of apples.'"

H 11698, Ch. 5, h 9

A number of our people have narrated from Ahmad Ibn abu 'Abd Allah from Ya'qub ibn Yazid from al-Qandiy from al-Mufaddal ibn 'Umar who has said the following:

"Once, fever was mentioned before abu 'Abd Allah, *'Alayhi al-Salam.* He (the Imam) said, 'We are the people of the family who do not use any medicine for it except pouring cold water on us and eating apples.'"

H 11699, Ch. 5, h 10

It is narrated from the narrator of the previous *Hadith* from Yunus from those whom he has mentioned who has said the following:

"Abu 'Abd Allah, *'Alayhi al-Salam,* has said, 'Had people known that which is in apples they would not treat their patients with anything other than apples.'

He (the narrator) has said that certain ones have narrated from abu 'Abd Allah, *'Alayhi al-Salam,* who has said the following: "Feed apples to your people suffering from fever; no other thing is more beneficial than apples.'"

H 11700, Ch. 5, h 11

A number of our people have narrated from Sahl ibn Ziyad from Muhammad ibn al-Hassan Shammun from 'Abd Allah ibn 'Abd al-Rahman from Misma' ibn 'Abd al-Malik who has said the following:

"Abu 'Abd Allah, *'Alayhi al-Salam,* has said that `Amir al-Mu'minin has said, 'Eat apples; it tans (cleanses) the stomach.'"

Chapter 6 - Quince

H 11701, Ch. 6, h 1

Muhammad ibn Yahya has narrated from Ahmad ibn Muhammad from al-Qasim ibn Yahya from his grandfather al-Hassan ibn Rashid who has said the following:

"Abu 'Abd Allah, *'Alayhi al-Salam,* has said that `Amir al-Mu'minin has said, 'Eating quince strengthens the weak heart, cleanses the stomach, purifies the mind and emboldens the coward.'"

H 11702, Ch. 6, h 2

Ali ibn Ibrahim has narrated from his father from al-Nawfaliy from al-Sakuniy who has said the following:

"Abu 'Abd Allah, *'Alayhi al-Salam,* has said that Ja'far ibn abu Talib was with the Holy Prophet, *O Allah, grant compensation to Muhammad and his family worthy of their services to Your cause,* and he presented quince to the Holy Prophet. The Holy Prophet cut one piece from it and gave it to Ja'far but he declined to eat it. The Holy Prophet said, 'Take and eat it. It makes the heart (mind) intelligent and emboldens a coward heart.' In another *Hadith* it is said, 'Eat it; it clears the color and beautifies the child (to be born).'"

H 11703, Ch. 6, h 3

Al-Husayn ibn Muhammad has narrated from Mu'alla' ibn Muhammad in a marfu' manner who has said the following:

"Abu 'Abd Allah, *'Alayhi al-Salam,* has said, 'If one eats quince before breakfast his seed becomes fine and his child well-formed.'"

H 11704, Ch. 6, h 4

Muhammad ibn Yahya has narrated from Ahmad ibn Muhammad from Muhammad ibn 'Isma'il ibn Bazi' from his uncle Hamzah ibn Bazi' who has said the following:

"Abu Ibrahim, *'Alayhi al-Salam,* has said that the Messenger of Allah, *O Allah, grant compensation to Muhammad and his family worthy of their services to Your cause,* said to Ja'far, 'O Ja'far, eat quince; it strengthens the heart and emboldens the coward heart.'"

H 11705, Ch. 6, h 5

Ahmad ibn Muhammad from al-Hassan ibn Ali from Jamil ibn Darraj who has said the following:

"Abu 'Abd Allah, *'Alayhi al-Salam,* has said, 'If one eats quince Allah, most Majestic, most Glorious, makes his tongue to speak wisdom for forty mornings.'"

H 11706, Ch. 6, h 6

Muhammad ibn 'Abd Allah ibn Ja'far has narrated from his father from Ali ibn Sulayman ibn Rashid from Marwak ibn 'Ubayd from those whom he has mentioned who has said the following:

"Abu 'Abd Allah, *'Alayhi al-Salam,* has said, 'There has not been any Prophet sent from Allah, most Majestic, most Glorious, who did not have the fragrance of quince.'"

H 11707, Ch. 6, h 7

A number of our people have narrated from Ahmad ibn abu 'Abd Allah from A number of his people from Ali ibn Asbat from abu Muhammad al-Jawhariy from Sufyan ibn 'Uyaynah who has said the following:

"I once heard Ja'far ibn Muhammad, *'Alayhi al-Salam,* saying, 'Eating quince removes the intensity of sadness just as the hand wipes perspiration from the forehead.'"

Chapter 7 - The Fig

H 11708, Ch. 7, h 1

Ali ibn Ibrahim has narrated from his father from Ahmad ibn Muhammad from ibn abu Nasr who has said the following:

"Abu al-Hassan, al-Rida', *'Alayhi al-Salam,* has said, 'Figs remove bad-breath (halitosis), brings firmness to the teeth and bones, grows hairs and dispels illness and with it medicine is not needed.' He (the Imam) has said, 'The fig is most similar to the plants of paradise.'"

Sahl ibn Ziyad has narrated from Ahmad ibn al-Ash'ath from Ahmad ibn Muhammad ibn abu Nasr a similar *Hadith.*"

Chapter 8 - The Pear

H 11709, Ch. 8, h 1
Muhammad ibn Yahya has narrated from Ahmad ibn Muhammad from al-Qasim ibn Yahya from his grandfather al-Hassan ibn Rashid from abu Basir who has said the following:

"Abu 'Abd Allah, *'Alayhi al-Salam,* has said, 'You can eat pears; it brightens the heart (mind) and calms down pains by the permission of Allah.'"

H 11710, Ch. 8, h 2
Muhammad ibn Yahya has narrated from Ahmad ibn Muhammad from 'Abd Allah ibn Ja'far from Muhammad ibn 'Isa from al-Washsha' from certain persons of our people who has said the following:

"Abu 'Abd Allah, *'Alayhi al-Salam,* has said, 'Pears tan (cleanses) the stomach and makes it strong. Pears and quince are the same. On a full stomach, it is more beneficial than before breakfast. If one feels depression and sadness in his heart he should eat pears after food.'"

Chapter 9 - The Plum

H 11711, Ch. 9, h 1
Muhammad ibn Yahya has narrated from 'Abd Allah ibn Ja'far from Ya'qub ibn Yazid from Ziyad al-Qandiy who has said the following:

"I once went to see abu al-Hassan, al-Awwal, *'Alayhi al-Salam,* and before him (the Imam) there was a bowl with black plums in its time (season). He (the Imam) said, 'It is because fever increased in my body and fresh plums lower down fever, calm down yellowness (stomach acid). Dry plums calm down blood (excitement) and remove reverberating illnesses.'"

Chapter 10 - The Citron

H 11712, Ch. 10, h 1
Muhammad ibn Yahya has narrated from Ahmad ibn Muhammad from Ali ibn al-Hakam from al-Washsha' all from Ali ibn abu Hamzah from abu Basir who has said the following:

"There was a guest in my house who liked citron with honey. I served him and I ate with him; then I went to visit abu 'Abd Allah, *'Alayhi al-Salam,* when the table-spread with food was before him (the Imam). He (the Imam) asked me to come close and eat. I said, 'I just had citron with honey before coming and I feel heavy because I overate.' He (the Imam) said, 'O boy, go to the girl and tell her to send for me pieces of dry loaves of bread of that which she dries up in the oven.' He brought it and he (the Imam) said to me, 'Eat from this dry bread; it helps one to digests citron.' I ate it, then left and I felt as if I had not eaten anything.'"

H 11713, Ch. 10, h 2
Muhammad ibn Yahya has narrated from Ahmad ibn Muhammad from Bakr ibn Salih from 'Abd Allah ibn Ibrahim al-Ja'fariy who has said the following:

"Abu 'Abd Allah, *'Alayhi al-Salam,* once asked, 'What do your physicians recommend for you about citron?' I replied, 'They recommend us to eat citron before food.' He (the Imam) said, 'I recommend you to eat it after food.'"

H 11714, Ch. 10, h 3

A number of our people have narrated from Ahmad ibn Muhammad ibn Khalid, from al-Qasim ibn Yahya, from his grandfather, al-Hassan ibn Rashid, from abu Basir who has said the following:

"Abu 'Abd Allah, *'Alayhi al-Salam,* has said, 'Eat citron after food; because Ale Muhammad, *O Allah, grant compensation to Muhammad and his family worthy of their services to Your cause,* do so.'"

H 11715, Ch. 10, h 4

A number of our people have narrated from Sahl ibn Ziyad from Ahmad ibn Muhammad from ibn abu Nasr who has said the following:

"Abu al-Hassan, al-Rida', *'Alayhi al-Salam,* has said, 'Dry bread helps one to digests citron.'"

H 11716, Ch. 10, h 5

Muhammad ibn Yahya has narrated from Ahmad ibn Muhammad from al-Husayn ibn Sa'id from Hammad ibn 'Isa from Ibrahim ibn 'Umar al-Yamaniy who has said the following:

"I once said to abu 'Abd Allah, *'Alayhi al-Salam,* 'They think that citron before breakfast is in its best.' Abu 'Abd Allah, *'Alayhi al-Salam,* said, 'Before food it is good after food it better and best.'"

H 11717, Ch. 10, h 6

Ali ibn Ibrahim has narrated from his father from Ali ibn Muhammad al-Qasaniy from abu Ayyub al-Madiniy from Sulayman ibn Ja'far al-Ja'fariy who has said the following:

"Abu al-Hassan, al-Rida', has said that the Messenger of Allah, *O Allah, grant compensation to Muhammad and his family worthy of their services to Your cause,* liked to look at the green citron and red apple.'"

Chapter 11 - The Bananas

H 11718, Ch. 11, h 1

A number of our people have narrated from Ahmad ibn abu 'Abd Allah from his father from Muhammad ibn abu 'Umayr from Yahya ibn Musa, San'aniy who has said the following:

"I once visited abu al-Hassan, al-Rida', *'Alayhi al-Salam,* in Mina and abu Ja'far, al-Thaniy was in his lap. He (the Imam) peeled banana and fed him (abu Ja'far, al-Thaniy).'"

H 11719, Ch. 11, h 2

Abu Ali al-Ash'ariy has narrated from Muhammad ibn 'Abd al-Jabbar from Safwan from abu 'Usamah who has said the following:

"I once visited abu 'Abd Allah, *'Alayhi al-Salam.* He brought banana nearer to me and I ate.'"

H 11720, Ch. 11, h 3

A number of our people have narrated from Sahl ibn Ziyad Ali ibn Asbat from Yahya al-San'aniy who has said the following:

"I once visited abu al-Hassan, al-Rida', *'Alayhi al-Salam,* in Makkah. He (the Imam) peeled banana and fed it to abu Ja'far, al-Thaniy, *'Alayhi al-Salam.* I then said, 'I pray to Allah to keep my soul in service for your cause, is this the blessed newborn?' He (the Imam) said, 'Yes, O Yahya, this is the new born, the like of whom in greatness of blessing is not born in Islam for our Shi'a.'"

Chapter 12 - The Rowan, Mountain Ash

H 11721, Ch. 12, h 1

Muhammad ibn Yahya has narrated from Muhammad ibn Musa from Ahmad ibn al-Hassan ibn Ali from his father from ibn Bukayr who has said the following:

"I once heard abu 'Abd Allah, *'Alayhi al-Salam,* saying, 'The flesh of *Rowan,* mountain ash berry grows flesh, its bones grow bones and its peels grow skin, besides it warms up kidneys, tans (cleanses) the stomach and it is protection against hemorrhoid and *al-Taqtir* (intense anger, stint). It brings firmness to the legs and uproots the vein of leprosy.'"

Chapter 13 - The Melons

H 11722, Ch. 13, h 1

Ali ibn Ibrahim has narrated from Yasar al-Khadim who has said the following:

"Abu al-Hassan, al-Rida', *'Alayhi al-Salam,* has said, 'Eating melons before breakfast causes paralysis, may Allah grant us protection against it!'"

H 11723, Ch. 13, h 2

Muhammad ibn Yahya has narrated from Ahmad ibn Muhammad from ibn Faddal from certain persons of his people who have said the following:

"Abu 'Abd Allah, *'Alayhi al-Salam,* has said that the Messenger of Allah, *O Allah, grant compensation to Muhammad and his family worthy of their services to Your cause,* would eat fresh dates with melons.'"

H 11724, Ch. 13, h 3

Ali ibn Ibrahim has narrated from his father from al-Nawfaliy from al-Sakuniy who has said the following:

"Abu 'Abd Allah, *'Alayhi al-Salam,* has said that the Messenger of Allah, *O Allah, grant compensation to Muhammad and his family worthy of their services to Your cause,* would eat melons with dates.'"

H 11725, Ch. 13, h 4

A number of our people have narrated from Sahl ibn Ziyad from Ja'far ibn Muhammad al-Ash'ariy from ibn al-Qaddah who has said the following:

"Abu 'Abd Allah, *'Alayhi al-Salam,* has said that the Messenger of Allah, *O Allah, grant compensation to Muhammad and his family worthy of their services to Your cause,* liked fresh dates with melons.'"

H 11726, Ch. 13, h 5

A number of our people have narrated from Ahmad ibn abu 'Abd Allah from Muhammad ibn 'Isa from 'Ubayd Allah ibn 'Abd Allah al-Dihqan from Durust from Ibrahim ibn 'Abd al-Hamid who has said the following:

"Abu al-Hassan, al-Awwal, *'Alayhi al-Salam,* has said that the Messenger of Allah, *O Allah, grant compensation to Muhammad and his family worthy of their services to Your cause,* ate melons with sugar. He (the Messenger of Allah) ate melons with fresh dates.'"

Chapter 14 - The Herbs

H 11727, Ch. 14, h 1
A number of our people have narrated from Sahl ibn Ziyad from Ahmad ibn Harun from Muwaffaq al-Madiniy from his father from his grandfather who has said the following:
"Abu al-Hassan, al-Madiy, 'Alayhi al-Salam, once sent for me and he made me to stay for lunch. When they brought the table-spread with food there were no herbs in it. He (the Imam) held his hand and said to the boy, 'Did you not know that I do not eat until there are green herbs on the table-spread, so bring for me fresh herbs.' The boy went, brought fresh herbs and placed it on the table-spread then he (the Imam) extended his hand and ate his lunch.'"

H 11728, Ch. 14, h 2
Ali ibn Ibrahim has narrated from his father from Hanan who has said the following:
"Once I was with abu 'Abd Allah, 'Alayhi al-Salam, on the table-spread of food and he (the Imam) ate fresh herbs but I abstained because of a certain illness. He (the Imam) turned to me and said, 'O Hanan, did you not know that whenever a package of food was brought to 'Amir al-Mu'minin it neccessarily had herbs in it?' I then asked, 'I pray to Allah to keep my soul in service for your cause, why did it have to be as such?' He (the Imam) said, 'It is because the hearts of the believers are fresh, green and they incline to what is similar to it.'"

Chapter 15 - The Endives

H 11729, Ch. 15, h 1
Muhammad ibn Yahya has narrated from Ahmad ibn Muhammad from Ali ibn al-Hakam from al-Muthanna' ibn al-Walid who has said the following:
"Abu 'Abd Allah, 'Alayhi al-Salam, has said, 'If one goes to sleep with seven leaves of endives in his belly he will remain safe from colic (colitis) pain that night by the will of Allah.'"

H 11730, Ch. 15, h 2
It is narrated from the narrator of the previous *Hadith* from Ahmad ibn Muhammad from Ali ibn al-Hakam from Khalid ibn Muhammad from his grandfather, Sufyan ibn al-Simt who has said the following:
"Abu 'Abd Allah, 'Alayhi al-Salam, has said, 'If one likes to increase his seed and children he should eat endives very often.'"

H 11731, Ch. 15, h 3
Ali ibn Ibrahim has narrated from his father from al-Nawfaliy from al-Sakuniy who has said the following:
"Abu 'Abd Allah, 'Alayhi al-Salam, has said, 'If one likes to increase his seed and children he should eat endives very often.'"

H 11732, Ch. 15, h 4
Ali ibn Ibrahim has narrated from his father from al-Nawfaliy from al-Sakuniy who has said the following:
"Abu 'Abd Allah, 'Alayhi al-Salam, has said, 'The endive is a very good herb. On every one of its leaves there is a drop of paradise, so you should eat it and do

not shake it off when eating.' He (the Imam) has said, 'My father, *'Alayhi al-Salam*, prohibited us from shaking off when we were eating it.'"

H 11733, Ch. 15, h 5
Ali ibn Ibrahim has narrated from his father from Harun ibn Muslim from Mas'adah ibn Sadaqah from Ziyad who has said the following:

"Abu 'Abd Allah, *'Alayhi al-Salam*, has said, 'The endive is the master of herbs.'"

H 11734, Ch. 15, h 6
Muhammad ibn Yahya has narrated from Ahmad ibn Muhammad and Abu Ali al-Ash'ariy has narrated from Muhammad ibn 'Abd al-Jabbar all from *al-Hajj*al from Tha'labah from a man who has said the following:

"Abu 'Abd Allah, *'Alayhi al-Salam*, once said, 'You must eat endives because it increases one's seed and forms children well. It is hot, soft and increases male children.'"

H 11735, Ch. 15, h 7
A number of our people have narrated from Ahmad ibn abu 'Abd Allah from abu Sulayman al-Hadhdha' al-Jabaliy from Muhammad ibn al-Fayd who has said the following:

"I once had lunch with abu 'Abd Allah, *'Alayhi al-Salam*, and on the table-spread there were herbs and with us: there was an old man who avoided endive. Abu 'Abd Allah, *'Alayhi al-Salam*, said, 'You think that endive is of cold nature, in fact, it is not the way you think it is. It is balanced and its excellence over other herbs is like our excellence over other people.'"*

H 11736, Ch. 15, h 8
It is narrated from the narrator of the previous *Hadith* from certain persons of our people from al-Asamm from Shu'ayb from abu Basir who has said the following:

"Abu 'Abd Allah, *'Alayhi al-Salam*, has said that `Amir al-Mu'minin has said, 'You should eat endives. Every morning one drop descends on it from paradise and when you eat it do not shake it off.' Abu 'Abd Allah, *'Alayhi al-Salam*, has said, 'My father, *'Alayhi al-Salam*, prohibited us from shaking off when we ate endives.'"

H 11737, Ch. 15, h 9
A number of our people have narrated from Sahl ibn Ziyad from Muhammad ibn `Isma'il who has said the following:

"I once heard al-Rida', *'Alayhi al-Salam*, saying, 'The endive is cure for a thousand illnesses. There is no illness in the belly of the sons of Adam that endives cannot dispel.' He (the narrator) has said, 'One day he asked for it because one of the servants suffered from fever and headache. He ordered to make it thin, spread it on a piece of paper then a certain amount of viola oil was poured on it and placed on his forehead. He (the Imam) then said, 'This removes fever and is beneficial in headaches and to dispel it off.'"

H 11738, Ch. 15, h 10
Muhammad ibn Yahya has narrated from Ahmad ibn Muhammad from abu Yahya al-Wasitiy from certain persons of our people who has said the following:

"Abu 'Abd Allah, *'Alayhi al-Salam*, has said, 'The endive is the herb of the

Messenger of Allah, *O Allah, grant compensation to Muhammad and his family worthy of their services to Your cause.* The herb of `Amir al-Mu'minin, *'Alayhi al-Salam,* is al-Badharuj (sweet basil) and the herb of Fatimah, *'Alayha al-Salam,* is al-*Farfakh* (purslane).

Chapter 16 - The Sweet Basil

H 11739, Ch. 16, h 1
Ali ibn Ibrahim has narrated from his father from al-Nawfaliy from al-Sakuniy who has said the following:

"Abu 'Abd Allah, *'Alayhi al-Salam,* has said that `Amir al-Mu'minin has said the Messenger of Allah, *O Allah, grant compensation to Muhammad and his family worthy of their services to Your cause,* liked sweet basil.'"

H 11740, Ch. 16, h 2
Muhammad ibn Yahya has narrated from Ahmad ibn Muhammad ibn 'Isa from ibn abu 'Umayr from Hammad ibn 'Uthaman who has said the following:

"Abu 'Abd Allah, *'Alayhi al-Salam,* has said that `Amir al-Mu'minin, *'Alayhi al-Salam,* liked al-*Badharuj* (sweet basil).'"

H 11741, Ch. 16, h 3
A number of our people have narrated from Sahl ibn Ziyad from Ayyub ibn Nuh who has said the following:

"I once was with abu al-Hassan, al-Awwal on a table of food and he asked for sweet basil saying, 'I like to begin my food with it because it opens up blockages, and strengthens one's appetite for food and takes away *al-Subul* (the paths). If I begin my food with it I then do not mind what I eat thereafter of food; I will not be afraid of illness or calamity.' When we completed eating, he (the Imam) asked for it again and I saw him searching on the table-spread for its leaves. He (the Imam) ate them and gave to me saying, 'Finish eating with this; it makes what you ate pleasant, strengthens your appetite for what you may eat thereafter, takes away heaviness and makes burps pleasant as well as one's breath.'"

H 11742, Ch. 16, h 4
Muhammad ibn Yahya has narrated from Muhammad ibn Musa from 'Ishkib ibn 'Abdah al-Hamadaniy through his chain of narrators who has said the following:

"Abu 'Abd Allah, *'Alayhi al-Salam,* has said, '*Al-Hawk* (sweet basil) is the herb of the Prophets. There are eight qualities in it; It is pleasant, opens up blockages, makes burping pleasant, freshens one's breath, increases appetite for food, pulls out illness and it is protection against leprosy and when it settles down in one's stomach it suppresses illness.'"

Chapter 17 - The Leek

H 11743, Ch. 17, h 1
A number of our people have narrated from Sahl ibn Ziyad from Ali ibn Hassan from Musa ibn Bakr who has said the following:

"Once, a slave of abu al-Hassan complained of illness. He (the Imam) asked about him and it was said that he has spleen trouble. He (the Imam) said, 'Feed him leeks for three days.' We fed him, blood formed and he became well.'"

H 11744, Ch. 17, h 2
It is narrated from the narrator of the previous *Hadith* has said the following:
"One who had seen abu al-Hassan, *'Alayhi al-Salam,* narrated to me that abu al-Hassan, *'Alayhi al-Salam,* ate leeks from the carriage from the farm and washed it with water.'"

H 11745, Ch. 17, h 3
Sahl ibn Ziyad has narrated from Muhammad ibn al-Walid from Yunus ibn Ya'qub who has said the following:
"I saw abu al-Hassan, *'Alayhi al-Salam,* cut leeks from their roots, wash with water and eat."

H 11746, Ch. 17, h 4
Ali ibn Muhammad ibn Bandar has narrated from his father from Muhammad ibn Ali al-Hamadaniy from 'Amr ibn 'Isa from Furat ibn Ahnaf who has said the following:
"Abu 'Abd Allah, *'Alayhi al-Salam,* was asked about leeks and he (the Imam) said, 'Eat it because it has four qualities. It refreshes one's breath, dispels gases, cuts down hemorrhoids and it is protection against leprosy for one who eats it very often.'"

H 11747, Ch. 17, h 5
A number of our people have narrated from Ahmad ibn abu 'Abd Allah from Muhammad ibn 'Isa or others from 'Abd al-Rahman from Hammad ibn Zakariya who has said the following:
"Abu 'Abd Allah, *'Alayhi al-Salam,* has said that herbs were mentioned before the Messenger of Allah, *O Allah, grant compensation to Muhammad and his family worthy of their services to Your cause,* he (the Messenger of Allah) said, 'Eat leeks because its likeness in herbs is like bread in other foods' or he said 'sauce.'" Uncertainty is from Muhammad ibn Ya'qub.

H 11748, Ch. 17, h 6
It is narrated from the narrator of the previous *Hadith* from Dawud ibn abu Dawud who has said the following:
"A man had seen abu al-Hassan, *'Alayhi al-Salam,* in Khurasan eating leeks from the garden as it was and it was said to him (the Imam), 'There is fertilizer with it.' He (the Imam) said, 'It does not stick to it and it is very good for hemorrhoids.'"

H 11749, Ch. 17, h 7
It is narrated from the narrator of the previous *Hadith* from certain persons of his people from Hanan ibn Sadir who has said the following:
"I once was with abu 'Abd Allah, *'Alayhi al-Salam,* around the table-spread of food. I reached for the endives and he (the Imam) said to me, 'O Hanan, why do you not eat leeks?' I replied, 'It is because of what is narrated from you in the *Hadith* about endives.' He (the Imam) then asked, 'What is narrated about it from us?' I replied, 'It is narrated from you as having said, "Every day one drop falls on it."' He (the Imam) said, 'On leeks it is seven drops.' I then asked, 'How

should I eat it?' He (the Imam) said, 'Cut their roots and throw away their heads.'"

H 11750, Ch. 17, h 8

It is narrated from the narrator of the previous *Hadith* from certain persons of his people in a marfu' manner who has said the following:

"'Amir al-Mu'minin, *'Alayhi al-Salam,* would eat leeks with not so finely powdered salt.'"

Chapter 18 - The Celery

H 11751, Ch. 18, h 1

A number of our people have narrated from Ahmad ibn abu 'Abd Allah from Muhammad ibn 'Isa or others from Qutaybah ibn Mehran from Hammad ibn Zakariya who has said the following:

"Abu 'Abd Allah, *'Alayhi al-Salam,* has said that the Messenger of Allah, *O Allah, grant compensation to Muhammad and his family worthy of their services to Your cause,* has said, 'You must eat celery because it is the food of Elias, al-Yasa' and Usha' ibn Nun (names of Israelite prophets).'"

H 11752, Ch. 18, h 2

It is narrated from the narrator of the previous *Hadith* Nuh ibn Shu'ayb al-Naysaburiy from Muhammad ibn al-Hassan ibn Ali Yaqtin as I know from Nadir al-Khadim who has said the following:

"Abu al-Hassan, *'Alayhi al-Salam,* once mentioned celery and said, 'You desire to eat celery and there is no living thing that does not rub against it.'" (It can be for or against it depending on if, they rub for cure or to leave poison).

Chapter 19(a) - Coriander

H 11753, Ch. 19a, h 1

Muhammad ibn Yahya has narrated from Ahmad ibn Muhammad ibn 'Isa from al-Dihqan from Durust from Ibrahim from 'Abd al-Hamid who has said the following:

"Abu al-Hassan, *'Alayhi al-Salam,* has said, 'Eating apple and coriander causes forgetfulness.'"

Chapter 19(b) - Purslane

H 11754, Ch. 19b, h 1

Muhammad ibn Yahya has narrated from Ahmad ibn Muhammad, from 'Uthman ibn 'Isa, from Furat ibn Ahnaf who has said the following:

"I once heard abu 'Abd Allah, *'Alayhi al-Salam,* saying, 'On the face of earth there is no herb more beneficial and graceful than *al-Farfakh* (purslane) and it is the herb of Fatimah, *'Alayha al-Salam.*' He (the Imam) then said, 'May Allah condemn banu 'Umayyah who named it foolish herb due to their animosity toward Fatimah, *'Alayhi al-Salam.*'"

H 11755, Ch. 19b, h 2

Ali ibn Ibrahim has narrated from his father from ibn abu 'Umayr from certain persons of our people who has said the following:

"Abu 'Abd Allah, *'Alayhi al-Salam,* has said that once the Messenger of Allah,

O Allah, grant compensation to Muhammad and his family worthy of their services to Your cause, set foot on a sun-baked ground which burned him. He (the Messenger of Allah) then set foot on purslane and it calmed down the heat and he (the Messenger of Allah) prayed for the herb. He liked it and would say, 'How blessed an herb it is!'"

Chapter 20 - The Lettuce

H 11756, Ch. 20, h 1
A number of our people have narrated from Ahmad ibn abu 'Abd Allah from his father from certain persons of his people from abu Hafs ibn al-Abbar who has said the following:
"Abu 'Abd Allah, *'Alayhi al-Salam,* has said, 'You must eat lettuce because it cleanses blood.'"

Chapter 21 - *Al-Sadab* (Rue Herb of Grace)

H 11757, Ch. 21, h 1
Muhammad ibn Yahya has narrated from Ahmad ibn Muhammad ibn 'Isa from Ya'qub ibn 'Amir from a man who has said the following:
"Abu al-Hassan, *'Alayhi al-Salam,* has said, *'Al-Sadab* (Rue herb of grace) increases the power of understanding.'"

H 11758, Ch. 21, h 2
It is narrated from the narrator of the previous *Hadith* from Muhammad ibn Musa from Ali ibn al-Hassan al-Hamadaniy from Muhammad ibn 'Amr ibn Ibrahim who has said the following:
"Abu Ja'far, or abu al-Hassan, *'Alayhim al-Salam,* -uncertainty is from Muhammad ibn Musa- has said, 'Once *al-Sadab* was mentioned and He (the Imam) said, 'There are benefits in it. It increases the power of understanding, increases in the brain except that it putrefies one's back's water.' It is narrated that it is very good for ear ache."

Chapter 22 - The Watercress

H 11759, Ch. 22, h 1
A number of our people have narrated from Ahmad ibn abu 'Abd Allah from Muhammad ibn 'Isa and others from Qutaybah al-A'sha' or he said, Qutaybah ibn Mehran from Hammad ibn Zakariya who has said the following:
"Abu 'Abd Allah, *'Alayhi al-Salam,* has said, 'If one fills himself up with watercress after performing *Salat* (prayer) of al-'Isha' he will spend the night while his soul invites him to leprosy.'"

H 11760, Ch. 22, h 2
Ali ibn Ibrahim has narrated from his father from al-Nawfaliy from al-Sakuniy who has said the following:
"Abu 'Abd Allah, *'Alayhi al-Salam,* has said, 'If one eats watercress during the night the vein of leprosy will hit him from his nose and blood will flow thereof.'"

H 11761, Ch. 22, h 3

Muhammad ibn Yahya has narrated from Musa ibn al-Hassan from Ahmad ibn Sulayman from his father from abu Basir who has said the following:

"Once, a man asked abu 'Abd Allah, *'Alayhi al-Salam,* about endives, sweet basil and watercress. He (the Imam) said, 'Endives and sweet basil are for us and watercress is for banu 'Umayyah.'"

H 11762, Ch. 22, h 4

A number of our people have narrated from Ahmad ibn abu 'Abd Allah from Muhammad ibn 'Isa from al-Husayn ibn Sa'id from Nusayr Mawla' abu 'Abd Allah, *'Alayhi al-Salam,* from Muwaffaq Mawla' abu al-Hassan, *'Alayhi al-Salam,* who has said the following:

"When my master ordered buying herbs he ordered quite a large amount and also watercress. It then would have been purchased for him and he (the Imam) would say, 'How dimwitted certain people are when they say that it grows in a valley of hell and Allah, most Majestic, most Glorious, says, 'Its fuel is people and stones' (2:24); then how can herbs grow therein?'"

Chapter 23 - The White Beet

H 11763, Ch. 23, h 1

A number of our people have narrated from Ahmad ibn abu 'Abd Allah from al-Hassan ibn Ali from abu 'Uthman in a *marfu'* manner who has said the following:

"Abu 'Abd Allah, *'Alayhi al-Salam,* has said, 'Allah, most Majestic, most Glorious, removed leprosy from Jews because of their eating beets and their cutting the veins.'"

H 11764, Ch. 23, h 2

It is narrated from the narrator of the previous *Hadith* from Muhammad ibn 'Abd al-Hamid from Safwan ibn Yahya who has said the following:

"Abu al-Hassan, *'Alayhi al-Salam,* has said, 'The white beet is a very good vegetable.'"

H 11765, Ch. 23, h 3

It is narrated from the narrator of the previous *Hadith* from Ali ibn al-Hassan al-Tamimiy from Sulayman ibn 'Abbad from 'Isa ibn abu al-Ward from Muhammad ibn Qays who has said the following:

"Abu Ja'far, *'Alayhi al-Salam,* has said that banu Israel complained before Musa, *'Alayhi al-Salam,* because of whiteness (vitiligo) they experienced and he complained about it before Allah, most Blessed, most High. Allah sent him revelation that said, 'Command them to eat cow meat with beets.'"

H 11766, Ch. 23, h 4

Muhammad ibn Yahya has narrated from 'Abd Allah ibn Ja'far from Muhammad ibn 'Isa who has said the following:

"Abu al-Hassan, al-Rida', *'Alayhi al-Salam,* has said, 'Feed your patients beets, the leaves, because there is cure in it without illness or shock and it makes sleep of a patient more relaxing; but abstain from its roots because it stirs up *al-Sawada'* (a certain illness).'"

H 11767, Ch. 23, h 5

It is narrated from the narrator of the previous *Hadith* from Muhammad ibn 'Isa from certain al-Husayniyin who has said the following:

"Abu al-Hassan, *'Alayhi al-Salam,* has said, 'Beets uproot the vein of leprosy and no other thing is as beneficial as leaves of beets that enter the belly of one suffering from leprosy.'"

Chapter 24 - The Truffle

H 11768, Ch. 24, h 1

Muhammad ibn Yahya has narrated from 'Abd Allah ibn Muhammad ibn 'Isa from Ali ibn al-Hakam, from Aban ibn 'Uthman from abu Basir from Fatimah daughter Ali from 'Umamah daughter of abu al-'Ass ibn al-Rabi' and her mother, Zaynab daughter the Messenger of Allah who has said the following:

"Once 'Amir al-Mu'minin, Ali, *'Alayhi al-Salam,* in the month of Ramadan came to me. For dinner, he brought dates and truffles. He (the Imam) ate it and he liked truffles.'"

H 11769, Ch. 24, h 2

A number of our people have narrated from Ahmad ibn abu 'Abd Allah from Muhammad ibn Ali from Muhammad ibn al-Fudayl from 'Abd al-Rahman ibn Zayd who has said the following:

"Abu 'Abd Allah, *'Alayhi al-Salam,* has said that the Messenger of Allah, *O Allah, grant compensation to Muhammad and his family worthy of their services to Your cause,* has said, 'The truffle is from Manna (honeydew, a kind of tree sap) which is from paradise and its water is cure for the eye.'"

Chapter 25 - Squash

H 11770, Ch. 25, h 1

Ali ibn Ibrahim has narrated from his father from al-Nawfaliy from al-Sakuniy who has said the following:

"Abu 'Abd Allah, *'Alayhi al-Salam,* has said that 'Amir al-Mu'minin was asked about squash if it needs to be slaughtered. He (the Imam) said, 'Squash does not need slaughtering. Do not slaughter it and do not allow Satan, may Allah condemn him, to seduce you.'"

H 11771, Ch. 25, h 2

Through the same chain of narrators as that of the previous *Hadith*, the following is narrated:

"Abu 'Abd Allah, *'Alayhi al-Salam,* has said that the Messenger of Allah, *O Allah, grant compensation to Muhammad and his family worthy of their services to Your cause,* liked calabash, gourd in the cooking pot. It is squash.'"

H 11772, Ch. 25, h 3

Muhammad ibn Yahya has narrated from Ahmad ibn Muhammad ibn 'Isa from ibn Faddal from 'Abd Allah ibn Maymun al-Qaddah who has said the following:

"Abu 'Abd Allah, *'Alayhi al-Salam,* has said that the Messenger of Allah liked gourd, calabash, and picked it up from the dish.'"

H 11773, Ch. 25, h 4

A number of our people have narrated from Sahl ibn Ziyad from Ahmad ibn Muhammad from ibn abu Nasr from 'Abd Allah ibn Muhammad al-Shamiy from al-Husayn ibn Hanzalah who has said the following:

"One of the two Imam, (abu Ja'far or abu 'Abd Allah), *'Alayhim al-Salam,* has said, 'Gourd, squash increases al-Damagh (abilities of the brain).'"

H 11774, Ch. 25, h 5

It is narrated from the narrator of the previous *Hadith* from Ali ibn Hassan from Musa ibn Bakr who has said the following:

"I once heard abu al-Hassan, *'Alayhi al-Salam,* saying, 'Squash, gourd increases power of reason.'"

H 11775, Ch. 25, h 6

Al-Husayn from Muhammad has narrated from al-Sayyariy in a *marfu'* manner who has said the following:

"The Messenger of Allah, *O Allah, grant compensation to Muhammad and his family worthy of their services to Your cause,* liked gourd and would order his wives to increase gourd when they cooked a dish. It is squash."

H 11776, Ch. 25, h 7

A number of our people have narrated from Ahmad ibn abu 'Abd Allah from his father from certain persons of our people who has said the following:

"Abu al-Hassan, Musa, *'Alayhi al-Salam,* has stated this *Hadith.* 'Of the things about which the Messenger of Allah, *O Allah, grant compensation to Muhammad and his family worthy of their services to Your cause,* recommended Ali, *'Alayhi al-Salam,* was his saying, 'O Ali, you must eat gourd, squash; it increases, al-Damagh, the abilities of the brain and the power of reason.'"

Chapter 26 - The Radish

H 11777, Ch. 26, h 1

Ali ibn Muhammad ibn Bandar from his father from Muhammad ibn Ali al-Hamadaniy from Hanan who has said the following:

"I once heard abu 'Abd Allah, *'Alayhi al-Salam,* saying; when I was with him at the table of food, he gave me a piece of radish and said, 'O Hanan, you must eat radish because there are three qualities in it; its leaves repel gas, its essence quickens urine, and its root cuts off phlegm.' In another *Hadith* it is said that its leaves make it pleasant."

H 11778, Ch. 26, h 2

It is narrated from the narrator of the previous *Hadith* from al-Sayyariy from Ahmad ibn Muhammad ibn Khalid from ibn al-Mubarak from abu 'Uthman from Durust who has said the following:

"Abu 'Abd Allah, *'Alayhi al-Salam,* has said, 'The essence, roots of radish cuts off phlegm, its core helps digest food and its leaves quicken urine fast.'"

Chapter 27 - The Carrot

H 11779, Ch. 27, h 1
Muhammad ibn Yahya has narrated from Ahmad ibn Muhammad from al-Hassan ibn Ali and others from Dawud ibn Farqad who has said the following:
"Abu 'Abd Allah, *'Alayhi al-Salam,* has said, 'Eating carrot warms up the kidneys and causes erection.'"

H 11780, Ch. 27, h 2
Muhammad ibn Yahya has narrated from Muhammad ibn Musa from Ahmad ibn al-Hassan al-Jallab from Musa ibn 'Isma'il from ibn abu 'Umayr from certain persons of our people who has said the following:
"Abu 'Abd Allah, *'Alayhi al-Salam,* has said, 'Carrot is protection against colic pain, hemorrhoid, and helps in going to bed with one's wife.'"

H 11781, Ch. 27, h 3
A number of our people have narrated from Sahl ibn Ziyad from Ibrahim ibn 'Abd al-Rahman from his father from Dawud ibn Farqad who has said the following:
"I once heard abu al-Hassan, *'Alayhi al-Salam,* saying, 'Eating carrot warms up the kidneys and causes erection.' He (the narrator) has said that he asked, 'I pray to Allah to keep my soul in service for your cause, how should I eat it when I have no teeth?' He (the Imam) said, 'Order the girl to boil it, then eat.'"

Chapter 28 - The Turnip

H 11782, Ch. 28, h 1
Muhammad ibn Yahya has narrated from 'Abd Allah ibn Ja'far from Muhammad ibn 'Isa from Ali ibn Musayyib who has said the following:
"The virtuous servant (of Allah) has said, 'You must eat *al-Luft*, that is, turnips; everyone has a vein of leprosy and al-Luft dissolves it.'"

H 11783, Ch. 28, h 2
A number of our people have narrated from Ahmad ibn abu 'Abd Allah from 'Abd 'Abd al-'Aziz al-Muhtadiy in a *marfu'* manner who has said the following:
"Abu 'Abd Allah, *'Alayhi al-Salam,* has said, 'Everyone has a vein of leprosy, so you should dissolve it with turnips.'"

H 11784, Ch. 28, h 3
It is narrated from the narrator of the previous *Hadith* from Ya'qub ibn Yazid from Yahya ibn al-Mubarak [from 'Abd Allah ibn al-Mubarak] from 'Abd Allah ibn Jabalah from Ali ibn abu Hamzah who has said the following:
"Abu al-Hassan or abu 'Abd Allah, *'Alayhim al-Salam,* has said, 'Everyone has a vein of leprosy so you should dissolve it with turnips.'"

H 11785, Ch. 28, h 4
It is narrated from the narrator of the previous *Hadith* from al-Hassan ibn al-Husayn from Muhammad ibn Sinan from those whom he has mentioned who has said the following:
"Abu 'Abd Allah, *'Alayhi al-Salam,* has said, 'You must eat turnips and continue to do so. You must keep it a secret except from its people; all people have a vein of leprosy so you must dissolve it with turnips.'"

Chapter 29 - The Cucumbers

H 11786, Ch. 29, h 1

A number of our people have narrated from Ahmad ibn Muhammad from *al-Hajj*al from those whom he has mentioned who has said the following:

"Abu 'Abd Allah, *'Alayhi al-Salam,* has said that the Messenger of Allah, *O Allah, grant compensation to Muhammad and his family worthy of their services to Your cause,* would eat cucumber with salt.'"

H 11787, Ch. 29, h 2

Muhammad ibn Yahya has narrated from 'Abd Allah ibn Ja'far from Muhammad ibn 'Isa from 'Abd Allah al-Dihqan from Durust al-Wasitiy from 'Abd Allah ibn Sinan who has said the following:

"Abu 'Abd Allah, *'Alayhi al-Salam,* has said, 'When you eat cucumber, eat it from the bottom because it is greater for blessing.'"

Chapter 30 - The Eggplant (Aubergine)

H 11788, Ch. 30, h 1

A number of our people have narrated from Ahmad ibn Muhammad from 'Abd Allah ibn Ali ibn 'Amir from Ibrahim ibn al-Fadl from Ja'far ibn Yahya from his father who has said the following:

"Abu 'Abd Allah, *'Alayhi al-Salam,* has said, 'Eat eggplant because it removes illnesses and does not cause any illness.'"

H 11789, Ch. 30, h 2

A number of our people have narrated from Sahl ibn Ziyad from certain persons of our people who have said the following:

"Abu al-Hassan, al-Thalith, *'Alayhi al-Salam,* would say to certain ones of his workers, 'Bring more eggplant for us because it is warm in hot season and it is cool in cold season and it is balanced in all seasons. It is fine in all conditions.'"

H 11790, Ch. 30, h 3

Al-Husayn from Muhammad from Mu'alla' ibn Muhammad, from Ahmad ibn Muhammad, from and 'Abd Allah ibn al-Qasim from 'Abd al-Rahman al-Hashimiy who has said the following:

"He (the Imam), *'Alayhi al-Salam,* once said to a certain one of his servants, 'You must bring for us less onion and more eggplant.' He inquired saying, 'Do you mean eggplant?' He (the Imam) said, 'Yes, eggplant, it is wholesome in taste, removes illness, is suitable for one's health, balanced in its condition and it is suitable for the old people. It is balancing in hot and cold seasons; it is hot in hot places and it is cool in cold places.'"

Chapter 31 - The Onions

H 11791, Ch. 31, h 1

A number of our people have narrated from Sahl ibn Ziyad from Mansur ibn al-'Abbas from 'Abd 'Abd al-'Aziz ibn Hassan from Salih ibn 'Uqbah from 'Abd Allah ibn Muhammad al-Al-Ju'fiy who has said the following:

"Abu 'Abd Allah, *'Alayhi al-Salam,* once mentioned onion and said, 'It is well flavored and it dissolves phlegm and increases one's ability to go to bed with his wife.'"

H 11792, Ch. 31, h 2

Abu Ali al-Ash'ariy has narrated from Muhammad ibn Salim from Ahmad ibn abu al-Nadr from 'Amr ibn Shamir from Jabir who has said the following:

"Abu 'Abd Allah, *'Alayhi al-Salam,* has said, 'Onion removes illness, strengthens nerves, increases the ability to walk, increases one's seed and removes fever.'"

H 11793, Ch. 31, h 3

Ali ibn Muhammad ibn Bandar from his father from Muhammad ibn Ali al-Hamadaniy from al-Hassan ibn Ali al-Kaslan from Muyassir Bayya' al-Zuttiy who was his maternal uncle has said the following:

"I once heard abu 'Abd Allah, *'Alayhi al-Salam,* saying, 'You must eat onion; it has three qualities; it is well flavored, brings firmness to one's gums, increases one's seeds and the ability to go to bed with one's wife.'"

H 11794, Ch. 31, h 4

It is narrated from the narrator of the previous *Hadith* from al-Sayyariy from Ahmad ibn Muhammad ibn Khalid from Ahmad ibn al-Mubarak al-Daynawariy from abu 'Uthman from Durust who has said the following:

"Abu 'Abd Allah, *'Alayhi al-Salam,* has said, 'Onion gives fine flavor, strengthens one's back and clears the skin.'"

H 11795, Ch. 31, h 5

A number of our people have narrated from Ahmad ibn Muhammad ibn Khalid from Muhammad ibn Ahmad from 'Abd al-Rahman ibn Zayd ibn Aslam who has said the following:

"Abu 'Abd Allah, *'Alayhi al-Salam,* has said that the Messenger of Allah, *O Allah, grant compensation to Muhammad and his family worthy of their services to Your cause,* has said, 'When you enter a town eat its onion, it keeps plague away from you.'"

Chapter 32 - The Garlic

H 11796, Ch. 32, h 1

Ali ibn Ibrahim has narrated from his father from ibn abu 'Umayr from 'Umar ibn 'Udhaynah from Muhammad ibn Muslim who has said the following:

"I once asked abu Ja'far, *'Alayhi al-Salam,* about garlic. He (the Imam) said, 'The Messenger of Allah, *O Allah, grant compensation to Muhammad and his family worthy of their services to Your cause,* prohibited it only because of its smell, saying, "Whoever eats this filthy vegetable must not come near our Masjid, however, for those who eat it and do not come to the Masjid it is not unlawful."'"

H 11797, Ch. 32, h 2

Muhammad ibn Yahya has narrated from Ahmad ibn Muhammad from al-Husayn ibn Sa'id from Hammad from Shu'ayb from abu Basir who has said the following:

"Once abu 'Abd Allah, *'Alayhi al-Salam,* was asked about garlic, onion and leek. He (the Imam) said, 'Eating them is not unlawful and in cooking pots, or for treating illnesses with garlic, however, if anyone of you eats it he must not go out to Masjid.'"

H 11798, Ch. 32, h 3

A number of our people have narrated from Ahmad ibn Muhammad ibn Khalid from 'Uthman ibn 'Isa from 'Abd Allah ibn Muskan from al-Hassan al-Zayyat who has said the following:

"I completed the acts of *al-Hajj* or 'Umrah, I passed by al-Madinah and asked about abu Ja'far, *'Alayhi al-Salam.* He said that he (the Imam) is in Yanbu'. I then went there and he (the Imam) asked, 'O Hassan, have you come walking here?' I replied, 'Yes, I pray to Allah to keep my soul in service for your cause, I disliked leaving without visiting you.' He (the Imam) said, 'I had eaten this vegetable, that is, garlic, so I wanted to keep away from the Masjid of the Messenger of Allah, *O Allah, grant compensation to Muhammad and his family worthy of their services to Your cause.*'"

Chapter 33 - The Wild Thyme

H 11799, Ch. 33, h 1

Muhammad ibn Yahya has narrated from Ahmad ibn Muhammad ibn 'Isa from Ziyad al-Qandiy who has said the following:

"Abu al-Hassan, al-Awwal, *'Alayhi al-Salam,* has said that the medicine of 'Amir al-Mu'minin was wild thyme, 'Amir al-Mu'minin would say, 'Thyme becomes fuzz and fluff for the stomach like that of velvet.'"

H 11800, Ch. 33, h 2

It is narrated from the narrator of the previous *Hadith* from Musa ibn al-Hassan from Ali ibn Sulayman from certain ones of al-Wasit who has said the following:

"I once complained before abu al-Hassan, *'Alayhi al-Salam,* about *rutubah* (acidity) and he (the Imam) commanded me to eat thyme complete and uncrushed."

Chapter 34 - The Toothpick

H 11801, Ch. 34, h 1

Ali ibn Ibrahim has narrated from his father from ibn abu 'Umayr from Hisham ibn Salim who has said the following:

"Abu 'Abd Allah, *'Alayhi al-Salam,* has said that the Messenger of Allah, *O Allah, grant compensation to Muhammad and his family worthy of their services to Your cause,* has said, 'Jibril came to me with the toothpick.'"

H 11802, Ch. 34, h 2

A number of our people have narrated from Ahmad ibn Muhammad from ibn Faddal from abu Jamilah who has said the following:

"Abu 'Abd Allah, *'Alayhi al-Salam,* once said to me, 'Jibril came to the Messenger of Allah, *O Allah, grant compensation to Muhammad and his family worthy of their services to Your cause,* with the toothbrush, toothpick and cupping.'"

H 11803, Ch. 34, h 3

Muhammad ibn Yahya has narrated from Ahmad ibn Muhammad ibn 'Isa from ibn Mahbub from Wahab ibn 'Abd Rabbibhi who has said the following:

"I once saw abu 'Abd Allah, *'Alayhi al-Salam,* using toothpicks and I looked at him (the Imam). He (the Imam) said, 'The Messenger of Allah would use a toothpick; it cleanses the mouth.'"

H 11804, Ch. 34, h 4

Muhammad ibn Yahya has narrated from Ahmad ibn Muhammad from Ibrahim al-Hadhdha' from Ahmad ibn 'Abd Allah al-Asadiy from a man who has said the following:

"Abu 'Abd Allah, *'Alayhi al-Salam,* has said that the Messenger of Allah, *O Allah, grant compensation to Muhammad and his family worthy of their services to Your cause,* once gave a toothpick to Ja'far ibn abu Talib, *'Alayhi al-Salam,* and said, 'O Ja'far use a toothpick. It is beneficial for the mouth ' or he said, 'It is beneficial for the gums and attracts sustenance.'"

H 11805, Ch. 34, h 5

A number of our people have narrated from Sahl ibn Ziyad from Ja'far ibn Muhammad al-Ash'ariy from ibn al-Qaddah who has said the following:

"Abu 'Abd Allah, *'Alayhi al-Salam,* has said that the Messenger of Allah has said, 'You must use a toothpick it is beneficial for the gum (gingival) and the back teeth.'"

H 11806, Ch. 34, h 6

A number of our people have narrated from Ahmad ibn abu 'Abd Allah from his father from Ali ibn al-Nu'man from Ya'qub ibn Shu'ayb from those who narrated to him who has said the following:

"Once, prepared toothpicks were brought to abu al-Hassan, *'Alayhi al-Salam,* when he was in the house of Fadl ibn Yunus. He (the Imam) took a fragment (piece) and left the rest.'"

H 11807, Ch. 34, h 7

Ali ibn Ibrahim has narrated from his father from ibn abu 'Umayr from Ibrahim ibn 'Abd al-Hamid who has said the following:

"Abu al-Hassan, *'Alayhi al-Salam,* has said, 'Do not use sticks of sweet basil or pomegranate as a toothpick because they stir up the vein of leprosy.'"

H 11808, Ch. 34, h 8

Ali has narrated from Muhammad ibn 'Isa from Yunus ibn 'Abd al-Rahman from those whom he has mentioned who has said the following:

"Abu 'Abd Allah, *'Alayhi al-Salam,* has said, 'If one uses reeds as toothpicks none of his wishes can come true for six days.'"

H 11809, Ch. 34, h 9

Ali ibn Ibrahim has narrated from his father from al-Nawfaliy from al-Sakuniy who has said the following:

"Abu 'Abd Allah, *'Alayhi al-Salam,* has said that the Messenger of Allah, *O Allah, grant compensation to Muhammad and his family worthy of their services to Your cause,* prohibited using reeds or sweet basil sticks for toothpicks.'"

H 11810, Ch. 34, h 10

A number of our people have narrated from Ahmad ibn abu 'Abd Allah from Muhammad ibn 'Isa from al-Dihqan from Durust from 'Abd Allah ibn Sinan who has said the following:

"Abu 'Abd Allah, *'Alayhi al-Salam,* has said that the Messenger of Allah, *O Allah, grant compensation to Muhammad and his family worthy of their services*

to Your cause, would use for a toothpick all kinds of wooden fragments except the leaves of palm trees and reeds.'"

H 11811, Ch. 34, h 11
It is narrated from the narrator of the previous *Hadith* from certain ones who narrated who has said the following:

"Abu 'Abd Allah, *'Alayhi al-Salam,* has said that the Messenger of Allah, *O Allah, grant compensation to Muhammad and his family worthy of their services to Your cause,* prohibited using pomegranate fragments as toothpicks, as well as myrtle and reeds, saying that they stir up the erosive vein.'"

Chapter 35 - Throwing away what Comes out with Toothpicks from Between the Teeth

H 11812, Ch. 35, h 1
A number of our people have narrated from Ahmad ibn Muhammad ibn Khalid from 'Uthman ibn 'Isa from Ishaq ibn Jarir who has said the following:

"I once asked abu 'Abd Allah, *'Alayhi al-Salam,* about the meat that remains between the teeth. He (the Imam) said, 'What is between the front teeth you can eat; but what is between the back teeth you must throw it away.'"

H 11813, Ch. 35, h 2
It is narrated from the narrator of the previous *Hadith* from ibn Mahbub from ibn Sinan who has said the following:

"Abu 'Abd Allah, *'Alayhi al-Salam,* has said, 'What is in gingival (front gums) swallow it and what is between the other teeth throw it away.'"

H 11814, Ch. 35, h 3
It is narrated from the narrator of the previous *Hadith* from his father from 'Abd Allah ibn al-Fadl al-Nawfaliy from al-Fadl ibn Yunus who has said the following:

"Once, abu al-Hassan, *'Alayhi al-Salam,* had lunch with me. When lunch was complete, toothpicks were brought and I asked, 'I pray to Allah to keep my soul in service for your cause, what are the limits of toothpicks?' He (the Imam) said, 'O Fadl, whatever remains in your mouth when you turn your tongue on it you can eat it; but whatever does not come out with the tongue, then take it out with a toothpick; and you have the choice to eat or throw it away.'"

H 11815, Ch. 35, h 4
Muhammad ibn Yahya has narrated from Ahmad ibn Muhammad in a *marfu'* manner who has said the following:

"Abu 'Abd Allah, *'Alayhi al-Salam,* has said, 'Do not take light what you use as a toothpick, it can cause a boil in one's belly (that may cause one's death).'"

Chapter 36 - The Saltwort and Cyperus

H 11816, Ch. 36, h 1
Muhammad ibn Yahya has narrated from Ahmad ibn Muhammad from al-Husayn ibn Sa'id from Ahmad ibn Yazid who has said the following:

"Abu al-Hassan al-Awwal, *'Alayhi al-Salam,* has said, 'Eating saltwort disinfects the mouth.'"

H 11817, Ch. 36, h 2

Certain persons of our people have narrated from Ja'far ibn Ibrahim al-Hadramiy from Sa'd ibn Sa'd who has said the following:

"I once said to abu al-Hassan, *'Alayhi al-Salam,* 'I eat saltwort.' He (the Imam) said, 'Abu al-Hassan, *'Alayhi al-Salam,* when washing his hands and mouth (with saltwort) would keep his lips closed. There is a quality in it, which is disliked. It can cause tuberculoses, it takes away the water of the back and weakens the knees.' I then asked about clay. He (the Imam) said, 'Eating clay is unlawful like dead bodies, blood and pork except the clay and soil of the grave of al-Husayn, *'Alayhi al-Salam,* in which there is cure for all illnesses, however, do not be excessive, and there is immunity in it against all kinds of fear.'"

H 11818, Ch. 36, h 3

Muhammad ibn Yahya has narrated from Ali ibn al-Hassan ibn Ali from Ahmad ibn al-Husayn ibn 'Umar from his uncle Muhammad ibn 'Umar from a man who has said the following:

"If one washes the outlet of his feces and his mouth after food with cyperus no illness will occur in his mouth and he will have no fear of gases or hemorrhoid.'"

H 11819, Ch. 36, h 4

A number of our people have narrated from Ahmad ibn abu 'Abd Allah from abu al-Khazraj al-Hassan ibn al-Zabarqan al-Ansariy from al-Fadl ibn 'Uthman from abu 'Aziz al-Muradiy who is maternal uncle of my mother who has said the following:

"I once heard abu 'Abd Allah, *'Alayhi al-Salam,* saying, 'Keep cyperus in your teeth; it gives the mouth pleasant smell and increases one's ability to go to bed with his wife.'"

H 11820, Ch. 36, h 5

Muhammad ibn Yahya has narrated from Ahmad ibn Muhammad from certain persons of his people from Ibrahim ibn Ibrahim ibn abu al-Balad who have said the following:

"Al-'Abbas ibn Musa took me and commanded to hit my mouth, so my teeth became shaky and I could not chew food. I then saw my father in my dream. There was an old man with him whom I could not recognize. My father, may Allah grant him mercy, said to me to offer greeting of peace to him.' I then asked, 'Father, who is he?' He replied, 'He is abu Shaybah al-Khurasaniy (of companions of abu Ja'far, *'Alayhi al-Salam*).' I offered him greeting of peace and he asked, 'Why do I see you in this condition?' I replied, 'Sinful al-'Abbas ibn Musa commanded to hit on my mouth and my teeth have become shaky.' He said, 'Tie them down with cyperus.' In the morning I rinsed my teeth with *al-Sa'd* and my teeth calmed down.'"

H 11821, Ch. 36, h 6

It is narrated from the narrator of the previous *Hadith* from ibn Mahbub from abu Wallad who has said the following:

"I once saw abu al-Hassan sitting in al-Hijr (near al-Ka'bah) along with a group of his family members and I heard him saying, 'I had a toothache so I took cyperus and rubbed with it my teeth, it benefited me and the pain calmed down.'"

End of the Book of Foods followed by the Book of Drinks, by the will of Allah, and all praise belongs to Allah alone, O Allah, grant compensation to Muhammad and his family worthy of their services to Your cause.

Part Six:
The Book of Drinks

Chapter 1 - The Excellence of Water

H 11822, Ch. 1, h 1
Muhammad ibn Yahya Ahmad ibn Muhammad ibn 'Isa from Bakr ibn Salih from 'Isa ibn 'Abd Allah ibn Muhammad ibn 'Umar ibn Ali from his father from his grandfather who has said the following:

"'Amir al-Mu'minin, *'Alayhi al-Salam,* has said, 'Water is the master of drinks in this world and in the next world.'"

A number of our people have narrated from Ahmad ibn abu 'Abd Allah al-Barqiy from Muhammad ibn Ali from 'Isa ibn 'Abd Allah through the chain of his narrators has narrated a similar *Hadith.*

H 11823, Ch. 1, h 2
Abu Ali al-Ash'ariy has narrated from Muhammad ibn 'Abd al-Jabbar and Muhammad ibn Yahya has narrated from Ahmad ibn Muhammad all from ibn Faddal from Tha'labah ibn Maymun from 'Ubayd ibn Zurarah who has said the following:

"I once heard abu 'Abd Allah, *'Alayhi al-Salam,* saying, upon mentioning the Messenger of Allah, *O Allah, grant compensation to Muhammad and his family worthy of their services to Your cause,* 'O Lord, You know that he (the Messenger of Allah) is more beloved to us than (our) fathers and mothers and cool water.'"

H 11824, Ch. 1, h 3
Muhammad ibn Yahya and more than one person has narrated from al-'Abbas ibn Ma'ruf from Sa'dan ibn Muslim from 'Abd al-Rahman ibn *al-Hajj*aj who has said the following:
"Abu 'Abd Allah, *'Alayhi al-Salam,* has said, 'The first thing that Allah, most Majestic, most Glorious, will ask the servants will be, 'Did I not quench your thirst with sweet water of al-Furat?'"

H 11825, Ch. 1, h 4
A number of our people have narrated from Ahmad ibn abu 'Abd Allah from Ali ibn al-Rayyan ibn al-Salt in a *marfu'* manner who has said the following:
"Abu 'Abd Allah, *'Alayhi al-Salam,* has said that the Messenger of Allah, *O Allah, grant compensation to Muhammad and his family worthy of their services to Your cause,* has said, 'The master of the drink in paradise is water.'"

H 11826, Ch. 1, h 5
It is narrated from the narrator of the previous *Hadith* from Muhammad ibn Ali from 'Isa ibn 'Abd Allah ibn Muhammad ibn 'Umar ibn Ali from his father from his grandfather who has said the following:
"'Amir al-Mu'minin, *'Alayhi al-Salam,* has said, 'Water is the master of drinks in this world and in the next world.'"

H 11827, Ch. 1, h 6
Muhammad ibn Yahya has narrated from Ahmad ibn Muhammad from Ya'qub ibn Yazid from ibn Faddal from those who narrated to him who has said the following:
"Abu 'Abd Allah, *'Alayhi al-Salam,* has said, 'If one enjoys and appreciates the taste of water in this world Allah, most Majestic, most Glorious, will give him water in paradise.'"

H 11828, Ch. 1, h 7
Ahmad ibn Muhammad al-Kufiy has narrated from Ali ibn al-Hassan al-Mithamiy from Ali ibn Asbat from 'Abd al-Samad ibn Bandar from al-Husayn ibn 'Ulwan who has said the following:
"Once, a man asked abu 'Abd Allah, *'Alayhi al-Salam,* about the taste of water. He (the Imam) said, 'Ask to understand not to harass. The taste of water is the taste of life.'"

Chapter 2 - Another Chapter on the same Issue

H 11829, Ch. 2, h 1
A number of our people have narrated from Sahl ibn Ziyad from Ja'far ibn Muhammad al-Ash'ariy from ibn al-Qaddah who has said the following:
"Abu 'Abd Allah, *'Alayhi al-Salam,* has said that the Messenger of Allah, *O Allah, grant compensation to Muhammad and his family worthy of their services to Your cause,* has said, 'Drink water in a sipping manner but do not gulp and pour it down at once; it may cause liver illness.'"

H 11830, Ch. 2, h 2
Sahl ibn Ziyad has narrated from Muhammad ibn al-Hassan ibn Shammun al-Basriy from abu Tayfur al-Mutatabib who has said the following:
"I once visited abu al-Hassan, al-Madiy, *'Alayhi al-Salam,* and I prohibited him from drinking water. He (the Imam) said, 'What is wrong with water when it turns food in the stomach, calms down the anger, increases marrows (learning ability) and removes bitterness?'"

H 11831, Ch. 2, h 3
Al-Husayn from Muhammad has narrated from Mu'alla' ibn Muhammad al-Basriy from Dawud al-Mustariq from the one who narrated to him who has said the following:
"I once was with abu 'Abd Allah, *'Alayhi al-Salam,* and he asked for dates which he ate and then he kept drinking water. I then said, 'I pray to Allah to keep my soul in service for your cause, I wish you refrain from drinking water.' He (the Imam) said, 'I eat dates only to make water taste more delicious.'"

H 11832, Ch. 2, h 4
Ali ibn Muhammad has narrated from certain persons of his people from Yasir who have said the following:
"Abu al-Hassan, *'Alayhi al-Salam,* once said, 'I wonder about the one who eats 'this much,' making a hand gesture, 'and does not drink any water on it, how is it that his stomach does not burst.'"

Chapter 3 - Drinking Water Excessively

H 11833, Ch. 3, h 1

Ali ibn Ibrahim has narrated from his father from ibn abu 'Umayr from Hisham ibn al-Hakam who has said the following:

"Abu al-Hassan, *'Alayhi al-Salam,* has said, 'Drinking cold water is more delicious.'"

H 11834, Ch. 3, h 2

A number of our people have narrated from Sahl ibn Ziyad from Sa'id ibn Junah from Ahmad ibn 'Umar al-Halabiy who has said the following:

"Abu 'Abd Allah, *'Alayhi al-Salam,* when giving advice to a man said, 'Reduce drinking water; it may stretch all illness and refrain from taking medicine as long as your body can take the pain.'"

H 11835, Ch. 3, h 3

Ali ibn Ibrahim has narrated from his father from Yasar al-Khadim who has said the following:

"Abu al-Hassan, al-Rida', *'Alayhi al-Salam,* has said, 'It is not harmful to drink water after food but do not drink water excessively on things other than food.' He (the Imam) said, 'Consider, the man who eats this much' -- he brought his hands close to each other and did not join them and did not keep them much apart – 'then he does not drink water, his stomach may burst.'"

H 11836, Ch. 3, h 4

A number of our people have narrated from Sahl ibn Ziyad from Ali ibn Hassan from Musa ibn Bakr from certain persons of our people who have said the following:

"Abu 'Abd Allah, *'Alayhi al-Salam,* has said, 'Do not drink water excessively, it is the substance of every illness.'"

Chapter 4 - Drinking Water Standing and Drinking it in One Breath

H 11837, Ch. 4, h 1

Ali ibn Ibrahim has narrated from his father from al-Nawfaliy from al-Sakuniy who has said the following:

"Abu 'Abd Allah, *'Alayhi al-Salam,* has said, 'During the day drinking water when standing gives the body more power and good health.'"

H 11838, Ch. 4, h 2

Ali ibn Muhammad has narrated from Muhammad ibn abu Mahmud in a *marfu'* manner has said the following:

"Abu 'Abd Allah, *'Alayhi al-Salam,* has said, 'During the day drinking water when standing makes the food more pleasant; but drinking water during the night when standing causes *al-Safra'* (yellowness, acidity).'"

H 11839, Ch. 4, h 3

A number of our people have narrated from Ahmad ibn Muhammad from Muhammad ibn Ali from 'Abd al-Rahman ibn abu Hashim [from abu Hashim] ibn Yahya al-Mada'iniy who has said the following:

"Abu 'Abd Allah, *'Alayhi al-Salam,* has said that 'Amir al-Mu'minin went to the water container and drank water standing.'"

H 11840, Ch. 4, h 4

Ali ibn Ibrahim has narrated from his father and Muhammad ibn 'Isma'il has narrated from al-Fadl ibn Shadhan from all from ibn abu 'Umayr from 'Abd al-Rahman ibn *al-Hajj*aj who has said the following:

"Once I was with abu 'Abd Allah, *'Alayhi al-Salam,* when 'Abd al-Malik al-Qummiy came and said, 'I pray to Allah to keep you well, can I drink water standing?' He (the Imam) said, 'You can do so if you like.' He then asked, 'Can I drink in one breath until I am satisfied?' He (the Imam) said, 'If you like you can do so.' He then asked, 'Can I perform *Sajdah* (prostration) with my hand in my pocket?' He (the Imam) said, 'You can do so if you like.' Abu 'Abd Allah, *'Alayhi al-Salam,* then said, 'I, by Allah, am not afraid for you of this and similar things (as long as your belief is proper).'"

H 11841, Ch. 4, h 5

A number of our people have narrated from Ahmad ibn abu 'Abd Allah from his father from his grandfather from 'Abd Allah ibn al-Mughirah from 'Amr ibn abu al-Miqdam who has said the following:

"Once my father and I were with abu Ja'far, *'Alayhi al-Salam,* when a bowl made of pottery with water was brought. He (the Imam) drank standing. He then gave it to my father who also drank standing and gave it to me and I also drank standing.'"

H 11842, Ch. 4, h 6

A number of our people have narrated from Ahmad ibn abu 'Abd Allah from ibn al-'Arzamiy from Hatim ibn 'Isma'il al-Madiniy who has said the following:

"Abu 'Abd Allah, *'Alayhi al-Salam,* has said that 'Amir al-Mu'minin once drank water standing. He then drank the water left from his wudu standing; then he turned to Al-Husayn, *'Alayhi al-Salam,* and said, 'Son, I saw your grandfather, the Messenger of Allah, *O Allah, grant compensation to Muhammad and his family worthy of their services to Your cause,* doing as I just did.'"

H 11843, Ch. 4, h 7

Ali ibn Ibrahim has narrated from his father from ibn abu 'Umayr from Hammad from al-Halabiy who has said the following:

"Abu 'Abd Allah, *'Alayhi al-Salam,* has said, 'Drinking water in three breaths is better than in one breath.'"

H 11844, Ch. 4, h 8

Abu Ali al-Ash'ariy has narrated from Muhammad ibn 'Abd al-Jabbar from Safwan ibn Yahya from Mu'alla' ibn 'Uthman from Mu'alla' ibn Khunayth who has said the following:

"Abu 'Abd Allah, *'Alayhi al-Salam,* has said, 'Drinking water in three breaths is better than in one breath.'"

H 11845, Ch. 4, h 9

Muhammad ibn Yahya has narrated from certain persons of his people from 'Uthman ibn 'Isa from an old man from the people of al-Madinah who has said the following:

"I once asked abu 'Abd Allah, *'Alayhi al-Salam,* about the case of a man who drinks water in one breath until he is satisfied. He (the narrator) has said that he (the Imam) said, 'Is the pleasure of taste anything but that?' I then said, 'People say that it is the thirsty camel's way of drinking.' He (the Imam) said, 'They have spoken a lie. The thirsty camel's way of drinking is when the name of Allah, most Majestic, most Glorious, is not mentioned.'"

Chapter 5 - The Words to Say When Drinking Water

H 11846, Ch. 5, h 1

Muhammad ibn Yahya has narrated from Ahmad ibn Muhammad from ibn Mahbub from 'Abd Allah ibn Sinan who has said the following:

"I once heard abu 'Abd Allah, *'Alayhi al-Salam,* saying, 'A man only drinks water but Allah, most Majestic, most Glorious, for that reason admits him in paradise.' I then asked, 'How can that happen, O child of the Messenger of Allah?' He (the Imam) said, 'The man drinks water, stops drinking, moves the bowl away when he still has the desire for water, and he praises Allah, most Majestic, most Glorious. He then drinks again, then moves the bowl of water away when he still has the desire for water, then praises Allah, most Majestic, most Glorious, then drinks more water and, thus, Allah, most Majestic, most Glorious, makes paradise necessary for him.'"

H 11847, Ch. 5, h 2

Muhammad ibn Yahya has narrated from Sahl ibn Ziyad from Ja'far ibn Muhammad al-Ash'ariy from ibn al-Qaddah who has said the following:

"Abu 'Abd Allah, *'Alayhi al-Salam,* has stated this *Hadith.* 'The Messenger of Allah, *O Allah, grant compensation to Muhammad and his family worthy of their services to Your cause,* when drinking water would say, 'All praise belongs to Allah, who has given us cool and clear water and not of salty and foul smelling kind, and has not yet questioned us because of our sins.'"

H 11848, Ch. 5, h 3

A number of our people have narrated from Ahmad ibn abu 'Abd Allah from Ya'qub ibn Yazid from the son of uncle of 'Umar ibn Yazid from daughter of 'Umar ibn Yazid from her father who has said the following:

"Abu 'Abd Allah, *'Alayhi al-Salam,* has stated this *Hadith.* 'If one of you drinks water, and says , 'In the name of Allah,' then drinks, then stops and say, 'All praise belongs to Allah,' He then drinks and says, 'In the name of Allah' then stops, and says, 'All praise belongs to Allah' then drinks and says, 'In the name of Allah' then stops and says, 'All praise belongs to Allah,' that water keeps saying *Tasbih* (Allah is free of all defects) for him as long as it is in his belly until it goes out.'"

H 11849, Ch. 5, h 4

Ali ibn Muhammad has narrated from in a *marfu'* manner the following:

"Abu 'Abd Allah, *'Alayhi al-Salam,* has said, 'When you decide to drink water during the night move the water and say, 'O water, water of Zamzam says greeting of peace to you and so also does water of Furat.'"

Chapter 6 - The Utensils, Pots, Pans, Bowls and Cups

H 11850, Ch. 6, h 1

Muhammad ibn Yahya has narrated from Ahmad ibn Muhammad from ibn Mahbub from Ibrahim al-Karkhiy from Talhah ibn Zayd who has said the following:

"Abu 'Abd Allah, *'Alayhi al-Salam,* has said that the Messenger of Allah, *O Allah, grant compensation to Muhammad and his family worthy of their services to Your cause,* would drink water in bowls from Syria that were brought from there and given as gifts to him (the Messenger of Allah).'"

H 11851, Ch. 6, h 2

Abu Ali al-Ash'ariy has narrated from Muhammad ibn 'Abd al-Jabbar from Muhammad ibn Salim from Ahmad ibn abu al-Nadr from 'Amr ibn abu al-Miqdam who has said the following:

"I saw abu Ja'far, *'Alayhi al-Salam,* drink water from a pottery bowl.'"

H 11852, Ch. 6, h 3

A number of our people have narrated from Ahmad ibn Muhammad from 'Uthman ibn 'Isa from Sama'ah ibn Mehran who has said the following:

"Abu 'Abd Allah, *'Alayhi al-Salam,* has said, 'It is not proper to drink water with bowl made of gold or silver.'"

H 11853, Ch. 6, h 4

It is narrated from the narrator of the previous *Hadith* from Muhammad ibn Ali from Yunus ibn Ya'qub from his brother Yusuf who has said the following:

"Once I was with abu 'Abd Allah, *'Alayhi al-Salam,* in al-Hijr (near al-Ka'bah) and he asked for water. Water was brought in a yellow bowl (made of brass) and a man said, ''Abbad ibn Kathir dislikes drinking water from yellow.' He (the Imam) said, 'It is not unlawful.' He (the Imam) said to the man, 'Did you ask him ('Abbad ibn Kathir) if it was made of gold or silver?'"

H 11854, Ch. 6, h 5

Muhammad ibn Yahya has narrated from Ahmad ibn Muhammad from Muhammad ibn Yahya from Ghiyath ibn Ibrahim who has said the following:

"Abu 'Abd Allah, *'Alayhi al-Salam,* has said that `Amir al-Mu'minin has said, 'Do not drink water from the broken part of a bowl or from its handle because Satan sits on the broken part and on the handle (ring).'"

H 11855, Ch. 6, h 6

Muhammad ibn Yahya has narrated from Muhammad ibn al-Hassan from 'Abd al-Rahman ibn abu Hashim from Salim ibn Mukram who has said the following:

"Abu 'Abd Allah, *'Alayhi al-Salam,* has said, 'My father once said to 'Amr ibn 'Ubayd, Bashir ibn al-Rahhal and Wasil in a *Hadith,* "Do not drink water from the ear (handle) of a bowl or its broken part if there is any, because it is the place from which Satan drinks."'"

H 11856, Ch. 6, h 7

A number of our people have narrated from Sahl ibn Ziyad from Ja'far ibn Muhammad al-Ash'ariy from ibn al-Qaddah who has said the following:

"Abu 'Abd Allah, *'Alayhi al-Salam,* has said that the Messenger of Allah, *O Allah, grant compensation to Muhammad and his family worthy of their services*

to Your cause, once passed by a people who drank water with their mouths during the war of Tabuk. The Holy Prophet said to them, 'Drink with your hands; it is the best of your utensils.'"

H 11857, Ch. 6, h 8

Muhammad ibn Yahya has narrated from Ahmad ibn Muhammad from ibn Mahbub from Ibrahim ibn Talhah ibn Zayd who has said the following:

"Abu 'Abd Allah, *'Alayhi al-Salam,* has said that the Messenger of Allah, *O Allah, grant compensation to Muhammad and his family worthy of their services to Your cause,* liked to drink water with bowls made in Syria and said, 'It is the best of your utensils.'"

H 11858, Ch. 6, h 9

Ali ibn Ibrahim has narrated from his father from and al-Husayn from Muhammad from Mu'alla' ibn Muhammad all from Ali ibn Asbat who has said the following:

"I once heard abu al-Hassan, al-Rida', *'Alayhi al-Salam,* saying, 'When a city (Egypt) was mentioned, the Holy Prophet, said, 'You must not eat in its pottery bowls; do not wash your head with its clay because it takes away one's courage (protective feeling) and causes one to become a pimp.'"

Chapter 7- Excellence of the Water of Zamzam and the Water of al-Mizab

H 11859, Ch. 7, h 1

A number of our people have narrated from Ahmad ibn Muhammad from ibn Faddal from Ali ibn 'Uqbah from those whom he has mentioned who has said the following:

"Abu 'Abd Allah, *'Alayhi al-Salam,* has said that the water of Zamzam was whiter than milk, sweeter than honey and it flowed. It then oppressed other waters. Allah, most Majestic, most Glorious, made it to sink and a fountain of *Sabere* (aloe) to flow on it.'"

H 11860, Ch. 7, h 2

Through the same chain of narrators as that of the previous *Hadith,* the following is narrated:

"Once, Zamzam was mentioned before abu 'Abd Allah, *'Alayhi al-Salam.* He (the Imam) said, 'A fountain from under the stone was made to flow on it. When the water of the fountain overwhelms it, water of Zamzam becomes sweet.'"

H 11861, Ch. 7, h 3

A number of our people have narrated from Sahl ibn Ziyad from Ja'far ibn Muhammad al-Ash'ariy from ibn al-Qaddah who has said the following:

"Abu 'Abd Allah, *'Alayhi al-Salam,* has said that 'Amir al-Mu'minin has said, 'The water of Zamzam is the best water on earth. The worst water on earth is the water of *Barhut* which is in *Hadra mawt* upon which wandering unbelievers roam during the night.'"

H 11862, Ch. 7, h 4

Muhammad ibn Yahya has narrated from Ahmad ibn Muhammad ibn 'Isa from Muhammad ibn Sinan from 'Isma'il ibn Jabir who has said the following:

"I once heard abu 'Abd Allah, *'Alayhi al-Salam,* saying, 'The water of Zamzam is a cure for all illnesses,' I think he said, 'no matter whatever it may be.'"

H 11863, Ch. 7, h 5

A number of our people have narrated from Sahl ibn Ziyad from Ja'far ibn Muhammad al-Ash'ariy from ibn al-Qaddah who has said the following:

"Abu 'Abd Allah, *'Alayhi al-Salam,* has said that `Amir al-Mu'minin has said, 'The Messenger of Allah, *O Allah, grant compensation to Muhammad and his family worthy of their services to Your cause,* has said, "The water of Zamzam is a cure for whatever reason it is drunk ."'"

H 11864, Ch. 7, h 6

Muhammad ibn Yahya has narrated from 'Abd Allah ibn Ja'far and other and certain persons of our people from Ahmad ibn abu 'Abd Allah all from Ya'qub ibn Yazid from Yahya ibn al-Mubarak from 'Abd Allah ibn Jabalah from Musadif who has said the following:

"Once in Makkah one of our brothers (in belief) fell ill and was near death. We met abu 'Abd Allah, *'Alayhi al-Salam,* on the way and he (the Imam) asked, 'O Musadif, how is so and so doing?' I replied, 'I left him for death, I pray to Allah to keep my soul in service for your cause.' He (the Imam) said, 'Were I in your place I would make him drink water from al-Mizab.' We then searched if anyone had such water but we did not find it. At this time, a cloud rose with thunder and lightning. I then went to those in al-Masjid, gave a dirham and took a bowl from someone, then took water from al-Mizab, took it to our patient, made him drink from it and I still was with him that he began drinking *sawiq.* He became well and in good health.'"

Chapter 8 - Water from the Sky

H 11865, Ch. 8, h 1

Muhammad ibn Yahya has narrated from Muhammad ibn Ahmad from Ya'qub ibn Yazid from Ali ibn Yaqtin from 'Amr ibn Ibrahim from Khalaf ibn Hammad from Muhammad ibn Muslim who has said the following:

"I once heard abu Ja'far, *'Alayhi al-Salam,* saying that the Messenger of Allah, *O Allah, grant compensation to Muhammad and his family worthy of their services to Your cause,* about the meaning of the words of Allah, most High, '. . .We sent blessed water from the sky.' (50:9) has said, there is no water on earth with which water of the sky is not mixed.'"

H 11866, Ch. 8, h 2

Muhammad ibn Yahya has narrated from Ahmad ibn Muhammad from al-Qasim ibn Yahya from his grandfather al-Hassan ibn Rashid from abu Basir who has said the following:

"Abu 'Abd Allah, *'Alayhi al-Salam,* has stated this *Hadith.* `Amir al-Mu'minin has said, 'You should drink of the water of the sky, it cleanses the body and removes illnesses as Allah, most Majestic, most Glorious, has said, "He sends water from the sky to cleanse you with it and remove the filth of Satan from you and to make your hearts firmly related and to make you steadfast." (8:11)'"

H 11867, Ch. 8, h 3

Muhammad ibn Yahya has narrated from 'Imran ibn Musa from Ali ibn Asbat from his father who has said the following:

"Abu 'Abd Allah, *'Alayhi al-Salam,* has said, 'Hail is not edible because Allah, most Majestic, most Glorious, has said, ". . . with it (hail) He causes whomever He wants to suffer." (13:13)'"

Chapter 9 - Excellence of the Water of al-Furat (Euphrates)

H 11868, Ch. 9, h 1

Ali ibn Ibrahim has narrated from his father from ibn abu 'Umayr from al-Husayn ibn 'Uthman from Muhammad ibn abu Hamzah from those whom he has mentioned who has said the following:

"In whoever's mouth water of Euphrates is dropped in childhood, I do not think he will not love us, people of the house.' He (the Imam) said, 'People of al-Kufah were not made to drink water of Euphrates except for a certain matter.' He (the Imam) said, 'Two shoots of water fall in it (Euphrates) from the garden (paradise).'"

H 11869, Ch. 9, h 2

Muhammad ibn Yahya has narrated from Ahmad ibn Muhammad from ibn Faddal from ibn Bukayr from certain persons of our people who have said the following:

"Abu 'Abd Allah, *'Alayhi al-Salam,* has said, 'Everyday several fluxes flow from the garden (paradise) into Euphrates.'"

H 11870, Ch. 9, h 3

Muhammad ibn Yahya has narrated from Ali ibn al-Husayn from ibn 'Uramah from al-Husayn ibn Sa'id in a *marfu'* manner who has said the following:

"'Amir al-Mu'minin, *'Alayhi al-Salam,* has said, 'In your canal, this one, that is, Euphrates, there are two shoots of the shoots of the garden (paradise).' He (the narrator) has said that abu 'Abd Allah, *'Alayhi al-Salam,* has said, 'Had there not been many miles in between we would drink water from it (Euphrates).'"

H 11871, Ch. 9, h 4

Muhammad ibn Yahya has narrated from Ali ibn al-Husayn in a marfu' manner the following:

"He (the narrator) has said that abu 'Abd Allah, *'Alayhi al-Salam,* once asked, 'What is the distance between you and Euphrates?' I then informed him (the Imam) and he (the Imam) said, 'Were I there near it I would go to it during both ends of the day.'"

H 11872, Ch. 9, h 5

Al-Husayn from Muhammad and Muhammad ibn Yahya all from Ahmad ibn Ishaq from Sa'dan from more than one person in a marfu' manner has said the following:

"'Amir al-Mu'minin, *'Alayhi al-Salam,* has said, 'If people of al-Kufah drop water of Euphrates in the mouth of their new born, they would become of our followers.'"

H 11873, Ch. 9, h 6

Al-Husayn ibn Muhammad has narrated from certain persons of our people from al-Hassan ibn Ali ibn Faddal from Hanan ibn Sadir from his father from Hakim ibn Jubayr who has said the following:

"I once heard our master, Ali ibn al-Husayn, *'Alayhim al-Salam*, saying, 'Every night an angel from the heaven descends with three ounces of musk of the ounces of the garden (paradises) and throws it in the Euphrates. There is no other canal in the east or west of earth more blessed than Euphrates.'"

Chapter 10 - The Prohibited Waters

H 11874, Ch. 10, h 1
Ali ibn Ibrahim has narrated from his father from Harun ibn Muslim from Mas'adah ibn Sadaqah who has said the following:

"Abu 'Abd Allah, *'Alayhi al-Salam,* has said that the Messenger of Allah, *O Allah, grant compensation to Muhammad and his family worthy of their services to Your cause,* prohibited seeking cures from the hot fountains which are in mountains in which the smell of sulfur is found.' It is said that it is of the smell of hell."

H 11875, Ch. 10, h 2
A number of our people have narrated from Sahl ibn Ziyad from ibn Mahbub from 'Abd Allah ibn Sinan who has said the following:

"Abu 'Abd Allah, *'Alayhi al-Salam,* has said, 'Nuh, *'Alayhi al-Salam,* in the days of flood called all waters and they all replied except water of the sulfur and bitter water which then he condemned.'"

H 11876, Ch. 10, h 3
Muhammad ibn Yahya has narrated from Hamdan ibn Sulayman al-Naysaburiy from Muhammad ibn Yahya from Zakariya and a number of our people have narrated from Ahmad ibn abu 'Abd Allah from his father all from Muhammad ibn Sinan from abu al-Jarud from abu Sa'id 'Aqisa' al-Tamimiy who has said the following:

"I once passed by al-Hassan and al-Husayn, *'Alayhim al-Salam,* who were in soaked wraparound cloths. I then said to them, 'Grandchildren of the Messenger of Allah, you have ruined your wraparound cloths.' They said to me, 'O abu Sa'id, ruining our wraparound cloths is more preferable to us than ruining the religion. Water has inhabitants like earth.' They then asked, 'What do you want?' I replied, 'I want to go in this water.' They asked, 'What is this water?' I replied, 'I need a cure for an illness and I want to drink this bitter one, perhaps the body becomes light and the belly soft.' They said, 'We do not think Allah, most Majestic, most Glorious, has placed cure in a thing which He has condemned.' I then asked, 'Why is that so?' They said, 'When Allah, most Blessed, most High, was angered with the people of Noah, *'Alayhi al-Salam,* He opened the sky with pouring water and sent revelation to earth, but certain fountains disobeyed and He then condemned them and turned them into salty and bitter ones.' In the *Hadith* from Hamdan ibn Sulayman it is said that they said, 'O abu Sa'id, you come to something which rejects our divine authority three times a day. Allah, most Majestic, most Glorious, presents our divine authority before waters and that which accepts it becomes sweet and fine, but what rejects it Allah, most Majestic, most Glorious, makes it bitter, salty and burning.'"

H 11877, Ch. 10, h 4
A number of our people have narrated from Sahl ibn Ziyad from Muhammad ibn Sinan from those whom he has mentioned who has said the following:

"Abu 'Abd Allah, *'Alayhi al-Salam,* has said, 'My father, *'Alayhi al-Salam,* disliked seeking cures from bitter water and water of sulfur and would say, 'Noah, *'Alayhi al-Salam,* in the days of the flood called the waters and all of them answered except bitter water and sulfur water, so he prayed against them.'"

Chapter 11 - The Rare Ahadith

H 11878, Ch. 11, h 1

A number of our people have narrated from Ahmad ibn Muhammad from Muhammad ibn `Isma'il from Mansur ibn Yunus from al-'Arzamiy who has said the following:

"Abu 'Abd Allah, *'Alayhi al-Salam,* has said, 'The fountains gushed from under the al-Ka'bah.'"

H 11879, Ch. 11, h 2

Muhammad ibn Yahya has narrated from Muhammad ibn 'Isa from Zakariya al-Mu'min from abu Sa'id al-Mukariy from abu Hamzah al-Thumaliy who has said the following:

"I once was near the pond of Zamzam when a man came and said, 'O abu Hamzah, do not drink from this water because it is shared by both al-Jin and man, and this one is just for human beings.' I found his words strange and then thought, 'How did he know it?' I then asked abu Ja'far, *'Alayhi al-Salam,* about it and he (the Imam) said, 'He was a male Jinn who wanted to give you this information.'"

H 11880, Ch. 11, h 3

Muhammad ibn Yahya has narrated from Ahmad ibn Muhammad from ibn Ya'qub ibn Yazid in a *marfu'* manner has said the following:

"'Amir al-Mu'minin, has said, 'Water of the Nile of Misr (Egypt) deadens the heart.'"

H 11881, Ch. 11, h 4

It is narrated from the narrator of the previous *Hadith* from Ahmad ibn Muhammad from al-'Abbas ibn Ma'ruf from Nawfaliy from al-Ya'qubiy from "Isa ibn 'Abd Allah from Sulayman ibn Ja'far who has said the following:

"About the meaning of the words of Allah, most Majestic, most Glorious, 'We sent water from the sky in measures and placed it on earth and We have the power to take it away,' (23:18) abu 'Abd Allah, *'Alayhi al-Salam,* has said, 'It means canyons and ravines.'"

H 11882, Ch. 11, h 5

A number of our people have narrated from Ahmad ibn Muhammad from 'Abd Allah ibn Ibrahim al-Mada'iniy who has said the following:

"Abu al-Hassan, *'Alayhi al-Salam,* has said, 'There are two unbelieving canals and two believing ones. The two believing canals are Euphrates and Nile of Misr (Egypt) and the unbelieving canals are Tigris and the canal of Balkh.'"

H 11883, Ch. 11, h 6

Muhammad ibn Yahya has narrated from Ahmad ibn Muhammad from Muhammad ibn Ja'far from those whom he has mentioned from al-Khashshab from Ali ibn Hassan from 'Abd al-Rahman ibn Kathir from Dawud al-Riqqiy who has said the following:

"I once was with abu 'Abd Allah, *'Alayhi al-Salam,* when he asked for water and when he drank water, I saw him (the Imam) weeping and tears come out of his eyes. He (the Imam) said to me, 'May Allah condemn those who murdered al-Husayn, *'Alayhi al-Salam*. Whoever of the servants (of Allah) when drinking water, remembers al-Husayn, *'Alayhi al-Salam,* and his family and condemns his murderers, Allah, most Majestic, most Glorious, writes for him one hundred thousand good deeds. He deletes one hundred thousand of his bad deeds, raises his position one hundred thousand degrees and it is as if he has set free one hundred thousand slaves. Allah, most Majestic, most Glorious, will raise him with his heart filled with comfort and serenity.'"

Chapters about Wine and Substances from which Wine is Taken

Chapter 1 - Substances from which Wine is Made

H 11884, Ch. 1, h 1
Ali ibn Ibrahim has narrated from his father and Muhammad ibn 'Isma'il has narrated from al-Fadl ibn Shadhan from all ibn abu 'Umayr from 'Abd al-Rahman ibn *al-Hajj*aj who has said the following:
"Abu 'Abd Allah, *'Alayhi al-Salam,* has said that the Messenger of Allah, *O Allah, grant compensation to Muhammad and his family worthy of their services to Your cause,* has said, 'Intoxicating liquors are made from five kinds of substances: grape juice, extracts of raisins, *al-Bit'* (mead) from honey, *al-Mizru* (beer) from barley and wine from dates.'"

H 11885, Ch. 1, h 2
Ali ibn Ibrahim has narrated from his father from ibn abu 'Umayr from al-Hassan al-Hadramiy from the one who narrated to him who has said the following:
"Ali ibn al-Husayn, *'Alayhi al-Salam,* has said, 'Wine is made of five substances: Dates, raisins, wheat, barley and honey.'"

Muhammad ibn Yahya from Muhammad ibn Ahmad has narrated from ibn abu Najran Safwan al-Jammal from 'Amir ibn al-Simt from Ali ibn al-Husayn, *'Alayhi al-Salam,* a similar *Hadith.*

H 11886, Ch. 1, h 3
Abu Ali al-Ash'ariy has narrated from Muhammad ibn 'Abd al-Jabbar from Safwan ibn Yahya from 'Abd al-Rahman ibn *al-Hajj*aj from Ali ibn Ja'far ibn Ishaq al-Hashimiy who has said the following:
"Abu 'Abd Allah, *'Alayhi al-Salam,* has said that the Messenger of Allah, *O Allah, grant compensation to Muhammad and his family worthy of their services to Your cause,* has said, 'Wine is made of five substances: it is made from grape juice, extracts of raisins, *al-Bit'* (mead) from honey, al-Mizru (beer) from barley and wine from dates.'"

Chapter 2 - The Origin of the Prohibition on Wine

H 11887, Ch. 2, h 1

Ali ibn Ibrahim has narrated from his father and a number of our people have narrated from Ahmad ibn Muhammad and Sahl ibn Ziyad all from ibn Mahbub from Khalid ibn Jarir from abu al-Rabi' al-Shamiy who has said the following:

"I once asked abu 'Abd Allah, *'Alayhi al-Salam,* about the origin of wine and how in the beginning it was lawful and its unlawfulness and when it was found. He (the Imam) said, 'When Adam, *'Alayhi al-Salam,* descended from the garden (paradises) he desired its fruits; and Allah, most Majestic, most Glorious, sent him two twigs of grape vine which he planted. When they grew leaves and fruits came out and ripened, Satan, may Allah condemn him built a wall around them. Adam, *'Alayhi al-Salam* asked how is your condition, O condemned one?' He said, 'They are for me.' He said, 'You are lying.' They agreed to go for Judgment before the Holy spirit. When they arrived before him, Adam, *'Alayhi al-Salam* told his side of the story. The holy spirit took a certain amount of fire and threw it on them, when there were grapes on their branches. Adam, *'Alayhi al-Salam* thought that nothing is left from them and so also thought Satan, may Allah condemn him.' He (the Imam) said, 'The fire worked as it did but two-third were gone and one-third was left. The Holy Spirit said, 'Whatever is gone is the share of Iblis, may Allah condemn him, and what is left is the share of Adam, *'Alayhi al-Salam.*'"

Al-Hassan ibn Mahbub has narrated from Khalid ibn Nafi' from abu 'Abd Allah, *'Alayhi al-Salam,* has narrated a similar *Hadith.*

H 11888, Ch. 2, h 2

Ali ibn Muhammad has narrated from Salih ibn abu Hammad from al-Husayn ibn Yazid from Ali ibn abu Hamzah from Ibrahim who has said the following:

"Abu 'Abd Allah, *'Alayhi al-Salam,* has said, 'When Allah, most Majestic, most Glorious, made Adam, *'Alayhi al-Salam* to descend, He commanded him to farm and plant and threw to him a plant from the plant of the garden (paradises). He gave him palm trees, grape vines, olives and pomegranates. He planted them for his offspring and descendents. He ate from its fruits. Iblis, may Allah condemn him, asked, 'What are these plantations, O Adam, which I did not know of on earth even though I was here before you? Will you allow me to eat from them something?' Adam, *'Alayhi al-Salam* did not allow him. Iblis came during the end of the life of Adam, *'Alayhi al-Salam,* to Eve saying, 'I am in a very bad condition because of hunger and thirst.' Eve asked, 'What do you want?' He said, 'I want you to allow me taste these fruits.' She said, 'Adam, *'Alayhi al-Salam,* has made me to promise not to feed you anything from these plantations because it is from the garden (paradises) and it is not proper for you to eat anything from them. He said to her, 'Squeeze something from them on my palm.' She refused. He said, 'Allow me to suck but I will not eat.' She took one bunch of grapes and gave it to him who sucked but did not eat from it because Eve had stressed on him not to eat. When he was about to bite Eve pulled it out from his mouth and Allah, most Blessed, most High, revealed to Adam, *'Alayhi al-Salam* that My enemy and your enemy, Iblis, has sucked the grape and the juice of wine is unlawful for you which is mixed with the breath of Iblis. Wine became unlawful because of the enemy of Allah, Iblis deceived Eve until he sucked the grape, but if he would eat, grapes would have become unlawful from the beginning to end and all of its fruits and what comes out of it. He then said to Eve, 'I wish you to allow me to suck from this date as you allowed me to suck the grape. She gave him one date and he sucked it. Grapes and dates had strong smells, finer than musk al-*Adhfar* (sweet smelling) and sweeter than honey. When the condemned enemy of Allah, Iblis sucked them, their fragrance went away and sweetness reduced.' Abu 'Abd Allah, *'Alayhi al-Salam,* has said, 'Iblis, may Allah condemn him, went after the death of Adam, *'Alayhi al-Salam,* and urinated on the root of grape vines and palm trees. Water flowed in their veins of the urine of Iblis, the enemy of Allah; and thereafter grape and dates ferment. Allah, most Majestic, most Glorious, has made it unlawful for the offspring of Adam, *'Alayhi al-Salam,* all intoxicating things because water carried the urine of the enemy of Allah in the palm tree and grape vines. Every fermenting thing becomes wine because water fermented in the palm tree and grape vines and it is because of the urine of the enemy of Allah, Iblis, may Allah condemn him.'"

H 11889, Ch. 2, h 3

Ali ibn Ibrahim has narrated from his father from Ahmad ibn Muhammad from ibn abu Nasr from Aban from Zurarah who has said the following:

"Abu Ja'far, *'Alayhi al-Salam,* has said, 'When Noah, *'Alayhi al-Salam,* disembarked from the ark, he established a plantation and of the things that he planted was a vine of grapes. He went back to his family and Iblis, may he be condemned, uprooted it. Noah, *'Alayhi al-Salam,* went to his plantation. He found everything in its condition except the grape vine that was uprooted. He found Iblis, may he be condemned, nearby. Jibril *'Alayhi al-Salam,* came and informed him that Iblis, may he be condemned, has uprooted it. Noah asked Iblis, 'What made you to uproot it? None of my plantations is more beloved to me than this. I by Allah will not allow it without being planted.' Iblis said, 'I, by Allah, will not allow it to grow without my uprooting.' He asked Noah to give him a share.' He (the Imam) said, 'Noah then gave him a share of one-third but he rejected. He gave him one-half and he rejected. Noah also refused to increase but Jibril *'Alayhi al-Salam* said to Noah, 'O Messenger of Allah, you should do him a favor because it comes from you.' Noah then noticed that the authority over it is given to him so Noah, *'Alayhi al-Salam* left two-thirds for him.' Abu Ja'far, *'Alayhi al-Salam,* has said, 'If you have grape juice; boil it until two-thirds of it evaporates; then eat and drink and that (which is gone evaporated) is the share of Satan.'"

H 11890, Ch. 2, h 4

Abu Ali al-Ash'ariy has narrated from al-Hassan ibn Ali al-Kufiy from 'Uthman ibn 'Isa from Sa'id ibn Yasar who has said the following:

"Abu 'Abd Allah, *'Alayhi al-Salam,* has said, 'Iblis, may Allah condemned him, disputed with Noah, *'Alayhi al-Salam* about the grape vine and Jibril, *'Alayhi al-Salam,* came and said, 'He has a right, so give him.' He gave him one-third but he did not agree. He gave one-half but he did not agree. Jibril then threw a fire, which burnt two-thirds and one-third was left. He said, 'Whatever fire has burnt is his share and what has remained, O Noah, is lawful for you.'"

Chapter 3 - Wine is Still Unlawful

H 11891, Ch. 3, h 1
Ali ibn Ibrahim has narrated from his father from Hammad ibn 'Isa from Ibrahim ibn 'Umar al-Yamaniy who has said the following:

"Abu 'Abd Allah, *'Alayhi al-Salam,* has said, 'Every time Allah, most Majestic, most Glorious, sent a Prophet it was in the knowledge of Allah, most Majestic, most Glorious, that in the case of completing His religion wine must have been made unlawful. It had to remain unlawful, however, religion is to change the habits one after the other. Were such change to take place all at once, people would boycott religion as a whole.'"

H 11892, Ch. 3, h 2
A number of our people have narrated from Ahmad ibn Muhammad from al-Husayn ibn Sa'id from Fadalah abu Ayyub from Musa ibn Bakr from Zurarah who has said the following:

"Abu Ja'far, *'Alayhi al-Salam,* has said, 'Every time Allah, most Majestic, most Glorious, sent a Prophet, it was in the knowledge of Allah, most Majestic, most Glorious, that in the case of completing His religion wine must have been made unlawful. It had to remain unlawful, however, religion is to change the habits one after the other. Were such change to take place at once people would boycott religion as a whole.'"

H 11893, Ch. 3, h 3
Ali ibn Ibrahim has narrated from his father from Hammad from Hariz from Zurarah who has said the following:

"Abu 'Abd Allah, *'Alayhi al-Salam,* has said, 'Every time Allah, most Majestic, most Glorious, sent a Prophet, it was in the knowledge of Allah, most Majestic, most Glorious, that in the case of completing his religion wine must have been made unlawful. It had to remain unlawful, however, religion is to change the habits one after the other. Were such change to take place at once people would boycott religion as a whole.' Abu Ja'far, *'Alayhi al-Salam,* has said, 'No one is more kind than Allah, most Majestic, most Glorious, and it is of the kindness of Allah, most Blessed, most High, that He transfers them from one habit to the other. Were He to change them at once they would have been destroyed.'"

Chapter 4 - The Wine Drinker

H 11894, Ch. 4, h 1
Ali ibn Ibrahim has narrated from his father and Muhammad ibn Yahya has narrated from Ahmad ibn Muhammad and a number of our people have narrated from Sahl ibn Ziyad all from ibn Mahbub from Khalid ibn Jarir from abu al-Rabi' al-Shamiy who has said the following:

"Once abu 'Abd Allah, *'Alayhi al-Salam,* was asked about wine. Abu 'Abd Allah, *'Alayhi al-Salam,* said that the Messenger of Allah, *O Allah, grant compensation to Muhammad and his family worthy of their services to Your cause,* has said, 'Allah, most Majestic, most Glorious, sent me as mercy for the worlds. (Allah sent me) to eradicate playing tools, musical pipes and matters of the age of darkness, ignorance and idols.' He (the Messenger of Allah) has said, 'My Lord swears and says, "If any of My servants in the world drinks wine I will make him drink al-Hamim (boiling water of hell, that roasts the face when drinking) on the Day of Judgment, regardless of whether he will be made to suffer or will be forgiven. If anyone makes a child to drink wine or a slave, I will make him drink the same amount of al-Hamim, regardless of whether he will be made to suffer or will be forgiven."'

H 11895, Ch. 4, h 2

Ibn Mahbub has narrated from Khalid ibn Jarir from abu al-Rabi' al-Shamiy who has said the following:

"The Messenger of Allah, *O Allah, grant compensation to Muhammad and his family worthy of their services to Your cause,* has said, 'If one drinks wine after Allah, most Majestic, most Glorious, has made it unlawful through my tongue, he does not deserve to receive acceptance to his marriage proposal. His intercession is not accepted. He is not considered truthful when speaking and is not trusted about a trust. If one trusts him after knowing his condition, he has no guarantee from Allah, most Majestic, most Glorious, or reward or replacement and compensation.'"

H 11896, Ch. 4, h 3

A number of our people have narrated from Sahl ibn Ziyad from 'Amr ibn 'Uthman from al-Husayn ibn Sadir from his father who has said the following:

"Abu Ja'far, *'Alayhi al-Salam,* has said, 'The wine drinker on the Day of Judgment will be brought with his face all black, his tongue hanging down and his saliva flowing on his chest. It is a right on Allah, most Majestic, most Glorious, to make him drink from *tinah* of *Khabal* or that he (the Imam) said, 'from the well of *Khabal*'. I (the narrator) then asked, 'What is well of *Khabal*?' He (the Imam) said, 'It is a well in which the puss from the bottom of fornicators flows.'"

H 11897, Ch. 4, h 4

Ali ibn Ibrahim has narrated from his father from ibn abu 'Umayr from certain persons of his people who has said the following:

"Abu 'Abd Allah, *'Alayhi al-Salam,* has said that the Messenger of Allah, *O Allah, grant compensation to Muhammad and his family worthy of their services to Your cause,* has said, 'The wine drinker must not be visited when he is sick. His funeral must not be attended, he must not be relied on when he testifies and must not be married when he proposes for marriage. You must not trust him about a trust.'"

H 11898, Ch. 4, h 5

Abu Ali al-Ash'ariy has narrated from Muhammad ibn 'Abd al-Jabbar from Safwan from al-'Ala' from certain persons of our people who has said the following:

"Abu 'Abd Allah, *'Alayhi al-Salam,* has stated this *Hadith*. "The Messenger of Allah, *O Allah, grant compensation to Muhammad and his family worthy of their services to Your cause,* has said, 'If a wine drinker becomes ill do not visit him. If he dies do not attend his funeral, if he testifies do not rely his testimony, if he proposes marriage do not marry him and if he asks to trust him about a trust do not trust him.'"

H 11899, Ch. 4, h 6
A number of our people have narrated from Ahmad ibn Muhammad from al-Husayn ibn Sa'id from Fadalah abu Ayyub from Bashir al- Hudhaliy from 'Ajlan abu Salih who has said the following:
"I once asked abu 'Abd Allah, *'Alayhi al-Salam,* if we can make a new born drink wine. He (the Imam) said, 'If one makes a child drink wine' or he said, 'intoxicating liquor, Allah, most Majestic, most Glorious, will make him drink al-Hamim (boiling water that roasts the face when drinking) of hell even if He forgives him.'"

H 11900, Ch. 4, h 7
Ali ibn Ibrahim has narrated from his father and Muhammad ibn 'Isma'il has narrated from al-Fadl ibn Shadhan from ibn abu 'Umayr from Hafs ibn al-Bakhtariy and Durust and Hisham ibn Salim all from 'Ajlan abu Salih who has said the following:
"I once heard abu 'Abd Allah, *'Alayhi al-Salam,* saying, 'Allah, most Majestic, most Glorious, says, "If one drinks an intoxicating liquor or makes a child, who does not understand, to drink it, I will make him to drink al-Hamim, regardless of whether he will suffer punishment or will be forgiven. One who quits intoxicating substances for My sake I will admit him in the garden (paradises) and give him sealed *Rahiq* (exquisite nectar in a sealed container) for a drink and will honor him as I will honor my friends.'"

H 11901, Ch. 4, h 8
Muhammad ibn Yahya has narrated from Ahmad ibn Muhammad from al-Fadl from certain persons of his people who has said the following:
"Abu 'Abd Allah, *'Alayhi al-Salam,* has said, 'On the Day of Judgment, the wine drinker will come with a black face, with his one-half bent and his tongue hanging out crying, "Thirsty, thirsty."'"

H 11902, Ch. 4, h 9
Humayd ibn Ziyad has narrated from al-Hassan ibn Muhammad ibn Sama'ah from more than one person from Aban ibn 'Uthman from Hammad ibn Bashir who has said the following:
"Abu 'Abd Allah, *'Alayhi al-Salam,* has stated this *Hadith.* 'The Messenger of Allah, *O Allah, grant compensation to Muhammad and his family worthy of their services to Your cause,* has said, 'If one drinks wine after Allah, most High, has made it unlawful through my tongue, he then does not deserve to be married if he proposes marriage. He is not considered truthful if he speaks, his intercession is not accepted and he is not trusted about a trust. If one trusts him about a trust and he missappropriates it or loses it, then the one who has trusted him will have no reward with Allah, most Majestic, most Glorious, or replacement or compensation.'

"Abu 'Abd Allah, *'Alayhi al-Salam,* has said, 'I once visited abu Ja'far, *'Alayhi al-Salam,* and said, 'I like to give a certain amount of asset to so and so to buy for me certain goods from Yemen.' He (the Imam) said, 'Do you not know that he drinks wine?' I replied, 'I have heard from believing people who say so.' He (the Imam) said to me, 'You must believe them because Allah, most Majestic, most Glorious, says, ". . . he believes in Allah and in the believing people."'" He (the Imam) then said, 'If you give a certain amount of assets and it is destroyed or lost, you will not have any reward or compensation for it with Allah, most Majestic, most Glorious. For example, you give him your asset and he loses it. You then pray to Allah, most Majestic, most Glorious, for reward.' He (the Imam) said, 'Never, my son, Allah will not reward you or compensate you for such loss.' He (the Imam) has said, 'I asked him (the Imam), 'Why is it so?' He (the Imam) said to me, 'Allah, most Majestic, most Glorious, says, "Do not give to the dimwitted ones your assets which Allah has given you for your sustenance," (4:5) do you see anyone more dimwitted than a wine drinker?' He (the Imam) has said that he (the Imam) said, 'A servant has a chance before Allah, most Majestic, most Glorious, until he drinks wine. When he drinks wine Allah, most Majestic, most Glorious, tears down his covering, then Satan, may Allah condemn him, becomes his guardian and brother, his ears, his eyes, his hands, his legs and he drives him to all misguidance and turns him away from all good things.'"

H 11903, Ch. 4, h 10
A number of our people have narrated from Ahmad ibn Muhammad ibn 'Isa from al-Husayn ibn Sa'id from al-Husayn ibn al-'Ulwan from 'Amr ibn Khalid from Zayd ibn Ali from his ancestors who have said the following:

"The Messenger of Allah, *O Allah, grant compensation to Muhammad and his family worthy of their services to Your cause,* has condemned wine. He has condemned those who squeeze the juice for it, those who want it be squeezed, those who sell it, those who buy it, those who serve it, those who receive payment for it, those who drink it, those who carry it for delivery and those to whom it is delivered.'"

H 11904, Ch. 4, h 11
Al-Husayn ibn Muhammad has narrated from Ja'far ibn Muhammad from Muhammad ibn al-Husayn from Ali al-Sufiy from Khadir al-Sayrafiy who has said the following:

"Abu 'Abd Allah, *'Alayhi al-Salam,* has said, 'If one drinks wine considering it lawful, he will be in hell forever, and one who drinks believing that it is unlawful will be punished in the fire.'"

H 11905, Ch. 4, h 12
A number of our people have narrated from Sahl ibn Ziyad from Yusuf ibn Ali from Nasr ibn Muzahim and Durust al-Wasitiy from Zurarah and others who has said the following:

"Abu 'Abd Allah, *'Alayhi al-Salam,* has said, 'Those who drink wine will not receive any protection from us.'"

H 11906, Ch. 4, h 13
Muhammad ibn Yahya has narrated from Ahmad ibn Muhammad from Ali ibn al-Hakam from 'Isma'il ibn Muhammad al-Minqariy from Yazid ibn abu Ziyad who has said the following:

"Abu Ja'far, *'Alayhi al-Salam,* has said, 'If one drinks intoxicating liquor and dies when there is something of wine inside him because of which he has not repented, he will be raised from his grave confused, his mouth bent to one side, his saliva flowing and crying woes and destruction.'"

H 11907, Ch. 4, h 14

A number of our people have narrated from Sahl ibn Ziyad from Ya'qub ibn Yazid from 'Amr ibn Ibrahim from Khalaf ibn Hammad from 'Umar ibn Aban who has said the following:

"Abu 'Abd Allah, *'Alayhi al-Salam,* has said, 'If one drinks intoxicating liquor, it is a right on Allah, most Majestic, most Glorious, to make him drink from tinah of Khabal.' I asked, 'What is it?' He (the Imam) said, 'It is puss from the vagina of fornicators.'"

H 11908, Ch. 4, h 15

Ali ibn Ibrahim has narrated from his father from Khalaf ibn Hammad from Muhriz from abu Basir who has said the following:

"Abu 'Abd Allah, *'Alayhi al-Salam,* has said that the Messenger of Allah, *O Allah, grant compensation to Muhammad and his family worthy of their services to Your cause,* has said, 'I do not perform *Salat* (prayer) on the dead body of one drowned in wine (a wine drinker).'"

H 11909, Ch. 4, h 16

A number of our people have narrated from Sahl ibn Ziyad from Bakr ibn Salih from al-Shaybaniy from Yunus ibn Zabayan who has said the following:

"Abu 'Abd Allah, *'Alayhi al-Salam,* once said to me, 'O Yunus ibn Zabayan, convey my words to 'Atiyyah that if one drinks one sip of wine Allah, most Majestic, most Glorious, condemns him and so also do His angels, His Messengers and the believing people. If he drinks until he becomes drunk, the spirit of belief is taken away from his body and a filthy condemned spirit rides him. He then stops performing *Salat* (prayer). When he stops performing *Salat* (prayer) the angels scold him and Allah, most Majestic, most Glorious, says to him, 'My servant, you have disbelieved and the angels have scolded you because of your evilness, My servant.' Abu 'Abd Allah, *'Alayhi al-Salam,* then said, 'It is evil, an evil that is real. By Allah, it is a great scolding, His name is glorious, His scolding of one hour is more severe than suffering for one thousand years.' He (the narrator) has said that abu 'Abd Allah, *'Alayhi al-Salam,* then said, '. . . they are condemned wherever they live, they are taken and killed entirely.' (33:61) He (the Imam) then said, 'O Yunus, condemned is one who overlooks the command of Allah, most Majestic, most Glorious. If he goes on land, he is destroyed and if he goes in the sea, he is drowned. He is subjected to anger because of the anger of the glorious One whose name is majestic.'"

H 11910, Ch. 4, h 17

A number of our people have narrated from Sahl ibn Ziyad from Muhammad ibn Khalid from Marwak from a man who has said the following:

"Abu 'Abd Allah, *'Alayhi al-Salam,* has said, 'People who quench themselves with intoxicating liquors in this world, die thirsty, will be raised thirsty, and will be sent in the fire thirsty.'"

H 11911, Ch. 4, h 18

Ali ibn Ibrahim has narrated from his father from al-Hassan ibn Ali, from his father from abu 'Abd Allah, *'Alayhi al-Salam,* a similar *Hadith.*

He has added, 'If a man uses wine of an amount equal to the amount of the kohl (eyeliner) powder picked up by an kohl (eyeliner) powder applicator, it becomes a right on Allah to apply the same amount of kohl (eyeliner) of the fire on him.'"

H 11912, Ch. 4, h 19
Ali ibn Ibrahim has narrated from his father from ibn abu 'Umayr from al-Hassan al-'Attar from abu Basir who has said the following:

"Abu 'Abd Allah, *'Alayhi al-Salam*, has said that the Messenger of Allah, *O Allah, grant compensation to Muhammad and his family worthy of their services to Your cause*, has said, 'My intercession will not apply to those who take their *Salat* (prayer) lightly and he will not be able to reach before me on the pond. No, by Allah my intercession will not apply to those who drink intoxicating liquor and will not be able to come to me on the pond, no, by Allah (it will not happen).'"

Chapter 5 - Another Chapter on the above Topic

H 11913, Ch. 5, h 1
Al-Husayn ibn Muhammad has narrated from Mu'alla' ibn Muhammad from al-Washsha' from Aban ibn 'Uthman from 'Abd al-Rahman ibn abu 'Abd Allah who has said the following:

"Abu 'Abd Allah, *'Alayhi al-Salam*, has said, 'If one drinks intoxicating liquor his *Salat* (prayer) is withheld for forty days, and if he dies within the forty days he dies like the people of the time of ignorance, but if he repents (turns to) Allah, most Majestic, most Glorious, also turns to him.'"

H 11914, Ch. 5, h 2
Abu Ali al-Ash'ariy has narrated from al-Hassan ibn Ali al-Kufiy from al-'Abbas ibn 'Amir from Dawud ibn al-Husayn who has said the following:

"Abu 'Abd Allah, *'Alayhi al-Salam*, has said, 'If one drinks intoxicating liquor his *Salat* (prayer) is not accepted for forty days. If he dies within the forty days, he dies as one of the ignorant people (pagans) and if he repents (turns to), Allah also turns to him.'"

H 11915, Ch. 5, h 3
Ali ibn Ibrahim has narrated from his father from ibn abu 'Umayr from Mehran ibn Muhammad from a man from Sa'd al-'Iskaf who has said the following:

"Abu Ja'far, *'Alayhi al-Salam*, has said, 'If one drinks intoxicating liquor his *Salat* (prayer) is not accepted for forty days. If he returns to drink again Allah will make him drink from *Tinah* of *Khabal*, which he (the Imam) said, is a liquid that comes out of the vagina of fornicators.'"

H 11916, Ch. 5, h 4
Ali ibn Ibrahim has narrated from his father from ibn abu 'Umayr from 'Abd al-Rahman ibn *al-Hajj*aj who has said the following:

"Abu 'Abd Allah, *'Alayhi al-Salam*, has said, 'If one drinks wine his *Salat* (prayer) is not accepted for forty days.'"

H 11917, Ch. 5, h 5
Abu Ali al-Ash'ariy has narrated from Muhammad ibn 'Abd al-Jabbar from Safwan from al-'Ala' from Muhammad ibn Muslim who has said the following:

"One of the two Imam, (abu Ja'far or abu 'Abd Allah), *'Alayhim al-Salam,* has said, 'If one drinks one sip of wine his *Salat* (prayer) is not accepted forty days.'"

H 11918, Ch. 5, h 6
Muhammad ibn Yahya has narrated from Ahmad ibn Muhammad from Ali ibn al-Hakam from Sayf ibn 'Amirah from Muhammad ibn Marwan from al-Fudayl ibn Yasar who has said the following:
"Abu Ja'far, *'Alayhi al-Salam,* has said, 'In the month of Ramadan at the time of iftar (at sunset) Allah, most Majestic, most Glorious, every night frees people from the fire except those who break their fast with intoxicating liquor. If a person drinks intoxicating liquor none of his *Salat* (prayer) is counted for forty days and if he dies in those forty days he has died like as an ignorant (pagan) person.'"

H 11919, Ch. 5, h 7
Ahmad ibn Muhammad has narrated from Muhammad ibn 'Isma'il from ibn Muskan from abu Basir who has said the following:
"Abu al-Hassan, *'Alayhi al-Salam,* has said, 'When my father was about to pass away he said to me, 'My son, our intercession will not apply to those who take their *Salat* (prayer) lightly and the addicts of these drinks will not be able to come to us at the pond. I then asked, 'What are these drinks, O father?' He (the Imam) said, 'It is all intoxicating liquor.'"

H 11920, Ch. 5, h 8
A number of our people have narrated from Ahmad ibn Khalid from 'Uthman ibn 'Isa from Sama'ah ibn Mehran who has said the following:
"Abu 'Abd Allah, *'Alayhi al-Salam,* has said that the Messenger of Allah, *O Allah, grant compensation to Muhammad and his family worthy of their services to Your cause,* has said, 'If one [of you] drinks intoxicating liquor his *Salat* (prayer) is not accepted for forty days.'"

H 11921, Ch. 5, h 9
Ali ibn Ibrahim has narrated from his father from Hammad ibn 'Isa from al-Husayn ibn al-Mukhtar from 'Amr ibn Shamir who has said the following:
"I once heard abu 'Abd Allah, *'Alayhi al-Salam,* saying, 'If one drinks one sip of wine Allah will not accept his *Salat* (prayer) for seven (days) and if one becomes drunk his *Salat* (prayer) is not accepted for forty days.'"

H 11922, Ch. 5, h 10
A number of our people have narrated from Ahmad ibn Muhammad from n Khalid from 'Uthman ibn 'Isa from Sama'ah ibn Mehran from abu Basir who has said the following:
"Abu 'Abd Allah, *'Alayhi al-Salam,* has said that the Messenger of Allah, *O Allah, grant compensation to Muhammad and his family worthy of their services to Your cause,* has said, 'If one drinks wine till he becomes drunk Allah, most Majestic, most Glorious, will not accept his *Salat* (prayer) for forty days.'"

H 11923, Ch. 5, h 11
Ali has narrated from his father from al-Nadr ibn Suwayd from Hisham ibn Salim from Sulayman ibn Khalid who has said the following:
"Abu 'Abd Allah, *'Alayhi al-Salam,* has said, 'If one drinks one sip of wine his

Salat (prayer) is not accepted for forty days.'"

H 11924, Ch. 5, h 12
Muhammad ibn Yahya has narrated from Ahmad ibn Muhammad ibn 'Isa from ibn abu Nasr from al-Husayn ibn Khalid who has said the following:

"I once said to abu al-Hassan, *'Alayhi al-Salam*, 'It is narrated to us from the Holy Prophet, *O Allah, grant compensation to Muhammad and his family worthy of their services to Your cause*, that he has said, "If one drinks wine his *Salat* (prayer) is not counted for forty days."' He (the Imam) said, 'They have spoken the truth.' I then asked, 'How is it that his *Salat* (prayer) is not counted for forty days: no less and no more?' He (the Imam) said, 'Allah, most Majestic, most Glorious, determined the creation of human beings so it becomes *nutfah* (seed, sperm) in forty days, then it changes and becomes a clot of blood in forty days, then it changes and becomes a lump of flesh (embryo) in forty days. If he drinks wine it remains in his bone joints for forty days proportionate to the changes in his creation.' He (the narrator) has said that he (the Imam) then said, 'In the same away all of his other food and drinks remain in his bone joints for forty days.'"

Chapter 6 - Wine is the Head of all Sins and Evil

H 11925, Ch. 6, h 1
Ali ibn Ibrahim has narrated from his father from ibn abu 'Umayr from 'Isma'il ibn Bashshar who has said the following:

"Once a man asked abu 'Abd Allah, *'Alayhi al-Salam*, saying, 'I pray to Allah to keep my soul in service for your cause, is drinking wine more evil or not performing *Salat* (prayer)?' He (the Imam) said, 'Drinking wine is more evil.' He (the Imam) then said, 'Do you know why?' The man said, 'No, I do not know.' He (the Imam) said, 'It is because he ends up in a condition in which he does not know his Lord.'"

H 11926, Ch. 6, h 2
Abu Ali al-Ash'ariy has narrated from Muhammad ibn Hassan from Muhammad ibn Ali from abu Jamilah from al-Halabiy and Zurarah and Muhammad ibn Muslim and Humran ibn 'A'yan who have said the following:

"Abu 'Abd Allah, and abu Ja'far, *'Alayhim al-Salam*, have made it clear that wine is the head of all sins.'"

H 11927, Ch. 6, h 3
A number of our people have narrated from Sahl ibn Ziyad from al-'Abbas ibn 'Amir from abu Jamilah from Zayd al-Shahham who has said the following:

"Abu 'Abd Allah, *'Alayhi al-Salam*, has said that the Messenger of Allah, *O Allah, grant compensation to Muhammad and his family worthy of their services to Your cause*, has said, 'Wine is the head of all sins.'"

H 11928, Ch. 6, h 4
It is narrated from the narrator of the previous *Hadith* from Muhammad ibn Ali from abu Jamilah from abu 'Usamah who has said the following:

"Abu 'Abd Allah, *'Alayhi al-Salam*, has said, 'Drinking wine is the key to all evil and a wine addict is like an idol worshipper. Wine is the head of all sins and a wine drinker is a rejecter of the book of Allah, most High; had he accepted the book of Allah he would consider what it declares unlawful as unlawful.'"

H 11929, Ch. 6, h 5
Abu Ali al-Ash'ariy has narrated from al-Hassan ibn Ali al-Kufiy from 'Uthman ibn 'Isa from ibn Muskan from those who narrated to him who has said the following:

"Abu 'Abd Allah, *'Alayhi al-Salam,* has said, 'Allah, most Majestic, most Glorious, has made for every evil thing a lock and He has made its keys' or he (the Imam) said, 'the keys to those locks to be wine.'"

H 11930, Ch. 6, h 6
A number of our people have narrated from Ahmad ibn abu 'Abd Allah from his father Ahmad ibn Muhammad from Muhammad ibn 'Isa from al-Nadr ibn Suwayd from Ya'qub ibn Shu'ayb from abu Basir who has said the following:

"One of the two Imam, (abu Ja'far or abu 'Abd Allah), *'Alayhim al-Salam,* has said that Allah, most Majestic, most Glorious, has made a house for sins. For this house He has made a door, for the door He has made a lock and for the lock He has made a key, the key to disobedience is wine.'"

H 11931, Ch. 6, h 7
Muhammad ibn Yahya has narrated from Ahmad ibn Muhammad from al-Husayn ibn Sa'id from Ibrahim ibn abu al-Balad from his father who has said the following:

"One of the two Imam, (abu Ja'far or abu 'Abd Allah), *'Alayhim al-Salam,* has said, 'Allah is not disobeyed by anything more severely than by drinking wine. One of them may neglect obligatory *Salat* (prayer), fall on his mother, sister or daughter when drunk and be devoid of reason.'"

H 11932, Ch. 6, h 8
Muhammad ibn Yahya has narrated from Muhammad ibn al-Husayn in a marfu' manner has said the following:

"It was said to `Amir al-Mu'minin, *'Alayhi al-Salam,* 'You think that drinking wine is a sin which is more serious than fornication and theft.' He (the Imam) said, 'Yes, because a fornicator perhaps does not extend it to other sins but a wine drinker when he drinks, fornicates, steals and murders a soul which Allah, most Majestic, most Glorious, has made unlawful to kill, and neglects *Salat* (prayer).'"

H 11933, Ch. 6, h 9
Muhammad ibn Yahya has narrated from certain persons of our people in a *marfu'* manner has said the following:

"Abu 'Abd Allah, *'Alayhi al-Salam,* has said, 'Drinking wine is the key to all evil.'"

Chapter 7 - The Wine Addict

H 11934, Ch. 7, h 1
Ali ibn Ibrahim has narrated from his father from ibn abu 'Umayr from abu Ayyub al-Khazzaz from 'Ajlan abu Salih who has said the following:

"Abu 'Abd Allah, *'Alayhi al-Salam,* has said, 'If one drinks intoxicating liquor until his life ends he is like an idol worshipper. If one quits drinking intoxicating liquor for fear of Allah, most Majestic, most Glorious, He will admit him in the garden (paradises) and give him drinks from exquisite, sealed nectar (containers)."'

H 11935, Ch. 7, h 2

A number of our people have narrated from Sahl ibn Ziyad from al-'Abbas ibn 'Amir from abu Jamilah from Zayd al-Shahham who has said the following:

"Abu 'Abd Allah, *'Alayhi al-Salam,* has said that the Messenger of Allah, *O Allah, grant compensation to Muhammad and his family worthy of their services to Your cause,* has said, 'A wine addict will meet Allah, most Majestic, most Glorious, as a worshipper of idols will do.'"

H 11936, Ch. 7, h 3

Abu Ali al-Ash'ariy has narrated from Muhammad ibn 'Abd al-Jabbar from Safwan from al-'Ala' from Muhammad ibn Muslim who has said the following:

"One of the two Imam, (abu Ja'far or abu 'Abd Allah), *'Alayhim al-Salam,* has said, 'A wine addict will meet Allah, most Majestic, most Glorious, when he will meet Him, as a worshipper of idols will do.'"

H 11937, Ch. 7, h 4

Ali ibn Ibrahim has narrated from his father from Hammad ibn 'Isa from al-Husayn ibn al-Mukhtar from 'Amr ibn 'Uthman who has said the following:

"I once heard abu 'Abd Allah, *'Alayhi al-Salam,* saying, 'A wine addict will meet Allah, most Majestic, most Glorious, when he meets Him, as a worshipper of idols will do.'"

H 11938, Ch. 7, h 5

Al-Husayn ibn Muhammad has narrated from Mu'alla' ibn Muhammad from al-Hassan ibn Ali al-Washsha' from 'Abd Allah ibn Sinan who has said the following:

"Abu 'Abd Allah, *'Alayhi al-Salam,* has said that the Messenger of Allah, *O Allah, grant compensation to Muhammad and his family worthy of their services to Your cause,* has said, 'A wine addict will meet Allah, most Majestic, most Glorious, as a worshipper of idols will do.'"

H 11939, Ch. 7, h 6

Ali ibn Ibrahim has narrated from his father from ibn abu 'Umayr from 'Abd al-Rahman ibn al-*Hajj*aj who has said the following:

"Abu 'Abd Allah, *'Alayhi al-Salam,* has said, 'A wine addict will meet Allah, most Majestic, most Glorious, as a worshipper of idols will do.'"

H 11940, Ch. 7, h 7

Abu Ali al-Ash'ariy has narrated from Muhammad ibn Hassan from Muhammad ibn Ali from abu Jamilah from al-Halabiy and Zurarah also and Muhammad ibn Muslim and Humran ibn 'A'yan who have said the following:

"Abu Ja'far, and abu 'Abd Allah, *'Alayhim al-Salam,* have said, 'A wine addict is like an idol worshipper.'"

H 11941, Ch. 7, h 8

A number of our people have narrated from Ahmad ibn Muhammad ibn Khalid from 'Uthman ibn 'Isa from Sama'ah from abu Basir who has said the following:

"Abu 'Abd Allah, *'Alayhi al-Salam,* has said that the Messenger of Allah, *O Allah, grant compensation to Muhammad and his family worthy of their services to Your cause,* has said, 'A wine addict is like an idol worshipper. When he dies as a wine addict and he will meet Allah, most Majestic, most Glorious, he will meet Him as a worshipper of idols will do.'"

H 11942, Ch. 7, h 9

A number of our people have narrated from Sahl ibn Ziyad and Ya'qub ibn Yazid from Muhammad ibn Dadhawayh who has said the following:

"I once wrote to abu al-Hassan, asking him (the Imam) about drinking intoxicating liquor. He (the Imam) wrote back in answer, 'A wine drinker is an unbeliever.'"

H 11943, Ch. 7, h 10

Ali ibn Ibrahim has narrated from his father from 'Amr ibn 'Uthman from Muhammad ibn 'Abd Allah from a man who has said the following:

"Abu 'Abd Allah, *'Alayhi al-Salam,* has said, 'A wine addict is like a worshipper of idols.'"

Chapter 8 - Another Chapter on the above Topic

H 11944, Ch. 8, h 1

Ali ibn Ibrahim has narrated from Muhammad ibn 'Isa from Yunus from Hammad from abu al-Jarud who has said the following:

"I once heard abu 'Abd Allah, *'Alayhi al-Salam,* saying, 'My father narrated to me from his father, *'Alayhi al-Salam,* that the Messenger of Allah, *O Allah, grant compensation to Muhammad and his family worthy of their services to Your cause,* has said, 'A wine addict is like an idol worshipper.' I (the narrator) then asked, 'What is a 'Mudmin'?' He (the Imam) said, 'He is one who drinks whenever he finds.'"

H 11945, Ch. 8, h 2

Muhammad ibn Ja'far has narrated from Muhammad ibn 'Ibn abu Ya'fur ibn abu Ya'fur-Hamid from Sayf ibn 'Amirah from Mansur ibn Hazim who has said that narrated to me abu Basir from ibn abu Ya'fur who have said the following:

"We once heard abu 'Abd Allah, *'Alayhi al-Salam,* saying, 'A wine addict is not one who drinks every day, he however, is one who settles his soul upon drinking it whenever he finds it.'"

H 11946, Ch. 8, h 3

A number of our people have narrated from Sahl ibn Ziyad from Mansur ibn al-'Abbas from Ali ibn Yaqtin from Hashim ibn Khalid from Nu'aym al-Basriy who has said the following:

"Abu 'Abd Allah, *'Alayhi al-Salam,* has said, 'A wine addict is one who drinks whenever he finds.'"

Chapter 9 - Unlawfulness of Wine in the Book

H 11947, Ch. 9, h 1

Abu Ali al-Ash'ariy has narrated from certain persons of our people and Ali ibn Ibrahim has narrated from his father 'Abd Allah from al-Hassan ibn Ali ibn abu Hamzah from his father from Ali ibn Yaqtin who has said the following:

"Al-Mahdiy once asked abu al-Hassan, *'Alayhi al-Salam,* about wine; if it is made unlawful in the book of Allah, most Majestic, most Glorious, because people know it is prohibited and they do not know if it is unlawful. Abu al-Hassan, *'Alayhi al-Salam,* said to him, 'Yes, it is unlawful in the book of Allah, most Majestic, most Glorious, O `Amir al-Mu'minin.' He then asked, 'Where in the book of Allah, majestic is whose name, it is unlawful, O abu al-Hassan?' He (the Imam) said, 'It is in these words of Allah, most Majestic, most Glorious, "Say, (O Muhammad) my Lord has made unlawful the sinful things, that which is clearly known and that which is not so clearly known, the sin and rebellion without right.' (7:33) His words, *'that which is clearly known'* is a reference to openly committed fornication with flags hoisted like the ones at the time of ignorance, the prostitutes did. The words of Allah majestic is whose name, *'that which is not clearly known'* is a reference to marrying the wife of one's father as it was done among people before the Holy Prophet, *O Allah, grant compensation to Muhammad and his family worthy of their services to Your cause,* was commanded to preach the death of a man who left a widow behind, his son married his own stepmother and Allah, most Majestic, most Glorious, made it unlawful. *'al-'Ithm'* (sin) in the words of Allah stands for wine exactly. Allah, most Majestic, most Glorious, has said in another passage, 'They ask you about wine and gambling. Say, "There is great sin in them and benefits for people" (2:216) The word *'al-'Ithm'* (sin) stands for wine in the book of Allah and for gambling. The sin in them is greater as Allah most High has said.' Al-Mahdiy then said, 'O Ali ibn Yaqtin, this by Allah, is a Hashimiy fatwa.' I (the narrator) then said, 'You have spoken the truth, O `Amir al-Mu'minin. All praise belongs to Allah who has not taken knowledge away from you *Ahl al-Bayt* (people of the family of the Holy Prophet).' He (the narrator) has said that al-Mahdiy could not wait but to say to me, 'You have spoken the truth, O Rafidiy (rejecter).'"

H 11948, Ch. 9, h 2

Certain persons of our people have, in *mursal* manner, narrated the following:

"He (the Imam), *'Alayhi al-Salam,* has said, 'The first thing about the unlawfulness of wine is in the words of Allah, most Majestic, most Glorious, "They ask you about wine and gambling. Say, 'There is great sin in them and benefits for people but the sin in them is greater than their benefits.'" (2:219) When this verse was revealed people sensed the prohibition on it and prohibition on gambling. They learned that one must stay away from sins and that Allah, most Majestic, most Glorious, does not impose on them both ways because of His saying, "and benefits for people". Thereafter Allah, most Majestic, most Glorious, sent another verse, "Wine, gambling, signs (indicators of sins), and gambling arrows are filthy matters of the acts of Satan, therefore, you must stay away from them, perhaps you attain salvation." (5:90) This verse is more intense than the previous one in being more forceful about the unlawfulness. Then is the third stage and the third verse which is even more forceful than the first and the second verses as Allah, most Majestic, most Glorious, has said, "Satan only wants to place animosity and hatred among you in wine and gambling and prevent you from speaking of Allah and from *Salat* (prayer). Why then do you not stay away from them?" (5:91) Allah, most Majestic, most Glorious, has commanded to stay away from them and has explained the reason because of which they are unlawful. Allah, most Majestic, most Glorious, then in the fourth verse has stated, besides these verses, saying, "Say (O Muhammad) my Lord has made unlawful only the sins which are clearly known and that which is not clearly known, the sin and rebellion without right." In the first verse Allah, most Majestic, most Glorious, has said, "They ask you about wine and gambling. Say, 'There are great sins in them and there is benefit for people.'" In the fourth verse He has said to say, "My Lord has made unlawful only the sins which are clearly known and that which is not clearly known." Allah, most Majestic, most Glorious, has informed that there is sin in wine and other things and that it is unlawful because when Allah, most Majestic, most Glorious, decides to sanction an obligation He explains in gradual steps. This, on the part of Allah, most Majestic, most Glorious, is a plan which is more correct and closer to them for acceptance and of less dislike on their part.'"

Chapter 10 - The Messenger of Allah, *O Allah, grant compensation to Muhammad and his family worthy of their services to Your cause,* has Prohibited all Intoxicating Liquor of a Small or Large Quantity

H 11949, Ch. 10, h 1
Ali ibn Ibrahim has narrated from his father from ibn abu 'Umayr from Kulayb al-Saydawiy who has said the following:
"I once heard abu 'Abd Allah, *'Alayhi al-Salam,* saying, 'The Messenger of Allah, *O Allah, grant compensation to Muhammad and his family worthy of their services to Your cause,* addressed the people in which he (the Messenger of Allah) said, "Every intoxicating liquor is unlawful for consumption."'"

H 11950, Ch. 10, h 2
Ali ibn Ibrahim has narrated from his father and Muhammad ibn Yahya has narrated from Ahmad ibn Muhammad all from ibn Mahbub from Khalid ibn Jarir from abu al-Rabi' al-Shamiy who has said the following:
"Abu 'Abd Allah, *'Alayhi al-Salam,* has said, 'Allah, most Majestic, most Glorious, has made the very substance of wine unlawful, in a small or large quantity. It is unlawful just as dead animals, blood and pork are unlawful. The Messenger of Allah, *O Allah, grant compensation to Muhammad and his family worthy of their services to Your cause,* made wine unlawful and all intoxicating liquor. Whatever the Messenger of Allah has made unlawful, Allah, most Majestic, most Glorious, also has made it unlawful.'"

H 11951, Ch. 10, h 3

Humayd ibn Ziyad has narrated from has narrated from al-Hassan ibn Muhammad ibn Sama'ah from Ahmad ibn al-Hassan al-Mithamiy from 'Abd al-Rahman ibn Zayd ibn Aslam from his father from 'Ata' ibn Yasar who has said the following:

"Abu Ja'far, *'Alayhi al-Salam,* has said that the Messenger of Allah, *O Allah, grant compensation to Muhammad and his family worthy of their services to Your cause,* has said, 'All intoxicating liquor is unlawful and every intoxicating liquor is wine.'"

H 11952, Ch. 10, h 4

Muhammad ibn Yahya has narrated from Ahmad ibn Muhammad from Ali ibn al-Hakam from Mu'awiyah ibn Wahab who has said the following:

"I once said to abu 'Abd Allah, *'Alayhi al-Salam,* that a man of the virtuous ones among your followers has asked me to ask you about al-Nabidh (wine) so I can describe it for him from you. He (the Imam) said, 'I describe it for you as the Messenger of Allah has said, 'Every intoxicating liquor is unlawful and whatever in a large quantity is intoxicating liquor, it in a small amount is unlawful.' I then asked, 'Can a large quantity of water make a small quantity of what is unlawful as lawful?' He (the Imam) then shook his hand like moving back something with the palm of his hand twice, saying, 'No, no.'"

H 11953, Ch. 10, h 5

Abu Ali al-Ash'ariy has narrated from Muhammad ibn 'Abd al-Jabbar from Muhammad ibn 'Isma'il from Ali ibn al-Nu'man from Muhammad ibn Marwan from al-Fudayl ibn Yasar who has said the following:

"I once asked abu Ja'far, *'Alayhi al-Salam,* about al-Nabidh. He (the Imam) said, 'Allah, most Majestic, most Glorious, had made the very substance of wine unlawful and the Messenger of Allah, *O Allah, grant compensation to Muhammad and his family worthy of their services to Your cause,* has made every intoxicating liquor unlawful.'"

H 11954, Ch. 10, h 6

It is narrated from the narrator of the previous *Hadith* from Muhammad ibn 'Abd Jabbar from Safwan ibn Yahya from Kulayb al-Asadiy who has said the following:

"I once asked abu 'Abd Allah, *'Alayhi al-Salam,* about al-Nabidh. He (the Imam) said that once the Messenger of Allah addressed the people and said, 'O people, all intoxicating liquor is unlawful. You must take notice that whatever in large quantity is intoxicating liquor, it in a small quantity also is unlawful.'"

H 11955, Ch. 10, h 7

Muhammad ibn Yahya has narrated from Ahmad ibn Muhammad from Ali ibn al-Hakam from Safwan al-Jammal who has said the following:

"I liked al-Nabidh a great deal and I said to abu 'Abd Allah, *'Alayhi al-Salam,* 'I pray to Allah to keep my soul in service for your cause, I want to describe al-Nabidh before you.' He (the Imam) said, 'No, allow me to describe it for you. The Messenger of Allah, *O Allah, grant compensation to Muhammad and his family worthy of their services to Your cause,* has said, "Every intoxicating liquor is unlawful and whatever in large quantity is intoxicating liquor, it in a small quantity is also unlawful."' I then asked, 'What is this al-Nabidh for drinking in the courtyard of al-Ka'bah?' He (the Imam) said to me, 'This was not the drinking place. The drinking place is Zamzam. Do you know who first changed it?' I replied, 'No' He (the Imam) said, 'Al-'Abbas ibn 'Abd al-Muttalib had a Habalah. Do you know what a Habalah is?' I replied, 'No, I do not know.' He (the Imam) said, 'It is grapes. He would soak raisins in the morning for them to drink it in the evening and soak it in the evening for them to drink in the morning. It was done to reduce the thickness of water for people but these people have crossed the limits so do not drink or go near it.'"

H 11956, Ch. 10, h 8

A number of our people have narrated from Ahmad ibn abu 'Abd Allah from 'Uthman ibn 'Isa from Sama'ah who has said the following:

"I once asked him (the Imam), *'Alayhi al-Salam,* if dates and raisins can be cooked for al-Nabidh. He (the Imam) said, 'No.' He (the Imam) said, 'All intoxicating liquor is unlawful and the Messenger of Allah, *O Allah, grant compensation to Muhammad and his family worthy of their services to Your cause,* has said, "Whatever in large quantity is intoxicating liquor, it in a small quantity is also unlawful."' He (the Imam) said, 'Al-Khamirah (yeast) which is murky is not proper for al-Nabidh.'"

H 11957, Ch. 10, h 9

Ali ibn Ibrahim has narrated from his father from ibn abu 'Umayr from 'Umar ibn 'Udhaynah from al-Fudayl ibn Yasar who has said the following:

"One day abu 'Abd Allah, *'Alayhi al-Salam,* initiating from himself and without my asking said, 'The Messenger of Allah, *O Allah, grant compensation to Muhammad and his family worthy of their services to Your cause,* has said, all intoxicating liquor is unlawful.' I then asked saying, 'I pray to Allah to keep you well, is all of it unlawful?' He (the Imam) said, 'Yes, even one sip is unlawful.'"

H 11958, Ch. 10, h 10

Muhammad ibn Yahya has narrated from Ahmad ibn Muhammad ibn 'Isa from al-Husayn ibn Sa'id and Muhammad ibn 'Isma'il all from Muhammad ibn al-Fudayl from abu al-Sabbah al-Kinaniy who has said the following:

"Abu 'Abd Allah, *'Alayhi al-Salam,* has said, 'Allah has made wine unlawful, regardless of its being a small or large quantity as He has made dead animals, blood and pork unlawful. The Messenger of Allah, *O Allah, grant compensation to Muhammad and his family worthy of their services to Your cause,* of drinks, has made intoxicating liquor unlawful. Whatever the Messenger of Allah has made unlawful Allah, most Majestic, most Glorious, has also made unlawful', and he (the Imam) said, 'Whatever in large quantity is intoxicating liquor, it is unlawful in small quantity also.'"

H 11959, Ch. 10, h 11

Ali ibn Ibrahim has narrated from his father from ibn abu 'Umayr from 'Abd al-Rahman ibn al-*Hajj*aj who has said the following:

"I once asked for permission from abu 'Abd Allah, *'Alayhi al-Salam,* for a certain person of our people and he asked him (the Imam) about al-Nabidh. He (the Imam) said, 'It is lawful.' He said, 'I pray to Allah to keep you well, I asked about al-Nabidh which is placed in al-'Akr (murky) to boil until it becomes intoxicating.' Abu 'Abd Allah, *'Alayhi al-Salam,* said that the Messenger of Allah has said, 'All intoxicating liquor is unlawful.' He said, 'I pray to Allah to keep you well, among us in Iraq they say that the Messenger of Allah thereby meant the cup that is intoxicating liquor.' Abu 'Abd Allah, *'Alayhi al-Salam,* said, 'Whatever is intoxicating liquor in large quantity, it is unlawful in small quantity also.' He (the man) then said, 'Can I break it (intoxicating effect) with water?' Abu 'Abd Allah, *'Alayhi al-Salam,* said, 'No, how can water make lawful what is unlawful? Have fear of Allah, most Majestic, most Glorious, and do not drink it.'"

H 11960, Ch. 10, h 12

Ali ibn Ibrahim has narrated from his father from Hanan who has said the following:

"I once heard a man asking abu 'Abd Allah, *'Alayhi al-Salam,* about al-Nabidh and that abu Maryam drinks it and that he thinks he (the Imam) has commanded him to drink it. He (the Imam) said, 'I seek protection with Allah, most Majestic, most Glorious, against commanding to drink intoxicating liquor. This by Allah is something about which I do not fear (Taqiyah, use caution before) the Sultan or people other than the Sultan. The Messenger of Allah, *O Allah, grant compensation to Muhammad and his family worthy of their services to Your cause,* has said, 'All intoxicating liquor is unlawful. What is intoxicating in large quantity, it is unlawful in small quantity also.'"

H 11961, Ch. 10, h 13

A number of our people have narrated from Sahl ibn Ziyad from Muhammad ibn 'Abd al-Hamid from Yunus ibn Ya'qub from 'Amr ibn Marwan who has said the following:

"I once said to abu 'Abd Allah, *'Alayhi al-Salam,* 'I may go with these people for dinner and they bring al-Nabidh thereafter. If I do not drink I fear they may say, 'He is of so and so (Ja'fariy). What must I do in such case?' He (the Imam) said, 'You can break it with water.' I then asked, 'When I break it with water can I then drink it?' He (the Imam) said, 'No, you cannot drink.'"

H 11962, Ch. 10, h 14

Sahl ibn Ziyad has narrated from Ali ibn Ma'bad from al-Hassan ibn Ali from abu Khidash from Ali ibn 'Isma'il from Muhammad ibn 'Abdah al-Naysaburiy who has said the following:

"I once asked abu 'Abd Allah, *'Alayhi al-Salam,* if a cup of wine and a cup of al-Nabidh are equal. He (the Imam) said, 'Yes, they are equal.' I then asked if the penalty is also the same. He (the Imam) said, 'It is equal.'"

H 11963, Ch. 10, h 15

A number of our people have narrated from Sahl ibn Ziyad and Muhammad ibn Yahya has narrated from Ahmad ibn Muhammad all from Ali ibn al-Hakam from abu al-Mighra' from 'Umar ibn Hanzalah who has said the following:

"I once asked abu 'Abd Allah, *'Alayhi al-Salam,* about the case of a cup of intoxicating liquor on which water is poured until its bad effect is gone and also its intoxicating effect. He (the Imam) said, 'No, by Allah, even if one drop of it is dropped in a *hub* (a large water container) the whole *hub* must be thrown out.'"

H 11964, Ch. 10, h 16

Muhammad ibn Yahya has narrated from Ahmad ibn Muhammad from Muhammad ibn `Isma`il and Ali ibn Ibrahim has narrated from his father from Hanan ibn Sadir from Yazid ibn Khalifah and he is a man from banu al-Harith ibn Ka`b who has said the following:

"I once went to al-Madinah when Ziyad ibn 'Ubayd Allah al-Harithiy was the governor. I asked permission to visit abu 'Abd Allah, *'Alayhi al-Salam.* I then visited and offered him (the Imam) the greeting of peace and took my place. I then said to abu 'Abd Allah, *'Alayhi al-Salam,* 'I am from banu al-Harith ibn Ka`b and Allah, most Majestic, most Glorious, has granted me guidance to your love and affection toward *Ahl al-Bayt.* He (the narrator) has said that abu 'Abd Allah, *'Alayhi al-Salam,* then asked, 'How were you guided to love of Ahl al-Bayt? By Allah our love in banu al-Harith ibn Ka`b is very little.' He (the narrator) has said that I then said, 'I pray to Allah to keep my soul in service for your cause, I have a Khurasaniy slave. He works as bleacher and he has four fellows from his town. They invite each other every Friday to the place of one of them. In every five Fridays, my slave has one day and he prepares al-Nabidh and meat for them. When they finish food and meat he brings a bowl and fills it with al-Nabidh, then brings a jug, when one of them wants to drink he is told not to drink until he says, *'O Allah, grant compensation to Muhammad and his family worthy of their services to Your cause.'* I received guidance to loving you because of this slave. He (the narrator) has said that he (the Imam) said to me, 'Give him good advice, convey my greeting of peace to him and say to him, 'Ja`far ibn Muhammad says to you, "You must look into the drink that you drink. If a large quantity of it is intoxicating liquor then do not go close to its small quantity also; the Messenger of Allah, *O Allah, grant compensation to Muhammad and his family worthy of their services to Your cause,* has said, 'All intoxicating liquor is unlawful.' He (the Messenger of Allah) said, 'Whatever is intoxicating liquor in large quantity, it in a small quantity is also unlawful.'"" He (the narrator) has said that I went to al-Kufah and conveyed the greeting of peace to him from Ja`far ibn Muhammad, *'Alayhi al-Salam.* He wept and asked me, 'Did Ja`far ibn Muhammad pay this much attention to me? He (the Imam) offered to me the greeting of peace!' I then said, 'Yes, he (the Imam) did and he (the Imam) instructed me to inform you that you must look to the drink which you drink. If it is intoxicating liquor in large quantity, then do not go near to its small quantity; the Messenger of Allah, *O Allah, grant compensation to Muhammad and his family worthy of their services to Your cause,* has said, "All intoxicating liquor is unlawful and whatever is intoxicating liquor in large quantity is unlawful in small quantity also." He (the Imam) has recommended me to be good to you. Therefore, I set you free. You can go free for the sake of Allah, most High.' The slave then said, 'It is the kind of drink that will never go in my belly as long as I live in this world.'"

H 11965, Ch. 10, h 17

Muhammad ibn Yahya has narrated from Ahmad ibn Muhammad from Ali ibn al-Hakam from Kulayb ibn Mu`awiyah has said the following:

"Abu Basir and his friends drank al-Nabidh and they broke it with water. I mentioned it before abu 'Abd Allah, *'Alayhi al-Salam,* and he (the Imam) said to me, 'How can water make intoxicating liquor lawful? Command them not to drink from it in large or small quantities.' I then said that they say, 'The approval of the family of Muhammad makes it lawful for them.' He (the Imam) said, 'Why should family of Muhammad make intoxicating liquor lawful when they do not drink it in large or small quantities? You must refrain from drinking it.' We then came together before abu 'Abd Allah, *'Alayhi al-Salam,* and abu Basir said, 'This has come to us from you as such and such.' He (the Imam, *'Alayhi al-Salam*) said, 'You must accept it as true, O abu Muhammad, water does not make intoxicating liquor lawful. You must not drink it in large or small quantities.'"

Chapter 11 - Wine is Prohibited because of its Effects; whatever has an Effect as the Effect of Wine. it is Wine

H 11966, Ch. 11, h 1

A number of our people have narrated from Sahl ibn Ziyad from al-Hassan ibn Ali ibn Yaqtin from Ya'qub ibn Ali ibn Yaqtin from his brother Ali ibn Yaqtin who has said the following:

"Abu Ibrahim, *'Alayhi al-Salam,* has said, 'Allah, the most Blessed, the most High, has not made wine unlawful because of its name. He has made it unlawful because of its consequences, therefore, whatever, works as wine does, it then is wine.'"

H 11967, Ch. 11, h 2

Muhammad ibn Yahya has narrated from Ahmad ibn Muhammad from al-Hassan ibn Ali ibn Yaqtin from his brother Al-Husayn ibn Ali ibn Yaqtin from his father Ali ibn Yaqtin who has said the following:

"Abu al-Hassan, al-Madiy, *'Alayhi al-Salam,* has said, 'Allah, most Majestic, most Glorious, has not made wine unlawful because of its name. He has made it unlawful because of its consequences, therefore, whatever, has the same consequence as that of wine, it then is wine.'"

H 11968, Ch. 11, h 3

A number of our people have narrated from Sahl ibn Ziyad and Ali ibn Ibrahim has narrated from his father all from 'Amr ibn 'Uthman from Muhammad ibn 'Abd Allah from certain persons of our people who has said the following:

"I once asked abu 'Abd Allah, *'Alayhi al-Salam,* 'Why has Allah prohibited wine?' He (the Imam) said, 'He has prohibited it because of its effects and the destructive effects that it leaves behind.'"

H 11969, Ch. 11, h 4

A number of our people have narrated from Sahl ibn Ziyad from Mu'awiyah ibn Hakim from abu Malik al-Hadramiy from abu al-Jarud who has said the following:

"I once asked abu Ja'far, *'Alayhi al-Salam,* 'Why Allah has prohibited wine?' He (the Imam) said, 'He has prohibited it because of what it does and its destructive effects.'"

H 11970, Ch. 11, h 5

A number of our people have narrated from Sahl ibn Ziyad from Mu'awiyah ibn Hakim from abu Malik al-Hadramiy from abu al-Jarud who has said the following:

"I once asked abu Ja'far, *'Alayhi al-Salam,* about al-Nabidh; if it is wine. He (the Imam) said, 'Whatever upon drinking is more pleasurable than not drinking, it is wine.'"

Chapter 12 - Compulsion to Drink Wine as Medicine, in Thirst or in Fear (Taqiyah)

H 11971, Ch. 12, h 1

Muhammad ibn al-Hassan has narrated from certain persons of our people from Ibrahim ibn Khalid from 'Abd Allah ibn Waddah from abu Basir who has said the following:

"Once I was with abu 'Abd Allah, *'Alayhi al-Salam* when the mother of Khalid al-'Abdiyah visited him (the Imam). She said, 'I pray to Allah to keep my soul in service for your cause. I have a growling condition in my belly [I asked a women with such condition about it and she said] the physicians of Iraq have prescribed for her al-Nabidh with sawiq; but I have learned and I know that you dislike it and I like to ask you about it. He (the Imam) asked, 'What stops you from drinking it?' She replied, 'I have taken upon myself to follow your instructions in matters of my religion so upon my meeting with Allah, most Majestic, most Glorious, I will be able to tell Him that Ja'far ibn Muhammad commanded and prohibited me.' He (the Imam) asked, 'O abu Muhammad, do you hear this woman and these issues? No, by Allah, I will not give you permission, not even for one drop of it and you must not taste even one drop of it because you, otherwise, will regret when the soul reaches here', pointing to his throat, 'Did you understand?' She replied, 'Yes, I understand.' He (the Imam) then said, 'A small amount of it (wine) that can hardly moisten an applicator of kohl (eyeliner) to the eye can make a whole *hub* (a large water container) filthy.' He (the Imam) said it three times.'"

H 11972, Ch. 12, h 2

Ali ibn Ibrahim has narrated from his father from ibn abu 'Umayr from 'Umar ibn 'Udhaynah who has said the following:

"I once wrote to abu 'Abd Allah, *'Alayhi al-Salam,* and asked about a man to whom a medicine for curing hemorrhoid gases is sent to drink in an amount that in the form of hard al-Nabidh makes one drunk. He does not drink it for pleasure but as medicine.' He (the Imam) said, 'No, not even one sip of it is lawful.' He (the Imam) then said, 'Allah, most Majestic, most Glorious, has not placed any cure as medicine in what He has prohibited.'"

H 11973, Ch. 12, h 3

A number of our people have narrated from Sahl ibn Ziyad from Ali ibn Asbat who has said the following:

"My father has informed me that he once was with abu 'Abd Allah, *'Alayhi al-Salam,* when a man said to him (the Imam), 'I pray to Allah to keep my soul in service for your cause, (I suffer from the) gases of hemorrhoids. Nothing suits me except drinking al-Nabidh.' He (the narrator) has said that he (the Imam) said, 'What do you have to do with what Allah, most Majestic, most Glorious, and the Messenger of Allah have made unlawful?' He (the Imam) said it three times. He (the Imam) then said, 'You must use this immersed (dates) which is immersed in water in the evening to drink in the morning and immersed in the morning to drink in the evening.' He said, 'This causes bloating in the belly.' He (the Imam) said, 'I can guide you to what is more beneficial than this. You must pray because it is cure for all illnesses.' He (the narrator) has said that we then asked him (the Imam), 'Is all of it, small and large quantities unlawful?' He (the Imam) said, 'Yes, it is unlawful in large quantity as well as in small quantity.'"

H 11974, Ch. 12, h 4
Abu Ali al-Ash'ariy has narrated from Muhammad ibn 'Abd al-Jabbar from Safwan ibn Yahya from ibn Muskan from al-Halabiy who has said the following:

"I once asked abu 'Abd Allah, *'Alayhi al-Salam,* about a medicine which is made in dough with wine. He (the Imam) said, 'No, by Allah I do not like to look at it, so how will I use it as medicine? It is like the fat of pork or flesh of pork. Why then certain people use it as medicine?'"

H 11975, Ch. 12, h 5
Muhammad ibn Yahya has narrated from Ahmad ibn Muhammad from Muhammad ibn Khalid and al-Husayn ibn Sa'id all from al-Nadr ibn Suwayd from al-Husayn ibn 'Abd Allah ibn 'Abd al-Hamid from 'Amr from ibn al-Jumhur who has said the following:

"I once visited abu 'Abd Allah, *'Alayhi al-Salam,* during the days that he had come to Iraq. He (the Imam) told me to visit `Isma'il ibn Ja'far because he complains and see what kind of pain has made him suffer then describe for him (the Imam) the pain he feels. I then left him (the Imam) to see `Isma'il and asked him about his pain that he felt. He explained it to me and I prescribed a medicine in which al-Nabidh existed. `Isma'il said, 'Al-Nabidh is unlawful and I belong to a family who do not use unlawful things as medicine.'"

H 11976, Ch. 12, h 6
Muhammad ibn Yahya has narrated from Muhammad ibn Ahmad from Ya'qub ibn Yazid from Muhammad ibn al-Hassan al-Mithamiy from Mu'awiyah ibn 'Ammar who has said the following:

"A man once asked abu 'Abd Allah, *'Alayhi al-Salam,* about a medicine which is made into dough to be used as Kohl (eyeliner) for the eyes. Abu 'Abd Allah, *'Alayhi al-Salam,* said, 'Allah, most Majestic, most Glorious, has not placed cures in things that He has made unlawful.'"

H 11977, Ch. 12, h 7
It is narrated from the narrator of the previous *Hadith* from Ahmad ibn Muhammad from Marwak ibn 'Ubayd from a man who has said the following:

"Abu 'Abd Allah, *'Alayhi al-Salam,* has said, 'If one uses intoxicating things as eye medicine with an applicator of medicine to the eye Allah, most Majestic, most Glorious, will apply as such with an applicator of fire.'"

H 11978, Ch. 12, h 8
Muhammad ibn Yahya has narrated from Ahmad ibn Muhammad from al-Husayn ibn Sa'id from al-Nadr ibn Suwayd from al-Husayn ibn 'Abd Allah al-Arjaniy from Malik al-Misma'iy from Qayed ibn Talhah who has said the following:

"I once asked abu 'Abd Allah, *'Alayhi al-Salam,* about al-Nabidh which is placed in medicine. He (the Imam) said, 'No, it is not proper for one to seek cure from unlawful things.'"

H 11979, Ch. 12, h 9

Ali ibn Muhammad ibn Bandar has narrated from Ahmad ibn abu 'Abd Allah from a number of our people from Ali ibn Asbat from Ali ibn Ja'far who has said the following:

"I once asked my brother, abu al-Hassan *'Alayhi al-Salam,* about kohl made into dough with al-Nabidh; if it is proper. He (the Imam) said, 'No, it is not proper.'"

H 11980, Ch. 12, h 10

A number of our people have narrated from Sahl ibn Ziyad from ibn Mahbub from ibn Ri'ab from al-Halabiy who has said the following:

"Once abu 'Abd Allah, *'Alayhi al-Salam,* was asked about a medicine which is made into dough with wine. He (the Imam) said, 'I do not like to look at it or smell it; so why should I use it as medicine?'"

H 11981, Ch. 12, h 11

Abu Ali al-Ash'ariy has narrated from al-Hassan ibn Ali al-Kufiy from 'Uthman ibn 'Isa from Sa'id ibn Yasar who has said the following:

"Abu 'Abd Allah, *'Alayhi al-Salam,* has said, 'There is no Taqiyah (maintaining caution because of fear) in the case of al-Nabidh (wine).'"

H 11982, Ch. 12, h 12

Ali ibn Ibrahim has narrated from his father from Hammad from Hariz from Zurarah from more than one person who has said the following:

"I once asked abu Ja'far, *'Alayhi al-Salam,* about wiping on slippers because of Taqiyah (caution due to fear). He (the Imam) said, 'There is no Taqiyah (caution because of fear) in three things.' I then asked, 'What are they?' He (the Imam) said, 'It is drinking wine,' or he said, 'Drinking intoxicating liquor, wiping on slippers and Mut'ah (advantage) of *al-Hajj.*'"

Chapter 13 - Al-Nabidh (A kind of Wine)

H 11983, Ch. 13, h 1

Muhammad ibn Yahya has narrated from Ahmad ibn Muhammad from Muhammad ibn 'Isma'il from Hanan ibn Sadir who has said the following:

"I once heard a man who asked abu 'Abd Allah, *'Alayhi al-Salam,* 'What do you say about al-Nabidh? Abu Maryam drinks it and he thinks that you have commanded him to drink.' He (the Imam) said, 'Abu Maryam has spoken the truth. He asked me about al-Nabidh but not about intoxicating liquor.' He (the Imam) then said, 'Intoxicating liquor is as such that one must not even seek Taqiyah (caution because of fear) before al-Sultan or others. The Messenger of Allah, *O Allah, grant compensation to Muhammad and his family worthy of their services to Your cause,* has said, "Intoxicating liquor is unlawful and whatever is intoxicating in large quantity is unlawful in small quantity also."' The man then said, 'I pray to Allah to keep my soul in service for your cause, what is al-Nabidh which you allowed abu Maryam to use?' He (the Imam) said, 'My father, *'Alayhi al-Salam,* would order the servant to bring a bowl and place raisins in it; wash them clean, place it in a bowl then pour on it three or four times as much water. Then keep it overnight to drink it in the morning and place it in a bowl in the morning to drink it in the evening. He (the Imam) commanded the servant to wash the bowl after every three days to remove the stain, if it had formed. If you want al-Nabidh, this is al-Nabidh.'"

H 11984, Ch. 13, h 2

Muhammad ibn Yahya has narrated from Ahmad ibn Muhammad from Ali ibn al-Hakam from and Muhammad ibn `Isma`il Ahmad ibn Muhammad from Muhammad ibn Ja`far abu al-`Abbas al-Kufiy from Muhammad ibn Khalid all from Sayf ibn `Amirah from Mansur who has said that narrated to me Ayyub ibn Rashid who has said the following:

"I once heard abu al-Balad ask abu 'Abd Allah, *'Alayhi al-Salam,* about al-Nabidh and he (the Imam) said, 'It is not unlawful.' He then said, 'The residue is placed in it.' Abu 'Abd Allah, *'Alayhi al-Salam,* then said, 'It is the worst drink, however, you can soak it in water in the morning to drink in the evening.' He then said, 'I pray to Allah to keep my soul in service for your cause, it is bad for our bellies.' He (the Imam) said, 'It is much worse for your bellies if you drink what is unlawful.'"

H 11985, Ch. 13, h 3

Al-Husayn ibn Muhammad has narrated from Mu`alla' ibn Muhammad and A number of our people have narrated from Sahl ibn Ziyad all from Muhammad ibn Ali al-Hamadaniy from Ali ibn 'Abd Allah al-Hannat from Sama`ah ibn Mehran from al-Kalbiy al-Nassabah who has said the following:

"I once asked abu 'Abd Allah, *'Alayhi al-Salam,* about al-Nabidh. He (the Imam) said, 'It is lawful.' I said, 'We soak it, then place the residue in it and other things.' He (the Imam) said, 'Shashsh! That is putrid wine.' I then asked, 'I pray to Allah to keep my soul in service for your cause, what kind of al-Nabidh is what you mention?' He (the Imam) said, 'People of al-Madinah once complained before the Holy Prophet, *O Allah, grant compensation to Muhammad and his family worthy of their services to Your cause,* about the change in their water and the ruined condition of their health. He commanded them to make al-Nabidh. A man commanded his servant to make al-Nabidh for him. He would take a handful of dates and throw it in *al-Shin* (water container) and from this they would drink and cleanse themselves.' I then asked, 'How many dates they would use?' He (the Imam) said, 'Whatever a handful picks or perhaps two handfuls.' He (the Imam) then said, 'Perhaps it was one handful or two handfuls.' I then asked, 'What was the size of *al-Shin* (water container)?' He (the Imam) said, 'Between forty to eighty or more.' I then asked, 'Is it in *ritl*?' He (the Imam) said, 'Yes, it is in *ritl* of Iraqi measurement.'"

H 11986, Ch. 13, h 4

Muhammad ibn Yahya has narrated from Ahmad ibn Muhammad from al-Husayn ibn Sa`id from Ibrahim ibn abu al-Bald from his father [from more than one person who were with him] who has said the following:

"I once was with abu Ja`far, *'Alayhi al-Salam,* and I said, 'O Jariyah (girl or slave-girl) give me some water.' He (the Imam) said to her, 'Give him from my al-Nabidh.' She then brought al-Nabidh which was a dry date in a cup of brass.' I then said, 'People of al-Kufah do not agree with it.' He (the Imam) asked, 'What is their al-Nabidh?' I said, 'They place in it al-Qa`wah.' He (the Imam) asked, 'What is al-Qa`wah?' I said, 'It is al-Dadhiy.' He (the Imam) asked, 'What is al-Dadhiy?' I said, 'It is residue of dates.' He (the Imam) said, 'It stains the pot by the time it rises, then boils, then it becomes intoxicating liquor; then it is used for drink.' He (the Imam) then said, 'This is unlawful.'"

H 11987, Ch. 13, h 5

A number of our people have narrated from Sahl ibn Ziyad from Ja'far ibn Muhammad from Ibrahim ibn abu al-Balad who has said the following:

"I once visited abu Ja'far, ibn al-Rida', *'Alayhi al-Salam,* and said to him, 'I want to touch your belly with my belly.' He (the Imam) said, 'Here O abu 'Isma'il,' He uncovered his belly and I uncovered my belly and touched his belly with my belly. He then made me sit and called for a plate of raisins. I ate and he began to speak and complained about his stomach. I felt thisty and asked for water. He (the Imam) said, 'O Jariyah, give him from my al-Nabidh. She brought for me al-Nabidh of Maris (soaked) in a cup of brass. I drank and found it sweeter than honey. I then said to him, 'This has made your stomach upset.' He (the Imam) said, 'This is dates from the charity of the Holy Prophet, *O Allah, grant compensation to Muhammad and his family worthy of their services to Your cause.* It is taken in the morning and water is poured on it. The girl soaks it and I drink it after food and during the day. In the evening the girl takes it and the people of the house drink.' I then said, 'People of al-Kufah do not agree with it.' He (the Imam) asked, 'What is their al-Nabidh?' I said, 'It is taken from dates of finiqiy and al-Qa'wah is placed in it.' He (the Imam) asked, 'What is al-Qa'wah?' I said, 'It is al-Dadhiy.' He (the Imam) asked, 'What is al-Dadhiy?' I said, 'It is grain which is brought from al-Basrah. It is thrown in al-Nabidh until it boils and becomes intoxicating liquor; then it is used as a drink.' He (the Imam) said, 'That is unlawful.'"

H 11988, Ch. 13, h 6

Ali ibn Ibrahim has narrated from his father from ibn abu 'Umayr from 'Abd al-Rahman ibn *al-Hajj*aj who has said the following:

"I once asked for permission to visit abu 'Abd Allah, *'Alayhi al-Salam,* for a certain person of our people and he asked him (the Imam) about al-Nabidh. He (the Imam) said, 'It is lawful.' He then said, 'I pray to Allah to keep you well, I ask about al-Nabidh in which residue is placed, then is boiled until it becomes intoxicating liquor.' Abu 'Abd Allah, *'Alayhi al-Salam,* said that the Messenger of Allah, *O Allah, grant compensation to Muhammad and his family worthy of their services to Your cause,* has said, 'All intoxicating liquor is unlawful.'"

H 11989, Ch. 13, h 7

Muhammad ibn al-Hassan and Ali ibn Muhammad ibn Bandar all from Ibrahim ibn Ishaq from 'Abd Allah ibn Hammad from Muhammad ibn Ja'far from his father who has said the following:

"Once a people from Yemen came to the Messenger of Allah, *O Allah, grant compensation to Muhammad and his family worthy of their services to Your cause,* to ask him (the Messenger of Allah) for the guidance of their religion and he (the Messenger of Allah) answered them. All of the people then left. When they went a certain distance certain ones among them said, 'We forgot to ask the Messenger of Allah about what is important to us.' The people disembarked and sent a delegate to the Messenger of Allah who said, 'O Messenger of Allah, people have sent us to you to ask about al-Nabidh.' The Messenger of Allah asked. 'What is al-Nabidh? Describe it for me.' They said it is taken from dates which is placed in a pot, then water is pour on it until it is full, then fire is lit beneath. It is cooked, then it is taken to be placed it in another pot, then water is poured on it to soak, then it is filtered with a cloth, then it is placed in another pot and the residue from before is poured in it. It then rises and boils, then it sits down on the residue.' The Messenger of Allah then said, 'O you, you have said a great deal. Is it intoxicating?' He replied, 'Yes, it is intoxicating.' He (the Messenger of Allah) said, 'All intoxicating substances are unlawful.' The delegate left and informed their people of what the Messenger of Allah had said. The people said, 'We must go back to the Messenger of Allah so we can hear what he (the Messenger of Allah) has said without anyone in between.' So all of the people came back and said, 'O Messenger of Allah, our land is vast and we farm. We cannot work without al-Nabidh.' The Messenger of Allah, *O Allah, grant compensation to Muhammad and his family worthy of their services to Your cause,* asked them to describe it for him (the Messenger of Allah). They described it for him (the Messenger of Allah) as their delegate had done. The Messenger of Allah asked, 'Does it intoxicate?' They replied, 'Yes, it does.' He (the Messenger of Allah) then said, 'All intoxicating substances are unlawful. It is a right on Allah to make the drinker of intoxicating liquor to drink of Tinah of Khabal. Do you know what Tinah of Khabal is?' They replied, 'No, we do not know.' He (the Messenger of Allah) said, 'It is the puss from the people of hellfire.'"

Chapter 14 - The Utensils

H 11990, Ch. 14, h 1
A number of our people have narrated from Ahmad ibn Muhammad ibn 'Isa from al-Husayn ibn Sa'id from Fadalah ibn Ayyub from 'Umar ibn Aban al-Kalbiy from Muhammad ibn Muslim who has said the following:

"I once asked one of the two Imam, (abu Ja'far or abu 'Abd Allah), *'Alayhim al-Salam,* about al-Nabidh which has stopped boiling. He (the Imam) said that the Messenger of Allah has said, 'All intoxicating substances are unlawful.' I then asked him (the Imam) about utensils. He (the Imam) has stated this *Hadith.* 'The Messenger of Allah, *O Allah grant compensation to Muhammad and his family worthy of their services to your cause,* has prohibited the use of al-Diba' (pumpkins) used in fermenting al-Nabidh. Also prohibited for such use is al-Hantam (the pot made of asphalt-coated clay), to which you have added oiled pottery, and al-Ghadar (what is made of palm tree trunks coated with asphalt) in which wine is brewed to make it of better quality.' I asked him (the Imam) about large green containers and lead. He (the Imam) said, 'It is not unlawful.'"

H 11991, Ch. 14, h 2
Ahmad ibn Muhammad has narrated from al-Husayn ibn Sa'id from al-Nadr ibn Suwayd from al-Qasim ibn Sulayman from Jarrah al-Mad'iniy who has said the following:

"Abu 'Abd Allah, *'Alayhi al-Salam,* prohibited all of intoxicating substances. He (the Imam) prohibited the use of containers made of curved palm tree trunks and pumpkins used as containers for fermentation of al-Nabidh. He (the Imam) said that the Messenger of Allah, *O Allah, grant compensation to Muhammad and his family worthy of their services to Your cause,* has said, 'Whatever is intoxicating in large quantity it is unlawful in small quantity also.'"

H 11992, Ch. 14, h 3

Ali ibn Ibrahim has narrated from his father from al-Hassan ibn Mahbub from Khalid ibn Jarir from abu al-Rabi' al-Shamiy who has said the following:

"Abu 'Abd Allah, *'Alayhi al-Salam,* has said that the Messenger of Allah, *O Allah, grant compensation to Muhammad and his family worthy of their services to Your cause,* prohibited all intoxicating substances, thus, all intoxicating substances are unlawful for consumption. I then asked about utensils in which such things are made. He (the Imam) said, 'The Messenger of Allah prohibited the use of pumpkins as pots (used in fermentation of raw material for liquor), *al-Danan,* casks (a large container coated with asphalt), containers of pottery and palm tree trunks (curved as a container used in fermentation of raw material for intoxicating substances) in the time of ignorance before Islam.'"

Chapter 15 - The Juice (grape juice)

H 11993, Ch. 15, h 1

Ali ibn Ibrahim has narrated from his father from Ahmad ibn Muhammad from ibn abu Nasr from Hammad ibn 'Uthaman who has said the following:

"Abu 'Abd Allah, *'Alayhi al-Salam,* has said, 'Juice (grape juice) is not unlawful until it boils.'"

H 11994, Ch. 15, h 2

Ali ibn Ibrahim has narrated from his father from ibn abu 'Umayr from Muhammad ibn 'Asem who has said the following:

"Abu 'Abd Allah, *'Alayhi al-Salam,* has said, 'It is not unlawful to drink juice (grape juice) up to six days.' Ibn abu 'Umayr has said, 'It means that it does not become intoxicating liquor and unlawful before it comes to a boil.'"

H 11995, Ch. 15, h 3

Muhammad ibn Yahya has narrated from Ahmad ibn Muhammad from abu Yahya al-Wasitiy from Hammad ibn 'Uthaman who has said the following:

"I once asked abu 'Abd Allah, *'Alayhi al-Salam,* about drinking juice (grape juice). He (the Imam) said, 'You can drink it before it is boiled. Once it is boiled then do not drink.' I then asked saying, 'I pray to Allah to keep my soul in service for your cause, what is boiling?' He (the Imam) said, 'It is fluctuation (fermentation) and change.'"

H 11996, Ch. 15, h 4

Muhammad ibn Yahya has narrated from Ahmad ibn Muhammad from ibn Faddal from al-Hassan ibn al-Jahm from Dharih who has said the following:

"I once heard abu 'Abd Allah, *'Alayhi al-Salam,* saying, 'When juice (grape juice) begins to simmer or boil it becomes unlawful to use it for drink.'"

Chapter 16 - The Juice which Fire has Touched

H 11997, Ch. 16, h 1

Ali ibn Ibrahim has narrated from his father from ibn Mahbub from 'Abd Allah ibn Sinan who has said the following:

"Abu 'Abd Allah, *'Alayhi al-Salam,* has said, 'Any juice (grape juice) which fire has touched is unlawful to use until two-thirds of it is evaporated and only one-third has remained.'"

H 11998, Ch. 16, h 2
Muhammad ibn Yahya has narrated from Ahmad ibn Muhammad ibn abu Najran from Muhammad ibn al-Haytham from a man who has said the following:

"I once asked abu 'Abd Allah, *'Alayhi al-Salam,* about grape juice which is cooked on fire until it boils for one hour; then the owner drinks it. He (the Imam) said, 'If it changes and boils, it then becomes devoid of goodness until two-thirds of it is evaporated and only one-third has remained.'"

Chapter 17 - Al-Tila' (The One-Third Juice (grape juice) that has Remained after the Evaporation of the other Two-Thirds)

H 11999, Ch. 17, h 1
Muhammad ibn Yahya has narrated from Ahmad ibn Muhammad Ali ibn al-Hakam from Ali ibn abu Hamzah from abu Basir who has said the following:

"I once heard abu 'Abd Allah, *'Alayhi al-Salam,* saying, when he was asked about al-Tila'; 'If it is cooked and boiled until its two-thirds have evaporated and only one-third has remained it then is lawful for use and if it has evaporated less it is devoid of goodness.'"

H 12000, Ch. 17, h 2
Ali ibn Ibrahim has narrated from his father from 'Abd Allah ibn al-Mughirah from 'Abd Allah ibn Sinan who has said the following:

"Abu 'Abd Allah, *'Alayhi al-Salam,* has said, 'If juice (grape juice) is boiled until its two-thirds are evaporated and only one-third has remained, it then is lawful for use.'"

H 12001, Ch. 17, h 3
Abu Ali al-Ash'ariy has narrated from Muhammad ibn 'Abd al-Jabbar from Mansur ibn Hazim from ibn abu Ya'fur who has said the following:

"Abu 'Abd Allah, *'Alayhi al-Salam,* has said, 'If *al-Tila'* (the remaining boiled juice) is more than one-third it is unlawful for use.'"

H 12002, Ch. 17, h 4
Ali ibn Ibrahim has narrated from his father from ibn abu 'Umayr from al-Hassan ibn 'Atiyyah from 'Umar ibn Yazid who has said the following:

"I once asked abu 'Abd Allah, *'Alayhi al-Salam,* about the case of a man who recommends the use of boiled juice (grape juice) and he is not one of our people. He (the Imam) said, 'If he is one who considers intoxicating substances lawful, then do not use it but if he considers it unlawful then you can use it for drink,' or that he (the Imam) said, 'You can drink it.'"

H 12003, Ch. 17, h 5
Ibn abu 'Umayr has narrated from 'Umar ibn Yazid who has said the following:

"Abu 'Abd Allah, *'Alayhi al-Salam,* has said, 'When two-thirds of juice (grape juice) is evaporated (because of boiling) then you can drink it.'"

H 12004, Ch. 17, h 6

Muhammad ibn Yahya has narrated from Ahmad ibn Muhammad from Ali ibn al-Hakam from Mu'awiyah ibn Wahab who has said the following:

"I once asked abu 'Abd Allah, *'Alayhi al-Salam,* about *al-Bakhtaj* (boiled juice). He (the Imam) said, 'If it is sweet with an indication of two-thirds being evaporated and the owner also says that two-thirds have been evaporated, only one-third has remained, then you can drink it.'"

H 12005, Ch. 17, h 7

Muhammad ibn Yahya has narrated from Ahmad ibn Muhammad from Muhammad ibn 'Isma'il from Yunus ibn Ya'qub from Mu'awiyah ibn 'Ammar who has said the following:

"I once asked abu 'Abd Allah, *'Alayhi al-Salam,* about the case of a man who knows the truth and brings boiled juice (grape juice). He says that it is cooked until two-thirds are evaporated but I know that he drinks even when only half is evaporated; if I can drink it while he drinks only when one-half is evaporated. He (the Imam) said, 'Do not drink it.' I then asked about the case of a man who is not of the people who know the truth, and we do not know him but he drinks only when two-thirds of juice are evaporated. He does not consider it lawful to drink after one-half is evaporated and he informs us about a boiled juice (grape juice), says that its two-thirds have evaporated and only one-third is left; if we can drink it. He (the Imam) said, 'Yes, you can drink it.'"

H 12006, Ch. 17, h 8

Al-Husayn ibn Muhammad has narrated from Ahmad ibn Ishaq from Bakr ibn Muhammad from ibn abu Ya'fur who has said the following:

"Abu 'Abd Allah, *'Alayhi al-Salam,* has said, 'If one drinks intoxicating al-Nabidh his testimony is not acceptable in any of the drinks, even if he believes in what you believe.'"

H 12007, Ch. 17, h 9

Certain persons of our people have narrated from Muhammad ibn 'Abd al-Hamid from Sayf ibn 'Amirah from Mansur from ibn abu Ya'fur who has said the following:

"If *al-Tila*' is more than one-third even by one *ritl* (a certain unit of measurement) it then is unlawful.'"

H 12008, Ch. 17, h 10

A number of our people have narrated from Sahl ibn Ziyad from Musa ibn al-Qasim from Ali ibn Ja'far from his brother abu al-Hassan, *'Alayhi al-Salam,* who has said the following:

"I once asked abu al-Hassan, *'Alayhi al-Salam,* about raisins; if it can be boiled to extract its sweetness, then that water is boiled until its two-thirds are evaporated and only one-third is left; then it is taken away to use for drink during the year. He (the Imam) said, 'It is not unlawful.'"

H 12009, Ch. 17, h 10

Muhammad ibn Yahya has narrated from Muhammad ibn al-Husayn from Muhammad ibn 'Abd Allah from 'Uqbah ibn Khalid who has said the following:

"About the case of a man who takes ten *ritl* of grape juice, then pours in it twenty *ritl* of water, then boils it until twenty *ritl* of it is evaporated and only ten *ritl* is left; if it can be used for drink or not. He (the Imam) said, 'What is cooked until only one-third remains it is lawful.'"

Chapter 18 - The Drops of Intoxicating Substances in Food

H 12010, Ch. 18, h 1

Muhammad ibn Yahya has narrated from Muhammad ibn Musa from al-Hassan ibn al-Mubarak from Zakariya ibn Adam who has said the following:

"I once asked abu 'Abd Allah, *'Alayhi al-Salam,* about a large cooking pot with a large amount of meat and broth in it and a drop of wine or al-Nabidh is dropped therein. He (the Imam) said, 'It must be thrown away or fed to the taxpayers or dogs. You can wash the meat and eat it.' I then asked about what happens if one drop of blood is dropped in it. 'The fire, if Allah wills, eats the blood,' said the Imam. I then asked about if wine or al-Nabidh by a drop is dropped in flour dough or a drop of blood. He (the Imam) said, 'It is destroyed.' I then asked if I can sell it to Jews or Christians and tell all about it because they consider drinking it lawful.' He (the Imam) said, 'Yes, you can do so.' I then asked about *al-Fuqa'* (beer) if it is like wine, and al-Nabidh when one drop of it is dropped in something. He (the Imam) said, 'I do not like to eat it if anything thereof is dropped in my food.'"

Chapter 19 - *Al-Fuqa'* (Beer)

H 12011, Ch. 19, h 1

A number of our people have narrated from Sahl ibn Ziyad from Muhammad ibn 'Isma'il from Sulayman ibn Ja'far al-Ja'fariy who has said the following:

"I once asked abu al-Hassan, al-Rida', *'Alayhi al-Salam,* about *al-Fuqa'* (beer). He (the Imam) said, 'It is unknown wine. Do not drink it, O Sulayman. If the house and command were in my hand I would execute its seller and whip its drinker.'"

H 12012, Ch. 19, h 2

It is narrated from the narrator of the previous *Hadith* from 'Amr ibn Sa'id al-Mad'iniy from Musaddiq ibn Sadaqah from 'Ammar ibn Musa who has said the following:

"I once asked abu 'Abd Allah, *'Alayhi al-Salam,* about *al-Fuqa'*. He (the Imam) said, 'It is wine.'"

H 12013, Ch. 19, h 3

Muhammad ibn Yahya has narrated from Ahmad ibn Muhammad ibn 'Isa from Muhammad ibn Sinan from Husayn al-Qalanisiy who has said the following:

"Once I asked abu al-Hassan, al-Madiy, *'Alayhi al-Salam,* in writing and asked about *al-Fuqa'* (beer). He (the Imam) wrote to me saying, 'Do not go close to it; it is wine.'"

H 12014, Ch. 19, h 4

Muhammad ibn Yahya has narrated from Ahmad ibn Muhammad [ibn 'Isa] from Muhammad ibn Sinan who has said the following:

"I once asked abu al-Hassan, al-Rida', *'Alayhi al-Salam,* about *al-Fuqa'*. He (the Imam) said, 'It is wine exactly.'"

H 12015, Ch. 19, h 5

Abu Ali al-Ash'ariy has narrated from Muhammad ibn 'Abd al-Jabbar from ibn Faddal who has said the following:

"I once wrote to abu al-Hassan, *'Alayhi al-Salam,* asking about *al-Fuqa'* and he (the Imam) prohibited me to use it."

H 12016, Ch. 19, h 6

Muhammad ibn Yahya and others have narrated from Muhammad ibn Ahmad from al-Husayn ibn 'Abd Allah al-Qarashiy certain persons of our people from abu 'Abd Allah al-Nawfaliy from Zadhan who has said the following:

"Abu 'Abd Allah, *'Alayhi al-Salam,* has said, 'If I had control over the market places of the Muslims I would ban this wine, that is, *al-Fuqa'* (beer).'"

H 12017, Ch. 19, h 7

Muhamad ibn Yahya has narrated from certain persons of our people from those whom he has mentioned from abu Jamilah al-Basriy who have said the following:

"Once Yunus and I were in Baghdad, as we were walking, an *al-Fuqa'* seller opened his shop and the cloth of Yunus came in contact with *al-Fuqa'*. I saw him depressed until the sun declined to the west and I asked, 'Do you not want to perform *Salat* (prayer), O abu Muhammad?' He replied, 'I do not want to perform *Salat* (prayer) until I return home so I can wash this wine from my clothes.' I then asked, 'Is it your own opinion or something that you narrate?' He said, 'Hisham ibn al-Hakam informed me that he asked abu 'Abd Allah, *'Alayhi al-Salam,* about *al-Fuqa'* and he (the Imam) said, 'Do not drink it; it is unknown wine and if your clothes come in contact with it wash them clean.'"

H 12018, Ch. 19, h 8

A number of our people have narrated from Sahl ibn Ziyad from 'Amr ibn Sa'id from al-Hassan ibn al-Jahm and ibn Faddal all have said the following:

"We asked abu al-Hassan, *'Alayhi al-Salam,* about *al-Fuqa'*. He (the Imam) said, 'It is unlawful, it is an unknown wine and its penalty is the same as that which is for wine.'"

H 12019, Ch. 19, h 9

Muhammad ibn Yahya has narrated from Muhammad ibn Ahmad from Muhammad ibn 'Isa from al-Washsha' who has said the following:

"I once wrote to al-Rida', *'Alayhi al-Salam,* and asked about *al-Fuqa'*. He (the Imam) wrote back, 'It is unlawful and it is wine. If one drinks it he is like a wine drinker.' He (the narrator) has said that abu al-Hassan, al-Akhir, *'Alayhi al-Salam,* has said, 'Had the house been my house I would execute its seller and whip its drinker.' He (the Imam) has also said, 'The penalty for drinking *al-Fuqa'* is the same as for drinking wine.' He (the Imam) has said, 'It is intoxicating liquor which people have taken lightly.'"

H 12020, Ch. 19, h 10

Muhammad ibn Yahya and others have narrated from Muhammad ibn Ahmad from Ahmad ibn al-Hassan from Muhammad ibn 'Isma'il from Sulayman ibn Ja'far who has said the following:

"I once asked abu al-Hassan, al-Rida', *'Alayhi al-Salam,* about *al-Fuqa'*. He (the Imam) said, 'It is an unknown wine, O Sulayman and do not drink it. Had the command been in my hand and the house was my house, I would whip its drinker and execute its seller.'"

H 12021, Ch. 19, h 11
Muhammad ibn Yahya has narrated from Ahmad ibn Muhammad from al-Husayn ibn Sa'id from Muhammad ibn 'Isma'il who has said the following:

"I once asked abu al-Hassan, *'Alayhi al-Salam,* about drinking *al-Fuqa'* and he (the Imam) disliked it very intensely." Ahmad ibn Muhammad has narrated from ibn Faddal from Muhammad ibn 'Isma'il a similar *Hadith.*"

H 12022, Ch. 19, h 12
Muhammad ibn Yahya has narrated from Ahmad ibn Muhammad from Bakr ibn Salih from Zakariya abu Yahya who has said the following:

"I once wrote to abu al-Hassan, *'Alayhi al-Salam,* asked about *al-Fuqa'* and described it for him (the Imam) how it is made. He (the Imam) said, 'Do not drink it and do not come back to me about it again.'"

H 12023, Ch. 19, h 13
Muhammad ibn Yahya has narrated from Muhammad ibn Ahmad from Ahmad ibn al-Hassan from 'Abd Allah ibn 'Amir ibn Sa'id from Musaddiq ibn Sadaqah from Mu'awiyah ibn Musa who has said the following:

"I once asked abu 'Abd Allah, *'Alayhi al-Salam,* about *al-Fuqa'*. He (the Imam) said to me, 'It is wine.'"

H 12024, Ch. 19, h 14
Muhammad ibn Yahya has narrated from Muhammad ibn Musa from Muhammad ibn 'Isa from al-Hassan ibn Ali al-Washsha' who has said the following:

"Abu al-Hassan, al-Rida', *'Alayhi al-Salam,* has said, 'All intoxicating substances are unlawful, everything confusing the power of reason is unlawful and *al-Fuqa'* (beer) is unlawful.'"

H 12025, Ch. 19, h 15
Muhammad ibn Yahya has narrated from Ahmad ibn Muhammad from ibn Faddal who has said the following:

"I once wrote to abu al-Hassan and asked about *al-Fuqa'*. He (the Imam) said in writing, 'It is wine and the penalty for drinking it is like that for drinking wine.'"

Chapter 20 - The Quality of Lawful Drinks

H 12026, Ch. 20, h 1
Muhammad ibn Yahya has narrated from Ali ibn al-Hassan or a man from Ali ibn Faddal from 'Amr ibn Sa'id from Musaddiq ibn Sadaqah from 'Ammar ibn Musa al-Sabatiy who has said the following:

"Abu 'Abd Allah, *'Alayhi al-Salam,* once explained for me how to cook raisins until the brew becomes lawful. He (the Imam) said, 'Take one quarter of raisins and clean them. Pour twelve *ritl* of water on them, then soak for one night. If it is summer and you are afraid of its simmering, keep it in an oven, which is full a little so it does not simmer, then remove all the water from it. In the morning, pour water on it so that it is covered with water. Thereafter, boil it until its sweetness is gone. Thereafter, remove the other water and pour on it the first water. Thereafter, measure all of it and see how much the water is. Thereafter, measure one-third of it and pour it in the pot in which you want to cook it. Pour enough water to cover it, then measure it with a stick and keep its size and measurement by a stick or reed and mark it at the surface of the water. Thereafter, boil the other third until the remaining water goes, then boil it on fire and keep boiling until two-thirds are gone and only one-third is left. Thereafter, for every quarter take one *ritl* of honey and boil it until its scum and suds and blur of honey is gone from the cooking. Thereafter, beat it with a stick or such thing firmly until it is mixed and if you like, you can mix fragrance with saffron or ginger, you can do so, then you can drink it. If you like it to remain with you for a longer time then clean it properly.'"

H 12027, Ch. 20, h 2

Muhammad ibn Yahya has narrated from Ahmad ibn Muhammad from Ahmad ibn al-Hassan from 'Amr ibn Sa'id from Musaddiq ibn Sadaqah from 'Ammar al-Sabatiy who has said the following:

"Once abu 'Abd Allah, *'Alayhi al-Salam,* was asked about raisins and how to cook them to become clean for drinking. He (the Imam) said, 'Take one quarter of raisins and clean it. Thereafter pour twelve *ritl* of water on it, then leave it for the night to soak. In the morning remove its suds, then pour on it enough water so it is covered thereby. Thereafter, boil it on fire for a boil then remove the water, then pour it on the first water, then place all of it in one pot. Then, ignite fire beneath it until two-thirds are evaporated and only one-third has remained with the fire underneath. Then take one *ritl* of honey and boil it on fire for a boil, remove its blur, pour it on the cooked (preparation), beat it until it is mixed, then pour saffron or a little ginger for fragrance.

"You can also divide it in three parts to cook. First, you should measure it by a certain measurement so you know how much it is. Then place the first one in a pot in which you want to boil it. Then pour in it one-third as much as water reaches and mark its level, then pour the other third part, then mark it where water reaches then pour the last third part, then mark it where this other reaches; then fire underneath gently until its two-thirds are gone and only one-third is left.'"

H 12028, Ch. 20, h 3

Muhammad ibn Yahya has narrated from Musa ibn al-Hassan from al-Sayyariy from Muhammad ibn al-Husayn from those who narrated to him from 'Isma'il ibn al-Fadl al-Hashimy who has said the following:

"I once complained before abu 'Abd Allah, *'Alayhi al-Salam,* about growling in my stomach and my not being able to digest food. He (the Imam) said, 'Why do you not drink al-Nabidh which we drink? It digests food and takes away abdominal growling and gases.' I then asked, 'Please describe it for me, I pray to Allah to keep my soul in service for your cause.' He (the Imam) said, 'Take one Sa' of raisins, clean it of seeds and other things in it, then wash it properly, then soak it with an equal amount of water or a quantity that covers it. In winter leave it for three days and nights, and in summer one day and night. Thereafter clean it and take the cleaned amount, place it in a pot and take its measurement with a piece of wood then cook it gently until its two-thirds are gone and one-third is left. Then place in it one-half *ritl* of honey. Take this honey and cook it until the extra is gone then take ginger, Khulinjana (a certain Indian plant) and cinnamon, saffron, dianthus and Mustakiy (Mastic tree) powder them and place them in a piece of fine cloth. Place it in to cook and boil it with the rest, then take it away from the fire. When it is cool clean it. You can take from it after your lunch and dinner.' He (the narrator) has said, 'I followed the instruction and my condition that I had was gone. It is a fine drink and does not change if it remains for a time, by the will of Allah.'"

H 12029, Ch. 20, h 4

Muhammad ibn Yahya has narrated from 'Abd Allah ibn Ja'far from al-Sayyariy from those whom he has mentioned from Ishaq ibn 'Ammar who has said the following:

"I once complained before abu 'Abd Allah, *'Alayhi al-Salam,* about a certain pain and that a physician has prescribed for me a drink from raisins with water twice as much, and that honey must be poured on it and cooked until two-thirds are gone and only one-third is left.' He (the Imam) said, 'Is it not sweet?' I replied, 'Yes, it is sweet.' He (the Imam) said, 'You can drink it.' I did not tell him how much the amount of honey was.'"

Chapter 21 - Also about Drinks

H 12030, Ch. 21, h 1

A number of our people have narrated from Sahl ibn Ziyad from Mansur ibn al-'Abbas from Ja'far ibn Ahmad al-Makfuf who has said the following:

"I once wrote to him, meaning, abu al-Hassan, al-Awwal, *'Alayhim al-Salam,* and asked about oxymel, rose water, jam of mulberry, apple, quince and pomegranate. He (the Imam) said in writing, 'It is lawful.'"

H 12031, Ch. 21, h 2

Muhammad ibn Yahya has narrated from Hamdan ibn Sulayman from Ali ibn al-Hassan from Ja'far ibn Ahmad al-Makfuf who has said the following:

"I once wrote to abu al-Hassan, al-Awwal, *'Alayhi al-Salam,* and asked about drinks like oxymel, rose-water, jam of mulberry, pomegranate, quince and apple; if the seller is not knowledgeable when they are sold in our market places. He (the Imam) wrote, 'It is permissible and it is not harmful.'"

H 12032, Ch. 21, h 3

Muhammad ibn Yahya has narrated from Ahmad ibn Muhammad from Ibrahim ibn Mahziyar from Khalilan ibn Hisham who has said the following:

"I once wrote to abu al-Hassan, *'Alayhi al-Salam,* saying, 'I pray to Allah to keep my soul in service for your cause, in our area there is a drink called *al-Myabeh* which is taken from quince which is peeled then is placed in water. Juice (grape juice) then is boiled until one-third (is left), then the quince is crushed. Its juice then is taken. Then the one-third water and quince, musk, spices and condiment, saffron and honey are cooked until its two-thirds are evaporated and only one-third is left; if it is lawful to drink it. He (the Imam) wrote, 'It is not unlawful as long as it is not changed.'"

Chapter 22 - The Utensils in which Wine is Kept, then Vinegar is poured in it or is used for Drink

H 12033, Ch. 22, h 1

Muhammad ibn Yahya has narrated from Muhammad ibn Ahmad from Ahmad ibn al-Hassan from 'Amr ibn Sa'id from Musaddiq ibn Sadaqah from 'Ammar ibn Musa who has said the following:

"I once asked abu 'Abd Allah, *'Alayhi al-Salam*, about a large jug in which there is wine; if it is suitable for vinegar, or water, sauce or olives. He (the Imam) said, 'If it is washed then it is not unlawful.' I asked about a pitcher in which there is wine; if it is suitable to use it for keeping water. He (the Imam) said, 'If it is washed then it is not harmful.' (I asked) about a cup or bowl, which is used to drink wine, he (the Imam) said, 'You must wash it three times.' It was asked if just pouring water in it is sufficient. He (the Imam) said, 'No, it is not sufficient until he rubs it with his hand and washes it three times.'"

H 12034, Ch. 22, h 2

Abu Ali al-Ash'ariy has narrated from Muhammad ibn 'Abd al-Jabbar and Muhammad ibn Yahya has narrated from Ahmad ibn Muhammad all from *al-Hajj*al from Tha'labah from Hafs ibn al-A'war who has said the following:

"I once asked abu 'Abd Allah, *'Alayhi al-Salam*, about a large jug in which there is wine, then it dries up if vinegar can be kept in it. He (the Imam) said, 'Yes, one can do so.'"

Chapter 23 - The Wine Placed in Vinegar

H 12035, Ch. 23, h 1

Muhammad ibn Yahya has narrated from Ahmad ibn Muhammad ibn Khalid from ibn Bukayr from abu Basir who has said the following:

"I once asked abu 'Abd Allah, *'Alayhi al-Salam*, about wine to which something is done until it is turned sour. He (the Imam) said, 'If what is done in it (the wine) overwhelms it, then is not harmful.'"

H 12036, Ch. 23, h 2

Ali ibn Ibrahim has narrated from his father from ibn abu 'Umayr from Jamil ibn Darraj and ibn Bukayr from Zurarah who has said the following:

"I once asked abu 'Abd Allah, *'Alayhi al-Salam*, about *al-'Atiqah* (old) wine which is turned into vinegar. He (the Imam) said, 'It is not harmful.'"

H 12037, Ch. 23, h 3

A number of our people have narrated from Ahmad ibn Muhammad ibn 'Isa from al-Husayn ibn Sa'id from Fadalah ibn Ayyub from ibn Bukayr from 'Ubayd ibn Zurarah who has said the following:

"I once asked abu 'Abd Allah, *'Alayhi al-Salam*, about the case of a man who takes wine and turns it into vinegar. He (the Imam) said, 'It is not harmful.'"

H 12038, Ch. 23, h 4

It is narrated from the narrator of the previous *Hadith* from Fadalah ibn Ayyub from 'Abd Allah ibn Bukayr from abu Basir who has said the following:

"I once asked abu 'Abd Allah, *'Alayhi al-Salam*, about wine which is turned into vinegar. He (the Imam) said, 'It is not harmful if one has not placed in it what overwhelms it.'"

Chapter 24 - The Rare Ahadith

H 12039, Ch. 24, h 1

Muhammad ibn Yahya has narrated from certain persons of our people from al-Hassan ibn Ali ibn Yaqtin from Bakr ibn Muhammad from 'Aythamah who has said the following:

"I once visited abu 'Abd Allah, *'Alayhi al-Salam,* when his women were with him and he (the Imam) sensed a smell and asked what it was. They said, 'It is a kind of perfume which is placed in one's hairs.' He (the narrator) has said, that he (the Imam) commanded to throw it in the sewage.'"

H 12040, Ch. 24, h 2

Muhammad ibn Yahya has narrated from Ahmad ibn Muhammad from Ahmad ibn al-Hassan ibn Ali from 'Amr ibn Sa'id from Musaddiq ibn Sadaqah from 'Ammar ibn Musa who has said the following:

"Once abu 'Abd Allah, *'Alayhi al-Salam,* was asked about the table on which wine or intoxicating substances is served. He (the Imam) said, 'The table becomes unlawful.' It then was asked, 'If one is on a table from which he eats and there is a man who has wine with him and no one has drunk from it. He (the Imam) said, 'It does not become unlawful until wine is drunk on it. If after drinking wine on the table, then sweet is served, one can eat it because it is another table, that is, one can eat the sweet.'"

H 12041, Ch. 24, h 3

Ali ibn Ibrahim has narrated from his father from 'Amr ibn 'Uthman from Ahmad ibn 'Isma'il al-Katib from his father who has said the following:

"Once abu Ja'far, *'Alayhi al-Salam,* went to Masjid al-Haram (the Sacred area). A group of Quraysh saw him. They asked, 'Who is he?' It was said to them, 'He is the Imam of the people of Iraq.' Certain ones among them said, 'You may send someone to ask him questions.' One young man from among them went and asked, 'Son of my uncle, what is the greatest of the great sins?' He (the Imam) said, 'It is drinking wine.' He went back and informed them about it. They said, 'Go back and ask again.' He went back and he (the Imam) said, 'Did I not say, O son of a brother, that it is drinking wine?' He went back and informed them and they told him to go back again. They were there that he went back to him (the Imam) and asked him. He (the Imam) said, 'Did I not say, O son of a brother that it is drinking wine? Drinking wine takes the drinker to fornication, theft, murder of what Allah has prohibited, paganism and the effects of wine goes above all sins like trees that go above all other trees.'"

H 12042, Ch. 24, h 4

Abu Ali al-Ash'ariy has narrated from Muhammad ibn Salim from Ahmad ibn al-Nadr from 'Amr ibn Shamir from Jabir who has said the following:

"Abu Ja'far, *'Alayhi al-Salam,* has said that the Messenger of Allah, *O Allah, grant compensation to Muhammad and his family worthy of their services to Your cause,* has condemned because of wine ten characters. Of such characters is the planter, the keeper, the seller, the buyer, the drinker, the payment receiver, the squeezer, the carrier, the one being carried to and the server of wine.'"

H 12043, Ch. 24, h 5

Muhammad ibn Yahya has narrated from Ahmad ibn Muhammad from Muhammad ibn Khalid al-Barqiy in a marfu' manner from Hafs ibn al-A'war who has said the following:

"I once said to abu 'Abd Allah, *'Alayhi al-Salam,* that I use a small water container. It is said that if wine is kept in it (water container), then *al-Bakhtaj* (a certain liquid item for personal use) is kept in it, it is better for it. In the small water container, wine is kept and it then is shaken, then it is poured out and then *al-Bakhtaj* is kept in it. He (the Imam) said, 'It is not harmful (after washing it clean).'"

H 12044, Ch. 24, h 6

A number of our people have narrated from Sahl ibn Ziyad from Harun ibn Muslim from Mas'adah ibn Sadaqah who has said the following:

"Abu 'Abd Allah, *'Alayhi al-Salam,* has said, 'Once there was a group of people with my father and they had different views about al-Nabidh. Certain ones among them said, "The cupful (of al-Nabidh) which is intoxicating is unlawful." Others said, "Al-Nabidh in small quantity does not intoxicate but it is unlawful in large quantity." They referred the matter to my father, *'Alayhi al-Salam,* who said, "On the basis of fairness and justice if nothing has been placed in the cup it would never become full. This applies to the other cup also. If nothing has been placed in, it would not intoxicate." He (the Imam) said that the Messenger of Allah, *O Allah, grant compensation to Muhammad and his family worthy of their services to Your cause,* has said, 'If a small quantity of that which in large quantity intoxicates, enters one's vein, Allah will make that vein suffer because of three hundred sixty kinds of torments.'"'"

H 12045, Ch. 24, h 7

A number of our people have narrated from Ahmad ibn Muhammad ibn Khalid from his father from Ghiyath who has said the following:

"Abu 'Abd Allah, *'Alayhi al-Salam,* has said that 'Amir al-Mu'minin, *'Alayhi al-Salam,* disliked one's making the animals drink wine.'"

H 12046, Ch. 24, h 8

Ali ibn Ibrahim has narrated from his father from ibn abu 'Umayr from certain persons of his people who has said the following:

"I once heard abu 'Abd Allah, *'Alayhi al-Salam,* saying, 'If one refrains from drinking wine for the sake of something other than Allah, most Majestic, most Glorious, Allah will provide him drink from the sealed wine of the garden (paradises). He (the narrator) then said, 'He does not refrain from it for the sake of Allah.' He (the Imam) said, 'Yes, it is (just as I said it is) to protect his soul.'"

H 12047, Ch. 24, h 9

Ali ibn Muhammad ibn Bandar has narrated from Ibrahim ibn Ishaq, from 'Abd Allah ibn Ahmad, from Muhammad ibn 'Abd Allah, from Mehzam who has said the following:

"I once heard abu 'Abd Allah, *'Alayhi al-Salam,* saying, 'If one refrains from drinking wine for his own protection Allah, most Majestic, most Glorious, will provide him drink from the sealed wine of the garden (paradises).'"

Chapter 25 - Music and Singing

H 12048, Ch. 25, h 1

A number of our people have narrated from Sahl ibn Ziyad from Yahya ibn al-Mubarak from 'Abd Allah ibn Jabalah from Sama'ah ibn Mehran from abu Basir who has said the following:

"I once asked abu 'Abd Allah, *'Alayhi al-Salam,* about the meaning of the words of Allah, most Majestic, most Glorious, 'Stay away from wickedness, idols, and false words.' (22:30) He (the Imam) said, 'It is music and singing.'"

H 12049, Ch. 25, h 2

It is narrated from the narrator of the previous *Hadith* from Muhammad ibn Ali from abu Jamilah from abu 'Usamah who has said the following:

"Abu 'Abd Allah, *'Alayhi al-Salam,* has said, 'Music (and singing) is the nest of hypocrisy.'"

H 12050, Ch. 25, h 3

It is narrated from the narrator of the previous *Hadith* from Sulayman ibn Sama'ah from 'Abd Allah ibn al-Qasim from Sama'ah who has said the following:

"Abu 'Abd Allah, *'Alayhi al-Salam,* has said that when Adam, *'Alayhi al-Salam,* died, Iblis and Qabil expressed joy and came together in the land. Thereafter Iblis and Qabil set up musical instruments and means of amusement to rejoice at the death of Adam, *'Alayhi al-Salam.* Thus whatever is there on earth of this sort in which people take pleasure is because of that."

H 12051, Ch. 25, h 4

Ali ibn Ibrahim has narrated from his father from ibn abu 'Umayr from Ali ibn 'Isma'il from ibn Muskan from Muhammad ibn Muslim who has said the following:

"I once heard abu Ja'far, *'Alayhi al-Salam,* saying, 'music (and singing) is of such things for which Allah, most Majestic, most Glorious, has warned with punishment in the fire.' He (the Imam) then read this verse, 'There are people who pay for worthless tales (or activities) that deviates them from the path of Allah without their realizing such bad results. They treat the signs of Allah with ridicule. It is such people who will suffer a humiliating torment.' (31:6)"

H 12052, Ch. 25, h 5

Ibn abu 'Umayr has narrated from Mehran ibn Muhammad who has said the following:

"I once heard abu 'Abd Allah, *'Alayhi al-Salam,* saying, 'music (and singing) are of the things about which Allah has said, 'Among people there are those who buy useless things in the form of words to mislead people from the path of Allah.'"

H 12053, Ch. 25, h 6

Abu Ali al-Ash'ariy has narrated from Muhammad ibn 'Abd al-Jabbar from Safwan from abu Ayyub al-Khazzaz from Muhammad ibn Muslim from abu al-Sabbah al-Kinaniy who has said the following:

"About the meaning of the words of Allah, most Majestic, most Glorious, '. . . those who do not attend al-Zur,' (25:72) abu 'Abd Allah, *'Alayhi al-Salam,* has said, 'It (al-Zur'ah) is music (and singing).'"

H 12054, Ch. 25, h 7

Ali ibn Ibrahim has narrated from his father from al-Nawfaliy from al-Sakuniy who has said the following:

"Abu 'Abd Allah, *'Alayhi al-Salam,* has said that the Messenger of Allah, *O Allah, grant compensation to Muhammad and his family worthy of their services to Your cause,* has said, 'I forbid dancing, use of flutes, smaller and bigger drums.'"

H 12055, Ch. 25, h 8

A number of our people have narrated from Sahl ibn Ziyad from al-Washsha' who has said the following:

"I once heard abu al-Hassan, al-Rida', *'Alayhi al-Salam,* saying that once abu 'Abd Allah, *'Alayhi al-Salam,* was asked about music (and singing). He (the Imam) said, 'It is in the words of Allah, most Majestic, most Glorious, '. . . among people there are those who buy useless things in the form of words to mislead others from the path of Allah.'"

H 12056, Ch. 25, h 9

Sahl ibn Ziyad has narrated from Sa'id ibn Junah from Hammad from abu Ayyub al-Khazzaz who has said the following:

"Once we arrived in al-Madinah and visited abu 'Abd Allah, *'Alayhi al-Salam,* who asked us, 'Where have you lodged?' We said, 'It is with so and so, the owner of singing slave-girls.' He (the Imam) said, 'You must remain honorable.' By Allah we did not understand what he (the Imam) meant and we thought perhaps he wants us to be kind to him (owner of the lodging). We returned to him (the Imam) and asked, 'We did not understand your words, 'Be honorable.' He (the Imam) said, 'Have you not heard the words of Allah, most Majestic, most Glorious, 'When they pass by useless things they pass honorably.' (25:72)"

H 12057, Ch. 25, h 10

Ali ibn Ibrahim has narrated from Harun ibn Muslim from Mas'adah ibn Ziyad who has said the following:

"Once I was with abu 'Abd Allah, *'Alayhi al-Salam,* when a man said, 'I pray to Allah to keep my soul and the souls of my parents in service for your cause, I enter my WC (water-closet) and I have neighbors who have singing slave-girls who play musical instruments and perhaps I sit longer, listening to them.' He (the Imam) said, 'You must not do so.' The man said, 'By Allah, I do not go to them; it is only my listening to them with my ears.' He (the Imam) said, 'For the sake of Allah, have you not heard Allah, most Majestic, most Glorious, saying, "...the ears, eyes, and hearts will all be held responsible for their deeds." (17:36)' He replied, 'Yes, by Allah, as if I have not heard this verse of the book of Allah from non-Arab or Arab people. However, I will not return to it if Allah so wills and I ask forgiveness from Allah. He (the Imam) said, 'You must go and take a shower, then ask what you want, because you were involved in a great thing and how terrible your condition could have been had you remained in such condition! Praise Allah and ask Him to forgive you because of what He dislikes and He dislikes only bad and indecent matters; and you must leave evil and indecent things to indecent people; everything has its associates.'"

H 12058, Ch. 25, h 11

Muhammad ibn Yahya has narrated from Salmah ibn al-Khattab from Ibrahim ibn Muhammad from 'Imran al-Za'faraniy who has said the following:

"Abu 'Abd Allah, *'Alayhi al-Salam*, has said, 'If Allah grants a bounty to a person and that person comes to that bounty with a flute, he has not appreciated it; and if one is affected by a misfortune and he comes in such condition with mourning (professional mourner) he has disregarded it also.'" (Expressing joy and grief through unlawful ways is harmful.)

H 12059, Ch. 25, h 12

Muhammad ibn Yahya has narrated from Ahmad ibn Muhammad from ibn Faddal from Yunus ibn Ya'qub from 'Abd al-'Ala' who has said the following:

"I once asked abu 'Abd Allah, *'Alayhi al-Salam*, about music (and singing). I said that they think the Messenger of Allah, *O Allah, grant compensation to Muhammad and his family worthy of their services to Your cause*, has granted permission in saying, 'We have come to you, we have come to you, so offer us greetings, offer us greetings, we will offer you greetings.' He (the Imam) said, 'They have spoken a lie. Allah, most Majestic, most Glorious, says, "We did not create the heavens and the earth just for fun. (21:16) Had We wanted to play games, We could have certainly done so with things at hand. (21:17) We bring forward the Truth to crush and destroy falsehood; it is doomed to be banished. Woe to you for your way of thinking about Allah!" (21:18)' He (the Imam) then said, 'Woe upon the one who ascribes something to one who is not present in the gathering.'"

H 12060, Ch. 25, h 13

Ali ibn Ibrahim has narrated from his father from ibn abu 'Umayr from abu Ayyub from Muhammad ibn Muslim and abu al-Sabbah al-Kinaniy who has said the following:

"About the meaning of the words of Allah, most Majestic, most Glorious, '. . . those who do not attend al-Zur . . .' (25:72) abu 'Abd Allah, *'Alayhi al-Salam*, has said, 'It is music (and singing).'"

H 12061, Ch. 25, h 14

A number of our people have narrated from Ahmad ibn Muhammad ibn Khalid from 'Uthman ibn 'Isa from Ishaq ibn Jarir who has said the following:

"I once heard abu 'Abd Allah, *'Alayhi al-Salam*, saying, 'There is Satan called *al-Qafandar*. If *barbat* (a musical instrument) is played in a house for forty days and men come to him then that Satan places every part of his (Satan's) body on every part of the body of the owner of the house, then blows a blow; and thereafter he will not mind even if people go in on to his women.'"

H 12062, Ch. 25, h 15

Muhammad ibn Yahya has narrated from Ahmad ibn Muhammad from al-Husayn ibn Sa'id from Ibrahim ibn abu al-Balad from Zayd al-Shahham who has said the following:

"Abu 'Abd Allah, *'Alayhi al-Salam*, has said, 'The house of music (and singing) is not safe from tragedy, prayers are not accepted and angels do not enter in it.'"

H 12063, Ch. 25, h 16

Ali ibn Ibrahim has narrated from his father from ibn abu 'Umayr from Mehran ibn Muhammad from al-Hassan ibn Harun who has said the following:

"I once heard abu 'Abd Allah, *'Alayhi al-Salam,* saying, '(The gathering for) music (and singing) is a gathering to the participant of which Allah does not look. Allah, most Majestic, most Glorious, has said, 'There are people who pay for worthless tales (or activities) that deviates them from the path of Allah without their realizing such bad results...' (31:6)"

H 12064, Ch. 25, h 17
Sahl ibn Ziyad has narrated from Muhammad ibn 'Isa or others from abu Dawud al-Mustariq who has said the following:

"He (the Imam), *'Alayhi al-Salam,* has said, 'If barbat is played in one's house for forty days Allah gives its control to a Satan called *al-Qafandar* who sits on every part of the body of the owner of the house. When this happens bashfulness (the sense to feel ashamed of one's indecent acts) is taken away from him and he does not mind whatever he says or is said about him.'"

H 12065, Ch. 25, h 18
Sahl ibn Ziyad has narrated from Ibrahim ibn Muhammad al-Madiniy from those whom he has mentioned who has said the following:

"Once abu 'Abd Allah, *'Alayhi al-Salam,* was asked about music (and singing) when I was present. He (the Imam) said, 'Do not enter the houses whose inhabitants Allah disregards.'"

H 12066, Ch. 25, h 19
It is narrated from the narrator of the previous *Hadith* from Yasir al-Khadim who has said the following:

"Abu al-Hassan, al-Rida', *'Alayhi al-Salam,* has said, 'If one keeps his soul clean of *al-Ghina'* (music (and singing)), Allah, most Majestic, most Glorious, commands the winds to move a tree in the garden (paradises). From this tree a sound is heard the like of which is never heard, and those who fail to keep their souls clean of *al-Ghina'* (music (and singing)) will not be able to hear it.'"

H 12067, Ch. 25, h 20
It is narrated from the narrator of the previous *Hadith* from Ali ibn Ma'bad from al-Hassan ibn Ali al-Khazzaz from Ali ibn 'Abd al-Rahman from Kulayb al-Saydawiy who has said the following:

"I once heard abu 'Abd Allah, *'Alayhi al-Salam,* saying, 'Playing *'Ud* (a certain musical instrument) grows hypocrisy just as water grows green plants.'"

H 12068, Ch. 25, h 21
It is narrated from the narrator of the previous *Hadith* from Ahmad ibn Yusuf ibn 'Aqil from his father from Musa ibn Habib who has said the following:

"Ali ibn al-Husayn, *'Alayhim al-Salam,* has said, 'Allah does not grant holiness to a nation in which *barbat* sounds and the (false) eulogies that cause pain.'"

H 12069, Ch. 25, h 22
Muhammad ibn Yahya has narrated from Ahmad ibn Muhammad from Muhammad ibn Sinan from Jahm from Hamid who has said the following:

"Abu 'Abd Allah, *'Alayhi al-Salam,* once asked me, 'Where have you been?' I then thought that he knows the place where I was. I then said, 'I pray to Allah to keep my soul in service for your cause, I was passing by so and so and he kept me, I went in his house and looked at his slave-girls.' He (the Imam) said, 'That is such a gathering to the inhabitants of which Allah, most Majestic, most Glorious, does not look. Have you placed your family and assets in the trust of Allah, most Majestic, most Glorious?'"

H 12070, Ch. 25, h 23
Ali ibn Ibrahim has narrated from his father from ibn Mahbub from 'Anbasah who has said the following:
"Abu 'Abd Allah, *'Alayhi al-Salam,* has said, 'Listening to *al-Ghina'* (music (and singing)) and useless things grows hypocrisy just as water grows green plants.'"

H 12071, Ch. 25, h 24
Al-Husayn ibn Muhammad has narrated from Mu'alla' ibn Muhammad from Ahmad ibn Muhammad from ibn Ibrahim al-Armaniy from al-Hassan ibn Ali ibn Yaqtin who has said the following:
"Abu Ja'far, *'Alayhi al-Salam,* has said, 'If one listens to a speaker he worships him. If the speaker conveys from Allah, most Majestic, most Glorious, he has worshipped Allah; but if he conveys from Satan he has worshipped Satan.'"

H 12072, Ch. 25, h 25
A number of our people have narrated from Sahl ibn Ziyad from Ali ibn al-Rayyan from Yunus who has said the following:
"I once asked al-Khurasaniy, *'Alayhi al-Salam,* saying, 'Al-'Abbasiy has said that you allow *al-Ghina'* (music (and singing)). He (the Imam) said, 'The infidel has spoken a lie. I did not say so to him. He asked me about *al-Ghina'* (music (and singing)) and I said, 'Once a man came to abu Ja'far, *'Alayhi al-Salam,* and asked him about *al-Ghina'* (music (and singing)). He (the Imam) said, "O so and so, if Allah distinguishes between truth and falsehood where is the place of *al-Ghina'* (music (and singing))?" He replied, 'It is in falsehood.' He (the Imam) said, 'So you have issued the judgment.'"

Chapter 26 - Dice and Chess

H 12073, Ch. 26, h 1
Muhammad ibn Yahya has narrated from Ahmad ibn Muhammad from Mu'ammar ibn Khallad who has said the following:
"Abu al-Hassan, *'Alayhi al-Salam,* has said, 'Dice, chess and checkers are all the same. Whatever is used in gambling (speculating) is gambling.'"

H 12074, Ch. 26, h 2
Muhammad ibn Yahya has narrated from Ahmad ibn Muhammad from Muhammad ibn Khalid and al-Husayn ibn Sa'id all from al-Nadr ibn Suwayd from Durust from Zayd al-Shahham who has said the following:
"I once asked abu 'Abd Allah, *'Alayhi al-Salam,* about the meaning of the words of Allah, most Majestic, most Glorious, '…Stay away from wickedness, idols, and false words.' (22:30) He (the Imam) said, ''The idols' is a reference to chess and 'false words' stands for *al-Ghina'* (music (and singing)).'"

H 12075, Ch. 26, h 3

A number of our people have narrated from Sahl ibn Ziyad from ibn abu Najran from Muthanna' al-Hannat from abu Basir who has said the following:

"Abu 'Abd Allah, *'Alayhi al-Salam,* has said that `Amir al-Mu'minin has said, 'Chess and dice are *al-Maysir* (gambling).'"

H 12076, Ch. 26, h 4

Ali ibn Ibrahim has narrated from his father from ibn abu 'Umayr from Hafs ibn al-Bakhtariy from those whom he has mentioned who has said the following:

"Abu 'Abd Allah, *'Alayhi al-Salam,* has said, 'Chess is of falsehood.'"

H 12077, Ch. 26, h 5

Ibn abu 'Umayr has narrated from Muhammad ibn al-Hakam brother of Hisham ibn al-Hakam from 'Umar ibn Yazid who has said the following:

"Abu 'Abd Allah, *'Alayhi al-Salam,* has said that every night in the month of Ramadan Allah sets free from fire certain people, except those who break their fast with intoxicating substances, a heretic in religion and *Sahib* of *Shahayn* (player of the game with two kings). I then asked, 'What is *Sahib* of *Shahayn?*' He (the Imam) said, 'It is chess.'"

H 12078, Ch. 26, h 6

Muhammad ibn Yahya has narrated from Ahmad ibn Muhammad from ibn Faddal from Ali ibn 'Uqbah from ibn Bukayr from Zurarah who has said the following:

"Once, abu 'Abd Allah, *'Alayhi al-Salam,* was asked about chess and about a game of youths called *'al-Amir* game' and the game called *'Thalathah'*. He (the Imam) said, 'Consider if right and wrong are made distinct from each other, where do these things fall?' He (the narrator) has said, 'I said that it falls in the wrong category.' He (the Imam) said, 'It then is devoid of goodness.'"

H 12079, Ch. 26, h 7

Ali ibn Ibrahim has narrated from his father from ibn abu 'Umayr from certain persons of his people who has said the following:

"About the meaning of the words of Allah, most Majestic, most Glorious, 'You must stay away from the filth of idols and you must stay away from false words,' abu 'Abd Allah, *'Alayhi al-Salam,* has said, '"The filth of idols" is a reference to chess and "false words" stands for *al-Ghina'* (music (and singing)).'"

H 12080, Ch. 26, h 8

Muhammad ibn Yahya has narrated from Ahmad ibn Muhammad from Muhammad ibn Sinan from 'Abd al-Malik al-Qummiy who has said the following:

"Once, my brother Idris and I were with abu 'Abd Allah, *'Alayhi al-Salam,* and Idris said, 'I pray to Allah to keep our souls in service for your cause, what is *al-Maysir?*' He (the Imam) said, 'It is chess.' I then said that they say it is dice.' He (the Imam) said, 'Dice also is *al-Maysir* (gambling).'"

H 12081, Ch. 26, h 9

A number of our people have narrated from Sahl ibn Ziyad from Muhammad ibn 'Isa from 'Abd Allah ibn 'Asem from Ali ibn `Isma'il al-Mithamiy from ibn Rib'iy ibn 'Abd Allah from al-Fudayl who has said the following:

"I once asked abu Ja'far, *'Alayhi al-Salam,* about these things with which people play, like dice, chess . . . until I mentioned *al-Sudar* (a certain game). He (the Imam) said, 'If Allah makes right distinct from wrong, where will it fall?' I said that it would fall in the wrong category. He (the Imam) said, 'What then do you have to do with anything which is wrong?'"

H 12082, Ch. 26, h 10
Sahl ibn Ziyad has narrated from Muhammad ibn 'Isa from Yunus from al-Husayn 'Umar ibn Yazid who has said the following:

"Abu 'Abd Allah, *'Alayhi al-Salam,* has said, 'In the month of Ramadan Allah forgives certain people except a drunk person, a chess playing person and a heretic.'"

H 12083, Ch. 26, h 11
It is narrated from the narrator of the previous *Hadith* from Muhammad ibn 'Isa from Yunus from abu Ayyub from 'Abd Allah ibn Jundab from those who narrated to him who has said the following:

"Abu 'Abd Allah, *'Alayhi al-Salam,* has said, 'Chess is *al-Maysir* (gambling) and dice is *al-Maysir* (gambling).'"

H 12084, Ch. 26, h 12
Ali ibn Ibrahim has narrated from his father from Hammad ibn 'Isa who has said the following:

"Once a man from the people of al-Basrah came to abu al-Hassan, al-Awwal, *'Alayhi al-Salam,* and said, 'I pray to Allah to keep my soul in service for your cause, I sit with people who play chess but I do not play. I only look at it.' He (the Imam) said, 'What do you have to do with a gathering to which Allah does not look?'"

H 12085, Ch. 26, h 13
Ali ibn Ibrahim has narrated from Harun ibn Muslim from Mas'adah ibn Ziyad who has said the following:

"Once abu 'Abd Allah, *'Alayhi al-Salam,* was asked about chess. He (the Imam) said, 'You must leave al-Majusiayah (the Zoroastrian thing) for its people, may Allah condemn it.'"

H 12086, Ch. 26, h 14
Muhammad ibn Yahya has narrated from Ahmad ibn Muhammad ibn 'Isa from Musa ibn al-Qasim from Muhammad ibn Ali ibn Ja'far who has said the following:

"Al-Rida', *'Alayhi al-Salam,* has said, that once a man came to abu Ja'far, *'Alayhi al-Salam,* and said, 'O abu Ja'far, what do you say about chess with which people play?' He (the Imam) said, 'My father narrated to me from Ali ibn al-Husayn, from al-Husayn ibn Ali from 'Amir al-Mu'minin, *'Alayhim al-Salam.* He (the Imam) has said that the Messenger of Allah, *O Allah, grant compensation to Muhammad and his family worthy of their services to Your cause,* has said, "If one speaks and his speech is something other than speaking of Allah, most Majestic, most Glorious, he is doing something useless. If one is silent and his silence is for something other than Allah he is forgetful."' He (the Imam) then remained calm and the man left.'"

H 12087, Ch. 26, h 15

A number of our people have narrated from Sahl ibn Ziyad from ibn Mahbub from ibn Ri'ab who has said the following:

"I once visited abu 'Abd Allah, *'Alayhi al-Salam,* and said, 'I pray to Allah to keep my soul in service for your cause, what do you say about chess?' He (the Imam) said, 'One who turns it from side to side is like one who turns pork from side to side.' I then asked, 'What must one who has turned pork from side to side do?' He (the Imam) said, 'He must wash his hands.'"

H 12088, Ch. 26, h 16

Sahl ibn Ziyad has narrated from Ali ibn Sa'id from Sulayman al-Ja'fariy who has said the following:

"Abu al-Hassan, al-Rida', *'Alayhi al-Salam,* has said, 'One who seeks cognizance with chess is like one seeking cognizance with the fire.'"

H 12089, Ch. 26, h 17

Ali ibn Ibrahim has narrated from his father from al-Nawfaliy from al-Sakuniy who has said the following:

"Abu 'Abd Allah, *'Alayhi al-Salam,* has said that the Messenger of Allah, *O Allah, grant compensation to Muhammad and his family worthy of their services to Your cause,* prohibited playing with chess and dice.'"

End of the Book of Drinks and all praise belongs to Allah, Cherisher of the worlds, *O Allah, grant compensation to our master Muhammad and his family worthy of their services to Your cause,* followed by the Book of Dresses, Beautification and Kindness, if Allah, most High, so wills.

Part Seven:
The Book of Dresses, Beautification and Kindness

Chapter 1 - Beautification and Showing the Bounty

H 12090, Ch. 1, h 1

Muhammad ibn Yahya has narrated from Ahmad ibn Muhammad from al-Qasim ibn Yahya from his grandfather al-Hassan ibn Rashid from abu Basir who has said the following:

"Abu 'Abd Allah, *'Alayhi al-Salam,* has said that `Amir al-Mu'minin has said, 'Allah is beautiful, He loves beauty and He loves to see the signs of bounty on His servant.'"

H 12091, Ch. 1, h 2

Ali ibn Muhammad has narrated from in a *marfu'* manner the following:

"Abu 'Abd Allah, *'Alayhi al-Salam,* has stated this *Hadith.* 'If Allah grants a bounty to one of His servants and such bounty appears on him, he is called the friend of Allah who speaks of the bounty of Allah. If Allah grants a bounty to one of His servants but it does not appear on him, he is called the anger of Allah and denying the bounty of Allah.'"

H 12092, Ch. 1, h 3

Muhammad ibn Yahya has narrated from Ahmad ibn Muhammad from Muhammad ibn Sinan from 'Uqbah ibn Muhammad from Salmah ibn Muhammad Bayya' al-Qalanisiy who has said the following:

"Once, abu 'Abd Allah, *'Alayhi al-Salam,* passed by a man whose voice had become very loud on another person when demanding something very little from him. He (the Imam) asked, 'How much do you demand from him?' he replied, 'So and so amount.' Abu 'Abd Allah, *'Alayhi al-Salam,* then said, 'Have you not heard the saying, 'One who has no kindness has no religion?'"

H 12093, Ch. 1, h 4

A number of our people have narrated from Sahl ibn Ziyad from Ali ibn Asbat from the one who narrated to him who has said the following:

"Abu 'Abd Allah, *'Alayhi al-Salam,* has said, 'When Allah grants a bounty to His servant He loves to see it on him; He is beautiful and loves beauty.'"

H 12094, Ch. 1, h 5

Sahl ibn Ziyad has narrated from Muhammad ibn al-Hassan ibn Shammun from 'Abd Allah ibn 'Abd al-Rahman from Misma' ibn 'Abd al-Malik who has said the following:

"Abu 'Abd Allah, *'Alayhi al-Salam,* has said that the Messenger of Allah, *O Allah, grant compensation to Muhammad and his family worthy of their services to Your cause,* once saw a man with his hairs untidy, his clothes dirty and his condition very bad. The Messenger of Allah said, 'It is of religion to enjoy and allow the bounty to show.'"

H 12095, Ch. 1, h 6

Through the same chain of narrators as that of the previous *Hadith* the following is narrated:

"He (the Imam)*'Alayhi al-Salam* has said that the Messenger of Allah, *O Allah, grant compensation to Muhammad and his family worthy of their services to Your cause,* has said, 'The worst servant is a dirty servant.'"

H 12096, Ch. 1, h 7

Ali ibn Ibrahim has narrated from his father from ibn abu 'Umayr from certain persons of his people from Mu'awiyah ibn Wahab who has said the following:

"Abu 'Abd Allah, *'Alayhi al-Salam,* once saw me carrying grass. He (the Imam) said, 'It is undesirable for a man of dignity to carry lowly things, thus people become bold against him.'"

H 12097, Ch. 1, h 8

A number of our people have narrated from Ahmad ibn Muhammad from Ali ibn Hadid from Murazim ibn Hakim from 'Abd al-'A'la' Mawla Ale Sam who has said the following:

"I once said to abu 'Abd Allah, *'Alayhi al-Salam,* 'People say you have a great wealth.' He (the Imam) said, 'It does not affect me badly because 'Amir al-Mu'minin one day passed by different groups of Quraysh with a very old shirt on him and they said, 'Ali has become very poor and has no assets.' 'Amir al-Mu'minin heard it. He then commanded the person in charge of charity to keep his share of dates, not to send to anyone but keep them. He (the Imam) then told him to sell to the first persons who wish to buy in exchange for dirham then place the dirhams as dates are placed, then hide them with dates so they are not seen. He then instructed the person in charge, "When I ask you for dates then climb on it, look at the asset and kick it with your foot as if you do not consider dirhams of any value and significance until they are scattered all over the place." He (the Imam) then sent someone to call the people (who had called him very poor and without any assets). He (the Imam) then asked for dates. When he went to bring dates he kicked with his foot and dirhams scattered all over the place. They asked, 'What is happening, O abu al-Hassan?' He (the Imam) replied, 'This is the assets of one who has become very poor and has no assets.' He (the Imam) then commanded to keep in mind the people to whom I have been sending dates. See how much were sent to each one then send that quantity to each one.'"

H 12098, Ch. 1, h 9

Ali ibn Ibrahim has narrated from his father from ibn abu 'Umayr in a marfu' manner has said the following:

"Abu 'Abd Allah, *'Alayhi al-Salam,* has said, 'I dislike to see a man who has received a bounty from Allah but does not show it.'"

H 12099, Ch. 1, h 10

A number of our people have narrated from Ahmad ibn Muhammad from al-Qasim ibn Yahya from his grandfather, al-Hassan ibn Rashid from abu Basir who has said the following:

"Abu 'Abd Allah, *'Alayhi al-Salam,* has said that 'Amir al-Mu'minin has said, 'You must dress up for your Muslim brother just as you dress up before a stranger; the Muslim brother who likes to see him (his Muslim brother) in the best dress.'"

H 12100, Ch. 1, h 11

A number of our people have narrated from Ahmad ibn Muhammad from ibn Mahbub from ibn Faddal all from Yunus ibn Ya'qub from abu Basir who has said the following:

"'Amir al-Mu'minin, *'Alayhi al-Salam,* was informed that Talhah and Zubayr say, 'Ali has no assets.' He (the Imam) said, 'It troubled him and he commanded his agents to collect his share of grains. They followed his instruction until the end of the year, then they brought it to him and it was worth one hundred thousand dirhams. It was spread before him. He sent for Talhah and Zubayr. When they came he told them, "This asset by Allah belongs to me and no one has any share in it." They had proof to verify it and they left saying, "He in fact does have assets."'"

H 12101, Ch. 1, h 12

It is narrated from the narrator of the previous *Hadith* from ibn Faddal and ibn Mahbub from Yunus ibn Ya'qub from abu Basir who has said the following:

"Abu 'Abd Allah, *'Alayhi al-Salam,* has said that in al-Madinah people said, 'Al-Hassan, *'Alayhi al-Salam,* has no assets.' Al-Hassan, *'Alayhi al-Salam,* sent to a man in al-Madinah, borrowed one thousand dirham from him and sent it to the charity collector saying, 'It is the charity due on our assets.' People said, 'Al-Hassan, *'Alayhi al-Salam,* has not sent it without a reason. This is because of a certain amount of assets.'"

H 12102, Ch. 1, h 13

It is narrated from the narrator of the previous *Hadith* from Ali ibn Hadid from Murazim ibn Hakim from 'Abd al-'A'la' Mawla'Ale Sam who has said the following:

"Ali ibn al-Husayn, *'Alayhim al-Salam,* lived in serious financial condition and people of al-Madinah began to speak about it. It came to his notice. He assigned one thousand dirham and sent it to the governor of al-Madinah saying, 'It is the charity due on our assets.'"

H 12103, Ch. 1, h 14

It is narrated from the narrator of the previous *Hadith* from Ahmad ibn Muhammad from ibn Faddal from abu Shu'ayb al-Mahamiliy from abu Hashim from certain persons of our people who has said the following:

"Abu 'Abd Allah, *'Alayhi al-Salam,* has said, 'Allah, most Majestic, most Glorious, loves beauty and beautification and dislikes misery and wretchedness.'"

H 12104, Ch. 1, h 15

Muhammad ibn Yahya has narrated from Muhammad ibn al-Husayn, from Muhammad ibn Aslam from Harun ibn Muslim from Burayd ibn Mu'awiyah who has said the following:

"Abu 'Abd Allah, *'Alayhi al-Salam,* once said to 'Ubayd ibn Ziyad, 'Showing the bounty is more beloved to Allah than its safekeeping. Therefore, you must live in your people with the best dress among them.' He (the narrator) has said that 'Ubayd was never seen except with the best dress among his people until he died.'"

Chapter 2 - The Dress

H 12105, Ch. 2, h 1

Muhammad ibn Yahya has narrated from Ahmad ibn Muhammad ibn 'Isa from Ali ibn al-Hakam from 'Abd Allah ibn Jundab from Sufyan ibn al-Simt who has said the following:

"I once heard abu 'Abd Allah, *'Alayhi al-Salam,* saying, 'Clean garments put down the enemy.'"

H 12106, Ch. 2, h 2

Abu Ali al-Ash'ariy has narrated from Muhammad ibn Salim from Ahmad ibn al-Nadr from 'Amr ibn Shamir from Jabir who has said the following:

"Abu Ja'far, *'Alayhi al-Salam,* has said that the Messenger of Allah, *O Allah, grant compensation to Muhammad and his family worthy of their services to Your cause,* dressed in *al-Taq,* (a certain garment) *al-Saj* (green pallium) and *al-Khama'is* (a black gown).'"

H 12107, Ch. 2, h 3

Ali ibn Ibrahim has narrated from his father from al-Nawfaliy from al-Sakuniy who has said the following:

"Abu 'Abd Allah, *'Alayhi al-Salam,* has said that the Messenger of Allah, *O Allah, grant compensation to Muhammad and his family worthy of their services to Your cause,* has said, 'One who chooses (makes use of) clothes, he must clean it.'"

H 12108, Ch. 2, h 4

A number of our people have narrated from Sahl ibn Ziyad from al-Jamuraniy from al-Hassan ibn Ali ibn abu Hamzah from Sayf ibn 'Amirah from Ishaq ibn 'Ammar who has said the following:

"I once asked abu 'Abd Allah, *'Alayhi al-Salam,* if a believing person can have ten shirts. He (the Imam) said, 'Yes, he can do so.' I then asked, 'Can he have twenty.' He (the Imam) said, 'Yes, he can do so.' I asked, 'Can he have thirty?' He (the Imam) said, 'Yes, he can do so. This is not profligacy and lavishness. Profligacy is when you make your dress to maintain your dignity the cloth of your disgraceful condition.'"

H 12109, Ch. 2, h 5

Al-Husayn ibn Muhammad has narrated from Mu'alla' ibn Muhammad from al-Hassan ibn Ali al-Washsha' who has said the following:

"I once heard al-Rida', *'Alayhi al-Salam,* saying, 'Ali ibn al-Husayn, *'Alayhim al-Salam,* would buy two dresses for summer, each valued at five hundred dirhams.'"

H 12110, Ch. 2, h 6

Muhammad ibn Yahya has narrated from 'Abd Allah ibn Muhammad from Ali ibn al-Hakam from Aban ibn 'Uthman from Yahya ibn al-'Ala' who has said the following:

"Abu 'Abd Allah, *'Alayhi al-Salam,* has said that 'Amir al-Mu'minin sent 'Abd Allah ibn al-'Abbas to ibn al-Kawwa' and his people. He was wearing a shirt of fine fabric and a gown. They looked at him and said, 'O ibn al-'Abbas, you are the better among us in our belief and you wear this kind of clothes.' He replied, 'This is the first thing about which I disagree with you. "Who has made it unlawful to maintain beauty and to eat the pure foods which Allah has created for His servants?" (7:32) and He also has said, "dress well when attending the mosques." (7:31)'"

H 12111, Ch. 2, h 7

A number of our people have narrated from Sahl ibn Ziyad from Muhammad ibn 'Isa from Safwan from Yusuf ibn Ibrahim who has said the following:

"I once visited abu 'Abd Allah, *'Alayhi al-Salam,* and I was wearing a *Jubbah* of silk and *al-Taylisan* (pallium) of silk. He (the Imam) looked at me and I asked saying, 'I pray to Allah to keep my soul in service for your cause, I am wearing a Taylisan of silk and a *Jubbah* of silk, what do you say about them?' He (the Imam) said, 'Silk is not unlawful.' I then said, 'Its warp is abrisam (silk from silk worm as opposed to that from certain plant fibers or synthetic). He (the Imam) said, 'Abrisam is not unlawful because when al-Husayn, *'Alayhi al-Salam,* was murdered, he was wearing abrisam and jubbah of silk.' He (the Imam) then said, 'Abd Allah ibn al-'Abbas was sent to al-Khawarij by `Amir al-Mu'minin and he stood before them wearing the best of his dresses with the best perfumes and with the best stumper. They said, 'O ibn al-'Abbas you are the best of people to us but you have come wearing the dress of the tyrants and riding the stumper of the tyrants.' He read to them this verse, 'Say, who has made unlawful the beauties that Allah has brought out for His servants and the best sustenance.' So dress up and beautify; Allah is beautiful and He loves beauty but it must be of the lawful ones.'"

H 12112, Ch. 2, h 8

Ali ibn Muhammad ibn Bandar Ahmad ibn abu 'Abd Allah from Muhammad ibn Ali in a *marfu'* manner has said the following:

"Once, Sufyan al-Thawriy passed by Masjid al-Haram (the sacred area) and he saw abu 'Abd Allah, *'Alayhi al-Salam,* dressed in fine expensive clothes. He decided to meet him (the Imam) and scold him. He went close and said, 'O child of the Messenger of Allah, the Messenger of Allah did not dress up with this kind of dress, Ali did not dress with this kind of dress nor any of your ancestors did.' Abu 'Abd Allah, *'Alayhi al-Salam,* said, 'The Messenger of Allah, *O Allah, grant compensation to Muhammad and his family worthy of their services to Your cause,* lived at a time when it was a financially serious and stringent condition. He (the Messenger of Allah) lived according to such conditions but the world thereafter has become financially relaxed. The most deserving in financial opportunities are the virtuous people.' He (the Imam) then read this verse, 'Say, who has made unlawful the beautiful things that Allah has brought out for His servants and the fine kinds of means of sustenance.' (7:31) We are the most deserving of what Allah has granted. However, O Thawriy, what you see I have dressed up with I have done so for people. He (the Imam) pulled his hand to himself and raised the outer layer of his dress. Underneath on his body was a layer of rough textured garment. He (the Imam) said, 'I wear this for my own soul and what you see (the outer layer) is for people.' He (the Imam) then raised the outer layer of the garment of Sufyan, which was of rough texture but the layer underneath on his body was of a fine quality. He (the Imam) said, 'You have dressed up for people with the outer layer and for yourself to enjoy with the fine quality layer underneath.'"

H 12113, Ch. 2, h 9
Al-Husayn ibn Muhammad has narrated from Mu'alla' ibn Muhammad from al-Washsha' from 'Abd Allah ibn Sinan who has said the following:

"I once heard abu 'Abd Allah, *'Alayhi al-Salam,* saying, 'When I was in *tawaf* (walking around al-Ka'bah) someone pulled my dress and he was 'Abbad ibn Kathir al-Basriy saying, "O Ja'far ibn Muhammad, you wear this kind of dress and your position to Ali, *'Alayhi al-Salam,* is so close."' I said, 'It is a material made in Furqubiy (a place in Egypt) which I have bought for a dinar. Ali, *'Alayhi al-Salam,* lived in a time when his kind of dress was suitable for him and if I wear that kind of dress now people will say, "He is another show off like 'Abbad."'"

H 12114, Ch. 2, h 10
A number of our people have narrated from Ahmad ibn Muhammad ibn Khalid from 'Uthman ibn 'Isa from Ishaq ibn 'Ammar who has said the following:

"I once asked abu 'Abd Allah, *'Alayhi al-Salam,* if a man can have ten shirts, changing them every day. He (the Imam) said, 'It is not unlawful.'"

H 12115, Ch. 2, h 11
Through the same chain of narrators as that of the previous *Hadith* the following is narrated from Ishaq ibn 'Ammar who has said the following:

"I once asked abu 'Abd Allah, *'Alayhi al-Salam,* if I can have three shirts. He (the Imam) said, 'It is not unlawful.' I asked again until I reached ten shirts and he (the Imam) said, 'Does exchanging give them more durability?' I said, 'It does, were I to wear one of them for a longer time, it would become less durable.' He (the Imam) said, 'It is not unlawful.'"

H 12116, Ch. 2, h 12
It is narrated from the narrator of the previous *Hadith* from Nuh ibn Shu'ayb from certain persons of his people who has said the following:

"I once asked abu 'Abd Allah, *'Alayhi al-Salam,* about the case of a man who is affluent and has a great deal of clothes and very fine ones, palliums, many shirts which are used to extend the life of each shirt and beautify himself; if it is profligacy and lavishness. He (the Imam) said, 'No, it is not lavishness because Allah, most Majestic, most Glorious, says, "The affluent can spend according to his affluent condition." (65:7)'"

H 12117, Ch. 2, h 13
A number of our people have narrated from Sahl ibn Ziyad from Ja'far ibn Muhammad al-Ash'ariy from ibn al-Qaddah who has said the following:

"Once abu 'Abd Allah, *'Alayhi al-Salam,* was leaning against me or he said, 'against my father' when 'Abbad ibn Kathir al-Basriy met him (the Imam) and he (the Imam) had a dress of fabrics made in Marw (name of place) of fine quality. He ('Abbad) said, 'O abu 'Abd Allah, you are of the family of the Holy Prophet, and your father was (so pious). What is this dress, made in Marw, on you? I wish you dressed in a lower quality dress.' Abu 'Abd Allah, *'Alayhi al-Salam,* said to him, 'Woe on you, O 'Abbad! Who has made unlawful the beautiful things that Allah, most Majestic, most Glorious, has brought out for His servants and the very fine kinds of means of sustenance. When Allah, most Majestic, most Glorious, grants bounties on His servant He loves to see it on him and it is not harmful. Woe on you, O 'Abbad, I am a piece of the Messenger of Allah, *O Allah, grant compensation to Muhammad and his family worthy of their services to Your cause,* do not trouble me.' 'Abbad wore two pieces of clothes made in Qitr (name of a place).'"

H 12118, Ch. 2, h 14

Muhammad ibn Yahya has narrated from Ahmad ibn Muhammad from al-Qasim ibn Yahya from his grandfather al-Hassan ibn Rashid from abu Basir who has said the following:

"Abu 'Abd Allah, *'Alayhi al-Salam,* has said that `Amir al-Mu'minin has said, 'Clean clothes remove sadness and it is of cleanliness for *Salat* (prayer).'"

H 12119, Ch. 2, h 15

Ahmad ibn Muhammad has narrated from Muhammad ibn Yahya from Hammad ibn 'Uthaman who has said the following:

"Once I was with abu 'Abd Allah, *'Alayhi al-Salam,* when a man said, 'I pray to Allah to keep you well, you have mentioned that Ali ibn abu Talib wore very rough-textured clothes. He wore a shirt valued at four dirham and similar items and we see you wear fine clothes.' Abu 'Abd Allah, *'Alayhi al-Salam,* said to him, 'Ali ibn abu Talib wore that kind of clothes in a time when it was not disliked. Were he to wear such clothes today he would have been defamed. The best dress in every period of time is what the people of that time use, however, when our al-Qa'im will rise, he will wear the kind of dress Ali, *'Alayhi al-Salam,* wore and follow his way of life.'"

H 12120, Ch. 2, h 16

A number of our people have narrated from Sahl ibn Ziyad from Ali ibn Asbat from the one who narrated to him who has said the following:

"Abu 'Abd Allah, *'Alayhi al-Salam,* has said, 'It is not unlawful if one has twenty shirts.'"

Chapter 3 - Dress Causing Public Abhorrence

H 12121, Ch. 3, h 1

Ali ibn Ibrahim has narrated from his father from ibn abu 'Umayr from abu Ayyub al-Khazzaz who has said the following:

"Abu 'Abd Allah, *'Alayhi al-Salam,* has said, 'Allah, most Blessed, most High, dislikes a dress that causes public abhorrence.'"

H 12122, Ch. 3, h 2

Muhammad ibn Yahya has narrated from Ahmad ibn Muhammad from Muhammad ibn `Isma'il from abu `Isma'il al-Sarraj from ibn Muskan from a man who has said the following:

"Abu 'Abd Allah, *'Alayhi al-Salam,* has said, 'It is enough humiliation for a man to wear a dress that causes public abhorrence or use such a stumper.'"

H 12123, Ch. 3, h 3

A number of our people have narrated from Ahmad ibn Muhammad ibn Khalid from 'Uthman ibn 'Isa from those whom he has mentioned who has said the following:

"Abu 'Abd Allah, *'Alayhi al-Salam,* has said, 'Something that causes public abhorrence is in the fire, regardless of being good or bad.'"

H 12124, Ch. 3, h 4
Muhammad ibn Yahya has narrated from Ahmad ibn Muhammad from Muhammad ibn Sinan from abu al-Jarud from abu Sa'id who has said the following:
"Al-Husayn, *'Alayhi al-Salam,* has said, 'If one wears a dress that causes public abhorrence, Allah on the Day of Judgment will make him to wear a dress of fire.'"

Chapter 4 - The Cotton White Dress

H 12125, Ch. 4, h 1
Muhammad ibn Yahya has narrated from Ahmad ibn Muhammad from ibn Faddal from ibn al-Qaddah who has said the following:
"Abu 'Abd Allah, *'Alayhi al-Salam,* has said that the Messenger of Allah, *O Allah, grant compensation to Muhammad and his family worthy of their services to Your cause,* has said, 'You must wear white because it is fine and pure; and shroud your dead people with it.'"

H 12126, Ch. 4, h 2
Al-Husayn ibn Muhammad has narrated from Mu'alla' ibn Muhammad from al-Hassan ibn Ali from Muthanna' al-Hannat who has said the following:
"Abu 'Abd Allah, *'Alayhi al-Salam,* has said that the Messenger of Allah, *O Allah, grant compensation to Muhammad and his family worthy of their services to Your cause,* has said, 'You must wear white; it is fine and pure; and shroud your dead people with it.'"

H 12127, Ch. 4, h 3
A number of our people have narrated from Ahmad ibn abu 'Abd Allah from certain persons of his people from Safwan al-Jammal who has said the following:
"I provided abu 'Abd Allah, *'Alayhi al-Salam,* transportation to al-Kufah for the second time and abu Ja'far al-Mansur was in it. When he (the Imam) arrived in al-Hashimiyah, the city of abu Ja'far, al-Mansur, he (the Imam) pulled out his feet from the saddle's stirrups and dismounted. He asked for *al-Shahba'* mule and dressed in white, with a white hat. When he (the Imam) entered the place of abu Ja'far al-Mansur he said, 'You have dressed like the Prophets.' Abu 'Abd Allah, *'Alayhi al-Salam,* said, 'Why do you want to distance me from the children of the Prophets?' Abu Ja'far al-Mansur said, 'I was planning to send to al-Madinah an army to uproot all its palm trees, take all of its inhabitants as captives.' He (the Imam) asked, 'Why did you want to do so, O 'Amir al-Mu'minin?' abu Ja'far al-Mansur said, 'Because I am informed that your slave Mu'alla' ibn Khunayth calls people to you and collects funds for you.' He (the Imam) said, 'By Allah it is not true.' Abu Ja'far al-Mansur said, 'I cannot agree with you unless it is swearing to divorce, setting free of slaves, sacrificial offering and walking (Sa'y).' He (the Imam) said, 'Are you commanding me to swear by things as partners of Allah? One who is not happy with Allah has no case with Allah.' Abu Ja'far al-Mansur said, 'Are you showing me how great your knowledge of the law is?' He (the Imam) said, 'Why do you distance me

from understanding and law when I am a child of the Messenger of Allah, *O Allah, grant compensation to Muhammad and his family worthy of their services to Your cause?*' Abu Ja'far al-Mansur said, 'I will bring the informer face to face with you.' He (the Imam) said, 'You can definitely do so.' The informer came and abu 'Abd Allah, *'Alayhi al-Salam,* asked him, 'O so and so.' He replied, 'Yes, by Allah, besides whom no one deserves to be worshipped, who knows the unseen and seen, the Beneficent, the Merciful that you have done so (called people to yourself . . .).' Abu 'Abd Allah, *'Alayhi al-Salam,* said to him, 'Woe is on you! Are you glorifying Allah so that He may feel embarrassed to punish you?' You must say, 'I denounce the means and power of Allah and I resort to my own means and power.' The man then took the oath the way he was told but before completing he dropped dead.' Abu Ja'far al-Mansur then said, 'I will not believe anyone thereafter against you.' He gave him (the Imam) good rewards and allowed him to go back.'"

H 12128, Ch. 4, h 4
Muhammad ibn Yahya has narrated from Ahmad ibn Muhammad from al-Qasim ibn Yahya from his grandfather al-Hassan ibn Rashid f, abu Basir who has said the following:
"Abu 'Abd Allah, *'Alayhi al-Salam,* has said that `Amir al-Mu'minin has said, 'You must wear cotton clothes because it is the clothes of the Messenger of Allah, *O Allah, grant compensation to Muhammad and his family worthy of their services to Your cause,* and our clothes.'"

Chapter 5 - Clothes Dyed with al-Mu'asfar (dye with safflower)

H 12129, Ch. 5, h 1
Muhammad ibn Yahya has narrated from Ahmad ibn Muhammad from Ali ibn al-Hakam from Mu'awiyah ibn Maysarah from al-Hakam ibn 'Utaybah who has said the following:
"I once visited abu Ja'far, *'Alayhi al-Salam,* in a well-furnished house. He (the Imam) was wearing a shirt which was not fully dry and a colored bed sheet which had left its color marks on his shoulder, and I was looking at the house and to him (the Imam). He (the Imam) said, 'O Hakam, what do you say about it?' I replied, 'I was about to say something about it after seeing it on you. With us it is used only by the youthful ones.' He (the Imam) said, 'O Hakam, 'Who has made unlawful the beautiful things that Allah, most Majestic, most Glorious, has brought out for His servants and the very fine kinds of means of sustenance.' (7:31) This is of the things that Allah has made to come out for His servants. This house which you see is the house of the woman and I am not far away from the time of the wedding, however, my house is that which you know.'"

H 12130, Ch. 5, h 2
Al-Husayn ibn Muhammad has narrated from Mu'alla' ibn Muhammad from al-Washsha' from Muhammad ibn Humran and Jamil ibn Darraj from Muhammad ibn Muslim who has said the following:
"One of the two Imam, (abu Ja'far or abu 'Abd Allah), *'Alayhim al-Salam,* has said, 'It is not unlawful to wear a cloth which is dyed with al-Mu'asfar (dye with safflower).'"

H 12131, Ch. 5, h 3

Ali ibn Ibrahim has narrated from his father from ibn abu 'Umayr from Hammad from Zurarah who has said the following:

"I once saw abu Ja'far, *'Alayhi al-Salam,* in al-Mu'asfar (dye with safflower) dress and he (the Imam) said that he has just married a woman from Quraysh.'"

H 12132, Ch. 5, h 4

A number of our people have narrated from Sahl ibn Ziyad from Ja'far ibn Muhammad from ibn al-Qaddah who has said the following:

"Abu 'Abd Allah, *'Alayhi al-Salam,* has stated this *Hadith.* ''Amir al-Mu'minin has said, 'The Messenger of Allah, *O Allah, grant compensation to Muhammad and his family worthy of their services to Your cause,* prohibited the dress causing public abhorrence and I do not say he (the Messenger of Allah) prohibited you from wearing clothes dyed with safflower, sharp red color.'"

H 12133, Ch. 5, h 5

Ali ibn Ibrahim has narrated from his father from ibn abu 'Umayr from a man who has said the following:

"Abu 'Abd Allah, *'Alayhi al-Salam,* has said, 'Wearing clothes of sharp color is not desirable except for weddings.'"

H 12134, Ch. 5, h 6

A number of our people have narrated from Sahl ibn Ziyad from Muhammad ibn 'Isa from al-Nadr ibn Suwayd from al-Qasim ibn Sulayman from Jarrah al-Mad'iniy who has said the following:

"Abu Ja'far, *'Alayhi al-Salam,* has said, 'Wearing clothes of sharp color is not desirable except for weddings.'"

H 12135, Ch. 5, h 7

Abu Ali al-Ash'ariy has narrated from Muhammad ibn 'Abd al-Jabbar from Safwan from Burayd from Malik ibn 'A'yan who has said the following:

"I once visited abu Ja'far, *'Alayhi al-Salam.* A sheet of sharp red color was on him. I smiled when I entered. He (the Imam) said, 'It seems I know why you are laughing. You laugh because of this cloth on me. It is because the Thaqafiy woman forced me to wear it and I love her.' He (the Imam) then said, 'We do not perform *Salat* (prayer) in a cloth of sharp color and you also must not perform *Salat* (prayer) with such clothes.' He (the narrator) has said, 'Afterward I went to see him when he had divorced her and he (the Imam) said, 'I divorced her because I heard her denounce Ali, *'Alayhi al-Salam,* so I could not keep her with such attitude.'"

H 12136, Ch. 5, h 8

Muhammad ibn Yahya has narrated from Ahmad ibn Muhammad from Muhammad ibn Sinan from abu al-Jarud who has said the following:

"Abu Ja'far, *'Alayhi al-Salam,* would wear al-Mu'asfar (dye with safflower) clothes and printed clothes."

H 12137, Ch. 5, h 9

A number of our people have narrated from Sahl ibn Ziyad from Ja'far ibn Muhammad from ibn al-Qaddah who has said the following:

"Abu 'Abd Allah, *'Alayhi al-Salam,* has said that the Messenger of Allah, *O*

Allah, grant compensation to Muhammad and his family worthy of their services to Your cause, had a sheet that was from *Wars* (a place in Yemen). He (the Messenger of Allah) would use it in the family. The color of the sheet had left marks on him (the Messenger of Allah).' Abu Ja'far, *'Alayhi al-Salam,* has said, 'We would use al-Mu'asfar (dye with safflower) clothes at home.'"

H 12138, Ch. 5, h 10
Abu Ali al-Ash'ariy has narrated from Muhammad ibn 'Abd al-Jabbar from ibn Faddal from ibn Bukayr from Zurarah who has said the following:

"Abu Ja'far, *'Alayhi al-Salam,* has said, 'We would dye our clothes al-Mu'asfar (dye with safflower) and banu 'Umayyah died with saffron dye.'"

H 12139, Ch. 5, h 11
A number of our people have narrated from Sahl ibn Ziyad from Muhammad ibn 'Isa from Yunus who has said the following:

"I saw abu al-Hassan, *'Alayhi al-Salam,* wearing al-Taylisan (pallium) of blue color.'"

H 12140, Ch. 5, h 12
Muhammad ibn 'Isa has narrated from Muhammad ibn Ali who has said the following:

"I saw Ali ibn al-Husayn, *'Alayhi al-Salam,* wearing clothes of lentil color.'"

H 12141, Ch. 5, h 13
A number of our people have narrated from Ahmad ibn Muhammad ibn Khalid from 'Uthman ibn 'Isa from 'Abd Allah ibn Muskan from al-Hassan al-Zayyat al-Basriy who has said the following:

"My friend and I once visited abu Ja'far, *'Alayhi al-Salam,* when he (the Imam) was in a well-furnished home. He had a flowery sheet on him, his beard was trimmed and kohl (metallic color eye powder) was applied to his eyes. We asked him (the Imam) certain questions and when we were to leave, he (the Imam) said to me, 'O Hassan,' and I replied, 'Yes, here I am, to obey your command.' He (the Imam) said, 'Tomorrow come to me with your friend.' I replied, 'Yes, I pray to Allah to keep my soul in service for your cause.' The next day we went to meet him (the Imam) and he (the Imam) was in a house with no furnishing except a mat and was wearing a rough-textured shirt. He (the Imam) turned to my friend and said, 'O brother from al-Basrah, yesterday you came to me when I was in the house of the woman. Yesterday was her day, the house is her house, and the furnishing is her furnishing. She had dressed up for me on condition that I dress up for her as she had dressed up for me. So do not think anything.' My friend said, 'I pray to Allah to keep my soul in service for your cause, by Allah there was something in my heart but now by Allah, Allah has removed what was in my heart. The truth is in what you just said.'"

Chapter 6 - Wearing Black

H 12142, Ch. 6, h 1
A number of our people have narrated from Ahmad ibn abu 'Abd Allah from certain persons of his people in a marfu' manner has said the following:

"The Messenger of Allah, *O Allah, grant compensation to Muhammad and his family worthy of their services to Your cause,* has said, 'It is detestable to wear black except three items such as slippers, turbans and gowns.'"

H 12143, Ch. 6, h 2

Abu Ali al-Ash'ariy has narrated from certain persons of his people from Muhammad ibn Sinan from Hudhafah ibn Mansur who has said the following:

"Once I was with abu 'Abd Allah, *'Alayhi al-Salam,* in al-Hirah (a city in Iraq) when the messenger of abu Ja'far al-Mansur, the caliph came to call him. He (the Imam) asked for a raincoat, one side black and the other side white, and abu 'Abd Allah, *'Alayhi al-Salam,* said, 'I wear it but I know that it is the dress of the people of fire.'" (Black was the emblem of al-'Abbaside rulers. Imam wore it due to Taqiyah (caution because of fear)

H 12144, Ch. 6, h 3

A number of our people have narrated from Sahl ibn Ziyad from Muhammad ibn 'Isa from Sulayman ibn Rashid from his father who has said the following:

"I once saw Ali ibn al-Husayn, *'Alayhim al-Salam,* wearing a black outer garment and a blue Taylisan (pallium).'"

Chapter 7 - Al-Kattan (Linen)

H 12145, Ch. 7, h 1

A number of our people have narrated from Ahmad ibn Muhammad from and Abu Ali al-Ash'ariy has narrated from Muhammad ibn 'Abd al-Jabbar all from ibn Faddal from Ali ibn 'Uqbah from his father who has said the following:

"Abu 'Abd Allah, *'Alayhi al-Salam,* has said, 'Al-Kattan (linen) is of the garment of the Prophets and it helps the flesh to grow,'"

Chapter 8 - Wearing Wool, Hairs and Fur

H 12146, Ch. 8, h 1

Muhammad ibn Yahya has narrated from Ahmad ibn Muhammad from al-Qasim ibn Yahya from his grandfather al-Hassan ibn Rashid from abu Basir who has said the following:

"Abu 'Abd Allah, *'Alayhi al-Salam,* has said, 'Do not wear wool or hairs unless because of illness.'"

H 12147, Ch. 8, h 2

A number of our people have narrated from Sahl ibn Ziyad from Muhammad ibn 'Isa from 'Abd Allah ibn 'Abd al-Rahman from Shu'ayb from abu Basir who has said the following:

"Abu 'Abd Allah, *'Alayhi al-Salam,* has said that `Amir al-Mu'minin has said, 'You must wear clothes of cotton because it is the cloth of the Messenger of Allah, *O Allah, grant compensation to Muhammad and his family worthy of their services to Your cause,* as well as our cloth. He (the Messenger of Allah) did not wear wool or hairs except because of illness.'"

H 12148, Ch. 8, h 3

A number of our people have narrated from Sahl ibn Ziyad from Muhammad ibn 'Isa from 'Uthman ibn Sa'id from 'Abd al-Karim al-Hamadaniy from abu Tamamah who has said the following:

"I once asked abu Ja'far, al-Thaniy, *'Alayhi al-Salam,* saying, 'Our land is cold. What do you say about wearing fur?' He (the Imam) said, 'Wear that which is from edible animals and verify (that it is from edible animals).'"

H 12149, Ch. 8, h 4

Abu Ali al-Ash'ariy has narrated from Muhammad ibn 'Abd al-Jabbar from ibn Faddal from Muhammad ibn al-Hassan ibn Kathir al-Khazzaz from his father who has said the following:

"I saw abu 'Abd Allah, *'Alayhi al-Salam,* wearing a shirt of rough texture underneath his clothes, over which was a woolen gown over which was a thick shirt and I felt it, and said, 'I pray to Allah to keep my soul in service for your cause, people dislike wearing wool.' He (the Imam) said, 'Not so, my father, Muhammad ibn Ali, *'Alayhi al-Salam,* would wear it as well as Ali ibn al-Husayn, *'Alayhi al-Salam,* did. They, *'Alayhim al-Salam,* wore their clothes of the roughest texture in their *Salat* (prayer) and we also do so.'"

H 12150, Ch. 8, h 5

Ali ibn Muhammad ibn Bandar has narrated from Ahmad ibn abu 'Abd Allah from Ahmad ibn Muhammad from ibn abu Nasr from abu Jarir al-Qummiy who has said the following:

"I once asked al-Rida', *'Alayhi al-Salam,* about feathers; if it is lawful. He (the Imam) said, 'My father would use a pillow of feathers.'"

Chapter 9 - Wearing al-Khazz (fur or skin of an animal that lives in water)

H 12151, Ch. 9, h 1

Ali ibn Ibrahim has narrated from his father from Hammad ibn 'Isa from Hariz from Zurarah who has said the following:

"Abu Ja'far, *'Alayhi al-Salam,* came out for *Salat* (prayer) and certain ones of his children had a gown of yellow al-Khazz (skin or fur of an animal that lives in water) with ribbon work of yellow al-Khazz.'"

H 12152, Ch. 9, h 2

A number of our people have narrated from Sahl ibn Ziyad from Ahmad ibn Muhammad from ibn abu Nasr who has said the following:

"Abu al-Hassan, al-Rida', *'Alayhi al-Salam,* has said, 'Ali ibn al-Husayn, *'Alayhim al-Salam,* wore a gown of al-Khazz (skin or fur of an animal that lives in water) valued at fifty dinar and al-Khazz ribbon work of fifty dinar.'"

H 12153, Ch. 9, h 3

Abu Ali al-Ash'ariy has narrated from Muhammad ibn 'Abd al-Jabbar from Safwan ibn Yahya from 'Abd al-Rahman ibn *al-Hajj*aj who has said the following:

"I, once, was with abu 'Abd Allah, *'Alayhi al-Salam,* when a man asked him (the Imam) about al-Khazz (skin or fur of an animal that lives in water). He (the Imam) said, 'Its use is not unlawful.' He then said, 'I pray to Allah to keep my soul in service for your cause, in our land they are dogs that come out of the water.' He (the Imam) asked, 'When they come out of the water do they then live on land?' The man replied, 'No, they do not live on land.' He (the Imam) then said, 'Its use is not unlawful.'"

H 12154, Ch. 9, h 4

A number of our people have narrated from Sahl ibn Ziyad from al-Hassan ibn Ali al-Washsha' who has said the following:

"I once heard abu al-Hassan, al-Rida', *'Alayhi al-Salam,* saying, 'Ali ibn al-

Husayn, *'Alayhim al-Salam,* in winter would wear al-Khazz (skin or fur of an animal that lives in water) decorated on both sides and a hat of al-Khazz for winter, then sell them in the summer and give its value in charity.' He (the Imam) then read, 'Who has made unlawful the beautiful things that Allah, most Majestic, most Glorious, has brought out for His servants and the very fine kinds of means of sustenance. (7:31)'"

H 12155, Ch. 9, h 5
Abu Ali al-Ash'ariy has narrated from Muhammad ibn 'Abd al-Jabbar from Safwan ibn Yahya from al-'Is ibn al-Qasim from abu Dawud, Yusuf ibn Ibrahim who has said the following:

"I once visited abu 'Abd Allah, *'Alayhi al-Salam,* and I was wearing a gown of al-Khazz (skin or fur of an animal that lives in water) with its lining of al-Khazz, a Taylisan (pallium) of al-Khazz of very fine texture. I then said, 'I am wearing a kind of clothing which I do not like.' He (the Imam) asked, 'Why is that so?' I replied, 'It is this Taylisan.' He (the Imam) asked, 'What is the matter with it?' I replied, 'It is of al-Khazz.' He (the Imam) asked, 'What is wrong with al-Khazz?' I then said, 'Its warp is of abrisam (silk from silk worm).' He (the Imam) asked, 'What is wrong with abrisam? It is not detestable if its warp is of abrisam, or its buttons or its emblems. Only all abrisam is detestable for men, and not for women.'"

H 12156, Ch. 9, h 6
A number of our people have narrated from Ahmad ibn abu 'Abd Allah from Musa ibn al-Qasim from 'Amr ibn 'Uthman from abu Jamilah from a man who has said the following:

"Abu Ja'far, *'Alayhi al-Salam,* has said, 'We the community of the family of Muhammad wear al-Khazz (skin or fur of an animal that lives in water) and al-Yumnah (that which is made in Yemen).'"

H 12157, Ch. 9, h 7
It is narrated from the narrator of the previous *Hadith* from Sa'd ibn Sa'd who has said the following:

"I once asked al-Rida', *'Alayhi al-Salam,* about the al-Khazz (skin or fur of an animal that lives in water). He (the Imam) said, 'It is al-Khazz that we wear.' I then said, 'I pray to Allah to keep my soul in service for your cause, that is fur.' He (the Imam) said, 'If its fur is lawful so also is its skin.'"

H 12158, Ch. 9, h 8
It is narrated from the narrator of the previous *Hadith* from Ja'far ibn 'Isa who has said the following:

"I once wrote to abu al-Hassan, al-Rida', *'Alayhi al-Salam,* about animals from the fur of which al-Khazz is made; if such animals are of predators.' He (the Imam) wrote in answer, 'Ali ibn al-Husayn, wore al-Khazz (garments made from skin or fur of an animal that lives in water) then my grandfather also did so.'"

H 12159, Ch. 9, h 9
Abu Ali al-Ash'ariy has narrated from Muhammad ibn Salim from Ahmad ibn al-Nadr from 'Amr ibn Shamir from Jabir who has said the following:

"Abu Ja'far, *'Alayhi al-Salam,* has said that when al-Husayn, *'Alayhi al-Salam,* was murdered, he wore a dark color Jubbah (gown) of al-Khazz (garments made of skin or fur of an animal that lives in water). They found thirty-three torn spots in it because of being hit with sword, spears or shooting arrows.'"

H 12160, Ch. 9, h 10
A number of our people have narrated from Sahl ibn Ziyad from Muhammad ibn 'Isa from Hafs ibn 'Umar ('Amr) abu Muhammad Mu'adhdhin Ali ibn Yaqtin who has said the following:
"I saw abu 'Abd Allah, *'Alayhi al-Salam,* performing *Salat* (prayer) in al-Rawdah and wore a jubbah (gown) of al-Khazz (garments made of skin or fur of an animal that lives in water) of the color of quince.'"

Chapter 10 - Garments made entirely of al-Washy (al-Khazz, garments made of skin or fur of an animal that lives in water)

H 12161, Ch. 10, h 1
A number of our people have narrated from Ahmad ibn Muhammad ibn 'Isa from ibn Faddal and Sahl ibn Ziyad from Muhammad ibn 'Isa from Yasir who has said the following:
"Abu al-Hassan, *'Alayhi al-Salam,* once said to me, 'Buy al-Khazz (garments made of skin or fur of an animal that lives in water) for yourself or if you like buy al-Washy.' I then asked, 'All with al-Washy?' He (the Imam) asked, '*What is al-Washy*?' I replied, 'It is that which has no cotton in it and they say it is unlawful.' He (the Imam) said, 'You can wear what has cotton in it.'"

H 12162, Ch. 10, h 2
It is narrated from the narrator of the previous *Hadith* from Yunus ibn Ya'qub from al-Husayn ibn Salim al-'Ijliy who delivered al-Washy to him (the Imam), *'Alayhi al-Salam.*

H 12163, Ch. 10, h 3
A number of our people have narrated from Ahmad ibn Muhammad from ibn Mahbub from Yunus ibn Ya'qub who has said that narrated to me the one whom I trust that he saw on the girls of abu al-Hassan al-Washy (al-Khazz, garments made of skin or fur of an animal that lives in water) .

Chapter 11 - Wearing Silk and al-Dibaj (Silk Brocade)

H 12164, Ch. 11, h 1
Muhammad ibn Yahya has narrated from Ahmad ibn Muhammad ibn 'Isa from ibn Faddal from ibn Bukayr from certain persons of our people who has said the following:
"Abu 'Abd Allah, *'Alayhi al-Salam,* has said, 'Men must not wear silk and clothes with brocades except during a war.'"

H 12165, Ch. 11, h 2
It is narrated from the narrator of the previous *Hadith* from ibn Faddal from abu Jamilah from Layth al-Muradiy who has said the following:
"Abu 'Abd Allah, *'Alayhi al-Salam,* has said that the Messenger of Allah, *O Allah, grant compensation to Muhammad and his family worthy of their services to Your cause,* made 'Usamah ibn Zayd dress in silk (during a war). He (after the war) came out in public in that dress. He (the Messenger of Allah), said, 'O

'Usamah, wait. Those who wear this (silk) do not have a share (in morality) so you must divide it among your women.'"

H 12166, Ch. 11, h 3
A number of our people have narrated from Ahmad ibn abu 'Abd Allah from 'Uthman ibn 'Isa from Sama'ah ibn Mehran who has said the following:

"I once asked abu 'Abd Allah, *'Alayhi al-Salam,* about dress of silk and brocades. He (the Imam) said, 'During war it is not unlawful even if it has prints and pictures on it.'"

H 12167, Ch. 11, h 4
Muhammad ibn Yahya has narrated from 'Abd Allah ibn Muhammad ibn 'Isa from Ali ibn al-Hakam from Aban 'Uthman from 'Isma'il ibn al-Fadl who has said the following:

"Abu 'Abd Allah, *'Alayhi al-Salam,* has said, 'It is not proper for men to wear silk, except during the time of war.'"

H 12168, Ch. 11, h 5
Humayd ibn Ziyad has narrated from Muhammad ibn 'Isa from al-'Abbas ibn Hilal al-Shamiy who has said the following:

"I once said to abu al-Hassan, *'Alayhi al-Salam,* 'I pray to Allah to keep my soul in service for your cause, those who eat tasteless food, wear garments of rough texture and appear very humble are very attractive to people.' He (the Imam) said, 'Has it not come to your notice that Yusuf was a prophet and the son of a prophet who wore gowns decorated with brocades and buttons of gold. He would sit in the gathering of the pharaohs and issue judgments. People did not need his dress. They however needed his justice. What is needed of an Imam is that when he speaks he must speak the truth, keep his promise and must rule with justice. Allah does not make food unlawful or drinks which are lawful. He however, has made unlawful the unlawful things of small or large quantity; and Allah, most Majestic, most Glorious, has said, 'Who has made unlawful the beautiful things that Allah has brought out for His servants of the fine and clean sustenance?' (7:32)"

H 12169, Ch. 11, h 6
Muhammad ibn Yahya Ahmad ibn Muhammad and others have narrated from Ahmad ibn Muhammad from al-Husayn ibn Sa'id fn al-Nadr ibn Suwayd from al-Qasim ibn Sulayman from Jarrah al-Mada'iniy who has said the following:

"Abu 'Abd Allah, *'Alayhi al-Salam,* disliked shirts with borders decorated with silk as well as garments of silk, clothes with embroideries, and cushions of red color; he called them the cushion of Satan.'"

H 12170, Ch. 11, h 7
Humayd ibn Ziyad has narrated from al-Hassan ibn Muhammad ibn Ahmad ibn Sama'ah from more than one person from Aban al-Ahmar from Muhammad ibn Muslim who has said the following:

"Abu Ja'far, *'Alayhi al-Salam,* has said, 'Silk garments are not proper, however, selling such garments is not unlawful.'"

H 12171, Ch. 11, h 8
Muhammad ibn Yahya has narrated from Ahmad ibn Muhammad from ibn Faddal from ibn Bukayr from certain persons of our people who have said the following:

"Abu 'Abd Allah, *'Alayhi al-Salam,* has said, 'Women can wear silk garments decorated with embroideries, except in the state of Ihram.'"

H 12172, Ch. 11, h 9
A number of our people have narrated from Ahmad ibn Muhammad ibn Khalid from Muhammad ibn Ali from al-'Abbas ibn Musa from his father who has said the following:
"I once asked him (the Imam), *'Alayhi al-Salam,* about abrisam and al-Qazz (kinds of silk from silk worm). He (the Imam) said, 'They are the same.'"

H 12173, Ch. 11, h 10
It is narrated from the narrator of the previous *Hadith* from his father from al-Qasim ibn 'Urwah from 'Ubayd ibn Zurarah who has said the following:
"Abu 'Abd Allah, *'Alayhi al-Salam,* has said, 'It is not unlawful to use a garments which are made of al-Qazz if its warp or weft is of cotton or kattan (linen, the fibers of certain plants).'"

H 12174, Ch. 11, h 11
It is narrated from the narrator of the previous *Hadith* from Ahmad ibn Muhammad from ibn abu Nasr who has said the following:
"Al-Hassan ibn Qiyaman once asked abu al-Hassan, *'Alayhi al-Salam,* about a garment with its weft of al-Qazz and cotton in which al-Qazz is more than half: if one can use for *Salat* (prayer). He (the Imam) said, 'It is not unlawful.' Abu al-Hassan, *'Alayhi al-Salam,* had such a gown.'"

H 12175, Ch. 11, h 12
Muhammad ibn Yahya has narrated from Ahmad ibn Muhammad from ibn Mahbub from abu Ayyub from Sama'ah who has said the following:
"Abu 'Abd Allah, *'Alayhi al-Salam,* has said, 'It is not proper for a woman to wear garments of all silk in the state of Ihram, however, in hot or cold weather it is not harmful.'"

H 12176, Ch. 11, h 13
Ali ibn Ibrahim has narrated from Salih ibn al-Sindy from Ja'far ibn Bashir from abu al-Hassan al-Ahmasiy who has said the following:
"Abu Sa'id once asked abu 'Abd Allah, *'Alayhi al-Salam,* about al-Khamisah (a square-shaped gown with prints), when I was there, with its warp of abrisam (silk from silk worm); if it can be used in very cold weather. He (the Imam) commanded him to wear it.'"

H 12177, Ch. 11, h 14
Humayd ibn Ziyad has narrated from al-Hassan ibn Muhammad ibn Sama'ah from more than one person from Aban from 'Isma'il ibn al-Fadl who has said the following:
"About the case of a cloth which has silk in it abu 'Abd Allah, *'Alayhi al-Salam,* has said, 'If it is mixed with other fibers it then it is not unlawful.'"

Chapter 12 - Lifting up Garments

H 12178, Ch. 12, h 1
Ali ibn Ibrahim has narrated from his father from ibn abu 'Umayr from 'Abd Allah ibn Sinan who has said the following:

"About the meaning of the words of Allah, most Majestic, most Glorious, '. . . and cleanse your clothes', (74:4) abu 'Abd Allah, *'Alayhi al-Salam,* has said, 'It means lift up (cut short) your clothes (instead of dragging them on the ground).'"

H 12179, Ch. 12, h 2
Al-Husayn ibn Muhammad has narrated from Mu'alla' ibn Muhammad from al-Hassan ibn Ali al-Washsha' from Ahmad ibn 'A'idh from abu Khadijah from Mu'alla' ibn Khunayth who has said the following:

"Abu 'Abd Allah, *'Alayhi al-Salam,* has said, ''Amir al-Mu'minin who lived among you once went to banu Diwan and bought three pieces of clothes for one dinar. One piece was a shirt, which in its length reached above his ankles, a loincloth, which in length reached to the middle of his leg, a gown that reached in his front side up to his breast and from the back down to his rump. He ('Amir al-Mu'minin) then raised his hand to the sky and continued praising Allah for providing him clothes until he ('Amir al-Mu'minin) reached his home and said, "This is the kind of clothes that is proper for the Muslims."' Abu 'Abd Allah, *'Alayhi al-Salam,* then said, 'However, today they (Muslims) are not able to wear that kind of clothes, and if we do so they will say, "They have become insane and show off." Allah, most Blessed, most High, says, ". . . and cleanse your clothes" meaning do not allow your clothes to be dragged on the ground. When our *al-Q'a'im* will rise this (the kind of clothes which 'Amir al-Mu'minin, *'Alayhi al-Salam,* would wear) will be kind of his clothes.'"

H 12180, Ch. 12, h 3
A number of our people have narrated from Sahl ibn Ziyad from Muhammad ibn 'Isa from Yunus ibn Ya'qub from 'Abd Allah ibn Ya'qub from 'Abd Allah ibn Hilal who has said the following:

"Abu 'Abd Allah, *'Alayhi al-Salam,* once commanded me to buy a loincloth for him. I said that I could only find wide ones. He (the Imam) said, 'You must cut it and stitch its borders.' He (the Imam) then said, 'My father has said, "Whatever of loincloth passes down the ankles is in the fire."'"

Muhammad ibn Yahya has narrated from Ahmad ibn Muhammad from ibn Faddal from Yunus ibn Ya'qub a similar *Hadith.*

H 12181, Ch. 12, h 4
Muhammad ibn Yahya has narrated from Ahmad ibn Muhammad from Ali ibn al-Hakam from 'Abd al-Rahman ibn 'Uthman from a man from the people of al-Yamamah who was with abu al-Hassan, *'Alayhi al-Salam,* in jail in Baghdad who has said the following:

"Abu al-Hassan, *'Alayhi al-Salam,* once said to me, 'Allah, most Blessed, most High, has said, to His Holy Prophet, '. . . and your clothes cleanse them,' (74:4) his clothes were clean but He commanded him to raise them instead of keeping them long (that drag on the ground).'"

H 12182, Ch. 12, h 5
Ali ibn Ibrahim has narrated from his father from ibn Mahbub from Hisham ibn Salim from abu Basir who has said the following:

"Abu Ja'far, *'Alayhi al-Salam,* has stated this *Hadith.* 'The Messenger of Allah, *O Allah, grant compensation to Muhammad and his family worthy of their services to Your cause,* once advised a man from banu Tamim and said to him, 'You must never allow the loincloth and shirt to hang down to drag; it is the sign of arrogance and Allah does not love arrogance.'"

H 12183, Ch. 12, h 6
Abu Ali al-Ash'ariy has narrated from al-Hassan ibn Ali al-Kufiy from 'Ubays ibn Hisham from ibn from abu Hamzah in a marfu' manner has said, the following:

"'Amir al-Mu'minin, *'Alayhi al-Salam,* once saw a young man with his loincloths hanging low, and said to him, 'Son, you must raise your loincloth; it will last longer and help clean your heart (from arrogance).'"

H 12184, Ch. 12, h 7
A number of our people have narrated from Sahl ibn Ziyad from Ja'far ibn Muhammad al-Ash'ariy from ibn al-Qaddah who has said the following:

"Abu 'Abd Allah, *'Alayhi al-Salam,* has said that 'Amir al-Mu'minin when wearing a shirt would extend his hands. If the sleeves reached his fingers he would cut them short.'"

H 12185, Ch. 12, h 8
A number of our people have narrated from Ahmad ibn Muhammad ibn Khalid from his father from Muhammad ibn Sinan from al-Hassan al-Sayqal who has said the following:

"Abu 'Abd Allah, *'Alayhi al-Salam,* once asked me, 'Do you like to see the shirt of 'Amir al-Mu'minin, Ali, *'Alayhi al-Salam* in which he sustained the injury, to show his blood (stain)?' I replied, 'Yes, I like to see it.' He (the Imam) asked for it and it was brought in a basket. He (the Imam) opened and spread it out and it was a shirt made of cotton similar to those of al-Sunbalaniy (a place in Rome) and from the spot for its pocket down to the ground there was a white blood mark like the strike of a sword. He (the Imam) said, 'This is the shirt of Ali, *'Alayhi al-Salam,* in which he was mortally wounded and these are the traces of his blood.' I measured it around his body; it was three shibr and around its bottom it was twelve shibr (the space between the tip of thump and the small finger when they are opened and stretched."

H 12186, Ch. 12, h 9
Abu Ali al-Ash'ariy has narrated from Muhammad ibn 'Abd al-Jabbar and Muhammad ibn Yahya has narrated from Ahmad ibn Muhammad all from *al-Hajja*l from Tha'labah Ibn Maymun from Zurarah ibn A'yan who has said the following:

"I saw the shirt of Ali, *'Alayhi al-Salam,* in which he was mortally wounded. It was with abu Ja'far, *'Alayhi al-Salam,* its bottom measured twelve shibr and around his body it was three shibr and I saw marks of blood splashed on it.'"

H 12187, Ch. 12, h 10
A number of our people have narrated from Ahmad ibn Muhammad ibn Khalid from Muhammad ibn Ali from a man from Salmah Bayya' al-Qalanis who has said the following:

"I once was with abu Ja'far, when abu 'Abd Allah, *'Alayhi al-Salam,* came. Abu Ja'far, said, 'You must cleanse your shirt.' He left and we thought his shirt might have come in contact with something unclean. He came back and he (the Imam) said, 'It just is as it was.' We then asked saying, 'We pray to Allah to keep our souls in service for your cause, what is wrong with his shirt?' He (the

Imam) said, 'His shirt is long and I commanded him to shorten it; because Allah, most Majestic, most Glorious, has said, '. . . and cleanse (shorten) your clothes.' (74:4)"

H 12188, Ch. 12, h 11

It is narrated from the narrator of the previous *Hadith* from al-Nadr ibn Suwayd from Yahya al-Halabiy from 'Abd al-Hamid al-Ta'iy from Muhammad ibn Muslim who has narrated the following:

"Once abu 'Abd Allah, *'Alayhi al-Salam,* looked at a man who had dressed in a shirt that dragged on the ground. He (the Imam) said, 'This cloth is not clean.'"

H 12189, Ch. 12, h 12

It is narrated from the narrator of the previous *Hadith* from 'Uthman ibn 'Isa from Sama'ah ibn Mehran who has said the following:

"About the case of a man who was dragging his clothes behind him on the ground, abu 'Abd Allah, *'Alayhi al-Salam,* said, 'I dislike one's making himself look like a woman.'"

H 12190, Ch. 12, h 13

It is narrated from the narrator of the previous *Hadith* from his father from Muhammad ibn Sinan from Hudhayfah ibn Mansur who has said the following:

"I once was with abu 'Abd Allah, *'Alayhi al-Salam,* and he asked for a piece of cloth. He (the Imam) took five yards from it, cut it, then measured it with his shibr and in width it was six shibr. He (the Imam) then asked to stitch its borders and trim its edges.'"

Chapter 13 - The Words to Say when Wearing New clothes

H 12191, Ch. 13, h 1

Muhammad ibn Yahya has narrated from Ahmad ibn Muhammad, from ibn Mahbub from al-'Ala' ibn Razin from Muhammad ibn Muslim who has said the following:

"I once asked abu Ja'far, *'Alayhi al-Salam,* about the case of a man who wears new clothes. He (the Imam) said, 'He must say, 'O Lord, make it the dress of good fortune and blessings. O Lord, grant me the opportunity to worship You properly and appreciate Your bounties. All praise belongs to Allah who has clothed me with something whereby I cover my private parts and dress up myself before the people.'"

H 12192, Ch. 13, h 2

Ali ibn Ibrahim has narrated from his father from al-Nawfaliy from al-Sakuniy who has said the following:

"Abu 'Abd Allah, *'Alayhi al-Salam,* has stated this *Hadith.* ''Amir al-Mu'minin has said, "The Messenger of Allah, *O Allah, grant compensation to Muhammad and his family worthy of their services to Your cause,* taught me when wearing new clothes to say, 'All praise belongs to Allah who has dressed me with clothes to beautify myself before the people. O Lord, make it the dress of blessings with which I will try to seek Your pleasure and build Your Masajid.'" He (the Messenger of Allah) then said to me, "O Ali whoever says it, before wearing a shirt Allah forgives him." Another version of this *Hadith* says, "He will not experience anything which he dislikes."''"

H 12193, Ch. 13, h 3

Al-Husayn ibn Muhammad has narrated from Mu'alla' ibn Muhammad from Ali al-Hamadaniy from al-Husayn ibn 'Uthman from Khalid al-Jawwan who has said the following:

"I once heard abu al-Hassan, Musa, *'Alayhi al-Salam,* saying, 'It is very proper for you when wearing a piece of new clothes to wipe it with your hand and say, "All praise belongs to Allah who has dressed me with something whereby I cover my privacy, beautify and decorate myself before the people.'"

H 12194, Ch. 13, h 4

Ali ibn Muhammad has narrated from Salih ibn abu Hammad from more than one person who has said the following:

"Abu 'Abd Allah, *'Alayhi al-Salam,* has said, 'If one reads Chapter 97 of the Quran thirty-two times on a bowl of water and sprinkles it on a new dress just before wearing it, he will continue to eat affluently as long as a fiber thereof is left with him.'"

H 12195, Ch. 13, h 5

Muhammad ibn Yahya has narrated from Ahmad ibn Muhammad from al-Qasim ibn Yahya from his grandfather al-Hassan ibn Rashid from Muhammad ibn Muslim who has said the following:

"Abu 'Abd Allah, *'Alayhi al-Salam,* has said that `Amir al-Mu'minin has said, 'When Allah, most High, dresses a believing man with a new clothe he must take wudu. He then should perform two *Rak'at Salat* (prayer) in which he should recite the first chapter of al-Quran, verse 255 of chapter two, Chapter 112 and Chapter 97 of al-Quran. He then should praise Allah who has covered his private parts and decorated him before people. He should say a great deal, "There is no means and power without Allah." He will not disobey Allah in such dress as long as a fiber thereof remains with him and an angel asks for him forgiveness and mercy.'"

H 12196, Ch. 13, h 6

Muhammad ibn Yahya has narrated from Ali ibn al-Husayn al-Naysaburiy from 'Abd Allah ibn Muhammad from Ali ibn al-Rayyan from Yunus from 'Umar ibn Yazid who has said the following:

"I once wanted to visit abu 'Abd Allah, *'Alayhi al-Salam.* I dressed up and spread my Taylisan (pallium) which was new and I liked it very much. Somewhere on the road the camel gave me a hard time and it (my dress) was torn in pieces all over. I became depress very much. I then met abu 'Abd Allah, *'Alayhi al-Salam,* he looked at my Taylisan and asked, 'Why do I see your cloth ripped apart?' I then informed him (the Imam) about what had happened. He (the Imam) said, 'O 'Umar, whenever you will wear a new pair of clothes say, "No one deserves worship except Allah. Muhammad is the Messenger of Allah.' You will remain safe from misfortunes and if you like something do not mention it very often because mentioning it causes you great damage. If you need something from a person do not revile him behind his back because Allah drops it in his heart.'"

Chapter 14 - Wearing Old clothes

H 12197, Ch. 14, h 1
Muhammad ibn Yahya has narrated from Ahmad ibn Muhammad from al-Hassan ibn Ali from Ali ibn 'Uqbah from Ishaq ibn 'Ammar who has said the following:

"Abu 'Abd Allah, *'Alayhi al-Salam,* has made this pronouncement: 'The least of squandering is throwing away the remaining water in a bowl, misuse of protective clothes and throwing away of nutlets.'"

H 12198, Ch. 14, h 2
Muhammad ibn Yahya Muhammad ibn al-Husayn from Muhammad ibn 'Isma'il from Salih ibn 'Uqbah from Sulayman ibn Salih who has said the following:

"I once asked abu 'Abd Allah, *'Alayhi al-Salam,* about the least degree of squandering. He (the Imam) said, 'It is misuse of protective clothes, throwing away the remaining water in your bowl and when eating dates throwing the date-stone here and there.'"

H 12199, Ch. 14, h 3
A number of our people have narrated from Sahl ibn Ziyad from Muhammad ibn 'Isa from al-Hassan ibn Ali ibn Yaqtin from Fadl ibn Kathir al-Mada'iniy from those whom he has mentioned who has said the following:

"Once certain person of his people came to him (the Imam) and he saw on him (the Imam) a shirt with a patch stitched on it and he kept looking at it. Abu 'Abd Allah, *'Alayhi al-Salam,* said, 'What is the matter; what are you looking at?' He replied, 'I look at the patch stitched on your shirt.' He (the Imam) said, 'Pick up this book and read what is in it.' There was a book before him (the Imam) or near him (the Imam). The man looked in it and there it said, 'There is no faith and belief in one who does not have any bashfulness, no wealth for one who has no planning and nothing new for one who does have any old item.'"

Chapter 15 - The Turbans

H 12200, Ch. 15, h 1
Ali ibn Ibrahim has narrated from his father from ibn abu 'Umayr from those whom he has mentioned who has said the following:

"Abu 'Abd Allah, *'Alayhi al-Salam,* has said, 'One who wears a turban without *tahannak* (allowing one end to hang down on one's front side and the other end down one's back side), if he faces an illness without cure he then must not blame anyone for it except his own-self.'"

H 12201, Ch. 15, h 2
Muhammad ibn Yahya has narrated from Ahmad ibn Muhammad from abu Hammam who has said the following:

"This is about the meaning of the words of Allah, most Majestic, most Glorious, 'marked angels.' (3:125) Abu al-Hassan, *'Alayhi al-Salam,* has said that it is a reference to turbans. The Messenger of Allah, *O Allah, grant compensation to Muhammad and his family worthy of their services to Your cause,* wore a turban and hanged down one end on his front side and the other end down his backside. Jibril wore a turban and hanged down one end on his front side and the other end down his back.'"

H 12202, Ch. 15, h 3
Muhammad ibn Yahya has narrated from Ahmad ibn Muhammad from ibn Faddal from abu Jamilah from Jabir who has said the following:
"Abu Ja'far, *'Alayhi al-Salam,* has said that the angels had turbans hanging on them on the day of Badr."

H 12203, Ch. 15, h 4
A number of our people have narrated from Ahmad ibn abu 'Abd Allah from al-Husayn ibn Ali al-'Aqiliy from Ali ibn abu Ali al-Lahbiy who has said the following:
"The Messenger of Allah, *O Allah, grant compensation to Muhammad and his family worthy of their services to Your cause,* made Ali, *'Alayhi al-Salam,* to wear turban and hanged one end down his front side but made it shorter for the end hanging down his back by four fingers. He (the Messenger of Allah) then asked him to go back which he did and then asked him to come forward which he also did and then he (the Messenger of Allah) said, 'This is how the Tijan (crown) of the angels is.'"

H 12204, Ch. 15, h 5
Ali ibn Ibrahim has narrated from his father from al-Nawfaliy from al-Sakuniy who has said the following:
"Abu 'Abd Allah, *'Alayhi al-Salam,* has said that the Messenger of Allah, *O Allah, grant compensation to Muhammad and his family worthy of their services to Your cause,* has said, 'Turbans are the crown of Arabs.'"

H 12205, Ch. 15, h 6
It is narrated that al-Tabiqiyah, a turban without *tahannak* (allowing one end to hang down on one's front side and the other end down one's backside), is the turban of Satan, may he be condemned.'"

H 12206, Ch. 15, h 7
A number of our people have narrated from Sahl ibn Ziyad from Musa ibn Ja'far al-Baghdadiy from 'Amr ibn Sa'id from "Isa ibn Hamzah who has said the following:
"Abu 'Abd Allah, *'Alayhi al-Salam,* has said, 'If one wears a turban but does not turn the turban under his chin and then suffers an incurable illness , he then must not blame anyone other than his own self.'"

Chapter 16 - The cape

H 12207, Ch. 16, h 1
Ali ibn Ibrahim has narrated from his father from al-Nawfaliy from al-Sakuniy who has said the following:
"Abu 'Abd Allah, *'Alayhi al-Salam,* has said that the Messenger of Allah, *O Allah, grant compensation to Muhammad and his family worthy of their services to Your cause,* would wear a white Yemeniy cape and a quilted one with two ears for the war time. His turban was *al-Sahab* and a hooded cloak which he would wear.'"

H 12208, Ch. 16, h 2

Ali ibn Ibrahim has narrated from his father from ibn abu 'Umayr from certain persons of his people who has said the following:

"Abu 'Abd Allah, *'Alayhi al-Salam,* has said that the Messenger of Allah, *O Allah, grant compensation to Muhammad and his family worthy of their services to Your cause,* wore a white cape which was quilted. And for the war time he would wear one which had two ears.'"

H 12209, Ch. 16, h 3

Humayd ibn Ziyad has narrated from al-Hassan ibn Muhammad from Sama'ah from Ahmad ibn al-Hassan al-Mithamiy from al-Husayn ibn al-Mukhtar who has said the following:

"Abu 'Abd Allah, *'Alayhi al-Salam,* once said, 'Make for me white capes and do not (make them of large size that require folding) break them; a master like me does not wear the broken one.'"

H 12210, Ch. 16, h 4

A number of our people have narrated from Ahmad ibn abu 'Abd Allah from Yahya ibn Ibrahim ibn abu al-Balad from his father from al-Husayn ibn al-Mukhtar who has said the following:

"Abu 'Abd Allah, *'Alayhi al-Salam,* once said to me, 'Find for me capes but do not color them; a master like me does not wear them, that is, you must not (make them of a large size to require you to) break (fold) them.'"

Chapter 17 - The Footgear

H 12211, Ch. 17, h 1

A number of our people have narrated from Sahl ibn Ziyad from Muhammad ibn 'Isa from 'Abd Allah ibn 'Abd al-Rahman from Shu'ayb from abu Basir who has said the following:

"Abu 'Abd Allah, *'Alayhi al-Salam,* has said that 'Amir al-Mu'minin has said, 'Good shoes (footgear) are protection for the body and helps for *Salat* (prayer) and al-Tahur (cleansing).'"

H 12212, Ch. 17, h 2

Ali ibn Ibrahim has narrated from his father from al-Nawfaliy from al-Sakuniy who has said the following:

"Abu 'Abd Allah, *'Alayhi al-Salam,* has said, 'The first one who used footgear was Ibrahim *'Alayhi al-Salam.'"

H 12213, Ch. 17, h 3

Through the same chain of narrators as that of the previous *Hadith* the following is narrated:

"Abu 'Abd Allah, *'Alayhi al-Salam,* has said that the Messenger of Allah, *O Allah, grant compensation to Muhammad and his family worthy of their services to Your cause,* has said, 'One who uses a sandal must find a good one.'"

H 12214, Ch. 17, h 4

Muhammad ibn Yahya has narrated from Ahmad ibn Muhammad from al-Qasim ibn Yahya from his grandfather, al-Hassan ibn Rashid who has said the following:

"Abu 'Abd Allah, *'Alayhi al-Salam,* has said that 'Amir al-Mu'minin has said, 'Do not use an *al-Mals* footgear (one without heels and strip between the toes); it is the kind of the footgear of the pharaoh who was the first to use such footgear.'"

H 12215, Ch. 17, h 5

Ali ibn Ibrahim has narrated from his father from ibn Mahbub, from al-'Ala' ibn Razin from Muhammad ibn Muslim who has said the following:

"Abu Ja'far, *'Alayhi al-Salam,* has said, 'I dislike a man whose footgear is without pursuer (the back part to support the back of the heels).'"

H 12216, Ch. 17, h 6

Muhammad ibn Yahya has narrated from Ahmad ibn Muhammad from Muhammad ibn 'Isma'il from 'Abd Allah ibn 'Uthman from a man from Minhal who has said the following:

"Once I was with abu 'Abd Allah, *'Alayhi al-Salam,* and I was wearing a sandal which was smooth. He (the Imam) said, 'This is of the kind of sandals that Jews wear.' Minhal then returned, took a knife and carved to narrow down its middle.'"

H 12217, Ch. 17, h 7

A number of our people have narrated from Ahmad ibn abu 'Abd Allah from abu al-Khazraj al-Hassan ibn al-Zabarqan al-Ansariy who has said that narrated to me Ishaq al-Hadhdha' who has said the following:

"Once abu 'Abd Allah, *'Alayhi al-Salam,* sent for me, when we were in Mina, to come to him with my tools. I went to his tent and offered him (the Imam) the greeting of peace to which he responded and made a hand gesture for me to sit down. I sat down. He (the Imam) took a new shoe and threw it to me. When I wanted to leave I said, 'I pray to Allah to keep my soul in service for your cause, I wish you gave this sandal to me as a present so I can use it as a model. He (the Imam) threw the other pair to me saying, 'How can you benefit from one pair?' He (the narrator) has said, 'It had a back support, a narrow middle part and two straps in their front part (to go between the toes). He (the Imam) said, 'It is the model of the footgear of the Messenger of Allah, *O Allah, grant compensation to Muhammad and his family worthy of their services to Your cause.*'"

H 12218, Ch. 17, h 8

It is narrated from the narrator of the previous *Hadith* who has said that narrated to him Dawud ibn Ishaq abu Sulayman al-Hadhdha' from Muhammad ibn al-Fayd from Taym al-Ribab who has said the following:

"I once heard abu 'Abd Allah, *'Alayhi al-Salam,* saying, 'I dislike a man when I see him wearing a sandal which does not have a narrow middle part. The first one who changed the model of the Messenger of Allah was so and so.' He (the Imam) then asked, 'What do you call this model?' I said, 'It is smooth.' He (the Imam) said, 'This smooth model (that I dislike).'"

H 12219, Ch. 17, h 9

Muhammad ibn Yahya has narrated from Ahmad ibn Muhammad from Ali ibn al-Hakam from Aban ibn 'Uthman from certain persons of our people from ibn Suwayd who has said the following:

"Once abu al-Hassan, looked at me when I was wearing sandals which were smooth. He (the Imam) took it in his hand and turned it, then said to me, 'Do you want to be like Jews?' I said, 'I pray to Allah to keep my soul in service for your cause, it is only what a human being has given to me as a gift.' He (the Imam) said, 'It then is not unlawful.'"

H 12220, Ch. 17, h 10

Ali ibn Ibrahim has narrated from his father from ibn abu 'Umayr from more than one person who has said the following:

"Abu 'Abd Allah, *'Alayhi al-Salam,* disliked tying of shoelaces. He (the Imam) took the sandals of one of them and opened its laces."

H 12221, Ch. 17, h 11

Muhammad ibn Yahya has narrated from Ahmad ibn Muhammad from Muhammad ibn Yahya from Ghiyath ibn Ibrahim who has said the following:

"Abu 'Abd Allah, *'Alayhi al-Salam,* has said, 'My father would keep *Dhawa'ib* (the clump) of his shoes longer.'"

H 12222, Ch. 17, h 12

A number of our people have narrated from Ahmad ibn abu 'Abd Allah from Muhammad ibn 'Isma'il from abu 'Isma'il al-Sarraj from 'Imran from a man who has said the following:

"Abu 'Abd Allah, *'Alayhi al-Salam,* once looked at a shoe which had laces that were tied down. He (the Imam) picked it up, opened its laces and said, 'This must not be tied down.'"

H 12223, Ch. 17, h 13

Al-Husayn ibn Muhammad has narrated from Mu'alla' ibn Muhammad, from Ali ibn Hassan, from 'Abd al-Rahman ibn Kathir who has said the following:

"I once was walking with abu 'Abd Allah, *'Alayhi al-Salam,* when the thong and strap of his shoe broke. I took out one from my bag with which he repaired his shoe. He (the Imam) touched my left shoulder saying, 'O 'Abd al-Rahman ibn Kathir, if one helps a believing person in the matters of his shoe thong Allah, most Majestic, most Glorious, will carry him on a fast running camel when he comes out of his grave until he will knock at the door of the garden (paradises).'"

H 12224, Ch. 17, h 14

A number of our people have narrated from Ahmad ibn Muhammad from ibn Mahbub from Ya'qub al-Sarraj who has said the following:

"Once we were walking with abu 'Abd Allah, *'Alayhi al-Salam,* to (the house of) one of his relatives for offering condolences because of the death of their child. The strap and thong of the shoe of abu 'Abd Allah, *'Alayhi al-Salam,* broke, so he took his shoes in his hand and began to walk barefoot. Ibn abu Ya'fur looked at him and took his shoes off, removed its strap and thong to give it to abu 'Abd Allah, *'Alayhi al-Salam,* who refused to accept it as if disappointed. He (the Imam) then said, 'The mourner has a greater responsibility to exercise patience.' He (the Imam) continued walking barefoot until he arrived at the house of the man whom he wanted to offer condolences.'"

H 12225, Ch. 17, h 15

Ahmad ibn Muhammad al-Kufiy has narrated from Ali ibn al-Hassan al-Taymiy from al-'Abbas ibn 'Amir from Aban ibn 'Uthman from 'Abd al-Rahman ibn abu 'Abd Allah who has said the following:

"Once I was with abu 'Abd Allah, *'Alayhi al-Salam,* when he visited a man. On his arrival he took off his shoes and then said, 'You must take off your shoes; when shoes are removed the feet receive more comfort and rest.'"

Chapter 18 - The Color of shoes

H 12226, Ch. 18, h 1

A number of our people have narrated from Ahmad ibn Muhammad from ibn Mahbub from those whom he has mentioned who has said the following:

"Once abu 'Abd Allah, *'Alayhi al-Salam,* looked at one of his people who wore a black shoe. He (the Imam) said, 'What have you to do with a black shoe, did you not know that it is harmful to the eyes, it slackens the penis, besides it is more expensive than others and whoever wears it, he shows arrogance in it?'"

H 12227, Ch. 18, h 2

A number of our people have narrated from Sahl ibn Ziyad from Muhammad ibn 'Isa from Muhammad ibn Ali al-Hamadaniy from Hanan ibn Sadir who has said the following:

"I once visited abu 'Abd Allah, *'Alayhi al-Salam,* and I wore a black shoe. He (the Imam) said, 'O Hanan, what do you have to do with black (color)? Did you not know that it has three disadvantages ? It weakens the eye sight, slackens the penis and causes anxieties [and besides it is of footgear of tyrants]?' I then asked, 'What kind of shoe must I wear?' He (the Imam) said, 'You must wear yellow because it has three qualities. It brightens eyesight, hardens the penis, dispels anxieties and besides it is of the footgear of the Prophets.'"

H 12228, Ch. 18, h 3

Muhammad ibn Yahya has narrated from Ahmad ibn Muhammad from al-Sayyariy from abu Sulayman al-Khawwas from al-Fadl ibn Dukin from Sadir al-Sayrafiy who has said the following:

"I once visited abu 'Abd Allah, *'Alayhi al-Salam,* and I was wearing a white shoe. He (the Imam) asked, 'O Sadir, are you wearing this shoe intentionally?' I replied, 'No, by Allah, I pray to Allah to keep my soul in service for your cause.' He (the Imam) said, 'Whoever goes to the market place to buy a white shoe, it will not become old before he earns an asset from a source that he never expected to earn.' Abu al-Nu'aym has narrated to me that Sadir said, 'That shoe did not become old until I earned one hundred dinar from an unexpected source.'"

H 12229, Ch. 18, h 4

Abu Ali al-Ash'ariy has narrated from Muhammad ibn 'Abd al-Jabbar from ibn Faddal from Burayd ibn Muhammad al-Ghadiriy from 'Ubayd ibn Zurarah who has said the following:

"Abu 'Abd Allah, *'Alayhi al-Salam,* saw me with a black shoe and said, 'O 'Ubayd, what have you to do with a black shoe? Did you not know that it has three negative qualities? It slackens the penis, weakens the eyesight and it is more expensive than other shoes. If a man, who does not have anything except his wife and children, wears it and Allah raises him an oppressor.'"

H 12230, Ch. 18, h 5

A number of our people have narrated from Ahmad ibn abu 'Abd Allah from Muhammad ibn Ali from abu al-Bakhtariy who has said the following:

"If one wears yellow shoes he continues with happiness until that shoe becomes old.'"

H 12231, Ch. 18, h 6

It is narrated from the narrator of the previous *Hadith* from certain persons of our people who received from Jabir al-Juhfiy who has said the following:

"Abu Ja'far, *'Alayhi al-Salam,* has said, 'If one wears yellow shoes he continues in happiness as long as he wears that shoes; Allah, most Majestic, most Glorious, says, "It is yellow which is delightful to the on-lookers." (2:69)*'"

H 12232, Ch. 18, h 7

Muhammad ibn Yahya has narrated from Ahmad ibn Muhammad from Muhammad ibn 'Isa from Sulayman ibn Sama'ah from Dawud al-Hadhdha' from 'Abd al-Malik ibn Bahr Sahib al-Lu'Lu who has said the following:

"He (the Imam), *'Alayhi al-Salam,* has said, 'If one wants to wear shoes and he finds yellow toward whiteness shoes, he will not live without property or children; but if one finds black shoes he will not live without sadness and anxieties.'"

Chapter 19 - Al-Khuff (the half-Boot)

H 12233, Ch. 19, h 1

A number of our people have narrated from Sahl ibn Ziyad from Muhammad ibn 'Isa from Salmah ibn abu Khadijah who has said the following:

"Abu 'Abd Allah, *'Alayhi al-Salam,* has said, 'If one wears *al-Khuff* (half-boot) his eyesight sharpens.'"

H 12234, Ch. 19, h 2

A number of our people have narrated from Ahmad ibn abu 'Abd Allah from al-'Awsiy from abu Ja'far, al-Musliy from Sulayman ibn Sa'd from Muni' who has said the following:

"Abu Ja'far, *'Alayhi al-Salam,* has said, 'Wearing *al-Khuff* (half-boot) provides immunity from tuberculoses.'"

H 12235, Ch. 19, h 3

It is narrated from the narrator of the previous *Hadith* from certain persons of our people from Mubarak Ghulam al-'Aqarqufiy who has said the following:

"Abu 'Abd Allah, *'Alayhi al-Salam,* has said, 'Continuously wearing *al-Khuff* (half-boot) provides immunity against tuberculoses.'"

H 12236, Ch. 19, h 4

It is narrated from the narrator of the previous *Hadith* from Salim ibn Mukram from Muhammad ibn Sinan from Dawud al-Riqqiy who has said the following:

"I once traveled with abu 'Abd Allah, *'Alayhi al-Salam,* to Yanbu'. When he (the Imam) came out, I saw him wearing a red *al-Khuff* (half-boot). I then said, 'I pray to Allah to keep my soul in service for your cause, what kind of shoe is this red shoe which I see you wearing?' He (the Imam) said, 'It is *al-Khuff* (half-boot) which I have found for traveling and it is good in clay (mud) and rain and more durable.' I then asked, 'Can I have such footgear?' He (the Imam) said, 'During a journey yes, you can have it, but not when you are at home; and do not exchange a black one for anything else.'" (Apparently it applies to *al-Khuff* (half-boot) only).

H 12237, Ch. 19, h 5

Muhammad ibn Yahya has narrated from Ahmad ibn Muhammad ibn 'Isa from Muhammad ibn Sinan from Ziyad ibn al-Mundhir who has said the following:

"I once visited abu Ja'far, *'Alayhi al-Salam,* and I was wearing *al-Khuff* (half-boot) which was Maqshurah. He (the Imam) said, 'O, Ziyad, what is this which I see you wearing?' I replied, 'It is *al-Khuff* (half-boot) that I have found.' He (the Imam) said, 'Did you know that the white one of *al-Khuff* (half-boot) that is, al-Maqshurah is of the footgear of the tyrants and they were the ones who made it? The red ones are of the footgear of Kisra's (Persian kings) and they were the first ones who made it. The black ones are of the footgear of banu Hashim and of the noble tradition.'"

H 12238, Ch. 19, h 6

A number of our people have narrated from Sahl ibn Ziyad from Muhammad ibn 'Abd Allah from Ali al-Baghdadiy from abu al-Hassan al-Darir from abu Salmah al-Sarraj who has said the following:

"Abu 'Abd Allah, *'Alayhi al-Salam,* has said, 'Continuously wearing *al-Khuff* (half-boot) is protection against dying badly.'"

Chapter 20 - The Tradition about Wearing al-Khuff (half-boot), al-Na'l (Shoes) and Taking them off

H 12239, Ch. 20, h 1

Muhammad ibn Yahya has narrated from Ahmad ibn Muhammad from ibn Mahbub from abu Ayyub from Muhammad ibn Muslim who has said the following:

"Abu Ja'far, *'Alayhi al-Salam,* has said, 'It is of the noble tradition to take off *al-Khuff* (half-boot) first from the left foot before the right foot and wear it on the right foot before the left foot.'"

H 12240, Ch. 20, h 2

Humayd ibn Ziyad has narrated from al-Hassan ibn Muhammad ibn Sama'ah from Wuhayb ibn Hafs from abu Basir who has said the following:

"Abu 'Abd Allah, *'Alayhi al-Salam,* has said, 'When wearing on begin with the right foot and when taking off your *al-Khuff* (half-boot) or shoe begin with the left foot.'"

H 12241, Ch. 20, h 3

A number of our people have narrated from Sahl ibn Ziyad from Ja'far ibn Muhammad al-Ash'ariy from ibn al-Qaddah who has said the following:

"Abu 'Abd Allah, *'Alayhi al-Salam,* has said, 'When one of you wears his shoes he must wear on the right foot first then the left foot, when taking off you should remove from the left before the right.'"

H 12242, Ch. 20, h 4

Muhammad ibn Yahya has narrated from Ahmad ibn Muhammad from Ali ibn al-Hakam from Aban from al-Halabiy who has said the following:

"Abu 'Abd Allah, *'Alayhi al-Salam,* has said, 'Do not walk with one pair of shoe.' I asked, 'Why I must not walk with one shoe?' He (the Imam) said, 'It is because if a touch of Satan reaches you, it will never go away, unless Allah wants otherwise.'"

H 12243, Ch. 20, h 5

It is narrated from the narrator of the previous *Hadith* from Ahmad ibn Muhammad from ibn Faddal from al-'Ala' from Muhammad ibn Muslim who has said the following:

"Abu Ja'far, *'Alayhi al-Salam,* has said, 'If one walks with one shoe and if a touch of Satan reaches, him it will not leave him unless Allah wants otherwise.'"

H 12244, Ch. 20, h 6

Ali ibn Ibrahim has narrated from his father from al-Nawfaliy from al-Sakuniy who has said the following:

"Abu 'Abd Allah, *'Alayhi al-Salam,* has said that Ali ibn al-Husayn, *'Alayhi al-Salam,* walked with one shoe while repairing the other one, and he did not consider it harmful.'"

Chapter 21 - The Rings (Insignia)

H 12245, Ch. 21, h 1

Ali ibn Ibrahim has narrated from his father from ibn abu 'Umayr from Hisham ibn Salim who has said the following:

"Abu 'Abd Allah, *'Alayhi al-Salam,* has said that the ring of the Messenger of Allah, *O Allah, grant compensation to Muhammad and his family worthy of their services to Your cause,* was made of leaf (dirham).'"

H 12246, Ch. 21, h 2

Muhammad ibn Yahya has narrated from Ahmad ibn Muhammad from ibn Mahbub from 'Abd Allah ibn Sinan and Mu'awiyah ibn Wahab who has said the following:

"Abu 'Abd Allah, *'Alayhi al-Salam,* has said that the ring (insignia) of the Messenger of Allah, was made of leaf (dirham).' I then asked if it had any stone, and he (the Imam) said, 'No, it did not have a stone.'"

H 12247, Ch. 21, h 3

Abu Ali al-Ash'ariy has narrated from al-Hassan ibn Ali al-Kufiy from 'Ubays ibn Hisham from Husayn ibn Ahmad al-Minqariy from Yunus ibn Zabayan who has said the following:

"Abu 'Abd Allah, *'Alayhi al-Salam,* has said, 'Wearing the ring (insignia) is of the noble tradition.'"

H 12248, Ch. 21, h 4

Muhammad ibn Yahya has narrated from Muhammad ibn al-Husayn from 'Abd al-Rahman ibn Hashim from abu Khadijah who has said the following:

"He (the Imam), *'Alayhi al-Salam,* has said, 'The stone of a ring is round and that is how the ring of the Messenger of Allah, *O Allah, grant compensation to Muhammad and his family worthy of their services to Your cause,* was.'"

H 12249, Ch. 21, h 5

Muhammad ibn Yahya has narrated from Ahmad ibn Muhammad from ibn Faddal from Ghalib ibn 'Uthman from Ruh ibn 'Abd al-Rahim who has said the following:

"Abu 'Abd Allah, *'Alayhi al-Salam,* has said that the Messenger of Allah, *O Allah, grant compensation to Muhammad and his family worthy of their services to Your cause,* said to 'Amir al-Mu'minin, 'Your ring must not be made of gold because it is your beautification in the next life.'"

H 12250, Ch. 21, h 6

Muhammad ibn Yahya has narrated from Ahmad ibn Muhammad from al-Qasim ibn Yahya from his grandfather al-Hassan ibn Rashid from abu Basir who has said the following:

"Abu 'Abd Allah, *'Alayhi al-Salam,* has said that `Amir al-Mu'minin has said, 'Do not use any ring other than what is made of silver, because the Messenger of Allah has said, "A hand which has a ring of iron does not become clean."'"

H 12251, Ch. 21, h 7

Ahmad ibn Muhammad from has narrated from al-Husayn ibn Sa'id from al-Nadr ibn Suwayd from al-Qasim ibn Sulayman from Jarrah al-Mada'iniy who has said the following:

"Abu 'Abd Allah, *'Alayhi al-Salam,* has said, 'Do not wear on your hand a ring of gold.'"

H 12252, Ch. 21, h 8

A number of our people have narrated from Ahmad ibn Muhammad ibn Khalid from Ali ibn al-Hakam from Aban from Yahya ibn abu al-'Ala' who has said the following:

"I once asked abu 'Abd Allah, *'Alayhi al-Salam,* about wearing the ring on the right hand saying, 'I have seen banu Hashim wearing rings on their right hands.' He (the Imam) said, 'My father would wear it on his left hand and he was the most excellent among them with more power of wisdom.'" (This is because of Taqiyah, according to al-Majlisy)

H 12253, Ch. 21, h 9

It is narrated from the narrator of the previous *Hadith* from Muhammad ibn Ali from Ali ibn Asbat from Ali ibn Ja'far who has said the following:

"I once asked my brother, Musa, *'Alayhi al-Salam,* about the ring; if it is worn on the right hand. He (the Imam) said, 'You can wear it on the right or left, as you wish.'"

H 12254, Ch. 21, h 10

Ali ibn Ibrahim has narrated from his father from ibn abu 'Umayr from Ali ibn 'Atiyyah who has said the following:

"Abu 'Abd Allah, *'Alayhi al-Salam,* has said that the Messenger of Allah used the ring for a very little time and then he (the Messenger of Allah) abandoned it.'"

H 12255, Ch. 21, h 11

A number of our people have narrated from Sahl ibn Ziyad from Ja'far ibn Muhammad al-Ash'ariy from ibn al-Qaddah who has said the following:

"Abu 'Abd Allah, *'Alayhi al-Salam,* has said that the Messenger of Allah, *O Allah, grant compensation to Muhammad and his family worthy of their services to Your cause,* would wear the ring on his right hand.'"

H 12256, Ch. 21, h 12

Through the same chain of narrators as that of the previous *Hadith* the following is narrated:

"Abu 'Abd Allah, *'Alayhi al-Salam,* has said that Ali, al-Hassan and al-Husayn, *'Alayhim al-Salam,* would wear the ring on their left hands.'"

H 12257, Ch. 21, h 13
Al-Husayn ibn Muhammad has narrated from Mu'alla' ibn Muhammad from al-Washsha' from Muthanna' al-Hannat from Hatim ibn 'Isma'il who has said the following:
"Abu 'Abd Allah, *'Alayhi al-Salam,* has said that al-Hassan and al-Husayn, *'Alayhim al-Salam,* wore the ring on their left hands.'"

H 12258, Ch. 21, h 14
A number of our people have narrated from Ahmad ibn Muhammad ibn Khalid from Ahmad ibn Muhammad from ibn abu Nasr from Aban from Yahya ibn abu al-'Ala' who has said the following:
"Abu 'Abd Allah, *'Alayhi al-Salam,* has said that al-Hassan and al-Husayn, *'Alayhim al-Salam,* wore the ring on their left hands.'"

H 12259, Ch. 21, h 15
Ali ibn Ibrahim has narrated from Salih ibn al-Sindiy from Ja'far ibn Bashir from 'Abd al-Rahman ibn Muhammad al-'Arzamiy who has said the following:
"Abu 'Abd Allah, *'Alayhi al-Salam,* has said that al-Hassan and al-Husayn, *'Alayhim al-Salam,* wore the ring on their right hands (fingers).'"

H 12260, Ch. 21, h 16
A number of our people have narrated from Ahmad ibn Muhammad ibn Khalid from Muhammad ibn Ali from al-'Arzamiy who has said the following:
"Abu 'Abd Allah, *'Alayhi al-Salam,* has said that 'Amir al-Mu'minin would wear the ring on his right hand.'"

H 12261, Ch. 21, h 17
Sahl ibn Ziyad has narrated from Muhammad ibn 'Isa from Safwan who has said the following:
"Abu al-Hassan, al-Rida', *'Alayhi al-Salam,* has said, 'They evaluated the ring of abu 'Abd Allah, *'Alayhi al-Salam,* and my father bought it for seven.' I then asked, 'Was it seven dirham?' He (the Imam) said, 'It was seven dinars.'"

Chapter 22 - The Carnelian (al-'Aqiq)

H 12262, Ch. 22, h 1
A number of our people have narrated from Ahmad ibn Muhammad ibn Khalid from Ahmad ibn Muhammad from ibn abu Nasr who has said the following:
"Al-Rida', *'Alayhi al-Salam,* has said, 'Carnelian disallows poverty and wearing carnelian dispels hypocrisy.'"

H 12263, Ch. 22, h 2
A number of our people have narrated from Ahmad ibn Muhammad from al-Washsha' who has said the following:
"Abu al-Hassan, al-Rida', has said, 'One who achieves a share of carnelian his share is a plentiful share.'"

H 12264, Ch. 22, h 3
It is narrated from the narrator of the previous *Hadith* from Muhammad ibn Ali from Muhammad ibn al-Fudayl from 'Abd al-Rahman ibn Zayd ibn Aslam al-Tanukiy who has said the following:
"Abu 'Abd Allah, *'Alayhi al-Salam,* has said that the Messenger of Allah, *O Allah, grant compensation to Muhammad and his family worthy of their services to Your cause,* has said, 'Wear a ring of carnelian; it is blessed and one who uses

a ring of carnelian has a good chance to end up in goodness.'"

H 12265, Ch. 22, h 4

It is narrated from the narrator of the previous *Hadith* from certain persons of his people from Salih ibn 'Uqbah from Fudayl ibn 'Uthman from Rabi'ah al-Ra'iy who has said the following:

"Once on the hand of abu al-Hassan, *'Alayhi al-Salam,* I saw carnelian as the stone of the ring, and asked, 'What is this stone?' He (the Imam) replied, 'It is a Roman carnelian. The Messenger of Allah has said, "If one uses carnelian as his ring his wishes come true."'"

H 12266, Ch. 22, h 5

It is narrated from the narrator of the previous *Hadith* from certain persons of his people in a *marfu'* manner has said the following:

"Abu 'Abd Allah, *'Alayhi al-Salam,* has said, 'Agate is safety on a journey.'"

H 12267, Ch. 22, h 6

Ali ibn Ibrahim has narrated from his father from Ali ibn Ma'bad from al-Husayn ibn Khalid who has said the following:

"Al-Rida', *'Alayhi al-Salam,* has said that abu 'Abd Allah, *'Alayhi al-Salam,* would say, 'One who uses 'Aqiq (carnelian) as the stone of his ring does not become poor and he ends up only in goodness.'"

H 12268, Ch. 22, h 7

Muhammad ibn Yahya has narrated from Ahmad ibn Muhammad from Ya'qub ibn Yazid from Ibrahim ibn 'Uqbah from Sayabah ibn Ayyub from Muhammad ibn al-Fadl from 'Abd al-Rahim al-Qasir who has said the following:

"Once, the governor summoned a man of Ale abu Talib in a criminal case, and he passed by abu 'Abd Allah, *'Alayhi al-Salam,* who said, 'Follow him with a ring of 'Aqiq (carnelian)'. 'Aqiq (carnelian) ring was brought and he did not experience any undesirable matters.'"

H 12269, Ch. 22, h 8

It is narrated from the narrator of the previous *Hadith* from Muhammad ibn Ahmad in a *marfu'* manner has said the following:

"He (the Imam), *'Alayhi al-Salam,* has said that once a man complained before the Messenger of Allah, *O Allah grant compensation to Muhammad and his family worthy of their services to your cause,* that on the road he was robbed. The Messenger of Allah said, 'Why did you not wear the ring of 'Aqiq (carnelian) which is protects from every evil matters?'"

Chapter 23 - The Ruby and Emerald

H 12270, Ch. 23, h 1

Ali ibn Ibrahim has narrated from his father from Ali ibn Ma'bad from al-Husayn ibn Khalid who has said the following:

"Al-Rida', *'Alayhi al-Salam,* has said that abu 'Abd Allah, *'Alayhi al-Salam,* would say, 'You must use ruby as a ring, it disallows poverty.'"

H 12271, Ch. 23, h 2

A number of our people have narrated from Ahmad ibn Muhammad ibn Khalid from Muhammad ibn al-Fudayl from abu al-Hassan from his father from his grandfather who has said the following:

"The Messenger of Allah, *O Allah, grant compensation to Muhammad and his family worthy of their services to Your cause,* has said, 'You must use rubies as rings; they disallow poverty.'"

H 12272, Ch. 23, h 3

A number of our people have narrated from Sahl ibn Ziyad from Harun ibn Muslim from a man from a certain persons of our people, al-Hassan ibn Ali ibn al-Fadl called Sikbaj from Ahmad ibn Muhammad from ibn abu Nasr, Sahib al-`Anzal who worked for certain tasks of al-Madiy, *'Alayhi al-Salam,* has said the following:

"He (the Imam), *'Alayhi al-Salam,* one day said to me dictating in a book, 'Using emerald in a ring is a comfort which is free of difficulties.'"

H 12273, Ch. 23, h 4

Sahl ibn Ziyad has narrated from al-Dihqan 'Ubayd Allah from al-Husayn ibn Khalid who has said the following:

"I once heard abu al-Hassan, *'Alayhi al-Salam,* saying, 'You must use ruby in the ring; it disallows poverty.'"

H 12274, Ch. 23, h 5

Ali ibn Ibrahim has narrated from his father from 'Uthman ibn 'Isa from Bakr ibn Muhammad who has said the following:

"Abu 'Abd Allah, *'Alayhi al-Salam,* has said, 'It is Mustahab (desirable) to use ruby as a ring.'"

Chapter 24 - The Turquoise

H 12275, Ch. 24, h 1

A number of our people have narrated from Sahl ibn Ziyad in a *marfu'* manner has said the following:

"Abu 'Abd Allah, *'Alayhi al-Salam,* has said, 'If one uses a ring of turquoise his palm does not become poor.'"

H 12276, Ch. 24, h 2

Ali ibn Muhammad ibn Bandar has narrated from Ibrahim ibn Ishaq al-Ahmar from al-Hassan ibn Sahl from al-Hassan ibn Ali ibn Mehran who has said the following:

"I once visited abu al-Hassan, Musa, *'Alayhi al-Salam,* and on his finger was a ring with a stone which was turquoise with an engraving that said, 'Allah is the owner'. I continued looking on it and he (the Imam) asked, 'Why do you continue looking at it?' I replied, 'I have received information that Ali, `Amir al-Mu'minin had a ring which had a stone of turquoise and its engraving said, "Allah is the owner".' He (the Imam) asked, 'Do you recognize it?' I replied, 'No, I do not recognize it.' He (the Imam) said, 'This is that ring; do you know what is the reason?' I replied, 'No, I do not know.' He (the Imam) said, 'This is a stone which Jibril gave as a gift to the Messenger of Allah, *O Allah, grant compensation to Muhammad and his family worthy of their services to Your cause,* and the Messenger of Allah gave it as a gift to `Amir al-Mu'minin, *'Alayhi al-Salam.* Do you know what its name is?' I replied, 'It is Firozaj (turquoise).' He (the Imam) said, 'That is in al-Farsiyah. What is its name in Arabic?' I replied, 'I do not know.' He (the Imam) said, 'Its name is *al-Zafar* (victory).'"

Chapter 25 - The Yemenite al-Jaza' (Carnelian) and The Crystals

H 12277, Ch. 25, h 1

A number of our people have narrated from Ahmad ibn abu 'Abd Allah from Muhammad ibn Ali from 'Ubayd ibn Yahya from Muhammad ibn al-Husayn ibn Ali ibn al-Husayn from his father from his grandfather has said the following:

"'Amir al-Mu'minin, *'Alayhi al-Salam,* has said, 'Use Yemenite carnelian as the ring; it dispels plots, the evil plans of defiant Satans.'"

H 12278, Ch. 25, h 2

Muhammad ibn Yahya has narrated from Ahmad ibn Muhammad from Ali ibn al-Rayyan from Ali ibn Muhammad known as ibn Wahbah al-'Abdasiy which is a town in Wasit in a marfu' manner has said the following:

"Abu 'Abd Allah, *'Alayhi al-Salam,* has said, *'Al-Billur* (crystal) is very good for the stone of a ring.'"

Chapter 26 - The Engraving on the Ring

H 12279, Ch. 26, h 1

A number of our people have narrated from Ahmad ibn Muhammad from al-Hassan ibn Mahbub from 'Abd Allah ibn Sinan who has said the following:

"Abu 'Abd Allah, *'Alayhi al-Salam,* has said that the engraving on the ring of the Holy Prophet, *O Allah, grant compensation to Muhammad and his family worthy of their services to Your cause,* said, 'Muhammad is the Messenger of Allah'. The engraving on the ring of 'Amir al-Mu'minin, *'Alayhi al-Salam,* said, 'Allah is the owner' and the engraving on the ring of my father said, 'All glory belongs to Allah'."

H 12280, Ch. 26, h 2

Ali ibn Ibrahim has narrated from his father from ibn abu 'Umayr from Jamil ibn Darraj from Yunus ibn Zabayan and Hafs ibn Ghiyath who has said the following:

"Once we asked abu 'Abd Allah, *'Alayhi al-Salam,* saying, 'We pray to Allah to keep our souls in service for your cause, is it undesirable to write on one's ring something other than one's name and the name of one's father?' He (the Imam) said, 'The writing on my ring says, *'Allah is the Creator of all things'.* On the ring of my father, Muhammad ibn Ali, *'Alayhi al-Salam,* who was the best Muhammadi, I saw with my own eyes, the writing said, *'All glory belongs to Allah.'* On the ring of Ali ibn al-Husayn, *'Alayhi al-Salam,* the writing said, *'All praise belongs to Allah, the most High, the most Great.'* On the ring of al-Hassan and al-Husayn, *'Alayhim al-Salam,* the writing said, *'Allah is sufficient for me.'* On the ring of 'Amir al-Mu'minin, *'Alayhi al-Salam,* the writing said, *'Allah is the owner'.'"

H 12281, Ch. 26, h 3

A number of our people have narrated from Ahmad ibn abu 'Abd Allah from 'Abd Allah ibn Muhammad al-Nuhaykiy from Ibrahim ibn 'Abd al-Hamid who has said that Mu'attib passed by me and there was a ring with him and I asked him what it was? He replied, 'It is the ring of abu 'Abd Allah, *'Alayhi al-Salam.'* I took it to read what was written on it and it said, 'O Lord, You are my protector so protect me from the mischief of Your creatures.'" (This may not be consider a *Hadith* directly from an Imam, but it speaks what was written on the ring of the Imam)

H 12282, Ch. 26, h 4

It is narrated from the narrator of the previous *Hadith* from Ahmad ibn Muhammad from ibn abu Nasr who has said the following:

"I once was with abu al-Hassan, al-Rida', *'Alayhi al-Salam,* and he (the Imam) showed us the ring of abu 'Abd Allah, and abu al-Hassan, *'Alayhim al-Salam.* On the ring of abu 'Abd Allah, *'Alayhi al-Salam,* it said, '*You are my trusty so protect me from people.*' The engraving on the ring of abu al-Hassan, *'Alayhi al-Salam,* said, '*Allah is sufficient for me*' and there was a flower and a crescent on its upper part.'"

H 12283, Ch. 26, h 5

It is narrated from the narrator of the previous *Hadith* from Yunus ibn 'Abd al-Rahman who has said the following:

"I once asked abu al-Hassan, al-Rida', *'Alayhi al-Salam,* about the engraving on his ring and the ring of his father. He (the Imam) said, 'The engraving on my ring says, '*It is whatever Allah wants and there is no power except the power of Allah*' and the engraving on the ring of my father said, '*Allah is sufficient for me*' and it is what I used for my ring.'"

H 12284, Ch. 26, h 6

Ali ibn Ibrahim has narrated from his father from Ali ibn Ma'bad from al-Husayn ibn Khalid who has said the following:

"Abu al-Hassan, *'Alayhi al-Salam,* has said, 'On the ring of Ali ibn al-Husayn, *'Alayhi al-Salam,* the writing said, '*Disgraced and destroyed are murderers of al-Husayn ibn Ali*' *'Alayhi al-Salam.*'"

H 12285, Ch. 26, h 7

Sahl ibn Ziyad has narrated from certain persons of his people from Wasil ibn Sulayman from 'Abd Allah ibn Sinan who has said the following:

"Once we mentioned the ring of the Messenger of Allah, *O Allah, grant compensation to Muhammad and his family worthy of their services to Your cause,* and he (the Imam) said, 'Will you like if I show you?' I replied, 'Yes, (I will be delighted to see it).' He (the Imam) then asked for a sealed package and took from it a pack of cotton in which there was a ring of silver. It had a piece of black stone with two lines of writing that said, '*Muhammad is the Messenger of Allah.*' He (the narrator) has said that he (the Imam) said, 'The stone of the ring of the Holy Prophet is black.'"

414

H 12286, Ch. 26, h 8

Sahl ibn Ziyad Muhammad ibn 'Isa from al-Husayn ibn Khalid who has said the following:

"I once said to abu al-Hassan, al-Thaniy, *'Alayhi al-Salam,* 'We narrate in *Hadith* that the Messenger of Allah, *O Allah, grant compensation to Muhammad and his family worthy of their services to Your cause,* after using the rest room performed cleansing while wearing his ring on his finger and so also did 'Amir al-Mu'minin. The engraving on the ring of the Messenger of Allah said, *'Muhammad is the Messenger of Allah'.* He (the Imam) said, 'They have spoken the truth.' I then asked, 'Is it proper for us to do so?' He (the Imam) said, 'They wore the ring on their right hand and you wear it on your left hand.' I then remained quiet and he (the Imam) asked, 'Do you know what the engraving on the ring of Adam, *'Alayhi al-Salam* was?' I replied, 'No, I do not know.' He (the Imam) said, 'It was *'No one deserves worship except Allah and Muhammad is the Messenger of Allah.'* The engraving on the ring of the last and seal of the prophets said, *'Muhammad is the Messenger of Allah'.* The engraving on the ring of 'Amir al-Mu'minin said, *'Allah is the owner.'* On the ring of al-Hassan, *'Alayhi al-Salam,* it said, *'All glory belongs to Allah.'* On the ring of al-Husayn, *'Alayhi al-Salam,* it said, *'Allah achieves His goals.'* On the ring of Ali ibn al-Husayn, *'Alayhim al-Salam,* it was like the ring of his father. On the ring of abu Ja'far, the great, it was like the ring of his grandfather. On the ring of Ja'far, *'Alayhi al-Salam,* it said, *'Allah is my Guardian and protector from His creatures.'* On the ring of abu al-Hassan, al-Awwal, *'Alayhi al-Salam,* it said, *'Allah is sufficient for me.'* On the ring of abu al-Hassan, al-Thaniy, *'Alayhi al-Salam,* it said, *'It is all what Allah wants, there is no power except Allah.'* Al-Husayn ibn Khalid has said that he (the Imam) then extended his hand to me and said, 'The engraving on my ring is like the engraving on the ring of my father, *'Alayhi al-Salam.'''* (Abu al-Hassan, al-Thaniy, *'Alayhi al-Salam,* it seems had two rings. One was his own ring with engraving that said, *'It is all what Allah wants, there is no power except Allah'* and his other ring was the ring of his father).

H 12287, Ch. 26, h 9

Muhammad ibn Yahya has narrated from Ahmad ibn Muhammad from al-Qasim ibn Yahya from his grandfather al-Hassan ibn Rashid from abu Basir who has said the following:

"Abu 'Abd Allah, *'Alayhi al-Salam,* has said that 'Amir al-Mu'minin has said, 'If one engraves the name of Allah on his ring he must change it from the hand with which one performs cleansing (washing one's bottom).'''

Chapter 27 - The Ornaments

H 12288, Ch. 27, h 1

Abu Ali al-Ash'ariy has narrated from Muhammad ibn 'Abd al-Jabbar from Muhammad ibn 'Isma'il from Ali ibn al-Nu'man from abu al-Sabbah al-Kinaniy who has said the following:

"I once asked abu 'Abd Allah, *'Alayhi al-Salam,* about the case of children; if they can use gold as ornaments. He (the Imam) said that Ali ibn al-Husayn, *'Alayhim al-Salam,* allowed his children and women to use gold and silver as ornaments.'''

H 12289, Ch. 27, h 2

A number of our people have narrated from Ahmad ibn Muhammad from al-Washsha' and Ahmad ibn Muhammad from ibn abu Nasr all from Dawud ibn Sarhan who has said the following:

"I once asked abu 'Abd Allah, *'Alayhi al-Salam,* about the case of children; if they can use gold as ornaments. He (the Imam) said, 'My father, *'Alayhi al-Salam,* allowed his children and women to use gold and silver as ornaments, so it is not unlawful.'"

H 12290, Ch. 27, h 3

Muhammad ibn Yahya has narrated from Ahmad ibn Muhammad from Ali ibn al-Hakam from al-'Ala' from Muhammad ibn Muslim who has said the following:

"I once asked abu 'Abd Allah, *'Alayhi al-Salam,* about women's using gold and silver as ornaments. He (the Imam) said, 'It is not unlawful.'"

H 12291, Ch. 27, h 4

Ali ibn Ibrahim has narrated from his father from al-Nawfaliy from al-Sakuniy who has said the following:

"Abu 'Abd Allah, *'Alayhi al-Salam,* has said that Na'l (the end of the sheath) *al-Qa'imah* (the handle) of the sword of the Messenger of Allah, *O Allah, grant compensation to Muhammad and his family worthy of their services to Your cause,* was of silver and in between there were rings of silver. I once wore the armor of the Messenger of Allah and I trailed it on the ground. It had three rings of silver, one in front and two on the back.'"

H 12292, Ch. 27, h 5

Ali ibn Ibrahim has narrated from his father from ibn abu 'Umayr from 'Abd Allah ibn Sinan who has said the following:

"Abu 'Abd Allah, *'Alayhi al-Salam,* has said, 'It is not unlawful to decorate the sword with gold and silver.'"

H 12293, Ch. 27, h 6

Al-Husayn ibn Muhammad has narrated from Mu'alla' ibn Muhammad from al-Washsha' from al-Muthanna' from Hatim ibn Sulayman who has said the following:

"Abu 'Abd Allah, *'Alayhi al-Salam,* has said, 'The sword of the Messenger of Allah, *O Allah, grant compensation to Muhammad and his family worthy of their services to Your cause,* was decorated with gold and silver, as well as its Qa'imah (handle) and Qiba' (hilt).'"

H 12294, Ch. 27, h 7

A number of our people have narrated from Sahl ibn Ziyad from Ahmad ibn Muhammad from ibn abu Nasr from Dawud ibn Sarhan who has said the following:

"Abu 'Abd Allah, *'Alayhi al-Salam,* has said, 'It is not unlawful to decorate *al-Musahaf* (Quran and books) and swords with gold and silver.'"

H 12295, Ch. 27, h 8

Humayd ibn Ziyad has narrated from al-Hassan ibn Muhammad ibn Sama'ah from more than one person from Aban from Muhammad ibn Muslim who has said the following:

"Abu Ja'far, *'Alayhi al-Salam,* has said, 'Women can continue wearing ornaments.'"

Muhammad ibn Yahya has narrated from 'Abd Allah ibn Muhammad from Aban from Muhammad ibn Muslim from abu Ja'far, *'Alayhi al-Salam,* a similar *Hadith.*

H 12296, Ch. 27, h 9

A number of our people have narrated from Sahl ibn Ziyad from Ja'far ibn Muhammad al-Ash'ariy from ibn al-Qaddah who has said the following:

"Abu 'Abd Allah, *'Alayhi al-Salam,* has said that the Messenger of Allah, *O Allah, grant compensation to Muhammad and his family worthy of their services to Your cause,* wore the ring on his left hand which was of gold then he appeared among people who continued staring at it. He (the Messenger of Allah) placed his right hand on the pinky (little finger) of his left hand until he returned home; then threw it and did not wear it again.'"

From abu 'Abd Allah, *'Alayhi al-Salam,* a narration, similar to the above *Hadith,* is also made by a number of our people from Ahmad ibn Muhammad, from al-Washsha', from al-Muthanna', from Hatim ibn `Isma'il.

H 12297, Ch. 27, h 10

A number of our people have narrated from Ahmad ibn abu 'Abd Allah from his father from Muhammad ibn Sinan from Hammad ibn 'Uthaman from Rib'iy from al-Fudayl ibn Yasar who has said the following:

"I once asked abu 'Abd Allah, *'Alayhi al-Salam,* about a bed which has gold in it; if it is proper to keep it in the house. He (the Imam) said, 'It is not unlawful if it is golden; but if it is gold then it is not lawful.'"

Chapter 28 - The Spreading, Furniture

H 12298, Ch. 28, h 1

A number of our people have narrated from Sahl ibn Ziyad from Mansur ibn al-'Abbas from Sa'id ibn Junah from ibn Khalid al-Zaydiy from Jabir who has said the following:

"Once a group of people visited al-Husayn ibn Ali, *'Alayhim al-Salam,* and said, 'O child of the Messenger of Allah, *O Allah, grant compensation to Muhammad and his family worthy of their services to Your cause,* in your house we see such things that we dislike.' In his home there were pleasing spreading and cushions. He (the Imam), *'Alayhi al-Salam,* said, 'We marry women and give them their mahr (dower). They buy whatever they want and we do not have anything to say about it.'"

H 12299, Ch. 28, h 2

A number of our people have narrated from Ahmad ibn Muhammad ibn Khalid from his father from 'Abd Allah ibn al-Mughirah from abu Malik al-Juhaniy from 'Abd Allah ibn 'Ata' who has said the following:

"I once visited abu Ja'far, *'Alayhi al-Salam,* and in his house I saw spreading, cushions, furnishings and pillows and I asked, 'What are these?' He (the Imam) said, 'These are the belongings of the woman (wife the Imam).'"

H 12300, Ch. 28, h 3

A number of our people have narrated from Sahl ibn Ziyad from Ahmad ibn Muhammad from ibn abu Nasr from Dawud ibn al-Haseen from al-Fadl abu al-'Abbas who has said the following:

"I once asked abu Ja'far, *'Alayhi al-Salam,* about the meaning of the words of Allah, most Majestic, most Glorious, 'They made for him whatever he wanted, such as *Salat* (prayer) niche, statues, basins like wells. . . .' (34:13) He (the Imam) said, 'They were not statues of men and women but they were the figures of trees and similar objects.'"

H 12301, Ch. 28, h 4

Ali ibn Ibrahim has narrated from Salih al-Sindiy from Ja'far ibn Bashir from those whom he has mentioned who has said the following:

"Abu 'Abd Allah, *'Alayhi al-Salam,* has said that Ali ibn al-Husayn, *'Alayhim al-Salam,* (in his house) had pillows and floor furnishings which had pictures (of sceneries) on which he (the Imam) sat.'"

H 12302, Ch. 28, h 5

A number of our people have narrated from Ahmad ibn abu 'Abd Allah from 'Uthman ibn 'Isa from 'Abd Allah ibn Muskan from al-Hassan al-Zayyat who has said the following:

"I once visited abu Ja'far, *'Alayhi al-Salam,* in a well-furnished house; and the next day I visited him in a house where there was nothing except a mat. He (the Imam) wore a thick and rough-textured shirt. He (the Imam) said, 'The house that you saw was not my house. It was the house of the woman and yesterday was her day.'"

H 12303, Ch. 28, h 6

Muhammad ibn Yahya has narrated from Ahmad ibn Muhammad from certain persons of his people from Ali ibn `Isma'il al-Maythamiy from abu al-Jarud who have said the following:

"I once visited abu Ja'far, *'Alayhi al-Salam.* He was sitting on a certain furnishing. I kept touching it with my hand. He (the Imam) said, 'What you are touching is from Armenia.' I then asked, 'What do you have to do with Armenia?' He (the Imam) said, 'This is what mother of Ali (wife of the Imam) has brought.' I then visited him at another time and kept touching what I was sitting on. He (the Imam) said, 'It seems you like to see what is underneath you.' I replied, 'No, but a blind only plays.' He (the Imam) said, to me, 'That item of belonging was owned by mother of Ali. She was of the opinion of al-Khawarij and I wanted that she can return from her opinion until the morning and accept the divine authority of Ali, *'Alayhi al-Salam,* but she refused; then in the morning I divorced her.'"

H 12304, Ch. 28, h 7

A number of our people have narrated from Ahmad ibn Muhammad ibn Khalid from `Isma'il ibn Mehran from 'Abd Allah ibn al-Mughirah who has said the following:

"I once heard abu 'Abd Allah, *'Alayhi al-Salam,* saying, 'Once a man asked abu Ja'far, *'Alayhi al-Salam,* if a man can sit on a furnishing which has pictures of things on it. He (the Imam) said, 'Al-'A'ajim (non-Arab) respect it, but we do not consider it important.'"

H 12305, Ch. 28, h 8

Muhammad ibn Yahya has narrated from al-'Amrakiy ibn Ali from Ali ibn Ja'far who has said the following:

"I once asked abu al-Hassan, *'Alayhi al-Salam,* about silk furnishings and similarly about brocaded items, prayer rugs of silk and of brocaded ones; if it is proper for a man to sleep on it, perform *Salat* (prayer) or lean against it. He (the Imam) said, 'He can spread it and stand on it but he cannot perform *Sajdah* (prostration) on it.'"

Chapter 29 - The Rare Ahadith

H 12306, Ch. 29, h 1

Muhammad ibn Yahya has narrated from Ahmad ibn Muhammad and A number of our people have narrated from Sahl ibn Ziyad all from ibn Mahbub from al-'Abbas ibn al-Walid ibn Sabiyh who has said the following:

"Once Shihab ibn 'Abd Rabbihi asked me to ask permission for him to visit abu 'Abd Allah, *'Alayhi al-Salam,* and I informed him (the Imam) about it. He (the Imam) said, 'He can visit if he likes.' I took him to the house of abu 'Abd Allah, *'Alayhi al-Salam.* It was during the night and Shihab had a mask on him. I found a furnishing for him to sit on and he sat down. Abu 'Abd Allah, *'Alayhi al-Salam,* said to him, 'O Shihab, remove your mask; it causes doubt during the night and disgrace in the day.'"

H 12307, Ch. 29, h 2

Ali ibn Ibrahim has narrated from his father from al-Nawfaliy from al-Sakuniy who has said the following:

"Abu 'Abd Allah, *'Alayhi al-Salam,* has said that 'Amir al-Mu'minin has said, 'When *al-Matrakah* (a certain kind of cape) becomes public, so also will become fornication.'"

H 12308, Ch. 29, h 3

Ali ibn Ibrahim has narrated from [his father] from Muhammad ibn 'Isa from 'Ubayd Allah ibn 'Abd Allah al-Dihqan from Durust ibn abu Mansur from Ibrahim ibn 'Abd al-Hamid who has said the following:

"Abu al-Hassan, *'Alayhi al-Salam,* has said, 'Folding clothes is giving them rest and durability.'"

H 12309, Ch. 29, h 4

Muhammad ibn Yahya has narrated from Ahmad ibn Muhammad from Mu'ammar ibn Khallad who has said the following:

"Abu al-Hassan, *'Alayhi al-Salam,* has said, 'Once I left home to visit Dawud ibn 'Isa ibn Ali who camped at Maymun well. I had two thick pieces of clothes on me and I saw an old woman and two girls with her. I asked her if she sells them. She said, 'Yes, but a man like you will not buy them.' I asked, 'Why is it so?' She replied, 'One is a singer and the other is a flute player.' I then met Dawud ibn 'Isa who treated me with high esteem and gave me my seat. When I left, he asked his companions, 'Do you know him? This is Ali ibn Musa. People of Iraq believe obedience to him is obligatory.'"

H 12310, Ch. 29, h 5

Ali ibn Ibrahim has narrated from his father from ibn abu 'Umayr from Hisham ibn al-Hakam who has said the following:

"Abu 'Abd Allah, *'Alayhi al-Salam,* disliked wearing *al-Burtalah* (a deep cape)."

H 12311, Ch. 29, h 6

Ali ibn Ibrahim has narrated from his father from Ali ibn Muhammad al-Qasaniy from al-Qasim ibn Muhammad from Sulayman ibn Dawud al-Minqariy from Hammad ibn 'Isa who has said the following:

"Abu 'Abd Allah, 'Alayhi al-Salam, once looked at the furnishings in the house of a man, and said, 'A spreading for the man, one for his wife, one for his guests and one for Satan.'"

H 12312, Ch. 29, h 7

Abu Ali al-Ash'ariy has narrated from certain persons of his people from Muhammad ibn Khalid al-Tayalisy from Ali ibn abu Hamzah from abu Basir who have said the following:

"Abu 'Abd Allah, 'Alayhi al-Salam, has said, 'If one wears a loincloth in a sitting position, he remains safe from lower back pain.'"

H 12313, Ch. 29, h 8

Al-Husayn ibn Muhammad has narrated from Mu'alla' ibn Muhammad from Mansur ibn al-'Abbas from al-Hassan ibn Ali ibn Yaqtin from 'Amr ibn Ibrahim from Khalaf ibn Hammad from Ali al-Qummiy who has said the following:

"Abu 'Abd Allah, 'Alayhi al-Salam, has said, 'Growing hairs in the nose and spacious shirt afford immunity from leprosy. Have you not heard a poet's saying, "You will not see my shirt other than being of wide sides and sleeves?"'"

H 12314, Ch. 29, h 9

Al-Husayn ibn Muhammad has narrated from Mu'alla' ibn Muhammad from Ahmad ibn Muhammad from al-Hassan ibn al-Husayn al-'Alawiy who has said the following:

"Abu al-Hassan, 'Alayhi al-Salam, has said, 'One sign of the manhood of a man is plumpness of his stumpers.' He (the narrator) has said that he heard him (the Imam) saying, 'Three things are of the signs of manhood of a man. One is liveliness of his stumper, good looking slaves and distinguished house furnishings.'"

H 12315, Ch. 29, h 10

A number of our people have narrated from Sahl ibn Ziyad from Muhammad ibn al-Hassan ibn Shammun from 'Abd Allah ibn 'Abd al-Rahman from Misma' who has said the following:

"Abu 'Abd Allah, 'Alayhi al-Salam, has said that the Messenger of Allah, *O Allah, grant compensation to Muhammad and his family worthy of their services to Your cause,* has said, 'You must not touch the clothes of one who has not yet worn them.'"

H 12316, Ch. 29, h 11

Sahl ibn Ziyad has narrated from Muhammad ibn Bakr from Zakariya al-Mu'min' from those who narrated to him who has said the following:

"Abu 'Abd Allah, 'Alayhi al-Salam, has said, 'Fold your clothes for the night because Satan wears during the night the spread out clothes.'"

H 12317, Ch. 29, h 12

Sahl ibn Ziyad has narrated from Yahya ibn al-Mubarak from 'Abd Allah ibn Jabalah al-Kinaniy who has said the following:

"Abu al-Hassan, 'Alayhi al-Salam, welcomed me and I was hanging a fish in my hand. He (the Imam) said, 'Throw it away; I dislike that a noble and high ranking man himself carry something unimportant.' He (the Imam) said, 'You are a people who have a large number of enemies. People are your enemies, O Shi'ah, because you have become their enemies, therefore, you must beautify yourselves before them to whatever degree you can.'"

Chapter 30 - The Dyes

H 12318, Ch. 30, h 1
Muhammad ibn Yahya has narrated from Ahmad ibn Muhammad from ibn Faddal from al-Hassan ibn al-Jahm who has said the following:
"Once I visited abu al-Hassan, *'Alayhi al-Salam.* He had applied black dye to his hairs. I said to him (the Imam), 'I see that you have applied black dye to your hairs.' He (the Imam) said, 'In applying dye there is reward. Applying dye and to be prepared is of matters by which Allah, most Majestic, most Glorious, increases the chastity of women. Women ignore chastity because of their husband's ignoring preparedness.' I then said, 'It is narrated to us that applying henna increases oldness.' He (the Imam) said, 'What else can you increase in oldness? Oldness increases every day.'"

H 12319, Ch. 30, h 2
Muhammad ibn Yahya has narrated from Ahmad ibn Muhammad from Ali ibn al-Hakam from Miskin ibn abu al-Hakam from a man who has said the following:
"Abu 'Abd Allah, *'Alayhi al-Salam,* has said that once a man came to the Holy Prophet, *O Allah, grant compensation to Muhammad and his family worthy of their services to Your cause.* He (the Messenger of Allah) looked at the signs of oldness in his beard. The Holy Prophet said, 'It is light.' He (the Messenger of Allah) then said, 'If one becomes white-headed because of oldness in Islam he will have a light on the Day of Judgment.' The man applied dye to his hair with henna, then visited the Holy Prophet. On seeing him the Holy Prophet, said, 'It is light and Islam.' He then applied black dye to his hairs and the Holy Prophet, said, 'It is light, Islam, belief and love from your women, and fear in the hearts of your enemies.'"

H 12320, Ch. 30, h 3
Ahmad ibn Muhammad has narrated from al-'Abbas ibn Musa al-Warraq who has said the following:
"Abu al-Hassan, *'Alayhi al-Salam,* has said that once a group of people visited abu Ja'far, *'Alayhi al-Salam,* and they saw him with black dye applied to his hairs. They asked him about it and he (the Imam) said, 'I am a man who loves women and I pretend before them.'"

H 12321, Ch. 30, h 4
Ahmad ibn Muhammad has narrated from Sa'id ibn Junah from abu Khalid al-Zaydiy from Jabir who has said the following:
"Abu Ja'far, *'Alayhi al-Salam,* has said that once a group of people visited al-Husayn, *'Alayhi al-Salam,* and saw black dye applied to his hairs. They asked him (the Imam) about it and he (the Imam) extended his hand to his beard and said, 'The Messenger of Allah, *O Allah, grant compensation to Muhammad and*

his family worthy of their services to Your cause, in an armed expedition commanded them to apply black dye so they can overpower the pagans.'"

H 12322, Ch. 30, h 5

Ali ibn Ibrahim has narrated from his father from ibn abu 'Umayr from Mu'awiyah ibn 'Ammar from Hafs ibn al-A'war who has said the following:

"I once asked abu 'Abd Allah, *'Alayhi al-Salam,* about the case of coloring the beard and head if it is of *Sunnah.* He (the Imam) said, 'Yes, it is of the *Sunnah.'* I then said, ''Amir al-Mu'minin, *'Alayhi al-Salam,* did not use dye.' He (the Imam) said, 'It is because of the words of the Messenger of Allah, *O Allah, grant compensation to Muhammad and his family worthy of their services to Your cause,* "This will be dyed with this".'"

H 12323, Ch. 30, h 6

Ali ibn Ibrahim has narrated from his father from Muhammad ibn 'Isma'il has narrated from al-Fadl ibn Shadhan from all from ibn abu 'Umayr from Ibrahim ibn 'Abd al-Hamid who has said the following:

"Abu al-Hassan, *'Alayhi al-Salam,* has said, 'In *al-Khidab* (applying hair dye) there are three positive qualities. It shows one's firmness in war, love of women and increase in sexual desire.'"

H 12324, Ch. 30, h 7

Ali ibn Ibrahim has narrated from his father from ibn abu 'Umayr from Hammad from al-Halabiy who has said the following:

"I once asked abu 'Abd Allah, *'Alayhi al-Salam,* about applying dye to the hairs. He (the Imam) said, 'The Messenger of Allah, *O Allah, grant compensation to Muhammad and his family worthy of their services to Your cause,* applied it as well as al-Husayn and abu Ja'far, *'Alayhim al-Salam,* with *al-Katam* (a plant that looks like myrtle and gives out a black dye).'"

H 12325, Ch. 30, h 8

Muhammad ibn Yahya has narrated from Ahmad ibn 'Isa from ibn Mahbub from 'Abd Allah ibn Sinan who has said the following:

"Abu 'Abd Allah, *'Alayhi al-Salam,* has said that the Messenger of Allah, *O Allah, grant compensation to Muhammad and his family worthy of their services to Your cause,* applied hair dye and 'Amir al-Mu'minin did not apply it because of the words of the Holy Prophet, *'This will be dyed with this'.* Al-Husayn and abu Ja'far, *'Alayhim al-Salam,* applied hair dye.'"

H 12326, Ch. 30, h 9

Abu al-'Abbas has narrated from Muhammad ibn Ja'far from Muhammad ibn 'Abd Hamid from Sayf ibn 'Amirah from abu Shaybah al-Asadiy who has said the following:

"I once asked abu 'Abd Allah, *'Alayhi al-Salam,* about *al-Khidab* (hair dye). He (the Imam) said, 'Al-Husayn and abu Ja'far, *'Alayhim al-Salam,* applied hair dye with henna and *al-Katam.'*"

H 12327, Ch. 30, h 10

Muhammad ibn Yahya has narrated from Ahmad ibn Muhammad, from ibn Khalid from Fadalah ibn Ayyub from Mu'awiyah ibn 'Ammar who has said the following:

"I saw abu Ja'far, *'Alayhi al-Salam,* had applied hair dye with henna of red color.'"

H 12328, Ch. 30, h 11
A number of our people have narrated from Ahmad ibn abu 'Abd Allah from Muhammad ibn 'Isma'il from Muhammad ibn 'Adhafir from 'Umar ibn Yazid who has said the following:

"Abu 'Abd Allah, *'Alayhi al-Salam,* has said, 'You must not allow the hair dye to wear off because it is despair.'"

H 12329, Ch. 30, h 12
Ali ibn Muhammad ibn Bandar and Muhammad ibn al-Hassan have narrated from Ibrahim ibn Ishaq al-Ahmar from Muhammad ibn 'Abd Allah ibn Mehran from his father in a *marfu'* manner has said the following:

"The Holy Prophet, *O Allah, grant compensation to Muhammad and his family worthy of their services to Your cause,* has said, 'Spending one dirham on hair dye is better than spending one dirham in the way of Allah. There are fourteen advantages in it. It dispels air from the ears, brightens gloominess from the eyes, softens the nose ducts, sweetens the fragrance, strengthens the gums, clears fainting and reduces temptation of Satan. It gives happiness to angels, gives good news to believers, disappoints the unbelievers, it is beautification, it is a perfume and freedom in one's grave because of which Mukar and Nakir (the two angels in one's grave) shy away.'"

Chapter 31 - The Black Dye and Woad

H 12330, Ch. 31, h 1
Muhammad ibn Yahya has narrated from Ahmad ibn Muhammad from Ali ibn al-Hakam from Sayf ibn 'Amirah from abu Bakr al-Hadramiy who has said the following:

"Once abu 'Alqamah, al-Harith ibn al-Mughirah, abu Hassan and I were with abu 'Abd Allah, *'Alayhi al-Salam,* and 'Alqamah had applied hair dye with henna, al-Harith had applied hair dye with woad and abu Hassan would not apply hair dye. Every man pointing to his beard asked him (the Imam), 'What do you say about it (hair dye), may Allah grant you kindness?' Abu 'Abd Allah, *'Alayhi al-Salam,* said, 'It is very good.' They asked, 'Did abu Ja'far, *'Alayhi al-Salam,* apply hair dye?' He (the Imam) said, 'Yes, when he married al-Thaqafiyah, her slave-girls applied hair dye to his hairs.'"

H 12331, Ch. 31, h 2
It is narrated from the narrator of the previous *Hadith* from ibn Mahbub from 'Abd Allah ibn Sinan who has said the following:

"I once asked abu 'Abd Allah, *'Alayhi al-Salam,* about applying Woad. He (the Imam) said, 'It is not harmful to an old man.'"

H 12332, Ch. 31, h 3
Ibn Mahbub has narrated from al-'Ala' ibn Razin from Muhammad ibn Muslim who has said the following:

"I once saw abu Ja'far, *'Alayhi al-Salam,* chewing gums and he (the Imam) said, 'O Muhammad, woad has loosened my molar teeth so I chew gums to strengthen them.' His teeth had become loose so he tied them with gold."

H 12333, Ch. 31, h 4

Abu Ali al-Ash'ariy has narrated from Muhammad ibn 'Abd al-Jabbar from ibn Faddal from Tha'labah ibn Maymun from Muhammad ibn Muslim who has said the following:

"Abu Ja'far, *'Alayhi al-Salam,* said, 'Woad has affected my molar teeth.'"

H 12334, Ch. 31, h 5

A number of our people have narrated from Ahmad ibn abu 'Abd Allah from a number of his people from Ali ibn Asbat from his uncle Ya'qub ibn Salim who has said the following:

"Abu 'Abd Allah, *'Alayhi al-Salam,* has said, 'At the time al-Husayn, *'Alayhi al-Salam,* was murdered he had applied hair dye with woad.'"

H 12335, Ch. 31, h 6

It is narrated from the narrator of the previous *Hadith* from his father from Yunus from abu Bakr al-Hadramiy who has said the following:

"I once asked abu 'Abd Allah, *'Alayhi al-Salam,* about applying hair dye with woad. He (the Imam) said, 'It is not harmful. At the time al-Husayn, *'Alayhi al-Salam,* was murdered he had applied hair dye with woad.'"

H 12336, Ch. 31, h 7

It is narrated from the narrator of the previous *Hadith* from his father from al-Qasim ibn Muhammad al-Jawhariy from al-Husayn ibn 'Umar ibn Yazid from his father who has said the following:

"I once heard abu 'Abd Allah, *'Alayhi al-Salam,* saying, 'Applying black hair dye is entertaining for women and show one's firmness to the enemy.'"

Chapter 32 - Dyeing Hairs with Henna

H 12337, Ch. 32, h 1

Ali ibn Ibrahim has narrated from his father from ibn abu 'Umayr from Hisham ibn al-Hakam who has said the following:

"Abu 'Abd Allah, *'Alayhi al-Salam,* has said, 'Applying hair dye with henna increases the beauty of the face as well as gray hairs.'"

H 12338, Ch. 32, h 2

Abu Ali al-Ash'ariy has narrated from Muhammad ibn 'Abd al-Jabbar from Safwan from al-'Ala' from Muhammad ibn Muslim who has said the following:

"Abu Ja'far, *'Alayhi al-Salam,* has said, 'Applying hair dye with henna stirs up gray hairs.'"

H 12339, Ch. 32, h 3

Ali ibn Ibrahim has narrated from his father from ibn abu 'Umayr from Mu'awiyah ibn 'Ammar who has said the following:

"I saw abu Ja'far, *'Alayhi al-Salam,* had applied hair dye with henna.'"

H 12340, Ch. 32, h 4

A number of our people have narrated from Ahmad ibn abu 'Abd Allah from his father from Fadalah ibn Ayyub from Hariz from a Mawla' of Ali ibn al-Husayn, *'Alayhim al-Salam,* who has said the following:

"I once heard Ali ibn al-Husayn, *'Alayhim al-Salam,* saying that the Messenger of Allah, *O Allah, grant compensation to Muhammad and his family worthy of their services to Your cause,* has said, 'Apply hair dye with henna, it increases eyesight, grows hair, sweetens the smell and comforts the wife.'"

H 12341, Ch. 32, h 5
It is narrated from the narrator of the previous *Hadith* from 'Ubdus ibn Ibrahim al-Baghdadiy in a *marfu'* manner has said the following:
"Abu 'Abd Allah, *'Alayhi al-Salam,* has said, 'Applying henna dispels bad odor, increases beauty of the face, sweetens the fragrance and beautifies the child.'"

H 12342, Ch. 32, h 6
It is narrated from the narrator of the previous *Hadith* from Ali ibn Sulayman ibn Rashid from Malik ibn 'Ushaym from 'Isma'il ibn Bazi' who has said the following:
"I once said to abu al-Hassan, *'Alayhi al-Salam,* 'My young daughter does not experience *Hayd* (menses) anymore.' He (the Imam) said, 'Apply hair dye to her head with henna; her *Hayd* (menses) will return.' He (the narrator) has said, 'She followed the instruction and her *Hayd* (menses) came back.'"

Chapter 33 - Clipping and Shaving Hairs

H 12343, Ch. 33, h 1
Muhammad ibn Yahya has narrated from Ahmad ibn Muhammad ibn 'Isa from Mu'ammar ibn Khallad who has said the following:
"Abu al-Hassan, *'Alayhi al-Salam,* has said, 'If one comes to know of three things he will not ignore them. They are clipping hairs, rolling up clothes and going to bed with slave-girls.'"

H 12344, Ch. 33, h 2
Ali ibn Ibrahim has narrated from his father from ibn abu 'Umayr from Muhammad ibn abu Hamzah from Ishaq ibn 'Ammar who has said the following:
"Abu 'Abd Allah, *'Alayhi al-Salam,* once said to me, 'You must clip your hairs; it reduces its smell, bugs (like flea etc.) and dirt. It thickens your neck and clears your eyesight.'"

In another *Hadith* it is said that it comforts your body.'"

H 12345, Ch. 33, h 3
A number of our people have narrated from Sahl ibn Ziyad Ahmad ibn Muhammad from ibn abu Nasr who has said the following:
"I once said to abu al-Hassan, *'Alayhi al-Salam,* 'Our people narrate that shaving one's head, except for *al-Hajj* or al-'Umrah, is like causing deformity.' He (the Imam) said, 'Abu al-Hassan, *'Alayhi al-Salam,* after *al-Hajj* and al-'Umrah would go to the town called Sayah and shave his head.'"

H 12346, Ch. 33, h 4
Ali ibn Muhammad has narrated from in a *marfu'* manner the following:
"I once said to abu 'Abd Allah, *'Alayhi al-Salam,* 'People say shaving of the head is like causing deformity.' He (the Imam) said, 'It is like performing al-'Umrah for us and deformity for our enemies.'"

H 12347, Ch. 33, h 5

Muhammad ibn Yahya has narrated from Ahmad ibn Muhammad ibn 'Isa and Ali ibn Ibrahim has narrated from his father from all from ibn abu 'Umayr from 'Abd al-Rahman ibn 'Umar ibn Aslam who has said the following:

"I once applied cupping. The cupping man shaved that area. Abu al-Hassan, *'Alayhi al-Salam,* saw me and asked, 'What is this? Go and shave your head.' I went and shaved my head.'"

H 12348, Ch. 33, h 6

Abu Ali al-Ash'ariy has narrated from Muhammad ibn 'Abd al-Jabbar from Safwan from ibn Sinan who has said the following:

"I once asked abu 'Abd Allah, *'Alayhi al-Salam,* about growing long hairs. He (the Imam) said that companions of the Holy Prophet, *O Allah, grant compensation to Muhammad and his family worthy of their services to Your cause,* clipped their hairs.'"

H 12349, Ch. 33, h 7

A number of our people have narrated from Ahmad ibn Muhammad from Ali ibn al-Hakam from Sa'dan from abu Basir who has said the following:

"Abu 'Abd Allah, *'Alayhi al-Salam,* has said, 'I shave every Friday from this to that duration.'"

H 12350, Ch. 33, h 8

A number of our people have narrated from Sahl ibn Ziyad from Yahya ibn al-Mubarak from 'Abd Allah ibn Jabalah from Ishaq ibn 'Ammar who has said the following:

"I once said to abu 'Abd Allah, *'Alayhi al-Salam,* 'I pray to Allah to keep my soul in service for your cause, at times hairs grow at my back and it causes great worries for me.' He (the Imam) said to me, 'O Ishaq did you not know that shaving one's back dispels anxieties?'"

Chapter 34 - Keeping Hairs and Parting them

H 12351, Ch. 34, h 1

A number of our people have narrated from Sahl ibn Ziyad from Ahmad ibn Muhammad from ibn abu Nasr from Dawud ibn al-Hassan from abu al-'Abbas al-Baqbaq who has said the following:

"I once asked abu 'Abd Allah, *'Alayhi al-Salam,* about the case of a man who has long hairs: if he must leave them or part them. He (the Imam) said, 'He must part them.'"

H 12352, Ch. 34, h 2

Ali ibn Ibrahim has narrated from his father from al-Nawfaliy from al-Sakuniy who has said the following:

"Abu 'Abd Allah, *'Alayhi al-Salam,* has said that the Messenger of Allah, *O Allah, grant compensation to Muhammad and his family worthy of their services to Your cause,* has said, 'If one keeps hairs he must maintain them properly or clip them.'"

H 12353, Ch. 34, h 3

Muhammad ibn Yahya has narrated from Ahmad ibn Muhammad from Yahya ibn Harun who has said the following:

"I once asked abu 'Abd Allah, *'Alayhi al-Salam,* if the Messenger of Allah, *O Allah, grant compensation to Muhammad and his family worthy of their services to Your cause,* parted his hairs. He (the Imam) said, 'No, the Messenger of Allah would keep his hairs long enough to reach his ear lobe only.'"

H 12354, Ch. 34, h 4

A number of our people have narrated from Sahl ibn Ziyad from Muhammad ibn 'Isa from 'Amr ibn Ibrahim from Khalaf ibn Hammad from 'Amr ibn Thabit who has said the following:

"I once said to abu 'Abd Allah, *'Alayhi al-Salam,* 'They narrated that parting the hairs is of *Sunnah.* He (the Imam) said, 'Of the *Sunnah!*' I said, 'They think that the Holy Prophet, *O Allah, grant compensation to Muhammad and his family worthy of their services to Your cause,* parted his hairs.' He (the Imam) said, 'The Holy Prophet did not part his hairs nor did the Prophets grow their hairs.'"

H 12355, Ch. 34, h 5

Muhammad ibn Yahya has narrated from Ahmad ibn Muhammad ibn 'Isa from ibn abu Nasr from Ali ibn abu Hamzah from abu Basir who has said the following:

"I once asked abu 'Abd Allah, *'Alayhi al-Salam,* if parting hairs is of *Sunnah.* He (the Imam) replied, 'No, it is not of *Sunnah.*' I then asked if the Messenger of Allah, *O Allah, grant compensation to Muhammad and his family worthy of their services to Your cause,* parted his hairs.' He (the Imam) said, 'Yes, he (the Messenger of Allah) did so.' I then asked, 'If the Messenger of Allah parted his hairs, then how is it that it is not part of the *Sunnah?*' He (the Imam) said, 'The Messenger of Allah experienced a certain condition which made him to part his hairs. If others experience such a condition, they also do as he (the Messenger of Allah) did and in so doing they follow the *Sunnah* of the Messenger of Allah, otherwise, they do not follow the *Sunnah.*' I then asked, 'How did that happen?' He (the Imam) said, 'When the Messenger of Allah was prevented from visiting the House, he had already driven his sacrificial animal to be offered as a sacrifice and had assumed the state of Ihram. Allah showed him in his dream, of which Allah has spoken in His book saying, "Allah certainly made the dream come true for the messenger in all truth. That is, you will enter al-Masjid al-Haram (the Sacred Masjid) if Allah so wills, in peace with your heads shaved, and Taqsir (cut or trim a part of his nails or hair) being done without any fear." (48:26) Thus, the Messenger of Allah learned that Allah would keep His promise about what He has shown him in the dream. For this reason he allowed his hairs that was on his head at the time of assuming the state of Ihram to grow, waiting for the time of shaving in al-Haram (the sacred area) as Allah, most Majestic, most Glorious, had promised. When he shaved his head as part of the acts of his *al-Hajj,* he (the Messenger of Allah) thereafter did not allow his hairs to grow. It (growing of his hairs) was not because of his intention to grow hairs.'"

Chapter 35 - The Beard and Mustache

H 12356, Ch. 35, h 1

Ali ibn Ibrahim has narrated from his father from ibn abu 'Umayr from Hisham ibn al-'Muthanna' from Sadir al-Sayrafiy who has said the following:

"I once saw abu 'Abd Allah, *'Alayhi al-Salam,* remove hairs from his cheek and from under his chin.'"

H 12357, Ch. 35, h 2

Al-Husayn ibn Muhammad has narrated from Mu'alla' ibn Muhammad and Ali ibn Muhammad from Salih ibn abu Hammad all from al-Washsha' from Ahmad ibn 'A'idh from abu Khadijah from Mu'alla' ibn Khunayth who has said the following:

"Abu 'Abd Allah, *'Alayhi al-Salam,* has said, 'Whatever of the beard exceeds one's fistful is in the fire.'"

H 12358, Ch. 35, h 3

A number of our people have narrated from Ahmad ibn abu 'Abd Allah from Ali ibn Ishaq ibn Sa'd ibn Yunus from certain persons of his people who has said the following:

"Abu 'Abd Allah, *'Alayhi al-Salam,* has said, 'The amount of beard that you must keep is what comes in inside your fist and you must clip off whatever exceeds you fist.'"

H 12359, Ch. 35, h 4

It is narrated from the narrator of the previous *Hadith* from 'Uthman ibn 'Isa from 'Abd Allah ibn Muskan from al-Hassan al-Zayyat who has said the following:

"I once saw abu Ja'far, *'Alayhi al-Salam,* had made his beard lighter.'"

H 12360, Ch. 35, h 5

It is narrated from the narrator of the previous *Hadith* from his father from al-Nadr ibn Suwayd from certain persons of his people from abu Ayyub al-Khazzaz from Muhammad ibn Muslim who has said the following:

"I once saw abu Ja'far, *'Alayhi al-Salam,* when the barber trimmed his beard, he (the Imam) said, 'Make it round.'"

H 12361, Ch. 35, h 6

Ali ibn Ibrahim has narrated from his father from al-Nawfaliy from al-Sakuniy who has said the following:

"Abu 'Abd Allah, *'Alayhi al-Salam,* has said that the Messenger of Allah, *O Allah, grant compensation to Muhammad and his family worthy of their services to Your cause,* has said, 'The mustache must be trimmed until the lips become visible.'"

H 12362, Ch. 35, h 7

Muhammad ibn Yahya has narrated from al-'Amrakiy ibn Ali from Ali ibn Ja'far from his brother, abu al-Hassan, *'Alayhi al-Salam,* who has said the following:

"I once asked abu al-Hassan, *'Alayhi al-Salam,* about trimming the mustache; if it is of *Sunnah.* He (the Imam) said, 'Yes, it is of *Sunnah.*'"

H 12363, Ch. 35, h 8

Muhammad ibn Yahya has narrated from Ahmad ibn Muhammad from ibn Faddal from those whom he has mentioned who has said the following:

"Once we mentioned trimming the mustache before abu 'Abd Allah, *'Alayhi al-Salam.* He (the Imam) said, 'It is a charm and trimming it is of *Sunnah.*'"

H 12364, Ch. 35, h 9

A number of our people have narrated from Ahmad ibn abu 'Abd Allah from certain persons of his people from Ali ibn Asbat from 'Abd Allah ibn 'Uthman who had seen abu 'Abd Allah, *'Alayhi al-Salam,* trim his mustache up to the root of the hairs.'"

H 12365, Ch. 35, h 10

Ali ibn Ibrahim has narrated from his father from ibn abu 'Umayr from Muhammad ibn abu Hamzah from those who narrated to him has said the following:

"Abu 'Abd Allah, *'Alayhi al-Salam,* has said, 'Whatever of beard exceeds the fist is in the fire.'"

H 12366, Ch. 35, h 11

Ali ibn Ibrahim has narrated from his father from al-Nawfaliy from al-Sakuniy who has said the following:

"Abu 'Abd Allah, *'Alayhi al-Salam,* has said that the Messenger of Allah, *O Allah, grant compensation to Muhammad and his family worthy of their services to Your cause,* has said, 'You must not allow your mustache to grow long; Satan makes it his hiding place and cover.'"

H 12367, Ch. 35, h 12

A number of our people have narrated from Sahl ibn Ziyad from certain persons of his people from al-Dihqan from Durust who have said the following:

"Abu 'Abd Allah, *'Alayhi al-Salam,* has said that a man with a long beard once passed by the Messenger of Allah, *O Allah, grant compensation to Muhammad and his family worthy of their services to Your cause,* who said, 'He would not look like that had he prepared his beard.' This remark reached that man and he prepared his beard, then visited the Holy Prophet. When he (the Messenger of Allah) saw him he said, 'This is how you must keep it.'"

Chapter 36 - Removing Hairs from the Nostrils

H 12368, Ch. 36, h 1

Muhammad ibn Yahya has narrated from Ahmad ibn Muhammad ibn 'Isa from Muhammad ibn Hamzah al-Ash'ariy in a *marfu'* manner has said the following:

"Abu 'Abd Allah, *'Alayhi al-Salam,* has said, 'Removing hairs from the nostrils (outside) beautifies the face.'"

Chapter 37 - Combing

H 12369, Ch. 37, h 1

Muhammad ibn Yahya has narrated from Ahmad ibn Muhammad from Ali ibn al-Hakam from 'Abd Allah ibn Jundab from Sufyan ibn al-Simt who has said the following:

"Abu 'Abd Allah, *'Alayhi al-Salam,* has said, 'Clean and fresh clothes saddens the enemy, using oil dispels despair and combing the head removes *al-Waba'*.' I then asked, 'What is *al-Waba'*?' He (the Imam) said, 'It is fever. Combing the beard strengthens molar teeth.'"

H 12370, Ch. 37, h 2

Humayd ibn Ziyad has narrated from al-Hassan ibn Sama'ah from Ahmad ibn al-Hassan al-Mithamiy from Muhammad ibn Ishaq from 'Ammar al-Nawfaliy from his father who has said the following:

"I once heard abu al-Hassan, *'Alayhi al-Salam,* saying, 'Combing dispels al-Waba'. Abu 'Abd Allah, *'Alayhi al-Salam,* had a comb in (for) the Masjid which he used after completing *Salat* (prayer).'"

H 12371, Ch. 37, h 3

Ali ibn Ibrahim has narrated from his father from ibn abu 'Umayr from al-Husayn ibn al-Hassan ibn 'Asem from his father who has said the following:

"I once visited abu Ibrahim, *'Alayhi al-Salam,* and he had an ivory comb in his hand which he used. I said, 'I pray to Allah to keep my soul in service for your cause, in Iraq there are people with us who think that using ivory comb is not permissible.' He (the Imam) said, 'For what reason it can be as you said it is, my father had one or two ivory combs.' He (the Imam) then said, 'You must use ivory comb; it removes al-Waba' (fever).'"

H 12372, Ch. 37, h 4

Ali ibn Ibrahim has narrated from Salih ibn al-Sindiy from Ja'far ibn Bashir from Musa ibn Bakr who has said the following:

"I saw abu al-Hassan, *'Alayhi al-Salam,* using an ivory comb and I bought it for him.'"

H 12373, Ch. 37, h 5

Al-Husayn ibn Muhammad has narrated from Mu'alla' ibn Muhammad from al-Washsha' from 'Abd Allah ibn Sulayman who has said the following:

"I once asked abu Ja'far, *'Alayhi al-Salam,* about ivory. He (the Imam) said, 'It is not unlawful and I have one ivory comb.'"

H 12374, Ch. 37, h 6

Muhammad ibn Yahya has narrated from Ahmad ibn Muhammad ibn 'Isa from ibn Mahbub from Nadr from 'Anbasah Sa'id in a *marfu'* manner has said the following:

"The Holy Prophet, *O Allah, grant compensation to Muhammad and his family worthy of their services to Your cause,* has said, 'Combing of the head very often removes *al-Waba'* (fever), attracts sustenance and increases one's ability to go to bed with one's wife.'"

H 12375, Ch. 37, h 7

Ali ibn Ibrahim has narrated from his father from 'Abd Allah ibn al-Mughirah who has said the following:

"About the meaning of the words of Allah, most Majestic, most Glorious, 'You must beautify yourselves near every Masjid' abu al-Hassan, *'Alayhi al-Salam,* has said, 'Of such matters one is combing at the time of every *Salat* (prayer).'"

H 12376, Ch. 37, h 8

A number of our people have narrated from Ahmad ibn Muhammad ibn Khalid from Nuh ibn Shu'ayb from ibn Mayyah from Yunus from those who narrated to him who has said the following:

"Abu al-Hassan, has said, 'When you comb your head and beard, then wipe the comb against your chest; it removes worries and al-Waba' (fever).'"

H 12377, Ch. 37, h 9

It is narrated from the narrator of the previous *Hadith* from his father who has said the following:

"Using the comb very often reduces phlegm.'"

H 12378, Ch. 37, h 10

A number of our people have narrated from Sahl ibn Ziyad from al-Hassan ibn 'Atiyyah from 'Isma'il ibn Jabir who has said the following:

"Abu 'Abd Allah, *'Alayhi al-Salam,* has said, 'If one uses his comb seventy times and counts it one by one, Satan will not come close to him for forty days.'"

H 12379, Ch. 37, h 11

Muhammad ibn Yahya has narrated from Ahmad ibn Muhammad from ibn Mahbub from Ibrahim ibn Mehzam from al-Qasim ibn al-Walid who has said the following:

"I once asked abu 'Abd Allah, *'Alayhi al-Salam,* about elephant bones, its oil (perfume) containers and combs. He (the Imam) said, 'It is not unlawful.'"

Chapter 38 - Clipping the finger Nails

H 12380, Ch. 38, h 1

Muhammad ibn Yahya has narrated from Ahmad ibn Muhammad ibn 'Isa from al-Qasim ibn Yahya from his grandfather al-Hassan ibn Rashid who has said the following:

"He (the Imam), *'Alayhi al-Salam,* has said, that the Messenger of Allah, *O Allah, grant compensation to Muhammad and his family worthy of their services to Your cause,* has said, 'Clipping fingernails repels great many pains and makes the sustenance flow.'"

H 12381, Ch. 38, h 2

Ali ibn Ibrahim has narrated from his father from ibn abu 'Umayr from Hisham ibn Salim who has said the following:

"Abu 'Abd Allah, *'Alayhi al-Salam,* has said, 'Clipping fingernails on Fridays is immunity from leprosy, vitiligo and blindness. If you do not need clipping then just scratch them.'"

H 12382, Ch. 38, h 3

Muhammad ibn Yahya has narrated from Ahmad ibn Muhammad from al-Hassan ibn Ali ibn Sulayman from his uncle 'Abd Allah ibn Hilal who has said the following:

"Abu 'Abd Allah, *'Alayhi al-Salam,* once said to me, 'You must clip your mustache and fingernails every Friday, if you do not need clipping then just scratch them. You will not be affected by insanity, leprosy and vitiligo.'"

H 12383, Ch. 38, h 4

It is narrated from the narrator of the previous *Hadith* from ibn Faddal from ibn Bukayr who has said the following:

"Abu 'Abd Allah, *'Alayhi al-Salam,* has said, 'Clipping fingernails and mustache every Friday is immunity from vitiligo and insanity.'"

H 12384, Ch. 38, h 5

A number of our people have narrated from Sahl ibn Ziyad from Ahmad ibn Muhammad from ibn abu Nasr from ibn 'Uqbah from his father who has said the following:

"Abu 'Abd Allah, *'Alayhi al-Salam,* has said, 'It is of *Sunnah* to clip one's fingernails.'"

H 12385, Ch. 38, h 6

A number of our people have narrated from Ahmad ibn abu 'Abd Allah from his father from those whom he has mentioned from Ayyub ibn al-Hurr from abu Hamzah who has said the following:

"Abu Ja'far, *'Alayhi al-Salam,* has said, 'There is clipping of fingernails; it reduces Satan; and because of it (unclipped fingernails) is forgetfulness.'"

H 12386, Ch. 38, h 7

It is narrated from the narrator of the previous *Hadith* from Muhammad ibn Ali from al-Hakam ibn Miskin from Hudhayfah ibn Mansur who has said the following:

"Abu 'Abd Allah, *'Alayhi al-Salam,* has said, 'The strongest cover and most secret place for Satan by which he dominates children of Adam, *'Alayhi al-Salam* is his hiding under the fingernails.'"

H 12387, Ch. 38, h 8

It is narrated from the narrator of the previous *Hadith* from Muhammad ibn Ali from Ali al-Hannat from Ali ibn abu Hamzah from al-Husayn ibn abu al-'Ala' from abu Basir who has said the following:

"I once asked abu 'Abd Allah, *'Alayhi al-Salam,* about the reward for clipping the mustache and fingernails every Friday. He (the Imam) said, 'He continues with cleanliness until the next Friday.'"

H 12388, Ch. 38, h 9

It is narrated from the narrator of the previous *Hadith* from ibn Faddal from Hafs ibn al-Jurjaniy from abu al-Khasib al-Rabi' ibn Bakr al-Azdiy from 'Abd al-Rahim al-Qasir who has said the following:

"Abu Ja'far, *'Alayhi al-Salam,* has stated this *Hadith.* 'There is one's clipping his mustache and fingernails every Friday. When clipping, one should say, "In the name of Allah, with Allah, and on the *Sunnah* of Muhammad, the Messenger of Allah, *O Allah, grant compensation to Muhammad and his family worthy of their services to Your cause.*" For every piece of clipped hair Allah writes for him the reward of setting free one enslaved soul. He will not become ill except the illness because of which he will die.'"

H 12389, Ch. 38, h 10

Ali ibn Ibrahim has narrated from his father from ibn abu 'Umayr from Muhammad ibn Talhah who has said the following:

"Abu 'Abd Allah, *'Alayhi al-Salam,* has said, 'Clipping fingernails, mustache and washing one's head with hollyhock (marshmallow plant) every Friday banishes poverty and increases one's sustenance.'"

H 12390, Ch. 38, h 11

Muhammad ibn Yahya has narrated from Ahmad ibn Muhammad ibn 'Isa from al-Hassan ibn Ali ibn 'Uqbah from abu Kahmas who has said the following:

"A man once asked 'Abd Allah ibn al-Hassan to teach him something for increased sustenance. He said, 'Remain in the place of your *Salat* (prayer) after the morning *Salat* (prayer) until sunrise; it is more useful for seeking increased sustenance than traveling in the land.' I informed abu 'Abd Allah, *'Alayhi al-*

Salam, about it and he (the Imam) said, 'Will you like if I teach you for increased sustenance what is more useful than that?' I replied, 'Yes, I will like it.' He (the Imam) said, 'Clip your fingernails and mustache every Friday.'"

H 12391, Ch. 38, h 12

It is narrated from the narrator of the previous *Hadith* from ibn Faddal from Ali ibn 'Uqbah from his father who has said the following:

"I once visited 'Abd Allah ibn al-Hassan and asked him to teach me a prayer for increased sustenance. He told me to say, 'O Lord, take charge of my affairs and do not make others the in-charge person of my affairs.' I mentioned it to abu 'Abd Allah, *'Alayhi al-Salam,* and he (the Imam) said, 'May I teach you something more useful than that for increased sustenance? Clip your fingernails and mustache every Friday.'"

H 12392, Ch. 38, h 13

A number of our people have narrated from Ahmad ibn abu 'Abd Allah from Ali ibn Asbat from Khalaf who has said the following:

"Abu al-Hassan, *'Alayhi al-Salam,* saw me in Khurasan and I complained of eye trouble. He (the Imam) said, 'May I teach you something which will remove your complaint because of your eyes?' I replied, 'Yes, I like to know it.' He (the Imam) said, 'Clip your fingernails every Thursday.' I followed the instruction and have not complained ever since of my eyes.'"

H 12393, Ch. 38, h 14

It is narrated from the narrator of the previous *Hadith* from his father from 'Abd Allah ibn al-Fadl al-Nawfaliy from his father from his uncle all has said the following:

"Abu 'Abd Allah, *'Alayhi al-Salam,* has said, 'Whoever continues clipping his fingernails every Thursday will not experience eye ache.'"

H 12394, Ch. 38, h 15

Ali ibn Ibrahim has narrated from his father from al-Nawfaliy from al-Sakuniy who has said the following:

"He (the Imam), *'Alayhi al-Salam,* has said that the Messenger of Allah, *O Allah, grant compensation to Muhammad and his family worthy of their services to Your cause,* has said, 'Men must clip their fingernails and women must keep them because it is more beautifying for them.'"

H 12395, Ch. 38, h 16

Ali ibn Ibrahim has narrated from his father from ibn abu 'Umayr from in a *marfu'* manner has said the following:

"When clipping fingernails you must begin with the little finger of the left hand and complete it with the right hand (little fingernail).'"

H 12396, Ch. 38, h 17

Al-Husayn ibn Muhammad has narrated from Mu'alla' ibn Muhammad from Ja'far ibn Muhammad al-Ash'ariy from ibn al-Qaddah who has said the following:

"Abu 'Abd Allah, *'Alayhi al-Salam,* has said, 'Once a lapse took place in coming of divine revelation to the Holy Prophet, *O Allah, grant compensation to Muhammad and his family worthy of their services to Your cause.* He (the Messenger of Allah) was asked, 'Has coming of divine revelation to you stopped?' He (the Messenger of Allah) said, 'Why should it not stop when you do not clip your fingernails and clean your finger joints?'"

Chapter 39 - Clipping or Pulling out Gray Hairs

H 12397, Ch. 39, h 1
A number of our people have narrated from Ahmad ibn Muhammad from al-Hassan ibn Ali al-Washsha' from 'Abd Allah ibn Sinan who has said the following:
"Abu 'Abd Allah, *'Alayhi al-Salam,* has said, 'It is not unlawful to clip or pull out gray from the head but clipping is more likable to me.'"

H 12398, Ch. 39, h 2
It is narrated from the narrator of the previous *Hadith* from ibn Faddal from those whom he has mentioned who has said the following:
"Abu 'Abd Allah, *'Alayhi al-Salam,* has said, 'It is not unlawful to pull up or clip gray from the beard.'"

H 12399, Ch. 39, h 3
Ali ibn Ibrahim has narrated from his father from al-Nawfaliy from al-Sakuniy who has said the following:
"Abu 'Abd Allah, *'Alayhi al-Salam,* has said that `Amir al-Mu'minin did not consider it harmful to clip gray hairs but disliked pulling it out.'"

H 12400, Ch. 39, h 4
Through the same chain of narrators as that of the previous *Hadith* the following is narrated:
"He (the Imam), *'Alayhi al-Salam,* has said, 'The first one who noticed gray hairs was Ibrahim *'Alayhi al-Salam*, and he asked, 'O Lord, what is this?' He said, 'It is light and reverence.' He then said, 'O Lord, increase it for me.'"

H 12401, Ch. 39, h 5
Ali ibn Ibrahim has narrated from his father from ibn abu 'Umayr from Hafs ibn al-Bakhtariy who has said the following:
"Abu 'Abd Allah, *'Alayhi al-Salam,* has said, 'People did not grow gray hairs but Ibrahim *'Alayhi al-Salam*, found gray in his beard and asked, 'O Lord, what is this?' He said, 'It is reverence.' He then said, 'O Lord, increase my reverence.'"

H 12402, Ch. 39, h 6
A number of our people have narrated from Ahmad ibn abu 'Abd Allah fn abu Ayyub al-Madiniy from Sulayman al-Ja'fariy who has said the following:
"Al-Rida', *'Alayhi al-Salam,* has narrated from his ancestors saying, 'Gray in front of the head is good fortune, on the sides is generosity, on top of the head is courage, and at the back is misfortune.'"

Chapter 40 - To Bury the Hairs and Fingernails

H 12403, Ch. 40, h 1
A number of our people have narrated from Sahl ibn Ziyad from ibn Faddal from certain persons of his people from abu Kahmas who have said the following:
"About the meaning of the words of Allah, most Majestic, most Glorious, 'Have

We not made the earth a collector (homes) of dead and living,' (77:25) abu 'Abd Allah, *'Alayhi al-Salam,* has said, 'It is a reference to burying of the hairs and fingernails.'"

Chapter 41 - Al-Kohl (The Eye Powder): Antimony

H 12404, Ch. 41, h 1

Ali ibn Ibrahim has narrated from his father from and Muhammad ibn Yahya has narrated from Ahmad ibn Muhammad ibn 'Isa from ibn abu 'Umayr from Salim al-Farra' from a man who has said the following:

"Abu 'Abd Allah, *'Alayhi al-Salam,* has said that the Messenger of Allah, *O Allah, grant compensation to Muhammad and his family worthy of their services to Your cause,* applied *al-Athmad* (antimony) to his eyes before going to bed, once in each eye.'"

H 12405, Ch. 41, h 2

Muhammad ibn Yahya has narrated from Ahmad ibn Muhammad from ibn Faddal from al-Hassan ibn al-Jahm who has said the following:

"Abu al-Hassan, *'Alayhi al-Salam,* once showed me a pin made of iron and a powder container of bones and said that this belonged to abu al-Hassan with which he applied eye powder and I also apply eye powder to my eyes.'"

H 12406, Ch. 41, h 3

A number of our people have narrated from Ahmad ibn abu 'Abd Allah from Musa ibn al-Qasim from Safwan from Zurarah who has said the following:

"Abu 'Abd Allah, *'Alayhi al-Salam,* has said, 'Applying eye powder to one's eyes is beneficial to the eyes and it is beautification during the day.'"

H 12407, Ch. 41, h 4

Ali ibn Ibrahim has narrated from his father from 'Abd Allah ibn al-Fadl al-Hashimiy from his father and uncle who have said the following:

"Abu Ja'far, *'Alayhi al-Salam,* has said, 'Applying eye powder with Athmad (antimony) sweetens the fragrance and strengthens the edge of the eyelid.'"

H 12408, Ch. 41, h 5

It is narrated from the narrator of the previous *Hadith* from ibn Faddal from Hammad ibn 'Isa who has said the following:

"Abu 'Abd Allah, *'Alayhi al-Salam,* has said, 'Applying eye powder sweetens the mouth.'"

H 12409, Ch. 41, h 6

It is narrated from the narrator of the previous *Hadith* from his father from Khalaf ibn Hammad from those whom he has mentioned who has said the following:

"Abu 'Abd Allah, *'Alayhi al-Salam,* has said, 'Applying eye powder grows hairs, sharpens eyesight and helps to perform longer Sujud (prostrations).'"

H 12410, Ch. 41, h 7

Muhammad ibn Yahya has narrated from Ahmad ibn Muhammad ibn 'Isa from ibn Faddal from Ali ibn 'Uqbah from a man who has said the following:

"Abu 'Abd Allah, *'Alayhi al-Salam,* has said, 'Al-Athmad (antimony) sharpens eye sight, grows hairs and banishes tears.'"

H 12411, Ch. 41, h 8

Ibn Faddal has narrated from certain persons of our people who have said the following:

"Abu 'Abd Allah, *'Alayhi al-Salam,* has said, 'Applying eye powder increases the desire to go to bed with ones' wife.'"

H 12412, Ch. 41, h 9

A number of our people have narrated from Ahmad ibn abu 'Abd Allah from Ahmad ibn Muhammad from ibn abu Nasr from Ahmad ibn al-Mubarak from al-Husayn ibn al-Hassan ibn 'Asem from his father who has said the following:

"Abu 'Abd Allah, *'Alayhi al-Salam,* has said, 'If one sleeps with eye powder containing Athmad (antimony) but without musk, he remains immune from *Ma' al-Aswad* (a certain eye illness) all the time as long as he sleeps with it.'"

H 12413, Ch. 41, h 10

A number of our people have narrated from Sahl ibn Ziyad from Muhammad ibn Sinan from Hammad ibn 'Isa who has said the following:

"Abu 'Abd Allah, *'Alayhi al-Salam,* has said, 'Applying eye powder grows hairs, dries up tears, sweetens saliva and sharpens eyesight.'"

H 12414, Ch. 41, h 11

A number of our people have narrated from Ahmad ibn abu 'Abd Allah from ibn Faddal from ibn al-Qaddah who has said the following:

"Abu 'Abd Allah, *'Alayhi al-Salam,* has said that 'Amir al-Mu'minin has said, 'If one applies eye powder, he must do it once because it is good; and if he did not do so it is not harmful.'"

H 12415, Ch. 41, h 12

It is narrated from the narrator of the previous *Hadith* from Musa ibn al-Qasim from Safwan from Zurarah who has said the following:

"Abu 'Abd Allah, *'Alayhi al-Salam,* has said that the Messenger of Allah, *O Allah, grant compensation to Muhammad and his family worthy of their services to Your cause,* applied eye powder before going to sleep-four times in the right and three in the left.'"

Chapter 42 - Brushing the Teeth

H 12416, Ch. 42, h 1

Ali ibn Ibrahim has narrated from his father from ibn abu 'Umayr from Ishaq ibn 'Ammar who has said the following:

"Abu 'Abd Allah, *'Alayhi al-Salam,* has said, 'It is of the moral discipline of the prophets to brush one's teeth.'"

H 12417, Ch. 42, h 2

Muhammad ibn Yahya has narrated from Ahmad ibn Muhammad ibn 'Isa from Muhammad ibn Khalid and al-Husayn ibn Sa'id all from al-Qasim ibn 'Urwah from Ishaq ibn 'Ammar who has said the following:

"Abu 'Abd Allah, *'Alayhi al-Salam,* has said, 'Brushing one's teeth is of the *Sunnah* and moral discipline of the prophets.'"

H 12418, Ch. 42, h 3

A number of our people have narrated from Sahl ibn Ziyad from Ja'far ibn Muhammad al-Ash'ariy from ibn al-Qaddah who has said the following:

"Abu 'Abd Allah, *'Alayhi al-Salam,* has said that the Messenger of Allah, *O Allah, grant compensation to Muhammad and his family worthy of their services to Your cause,* has said, 'Jibril continued urging me to brush so much so that I feared of becoming toothless or wearing them thin.'"

H 12419, Ch. 42, h 4

Through the same chain of narrators as that of the previous *Hadith* the following is narrated:

"He (the Imam) said that 'Amir al-Mu'minin has said, 'Brushing one's teeth cleanses the mouth and earns Allah's pleasure.'"

H 12420, Ch. 42, h 5

Sahl ibn Ziyad has narrated from Muhammad ibn 'Isa from al-Hassan ibn al-Bahr from Mehzam al-Asadiy who has said the following:

"I once heard abu 'Abd Allah, *'Alayhi al-Salam,* saying, 'Tooth brushing has ten qualities. One is its cleansing the mouth, its earning the pleasure of Allah, happiness of angels, it is an act of *Sunnah,* it strengthens the gums, sharpens eyesight, dispels phlegm and cavities.'"

H 12421, Ch. 42, h 6

It is narrated from the narrator of the previous *Hadith* from Muhammad ibn 'Isa from 'Ubayd al-Dihqan from Durust from ibn Sinan who has said the following:

"Abu 'Abd Allah, *'Alayhi al-Salam,* has said, 'In tooth brushing there are twelve qualities. It is an act of *Sunnah,* it cleanses the mouth, sharpens eyesight, earns Allah's pleasure, dispels phlegm, improves memory, whitens the teeth, amplifies the list of good deeds, banishes cavities, strengthens gums, increases appetite for food and it makes the angels happy.'"

H 12422, Ch. 42, h 7

Muhammad ibn Yahya has narrated from Ahmad ibn Muhammad from ibn Faddal from Hammad ibn 'Isa who has said the following:

"Abu 'Abd Allah, *'Alayhi al-Salam,* has said, 'Tooth brushing stops tears and sharpens eyesight.'"

H 12423, Ch. 42, h 8

Ali ibn Ibrahim has narrated from his father from ibn abu 'Umayr from Jamil ibn Darraj who has said the following:

"Abu 'Abd Allah, *'Alayhi al-Salam,* has said that the Messenger of Allah, *O Allah, grant compensation to Muhammad and his family worthy of their services to Your cause,* has said, 'Jibril recommend me to brush my teeth so much so that I began to fear for my teeth.'"

H 12424, Ch. 42, h 9

Muhammad ibn Yahya has narrated from Ahmad ibn Muhammad from Ali ibn al-Hakam from al-Marzaban ibn al-Nu'man in a *marfu'* manner has said the following:

"He (the Imam) has said that the Messenger of Allah, *O Allah, grant compensation to Muhammad and his family worthy of their services to Your cause,* once said, 'Why do I see you, people, with yellow teeth, what is the matter with you, why do you not brush your teeth?"

H 12425, Ch. 42, h 10
Ahmad ibn Muhammad has narrated from ibn Mahbub from 'Amr ibn abu al-Miqdam from Muhammad ibn Marwan who has said the following:
"Abu Ja'far, *'Alayhi al-Salam,* has said that it is in the will of the Messenger of Allah, *O Allah, grant compensation to Muhammad and his family worthy of their services to Your cause,* to `Amir al-Mu'minin that says, 'You must brush your teeth for every *Salat* (prayer).'"

Chapter 43 - Taking Shower or Bath

H 12426, Ch. 43, h 1
A number of our people have narrated from Ahmad ibn Muhammad ibn Khalid from his father or others from Muhammad ibn Aslam al-Jabaliy in a *marfu'* manner has said the following:
"Abu 'Abd Allah, *'Alayhi al-Salam,* has said that `Amir al-Mu'minin has said, 'The bathhouse is a very good house; it reminds of fire and banishes dirt.' 'Umar has said, 'A bathhouse is the worst house; it exposes private parts and violates secrets.' He (the Imam) said, 'People have ascribed the words of `Amir al-Mu'minin to 'Umar and vice versa.'"

H 12427, Ch. 43, h 2
It is narrated from the narrator of the previous *Hadith* from Ali ibn al-Hakam from and Ali ibn Hassan from Sulayman ibn al-Ja'fariy who has said the following:
"Abu al-Hassan, *'Alayhi al-Salam,* has said, 'Taking a bath one day and the day after does not increase flesh. Continuously taking a bath every day melts the fat of the kidneys.'"

H 12428, Ch. 43, h 3
Ali ibn Ibrahim has narrated from his father from ibn abu 'Umayr from Rifa'ah ibn Musa who has said the following:
"Abu 'Abd Allah, *'Alayhi al-Salam,* has said that the Messenger of Allah, *O Allah, grant compensation to Muhammad and his family worthy of their services to Your cause,* has said, 'If one believes in Allah and in the life hereafter, he must not enter a bathhouse without a loincloth.'"

H 12429, Ch. 43, h 4
Muhammad ibn Yahya has narrated from Ahmad ibn Muhammad from 'Abd Allah ibn Muhammad *al-Hajj*al from Sulayman al-Ja'fariy who has said the following:
"Once I became ill until I lost all of my flesh. I visited al-Rida', *'Alayhi al-Salam,* who asked, 'Will you like to see your flesh come back?' I replied, 'Yes, I like to see my flesh come back.' He (the Imam) said, 'You must continue taking a bath one day and on the day after the next day, your flesh will come back. You must not take a bath every day because it causes tuberculosis.'" (Perhaps if it is a public bathhouse)

H 12430, Ch. 43, h 5
Ahmad ibn Muhammad has narrated from Ali ibn al-Hakam from al-Muthanna' al-Hannat from abu Basir who has said the following:
"Abu 'Abd Allah, *'Alayhi al-Salam,* has said, 'Do not enter a bathhouse until

there is something in your belly to calm down the excitement of your stomach and it is more energizing for the body. Do not enter it with your stomach full of food.'"

H 12431, Ch. 43, h 6

Ali ibn al-Hakam from has narrated from Rifa'ah ibn Musa from those who narrated to him who has said the following:

"Abu 'Abd Allah, *'Alayhi al-Salam,* when about to take a bath would eat something. I once asked, 'People around us say that before eating anything is the best time for taking a bath.' He (the Imam) said, 'No, one must eat something before taking bath; it banished bitterness (acidity) and calms down the temperature in the belly.'"

H 12432, Ch. 43, h 7

A number of our people have narrated from Sahl ibn Ziyad from Mansur ibn al-'Abbas from Hamzah ibn 'Abd Allah from Rib'iy from 'Ubayd Allah al-Dabiqiy who has said the following:

"I once in al-Madinah entered a bathhouse and an old man was the manager of the bathhouse. I asked, 'O Shaykh to whom does this bathhouse belong?' He replied, 'It belongs to abu Ja'far, Muhammad ibn Ali ibn al-Husayn, *'Alayhim al-Salam.'* I then asked, 'Did he use it?' He replied, 'Yes, he did.' I then asked, 'How would he use it?' He said, 'First he applied lime to his pubic region and the surrounding area and to his urethra then he would call me to apply to the other parts of his body.' I then asked, 'Did you ever see what you do not like to see?' He replied, 'It never happened because lime is a cover.'"

H 12433, Ch. 43, h 8

Ali ibn Ibrahim has narrated from his father from Ahmad ibn Muhammad from Muhammad ibn Yahya has narrated from Ahmad ibn Muhammad from Muhammad ibn 'Isma'il ibn Bazi' all from Hanan ibn Sadir from his father who has said the following:

"My father, grandfather, uncle and I once entered a bathhouse in al-Madinah and there was a man in the room for undressing. He asked, 'From where are you people ?' We replied, 'We are from Iraq.' He then asked, 'From which part of Iraq are you?' We replied that we are from al-Kufah.' He said, 'Welcome, O people of al-Kufah, but you wear only one layer of clothes and why do you not have loincloths? The Messenger of Allah, *O Allah, grant compensation to Muhammad and his family worthy of their services to Your cause,* has said, "Private parts of believing people are unlawful for the believing people."' He then sent a piece of cotton fabric for my father and made it in four parts. Then each one of us took one piece. When we were in the hot room, he turned to my grandfather and said, 'Old man, what prevents you from using dyes?' My grandfather said, 'I lived with one who was better than me and you, and who did not use dyes.' He became angry so much so that we noticed it in the bathhouse. He asked, 'Who is that person better than you and me?' He replied, 'I lived with Ali ibn abu Talib, *'Alayhi al-Salam,* and he did not use dyes.' He looked down and perspired. He said, 'You have spoken the truth and proved your point.' 'O old man, if the Messenger of Allah used dyes, you should also use dyes because he is better than Ali ibn abu Talib, but if you will not use it you have followed the *Sunnah* of Ali ibn abu Talib.' He (the narrator) has said, 'When we left the bathhouse we asked about the man and found out that he was Ali ibn al-Husayn, along with his son, Muhammad ibn Ali, *'Alayhim al-Salam.'"*

H 12434, Ch. 43, h 9

Muhammad ibn Yahya has narrated from Ahmad ibn Muhammad ibn 'Isa from Ali ibn al-Hakam from Ali ibn abu Hamzah who has said the following:

"I once entered a bathhouse with abu Basir and saw abu 'Abd Allah, *'Alayhi al-Salam,* who had applied (lime) and on his underarms. I then informed abu Basir and he asked me to lead him so he can ask him about it. I said, 'I saw him.' He said, 'You saw him (the Imam) but I cannot see him (the Imam)? Lead me to where he is.' I then led him and he said, 'I pray to Allah to keep my soul in service for your cause, my lead has said that you have applied lime and on your underarms.' He (the Imam) said, 'Yes, O abu Muhammad, pulling up hairs of underarms weakens eyesight, so you must apply lime, O abu Muhammad.' He (the narrator) has said, 'I applied since that time and he (the Imam) said, 'Apply; it is cleansing.'"

H 12435, Ch. 43, h 10

Ahmad ibn Muhammad has narrated from Ali ibn al-Hakam from a man of banu Hashim who has said the following:

"I once entered in dark house where a group of banu Hashim were and I offered them greeting of peace with the phrase of offering greeting. A certain one among them said, 'Offer greeting of peace to abu al-Hassan, *'Alayhi al-Salam,* he is in the center.' He (the narrator) has said, 'I offered him (the Imam) greeting of peace and sat in front of him and said, "Since a long time I loved to visit you to ask about certain things."' He (the Imam) said, 'Ask whatever you like.' I then asked, 'What do you say about using a bathhouse?' He (the Imam) said, 'Do not enter a bathhouse without a loincloth, keep your eyes cast down, do not wash with used water because fornicators take a bath with it as well as those born out of wedlock, and enemies of *Ahl al-Bayt, 'Alayhim al-Salam,* who are the worst of them.'"

H 12436, Ch. 43, h 11

Ahmad ibn Muhammad has narrated from Ali ibn Ahmad ibn 'Ushaym from Sulayman al-Ja'fariy who has said the following:

"He (the Imam) has said, 'If one wants to gain weight he should use a bathhouse one day and the day after the next day but if one is heavy and wants to lose weight he should use a bathhouse every day.'"

H 12437, Ch. 43, h 12

Ali ibn Ibrahim has narrated from his father from ibn abu 'Umayr from 'Abd al-Rahman ibn al-*Hajj*aj who has said the following:

"I once asked abu 'Abd Allah, *'Alayhi al-Salam,* about the case of a man who applies lime, then mixes flour with oil then rubs it on him after lime to remove its smell. He (the Imam) said, 'It is not harmful.'"

H 12438, Ch. 43, h 13

In another *Hadith* it is narrated from 'Abd al-Rahman who has said the following:

"I once saw abu al-Hassan, *'Alayhi al-Salam,* rubbing with flour mixed with oil and I said that people dislike it. He (the Imam) said, 'It is not harmful.'"

H 12439, Ch. 43, h 14

A number of our people have narrated from Ahmad ibn Muhammad ibn Khalid from 'Uthman ibn 'Isa from Ishaq ibn 'Abd al-'Aziz who has said the following:

"Once abu 'Abd Allah, *'Alayhi al-Salam*, was asked about rubbing with flour after lime. He (the Imam) said, 'It is not harmful.' I then said, 'They think it is misuse of flour.' He (the Imam) said, 'Use of things for the benefit of body is not a misuse. I sometimes ask for bleached flour mixed with oil and rub. Misuse is when one's belongings are destroyed and the body is harmed.'"

H 12440, Ch. 43, h 15

Ali ibn Ibrahim has narrated from his father from and Muhammad ibn 'Isma'il has narrated from al-Fadl ibn Shadhan from all from ibn abu 'Umayr from Hisham ibn al-Hakam who has said the following:

"About the case of a man who rubs his body with flour and oil after lime, abu al-Hassan, *'Alayhi al-Salam*, has said, 'It is not harmful.'"

H 12441, Ch. 43, h 16

Ali has narrated from Ahmad ibn Muhammad from Muhammad ibn Aslam al-Jabaliy from Ali ibn abu Hamzah from Aban ibn Taghlib who has said the following:

"I once said to abu 'Abd Allah, *'Alayhi al-Salam*, 'Sometimes when on a journey we do not find bran; if we can rub with flour.' He (the Imam) said, 'It is not harmful. It is bad only when belongings are destroyed and the body is harmed. If body is benefited then it is not bad. I sometimes command my slave to prepare bleached flour with oil and I rub with it.'"

H 12442, Ch. 43, h 17

Muhammad ibn Yahya has narrated from Ahmad ibn Muhammad ibn 'Isa from Ali ibn al-Hakam from Sayf ibn 'Amirah who has said the following:

"Once abu 'Abd Allah, *'Alayhi al-Salam*, came out of the bathhouse, dressed, wore his turban and said to me, 'When you come out of bathhouse wear a turban.' He (the narrator) has said, 'I thereafter would always wear a turban after coming out of the bathhouse in winter and summer.'"

H 12443, Ch. 43, h 18

Ali ibn Ibrahim has narrated from his father from ibn abu 'Umayr from a man who has said the following:

"I once asked abu 'Abd Allah, *'Alayhi al-Salam*, about the case of a man who applies lime and urinates standing. He (the Imam) said, 'It is not harmful.'"

H 12444, Ch. 43, h 19

Muhammad ibn Yahya has narrated from Ali ibn al-Hassan al-Taymiy from Muhammad ibn abu Hamzah from 'Umar ibn Yazid who has said the following:

"Abu 'Abd Allah, *'Alayhi al-Salam*, has said that `Amir al-Mu'minin has said, 'You must not lie down on your back in the bathhouse; it melts the fat of kidneys and must not rub your feet with pottery because it may cause leprosy.'"

H 12445, Ch. 43, h 20

Muhammad ibn Yahya in a marfu' manner has narrated the following from 'Abd Allah ibn Muskan:

"Once we in a group of our people entered a bathhouse and when coming out we met abu 'Abd Allah, *'Alayhi al-Salam,* who asked us, 'Wherefrom are you coming?' We replied, 'We are coming from the bathhouse.' He (the Imam) said, 'May Allah make your bathing pure and clean.' We then said, 'We pray to Allah to keep our souls in service for your cause.' We then went with him (the Imam). He (the Imam) entered the bathhouse and we waited until he came out, then we said, 'May Allah make your bathing pure and clean.' He (the Imam) said, 'May Allah cleanse you.'"

H 12446, Ch. 43, h 21

Muhammad ibn al-Hassan and Ali ibn Muhammad ibn Bandar have narrated from Ibrahim ibn Ishaq al-Nahawandiy from 'Abd al-Rahman ibn Hammad from abu Maryam al-Ansariy in a *marfu'* manner has said the following:

"Once al-Hassan ibn Ali, *'Alayhim al-Salam,* came out of the bathhouse and someone met him and said, 'I wish you a fine bathing *Istihmam.*' He (the Imam) said, 'You are poor in vocabulary, why does the word ''Ist' (meaning your seeking bath or the word's other meaning which is 'buttock') need to be mentioned?' He then said, 'I wish you a good *'Humaym'.* He (the Imam) said, 'Did you not know that 'Humaym' means perspiration?' He then said, 'May your bathhouse be nice.' He (the Imam) said, 'If you wish a nice bathhouse then what is for me in it? You should instead say, 'I wish purity for what is nice of you and nicety of what is pure of you.'"

H 12447, Ch. 43, h 22

A number of our people have narrated from Sahl ibn Ziyad from Muhammad ibn 'Isa from 'Isma'il ibn Yasar from 'Uthman ibn 'Affan al-Sadusiy from Bashir al-Nabbal who has said the following:

"I once asked abu Ja'far, *'Alayhi al-Salam,* about using a bathhouse. He (the Imam) asked, 'Do you want to take a bath?' I replied, 'Yes, I like to take a bath.' He (the Imam) commanded to warm up the bathhouse. He then entered in it and wore a loincloth, which covered from his belly button down to his knees. Then he commanded the owner of the bathhouse to apply on him (lime or oil) on what was not covered by the loincloth. Then he (the Imam) asked him to move away. He (the Imam) then applied with his hand on the area under the loincloth and said, 'This is how you must take a bath.'"

H 12448, Ch. 43, h 23

Sahl in a *marfu'* manner has narrated the following:

"Abu 'Abd Allah, *'Alayhi al-Salam,* has said, 'A man must not enter a bathhouse with his son to allow him look at his private parts.'"

H 12449, Ch. 43, h 24

Ali ibn Muhammad ibn Bandar has narrated from Ibrahim ibn Ishaq from Yusuf ibn al-Sukht in a *marfu'* manner has said the following:

"Abu 'Abd Allah, *'Alayhi al-Salam,* has said, 'You must not lean in a bathhouse; it melts the fat of kidneys. You must not comb in it; it thins out the hairs, do not wash your head with clay; it destroys self-esteem, do not rub (your feet) with pottery; it may cause leprosy and do not wipe your face with loincloths; it destroys the beauty of the face.'"

H 12450, Ch. 43, h 25

Ali ibn Ibrahim has narrated from his father from Ali ibn Asbat who has said the following:

"Abu al-Hassan, al-Rida', *'Alayhi al-Salam,* has said that the Messenger of Allah, *O Allah, grant compensation to Muhammad and his family worthy of their services to Your cause,* has said, 'Do not wash your head with the clay of Misr (Egypt); it destroys self-esteem and may cause one to become a pimp.'"

H 12451, Ch. 43, h 26

Muhammad ibn Yahya has narrated from Ahmad ibn Muhammad ibn 'Isa from abu Yahya al-Wasitiy from certain persons of our people who has said the following:

"Abu al-Hassan, al-Madiy, *'Alayhi al-Salam,* has said, 'Private parts are two: the front and back. The back is covered with the rump. If you cover the penis and testicles you have covered your private parts.'"

In another *Hadith* it is said, 'The back is covered with the rump. You can cover the front with your hand.'

H 12452, Ch. 43, h 27

Ali ibn Ibrahim has narrated from his father from ibn abu 'Umayr from more than one person who has said the following:

"Abu 'Abd Allah, *'Alayhi al-Salam,* has said, 'Looking at the private parts of non-Muslims is like looking at the private parts of donkeys.'"

H 12453, Ch. 43, h 28

Muhammad ibn Yahya has narrated from Ahmad ibn Muhammad from Ali ibn al-Hakam from Aban ibn 'Uthman from ibn abu Ya'fur who has said the following:

"I once asked abu 'Abd Allah, *'Alayhi al-Salam,* if a nude person during pouring water on him can look at his own private parts, or water can be poured on him or he can look at the private parts of others. He (the Imam) said, 'My father disliked all of it on the part of everyone.'"

H 12454, Ch. 43, h 29

Ali ibn Ibrahim has narrated from his father from ibn abu 'Umayr from Rifa'ah who has said the following:

"Abu 'Abd Allah, *'Alayhi al-Salam,* has said, 'One who believes in Allah and in the Day of Judgment must not allow his wife to go to a bathhouse.'"

H 12455, Ch. 43, h 30

A number of our people have narrated from Ahmad ibn Muhammad ibn Khalid from 'Uthman ibn 'Isa from Sama'ah who has said the following:

"Abu 'Abd Allah, *'Alayhi al-Salam,* has said, 'One who believes in Allah and in the Day of Judgment must not send his wife to a bathhouse.'"

H 12456, Ch. 43, h 31

It is narrated from the narrator of the previous *Hadith* from 'Isma'il ibn Mehran from Muhammad ibn abu Hamzah from Ali ibn Yaqtin who has said the following:

"I once asked abu al-Hassan, *'Alayhi al-Salam,* 'Can I read Quran in a bathhouse or do sex?' He (the Imam) said, 'It is not harmful.'"

H 12457, Ch. 43, h 32

Ali ibn Ibrahim has narrated from his father from Hammad ibn 'Isa from 'Rib'iy ibn 'Abd Allah from Muhammad ibn Muslim who has said the following:

"I once asked abu Ja'far, *'Alayhi al-Salam*, if 'Amir al-Mu'minin prohibited reading al-Quran in a bathhouse. He (the Imam) said, 'No, he did not prohibit. He however, prohibited reading while nude but if one has a loincloth on him, then it is not harmful.'"

H 12458, Ch. 43, h 33

Ali ibn Ibrahim has narrated from his father from ibn abu 'Umayr from Hammad from al-Halabiy who has said the following:

"Abu 'Abd Allah, *'Alayhi al-Salam*, has said, 'It is not harmful if one reads al-Quran in a bathhouse if he does it for the sake of Allah, but not to find out how his voice is.'"

H 12459, Ch. 43, h 34

Certain persons of our people have narrated from ibn Jumhur from Muhammad ibn al-Qasim from ibn abu Ya'fur who has said the following:

"Abu 'Abd Allah, *'Alayhi al-Salam*, has said, 'Do not lie down in a bathhouse; it melts the fat of the kidneys.'"

H 12460, Ch. 43, h 35

Muhammad ibn Yahya has narrated from Ahmad ibn Muhammad from 'Umar ibn Ali ibn 'Umar ibn Yazid from his uncle Muhammad ibn 'Umar from those who narrated to him who has said the following:

"Abu Ja'far, *'Alayhi al-Salam*, would say, 'One who believes in Allah and in the Day of Judgment must not enter a bathhouse without a loincloth.' One day he entered a bathhouse and applied lime that covered his body. He (the Imam) then dropped the loincloth and one of his slaves said, 'I pray to Allah to keep my soul and the souls of my parents in service for your cause, you always instruct us about the necessity of loincloth but you have dropped it.' He (the Imam) said, 'Do you not know that lime has fully covered?'"

H 12461, Ch. 43, h 36

Al-Husayn ibn Muhammad has narrated from Mu'alla' ibn Muhammad from Ahmad ibn Muhammad from ibn 'Abd Allah from Muhammad ibn Ja'far from certain persons of his people who has said the following:

"Abu 'Abd Allah, *'Alayhi al-Salam*, has said that the Messenger of Allah, *O Allah, grant compensation to Muhammad and his family worthy of their services to Your cause*, has said, 'A man must not enter a bathhouse with his son where he can look at his private parts.' He (the Imam) said, 'Parents cannot look at the private parts of their children, and children cannot look at the private parts of their parents.' He (the Imam) then said, 'The Messenger of Allah has condemned the looking and the one being looked at in a bathhouse when one is without a loincloth.'"

H 12462, Ch. 43, h 37

Al-Husayn ibn Muhammad has narrated from Ahmad ibn Ishaq from Sa'dan from abu Basir who has said the following:

"Abu 'Abd Allah, *'Alayhi al-Salam*, once entered a bathhouse and the owner of the bathhouse asked him (the Imam), 'Must I vacate it for you?' He (the Imam) said, 'That is not necessary. A believing person (his needs) is lighter than that.'"

H 12463, Ch. 43, h 38

Al-Husayn ibn Muhammad and Muhammad ibn Yahya has narrated from Ali ibn Muhammad from Sa'd ibn Muhammad ibn Salim from Musa ibn 'Abd Allah ibn Musa who has said that narrated to us Ali ibn Ja'far the following:

"Abu al-Hassan, al-Rida', *'Alayhi al-Salam,* has said, 'If one picks up a piece of pottery from a bathhouse and rubs himself with it, then becomes ill with leprosy he must not blame anyone except himself. One who washes with the used water of a bathhouse and becomes ill with leprosy, he also must not blame anyone else except himself.'

Muhammad ibn Ali has said, 'I said to abu al-Hassan, *'Alayhi al-Salam,* that people of al-Madinah say, "There is cure (and protection) in it against the evil effect of the eyes."' He (the Imam) said, 'They have spoken a lie. In it people after unlawful sexual acts bathe and fornicators bathe. In it, the worst of all creatures that Allah has created, the enemies of *Ahl al-Bayt,* bathe and then they say that there is cure (and protection) in it against the evil effects of the eyes. Cure for the eyes because of such effect is in reading al-Hamd (Chapter one) and al-Ma'udhatayn (chapters One Hundred Thirteen and One Hundred Fourteen), Ayatu al-Kursi (2:255) and burning incense of *al-Qust,* (a certain Indian or Arabian wood), *al-Murr* (gum of a certain tree) and al-Luban (frankincense).'"

Chapter 44 - Washing the Head

H 12464, Ch. 44, h 1

Ali ibn Ibrahim has narrated from his father from ibn abu 'Umayr from Sufyan al-Simt who has said the following:

"Abu 'Abd Allah, *'Alayhi al-Salam,* has said, 'Cutting fingernails, trimming the mustache and washing the head with marshmallow plant banish poverty and increases one's sustenance.'"

H 12465, Ch. 44, h 2

Muhammad ibn Yahya has narrated from Ahmad ibn Muhammad ibn 'Isa from ibn Faddal from ibn Bukayr who has said the following:

"Abu 'Abd Allah, *'Alayhi al-Salam,* has said, 'Washing one's head every Friday with marshmallow plant is immunity from vitiligo and insanity.'"

H 12466, Ch. 44, h 3

Ahmad ibn Muhammad from has narrated from al-Qasim ibn Yahya from his grandfather al-Hassan ibn Rashid from abu Basir who has said the following:

"Abu 'Abd Allah, *'Alayhi al-Salam,* has said that 'Amir al-Mu'minin has said, 'Washing the head with marshmallow plant removes dirt and fine dust.'"

H 12467, Ch. 44, h 4

Muhammad ibn Yahya has narrated from Muhammad ibn al-Husayn from Musa ibn Sa'dan from 'Abd Allah ibn Sinan who has said the following:

"Abu 'Abd Allah, *'Alayhi al-Salam,* has said, 'One who trims his fingernails and washes his head with marshmallow plant every Friday is like one who sets free one human soul from bondage and slavery.'"

H 12468, Ch. 44, h 5
A number of our people have narrated from Ahmad ibn abu 'Abd Allah from Muhammad ibn Ali from al-Hassan ibn Muhammad al-Sayrafiy from 'Isma'il ibn 'Abd al-Khaliq who has said the following:

"Abu 'Abd Allah, *'Alayhi al-Salam,* has said, 'Washing the head with marshmallow plant is a protective charm.'"

H 12469, Ch. 44, h 6
It is narrated from the narrator of the previous *Hadith* from Muhammad ibn 'Isma'il from Mansur ibn Buzurj who has said the following:

"I once heard abu al-Hassan, *'Alayhi al-Salam,* saying, 'Washing the head with lotus tree leaves attracts sustenance with a strong attraction.'"

H 12470, Ch. 44, h 7
It is narrated from the narrator of the previous *Hadith* from Muhammad ibn Ali from 'Ubayd ibn Yahya al-Thawriy al-'Attar from Muhammad ibn al-Husayn al-'Alawiy from his father from his grandfather who has said the following:

"Ali, *'Alayhi al-Salam,* has said, 'When Allah, most Majestic, most Glorious, commanded the Messenger of Allah, *O Allah, grant compensation to Muhammad and his family worthy of their services to Your cause,* to publicly announce his mission, he saw the small number of Muslims and the large number of the pagans. He (the Messenger of Allah) felt strongly depressed. Then Allah, most Majestic, most Glorious, sent Jibril, *'Alayhi al-Salam,* with lotus tree leaves from the ultimate lotus tree. He washed with it his head and his depression went away.'"

Chapter 45 - Applying Lime Paste

H 12471, Ch. 45, h 1
Ali ibn Ibrahim has narrated from his father from ibn abu 'Umayr from Sulaym al-Farra' who has said the following:

"'Amir al-Mu'minin, *'Alayhi al-Salam,* has said, 'Lime is a cleansing (agent).'"

H 12472, Ch. 45, h 2
Muhammad ibn Yahya has narrated from Ahmad ibn Muhammad from *al-Hajj*al from Hammad ibn 'Uthaman from 'Abd al-Rahman ibn abu 'Abd Allah who has said the following:

"Once I went to a bathhouse with abu 'Abd Allah, *'Alayhi al-Salam.* He (the Imam) said, 'O 'Abd al-Rahman, you should apply lime.' I said, 'I had applied sometimes ago.' He (the Imam) said, 'Apply it again; it is cleansing.'"

H 12473, Ch. 45, h 3
Ahmad ibn Muhammad has narrated from ibn Faddal from Ali ibn 'Uqbah from abu Kahmas from Muhammad ibn 'Abd Allah ibn Ali ibn al-Husayn who has said the following:

"Once abu 'Abd Allah, *'Alayhi al-Salam,* entered a bathhouse when I was coming out. He (the Imam) said, 'O Muhammad, do you like to apply (lime)?' I replied, 'Just a few days ago I had applied it.' He (the Imam) said, 'Do you know that it is purifying?'"

H 12474, Ch. 45, h 4

A number of our people have narrated from Ahmad ibn abu 'Abd Allah from his father from Khalaf ibn Hammad from those who narrated to him who has said the following:

"Abu 'Abd Allah, *'Alayhi al-Salam,* once sent the son of his brother for something he needed. He returned when abu 'Abd Allah, *'Alayhi al-Salam,* had applied lime paste. He (the Imam) said, 'Apply lime paste.' He said, 'Only three days ago I had applied it.' Abu 'Abd Allah, *'Alayhi al-Salam,* said, 'Applying lime is purifying.'"

H 12475, Ch. 45, h 5

It is narrated from the narrator of the previous *Hadith* from 'Abd Allah ibn Muhammad al-Nuhaykiy from Ibrahim ibn 'Abd al-Hamid who has said the following:

"I once heard abu al-Hassan, *'Alayhi al-Salam,* saying, 'Remove hairs from yourselves; it beautifies.'"

H 12476, Ch. 45, h 6

Muhammad ibn Yahya has narrated from Ahmad ibn Muhammad ibn 'Isa from certain persons of his people from Ali ibn abu Hamzah from abu Basir who has said the following:

"I once led abu Basir to a bathhouse and I saw abu 'Abd Allah, *'Alayhi al-Salam,* apply lime. Abu Basir went close to him (the Imam) and offered greeting of peace. He (the Imam) asked, 'O abu Basir, do you like to apply lime paste?' He replied, 'Only three days ago I had applied it.' He (the Imam) said, 'Do you know that it is purification? So you should apply it.'"

H 12477, Ch. 45, h 7

Ahmad ibn Muhammad has narrated from al-Qasim ibn Yahya from his grandfather al-Hassan ibn Rashid from abu Basir who has said the following:

"Abu 'Abd Allah, *'Alayhi al-Salam,* has said that `Amir al-Mu'minin has said, 'Applying lime paste is a protective charm and purification (for the body).'"

H 12478, Ch. 45, h 8

Ahmad ibn Muhammad has narrated from al-Qasim ibn Yahya from his grandfather al-Hassan ibn Rashid from Muhammad ibn Muslim who has said the following:

"Abu 'Abd Allah, *'Alayhi al-Salam,* has said that `Amir al-Mu'minin has said, 'I like for the believers to apply (lime) paste after every fifteen days.'"

H 12479, Ch. 45, h 9

A number of our people have narrated from Sahl ibn Ziyad and Ali ibn Ibrahim has narrated from his father from all Ahmad ibn Muhammad from ibn abu Nasr from Ahmad ibn al-Mubarak from al-Husayn ibn Ahmad al-Minqariy who has said the following:

"Abu 'Abd Allah, *'Alayhi al-Salam,* has said, 'The *Sunnah* about lime paste is to apply it after every fifteen days. If it becomes twenty days but you do not have it, you must borrow on the account of Allah.'"

H 12480, Ch. 45, h 10

Ali ibn Ibrahim has narrated from Ahmad ibn abu 'Abd Allah in a *marfu'* has said the following:

"Once it was said to abu 'Abd Allah, *'Alayhi al-Salam,* that certain people think applying lime paste on Friday is detestable. He (the Imam) said, 'It is not as they think. Which cleansing agent is more cleansing than lime on Friday?'"

H 12481, Ch. 45, h 11

Ali ibn Ibrahim has narrated from his father from al-Nawfaliy from al-Sakuniy who has said the following:

"Abu 'Abd Allah, *'Alayhi al-Salam*, has said that the Messenger of Allah, *O Allah, grant compensation to Muhammad and his family worthy of their services to Your cause,* has said, 'One who believes in Allah and in the Day of Judgment, must not keep his pubic hairs for more than forty days. It is not lawful for a woman who believes in Allah and in the Day of Judgment to keep that in her case for more than twenty days.'"

H 12482, Ch. 45, h 12

Muhammad ibn Yahya has narrated from Ahmad ibn Muhammad ibn 'Isa from al-Hassan ibn Ali al-Washsha' from Ahmad ibn Tha'labah from 'Ammar al-Sabatiy who has said the following:

"Abu 'Abd Allah, *'Alayhi al-Salam*, has said, 'Applying (lime paste) once in summer is better than applying it ten times in winter.'"

H 12483, Ch. 45, h 13

Ali ibn Muhammad ibn Bandar has narrated from al-Sayyariy in a *marfu'* manner has said the following:

"Abu 'Abd Allah, *'Alayhi al-Salam*, has said, 'If one wants to apply lime paste, he must take from it with his finger, smell it, place it on the tip of his nose and say, 'O Allah, grant favors to Sulayman ibn Dawud who taught us applying lime paste' the lime will not burn him.'"

H 12484, Ch. 45, h 14

A number of our people have narrated from Sahl ibn Ziyad from Muhammad ibn Sinan from Hudhayfah ibn Mansur who has said the following:

"I once heard abu 'Abd Allah, *'Alayhi al-Salam*, saying that the Messenger of Allah, *O Allah, grant compensation to Muhammad and his family worthy of their services to Your cause,* would apply lime paste to the pubic region and under the rump every Friday.'"

H 12485, Ch. 45, h 15

A number of our people have narrated from Ahmad ibn Muhammad ibn Khalid from his father from Zurayq ibn al-Zubayr from Sadir who has said the following:

"I once heard Ali ibn al-Husayn, *'Alayhim al-Salam*, saying, 'When applying lime paste one should say, "O Lord, make pleasant what it has cleansed of me and cleanse what it has made pleasant of me. Replace it with clean hairs, which will not disobey You. O Lord, I have cleansed and sought to follow the *Sunnah* of the messengers, Your pleasure and forgiveness so make my hairs unlawful to the fire as well as my skin. O Lord, cleanse my body, my moral feelings, purify my acts and make me of those who meet You as a follower of the magnanimous religion of Ibrahim Your friend. Make me to meet You as a follower of the religion of Muhammad, *O Allah, grant compensation to Muhammad and his family worthy of their services to Your cause,* your beloved one, Your messenger. (O Lord), make me to abide by Your laws, subordinate to the *Sunnah* of Your prophet, accept it to find discipline by its disciplines and the discipline of Your friends whom You have fed with Your discipline, planted wisdom in their chest and have made them the mines of Your knowledge. Please grant them favors."' If one says the above Allah cleanses him from filth of the world and from sins and replaces his hairs with hairs, which will not disobey Allah. He will create with every hair of his body an angel who will say Tasbih (Allah is free of all defects) for him until the Day of Judgment. One Tasbih (Allah is free of all defects) of this angel is equal to one thousand Tasbih (Allah is free of all defects) of the inhabitants of earth."'

Chapter 46 - The Underarms

H 12486, Ch. 46, h 1
Ali ibn Ibrahim has narrated from his father from al-Nawfaliy from al-Sakuniy who has said the following:
"Abu 'Abd Allah, *'Alayhi al-Salam,* has said that the Messenger of Allah, *O Allah, grant compensation to Muhammad and his family worthy of their services to Your cause,* has said, 'No one of you must allow the hairs of his underarms to grow long; Satan makes it his hiding place and cover.'"

H 12487, Ch. 46, h 2
Muhammad ibn Yahya has narrated from Ahmad ibn Muhammad from ibn Faddal from Ali ibn 'Uqbah from abu Kahmas who has said the following:
"Abu 'Abd Allah, *'Alayhi al-Salam,* has said, 'Pulling out the hairs of the underarms weakens the shoulders.' Abu 'Abd Allah, *'Alayhi al-Salam,* applied lime paste as a hair remover.'"

H 12488, Ch. 46, h 3
Ali ibn Ibrahim has narrated from his father from and Muhammad ibn 'Isma'il has narrated from al-Fadl ibn Shadhan from all ibn abu 'Umayr from Hisham ibn al-Hakam from Hafs ibn al-Bakhtariy who has said the following:
"Abu 'Abd Allah, *'Alayhi al-Salam,* would apply lime paste on his underarms in the bathhouse.'"

H 12489, Ch. 46, h 4
A number of our people have narrated from Ahmad ibn abu as from Muhammad ibn Ali from Sa'dan who has said the following:
"I once was with abu Basir in a bathhouse and I saw abu 'Abd Allah, *'Alayhi al-Salam,* applying lime on his underarms. I informed abu Basir about it who asked saying, 'I pray to Allah to keep my soul in service for your cause, which is better; pulling out or shaving the hairs of the underarms?' He (the Imam) said, 'O abu Muhammad pulling out the hairs of the underarms weakens (the shoulders) so you must shave them.'"

H 12490, Ch. 46, h 5
Certain persons of our people has narrated from ibn Jumhur from Muhammad ibn al-Qasim Ahmad ibn Muhammad from Muhammad ibn Yahya from Muhammad ibn Ahmad from Yusuf ibn al-Sukht al-Basriy from Muhammad ibn Sulayman from Ibrahim ibn Yahya ibn abu al-Balad from al-Hassan ibn Ali ibn Mehran all from 'Abd Allah ibn abu Ya'fur who has said the following:
"Once in al-Madinah Zurarah argued about pulling out or shaving of the hairs of the underarms and I said that shaving is better. Zurarah said pulling out is better. We then asked permission to meet abu 'Abd Allah, *'Alayhi al-Salam.* Permission was granted and he (the Imam) was in the bathhouse applying lime

paste and it was applied to his underarms. I said to Zurarah that that is sufficient but Zurarah said, 'Perhaps he (the Imam) has done so because it is not permissible for me to do so.' He (the Imam) asked, 'What is the issue between you two?' I said, 'Zurarah argues with me about the pulling up of the hairs of underarms or shaving. I say that shaving is better than pulling it out and he says pulling out is better.' He (the Imam) said, 'You have followed the *Sunnah* correctly but Zurarah has missed it. Shaving is better than pulling out and applying lime paste is better than shaving.' He (the Imam) then said, 'Apply lime paste.' We said that we had done so three days ago. He (the Imam) said, 'Apply it again; it is a cleanser.'"

H 12491, Ch. 46, h 6

Muhammad ibn Yahya has narrated from Ahmad ibn Muhammad from ibn Mahbub from Yunus ibn Ya'qub who has said the following:

"Abu 'Abd Allah, *'Alayhi al-Salam,* whenever needed would go to the bathhouse only to apply lime paste to his underarms.'"

H 12492, Ch. 46, h 7

A number of our people have narrated from Sahl ibn Ziyad from Ahmad ibn Muhammad from ibn abu Nasr from Yunus ibn Ya'qub who has said the following:

"I am informed that abu 'Abd Allah, *'Alayhi al-Salam,* enters the bathhouse only to apply lime paste to his underarms alone.'"

Chapter 47 - Applying Henna after Lime Paste

H 12493, Ch. 47, h 1

Ali ibn Muhammad ibn Bandar and Muhammad ibn al-Hassan all have narrated from Ibrahim ibn Ishaq al-Ahmar from al-Husayn ibn Musa who has said the following:

"Al-Husayn ibn Musa has said, 'When my father, Musa ibn Ja'far, *'Alayhim al-Salam,* wanted to take a bath, he asked to fire the bathhouse for him by three (people). He could not enter the bathhouse until the servants spread for him the felt on the floor (because of heat). When he entered the bathhouse, he sat once, then stood up once. One day when he came out of the bathhouse, he met a man from the family of al-Zubayr called Kunayd who saw the marks of henna on his hand and asked about it. He (the Imam) said, 'This is the mark of henna.' He (the Imam) said, 'Woe up on you, O Kunayd, (for not knowing). My father was the most knowledgeable person of his time. He narrated from his father from his grandfather who has said that the Messenger of Allah, *O Allah, grant compensation to Muhammad and his family worthy of their services to Your cause,* has stated this *Hadith.* "If one goes to the bathhouse, applies lime paste, then applies henna from top to his toes, it is immunity for him from insanity, leprosy, vitiligo and erosion caused by lime paste."'"

H 12494, Ch. 47, h 2

Muhammad ibn Yahya has narrated from Ahmad ibn Muhammad ibn 'Isa from Ali ibn al-Hakam from Mu'awiyah ibn Maysarah from al-Hakam ibn 'Utaybah who has said the following:

"Once I saw abu Ja'far, *'Alayhi al-Salam,* who had placed henna on his finger nails and asked me, 'O Hakam, what do you say about it? I replied, 'I cannot say anything when you have done so. In our town young people do so.' He (the

Imam) said, 'O Hakam, when fingers touch lime paste their color change and they look like fingers of dead people but you can change that kind of change of color with henna.""""

H 12495, Ch. 47, h 3
A number of our people have narrated from Ahmad ibn abu 'Abd Allah from certain persons of our people in a *marfu'* manner has said the following:

"He (the Imam), *'Alayhi al-Salam,* has said, 'If one applies lime paste then rubs henna from his top to his toes, his poverty goes away.'"

H 12496, Ch. 47, h 4
It is narrated from the narrator of the previous *Hadith* from Ahmad ibn 'Ubdus ibn Ibrahim who has said the following:

"I once saw abu Ja'far, *'Alayhi al-Salam,* coming out of the bathhouse and he looked like a flower from his top to his toes because of applying henna.'"

H 12497, Ch. 47, h 5
Ali ibn Muhammad has narrated from Salih ibn abu Hammad from Ibrahim ibn 'Uqbah from Al-Husayn ibn Musa who has said the following:

"Once abu al-Hassan, *'Alayhi al-Salam,* was with a man near the grave of the Messenger of Allah, *O Allah, grant compensation to Muhammad and his family worthy of their services to Your cause.* He looked at him (the Imam) and found his hands had the color of henna on them. Certain ones of the people of al-Madinah said, 'Look at him. His hands are colored with henna.' He (the Imam) turned to him and said, 'In henna there is what you know as well as what you do not know.' He (the Imam) then said, 'If one after applying lime paste rubs henna all over his body, he gains immunity from three things, namely, insanity, leprosy and vitiligo.'"

Chapter 48 - The Perfumes

H 12498, Ch. 48, h 1
A number of our people have narrated from Sahl ibn Ziyad from Ahmad ibn Muhammad from ibn abu Nasr who has said the following:

"Abu al-Hassan, al-Rida', *'Alayhi al-Salam,* has said, 'Using perfume is of the moral discipline of the Prophets.'"

H 12499, Ch. 48, h 2
Muhammad ibn Yahya has narrated from Ahmad ibn Muhammad from ibn Faddal from Yunus ibn Ya'qub from abu Usamah who has said the following:

"Abu 'Abd Allah, *'Alayhi al-Salam,* has said, 'Using perfume is of the discipline of the Messengers *'Alayhim al-Salam.*'"

H 12500, Ch. 48, h 3
A number of our people have narrated from Sahl ibn Ziyad from ibn Mahbub from ibn Ri'ab who has said the following:

"I once was with abu 'Abd Allah, *'Alayhi al-Salam,* in the company of abu Basir. I heard abu 'Abd Allah, saying, 'The Messenger of Allah, *O Allah, grant compensation to Muhammad and his family worthy of their services to Your cause,* has said that good perfume strengthens the heart and increases the ability to go to bed with one's wife.'"

H 12501, Ch. 48, h 4

Muhammad ibn Yahya has narrated from Ahmad ibn Muhammad from Mu'ammar ibn Khallad who has said the following:

"Abu al-Hassan, *'Alayhi al-Salam,* has said, 'A man must not ignore using perfumes every day, or every other day, if he cannot afford. If he cannot afford this, he must use perfume every Friday.'"

H 12502, Ch. 48, h 5

Muhammad ibn Yahya has narrated from Ahmad ibn Muhammad ibn 'Isa from al-Qasim ibn Yahya from his grandfather al-Hassan ibn Rashid from abu Basir who has said the following:

"Abu 'Abd Allah, *'Alayhi al-Salam,* has said that `Amir al-Mu'minin has said, 'Applying perfume to one's mustache is of the discipline of the Prophets *'Alayhim al-Salam,* and honoring the scribes (the angels on one's shoulders).'"

H 12503, Ch. 48, h 6

Al-Husayn ibn Muhammad has narrated from Ahmad ibn Ishaq from Sa'dan from abu Basir who has said the following:

"Abu 'Abd Allah, *'Alayhi al-Salam,* has said that the Messenger of Allah, *O Allah, grant compensation to Muhammad and his family worthy of their services to Your cause,* has said, 'Applying perfume strengthens the heart.'"

H 12504, Ch. 48, h 7

Ali ibn Ibrahim has narrated in a *marfu'* manner has said the following:

"Abu 'Abd Allah, *'Alayhi al-Salam,* has said, 'If one uses perfume in the beginning of the day, his power of reason continues to work until the night.' He (the Imam) said, 'Performing one *Salat* (prayer) with perfume is better than seventy *Salat* (prayer) without perfume.'"

H 12505, Ch. 48, h 8

A number of our people have narrated from Ahmad ibn abu 'Abd Allah from Muhammad ibn Ali from al-'Abbas ibn Musa who has said the following:

I heard my father, *'Alayhi al-Salam,* saying, '*Al-'Atr* (perfume) is of the *Sunnah* of the messengers (of Allah).'"

H 12506, Ch. 48, h 9

Ali ibn Ibrahim has narrated from his father from Muhammad ibn Yahya from Talhah ibn Zayd who has said the following:

"Abu 'Abd Allah, *'Alayhi al-Salam,* has said, 'Three things were given to the Prophets. They are perfumes, marriage and toothbrushes.'"

H 12507, Ch. 48, h 10

A number of our people have narrated from Ahmad ibn abu 'Abd Allah from Muhammad ibn Musa ibn al-Furat from Ali ibn Matar from al-Sakan al-Khazzaz who has said the following:

"I once heard abu 'Abd Allah, *'Alayhi al-Salam,* saying, 'It is a right on every adult Muslim to trim his mustache every Friday, cut his fingernails and apply perfume. The Messenger of Allah, on Friday, when he could not find perfumes, soaked the scarf of one of his wives with water, then placed it on his face.'"

H 12508, Ch. 48, h 11

Al-Husayn ibn Muhammad has narrated from Mu'alla' ibn Muhammad and a number of our people have narrated from Sahl ibn Ziyad all from al-Hassan ibn Ali who has said the following:

"One could recognize the [place of *Sujud* (prostrations)] of abu 'Abd Allah, *'Alayhi al-Salam,* because of its perfumes.'"

H 12509, Ch. 48, h 12

Ali ibn Ibrahim has narrated from [his father] from Yasar who has said the following:

"Abu al-Hassan, *'Alayhi al-Salam,* has said that the Messenger of Allah, *O Allah, grant compensation to Muhammad and his family worthy of their services to Your cause,* has said, 'My friend Jibril has told me to apply perfume one day and not on the next day. On Friday it is necessary and it must not be ignored.'"

H 12510, Ch. 48, h 13

Ali ibn Ibrahim has narrated from his father from al-Nawfaliy from al-Sakuniy who has said the following:

"Abu 'Abd Allah, *'Alayhi al-Salam,* has said that the Messenger of Allah, *O Allah, grant compensation to Muhammad and his family worthy of their services to Your cause,* has said, 'On Friday you must apply perfume: even if it is from the perfumes of your wives.'"

H 12511, Ch. 48, h 14

A number of our people have narrated from Ahmad ibn abu 'Abd Allah from Ya'qub ibn Yazid in a *marfu'* manner has said the following:

"Abu 'Abd Allah, *'Alayhi al-Salam,* has said, ''Uthman ibn Maz'un once said to the Messenger of Allah, *O Allah, grant compensation to Muhammad and his family worthy of their services to Your cause,* "I had decided to give up certain things, of which one is perfumes and other things." The Messenger of Allah said, 'You must not give up perfume; the angels smell fine perfume from believing people, so you must not ignore applying perfumes on Fridays.'"

H 12512, Ch. 48, h 15

A number of our people have narrated from Sahl ibn Ziyad Muhammad ibn 'Isa from 'Abd Allah ibn 'Abd al-Rahman from Shu'ayb from abu Basir who has said the following:

"Abu 'Abd Allah, *'Alayhi al-Salam,* has said, 'Applying perfume is of moral discipline of the Prophets and honoring the scribes (the two angels on one's shoulders).'"

H 12513, Ch. 48, h 16

It is narrated from the narrator of the previous *Hadith* from Muhammad ibn 'Isa from Zakariya al-Mu'min in a marfu' manner has said the following:

"He (the Imam), *'Alayhi al-Salam,* has said, 'Your spending for perfumes is not useless spending.'"

H 12514, Ch. 48, h 17

Ali ibn Ibrahim has narrated from his father from al-Nawfaliy from al-Sakuniy who has said the following:

"Abu 'Abd Allah, *'Alayhi al-Salam,* has stated this *Hadith*. 'The Messenger of Allah, *O Allah, grant compensation to Muhammad and his family worthy of their services to Your cause,* has said, "Perfume for women is that which shows its color but hides its fragrance, and the perfume for men is that which spreads its fragrance but its color does not show.""'"

H 12515, Ch. 48, h 18
Muhammad ibn Yahya has narrated from Muhammad ibn al-Husayn from Sulayman from Muhammad al-Khath'amiy from Ishaq al-Tawil al-'Attar who has said the following:

"Abu 'Abd Allah, *'Alayhi al-Salam,* has said that the Messenger of Allah, *O Allah, grant compensation to Muhammad and his family worthy of their services to Your cause,* spent more on perfumes than his spending on food."

Chapter 49 - The Detestability of Rejecting Perfume

H 12516, Ch. 49, h 1
A number of our people have narrated from Ahmad ibn Muhammad ibn Khalid from 'Uthman ibn 'Isa from Sama'ah ibn Mehran who has said the following:

"I once asked abu 'Abd Allah, *'Alayhi al-Salam,* about the case of a man who refuses to accept perfumes. He (the Imam) said, 'It is not proper for him to reject an honor.'"

H 12517, Ch. 49, h 2
A number of our people have narrated from Sahl ibn Ziyad from Ja'far ibn Muhammad al-Ash'ariy from ibn al-Qaddah who has said the following:

"Abu 'Abd Allah, *'Alayhi al-Salam,* has said that once oil was brought to 'Amir al-Mu'minin when he had already applied oil (perfume). He applied the oil offered to him saying, "We do not reject perfumes.""'"

H 12518, Ch. 49, h 3
Muhammad ibn Yahya has narrated from Ahmad ibn Muhammad from ibn Faddal from al-Hassan ibn Jahm who has said the following:

"I once visited abu al-Hassan, *'Alayhi al-Salam.* He took out a container with musk in it and said, 'Apply it and place in your nostril.' He (the narrator) has said, 'I took a little and applied to my nostrils.' He (the Imam) said, 'Apply more.' I then took more from it and something from it remained on my hand. He (the Imam) said, 'Apply it to your nostril.' I applied it.' He (the Imam) said that 'Amir al-Mu'minin has said, 'No one rejects honor except a donkey.' He (the narrator) has said, 'I then asked, what it means?' He (the Imam) said, 'It is perfumes, pillows', and he (the Imam) counted certain other things.'"

H 12519, Ch. 49, h 4
Muhammad ibn Yahya Ahmad ibn Muhammad from ibn Hilal from 'Isa ibn 'Abd Allah from his father from his grandfather who has said the following:

"The Messenger of Allah, *O Allah, grant compensation to Muhammad and his family worthy of their services to Your cause,* would not refuse to accept perfume and sweet (fruit).'"

Chapter 50 - Kinds of Perfumes

H 12520, Ch. 50, h 1
Muhammad ibn Ja'far has narrated from Muhammad ibn Khalid fn Sayf ibn 'Amirah from 'Abd al-Ghaffar who has said the following:

"I once heard abu 'Abd Allah, *'Alayhi al-Salam,* saying, 'Of perfumes are, musk, ambergris, saffron and aloe wood.'"

Chapter 51 - The Origin of Perfumes

H 12521, Ch. 51, h 1
A number of our people have narrated from Sahl ibn Ziyad from Ali ibn Hassan from Musa ibn Bakr who has said the following:

"Abu 'Abd Allah, *'Alayhi al-Salam,* has said, 'When Adam, *'Alayhi al-Salam,* came down from the garden (paradises) at al-Safa' and Eve on al-Marwah, she wore a hairstyle from the garden (paradise) with the perfume of the garden (paradise). When she turned on earth she said, 'I have no hope in this hairstyling while I am being angered at.' She opened her braid. The perfume from her hairstyling that she had done in the garden (paradises) spread and the wind blew it away. The majority of it fell in India, thus perfume is in India.'"

A number of our people have narrated from Ahmad ibn abu 'Abd Allah from Ali ibn Hassan a similar *Hadith*. In another *Hadith* it is said that '. . . 'her braid' . . . ' Allah sent on what was there (in her braid) of perfumes a wind which blew to the east and west, thus the origin of perfume is thereof.

H 12522, Ch. 51, h 2
A number of our people have narrated from Ahmad ibn Muhammad from Ja'far ibn Yahya from Ali al-Qasir from a man who has said the following:

"I once asked abu 'Abd Allah, *'Alayhi al-Salam,* about the origin of perfumes and from where it has come. He (the Imam) asked, 'What do people say about it?' I replied, 'They think that when Adam, *'Alayhi al-Salam,* came down from the garden (paradises) he had a crown on his head.' He (the Imam) said, 'By Allah his preoccupation and trouble was beyond his condition to have a crown.' He (the Imam) then said, 'Eve wore a hairstyle in the garden (paradises) with perfumes before falling in the mistake and when she came down on earth she opened her braid and Allah, most High, sent a wind on what was in her braid. It blew the perfume to the east and west, thus, the origin of perfume is thereof.'"

H 12523, Ch. 51, h 3
Ali ibn Muhammad from Salih ibn abu Hammad from al-Husayn ibn Yazid from al-Hassan ibn Ali ibn abu Hamzah from Ibrahim who has said the following:

"Abu 'Abd Allah, *'Alayhi al-Salam,* has said that when Allah sent Adam, *'Alayhi al-Salam,* down, he began to hold the leaves of the garden (paradises) to himself, and his clothes which were of the dresses of the garden (paradises) that he wore flew away from him. He picked up a leaf to cover his private parts. When he came down the perfume of that leaf trapped in India; the wind from the south blew and its perfume reached to the west. It carried the perfume of the leaf in the air. When the wind became stagnant in India, it adhered to its trees and their plants. The first animal that grazed on such a plant was a deer of musk and from that is musk in the bellybutton of the deer; the fragrance of the plant moved in her body and blood until it gathered in the bellybutton of the deer.'"

Chapter 52 - The Musk

H 12524, Ch. 52, h 1
A number of our people have narrated from Sahl ibn Ziyad and Al-Husayn ibn Muhammad has narrated from Mu'alla' ibn Muhammad from al-Washsha' who has said the following:

"I once heard abu al-Hassan, *'Alayhi al-Salam,* saying Ali ibn al-Husayn, *'Alayhim al-Salam,* had an *Ashbidana* (musk container) of lead that was kept hanging with musk in it and when he wanted to go out he dressed up, took that container and musk to take musk thereof and rubbed on himself.'" (*Ashbidana* is an Arabicized word from the farsi word *Mushk-dan*)

H 12525, Ch. 52, h 2
A number of our people have narrated from Ahmad ibn abu 'Abd Allah from his father from abu al-Bakhtariy who has said the following:

"Abu 'Abd Allah, *'Alayhi al-Salam,* has said that the Messenger of Allah, *O Allah grant compensation to Muhammad and his family worthy of their services to your cause,* would use musk and its marks could be found on his joints.'"

H 12526, Ch. 52, h 3
Muhammad ibn Yahya has narrated from Ahmad ibn Muhammad from ibn Mahbub from 'Abd Allah ibn Sinan who has said the following:

"Abu 'Abd Allah, *'Alayhi al-Salam,* has said that the Messenger of Allah, *O Allah, grant compensation to Muhammad and his family worthy of their services to Your cause,* had a musk container. When making wudu he would take it in his hand while wet. When coming out people noticed his coming because of the perfume and fragrance.'"

H 12527, Ch. 52, h 4
Muhammad ibn Yahya has narrated from Ahmad ibn Muhammad from ibn Faddal from al-Hassan ibn al-Jahm who has said the following:

"Abu al-Hassan, *'Alayhi al-Salam,* once took out for me a musk container in which there was musk in an *Abnus* (a container made of a certain wood) container which had sections with things that women keep.'"

H 12528, Ch. 52, h 5
A number of our people have narrated from Ahmad ibn abu 'Abd Allah from his father from al-Muttalib ibn Ziyad from abu Bakr ibn 'Abd Allah al-Ash'ariy who has said the following:

"I once asked abu 'Abd Allah, *'Alayhi al-Salam,* about smelling musk. He (the Imam) said, 'We smell it.'"

H 12529, Ch. 52, h 6
It is narrated from the narrator of the previous *Hadith* from Ya'qub ibn Yazid from 'Abd Allah ibn al-Fadl al-Nawfaliy who has said that narrated to me my father from his father from his uncle Ishaq ibn 'Abd Allah from his father 'Abd Allah ibn al-Harith who has said the following:

"Ali ibn al-Husayn, *'Alayhim al-Salam,* had a bottle of musk in the Masjid. When he came for *Salat* (prayer) he would take it and rub on himself.'"

H 12530, Ch. 52, h 7
It is narrated from the narrator of the previous *Hadith* from Nuh ibn Shu'ayb from certain persons of our people who has said the following:

"Abu al-Hassan, *'Alayhi al-Salam,* has said, that marks and traces of musk could be seen on the joints of the Messenger of Allah, *O Allah, grant compensation to Muhammad and his family worthy of their services to Your cause.*'"

H 12531, Ch. 52, h 8

Muhammad ibn Yahya has narrated from al-'Amrakiy ibn Ali from Ali ibn Ja'far from his brother who has said the following:

"I once asked him (the Imam) about musk and if it can be applied with oil. He (the Imam) said, 'I apply it with oil and it is not harmful.' It is narrated that it is not harmful to use musk with food.'"

Chapter 53 - Al-Ghaliyah (A Perfume that is a Mix of Musk, Camphor and Ambergris)

H 12532, Ch. 53, h 1

A number of our people have narrated from Ahmad ibn Muhammad from 'Uthman ibn 'Isa from Ishaq ibn 'Ammar who has said the following:

"I once said to abu 'Abd Allah, *'Alayhi al-Salam,* that I work with the merchants and prepare myself for people because of my dislike for their seeing me as a destitute person; if I can use al-Ghaliyah. He (the Imam) said, 'O Ishaq, a small amount of it is enough just like a large amount. If one uses a small amount of al-Ghaliyah all the time it is sufficient.' Ishaq has said, 'I would buy for a whole year of al-Ghaliyah worth ten dirham and it was enough because its fragrance was constant all the time.'"

H 12533, Ch. 53, h 2

Muhammad ibn Yahya has narrated from Ahmad ibn Muhammad ibn 'Isa from Mu'ammar ibn Khallad who has said the following:

"Abu al-Hassan, al-Rida', *'Alayhi al-Salam,* once commanded me to prepare for him oil mixed with musk and ambergris and write on paper verse 2:255, 'Umm al-Kitab, al-Ma'udhatayn and al-Qawari' (verse that crush Satan) from al-Quran; then place it in a cover in a bottle. I did as I was told to do. I then brought it to him (the Imam). He (the Imam) placed it in a cover and I was looking at him (the Imam).'"

H 12534, Ch. 53, h 3

A number of our people have narrated from Ahmad ibn abu 'Abd Allah from Muhammad ibn Ali from Mawla' of Banu Hashim from Muhammad ibn Ja'far ibn Muhammad who has said the following:

"One night Ali ibn al-Husayn, *'Alayhim al-Salam,* came out wearing a robe and gown of fur of al-Khazz (garments made of skin or fur of an animal that lives in water), and his beard covered with al-Ghaliyah. They said, 'At this time and in this make-up!' He said, 'I like to propose to al-Hur al-'In before Allah, most Majestic, most Glorious, in this night.'"

Sahl ibn Ziyad has narrated from Ali ibn Asbat from Mawla of banu Hashim from Muhammad ibn Ja'far a similar *Hadith.*

H 12535, Ch. 53, h 4

It is narrated from the narrator of the previous *Hadith* from abu al-Qasim al-Kufiy from those who narrated to him from Muhammad ibn al-Walid al-Kirmaniy who has said the following:

"I once asked abu Ja'far, *'Alayhi al-Salam,* about musk. He (the Imam) said, 'My father once commanded to prepare for him musk in frankincense for seven hundred dirham. Fadl ibn Sahl then informed him (the Imam) that people scorn it. He (the Imam) wrote to him saying, 'O Fadl, did you not know that Yusuf *'Alayhi al-Salam,* a Prophet wore brocades with buttons of gold and sat on the chair made of gold and it did not reduce of his wisdom anything?' He (the Imam) said that he commanded to prepare for him al-Ghaliyah for four thousand dirham.'"

H 12536, Ch. 53, h 5

A number of our people have narrated from Sahl ibn Ziyad from al-Husayn ibn Yazid from certain persons of his people who has said the following:

"Abu 'Abd Allah, *'Alayhi al-Salam,* has said that 'Ali ibn al-Husayn, *'Alayhim al-Salam,* came face to face with one of his Mawla' in a cold night wearing a gown, a robe and a turban of al-Khazz (garments made of skin or fur of an animal that lives in water), covered with al-Ghaliyah. He said, 'I pray to Allah to keep my soul in service for your cause, where are you going in such a night and in such a dress?' He (the Imam) replied, 'I am going to the Masjid of my grandfather, the Messenger of Allah, *O Allah, grant compensation to Muhammad and his family worthy of their services to Your cause,* to propose marriage with al-Hur al-'In before Allah, most Majestic, most Glorious.'"

Chapter 54 - Al-Khuluq (a kind of Perfume of Yellow Color)

H 12537, Ch. 54, h 1

Muhammad ibn Yahya has narrated from Ahmad ibn Muhammad from ibn Faddal from ibn Bukayr from Zurarah who has said the following:

"I once asked abu Ja'far, *'Alayhi al-Salam,* about *al-Khuluq*; if I can use it. He (the Imam) said, 'It is not harmful but I do not like for you to continuously use it.'"

H 12538, Ch. 54, h 2

Abu Ali al-Ash'ariy has narrated from certain persons of his people from ibn abu Najran from 'Abd Allah ibn Sinan who has said the following:

"Abu 'Abd Allah, *'Alayhi al-Salam,* has said, 'It is not harmful to touch *al-Khuluq* in the bathhouse or touch to cure cracks in your hand, but I do not like to always use it.' He (the Imam) said, 'It is not harmful to use *al-Khuluq* but one must not sleep overnight with it.'"

H 12539, Ch. 54, h 3

Ali ibn Ibrahim has narrated from his father from ibn abu 'Umayr from 'Abd Allah ibn Sinan who has said the following:

"He (the Imam), *'Alayhi al-Salam,* has said, 'It is not harmful to touch al-Khuluq in the bathhouse or touch to cure cracks in your hand, but I do not like to always use it.'"

H 12540, Ch. 54, h 4

A number of our people have narrated from Sahl ibn Ziyad from Muhammad ibn 'Isa from a man from Muhammad ibn al-Fayd who has said the following:

"I once heard abu 'Abd Allah, *'Alayhi al-Salam,* saying, 'I like *al-Khuluq.*'"

H 12541, Ch. 54, h 5

Humayd ibn Ziyad has narrated from al-Hassan ibn Muhammad ibn Sama'ah from Ja'far ibn Sama'ah from Aban from a man whose name is he has confirmed who has said the following:

"Abu 'Abd Allah, *'Alayhi al-Salam,* has said, 'It is not harmful for one to use *al-Khuluq* for his wife, but he must not sleep overnight with it.'"

H 12542, Ch. 54, h 6

Ali ibn Ibrahim has narrated from Salih ibn al-Sindiy from Ja'far ibn Bashir from Aban from al-Fudayl from a man who has said the following:

"Abu Ja'far, *'Alayhi al-Salam,* has said, 'It is not harmful to use *al-Khuluq*, but one must not sleep overnight with it.'"

Chapter 55 - The Incense

H 12543, Ch. 55, h 1

Muhammad ibn Yahya has narrated from Ali ibn Ibrahim al-Ja'fariy from certain persons of his people in a *marfu'* manner has said the following:

"Abu 'Abd Allah, *'Alayhi al-Salam,* has said, 'The fragrance of aloe that is in the body remains for forty days but the fragrance of the prepared aloe remains for twenty days.'"

H 12544, Ch. 55, h 2

Al-Husayn ibn Muhammad has narrated from Mu'alla' ibn Muhammad from al-Washsha' from 'Abd Allah ibn Sinan who has said the following:

"Abu 'Abd Allah, *'Alayhi al-Salam,* has said, 'It is very proper for one to apply incense to his clothes if one can afford.'"

H 12545, Ch. 55, h 3

A number of our people have narrated from Ahmad ibn abu 'Abd Allah from Musa ibn al-Qasim from Ali ibn Asbat from al-Hassan ibn Jahm who has said the following:

"Once abu al-Hassan, *'Alayhi al-Salam,* came out and I felt the fragrance of incense from him (the Imam).'"

H 12546, Ch. 55, h 4

Ali ibn Ibrahim has narrated from his father from ibn abu 'Umayr from Murazim who has said the following:

"I once entered a bathhouse with abu al-Hassan, *'Alayhi al-Salam.* When he (the Imam) came out to the room for undressing, he asked for the incense stand, and applied incense in it then said, 'Allow them to the incense O Murazim.' I then asked, 'Can anyone who wants take a share?' He (the Imam) said, 'Yes, they can do so.'"

H 12547, Ch. 55, h 5

Muhammad ibn Yahya has narrated from Muhammad ibn Ahmad from Ali ibn al-Rayyan from Ahmad ibn abu Khalaf Mawla' of abu al-Hassan, *'Alayhi al-Salam,* whom he (the Imam) had bought along with his parents and brother then set them free but Ahmad made a contract with him (the Imam) and became his agent. He has said the following:

"Women of abu al-Hassan, *'Alayhi al-Salam,* when burning incense first took the date-stone of Sayhaniy (a certain kind of date of al-Madinah) date, clean of date fruit or sweetness and peel, then placed it on the fire before the incense. When the date-stones smoked the minimum they threw away the date-stones and burnt the incense. They said, 'It clings with better fragrance and nicer incense' and they instructed with this method."

Chapter 56 -Applying Oil

H 12548, Ch. 56, h 1
Muhammad ibn Yahya has narrated from Ahmad ibn Muhammad ibn 'Isa from al-Qasim ibn Yahya from his grandfather al-Hassan ibn Rashid from abu Basir who has said the following:
"Abu 'Abd Allah, *'Alayhi al-Salam,* has said that `Amir al-Mu'minin has said, 'Applying oil softens the skin, increases the ability of brain, opens the channels of water, removes the scaling and makes color to glow.'"

H 12549, Ch. 56, h 2
It is narrated from the narrator of the previous *Hadith* from Ahmad ibn Muhammad from Ali ibn al-Hakam from 'Abd Allah ibn Jundab from Sufyan ibn al-Simt who has said the following:
"Abu 'Abd Allah, *'Alayhi al-Salam,* has said, 'Applying oil removes wickedness (despair).'"

H 12550, Ch. 56, h 3
Ali ibn Ibrahim has narrated from his father from al-Nawfaliy from al-Sakuniy who has said the following:
"Abu 'Abd Allah, *'Alayhi al-Salam,* has said, 'Applying oil demonstrates wealth.'"

H 12551, Ch. 56, h 4
A number of our people have narrated from Sahl ibn Ziyad from Muhammad ibn 'Isa from 'Abd Allah ibn 'Abd al-Rahman from Shu'ayb from abu Basir who has said the following:
"Abu 'Abd Allah, *'Alayhi al-Salam,* has said that `Amir al-Mu'minin has said, 'Applying oil softens the skin, increases the abilities of the brain, opens the channels of water, removes the scaling and improves color (of the skin).'"

H 12552, Ch. 56, h 5
Muhammad ibn Yahya has narrated from Ahmad ibn Muhammad ibn 'Isa from ibn Mahbub 'Abd Allah ibn Sinan from abu Hamzah who has said the following:
"Abu Ja'far, *'Alayhi al-Salam,* has said, 'Applied oil at night flows in the veins, quenches the skin and brightens the face.'"

H 12553, Ch. 56, h 6
A number of our people have narrated from Ahmad ibn Muhammad ibn Khalid from his father from al-Hassan ibn Bahr from Mehzam al-Asadiy who has said the following:
"Abu 'Abd Allah, *'Alayhi al-Salam,* has said, 'When you take oil in your palm, say, 'O Lord, I ask You to grant me grace, beauty and love. I ask from You protection against abhorrence, disgrace and anger.' Then place it on your forehead and say whatever you can.'"

H 12554, Ch. 56, h 7

A number of our people have narrated from Sahl ibn Ziyad from Muhammad ibn Ahmad al-Daqqaq from Muhammad ibn 'Isma'il from Salih ibn 'Uqbah from Bashir al-Dahhan who has said the following:

"Abu 'Abd Allah, *'Alayhi al-Salam*, has said, 'If one applies oil on a believing person, Allah writes for every hair a light on the Day of Judgment.'"

Chapter 57 - Undesirability of Applying oil all the Time

H 12555, Ch. 57, h 1

Muhammad ibn Yahya has narrated from al-Husayn ibn 'Abd al-Rahman ibn abu Hashim from abu Khadijah who has said the following:

"Abu 'Abd Allah, *'Alayhi al-Salam*, has said, 'A man must not apply oil every day; a man should look shaggier and not polished and greasy like a woman.'"

H 12556, Ch. 57, h 2

Muhammad ibn Yahya has narrated from Ahmad ibn Muhammad from Muhammad ibn Sinan from Ishaq ibn 'Ammar who has said the following:

"I once said to abu 'Abd Allah, *'Alayhi al-Salam*, 'I associate with careful people and content myself with a small amount of oil which I use little by little every day.' He (the Imam) said, 'I do not like it for you.' I then asked, 'Should I then use one day and should not use the next day?' He (the Imam) said, 'I do not like that for you.' I then asked, 'Can I use once after every two days?' He (the Imam) said, 'You can apply oil every Friday, once or twice a week.'"

H 12557, Ch. 57, h 3

A number of our people have narrated from Ahmad ibn abu 'Abd Allah from 'Uthman ibn 'Isa from Ishaq ibn Jarir who has said the following:

"I once asked abu 'Abd Allah, *'Alayhi al-Salam*, about how many times should I apply oil?' He (the Imam) said, 'Apply oil only once a year.' I then said, 'People will consider me as living in destitution.' I continued asking if I can apply oil once a month or so but he (the Imam) did not increase.'"

Chapter 58 - The Viola Oil

H 12558, Ch. 58, h 1

Ali ibn Ibrahim has narrated from his father from ibn abu 'Umayr from Hisham ibn al-Hakam who has said the following:

"Abu 'Abd Allah, *'Alayhi al-Salam*, has said, 'Viola oil is the master of your oils.'"

H 12559, Ch. 58, h 2

Muhammad ibn Yahya has narrated from Ahmad ibn Muhammad ibn 'Isa from Ja'far ibn Muhammad ibn abu Zayd al-Raziy from his father from Salih ibn 'Uqbah from his father who has said the following:

"I once sent a mule as a gift to abu 'Abd Allah, *'Alayhi al-Salam*, but (on the way) it made the driver to fall off. I then decided to visit him (the Imam) and when we were in al-Madinah, we informed abu 'Abd Allah, *'Alayhi al-Salam*, about it. He (the Imam) said, 'You must make him (the driver) to sniff viola. He sniffed viola and recovered. He (the Imam) said, 'O 'Uqbah, viola is of cool

461

condition in summer and warm in winter. It is soft to our followers and dry to our enemies. If people had known what is in viola, every Awqiyah (a certain measurement) would cost one dinar.'"

H 12560, Ch. 58, h 3

Ahmad ibn Muhammad has narrated from Ali ibn al-Hakam from Yunus ibn Ya'qub who has said the following:

"Abu 'Abd Allah, *'Alayhi al-Salam,* once said, 'From your area no other thing comes more likable to us than viola.'"

H 12561, Ch. 58, h 4

Abu Ali al-Ash'ariy has narrated from Muhammad ibn 'Abd al-Jabbar from ibn Faddal from Tha'labah from Asbat ibn Salim from Israel ibn abu 'Usamah Bayya' al-Zuttiy who has said the following:

"Abu 'Abd Allah, *'Alayhi al-Salam,* has said, 'The likeness of voila oil among oils is like us among other people.'"

H 12562, Ch. 58, h 5

A number of our people have narrated from Ahmad ibn abu from Ali ibn Hassan from 'Abd al-Rahman ibn Kathir who has said the following:

"Abu 'Abd Allah, *'Alayhi al-Salam,* has said, 'The excellence of viola oil over other oils is like the excellence of Islam over other religions. Viola is very good; it banishes the pain from the head and eyes, so you must apply it.'"

H 12563, Ch. 58, h 6

Ali ibn Hassan has narrated from 'Abd al-Rahman ibn Kathir who has said the following:

"Once I was with abu 'Abd Allah, *'Alayhi al-Salam,* when Mehzam came to visit him (the Imam) and abu 'Abd Allah, *'Alayhi al-Salam,* said to me, 'Call the slave-girl to bring for us oil.' I called her, she brought a bottle of viola, and it was a cold day. Mehzam poured a certain amount on his palm, then said, 'I pray to Allah to keep my soul in service for your cause, this is viola and the day is very cold.' He (the Imam) asked, 'What about it, O Mehzam?' He replied, 'Our physicians in al-Kufah think that viola is of cold nature.' He (the Imam) said, 'It is cool in summer and it is soft and warm in winter.'"

H 12564, Ch. 58, h 7

Muhammad ibn Yahya has narrated from Ahmad ibn Muhammad from al-Qasim ibn Yahya from his grandfather al-Hassan ibn Rashid from Muhammad ibn Muslim who has said the following:

"Abu 'Abd Allah, *'Alayhi al-Salam,* has said that `Amir al-Mu'minin has said, 'You must try to sniff viola; the Messenger of Allah, *O Allah, grant compensation to Muhammad and his family worthy of their services to Your cause,* has said, "Had people known about what is in viola they would drink and slurp it."'"

H 12565, Ch. 58, h 8

A number of our people have narrated from Sahl ibn Ziyad from Ahmad ibn Muhammad from ibn abu Nasr from Hammad ibn 'Uthaman from Muhammad ibn Sawqah who has said the following:

"Abu 'Abd Allah, *'Alayhi al-Salam,* has said, 'Viola oil calms down the condition of the brain.'"

H 12566, Ch. 58, h 9

Sahl ibn Ziyad has narrated from Ali ibn Asbat in a *marfu'* manner has said the following:

"He (the Imam), *'Alayhi al-Salam,* has said, 'Applying viola oil to one's eyebrows dispels headaches.'"

H 12567, Ch. 58, h 10

Muhammad ibn Yahya has narrated from Ahmad ibn Muhammad ibn 'Isa from 'Uthman ibn 'Isa from Khalid ibn Najih who has said the following:

"Abu 'Abd Allah, *'Alayhi al-Salam,* has said, 'The likeness of viola oil among the oils is like our followers among the people.'"

H 12568, Ch. 58, h 11

Ahmad ibn Muhammad has narrated from al-Qasim ibn Yahya from his grandfather al-Hassan ibn Rashid from Muhammad ibn Muslim who has said the following:

"Abu 'Abd Allah, *'Alayhi al-Salam,* has said that `Amir al-Mu'minin has said, 'Curb the heat of fever with viola oil.'"

Chapter 59 - The Oil of Gillyflower

H 12569, Ch. 59, h 1

Muhammad ibn Yahya has narrated from Ahmad ibn Muhammad ibn 'Isa and Abu Ali al-Ash'ariy has narrated from Muhammad ibn 'Abd al-Jabbar all ibn Faddal from Tha'labah ibn Maymun from those whom he has mentioned who has said the following:

"Abu 'Abd Allah, *'Alayhi al-Salam,* mentioned viola oil and praised it; then he (the Imam) said that the oil of gillyflower is also very fine oil.'"

H 12570, Ch. 59, h 2

A number of our people have narrated from Ahmad ibn abu 'Abd Allah from his father and ibn Faddal from al-Hassan ibn al-Jahm who has said the following:

"I once saw abu al-Hassan, *'Alayhi al-Salam,* apply gillyflower oil and said to me to apply it.' I then said, 'Why do you not apply viola oil when there is narration about it from abu 'Abd Allah, *'Alayhi al-Salam?'* He, abu al-Hassan, *'Alayhi al-Salam,* said, 'I do not like its smell.' He (the narrator) has said that I said, 'I also do not like its smell, but I do not like to say it because of the narration from abu 'Abd Allah, *'Alayhi al-Salam,* about it.' He, abu al-Hassan, *'Alayhi al-Salam,* said, 'It is not harmful.'"

Chapter 60 - The Oil of Frankincense

H 12571, Ch. 60, h 1

Muhammad ibn Yahya has narrated from Ahmad ibn Muhammad ibn 'Isa from Ali ibn al-Hakam from Muhammad ibn al-Fayd who has said the following:

"I once mentioned oils and viola oil and its excellence before abu 'Abd Allah, *'Alayhi al-Salam.* He (the Imam) said, 'Viola oil is very good oil. You must apply it; its excellence over other oils is like our excellence over other people. Oil of frankincense is fine oil, I however like al-Khuluq oil.'"

H 12572, Ch. 60, h 2

Ali ibn Ibrahim has narrated from his father from ibn abu 'Umayr from Muhammad ibn abu Hamzah from Ishaq ibn 'Ammar and ibn abu 'Umayr from 'Umar ibn 'Udhaynah who has said the following:

"Once, a man complained before abu 'Abd Allah, *'Alayhi al-Salam,* about cracks in his hands and feet. He (the Imam) said, 'Take a piece of cotton, place frankincense oil in it and apply it in your belly button.' Ishaq ibn 'Ammar has said that I said, 'I pray to Allah to keep my soul in service for your cause, frankincense oil in cotton, then in his belly button?' He (the Imam) said, 'O Ishaq, to pour frankincense oil in your belly button it is a great task.' Ibn 'Udhaynah has said, 'Thereafter I met the man. He informed me that he followed the instruction only once and his problems went away.'"

H 12573, Ch. 60, h 3
A number of our people have narrated from Ahmad ibn abu 'Abd Allah from Dawud ibn Ishaq abu Sulayman al-Hadhdha' from Muhammad ibn al-Fayd who has said the following:
"Abu 'Abd Allah, *'Alayhi al-Salam,* has said, 'Frankincense oil is a fine oil.'"

Chapter 61 - The Oil of Gladiola (Lily)

H 12574, Ch. 61, h 1
Muhammad ibn Yahya has narrated from 'Abd Allah ibn Ja'far from al-Sayyariy in a *marfu'* manner has said the following:
"The Messenger of Allah, *O Allah, grant compensation to Muhammad and his family worthy of their services to Your cause,* has said, that no other thing is better for the body than the oil of gladiola (lily), that is *al-Raziqiy* (a certain plant).'"

H 12575, Ch. 61, h 2
Muhammad ibn Yahya has narrated from Ahmad ibn Muhammad ibn 'Isa from al-'Abbas ibn Ma'ruf from al-Ya'qubiy from 'Isa ibn 'Abd Allah from Ali ibn Ja'far who has said the following:
"Abu al-Hassan, *'Alayhi al-Salam,* would smell *al-Shalisha* (a certain mixture) and gladiola as medicine to cure the heat of his runny nose. I asked 'Ali ibn Ja'far about it. Ali said that I mentioned it to a certain physician who said that it is very good for going to bed with one's wife.'"

Chapter 62 - The Sesame Oil

H 12576, Ch. 62, h 1
Muhammad ibn Yahya has narrated from more than one person from al-Khashshab from Ghiyath ibn Kalub from Ishaq ibn 'Ammar who has said the following:
"Abu 'Abd Allah, *'Alayhi al-Salam,* has said that when the Messenger of Allah, *O Allah, grant compensation to Muhammad and his family worthy of their services to Your cause,* complained about his head he inhaled sesame oil.'"

H 12577, Ch. 62, h 2
A number of our people have narrated from Ahmad ibn abu 'Abd Allah from certain persons of his people from son of the daughter al-Awza'iy from Mas'adah ibn al-Yasa' from Qays al-Bahiliy who has said the following:
"Abu 'Abd Allah, *'Alayhi al-Salam,* has said that the Holy Prophet, *O Allah, grant compensation to Muhammad and his family worthy of their services to Your cause,* liked to inhale the fragrance of sesame oil.'"

Chapter 63 - The Oil of Sweet Basil

H 12578, Ch. 63, h 1

A number of our people have narrated from Ahmad ibn Muhammad ibn 'Isa and Ahmad ibn Muhammad ibn Khalid all from ibn Mahbub from Ibrahim ibn Mehzam from Talhah ibn Zayd from the one who has narrated it in a *marfu'* manner has said the following:

"The Messenger of Allah, *O Allah, grant compensation to Muhammad and his family worthy of their services to Your cause,* has said, 'If one brings you sweet basil you must smell it and place it on your eyes because it is from the garden (paradises); and if it is brought for you do not reject it.'"

H 12579, Ch. 63, h 2

Ibn Mahbub has narrated from 'Abd Allah ibn Sinan who has said the following:

"Abu 'Abd Allah, *'Alayhi al-Salam,* has said, 'If sweet basil is brought for one of you he must smell it and place it on his eyes because it is from the garden (paradises).'"

H 12580, Ch. 63, h 3

Muhammad ibn Yahya has narrated from in a marfu' manner the following:

"Abu 'Abd Allah, *'Alayhi al-Salam,* has said, 'Sweet basil is of twenty-one kinds and the master among them is myrtle.'"

H 12581, Ch. 63, h 4

A number of our people have narrated from Ahmad ibn abu 'Abd Allah from al-Hassan ibn Ali ibn Yaqtin from Yunus ibn Ya'qub who has said the following:

"I once visited abu 'Abd Allah, *'Alayhi al-Salam,* when there was a bucket for herbs in his hand with sweet basil therein.'"

H 12582, Ch. 63, h 5

Ali ibn Muhammad has narrated from certain persons of his people from abu Hashim al-Ja'fariy who has said the following:

"I once visited abu al-Hassan, Sahib al-'Askar, *'Alayhi al-Salam,* when one of his children came and give him a flower. He (the Imam) kissed it and placed it on his eyes. He (the Imam) then gave it to me and said, 'O abu Hashim, one on receiving a flower or a bunch of sweet basil should kiss and then place it on his eyes. Then he should say, *'O Allah, grant compensation to Muhammad and his family worthy of their services to Your cause,* and *'A'immah, 'Alayhim al-Salam.* Allah writes for him of merits equal to the sands of the wilderness and deletes of his bad deeds an equal number.'"

Chapter 64 - The Spaciousness of the House

H 12583, Ch. 64, h 1

Ali ibn Ibrahim has narrated from his father from and Muhammad ibn 'Isma'il has narrated from al-Fadl ibn Shadhan from all from ibn abu 'Umayr from Hisham ibn al-Hakam who has said the following:

"Abu 'Abd Allah, *'Alayhi al-Salam,* has said, 'Spaciousness of the house is of one's good fortune.'"

H 12584, Ch. 64, h 2

Muhammad ibn Yahya has narrated from Ahmad ibn Muhammad ibn 'Isa from Mu'ammar ibn Khallad who has said the following:

"Abu al-Hassan, *'Alayhi al-Salam,* purchased a house and instructed one of his Mawla' to move in saying, 'Your house is congested.' He said, 'My father has established this house.' He (the Imam) said, 'If your father was dimwitted, is it proper that you also be like him?'"

H 12585, Ch. 64, h 3

A number of our people have narrated from Sahl ibn Ziyad and Muhammad ibn Yahya has narrated from Ahmad ibn Muhammad all from Sa'id ibn Junah from Mutarrif Mawla' Ma'n who has said the following:

"Abu 'Abd Allah, *'Alayhi al-Salam,* has said, 'Three things provide comfort for a believing person. Of such matters one is a spacious house which provides him privacy for his bad conditions among people, a virtuous wife who helps him in the matters of this and the next life and a daughter or sister whom he sends out of his house in marriage or death.'"

H 12586, Ch. 64, h 4

A number of our people have narrated from Ahmad ibn abu 'Abd Allah from Nuh ibn Shu'ayb from Sulayman ibn Rashid from his father from Bashir who has said the following:

"I once heard abu al-Hassan, *'Alayhi al-Salam,* saying, 'Spaciousness of the house and extra help from the servants are of the means of happy living.'"

H 12587, Ch. 64, h 5

It is narrated from the narrator of the previous *Hadith* from Mansur ibn al-'Abbas from Sa'id from more than one person who has said the following:

"Abu al-Hassan, *'Alayhi al-Salam,* was asked about the excellence of the worldly life. He (the Imam) said, 'It is in spacious house and in the great number of friends.'"

H 12588, Ch. 64, h 6

Abu Ali al-Ash'ariy has narrated from Muhammad ibn 'Abd al-Jabbar from Muhammad ibn 'Isma'il from Ibrahim ibn abu al-Balad from Ali ibn abu al-Mughirah who has said the following:

"Abu Ja'far, *'Alayhi al-Salam,* has said, 'Of the misfortunes in the worldly life is a small and congested house.'"

H 12589, Ch. 64, h 7

Ali ibn Ibrahim has narrated from his father from al-Nawfaliy from al-Sakuniy who has said the following:

"Abu 'Abd Allah, *'Alayhi al-Salam,* has said that the Messenger of Allah, *O Allah, grant compensation to Muhammad and his family worthy of their services to Your cause,* has said, 'Of the good fortune for a Muslim man is spaciousness of the house.'"

H 12590, Ch. 64, h 8

Through the same chain of narrators as that of the previous *Hadith* the following is narrated:

"Once, a man of the people of al-Ansar complained before the Holy Prophet, *O Allah, grant compensation to Muhammad and his family worthy of their services to Your cause,* that houses have caused great congestions for him. The Holy

Prophet said to him, 'Raise your voice as much as you can and ask Allah to make it spacious for you.'"

Chapter 65 - Decorating the Houses

H 12591, Ch. 65, h 1

Muhammad ibn Yahya has narrated from Ahmad ibn Muhammad ibn 'Isa from Muhammad ibn Khalid and al-Husayn ibn Sa'id from al-Qasim ibn Muhammad al-Jawhariy from Ali ibn abu Hamzah from abu Basir who has said the following:

"Abu 'Abd Allah, *'Alayhi al-Salam,* has said that the Messenger of Allah, *O Allah, grant compensation to Muhammad and his family worthy of their services to Your cause,* has said, 'Once Jibril came to me and said, "O Muhammad, your Lord sends you greeting of peace and prohibits you to decorate the houses."' Abu Basir has said, 'I asked what is decorating the house?' He (the Imam) said, 'It is pictures and statues.'"

H 12592, Ch. 65, h 2

Abu Ali al-Ash'ariy has narrated from Muhammad ibn 'Abd al-Jabbar from Safwan ibn Yahya from ibn Muskan from Muhammad ibn Marwan who has said the following:

"Abu 'Abd Allah, *'Alayhi al-Salam,* has stated this *Hadith.* 'The Messenger of Allah, *O Allah, grant compensation to Muhammad and his family worthy of their services to Your cause,* has said, "Once Jibril came to me and said, 'We the community of angels do not enter a house in which there is a dog, statues or a pot in which people urinate.'"'"

H 12593, Ch. 65, h 3

Muhammad ibn Yahya has narrated from 'Abd Allah ibn Muhammad ibn 'Isa from Ali ibn al-Hakam from Aban 'Uthman from abu Basir who has said the following:

"Abu 'Abd Allah, *'Alayhi al-Salam,* has said that Jibril has said, 'We do not enter a house in which there are pictures, or a dog, that is, pictures of human beings or a house in which statues exist.'"

H 12594, Ch. 65, h 4

Ali ibn Ibrahim has narrated from his father from ibn abu 'Umayr from a man who has said the following:

"Abu 'Abd Allah, *'Alayhi al-Salam,* has said, 'If one forms a statue, he on the Day of Judgment will be held responsible to blow the spirit in it.'"

H 12595, Ch. 65, h 5

Ali ibn Ibrahim has narrated from his father from ibn abu 'Umayr from al-Muthanna' who has said the following:

"Abu 'Abd Allah, *'Alayhi al-Salam,* has said that Ali, *'Alayhi al-Salam,* disliked the existence of pictures in houses.'"

H 12596, Ch. 65, h 6

A number of our people have narrated from Ahmad ibn Muhammad ibn Khalid from 'Uthman ibn 'Isa from Sama'ah from abu Basir who has said the following:

"I once asked abu 'Abd Allah, *'Alayhi al-Salam,* about the pillow or furnishings which have pictures on them. He (the Imam) said, 'It is not unlawful if it is in the house.' He (the Imam) then said, 'Anything with pictures which is used

467

under the feet is not harmful.'"

H 12597, Ch. 65, h 7
Muhammad ibn Yahya has narrated from Ahmad and 'Abd Allah sons of Muhammad ibn 'Isa from Ali ibn al-Hakam from Aban ibn 'Uthman from abu al-'Abbas who has said the following:
"About the meaning of the words of Allah, most Majestic, most Glorious, '. . . they made for him whatever he wanted like prayer niche, statues . . .' (34:12) abu 'Abd Allah, *'Alayhi al-Salam,* has said, 'They (statues) by Allah were not the statues of man and women, they, however, were of trees and similar things.'"

H 12598, Ch. 65, h 8
Ali ibn Ibrahim has narrated from his father from ibn abu 'Umayr from Jamil ibn Darraj from Zurarah ibn 'A'yan who has said the following:
"Abu Ja'far, *'Alayhi al-Salam,* has said, 'The existence of *al-Tamathil* (pictures or statues) in a house is not harmful if their heads are changed and the rest is left.'"

H 12599, Ch. 65, h 9
Muhammad ibn Yahya has narrated from al-'Amrakiy ibn Ali from Ali ibn Ja'far who has said the following:
"I asked abu al-Hassan, *'Alayhi al-Salam,* about the house or a room in which there are pictures; if *Salat* (prayer) can be performed there. He (the Imam) said, 'Do not perform *Salat* (prayer) where in front of you there is something (as such), unless you have no choice then you must cut their heads, otherwise, do not perform *Salat* (prayer) there.'"

H 12600, Ch. 65, h 10
Abu Ali al-Ash'ariy has narrated from Ahmad ibn Muhammad and Humayd ibn Ziyad has narrated from al-Hassan ibn Muhammad ibn Sama'ah all from Ahmad ibn al-Hassan al-Mithamiy, from Aban ibn 'Uthman from al-Husayn ibn al-Mundhir who has said the following:
"Abu 'Abd Allah, *'Alayhi al-Salam,* has stated this *Hadith.* 'Three kinds of people will be in suffering on the Day of Judgment. Of such people, one is a man who lies about his dream. He will be held responsible to form a knot between two pieces of barley grains and he will never be able to do so. One is a man who builds statues. He will be held responsible to blow the spirit in it and he will never be able to do so.'" (The third according to al-Saduq is one who listens to a people who do not like him. Lead will be poured in his ears.)

H 12601, Ch. 65, h 11
A number of our people have narrated from Sahl ibn Ziyad Ja'far ibn Muhammad al-Ash'ariy from ibn al-Qaddah who has said the following:
"Abu 'Abd Allah, *'Alayhi al-Salam,* has said that 'Amir al-Mu'minin has said that the Messenger of Allah, *O Allah, grant compensation to Muhammad and his family worthy of their services to Your cause,* sent me to destroy the graves and pictures (forms).'"

H 12602, Ch. 65, h 12
Humayd ibn Ziyad has narrated from al-Hassan ibn Muhammad ibn Sama'ah from more than one person from Aban ibn 'Uthman from 'Amr ibn Khalid who has said the following:

"Abu Ja'far, *'Alayhi al-Salam,* has said that Jibril, *'Alayhi al-Salam*, once said, 'O Messenger of Allah, we do not enter a house in which picture of human beings exists or a house in which people urinate or a house in which a dog exists.'"

H 12603, Ch. 65, h 13

Abu Ali al-Ash'ariy has narrated from Muhammad ibn Salim from Ahmad ibn al-Nadr from 'Amr ibn Shamir from Jabir from 'Abd Allah ibn Yahya al-Kindiy from his father who provided water for 'Amir al-Mu'minin, *'Alayhi al-Salam,* for his wudu who has said the following:

"Amir al-Mu'minin, has said, that the Messenger of Allah, *O Allah, grant compensation to Muhammad and his family worthy of their services to Your cause,* has said that Jibril, *'Alayhi al-Salam*, has said, 'We do not enter a house in which a picture on which feet are not set exists . . . *Hadith* in brief.'"

H 12604, Ch. 65, h 14

Ali ibn Ibrahim has narrated from his father from al-Nawfaliy from al-Sakuniy who has said the following:

"Abu 'Abd Allah, *'Alayhi al-Salam,* has stated this *Hadith.* ''Amir al-Mu'minin has said, 'Once the Messenger of Allah, *O Allah, grant compensation to Muhammad and his family worthy of their services to Your cause,* sent me to al-Madinah saying, "Do not leave any picture without being deleted, any graves without being leveled and any dog without being put to sleep."'"

Chapter 66 - Construction of Buildings

H 12605, Ch. 66, h 1

A number of our people have narrated from Ahmad ibn Muhammad ibn Khalid from his father from 'Abd Allah ibn al-Fadl al-Nawfaliy, from Ziyad ibn 'Umar and al-Ju'fiy from those who narrated to him who has said the following:

"Abu 'Abd Allah, *'Alayhi al-Salam,* has said, 'Allah, most Majestic, most Glorious, has appointed an angel on buildings who says to those who raise a roof higher than eight yards (arms length), "Where do you want to go, O sinful person?"'"

H 12606, Ch. 66, h 2

Ali ibn Ibrahim has narrated from his father from ibn abu 'Umayr from Hisham ibn al-Hakam and others who has said the following:

"Abu 'Abd Allah, *'Alayhi al-Salam,* has said, 'If the roof of a house is higher than seven' or as he (the Imam) said, 'eight yards (arm-length), it is the residence of Satan or his living quarter.'"

H 12607, Ch. 66, h 3

Ali ibn Ibrahim and a number of our people have narrated from Ahmad ibn abu 'Abd Allah and Sahl ibn Ziyad all from Muhammad ibn 'Isa from abu Muhammad al-Ansariy from Aban ibn 'Uthman who has said the following:

"A man once complained before abu 'Abd Allah, *'Alayhi al-Salam,* about people of the land mocking at his family and children. He (the Imam) asked, 'How much is the height of your house?' He replied, 'It is ten yards.' He (the Imam) said, 'Make it eight yards, then write verse 2:255 between the eigth and tenth yards as you go around; a house with a roof higher than eight yards is an assembly place for Jinn who come and live there.'"

H 12608, Ch. 66, h 4
Ali ibn Ibrahim has narrated from his father from 'Isma'il ibn Marrar and Ahmad ibn abu 'Abd Allah from his father all from Yunus from those whom he has mentioned who has said the following:

"About the case of the roof of a house which is eight yards high, abu 'Abd Allah, *'Alayhi al-Salam,* has said that it is a residence. If it is higher than eight yards, then on the level of eight yard height you must write verse 2:255.'"

H 12609, Ch. 66, h 5
A number of our people have narrated from Ahmad ibn abu 'Abd Allah from Muhammad ibn Ali from Muhammad ibn Sinan from Hamzah ibn Humran who has said the following:

"Once, a man complained before abu Ja'far, *'Alayhi al-Salam,* saying, 'Jinn has expelled us from our homes.' He (the Imam) said, 'Keep the height of the roof of your houses seven yards (arm-length).' The man has said, 'We followed the instruction and thereafter we did not see anything that we dislike.'"

H 12610, Ch. 66, h 6
A number of our people have narrated from Sahl ibn Ziyad from Ja'far ibn Bashir from Al-Husayn Zurarah from Muhammad ibn Muslim who has said the following:

"Abu 'Abd Allah, *'Alayhi al-Salam,* has said, 'Build your house seven yards high; anything higher than this becomes residence of Satans. Satans do not live in the sky or on earth. They live in the air.'"

H 12611, Ch. 66, h 7
It is narrated from the narrator of the previous *Hadith* Ali ibn al-Hakam and Muhassan ibn Ahmad from Aban ibn 'Uthman from Muhammad ibn 'Isma'il who has said the following:

"Abu 'Abd Allah, *'Alayhi al-Salam,* has said, 'If the height of the house is more than eight yards (Zira' arm-length) then write verse 2:255 above that level.'"

Chapter 67 - Fencing Wall Around a Flat Roof of the House

H 12612, Ch. 67, h 1
Ali ibn Ibrahim has narrated from his father from ibn abu 'Umayr from Hisham ibn al-Hakam who has said the following:

"Abu 'Abd Allah, *'Alayhi al-Salam,* has said that the Messenger of Allah, *O Allah, grant compensation to Muhammad and his family worthy of their services to Your cause,* prohibited sleeping on the flat roof without a safety fencing wall around it.'"

H 12613, Ch. 67, h 2
Abu Ali al-Ash'ariy has narrated from Muhammad ibn 'Abd al-Jabbar from Ali ibn Ishaq from Sahl ibn al-Yasa' who has said the following:

"Abu 'Abd Allah, *'Alayhi al-Salam,* has said that the Messenger of Allah, *O Allah, grant compensation to Muhammad and his family worthy of their services to Your cause,* has said, 'One who sleeps on a flat roof without a safety fencing walls around it and if something happened to him, he must not blame anyone except his own soul.'"

H 12614, Ch. 67, h 3

It is narrated from the narrator of the previous *Hadith* from *al-Hajj*al from 'Abd Allah ibn Bukayr from Muhammad ibn Muslim who has said the following:

"Abu 'Abd Allah, *'Alayhi al-Salam,* disliked a man's sleeping overnight on a flat roof without safety fencing wall around it. It is the same for both men women.'"

H 12615, Ch. 67, h 4

Muhammad ibn Yahya has narrated from Ahmad ibn Muhammad ibn 'Isa from ibn Faddal from ibn Bukayr from Muhammad ibn Muslim who has said the following:

"Abu 'Abd Allah, *'Alayhi al-Salam,* disliked a man's sleeping alone overnight on a flat roof without safety fencing wall around it; and that it is the same for both men and women.'"

H 12616, Ch. 67, h 5

Ali ibn Ibrahim has narrated from his father from ibn abu 'Umayr from Muhammad ibn abu Hamzah and others who has said the following:

"About the case of a flat roof without fencing wall around it abu 'Abd Allah, *'Alayhi al-Salam,* has said, 'If the height of the fencing wall around a flat roof is two yards (Zira' arm-length) it is sufficient.'"

H 12617, Ch. 67, h 6

It is narrated from the narrator of the previous *Hadith* from his father from Safwan ibn Yahya from 'Is ibn al-Qasim who has said the following:

"I once asked abu 'Abd Allah, *'Alayhi al-Salam,* about sleeping overnight on a flat roof without fencing wall around it. He (the Imam) said, 'The Messenger of Allah, *O Allah, grant compensation to Muhammad and his family worthy of their services to Your cause,* prohibited it.' I then asked if three yards (Zira' arm-length) is sufficient for the height of such fencing wall. He (the Imam) said, 'No, it is four.' I then asked, 'How much is the length of the wall?' He (the Imam) said, 'The shortest is one yard (Zira' arm-length) and one Shibr. (the distance from the tip of the thump to the tip of the little finger with the thump and little finger open and stretched out).'"

Chapter 68 - The Rare Ahadith

H 12618, Ch. 68, h 1

A number of our people have narrated from Sahl ibn Ziyad from al-Sayyariy, from a shaykh from a certain persons of our people from those whom he has mentioned who has said the following:

"Of the bitterness in life is moving from one house to another house and eating bread made of colocynth.'"

H 12619, Ch. 68, h 2

Ali ibn Ibrahim has narrated from his father from ibn abu 'Umayr from Hisham ibn al-Hakam who has said the following:

"Abu 'Abd Allah, *'Alayhi al-Salam,* has said, 'If one earns an asset through unlawful means Allah overpowers him by means of building, water and clay.'"

H 12620, Ch. 68, h 3

Ibn abu 'Umayr has narrated from Husayn ibn 'Uthman man who has said the following:

"I once saw abu al-Hassan, *'Alayhi al-Salam,* in Mina where he built a structure, then destroyed it.'"

H 12621, Ch. 68, h 4

A number of our people have narrated from Sahl ibn Ziyad fn Ali ibn Asbat from Dawud al-Riqqiy who has said the following:

"I once asked abu 'Abd Allah, *'Alayhi al-Salam,* about the meaning of the words of Allah, most Majestic, most Glorious, 'There is not anything that does not say Tasbih (Allah is free of all defects) and praise Him but you do not understand their Tasbih (Allah is free of all defects).' (17:34) He (the Imam) said, 'The breaking down of a wall is its saying Tasbih (Allah is free of all defects).'"

H 12622, Ch. 68, h 5

Al-Husayn ibn Muhammad has narrated from Ahmad ibn Ishaq from Sa'dan ibn Muslim from Ishaq ibn 'Ammar who has said the following:

"Abu 'Abd Allah, *'Alayhi al-Salam,* has said, 'You must sweep the yard of your house and do not become similar to the Jews.'"

H 12623, Ch. 68, h 6

A number of our people have narrated from Sahl ibn Ziyad from Ali ibn Asbat from his uncle Ya'qub ibn Salim in a *marfu'* manner has said the following:

"'Amir al-Mu'minin, *'Alayhi al-Salam,* has said, 'You must not allow the dust to accumulate behind the door; it becomes a resort for Satans.'"

H 12624, Ch. 68, h 7

A number of our people have narrated from Ahmad ibn abu 'Abd Allah from Safwan ibn Yahya from abu Jamilah from Hamid al-Sayrafiy who has said the following:

"Abu 'Abd Allah, *'Alayhi al-Salam,* has said, 'The constructions that are not within owner's budget will be a burden for him on the Day of Judgment.'"

H 12625, Ch. 68, h 8

It is narrated from the narrator of the previous *Hadith* from certain persons of his people in a *marfu'* manner has said the following:

"Abu Ja'far, *'Alayhi al-Salam,* has said, 'Sweep the house, it removes poverty.'"

H 12626, Ch. 68, h 9

Ali ibn Ibrahim has narrated from his father from al-Nawfaliy from al-Sakuniy who has said the following:

"Abu 'Abd Allah, *'Alayhi al-Salam,* has said that the Holy Prophet, *O Allah, grant compensation to Muhammad and his family worthy of their services to Your cause,* prohibited entering a dark house without a lamp.'"

H 12627, Ch. 68, h 10

It is narrated from the narrator of the previous *Hadith* from Ibrahim ibn Ahmad al-Thaqafiy from Ali ibn al-Mu'alla' from Ibrahim ibn al-Khattab in a *marfu'* manner has said the following:

"Abu 'Abd Allah, *'Alayhi al-Salam,* has said, 'The lower parts of the wall complained before Allah because of the weight of the upper parts and Allah, most Majestic, most Glorious, inspired it saying, 'Certain parts of you must leave the other parts.'"

H 12628, Ch. 68, h 11

Muhammad ibn Yahya has narrated from Salmah ibn al-Khattab from Ibrahim ibn Maymun from 'Isa ibn 'Abd Allah from his grandfather who has said the following:

"'Amir al-Mu'minin, *'Alayhi al-Salam,* has said, that the Messenger of Allah, *O Allah, grant compensation to Muhammad and his family worthy of their services to Your cause,* has said, 'The house of Satans in your houses are the spider webs.'"

H 12629, Ch. 68, h 12

A number of our people have narrated from Ahmad ibn Muhammad from 'Uthman ibn 'Isa from Sama'ah who has said the following:

"I once asked abu 'Abd Allah, *'Alayhi al-Salam,* about closing the doors, turning the utensils around and turning-off the lamp. He (the Imam) said, 'Close your door; Satan does not open the door, turnoff the lamp against *al-Fuwaysaqah* which is the mouse, do not burn your house and secure the utensils (by means of cover and so on). It is narrated that Satan does not remove the cover.'"

H 12630, Ch. 68, h 13

Abu Ali al-Ash'ariy has narrated in a *marfu'* manner has said the following:

"Al-Rida', *'Alayhi al-Salam,* has said, 'Turning on the lamp before sunset banishes poverty.'"

H 12631, Ch. 68, h 14

Ali ibn Ibrahim has narrated from his father from al-Nawfaliy from al-Sakuniy who has said the following:

"Abu 'Abd Allah, *'Alayhi al-Salam,* has said that when the Holy Prophet, *O Allah, grant compensation to Muhammad and his family worthy of their services to Your cause,* wanted to travel in summer he would leave on Thursday, and in winter because of cold enter on Friday. It also is narrated that his leaving and entering took place on a Friday night.'"

H 12632, Ch. 68, h 15

Al-Husayn ibn Muhammad has narrated from Mu'alla' ibn Muhammad from Ahmad ibn Muhammad ibn 'Abd Allah who has said that abu Hashim al-Ja'fariy has said the following:

"Abu al-Hassan, al-Thalith, *'Alayhi al-Salam,* has said that Allah, most Majestic, most Glorious, has made certain areas of the earth called recipient of mercy. He has liked that He is asked for help therein so He might answer such prayers. Allah, most Majestic, most Glorious, has made certain parts of the earth as disliked, thus if a man earns a certain amount of assets therein through unlawful ways, Allah makes a certain area to control him and spend his earnings therein.'"

Chapter 69 - The Undesirable Case of One's Sleeping Alone and the Characteristics Prohibited because of its Frightfulness

H 12633, Ch. 69, h 1

Muhammad ibn Yahya has narrated from Ahmad ibn Muhammad from ibn Faddal from ibn al-Qaddah from his father who has said the following:

"I once visited abu Ja'far, *'Alayhi al-Salam,* and he asked saying, 'O Maymun, who sleeps near you in the night, is there a slave with you?' I replied, 'No, no one sleeps near me.' He (the Imam) said, 'Do not sleep alone; Satan becomes more daring against man when he finds him alone.'"

H 12634, Ch. 69, h 2

Ahmad ibn Muhammad has narrated from ibn Mahbub al-'Ala' ibn Razin from Muhammad ibn Muslim who has said the following:

"Abu Ja'far, *'Alayhi al-Salam,* has stated this *Hadith.* 'Unless Allah wills otherwise, something from Satan reaches very fast to one who defecates on a grave or urinates standing or urinates in stagnant water or walks in one shoe or drinks water standing, or stays in a house alone or sleeps overnight with his hands greasy with animal fat. The Messenger of Allah, *O Allah, grant compensation to Muhammad and his family worthy of their services to Your cause,* once travelled in a group of people during an armed expedition and reached in the valley where Jinns lived. He (the Messenger of Allah) called his companions saying, 'Every one of you must hold the hand of another one and no one must enter alone and no one must walk ahead.' One man moved forward alone, he completed the area of the valley but he became epileptic. The Messenger of Allah was informed about it and he (the Messenger of Allah) pressed his finger against him and touched, then said, 'In the name of Allah, O filthy (Jinn) move out, I am the Messenger of Allah.' He then stood up.'"

H 12635, Ch. 69, h 3

Muhammad ibn Yahya has narrated from 'Abd Allah ibn Muhammad from Ali ibn al-Hakam from Aban al-Ahmar from Muhammad ibn Muslim who has said the following:

"Abu Ja'far, *'Alayhi al-Salam,* has said that Satan is the strongest against man when he is alone without anything and I say that he must not sleep alone.'"

H 12636, Ch. 69, h 4

A number of our people have narrated from Ahmad ibn Muhammad ibn Khalid from 'Uthman ibn 'Isa from Sama'ah ibn Mehran who has said the following:

"I once asked abu 'Abd Allah, *'Alayhi al-Salam,* about the case of a man who sleeps in a house alone. He (the Imam) said, 'I dislike it but if it is an emergency, then it is not harmful, however, he must speak of Allah a great deal and as much as he can, when he goes to sleep.'"

H 12637, Ch. 69, h 5

It is narrated from the narrator of the previous *Hadith* from his father from 'Abd Allah ibn al-Mughirah and Muhammad ibn Sinan from Talhah ibn Zayd who has said the following:

"Abu 'Abd Allah, *'Alayhi al-Salam,* disliked one's sleeping in a house which does not have a door or a curtain.'"

H 12638, Ch. 69, h 6

Through the same chain of narrators as that of the previous *Hadith* the following is narrated:

"The Messenger of Allah, *O Allah, grant compensation to Muhammad and his family worthy of their services to Your cause,* disliked entering a dark house without a lamp."

H 12639, Ch. 69, h 7

A number of our people have narrated from Sahl ibn Ziyad from Ja'far ibn Muhammad al-Ash'ariy from ibn al-Qaddah from his father Maymun who has said the following:

"Abu Ja'far, *'Alayhi al-Salam,* once asked Muhammad ibn Sulayman, 'Where have you found lodging?' He replied, 'It is in so and so place.' He (the Imam) asked, 'Is there anyone else with you?' he replied, 'No, there is no one with me.' He (the Imam) said, 'Move from there, O Maymun and do not stay there alone; Satan is most daring against man when he is alone.'"

H 12640, Ch. 69, h 8

Sahl has narrated from Ahmad ibn Muhammad from ibn abu Nasr from Safwan from al-'Ala' from Muhammad ibn Muslim who has said the following:

"One of the two Imam, (abu Ja'far or abu 'Abd Allah), *'Alayhim al-Salam,* has stated this *Hadith.* 'You must not drink water when you are standing, must not urinate in stagnant water, must not spit on a grave, must not stay in a house alone, you must not walk in one shoe; Satan is the fastest against a servant when he is in one of such conditions.' He (the Imam) said, 'If one becomes affected in any one of such conditions, it will not leave him unless Allah, most Majestic, most Glorious, wants otherwise.'"

H 12641, Ch. 69, h 9

Ali ibn Ibrahim has narrated from his father from ibn abu 'Umayr from Hammad from al-Halabiy who has said the following:

"Abu 'Abd Allah, *'Alayhi al-Salam,* has said, 'Satan is the strongest against man when he is alone, thus one must not sleep alone or travel alone.'"

H 12642, Ch. 69, h 10

A number of our people have narrated from Sahl ibn Ziyad and Ali ibn Ibrahim all from Muhammad ibn 'Isa from al-Dihqan from Durust from Ibrahim ibn 'Abd al-Hamid who has said the following:

"Abu al-Hassan, Musa, *'Alayhi al-Salam,* has said, 'Three things are feared for causing insanity: defecating among the gravesites, walking in one shoe and a man's sleeping alone.' Such things are disliked because of such reasons but they are not unlawful." (The last sentence apparently is the words of the compiler).

End of the Book of Dresses, Beautification and Kindness followed by the Book of Domestic Animals by help of Allah, most High.

Part Eight:
The Book of Domestic Animals

Chapter 1 - The Relation between a Stumper and the Rider

H 12643, Ch. 1, h 1

Al-Husayn ibn Muhammad has narrated from Mu'alla' ibn Muhammad from Ahmad ibn Muhammad from those who narrated to him from ibn Tayfur al-Mutatabbib who has said the following:

"Once abu al-Hassan, *'Alayhi al-Salam,* asked me, 'What do you ride?' I replied, 'It is a donkey.' He (the Imam) asked, 'For how much have you bought it?' I replied, 'I have bought it for thirteen dinars.' He (the Imam) said, 'This is improper spending. You have bought a donkey for thirteen dinar and ignored buying a mule.' I then said, 'My master, maintenance of a mule is more than that for a donkey.' He (the Imam) said, 'The one who maintains a donkey maintains a mule also. Did you not know that if one rides a stumper expecting our cause to materialize and makes our enemies feel jealous because he is counted on us, Allah manages his affairs, opens his chest, makes his wishes to come true and He is a helper in his affairs.'"

H 12644, Ch. 1, h 2

Muhammad ibn Yahya has narrated from al-Husayn from Muhammad ibn Sinan from 'Abd Allah ibn Jundab has said that narrated to him certain persons of our people who have said the following:

"Abu 'Abd Allah, *'Alayhi al-Salam,* has said, 'Nine-tenths of sustenance is with the owner of a stumper.'"

H 12645, Ch. 1, h 3

A number of our people have narrated from Sahl ibn Ziyad and Ahmad ibn Muhammad all from ibn Bukayr ibn Salih from Sulayman al-Ja'fariy who has said the following:

"I once heard abu al-Hassan, *'Alayhi al-Salam,* saying, ''Amir al-Mu'minin, *'Alayhi al-Salam,* sent as present to the Messenger of Allah, *O Allah, grant compensation to Muhammad and his family worthy of their services to Your cause.* It comprised of four horses from Yemen. He (the Messenger of Allah) asked, 'Describe them for me.' He (the Imam) said, 'They are of different colors.' He (the Messenger of Allah) asked, 'Has anyone of them bright spots?' He (the Imam) replied, 'There is a blond more toward redness among them which has bright spots on it.' He (the Messenger of Allah) said, 'Keep it for me.' He (the Imam) said there are two blonds more toward yellowness which have bright spots on them.' He (the Messenger of Allah) said, 'Give these to your sons.' He (the Imam) said, 'The fourth one is of one color all over without spots on it.' He (the Messenger of Allah) said, 'Sell it for the expenses of your family. The good fortune in horses is in those with bright spots on them.' I heard abu al-Hassan, *'Alayhi al-Salam,* saying, 'We dislike all animals of one color, all over except donkeys and mules; and I dislike bright-hooved donkeys and mules of many colors. I dislike a white spot on the forehead of a mule unless it has expanded, however, I do not have the desires for it with such condition.'"

477

H 12646, Ch. 1, h 4

Ali ibn Ibrahim has narrated from his father from ibn abu 'Umayr from Ali ibn Ri'ab who has said the following:

"Abu 'Abd Allah, *'Alayhi al-Salam,* has said, 'Buy a stumper; its benefit is for you and its sustenance with Allah, most Majestic, most Glorious.'"

H 12647, Ch. 1, h 5

A number of our people have narrated from Sahl ibn Ziyad from Muhammad ibn al-Husayn from Ja'far ibn Bashir from Dawud al-Riqqiy who has said the following:

"Abu 'Abd Allah, *'Alayhi al-Salam,* has said, 'If one buys a stumper, he has the benefit of riding and its sustenance is with Allah.'"

H 12648, Ch. 1, h 6

Sahl ibn Ziyad has narrated from Muhammad ibn al-Walid from Yunus ibn Ya'qub who has said the following:

"Abu 'Abd Allah, *'Alayhi al-Salam,* once said, 'Buy a donkey which will carry your luggage and its sustenance is with Allah.' He (the narrator) has said, 'I then found a donkey. Yunus, my brother and I at the end of the year would do our accounts and we found that there was no difference in our budget and no increase over the expenses of other years.'"

H 12649, Ch. 1, h 7

Ali ibn Ibrahim has narrated from his father from Muhammad ibn 'Isa from Muhammad ibn Sama'ah from Muhammad ibn Marwan who has said the following:

"It is of the good fortune of a believing person to have a stumper that he can ride to meet his own needs and the needs of his brothers (in belief).'"

H 12650, Ch. 1, h 8

Ali ibn Ibrahim has narrated from his father from al-Nawfaliy from al-Sakuniy who has said the following:

"Abu 'Abd Allah, *'Alayhi al-Salam,* has said that the Messenger of Allah, *O Allah, grant compensation to Muhammad and his family worthy of their services to Your cause,* has said, 'It is of the good fortune of a Muslim man to have a healthy stumper.'"

H 12651, Ch. 1, h 9

Ali ibn Ibrahim a number of our people have narrated from Sahl ibn Ziyad all from Muhammad ibn 'Isa from Ziyad al-Qandiy from 'Abd Allah ibn Sinan who has said the following:

"Abu 'Abd Allah, *'Alayhi al-Salam,* has said, 'You must have a stumper; it is of beautification and helps meet one's needs and its sustenance is with Allah, most Majestic, most Glorious.' He (the narrator) has said that narrated to me 'Ammar ibn al-Mubarak with the addition of 'and ride it to meet your brothers (in belief).' It is also narrated that he (the Imam) said, 'How can one who has a stumper miss fulfilling his needs?'"

H 12652, Ch. 1, h 10

Ali ibn Ibrahim has narrated from Muhammad ibn 'Isa from certain persons of his people from Ibrahim ibn abu al-Balad from Ali ibn al-Mughirah who has said the following:

"Abu Ja'far, *'Alayhi al-Salam,* has said, 'It is a misfortune in life to have a bad stumper.'"

Chapter 2 - The Rare Ahadith about the Stumpers

H 12653, Ch. 2, h 1

Ali ibn Ibrahim has narrated from his father from al-Nawfaliy from al-Sakuniy who has said the following:

"Abu 'Abd Allah, *'Alayhi al-Salam*, has said, 'A stumper has six rights on its owner. He must not load more than its power. He must not take its back as a meeting place to keep talking from there. He must feed it as soon as he disembarks, must not mark it with burns, or hit it on its face because it says Tasbih (Allah is free of all defects) and offer it water whenever passing by water.'"

H 12654, Ch. 2, h 2

A number of our people have narrated from Ahmad ibn Muhammad from ibn Faddal from abu al-Mighra' from Sulayman ibn Khalid who has said the following as I thing from abu 'Abd Allah, *'Alayhi al-Salam*:

"Abu 'Abd Allah, *'Alayhi al-Salam*, has said that abu Dharr was seen offering water to a donkey at al-Rabadhah and certain people said to him, 'O abu Dharr do you not have someone who can offer water to your donkey?' He said, 'I once heard the Messenger of Allah, *O Allah, grant compensation to Muhammad and his family worthy of their services to Your cause*, saying, "Every stumper asks Allah every morning, 'O Lord, grant me an owner who will feed me sufficiently of feed, offer me water, will not load me more than my power.'" For this reason I personally offer it water.'"

H 12655, Ch. 2, h 3

Al-Husayn ibn Muhammad has narrated from Mu'alla' ibn Muhammad from al-Washsha' from Tarkhan al-Nakhkhas who has said the following:

"I once visited abu 'Abd Allah, *'Alayhi al-Salam*, when he had disembarked in al-Hirah and asked me, 'What do you do for a living?' I replied, 'I trade in animals.' He (the Imam) said, 'Find for me a mule which is *Fadha'*.' I then asked saying, 'I pray to Allah to keep my soul in service for your cause, what is *Fadha'*?' He (the Imam) said, 'It is of one color except for its white belly, white thighs of the back legs and of white harness area.' He (the narrator) has said, 'I said, by Allah I have not seen any mule as such.' After (a while), I entered the ditch and saw a slave riding a mule of such description. I asked, 'Whose mule is this?' The slave said that it belongs to his master. I then asked, 'Does he sell it?' He said, 'I do not know.' I went to his master, bought it from him, and brought it to him (the Imam). He (the Imam) said, 'This mule is of the qualities that I had asked for.' I then said, 'I pray to Allah to keep my soul in service for your cause, pray for me before Allah.' He (the Imam) said, 'O Allah, grant him a great deal of assets and children.' He (the narrator) has said, 'I then became the wealthiest of the people of al-Kufah as well in terms of children.'"

H 12656, Ch. 2, h 4

A number of our people have narrated from Ahmad ibn Muhammad from al-Qasim ibn Yahya from his grandfather al-Hassan ibn Rashid from Muhammad ibn Muslim who has said the following:

"Abu 'Abd Allah, *'Alayhi al-Salam*, has said that the Messenger of Allah, *O Allah, grant compensation to Muhammad and his family worthy of their services to Your cause,* has said, 'You must not hit the stumpers on their faces; they say Tasbih (Allah is free of all defects) with Tahmid, (all praise belongs to Allah).' He (the narrator) has said that in another *Hadith* it is said, 'You must not make burn marks on their faces.'"

H 12657, Ch. 2, h 5

A number of our people have narrated from Sahl ibn Ziyad from Ja'far ibn Muhammad ibn Yasar from 'Ubayd Allah al-Dihqan from Durust who has said the following:

"Abu 'Abd Allah, *'Alayhi al-Salam,* has said that the Messenger of Allah, *O Allah, grant compensation to Muhammad and his family worthy of their services to Your cause,* has said, 'When a stumper stumbles and man riding it says, 'May you be destroyed.' The stumper says, 'May the one of us who is most disobedient to the Lord be destroyed.'"

H 12658, Ch. 2, h 6

Muhammad ibn Yahya has narrated from Ali ibn Ibrahim al-Ja'fariy in a *marfu'* manner has said the following:

"I once asked al-Sadiq, *'Alayhi al-Salam,* 'When can I hit my stumper?' He (the Imam) said, 'You can do so when you are riding and it does not walk as it does when going to its manger, its feeding place.'"

H 12659, Ch. 2, h 7

It is narrated from the Holy Prophet, *O Allah, grant compensation to Muhammad and his family worthy of their services to Your cause,* who has said, 'You may hit your stumpers for running away in fright but not because of their stumbling.'"

H 12660, Ch. 2, h 8

Humayd ibn Ziyad has narrated from al-Khashshab from ibn Baqqah from Mu'adh al-Jawhariy from 'Amr ibn Jumay' who has said the following:

"Abu 'Abd Allah, *'Alayhi al-Salam,* has stated this *Hadith.* 'The Messenger of Allah, *O Allah, grant compensation to Muhammad and his family worthy of their services to Your cause,* has said, 'You must not sit on the stumper with both legs hanging from one side (causing imbalance) or make its back a meeting place (talking to someone with the stumper halted and kept on hold).'"

H 12661, Ch. 2, h 9

A number of our people have narrated from Sahl ibn Ziyad from ibn Mahbub from ibn Ri'ab from abu Hamzah who has said the following:

"Ali ibn al-Husayn, *'Alayhim al-Salam,* would say, 'Animals, no matter how unintelligent and dubious they may be, are not so in four issues: One is knowing the Lord, death, male and female, and what is a pasture and what is a barren land.'"

H 12662, Ch. 2, h 10

Ali ibn Ibrahim has narrated from his father from al-Nawfaliy from al-Sakuniy who has said the following:

"Abu 'Abd Allah, *'Alayhi al-Salam,* has said, 'Everything has honor. The honor of animals is in their faces.'"

H 12663, Ch. 2, h 11

Abu Ali al-Ash'ariy has narrated from Muhammad ibn 'Abd al-Jabbar from *al-Hajj*al and ibn Faddal from Tha'labah, from Ya'qub ibn Salim from a man who has said the following:

"Abu 'Abd Allah, *'Alayhi al-Salam,* has said, 'No matter how unintelligent the animals may be, they are not so about four issues. They know that they have a Creator, they know how to find sustenance, they know male and female and they are afraid of death.'"

H 12664, Ch. 2, h 12

Sahl ibn Ziyad has narrated from Muhammad ibn al-Hassan ibn Shammun from al-Asamm from Misma' ibn 'Abd al-Malik who has said the following:

"Abu 'Abd Allah, *'Alayhi al-Salam,* has said that the Messenger of Allah, *O Allah, grant compensation to Muhammad and his family worthy of their services to Your cause,* has said, 'You may hit your stumpers for their running away in fright, but do not do so for their stumbling.'"

H 12665, Ch. 2, h 13

A number of our people have narrated from Ahmad ibn Muhammad from al-Qasim ibn Yahya from his grandfather al-Hassan ibn Rashid from Ya'qub ibn Ja'far who has said the following:

"I once heard abu al-Hassan, *'Alayhi al-Salam,* saying, 'In the nostrils of every stumper there is a Satan. When you want to harness them you must say, "In the name of Allah, most Majestic, most Glorious."'"

H 12666, Ch. 2, h 14

Ahmad ibn Muhammad has narrated from ibn Mahbub from ibn Ri'ab from abu 'Ubaydah from one of the two Imam, (abu Ja'far or abu 'Abd Allah) who has said the following:

"If any stumper becomes difficult with the owner in harnessing or running away in fright, he must read in its ear or on it, 'Do you want something other than the religion of Allah, when all who are in the skies and earth are submitted to Him voluntarily, or by force and to Him they all return.' (3:83)"

H 12667, Ch. 2, h 15

Ali ibn Ibrahim has narrated from his father from ibn abu 'Umayr from Hisham ibn Salim who has said the following:

"Abu 'Abd Allah, *'Alayhi al-Salam,* has said, 'It is a matter of rights that a person riding say to the one walking, *'the road'* (meaning please open the road, to inform him of his presence).' In another copy it is said that a rider saying to one walking *'the road'* is of injustice.'"

H 12668, Ch. 2, h 16

Through the same chain of narrators as that of the previous *Hadith* the following is narrated:

"Once 'Amir al-Mu'minin, *'Alayhi al-Salam,* came out riding and people walked with him. He (the Imam) asked, 'Do you need me for something?' They replied, 'No, but we love to walk with you.' He (the Imam) said, 'You must go back; walking with a rider is harmful for the rider and humiliation for the walking people.'"

H 12669, Ch. 2, h 17

Ali ibn Ibrahim has narrated from Muhammad ibn 'Isa from al-Dihqan from Durust from Ibrahim ibn 'Abd al-Hamid who has said the following:

"Abu al-Hassan, *'Alayhi al-Salam,* has said that the Messenger of Allah, *O Allah, grant compensation to Muhammad and his family worthy of their services to Your cause,* has stated this *Hadith.* 'If one rides his stumper and mentions the name of Allah, an angel sits behind him to protect him until he disembarks; but if one rides his stumper without mentioning the name of Allah, a Satan sits behind him and says to him to sing. If he says, 'I do not know singing.' He says, 'Wish that you could sing.' He then continues wishing until he disembarks.' He (the Messenger of Allah) has said, 'If one says, "In the name of Allah, there is no means and power without Allah, all praise belongs to Allah who has guided us to this. . . ." (7:43) Then he reads, "Glory belongs to the One who has made this subservient to us when we could not bring it together," (43:13) he and his stumper will be protected until he disembarks.'"

H 12670, Ch. 2, h 18

Ali ibn Ibrahim and others in a *marfu'* manner has narrated the following:

"Once 'Abd al-Samad came out with a group of people and he saw abu al-Hassan, Musa ibn Ja'far, *'Alayhim al-Salam,* coming from the opposite direction on a mule. He then said to those with him, 'Wait until I will make you laugh at Musa ibn Ja'far.' When close nearby he said, 'What good is this stumper with which one cannot achieve any compensation for his losses and it is not of any use in a warfare struggle?' Abu al-Hassan, *'Alayhi al-Salam,* said, 'I have come down from the height of the horse and stepped up from lowliness of donkeys and the best of things is that which is of the middle and balanced status.' 'Abd al-Samad remained speechless and could not phrase any response.'"

H 12671, Ch. 2, h 19

A number of our people have narrated from Ahmad ibn abu 'Abd Allah A number of his people from Ali ibn Asbat from his uncle Ya'qub ibn Salim in a *marfu'* manner has said the following:

"'Amir al-Mu'minin, *'Alayhi al-Salam,* has said that the Messenger of Allah, *O Allah, grant compensation to Muhammad and his family worthy of their services to Your cause,* has said, 'Three people must not ride one stumper, one behind the other, because one of them is condemned.'"

Chapter 3 - The Tools for the Stumpers

H 12672, Ch. 3, h 1

Ali ibn Ibrahim has narrated from his father from ibn abu 'Umayr from certain persons of his people who has said the following:

"Abu 'Abd Allah, *'Alayhi al-Salam,* has said, 'The saddle is a condemned riding thing for women.'"

H 12673, Ch. 3, h 2

A number of our people have narrated from Ahmad ibn Muhammad ibn Khalid from 'Uthman ibn 'Isa from Sama'ah who has said the following:

"Once abu 'Abd Allah, *'Alayhi al-Salam,* was asked about the skins of beasts. He (the Imam) said, 'You can use them when riding but you must not use them during performing *Salat* (prayer).'"

H 12674, Ch. 3, h 3

Muhammad ibn Yahya has narrated from al-'Amrakiy ibn Ali from Ali ibn Ja'far from his brother abu al-Hassan, *'Alayhi al-Salam,* who has said the following:

"I once asked abu al-Hassan, *'Alayhi al-Salam,* about the saddle and the rein in which silver is used; if it can be used. He (the Imam) said, 'If it is in a whitewashing (painted) form which cannot be removed, then it is not harmful, otherwise, you must not ride with it.'"

H 12675, Ch. 3, h 4

Muhammad ibn Yahya has narrated from Ahmad ibn Muhammad from Muhammad ibn 'Isma'il from his father from Hanan ibn Sadir who has said the following:

"I once heard abu 'Abd Allah, *'Alayhi al-Salam,* saying that the Messenger of Allah, *O Allah, grant compensation to Muhammad and his family worthy of their services to Your cause,* once said to Ali, *'Alayhi al-Salam,* 'You must never use a red saddlecloth; it is the saddlecloth of Satan.'"

H 12676, Ch. 3, h 5

A number of our people have narrated from Ahmad ibn abu 'Abd Allah from Muhammad ibn Ali from 'Abd al-Rahman ibn abu Hashim from Ibrahim ibn abu Yahya al-Madiniy who has said the following:

"Abu 'Abd Allah, *'Alayhi al-Salam,* has said that 'Ali ibn al-Husayn, *'Alayhim al-Salam,* rode on a piece of marigold red color cloth.'"

H 12677, Ch. 3, h 6

A number of our people have narrated from Sahl ibn Ziyad from Muhammad ibn al-Hassan ibn Shammun from 'Abd Allah ibn 'Abd al-Rahman from Misma' ibn 'Abd al-Malik who has said the following:

"Abu 'Abd Allah, *'Alayhi al-Salam,* has said that the ring in the nostrils of the camel of the Messenger of Allah, *O Allah, grant compensation to Muhammad and his family worthy of their services to Your cause,* was made of silver.'"

Chapter 4 - Choosing the Camel

H 12678, Ch. 4, h 1

Ali ibn Ibrahim has narrated from his father from ibn abu 'Umayr from 'Abd Allah ibn Sinan who has said the following:

"Abu 'Abd Allah, *'Alayhi al-Salam,* has said that Ali ibn al-Husayn, *'Alayhi al-Salam,* bought a stumper for one hundred dinar in his own honor."

H 12679, Ch. 4, h 2

Abu Ali al-Ash'ariy has narrated from Muhammad ibn 'Abd al-Jabbar from *al-Hajj*al from Safwan al-Jammal who has said the following:

"Abu 'Abd Allah, *'Alayhi al-Salam,* has said, 'Had people known the fact of how Allah gives strength to the weak to carry the load, carry-animals would not become expensive.'"

H 12680, Ch. 4, h 3

Muhammad ibn Yahya has narrated from Ahmad ibn Muhammad from Muhammad ibn Yahya from Ghiyath ibn Ibrahim who has said the following:

"Abu 'Abd Allah, *'Alayhi al-Salam,* has said that the Messenger of Allah, *O*

Allah, grant compensation to Muhammad and his family worthy of their services to Your cause, has stated this *Hadith.* 'On the peak of every camel there is a Satan and you must degrade him before yourselves by mentioning the name of Allah, only Allah, most Majestic, most Glorious is He who carries loads.'"

H 12681, Ch. 4, h 4

Ali ibn Ibrahim has narrated from his father from ibn abu 'Umayr from Hisham ibn al-Hakam who has said the following:

"Abu 'Abd Allah, *'Alayhi al-Salam,* has said, 'Had the pilgrim to Makkah known what carries his load, camel would not become expensive.'"

H 12682, Ch. 4, h 5

A number of our people have narrated from Ahmad ibn abu 'Abd Allah from his father from Muhammad ibn 'Amr from Sulayman al-Rahhal from ibn abu Ya'fur who has said the following:

"Once, abu 'Abd Allah, *'Alayhi al-Salam,* passed by me and I was walking next to my camel. He (the Imam) asked, 'Why are you not riding?' I replied, 'My camel has become weak, thus I decided to provide it relief.' He (the Imam) said, 'May Allah grant you blessings. Ride your camel, Allah carries for both the weak and the strong.'"

H 12683, Ch. 4, h 6

It is narrated from the narrator of the previous *Hadith* from his father from those whom he has mentioned who has said the following:

"Abu 'Abd Allah, *'Alayhi al-Salam,* has said that the Messenger of Allah, *O Allah, grant compensation to Muhammad and his family worthy of their services to Your cause,* prohibited to cross and intersect the row of camels. Someone asked, 'Why is this, O Messenger of Allah?' He (the Messenger of Allah) said, 'In every row of camels between every two camels there is a Satan.'"

H 12684, Ch. 4, h 7

Muhammad ibn Yahya has narrated from Ahmad ibn Muhammad from ibn Mahbub from Husayn ibn 'Umar ibn Yazid from his father who has said the following:

"I once bought a camel, when I was living in al-Madinah, and I liked it very intensely. I then visited Ali ibn al-Husayn, *'Alayhim al-Salam,* and mentioned it to him. He (the Imam) said, 'What do you have to do with camels? Did you not know that camels have many troubles?' Because of my happiness with it I gave it for hire with two of my slaves to al-Kufah. He (the narrator) has said that all of them fell. I then visited him (the Imam) and informed him about what had happened. He (the Imam) said, '. . . thus, those who oppose His commands must remain afraid of being afflicted by mischief or painful suffering.' (24:63)"

H 12685, Ch. 4, h 8

A number of our people have narrated from Ahmad ibn Muhammad ibn Khalid from *al-Hajj*al from Safwan al-Jammal who has said the following:

"Abu 'Abd Allah, *'Alayhi al-Salam,* once said, 'Buy a camel for me, an ugly looking one, because it lives longer.' I then bought for him (the Imam) a camel for eighty dirham and brought it to him (the Imam)." In another *Hadith* it is said that he (the Imam) said, 'Buy the black and ugly looking one because it lives longer.'

H 12686, Ch. 4, h 9

A number of our people have narrated from Sahl ibn Ziyad from Ja'far ibn Muhammad from ibn al-Qaddah from abu 'Abd Allah, *'Alayhi al-Salam,* and from his father Maymun who has said the following:

"Once we left with abu Ja'far, *'Alayhi al-Salam,* to Ard of Taybah (name of a place between Makkah and al-Madinah) and 'Amr ibn Dinar was with him (the Imam) as well as other ones of his people. We stopped at Taybah as long as Allah willed, and abu Ja'far rode a difficult camel. 'Amr ibn Dinar said, 'Your camel is very difficult.' He (the Imam) said, 'You must take notice that the Messenger of Allah, *O Allah, grant compensation to Muhammad and his family worthy of their services to Your cause,* has said the following. 'On the peak of every camel there is a Satan, so you must degrade and make him lowly by mentioning the name of Allah on it because He is Allah who carries loads.' He (the Imam) then entered Makkah and we also entered Makkah without assuming the state of Ihram (because of entering before the passing of a month from his previous Ihram).'"

H 12687, Ch. 4, h 10

Muhammad ibn Yahya has narrated from Ahmad ibn Muhammad from Ahmad ibn Ali al-Sindiy from Muhammad ibn 'Amr ibn Sa'id from a man from ibn abu Ya'fur who has said the following:

"I once heard abu Ja'far, *'Alayhi al-Salam,* saying, 'Beware of red camels because the life of such camels is the shortest.'"

H 12688, Ch. 4, h 11

Al-Husayn ibn Muhammad has narrated from Mu'alla' ibn Muhammad from al-Washsha' from 'Abd Allah ibn Sinan who has said the following:

"I once heard abu 'Abd Allah, *'Alayhi al-Salam,* saying, 'Allah, most Majestic, most Glorious, has chosen something from everything and from camels, He has chosen she-camels and from sheep He has chosen ewes.'"

Chapter 5 - The Sheep

H 12689, Ch. 5, h 1

Al-Husayn ibn Muhammad has narrated from Mu'alla' ibn Muhammad from al-Washsha' from Ishaq ibn Ja'far who has said the following:

"Abu 'Abd Allah, *'Alayhi al-Salam,* once said to me, 'Son, keep sheep but do not keep camels.'"

H 12690, Ch. 5, h 2

Muhammad ibn Yahya has narrated from Ahmad ibn Muhammad from Ali ibn al-Hakam from 'Amr ibn Aban who has said the following:

"Abu 'Abd Allah, *'Alayhi al-Salam,* has said that the Messenger of Allah, *O Allah, grant compensation to Muhammad and his family worthy of their services to Your cause,* has said, 'The best asset is sheep.'"

H 12691, Ch. 5, h 3

Abu Ali al-Ash'ariy has narrated from al-Hassan ibn Ali from 'Ubays ibn Hisham from 'Abd Allah ibn Sinan who has said the following:

"Abu 'Abd Allah, *'Alayhi al-Salam,* has said that the Messenger of Allah, *O Allah, grant compensation to Muhammad and his family worthy of their services*

to Your cause, has said, 'You must clean the fold of the sheep and dust from them.'"

H 12692, Ch. 5, h 4

Through the same chain of narrators as that of the previous *Hadith* the following is narrated:

"Abu 'Abd Allah, *'Alayhi al-Salam,* has said, 'If a family keeps one sheep, Allah provides her sustenance, increases their sustenance and dispels poverty from them by a distance (of one day's journey). If a family keeps two sheep, Allah provides their sustenance and increases their sustenance and dispels poverty from them by two distances, when the family keeps three sheep Allah provides their sustenance and dispels poverty from the family in its totality.'"

H 12693, Ch. 5, h 5

Ali ibn Ibrahim has narrated from his father from ibn abu 'Umayr from 'Abd Allah ibn Sinan from Muhammad ibn al-'Ajlan who has said the following:

"I once heard abu Ja'far, *'Alayhi al-Salam,* saying, 'If a family keeps a milking sheep, such family is revered twice a day.' I (the narrator) then asked, 'What is said to such family?' He (the Imam) said, 'It is said to the family, "You have received blessings, you have received blessings."'"

H 12694, Ch. 5, h 6

Muhammad ibn Yahya has narrated from Ahmad ibn Muhammad ibn 'Isa from ibn Mahbub from Muhammad ibn Marid who has said the following:

"I once heard abu 'Abd Allah, *'Alayhi al-Salam,* saying, 'If a family keeps a milking goat, reverence and blessing is sent on them. If they are two, the family is revered and blessed twice a day.' Certain persons of our people then said, 'How are they revered?' He (the Imam) said, 'An angels stands on them every morning and says, "You are revered and blessed, you are fine and your sauce is fine.' I then asked, 'What is the meaning of *'qudistum'* (you are revered)?' He (the Imam) said, 'It means, 'You are cleansed.'"

H 12695, Ch. 5, h 7

A number of our people have narrated from Ahmad ibn Muhammad ibn Khalid from ibn abu Najran from abu Jamilah from Jabir who has said the following:

"Abu Ja'far, *'Alayhi al-Salam,* has said that the Messenger of Allah, *O Allah, grant compensation to Muhammad and his family worthy of their services to Your cause,* once said to his aunt, 'What keeps you from having a blessing in your home?' She asked, 'O Messenger of Allah, what is a blessing?' He (the Messenger of Allah) said, 'It is a sheep that you can milk. If one keeps a sheep in his home to milk or an ewe or a cow to milk they all are blessings.'"

H 12696, Ch. 5, h 8

Ali ibn Ibrahim has narrated from his father from Hammad from Hariz from abu al-Jarud who has said the following:

"Abu Ja'far, *'Alayhi al-Salam,* has said that once the Messenger of Allah, *O Allah, grant compensation to Muhammad and his family worthy of their services to Your cause,* went to the house of 'Umm Salamah and said to her, 'Why is it that I do not see blessing in your house?' She said, 'Yes, all praise belongs to Allah, there are blessings in my house.' He (the Messenger of Allah) said,

'Allah, most Majestic, most Glorious, has sent three kinds of blessings which are water, fire and sheep.'"

H 12697, Ch. 5, h 9

A number of our people have narrated from Ahmad ibn abu 'Abd Allah, from his father, from Sulayman al-Ja'fariy who in a *marfu'* manner has said the following:

"Abu 'Abd Allah, *'Alayhi al-Salam,* has said, 'If any family keeps thirty sheep in the evening in their house, angels continue to protect them until the morning.'"

Chapter 6 - The Marked Domestic Animals

H 12698, Ch. 6, h 1

Muhammad ibn Yahya has narrated from Ahmad ibn Muhammad from ibn Faddal from Yunus ibn Ya'qub who has said the following:

"I once asked abu 'Abd Allah, *'Alayhi al-Salam,* about if I can mark sheep on their faces. He (the Imam) said, 'Mark them on their ears.'"

H 12699, Ch. 6, h 2

Ahmad ibn Muhammad has narrated from ibn Mahbub from 'Abd Allah ibn Sinan who has said the following:

"I once asked abu 'Abd Allah, *'Alayhi al-Salam,* about marking the animals. He (the Imam) said, 'It is not harmful except their faces.'"

Chapter 7 - The Pigeons

H 12700, Ch. 7, h 1

Muhammad ibn Yahya has narrated from Ahmad ibn Muhammad from Ali ibn al-Hakam from an ibn Mahbub from Mu'awiyah ibn Wahab who has said the following:

"He (the Imam), *'Alayhi al-Salam,* has said, 'Pigeons are the birds of the Prophets, *'Alayhim al-Salam.'"

H 12701, Ch. 7, h 2

Al-Husayn ibn Muhammad has narrated from Mu'alla' ibn Muhammad from al-Washsha' from Hammad ibn 'Uthman from 'Abd al-'Ala' Mawla' Ale Sam who has said the following:

"I once heard abu 'Abd Allah, *'Alayhi al-Salam,* saying, 'The first pigeon in Makkah was the pigeon of 'Isma'il *'Alayhi al-Salam.'"

H 12702, Ch. 7, h 3

Ali ibn Ibrahim has narrated from his father from ibn abu 'Umayr from Hafs ibn al-Bakhtariy who has said the following:

"Abu 'Abd Allah, *'Alayhi al-Salam,* has said, 'The real free pigeon remaining is the pigeon that belonged to 'Isma'il ibn Ibrahim, *'Alayhima al-Salam,* who kept it for comfort. Abu 'Abd Allah, *'Alayhi al-Salam,* has said, 'It is preferable to keep a bird with clipped wings for comfort and for (to dispel) fear from vermin.'"

H 12703, Ch. 7, h 4

Ali ibn Muhammad has narrated from Salih ibn abu Hammad from al-Washsha' from Ahmad ibn 'A'idh from abu Khadijah who has said the following:

"I once heard abu 'Abd Allah, *'Alayhi al-Salam,* saying, 'These pigeons –the pigeons of al-Haram (the sacred area) – are of the offspring of the pigeon of 'Isma'il ibn Ibrahim, *'Alayhima al-Salam,* that belonged to him.'"

H 12704, Ch. 7, h 5

Ali ibn Muhammad has narrated from Salih ibn abu Hammad and Al-Husayn ibn Muhammad has narrated from Mu'alla' ibn Muhammad all from al-Washsha' from Ahmad ibn 'A'idh from abu Khadijah who has said the following:

"Abu 'Abd Allah, *'Alayhi al-Salam,* has said, 'A house in which pigeons exist, the people of that house do not receive any harm from Jinn. The dimwitted Jinns play in the house, thus they play with pigeons and the people are left alone.'"

H 12705, Ch. 7, h 6

Ali ibn Ibrahim has narrated from Muhammad ibn 'Isa from 'Ubayd Allah al-Dihqan from Durust from 'Abd Allah ibn Sinan who has said the following:

"Abu 'Abd Allah, *'Alayhi al-Salam,* has said that once a man complained before the Messenger of Allah, *O Allah, grant compensation to Muhammad and his family worthy of their services to Your cause,* about loneliness and fear. He (the Messenger of Allah) commanded him to keep a pair of pigeons in his house.'"

H 12706, Ch. 7, h 7

A number of our people have narrated from Sahl ibn Ziyad from abu 'Abd Allah, al-Jamuraniy from al-Hassan ibn Ali ibn abu Hamzah from his father from Sandal from Zayd al-Shahham who has said the following:

"I once mentioned pigeons before abu 'Abd Allah, *'Alayhi al-Salam,* and he (the Imam) said, 'You can keep them in your homes; it is a lovely (hobby). The prayer of Nuh (Noah), *'Alayhi al-Salam,* has arrived at them. It is the most comforting thing in the house.'"

H 12707, Ch. 7, h 8

Al-Husayn ibn Muhammad has narrated from Mu'alla' ibn Muhammad from al-Washsha' from a man from 'Umar ibn Yazid from abu Salamah who has said the following:

"Abu 'Abd Allah, *'Alayhi al-Salam,* has said that pigeons are of the birds of the Prophets, *'Alayhim al-Salam,* who kept them in their homes. Any home in which there is a pigeon, the people therein are not harmed by the dimwitted ones of Jinn who plays in the house, thus they play with the pigeons and leave the people alone.' I then saw in the house of abu 'Abd Allah, *'Alayhi al-Salam,* a pigeon that belonged to his son 'Isma'il."

H 12708, Ch. 7, h 9

A number of our people have narrated from Ahmad ibn Muhammad from al-Qasim ibn Yahya from his grandfather al-Hassan ibn Rashid from Ya'qub ibn Ja'far who has said the following:

"Abu al-Hassan, *'Alayhi al-Salam,* looked at pigeons in his house and said, 'With every vibration that it causes, Allah thereby dispels from the house the incantations and spells by the people on earth that may try to enter therein.'"

H 12709, Ch. 7, h 10

It is narrated from the narrator of the previous *Hadith* from al-Jamuraniy from ibn abu Hamzah from Sandal from Dawud ibn Farqad who has said the following:

"I once was sitting in the house of abu 'Abd Allah, *'Alayhi al-Salam,* and I looked at a pigeon of Ra''ibiy kind (name of a place) that made a long sound. Abu 'Abd Allah, *'Alayhi al-Salam,* looked at me and asked, 'O Dawud, do you know what this bird says?' I said, 'No, I pray to Allah to keep my soul in service for your cause.' He (the Imam) said, 'It prays against the people who murdered al-Husayn, *'Alayhi al-Salam,* so you must keep it in your homes.'"

H 12710, Ch. 7, h 11
It is narrated from the narrator of the previous *Hadith* from Muhammad ibn Ali from a man from Yahya al-Arzaq who has said the following:

I once heard abu 'Abd Allah, *'Alayhi al-Salam,* saying, 'The sound of the wings of pigeon dispels the devils.'"

H 12711, Ch. 7, h 12
A number of our people have narrated from Sahl ibn Ziyad in a *marfu'* manner has said the following:

"Abu 'Abd Allah, *'Alayhi al-Salam,* has said Allah, most Majestic, most Glorious, with pigeons, keeps a house safe from crumbling down.'"

H 12712, Ch. 7, h 13
Ali ibn Ibrahim has narrated from his father from al-Nawfaliy from al-Sakuniy who has said the following:

"Abu 'Abd Allah, *'Alayhi al-Salam,* has said, 'You must keep al-Ra''ibiy pigeon in your homes because it condemns the murderers of al-Husayn ibn Ali, *'Alayhim al-Salam*, and Allah has condemned his killer.'"

H 12713, Ch. 7, h 14
A number of our people have narrated from Sahl ibn Ziyad from Bakr ibn Salih from Muhammad ibn abu Hamzah from 'Uthman al-Asbahaniy who has said the following:

"'Isma'il ibn abu 'Abd Allah, *'Alayhi al-Salam,* asked me for a gift and I gave him a Ra''ibiy bird (a pigeon). Abu 'Abd Allah, *'Alayhi al-Salam,* came in and said, 'Keep this al-Ra''ibiy bird in the house with me for comfort.' 'Uthman has said, 'I once visited abu 'Abd Allah, *'Alayhi al-Salam,* when in front of him there was a pigeon for which he (the Imam) made the bread in pieces.'"

H 12714, Ch. 7, h 15
It is narrated from the narrator of the previous *Hadith* from Bakr ibn Salih from Ash'ath ibn 'Uthman ibn Muhammad al-Bariqiy from 'Abd al-Karim ibn Salih who has said the following:

"I once went to visit abu 'Abd Allah, *'Alayhi al-Salam,* and I saw three green pigeons on his furnishing which had made droppings on the furnishings and I said, 'I pray to Allah to keep my soul in service for your cause, these pigeons have dirtied the furnishings.' He (the Imam) said, 'No, it is preferable that they stay inside the house.'"

H 12715, Ch. 7, h 16
Ali ibn Ibrahim has narrated from his father from certain persons of his people from Aban from a man who has said the following:

"Abu 'Abd Allah, *'Alayhi al-Salam,* has said that in the house of the Messenger of Allah, *O Allah, grant compensation to Muhammad and his family worthy of their services to Your cause,* there was a pair of red pigeons.'"

489

H 12716, Ch. 7, h 17

Ali ibn Ibrahim has narrated from his father from ibn abu Najran from Muhammad ibn 'Amr [and] Ibrahim al-Sindiy from Yahya al-Azraq who has said the following:

"Abu 'Abd Allah, *'Alayhi al-Salam*, has said that `Amir al-Mu'minin had dug a well, then they threw things in it and it was reported to him (the Imam). He went, stood on the well and said, 'You must stop throwing things in it, otherwise, I will make the pigeons to use it as their living place.' Abu 'Abd Allah, *'Alayhi al-Salam*, then said, 'The sound of the pigeon repels Satans.'"

H 12717, Ch. 7, h 18

It is narrated from the narrator of the previous *Hadith* from his father from certain persons of our people who has said the following:

"Once, pigeons were mentioned before abu 'Abd Allah, *'Alayhi al-Salam*, and a man said, 'It has come to my knowledge that once 'Umar saw a pigeon flying and a man underneath was running. 'Umar then said, "One Satan runs under another Satan." Abu 'Abd Allah, *'Alayhi al-Salam*, then said, '(It is because) `Isma'il was not there with you.' Someone then asked, 'Was he (`Isma'il) a friend (of pigeons)?' He (the Imam) said, 'The pigeons of al-Haram (the sacred area) are of the remaining pigeons of `Isma'il.'"

H 12718, Ch. 7, h 19

A number of our people have narrated from Sahl ibn Ziyad and Ahmad ibn Muhammad from all from ibn abu Nasr who has said the following:

"Once a man asked al-Rida', *'Alayhi al-Salam*, about a pair of pigeons which hatched chicks with him; if a bird can mate a mother bird or daughter bird. He (the Imam) said, 'It is not harmful with what is in animals.'"

Chapter 8 - Setting Birds Free

H 12719, Ch. 8, h 1

A number of our people have narrated from Ahmad ibn Muhammad ibn Khalid from Muhammad ibn `Isma'il from Muhammad ibn 'Adhafir who has said the following:

"I once asked abu 'Abd Allah, *'Alayhi al-Salam*, about the case of a bird which is set free in a faraway area and the bird has never seen it but it comes back. He (the Imam) said, 'O ibn 'Udha'fir, birds can come to the house of its owner from a distance of thirty farsakh (90 miles) because of its knowledge and environment, but if it is more than thirty farsakh then the bird comes for the sustenance which is determined for it.'"

H 12720, Ch. 8, h 2

A number of our people have narrated from Sahl ibn Ziyad in a *marfu'* manner has said the following:

"Abu 'Abd Allah, *'Alayhi al-Salam*, has said, 'That (bird) which comes back from a distance of thirty farsakh is because of guidance and from a distance of more than this is because of food.'"

H 12721, Ch. 8, h 3

Muhammad ibn Yahya has narrated from Ahmad ibn Muhammad from Ali ibn al-Hakam from Sayf ibn 'Amirah from Ishaq ibn 'Ammar who has said the following:

"I once asked abu 'Abd Allah, *'Alayhi al-Salam,* about the case of a bird which comes back from a faraway place. He (the Imam) said, 'It comes back because of its sustenance.'"

H 12722, Ch. 8, h 4
Al-Husayn ibn Muhammad has narrated from Mu'alla' ibn Muhammad from Muhammad ibn Jumhur from Ali ibn Dawud al-Haddad from Hariz who has said the following:
"I once asked abu 'Abd Allah, *'Alayhi al-Salam,* about the case of birds that are set free in a faraway place come but not the ones released nearby. He (the Imam) said, 'When its sustenance in the area is depleted, then it does not come back.'"

Chapter 9 - The Rooster

H 12723, Ch. 9, h 1
A number of our people have narrated from Ahmad ibn Muhammad ibn Khalid from Muhammad ibn Ali from abu Jamilah from Jabir who has said the following:
"Abu Ja'far, *'Alayhi al-Salam,* has said that the Messenger of Allah, *O Allah, grant compensation to Muhammad and his family worthy of their services to Your cause,* has said, 'A white rooster which is called *afraq* (white) protects the house of its people and seven other houses around it.'"

H 12724, Ch. 9, h 2
A number of our people have narrated from Sahl ibn Ziyad from Ali ibn Sulayman ibn Rushayd from al-Qasim ibn 'Abd al-Rahman al-Hashimiy from Muhammad ibn Mukhallad al-Ahwaziy who has said the following:
"Abu 'Abd Allah, *'Alayhi al-Salam,* has said, 'A white rooster which is called afraq protects its house and seven houses around it, however, a vibration from a spotted pigeon is better than seven white roosters.'"

H 12725, Ch. 9, h 3
A number of our people have narrated from, Ahmad ibn Muhammad ibn Khalid, from al-Qasim ibn Yahya from his grandfather al-Hassan ibn Rashid, from Ya'qub ibn Ja'far ibn Ibrahim al-Ja'fariy who has said the following:
"Once, the beauty of peacock was mentioned before abu al-Hassan, *'Alayhi al-Salam,* who said, 'It cannot have any greater beauty over the white rooster.' He (the narrator) has said, 'I heard him (the Imam) saying, 'The voice of rooster is better than the voice of peacock. It is of greater blessing because it wakes you up for the time of *Salat* (prayer). The peacock says, 'Woe is me.' It says so because of the mistake that it fell in.'"

H 12726, Ch. 9, h 4
It is narrated from the narrator of the previous *Hadith* from certain persons of his people in a *marfu'* manner who has said the following:
"Abu 'Abd Allah, *'Alayhi al-Salam,* has said, 'The white rooster is my friend and the friend of every believing person.'"

H 12727, Ch. 9, h 5
It is narrated from the narrator of the previous *Hadith* from certain persons of his people from abu Shu'ayb al-Muhamiliy who has said the following:
"Abu al-Hassan, *'Alayhi al-Salam,* has said, 'In roosters there are five qualities

of the qualities of the Prophets, like bravery, contentment, knowledge of the times of *Salat* (prayer), the great deal of ability of mating and courage (to protect the female).'"

H 12728, Ch. 9, h 6

It is narrated from the narrator of the previous *Hadith* from A number of our people have narrated from Sahl ibn Ziyad all from Ja'far ibn Muhammad al-Ash'ariy from ibn al-Qaddah who has said the following:

"Abu 'Abd Allah, *'Alayhi al-Salam,* has said that 'Amir al-Mu'minin has said, 'Crowing of the rooster is its *Salat* (prayer) and flipping of its wings is its *Ruku'* (bowing down on one's knees) and *Sujud* (prostrations).'"

Chapter 10 - Al-Warshan (a kind of Pigeon)

H 12729, Ch. 10, h 1

A number of our people have narrated from Ahmad ibn Muhammad ibn Khalid from 'Isma'il ibn Mehran from Sayf ibn 'Amirah from abu Bakr al-Hadramiy who has said the following:

"Abu 'Abd Allah, *'Alayhi al-Salam,* has said, 'If one likes to keep birds in his house, he must keep Warshan (a kind of pigeon). It speaks of Allah, most Majestic, most Glorious, most often as well as Tasbih (Allah is free of all defects) and it is a bird that loves us, the Ahl al-Bayt (family of prophet Muhammad, *O Allah, grant compensation to Muhammad and his family worthy of their services to Your cause).'"

H 12730, Ch. 10, h 2

It is narrated from the narrator of the previous *Hadith* from Bakr ibn Salih from Muhammad ibn abu Hamzah 'Uthman al-Asbahaniy who has said the following:

"'Isma'il, ibn abu 'Abd Allah, *'Alayhi al-Salam,* once, asked me to give a bird of Iraq as a gift to him. I gave him a Warshan. Abu 'Abd Allah, *'Alayhi al-Salam,* came in. He (the Imam) saw it and said, 'Al-Warshan says, 'You are blessed, you are blessed', so you must keep it.'"

H 12731, Ch. 10, h 3

It is narrated from the narrator of the previous *Hadith* from al-Jamuraniy ibn abu Hamzah from Sayf from Ishaq ibn 'Ammar from abu Basir who has said the following:

"Abu 'Abd Allah, *'Alayhi al-Salam,* prohibited his son 'Isma'il from keeping *al-Fakhtah* (ring pigeon) and said if you must keep a bird, keep Warshan because it speaks of Allah, most Blessed, most High, very often.'"

Chapter 11 - *Al-Fakhtah* and *Al-Sulsul*

H 12732, Ch. 11, h 1

Ali ibn Ibrahim has narrated from his father from ibn abu 'Umayr from Hafs ibn al-Bakhtariy from a man who has said the following:

"Abu 'Abd Allah, *'Alayhi al-Salam,* has said that in the house of abu Ja'far, *'Alayhi al-Salam,* there was al-Fakhtah and he one day heard it crying. He (the Imam) said, 'Do you know what it (al-Fakhtah) says?' They replied, 'No, we do not know.' He (the Imam) said, 'It says, 'I have lost you, I have lost you.' He (the Imam) said, 'We will lose it before it will lose us.' He (the Imam) commanded to slaughter it (for food).'"

H 12733, Ch. 11, h 2
A number of our people have narrated from Ahmad ibn Muhammad ibn Khalid from Bakr ibn Salih from Muhammad ibn abu Hamzah from 'Uthman al-Asbahaniy who has said the following:

"I once gave a *Sulsul* as a gift to `Isma'il, son of abu 'Abd Allah, *'Alayhi al-Salam,* and abu 'Abd Allah, *'Alayhi al-Salam,* came in. When he (the Imam) saw it he said, 'This bird is an unfortunate bird, so you must send it away. It says, 'I have failed to find you, I have failed to find you.' You must lose it before it fails to find you.'"

H 12734, Ch. 11, h 3
It is narrated from the narrator of the previous *Hadith* from al-Jamuraniy ibn abu Hamzah from Sayf ibn 'Amirah from Ishaq ibn 'Ammar from abu Basir who has said the following:

"I once visited abu 'Abd Allah, *'Alayhi al-Salam,* and he said to me, 'O abu Muhammad, come with us to visit `Isma'il because of his illness. We left to visit `Isma'il and in his house we saw *al-Fakhtah* in a cage crying. Abu 'Abd Allah, *'Alayhi al-Salam,* said, 'Son, what has made you to keep this *al-Fakhtah*? Did you not know that it is a misfortune?' Do you know what it says?' `Isma'il replied, 'No, I do not know.' He (the Imam) said, 'It prays against its owners saying, 'May I fail to find you, may I fail to find you' so you must send it far and away.'"

Chapter 12 - The Dogs

H 12735, Ch. 12, h 1
Ali ibn Ibrahim has narrated from his father from ibn abu 'Umayr from Hammad from al-Halabiy who has said the following:

"Abu 'Abd Allah, *'Alayhi al-Salam,* has said, 'It is detestable for a Muslim to allow a dog to live in his house.'"

H 12736, Ch. 12, h 2
A number of our people have narrated from Ahmad ibn Muhammad from ibn Faddal from ibn Bukayr from Zurarah who has said the following:

"Abu 'Abd Allah, *'Alayhi al-Salam,* has said, 'Whoever keeps a dog, every day one *Qirat* (a certain unit of measurement) is reduced from the (good) deeds of his owner.'"

H 12737, Ch. 12, h 3
It is narrated from the narrator of the previous *Hadith* from 'Uthman from Sama'ah who has said the following:

"I once asked him (the Imam), *'Alayhi al-Salam,* if we can keep a dog in the house. He (the Imam) said, 'No, you must not do so.'"

H 12738, Ch. 12, h 4
Muhammad ibn Yahya has narrated from Ahmad ibn Muhammad ibn 'Isa from Yusuf ibn 'Aqil from Muhammad ibn Qays who has said the following:

"Abu Ja'far, *'Alayhi al-Salam,* has said that `Amir al-Mu'minin has said, 'There is nothing good in dogs except hunting dogs or that which guards cattle.'"

H 12739, Ch. 12, h 5

A number of our people have narrated from Ahmad ibn Muhammad ibn Khalid from his father from al-Nadr ibn Suwayd from al-Qasim ibn Sulayman from Jarrah al-Mada'iniy who has said the following:

"Abu 'Abd Allah, *'Alayhi al-Salam,* has said, 'You must not keep a hunting dog in the house unless there is a door between you and the dog.'"

H 12740, Ch. 12, h 6

It is narrated from the narrator of the previous *Hadith* from 'Uthman ibn 'Isa from Sama'ah who has said the following:

"I once asked him (the Imam), *'Alayhi al-Salam,* if a hunting dog can be kept in the house. He (the Imam) said, 'If a door can be closed in front of it, then it is not harmful.'"

H 12741, Ch. 12, h 7

A number of our people have narrated from Ahmad ibn Muhammad from and Muhammad ibn Yahya from 'Abd Allah ibn Muhammad from Ali ibn al-Hakam from Aban from Zurarah who has said the following:

"One of the two Imam, (abu Ja'far or abu 'Abd Allah), *'Alayhim al-Salam,* has said that dogs of one color, all black are from Jinn.'"

H 12742, Ch. 12, h 8

Muhammad ibn Yahya has narrated from Muhammad ibn al-Husayn from Muhammad ibn 'Isma'il from Ali ibn al-Hakam from Malik ibn 'Atiyyah from abu Hamzah al-Thumaliy who has said the following:

"Once I was with abu 'Abd Allah, *'Alayhi al-Salam,* on the road between Makkah and al-Madinah and I saw on his left side a dog of one color, all black. He (the Imam) said, 'What is the matter with you, may Allah disfigure you, how fiercely you rush!' It then resembled a bird. I then asked, 'What is this? I pray to Allah to keep my soul in service for your cause.' He (the Imam) said, 'It was *Ghuthaym*, mailman of Jinn. Hisham has died in this hour and it flies to spread this news in every town.'"

H 12743, Ch. 12, h 9

A number of our people have narrated from Sahl ibn Ziyad from Muhammad ibn al-Hassan ibn Shammun from 'Abd Allah ibn 'Abd al-Rahman from Misma' who has said the following:

"Abu 'Abd Allah, *'Alayhi al-Salam,* has said that the Messenger of Allah, *O Allah, grant compensation to Muhammad and his family worthy of their services to Your cause,* has said, 'Dogs are weak Jinns. If one of you eat food and something of it (dog or jinn) is in front of you, feed it or send it away because they have evil souls.'"*

H 12744, Ch. 12, h 10

Muhammad ibn Yahya has narrated from Muhammad ibn al-Husayn from 'Abd al-Rahman ibn abu Hashim from Salim ibn abu Salmah who has said the following:

"Once abu 'Abd Allah, *'Alayhi al-Salam,* was asked about dogs. He (the Imam) said, 'Every dog of one color, all black or all red or all white is a creature of Jinn in the form of dog; but that of spotted colors is a metamorphosed of Jinn and man.'"

H 12745, Ch. 12, h 11

Ali ibn Ibrahim has narrated from his father from al-Nawfaliy from al-Sakuniy who has said the following:

"Abu 'Abd Allah, *'Alayhi al-Salam,* has said that the Messenger of Allah, *O Allah, grant compensation to Muhammad and his family worthy of their services to Your cause,* granted permission to the people of al-Qasiyah (country side) to keep dogs.'"

H 12746, Ch. 12, h 12

It is narrated from the narrator of the previous *Hadith* from his father from ibn Mahbub from al-'Ala' ibn Razin from Muhammad ibn Muslim who has said the following:

"I once asked abu 'Abd Allah, *'Alayhi al-Salam,* about the dog from al-Saluqiy (name of a place in Yemen). He (the Imam) said, 'If you touch it you must then wash your hands.'"

Chapter 13 - Instigating Animals against each other

H 12747, Ch. 13, h 1

A number of our people have narrated from Ahmad ibn Muhammad from Ali ibn al-Hakam from Aban ibn 'Uthman from abu al-'Abbas who has said the following:

"I once asked abu 'Abd Allah, *'Alayhi al-Salam,* about instigating animals against each other. He (the Imam) said, 'All of it is detestable except dogs.'"

H 12748, Ch. 13, h 2

It is narrated from the narrator of the previous *Hadith* from Ali ibn al-Hakam from Aban from Misma' who has said the following:

"I once asked abu 'Abd Allah, *'Alayhi al-Salam,* about instigating animals against each other. He (the Imam) said, 'I dislike it except dogs.'"

End of the Book of Domestic Animals of the book of al-Kafi, and all praise belongs to Allah, in the beginning and at the end, followed by the Book of Wills by the Will of Allah.

CPSIA information can be obtained
at www.ICGtesting.com
Printed in the USA
BVHW020612030423
661648BV00025B/309